Microsoft Office 97 Professional Essentials

Laura Acklen
Linda Bird
Robert Ferrett
Donna M. Matherly
John Preston
Sally Preston
Michele Reader
Rob Tidrow
Thomas Underwood
Suzanne Weixel

An Imprint of
Macmillan Computer Publishing

Microsoft Office 97 Professional Essentials

Copyright ©1998 by Que® Education & Training.

All rights reserved. Printed in the United States of America. No part of this book may be used or reproduced in any form or by any means, or stored in a database or retrieval system, without prior written permission of the publisher except in the case of brief quotations embodied in critical articles and reviews. Making copies of any part of this book for any purpose other than your own personal use is a violation of United States copyright laws. For information, address Que Education and Training, Macmillan Computer Publishing, 201 W. 103rd Street, Indianapolis, IN 46290.

Library of Congress Catalog No: 97-68154

ISBN: 1-57576-787-2

This book is sold *as is*, without warranty of any kind, either express or implied, respecting the contents of this book, including but not limited to implied warranties for the book's quality, performance, merchantability, or fitness for any particular purpose. Neither Que Education and Training nor its dealers or distributors shall be liable to the purchaser or any other person or entity with respect to any liability, loss, or damage caused or alleged to be caused directly or indirectly by this book.

01 00 99 98 4 3

Screens reproduced in this book were created using Collage Plus from Inner Media, Inc., Hollis, NH.

Publisher: Robert Linsky

Executive Editor: Kyle Lewis

Brand Director, Education: Susan L. Kindel

Managing Editor: Caroline Roop

Cover Designer: Anne Jones

Book Designer: Louisa Klucznik

Production Team: Trina Brown, Cindy Fields, Rowena Rappaport, Susan Van Ness

Indexer: Tim Tate

Composed in *Stone Serif* and *MCPdigital* by Que Corporation

Trademark Acknowledgments

All terms mentioned in this book that are known to be trademarks or service marks have been appropriately capitalized. Que Education and Training cannot attest to the acccuracy of this information. Use of a term in this book should not be regarded as affecting the validity of any trademark or service mark.

This book was produced digitally by Macmillan Computer Publishing and manufactured using computer-to-plate technology (a film-less process) by GAC/Shepard Poorman, Indianapolis, Indiana.

Preface

Que Education and Training is the educational publishing imprint of Macmillan Computer Publishing, the world's leading computer book publisher. Macmillan Computer Publishing books have taught more than 20 million people how to be productive with their computers.

This expertise in producing high-quality computer tutorial and reference books is evident in every Que Education and Training title we publish. The same tried-and-true writing and product-development process that makes Macmillan Computer Publishing books bestsellers is used to ensure that educational materials from Que Education and Training provide the most accurate and up-to-date information. Experienced and respected computer application experts write and review every manuscript to provide class-tested pedagogy. Quality-assurance editors check every keystroke and command in Que Education and Training books to ensure that instructions are clear, accurate, and precise.

Above all, Macmillan Computer Publishing and, in turn, Que Education and Training have years of experience in meeting the learning demands of students across all disciplines.

The "Essentials" of Hands-on Learning

The *Essentials* applications tutorials are appropriate for use in both corporate training and college classroom settings. The *Essentials* workbooks are ideal for short courses—from a few hours to a full day or more—and meet the needs of a wide variety of students. They can also be used effectively as computer-lab applications modules to accompany Que Education and Training's computer concepts text, *Computers in Your Future, Second Edition*, by Marilyn Meyer and Roberta Baber, both of Fresno City College; and *Using Computers and Information*, by Jack Rochester of Plymouth State College. The *Essentials* workbooks enable users to become self-sufficient quickly; encourage self-learning after instruction; maximize learning through clear, complete explanations; and serve as future references. Each *Essentials* module is four-color throughout and is sized at 8-½×11 inches for maximum screen-shot visibility. Each text contains a disk with the data files needed to complete the tutorials and end-of-chapter exercises.

Project Objectives list what students will do and learn from the project.

"Why Would I Do This?" shows students why the material is essential.

Step-by-Step Tutorials simplify the procedures with large screen shots, captions, and annotations.

If you have problems... anticipates common pitfalls and advises students accordingly.

Inside Stuff provides tips and shortcuts for more effective applications.

Key Terms are highlighted in the text and defined in the margin when they first appear, as well as in an end-of-book glossary.

Jargon Watch offers a layperson's view of "technobabble" in easily understandable terms.

Checking Your Skills provides true/false, multiple choice, matching, screen identification, and completion exercises.

Applying Your Skills contains directed, hands-on exercises to check comprehension and reinforce learning, as well as self-directed challenge exercises requiring students to use critical thinking skills.

Data disks contain files for the text's step-by-step tutorials and end of project exercises.

Virtual Tutor CD-ROM

Virtual Tutor from Que Education and Training is a Lotus® ScreenCam driven CD-ROM product that displays every step-by-step tutorial via automated keystrokes and voice-over narration. It can be used as a self-study tool for reinforcement or review.

Instructor's Manual

If you have adopted this text for use in a college classroom, you will receive, upon request, an Instructor's Manual at no additional charge. The manual contains suggested curriculum guides for courses of varying lengths, teaching tips, answers to exercises in Checking Your Skills and Applying Your Skills sections, test questions and answers, a PowerPoint presentation, and data files and solutions for each tutorial and exercise. Please contact your local representative or write to us on school or business letterhead at Macmillan Computer Publishing, 201 West 103rd Street, Indianapolis, IN 46290-1097, Attention: Que Education and Training Sales Support.

Conventions Used in This Book

The Essentials series uses the following conventions to make it easier for yiou to understand the material:

- Text that you are to type appears in **`color`**, **`boldface`**, and **`special font`**.
- Underlined letters in menu names, menu commands, and dialog-box options appear in a different color or in **boldface**. Examples are the **F**ile menu, the **O**pen command and the File **n**ame list box.
- Important words or phrases appear in *italic* the first time they are discussed.
- *Key terms* are defined in the margin as soon as they are introduced.
- On-screen text and messages appear in a `special font`.

Table of Contents

Project 1

Getting Started with MS Office Professional

Getting to Know the Microsoft Office Applications

In this project, you learn how to:

- Open, Switch, and Close Microsoft Office Applications
- Create a New Office Document
- Save and Close an Office Document
- Open an Existing Office Document and Save It with a New Name
- Use the Microsoft Office Shortcut Bar
- Get Help

Why Would I Do This?

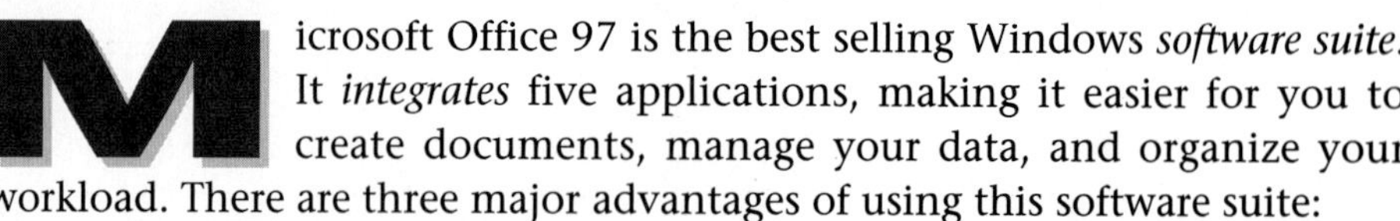

Microsoft Office 97 is the best selling Windows *software suite*. It *integrates* five applications, making it easier for you to create documents, manage your data, and organize your workload. There are three major advantages of using this software suite:

- Microsoft Office makes it easier for you to share data, documents, and graphics across applications.
- The applications look alike and work alike—thus reducing your learning curve and increasing your productivity.
- There is a substantial discount for buying the suite compared to purchasing the same products individually.

Software suite
A collection of full-featured, stand-alone programs. The programs share a common command structure and have similar interfaces to make them easy to learn.

Integration
The use two or more software applications together to create a single document.

There are different versions of Microsoft Office available. The basic Office 97 package contains four popular applications: Word 97, a word processor; Excel 97, an electronic spreadsheet; PowerPoint 97, a presentation graphics application; and Outlook 97, an information management program. In addition, Microsoft Office 97 Professional contains Access 97, a database manager.

In this project, you learn how to use some of the common features of Microsoft Office, including how to start and close applications and how to create, save, and close documents. You also learn how to get help and use the Microsoft Office Shortcut toolbar.

Lesson 1: Opening, Switching, and Closing Microsoft Office Applications

The first thing you need to know about Microsoft Office is how to start the applications. On some computers, Windows and Microsoft Office start automatically when you turn on the computer. On other computers, you must use the commands to start.

To Open, Switch, and Close Microsoft Office Applications

1 Turn on the computer and monitor by flipping their power switches.

The switches may be located on the front, side, or back of your computer and monitor. When you turn on the computer, you may see information displayed on-screen as the computer starts or boots. When all the startup commands are executed, you should see the Windows 95 desktop, as shown in Figure 1.1. Keep in mind that the appearance of the Windows 95 desktop depends on the way your computer system is set up, so your desktop may not look exactly like the desktop used in the illustrations for this book.

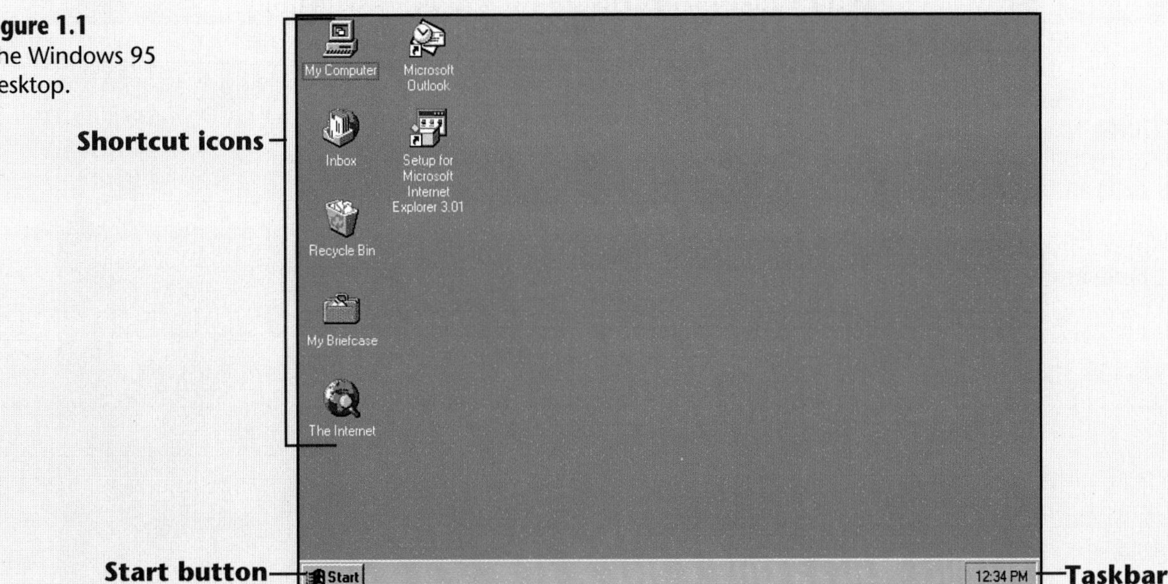

Figure 1.1
The Windows 95 desktop.

In some cases, you may have to choose Windows 95 from a menu (list of options) that has been set up for your system. If your machine is part of a network of computers, your startup procedure may include entering a user ID and password.

If You Have Problems...

If you see the DOS prompt on-screen (C:>), it means that you must type a command to start Windows 95. In the space immediately to the right of the symbol on your screen, type **WIN** and press ↵Enter. Windows should start, and you should see the Windows 95 desktop on your screen. For more information, consult your instructor.

2 Click the Start button on the Windows 95 taskbar.

The Start menu is displayed, as shown in Figure 1.2. The two commands at the top of the Start menu are used to create a new Office document or to open an existing Office document. However, to start an application, you use the Programs menu.

continues

To Open, Switch, and Close Microsoft Office Applications (continued)

Figure 1.2
You can use the Start menu to quickly create a new Office document, open an existing Office document, or open a menu of application programs.

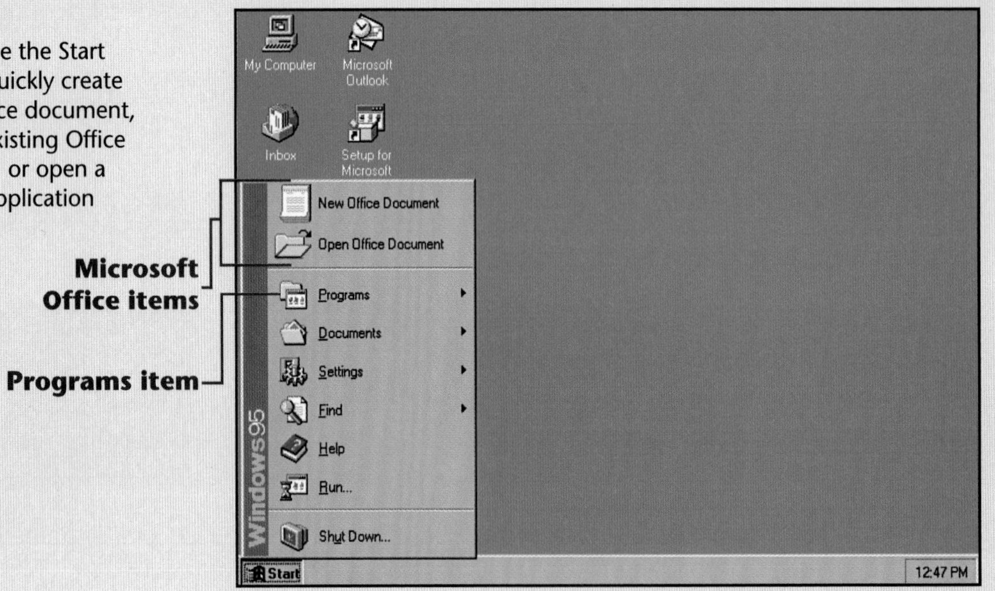

Microsoft Office items

Programs item

3 Move the mouse pointer up to highlight Programs on the Start menu.

The Programs menu is displayed, as shown in Figure 1.3. All of the Office applications that you have installed appear on the **P**rograms menu with other applications that are installed on your computer.

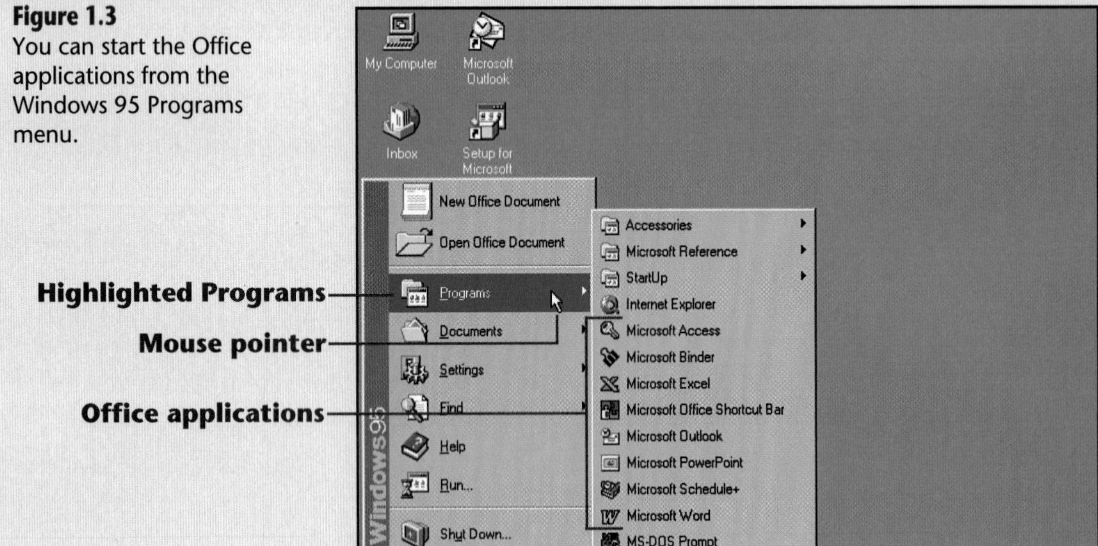

Figure 1.3
You can start the Office applications from the Windows 95 Programs menu.

4 Slide the mouse pointer to the right onto the Programs menu, then click Microsoft Word.

Word 97 starts, as shown in Figure 1.4. In Office, Word is the word processing application that you use to create text-based documents.

In the Word screen, you can see some of the typical Windows 95 screen elements as well as elements that appear in each of the Office applications. For example, the menu bar, the toolbars, and the status bar all appear in each Office application. Sometimes the commands are different, but the appearance and function of the elements remain the same. You learn about using the Word screen in Project 2, "Working with Word Documents." For more information about the Windows 95 elements, see Appendix A, "Working with Windows 95."

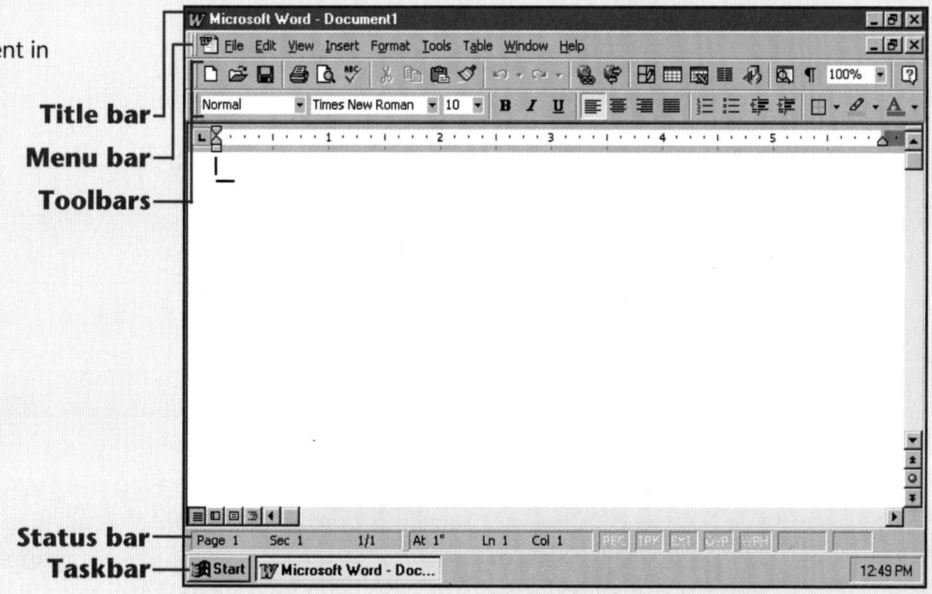

Figure 1.4
A blank document in Microsoft Word.

Title bar
Menu bar
Toolbars
Status bar
Taskbar

❺ Click the Start button on the taskbar again, then highlight Programs and click Microsoft Excel on the Programs menu.

Active application
The application in which you are working. Sometimes called the current application.

This starts Microsoft Excel, as shown in Figure 1.5. You can open more than one application at a time using Windows 95. Word remains running in the background, but Excel is the *active application*. Notice on the taskbar that the Excel button is pressed. All open applications appear as buttons on the taskbar, but the button for the active application appears pressed. Notice also that many elements you see on your screen are the same as elements in Word.

continues

To Open, Switch, and Close Microsoft Office Applications (continued)

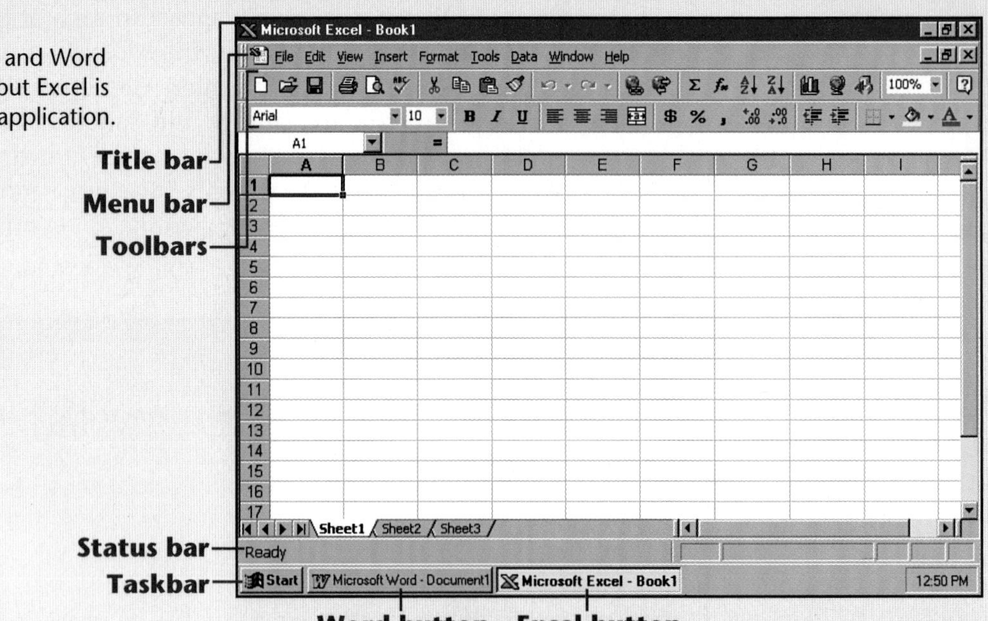

Figure 1.5
Both Excel and Word are open, but Excel is the active application.

If You Have Problems...

If the Excel window is not maximized, you may see the Word window on the screen behind it. You can resize the Excel window, or click the maximize button on the title bar to maximize it. For more information on using Windows 95 features to arrange and resize windows, see Appendix A, "Working with Windows 95."

6 Click the Microsoft Word button on the taskbar.

Word becomes the active application and Excel moves to the background. To change to any open application, click its button on the taskbar.

7 Click File on the Word menu bar.

This opens the File menu, as shown in Figure 1.6. The commands on the **F**ile menu are similar in all Office applications.

If You Have Problems...

The first time you start an Office application, the Office Assistant may appear on-screen. The Office Assistant is a feature designed to help you learn how to use Office and to access the Help files for each of the Office applications. By default, it appears as an animated paper clip with a caption balloon that lists options.

When the Office Assistant is open, you cannot select a menu command or close the application. If the Office Assistant is open in

Word, click the option that says Start Using Microsoft Word. The Office Assistant will close. If the Office Assistant is open in Excel, click Start Using Microsoft Excel to close it. You learn how to use the Office Assistant in Lesson 6.

Figure 1.6
All Office applications have a **F**ile menu.

Click File here

Choose Exit here

8 Click Exit on the File menu.

Word closes, and you see Excel on your screen. (Choosing E**x**it from the **F**ile menu closes any Office application.)

9 Click the application Close button on the right end of Excel's title bar.

Excel closes, and you see the Windows 95 Desktop. You can quickly close an Office application by clicking the Close button on the title bar. You have now learned how to open, close, and switch among Office applications. Keep Windows 95 running. In the next lesson, you learn how to create a new document for an Office application.

Another quick way to switch among open applications is to press and hold the Alt key as you press Tab. A window opens in the middle of the screen displaying icons for each of the open applications. The active application is surrounded by a red box. Each time you press Tab, the box moves to the next application icon. When the red box is around the application you want to use, release both keys.

If you can see the window you want to make active on the desktop, simply click in the window to make it active.

If you have problems...

If you find that your system is slow or locking up, you may have opened a program twice instead of simply switching to it. The **P**rograms menu allows you to open a program that is already running, which you might do accidentally. You can check the taskbar before opening new applications to make sure the program is not already running.

Random-Access Memory
The computer's main working memory. RAM is a temporary storage space in which program instructions and data are stored. When the computer is turned off, the data in RAM is lost.

Depending on how much *random-access memory* (RAM) is installed in your computer and the other applications that are running, you may not be able to launch a number of Microsoft Office programs simultaneously. You might get a message, such as `There is insufficient memory to start this application`. If this happens, close one of the applications before you start another.

Lesson 2: Creating a New Document

Template
A document set up for a specific purpose that you can use to create new documents. Templates usually include built-in settings for the page layout and appearance of text on the page, and may even include sample text, which you can use or replace.

Default
A setting that Office, or an Office application, assumes you want to use. You can change default settings if you want.

Each of the Office applications comes with built-in document types that are set up for a specific purpose. These documents types are called *templates*. You can use the templates to create new documents that are already configured with margins and other page elements, and may even contain sample text. For example, Word comes with templates for creating letters, memos, and forms (such as a fax cover sheet). Excel comes with templates for invoices, a loan manager, and so on.

All of the Office applications also come with Blank Document templates that you can use to create a general, or *default*, document type. For example, when you started Word and Excel in Lesson 1, each opened with a new, default document on-screen.

In this lesson, you use the New Office Document command to learn about the types of documents you can create with Office applications, and to create a new document.

To Create a New Document

1. **Click the Start button on the Windows taskbar.**

   The Start menu is displayed.

2. **Click New Office Document at the top of the Start menu.**

   The New Office Document dialog box is displayed, as shown in Figure 1.7. By default, the General tab is selected, and you see the icons for the blank documents.

If You Have Problems...

The New Office Document item is added to the Start menu when you install Microsoft Office. If it does not appear, consult your instructor.

If the General tab is not selected, click it.

Figure 1.7
In the New Office Document dialog box, click a tab to see other document types.

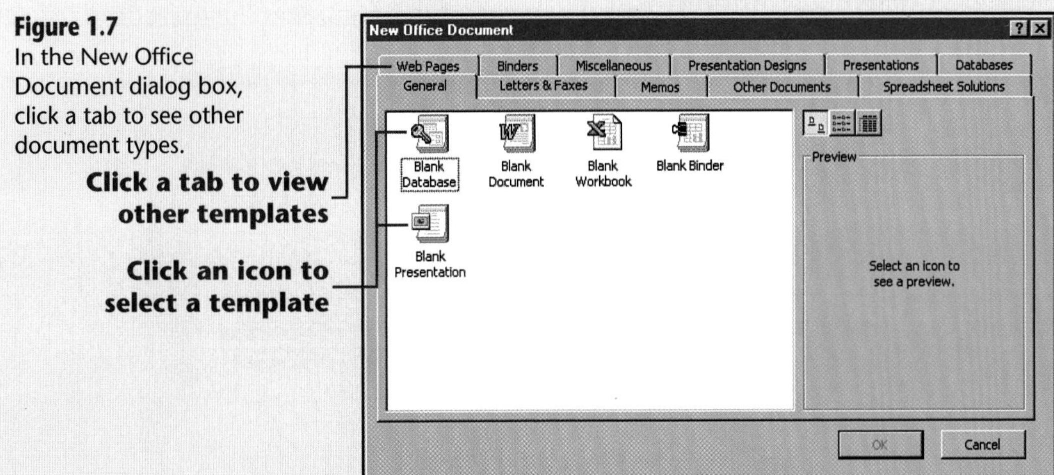

3 Click the Blank Presentation icon.

This selects the blank PowerPoint presentation type. A sample of the presentation is displayed in the Preview area.

4 Click the Presentation Designs tab at the top of the dialog box.

Icons representing the types of presentations you can create with Office appear in the dialog box. Most icons have samples available; when you click the icon, a sample of it is displayed in the Preview area.

5 Click the Spreadsheet Solutions tab.

You see icons representing the types of Excel worksheet documents you can create. Go ahead and explore the different documents. Don't worry if the templates in your New Office Document dialog box are different from the ones in the figures used to illustrate this book. The available templates depend on which templates you chose to install when you set up Office. You can go back and add templates using Office Setup at any time.

6 Click the Memos tab at the top of the dialog box, then click the Professional Memo icon.

A sample of the Professional Memo template is displayed in the preview area, as shown in Figure 1.8.

continues

To Create a New Document (continued)

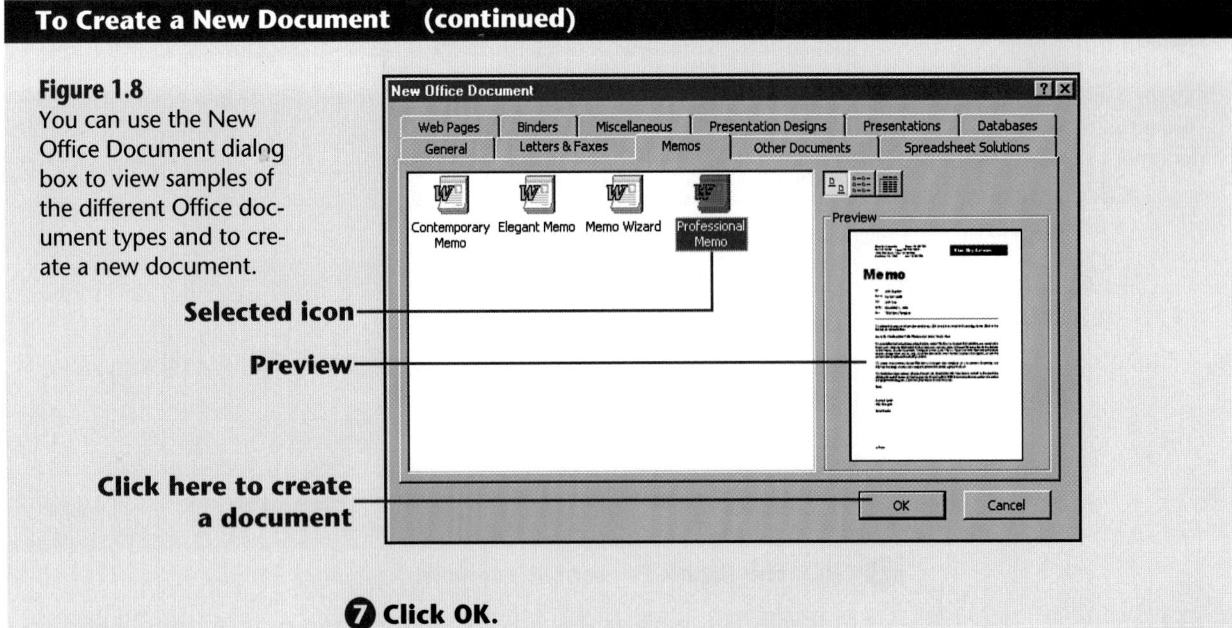

Figure 1.8
You can use the New Office Document dialog box to view samples of the different Office document types and to create a new document.

7 Click OK.

Word starts, and creates a new document based on the Professional Memo template, as shown in Figure 1.9. The sample text shows you where and what to type to complete the document. Leave the document open in Word. In the next lesson you learn how to save and close an Office document.

If You Have Problems...

Don't worry if the document on your screen doesn't look exactly the same as the one used in this book. The settings that control the size of the document and the way it is displayed on your screen may have been customized.

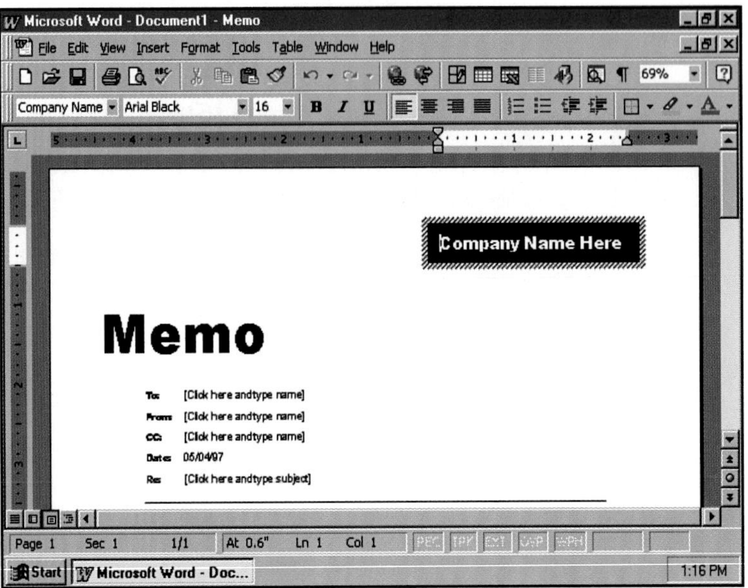

Figure 1.9
A Word document based on the Professional Memo template.

You can also create a new document in each Office application by choosing **N**ew from the **F**ile menu, or by clicking the New button on the Standard toolbar.

You may have noticed that some of the document icons in the New dialog box are labeled as *wizards*. You can use these template wizards to automatically create documents, including specific text. In Office applications, wizards are automated templates that lead you step by step through specific tasks: You answer questions or choose options, and the wizard performs the task. For example, with the Memo Wizard, Word prompts you to enter the name of the person the memo is going to as well as the topic and other information. When it creates the document, most of the text is filled in. You will have the chance to use wizards in many projects in this book. They are often the quickest and easiest way to accomplish specific tasks.

Lesson 3: Saving and Closing an Office Document

When you create documents in Office applications, the documents are stored in the computer's memory (RAM), which is only good for short-term storage because when you shut off the computer—or if it shuts off by accident because of a power failure, power surge, or other problem—everything stored in RAM is lost. To keep a document for future use, you must save it. When you save a document, it is stored in a file on your *hard disk* (also called the hard drive) inside the computer, or on a *floppy disk*. Once a document is saved, you can open it and use it again and again.

The steps for saving documents in Office applications are basically the same. Once you learn how to save a document in one application, you will be able to save a document in any application. In this lesson, you learn how to save a Word document and then close it.

To Save and Close an Office Document

1 With the document you created using the Professional Memo template open on your screen in Word, click File on the menu bar.

The **F**ile menu opens. As mentioned earlier, Office applications all have **F**ile menus.

2 Choose Save.

Save is the command that tells the application you want to store the document. Since this is the first time you are saving the document, the Save As dialog box is displayed, as shown in Figure 1.10.

In the Save As dialog box, choose the folder and disk where you want to store the file, and type a name for the new file. The suggested name is selected in the File **N**ame text box. By default, all Office

continues

To Learn Parts of the Screen (continued)

documents are stored in the My Documents folder. If any documents are already stored in the default folder, they appear listed in the dialog box. Your instructor may want you to store the documents you create in this book in a different folder, or on a floppy disk.

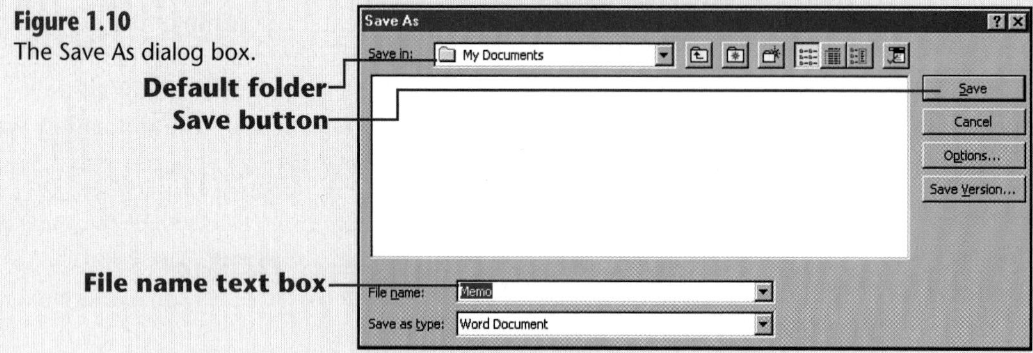

Figure 1.10
The Save As dialog box.

❸ **Type** `First Document`**.**

As soon as you begin to type, the characters replace the selected name in the File **N**ame text box. With Windows 95, you can give a file any name, using as many characters as you want, including spaces as well as upper- and lowercase letters.

❹ **Click the drop down arrow next to the Save In text box.**

A drop down list showing the disks and folders on your computer is displayed. You can select the folder or disk where you want to store the file. The default, My Documents folder, is appropriate, unless your instructor specifies a different location.

❺ **Click the Save In drop down arrow again.**

This closes the list without changing the name of the folder in the Save **I**n box. If your instructor wants you to store the file somewhere other than in the My Documents folder, click that location on this list. For example, to store the file on a floppy disk in drive A, click Drive A on this list. For more information, consult your instructor.

❻ **Click the Save button in the Save As dialog box.**

The First Document file is saved in the folder you selected. The document remains open on your screen. Now, try closing the document.

❼ **Open the File menu and choose Close.**

Word closes the document, leaving a blank Word document window open on your screen. If you have made any changes to the document, a message box is displayed, asking if you want to save the changes. Choose **Y**es. You have now learned how to save and close an Office document. You will find that you will use these commands in all of the Office 97 applications.

Keep Windows 95 open. In the next lesson, you learn how to open an existing document and save it with a new name.

The Save As dialog box only is displayed the first time you save a document, or if you choose the Save **A**s command from the **F**ile menu to save an existing document with a new name, as you learn in Lesson 4.

Once you have saved a new document, you can save it again quickly by clicking the Save button on the Standard toolbar or by pressing Ctrl+S.

To quickly close a document, click the document Close button on the right end of the menu bar, or on the right end of the document window title bar.

To close a document without saving it, simply choose **C**lose from the **F**ile menu, then choose **N**o when the application prompts you to save the changes.

Jargon Watch

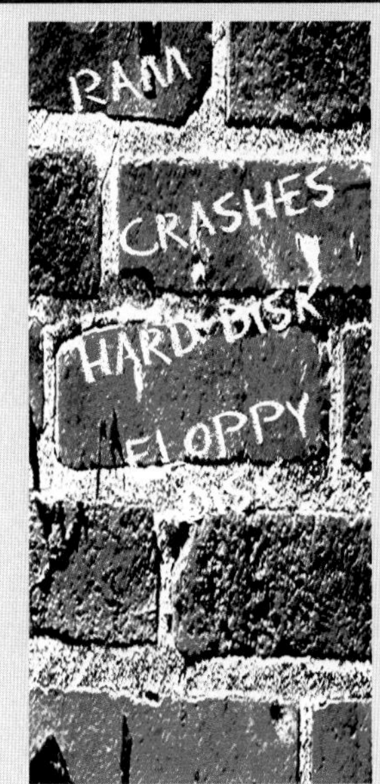

In this lesson, a number of technical terms have been used to describe how computers save information. **RAM** stands for *random-access memory*, which simply means the temporary storage space the computer uses for programs it's currently working with.

When a computer **crashes**, it means that an error—either with the software (a program or application) or with the hardware (any physical component, such as the power supply or disk drive)—has caused the computer to stop working. Everything stored in RAM is lost when a crash occurs. Remember, it's important to save your work to a **hard disk** or **floppy disk** frequently.

Floppy disks are small disks that you can carry around with you. They are usually 3.5-inch disks, but some older computers use 5.25-inch disks. Floppy disks are often used to keep backup copies of important information, or to transfer information from one computer to another. Although 3.5-inch floppies have a hard outer case, the disk inside it is flexible. Your hard disk (or hard drive) is made up of several rigid platters inside your computer that look similar to CDs. The bulk of the programs and information that your computer uses is stored on the computer's hard disk.

Lesson 4: Opening an Existing Document and Saving It with a New Name

One of the benefits of using a computer is that once a file is stored on a disk, you can work with it over and over again. For example, you can open a document to make corrections or changes, or to save it again with a new name. Throughout this book, you open existing documents, which you then save using different file names. Saving a document with a different name creates a copy, which you can use and modify without affecting the original file.

In this lesson, you learn how to open an existing file and save it with a new name.

To Open an Existing Document and Save It with a New Name

1 Click the Start button on the taskbar, then click Open Office Document on the Start menu.

The Open Office Document dialog box is displayed, as shown in Figure 1.11. All Office documents stored in the default folder appear listed in the dialog box.

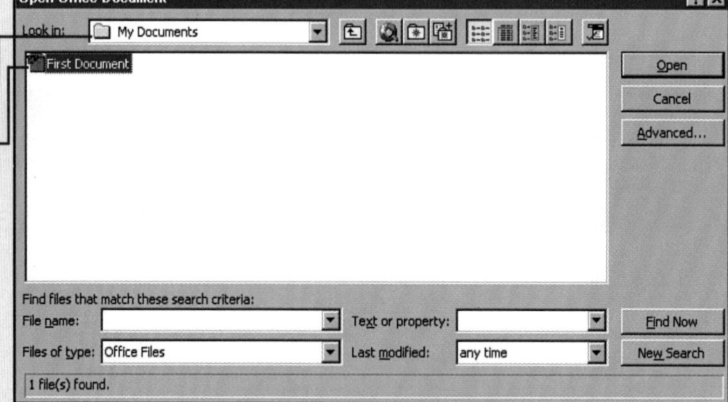

Figure 1.11 The Open Office Document dialog box.

2 Click the `First Document` file name to select it if it is not already selected.

You can open any file that appears in the dialog box.

If You Have Problems...

If the `First Document` file is not listed in the dialog box, it may be stored in a different folder. Ask your instructor where the file is stored (or refer to Step 4 and Step 5 in Lesson 3); then, click the drop down arrow next to the Look In drop down list, and choose that folder.

3 Click the Open button.

The `First Document` opens in Word, as shown in Figure 1.12. Notice the document name in the title bar. When you use the Open dialog box to open a file, the application associated with the selected file is launched at the same time if it is not already running. Now, try saving the document with a new name.

Figure 1.12
The `First Document` open in Word.

File name appears in title bar

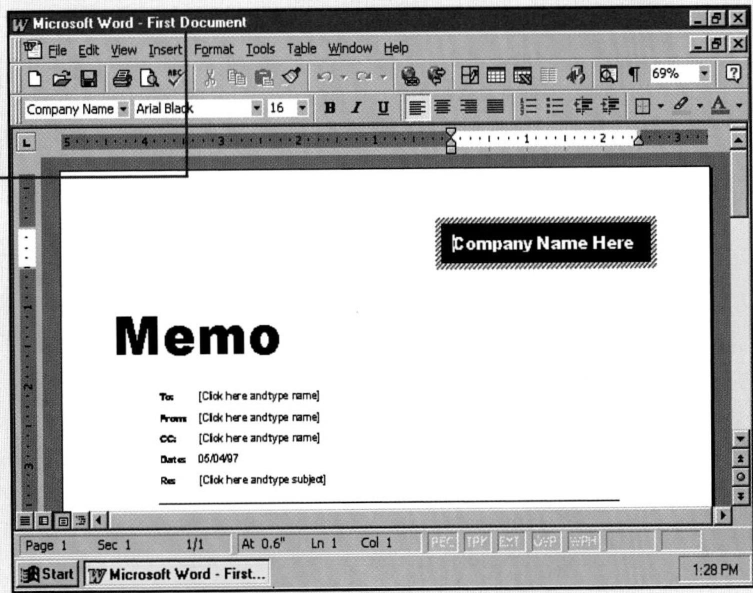

❹ **Open the File menu and choose Save As.**

The Save As dialog box is displayed. After a file is saved the first time, you use the Save As command to save it with a new name.

❺ **Type `Second Document`.**

The name replaces the current file name in the File Name text box.

❻ **Click the Save button in the Save As dialog box.**

Word saves a copy of the First Document in the My Documents folder with the name `Second Document`. The `Second Document` is displayed on your screen. Notice the file name in the title bar. The `First Document` is closed, and it remains unchanged and stored on the disk.

❼ **Open the File menu and choose the Exit command.**

This closes the `Second Document` file and the Word application. If prompted, choose **Y**es to save changes. Keep Windows 95 open to use in the next lesson, when you learn how to use the Microsoft Office Shortcut bar.

You can choose **O**pen on the **F**ile menu of any Office application to open the Open dialog box in that application. Only documents created with that application will be displayed, and only that application will be used to display the file. For example, to open a file in Word, choose File on Word's main menu bar, then choose **O**pen. Only Word documents are listed in the Open dialog box. Any document you select to open is displayed in Word.

In an application, click the Open button on the standard toolbar to quickly display the Open dialog box.

A list of recently opened files is displayed at the bottom of the **F**ile menu in Office applications. To quickly open a recently used file, click its name on the **F**ile menu.

You cannot use the Save **A**s command on the **F**ile menu to save a copy of an Access database with a new name. As you will learn in the Access projects of this book, database files are quite different from other types of files. To create a copy of an Access file with a new name, you must use the Windows file management features. For example, you can use the **E**dit menu in the Windows Explorer to **C**opy, **P**aste and Re**n**ame an Access file. For more information, consult your instructor.

Lesson 5: Using the Microsoft Office Shortcut Bar

To help you get the most out of Microsoft Office, use the Shortcut toolbar. The Microsoft Office Shortcut Bar provides buttons that enable you to quickly access some of the common Office features, including creating and opening documents. You can also use the Shortcut Bar to display other toolbars, including one that shows buttons for starting and switching to each of the Office applications.

If You Have Problems...

The Office Shortcut bar is not part of the typical Office installation. If it has not been installed on your computer, you can add it using Office Setup.

In this lesson you learn how to open the Office Shortcut Bar and display different toolbars within the Office Shortcut Bar.

To Use the Microsoft Office Shortcut Bar

1 Open the Start menu, slide the mouse pointer up until Programs is highlighted, then click Microsoft Office Shortcut Bar on the Programs menu.

The Microsoft Office Shortcut bar is started and displayed at the top of the Windows desktop, as shown in Figure 1.13. Remember, the toolbar on your computer may look different from the toolbar in the figures used to illustrate this book, depending on which Microsoft Office programs are installed and whether the toolbar has been customized.

If You Have Problems...

When you start the Microsoft Office Shortcut bar, Office may display a message asking if you would like to configure the Microsoft Office Shortcut bar to start automatically whenever Windows is started. Choose Yes to add the Shortcut bar to your Startup folder, so it appears whenever you start your computer. Choose No to keep it the way it is. Select the Please **D**o Not Ask Me This Question Again check box if you do not want the message to appear every time you start the Office Shortcut bar.

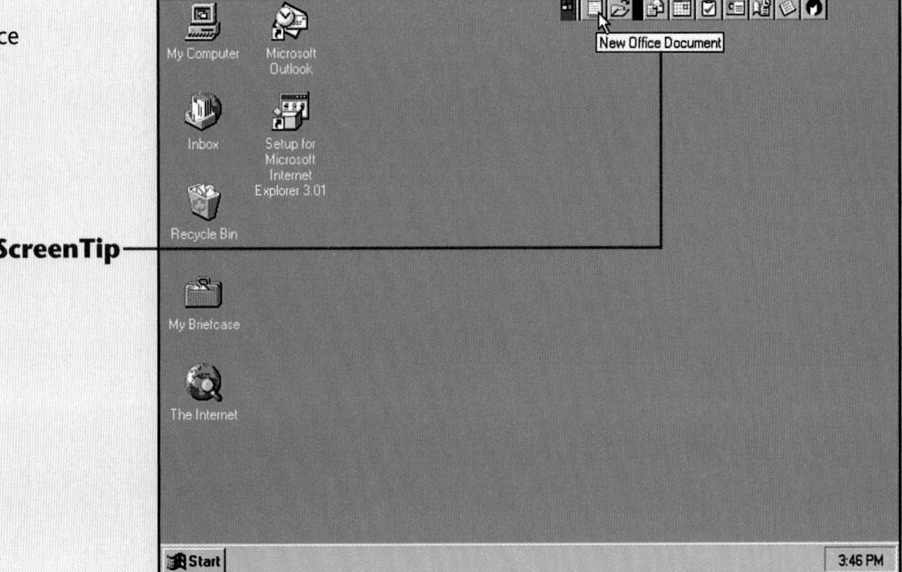

Figure 1.13 The Microsoft Office Shortcut bar.

2 With the mouse pointer, point to any icon on the Office Shortcut bar.

A ScreenTip is displayed, telling you the name of the button (see Figure 1.13). Whenever you point at an icon or button in an Office application, a ScreenTip is displayed.

If You Have Problems...

If a ScreenTip does not appear, click the Office Control icon at the left end of the Microsoft Office Shortcut Bar, and choose **C**ustomize from the menu that is displayed. In the Customize dialog box, click the View tab, then select the **S**how Tooltips check box and click OK.

3 Click the New Office Document button.

The New Office Document dialog box is displayed, just as it was when you selected the New Office Document command from the Start menu. You can use the buttons on the Office Shortcut bar to quickly execute common Office commands.

continues

To Use the Microsoft Office Shortcut Bar (continued)

4 Click the Cancel button in the New Office Document dialog box.

This closes the dialog box. Now, try customizing the buttons on the Office Shortcut toolbar.

5 Click the Office Control icon at the far left of the toolbar.

The Office Control menu is displayed, as shown in Figure 1.14. You can use the Control menu to customize the toolbar as well as to add or remove Office programs using Office Setup and to start Office Help.

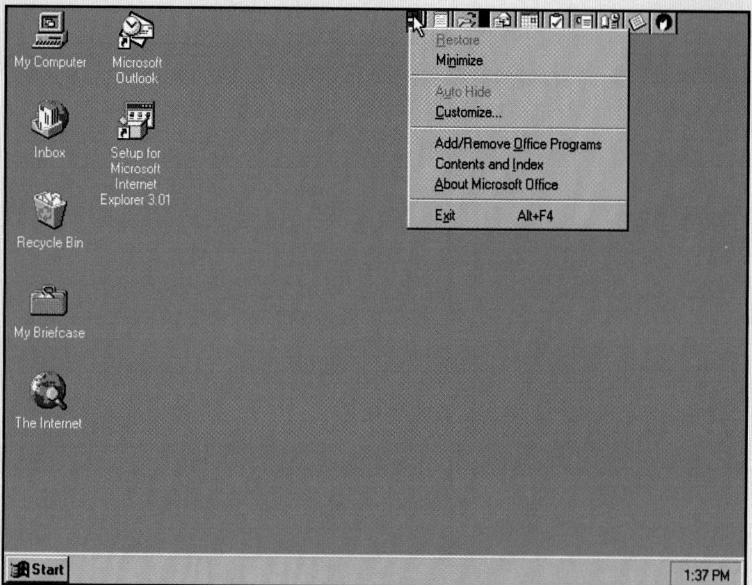

Figure 1.14 The Office Control menu.

6 Choose the Customize command.

The Customize dialog box is displayed, as shown in Figure 1.15. There are four pages in the Customize dialog box. The first, View, lets you change the appearance of the Shortcut bar. For example, you can change the background color and the size of the buttons. The second, Buttons, lets you choose the buttons you want displayed on the Shortcut bar. The third, Toolbars, lets you choose other Windows toolbars to include. The fourth, Settings, lets you change the default location of templates and files.

Figure 1.15
The Customize dialog box for the Office Shortcut bar.

Click a tab to change pages

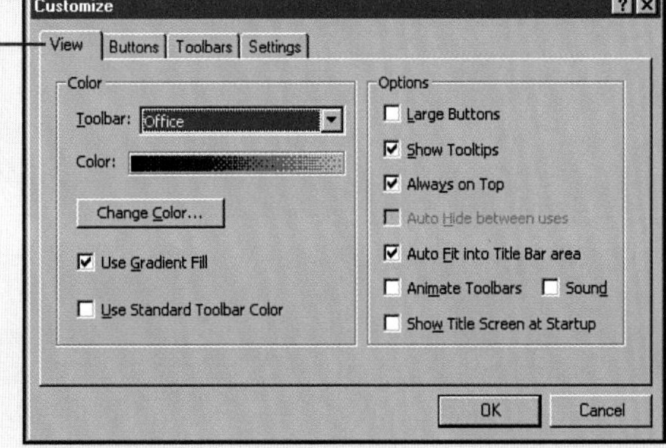

❼ **Click the Buttons tab at the top of the Customize dialog box.**

The Buttons page is displayed, as shown in Figure 1.16. A list of features and applications for which there are buttons available is displayed in the Show These Files as **B**uttons list. Use the scroll arrows to scroll down and see all of the available items. If a check mark appears in the checkbox beside an item, the item has a button on the toolbar. To add a button to the toolbar, click the checkbox so a check mark appears. To remove a button, click the checkbox to clear the check mark.

Figure 1.16
The Buttons page of the Customize dialog box.

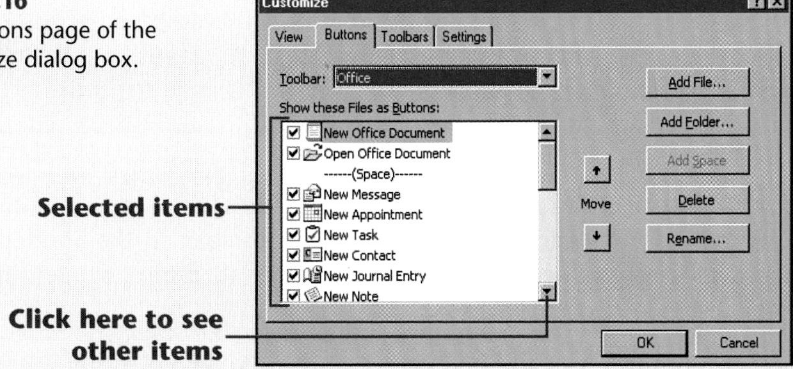

❽ **Click the checkbox beside the New Message item.**

Clicking a check box that has a check mark in it clears the check mark. Office removes the New Message button from the Office Shortcut bar.

❾ **Clear the check marks from the new Appointment, New Task, New Contact, New Journal Entry, and New Note check boxes.**

Office removes the corresponding buttons from the Shortcut bar. Now, add the buttons for the Office applications you use throughout this book.

❿ **Click the checkboxes beside Microsoft Word, Microsoft Excel, Microsoft PowerPoint, Microsoft Access, and Microsoft Binder.**

continues

To Learn Parts of the Screen (continued)

Clicking a blank checkbox marks it with a check mark. Office adds the buttons corresponding to the Office applications to the Shortcut bar. You can add and remove any of the buttons in the list, depending on which features you think you will use most often. Of course, if you find you need a button that you removed, you can easily come back and add it.

If You Have Problems...

Do not delete items from the list in the Buttons page of the Customize dialog box! If you do not want an item to appear on the toolbar, simply deselect it. If you select the button and choose **D**elete, you will remove the application files from your hard disk, and you will have to reinstall the program. If a message box is displayed asking you if you are sure you want to delete a button, select **N**o!

11 Click OK.

This closes the Customize dialog box. The Microsoft Office Shortcut toolbar now has buttons for starting the Office applications you use in this book. Simply click the button to start the application, or to switch to it if it is already running.

Leave the Office Shortcut bar open on the desktop. In the next lesson, you learn how to use the Office Assistant to get help while using an Office application.

If you want all of the programs on your Programs menu to appear on the Office Shortcut bar, you can display the Programs toolbar on the Shortcut bar, too. Right-click a blank space on the Shortcut bar to display a menu of available toolbars, then click Programs.

By default, the Office Shortcut bar fits inside the title bar at the top of the desktop. You can, however, move it anywhere on the screen. Open the Office menu and choose Customize. In the Customize dialog box, click the Auto **F**it into Title Bar Area check box to deselect it. You can then drag the toolbar anywhere you want, and resize it. To change back, select the Auto **F**it into Title Bar Area check box, then drag the toolbar back to the title bar area.

You can rearrange the buttons on the Shortcut bar using the Move up and Move down arrows on the Buttons page of the Customize dialog box. Simply select the button you want to move, then click the arrow to move it. To insert a blank space before a button, select the button, then click the Add **S**pace button in the Customize dialog box.

If you want the Microsoft Office Shortcut Bar to appear whenever you start Windows, you can add it to your Startup folder.

To close the Office Shortcut bar, click the Shortcut bar Control icon, and choose E**x**it from the menu.

Lesson 6: Getting Help

By now, you have probably realized that you may run into problems as you work with your computer and Office. If you find that you need a quick solution to a problem, you can use any one of Office's help features. Help is available for Office, as well as for each of the Office applications. For example, you can use the Help Contents or Index for information about an Office feature, such as the Shortcut bar. When you are working in a document, you can use the Office Assistant to find the answer to a specific question, or you can use the What's This? pointer to display a description of any feature on the screen.

In this lesson, you use the Office Assistant to learn more about getting help while working with Excel.

To Get Help

1 Click the Excel button on the Office Shortcut bar.

Excel starts. If you do not have an Office Shortcut bar, click the Start button on the taskbar, highlight **P**rograms on the Start menu, then choose Microsoft Excel from the Programs menu.

2 Click Help on the menu bar.

The **H**elp menu opens to display a number of options that you can use to get help information. Every Office application has a Help menu.

3 Choose the Microsoft Excel Help command.

The Office Assistant appears. It should look similar to the one shown in Figure 1.17, although it may not be exactly the same. Each time Office Assistant opens, it displays a balloon listing information it thinks you need to complete the current task. If it can't tell what you are trying to do, it suggests that you type a question and then click Search.

continues

To Get Help (continued)

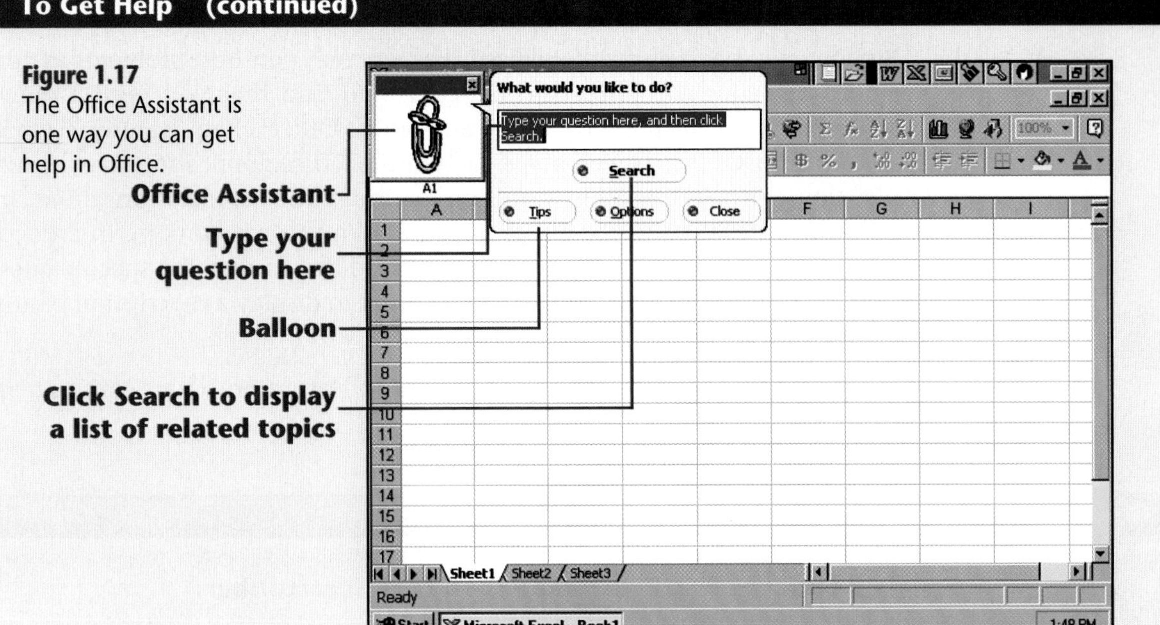

Figure 1.17
The Office Assistant is one way you can get help in Office.

If You Have Problems...

Sometimes the Office Assistant opens offering a list of topics because it tries to figure out what you need help with before you actually ask. If your Office Assistant opens looking different from the one in Figure 1.17, don't worry; the steps work the same.

4 Type `Get Help`.

As soon as you begin typing, the characters replace the highlighted text in the Office Assistant balloon.

5 Click the Search button in the Office Assistant balloon.

Office Assistant displays a new balloon listing topics related to the question you type, as shown in Figure 1.18. You can use the options in the balloon to select a topic, type a different question, display more topics, display tips or options, or close the Office Assistant without getting any help.

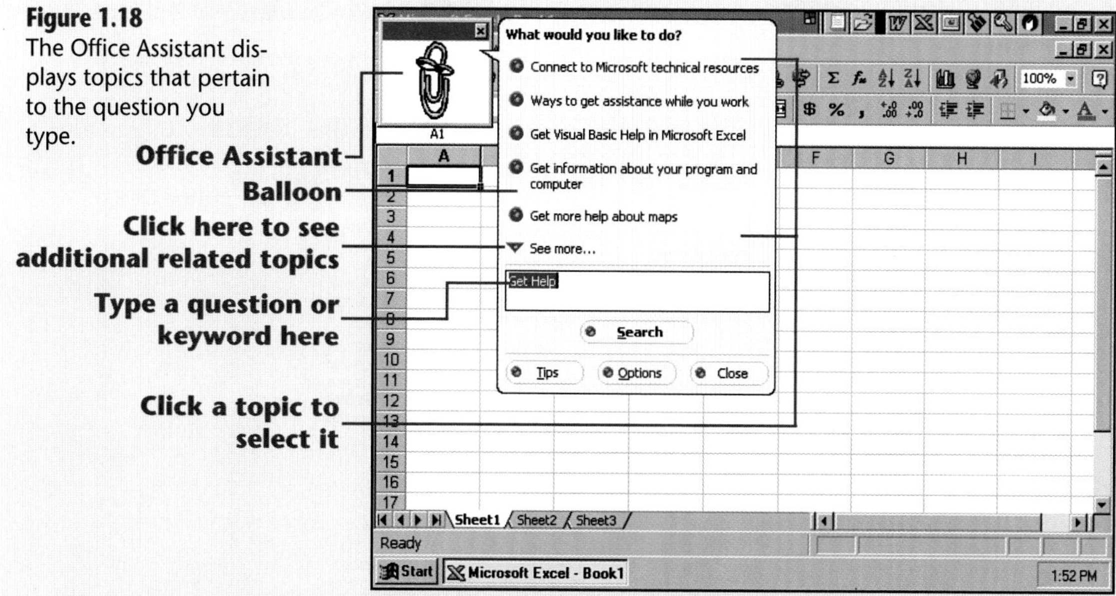

Figure 1.18
The Office Assistant displays topics that pertain to the question you type.

If You Have Problems...

If Office Assistant can't find topics related to the question you type, a balloon appears telling you so. Check to be sure you typed the question correctly, or try being more specific and then click Search again.

6 Click See More, then click the topic Get Help, Tips, and Messages Through the Office Assistant.

The Excel Help program starts, and a Help topic window is displayed on your screen, as shown in Figure 1.19. This window provides information about the many ways you can use the Office Assistant. Every Office application has a Help program. Notice the Help program button on the taskbar. You can leave the Help program window open or minimized while you work.

continues

To Get Help (continued)

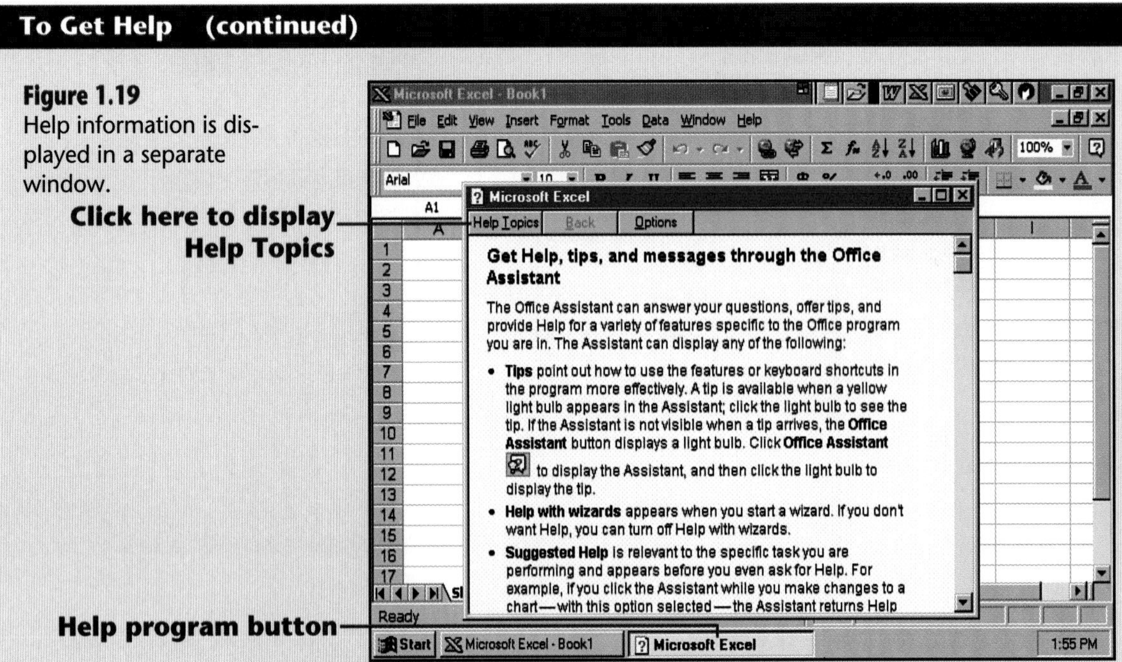

Figure 1.19
Help information is displayed in a separate window.

❼ **Click the Help Topics button in the Help window.**

The Help Topics: Microsoft Excel dialog box is displayed (see Figure 1.20). Here you can choose from three functions to help find the information you need: Contents, which displays a list of general topics; Index, which displays a comprehensive, alphabetical list of all topics; and Find, which enables you to search through all topics for a word or phrase.

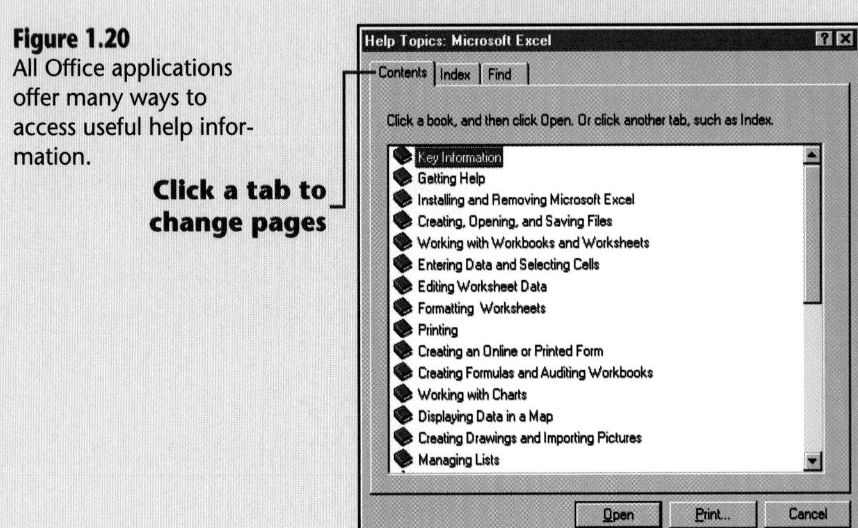

Figure 1.20
All Office applications offer many ways to access useful help information.

❽ **Click the Contents tab to make sure the Contents page is displayed.**

Clicking the Contents tab ensures that the list of general help topics is displayed (see Figure 1.20). The help information in the Contents tab is similar to a book with chapters: You open the chapter and read the pages.

9 In the list of topics, click Getting Help and then click the Open button.

This opens the topic Getting Help. Specific tasks related to getting help appear in the topic list, as shown in Figure 1.21.

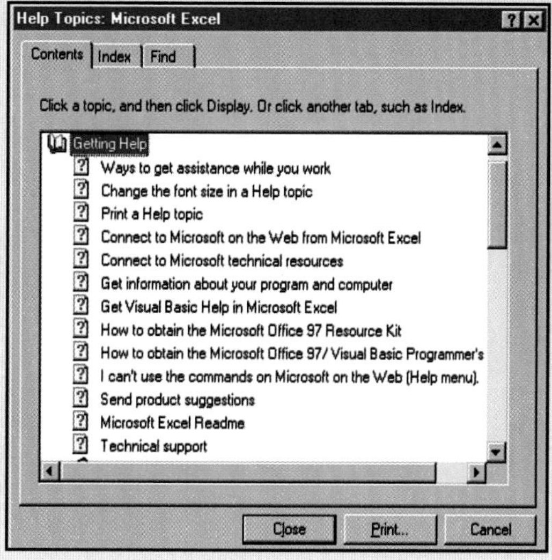

Figure 1.21
You can display any topic for more information.

Hypertext
Text that you can click to access additional information in another file. Often, hypertext appears in a different color from the surrounding text, and is underlined. When you point at hypertext, the mouse pointer appears as a hand with a pointing finger.

10 Click the topic Ways to Get Assistance While You Work, then click the Display button.

The Help program starts, and a Help screen is displayed, providing access to information about how to get assistance while you work in Excel (see Figure 1.22). Some help topics, like this one, provide at-a-glance information as well as *hypertext* labels that you can click for more information.

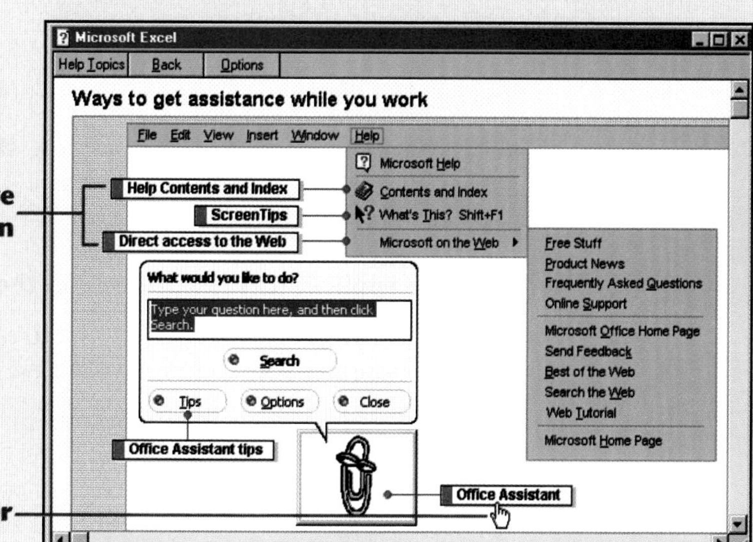

Figure 1.22
In some Help screens, you can click labels for additional information.

continues

To Get Help (continued)

⑪ **Click the label Office Assistant.**

A help box appears, providing information about how to use the Office Assistant while you work, as shown in Figure 1.23. Notice that when you move the mouse pointer to a label, the pointer becomes a hand with a pointing finger. This mouse pointer indicates that you are pointing at hypertext and that more information is available. Click any hypertext label on the Help screen to get information about using that feature.

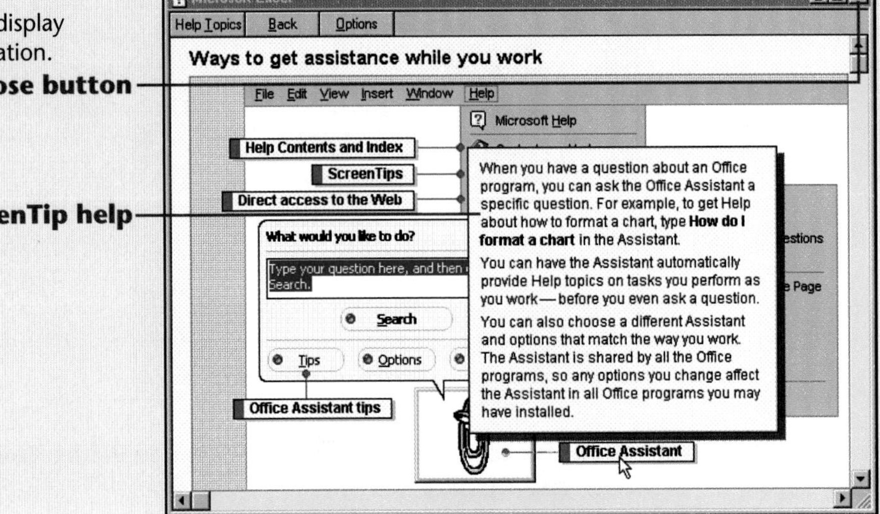

Figure 1.23
Use hypertext to display additional information.

⑫ **Click the Close button at the right end of the Help topic window's title bar.**

This closes Help. Excel is still open, and the Office Assistant is still displayed, although the balloon is not open.

⑬ **Click the Office Assistant.**

The balloon opens, so you can type a question.

⑭ **Click the Close button in the balloon, then click the Close button on the Office Assistant title bar.**

Office Assistant closes.

⑮ **Click the application Close button on the Excel window title bar.**

This closes Excel. If you are prompted to save the changes you have made, choose **N**o; you do not have to save the Excel document.

You have now completed the lessons in this project. If you have completed your session on the computer, close Windows 95 before turning off the computer. Otherwise, continue with the section "Checking Your Skills" at the end of this project.

To quickly open the Office Assistant in any Office Application, press F1 at any time or click the Office Assistant button on the Standard toolbar.

To change the icon used to represent the Office Assistant, click the **O**ptions button in any Office Assistant balloon, choose the **G**allery tab, and click **N**ext to display a series of available icons. Select from The Dot, The Genius, Hoverbot, Mother Nature, Power Pup, Scribble (the cat), Office Logo, and Shakespeare, then click OK.

To quickly open the Help Topics dialog box in any Office application, choose **H**elp, **C**ontents and Index. To print any help topic window, choose **O**ptions, **P**rint in the Help topic window.

To get help for Office, click the Office Control button on the Shortcut bar, and select Contents and **I**ndex from the Control menu.

To use the What's This? pointer in an application to display a ScreenTip about anything on the screen, choose **H**elp, What's **T**his, or press Shift+F1. When the pointer resembles a question mark with an arrow, point at the item for which you need information.

Checking Your Skills

True/False

For each of the following, check *T* or *F* to indicate whether the statement is true or false.

__T __F **1.** Six applications make up the Microsoft Office 97 Professional software suite.

__T __F **2.** The Office applications share many common features and screen elements.

__T __F **3.** Microsoft Word 97, Excel 97, PowerPoint 97, and Access 97 all have a **F**ile menu.

__T __F **4.** You can click the Office Shortcut Bar to close an Office application.

__T __F **5.** When more than one application is open at the same time, the active application runs in the background.

__T __F **6.** By default, the Microsoft Office applications you have installed on your computer appear listed on the Start menu.

__T __F **7.** You use the Office Assistant to switch between open applications.

__T __F **8.** To make a copy of an Office document, you can save an existing document with a new name.

__T __F **9.** If you want the Office Shortcut bar to be displayed whenever you start Windows 95, you can add it to your Startup folder.

__T __F **10.** When the mouse pointer touches hypertext, it changes to look like a hand with a pointing finger.

Multiple Choice

Circle the letter of the correct answer for each of the following questions.

1. What can you do to get help while using Office or an Office application?
   - **a.** Press F1.
   - **b.** Click the Office Assistant button on the Office Standard toolbar.
   - **c.** Open the **H**elp menu and choose **H**elp Topics.
   - **d.** All the above
2. Which command do you use to open an existing document in an Office application?
   - **a.** **F**ile, **O**pen
   - **b.** **F**ile, **D**ocument Open
   - **c.** **O**pen, **E**xisting File
   - **d.** **O**pen, **D**ocument
3. What can you use to create a new Office document?
   - **a.** Window
   - **b.** Text
   - **c.** Template
   - **d.** Presentation
4. The **F**ile menu contains which of the following menu items in all the Microsoft Office applications?
   - **a.** **S**tart
   - **b.** **P**rograms
   - **c.** E**x**it
   - **d.** Do**c**ument
5. On the taskbar, how does the button for the active application appear?
   - **a.** In italics
   - **b.** Pressed in
   - **c.** With a shadow
   - **d.** With a double-line border
6. Which Office application does not have a **F**ile, Save **A**s command for saving an existing document with a new name?
   - **a.** Microsoft Word
   - **b.** Microsoft Excel
   - **c.** Microsoft Powerpoint
   - **d.** Microsoft Access
7. What Office application should you use to create a text-based document?
   - **a.** Microsoft Word
   - **b.** Microsoft Excel
   - **c.** Microsoft Powerpoint
   - **d.** Microsoft Access
8. What Office application should you use to create a budget spreadsheet?
   - **a.** Microsoft Word
   - **b.** Microsoft Excel
   - **c.** Microsoft Powerpoint
   - **d.** Microsoft Access
9. What Office application should you use to create a slide show presentation?
   - **a.** Microsoft Word
   - **b.** Microsoft Excel
   - **c.** Microsoft Powerpoint
   - **d.** Microsoft Access
10. What button do you click to quickly close an application?
    - **a.** The Control button
    - **b.** The Minimize button
    - **c.** The Close button
    - **d.** The Shut Down button

Completion

In the blank provided, write the correct answer for each of the following statements.

1. To start an Office application, click its name on the ____________ menu.
2. To switch to an open application, click its button on the ___________ at the bottom of the screen.
3. Ask the ________ for help on using any Office application.
4. You can customize the ___________ to include buttons for all of the Office applications.
5. You can preview a sample document before you create it in the __________ dialog box.
6. The application name appears on the ____________ bar in every Office application.
7. You can create new documents that include formatting and sometimes text by selecting one of the built-in document ___________ that come with Microsoft Office.
8. Click on a ____________ label to display additional information about a help topic.
9. When you point at a toolbar button, Microsoft Office displays a ___________ providing the button's name or function.
10. Files are stored in your computer's __________ until you use the **F**ile, **S**ave command to store them on a disk.

Applying Your Skills

The following exercises enable you to practice the skills you have learned in this project. Take a few minutes to work through these exercises now.

Practice

1. Starting and Switching Applications

Now that you have been introduced to the basics of using the Microsoft Office applications, use these skills to continue to explore the programs. For this study, you practice opening, switching, and closing the different applications.

To Start, Switch, and Close Applications

1. Start Windows, and use the **P**rograms menu to open Excel.
2. Leave Excel open, and start PowerPoint.
3. Switch back to Excel, and close it.
4. Start Word.
5. Switch to PowerPoint, cancel the open dialog box if necessary, and close PowerPoint.
6. Start Access.
7. Switch to Word and close it.
8. Cancel the open dialog box in Access, and close Access.

2. Creating and Saving a New Document

Creating and saving documents is one of the most important skills·you can master. In this exercise, explore the available spreadsheet document templates, then create and save a blank Excel workbook.

To Create and Save a New Document

1. Use the New Office Document command on the Start menu to open the new dialog box.
2. Click the Spreadsheet Solutions page tab.
3. Preview the Purchase Order document template.
4. Click the General page tab.
5. Create a new document based on the Blank Workbook template.
6. In Excel, click **F**ile on the menu bar to open the **F**ile menu.
7. On the **F**ile menu, click **S**ave.
8. In the Save As dialog box, type the name `First Workbook` in the File **N**ame text box.
9. From the Save **I**n drop-down list, select the folder or file where you want to save the document.
10. Click **S**ave.
11. Close the First Workbook document.
12. Close Excel.

3. Opening a Document and Saving It with a New Name

Opening existing documents so you can work with them is possibly the greatest benefit of using a computer. Saving a document with a new name is one way to ensure that the original document remains unchanged, even if you want to edit the copy. In this exercise, practice opening a document, then save it with a new name.

To Open a Document and Save It With a New Name

1. In Windows 95, click the Start button, then click Open Office Document.
2. In the Open dialog box, click the file `First Workbook` that you created in the previous exercise.
3. Click **O**pen.
4. In Excel, click **F**ile on the menu bar to open the **F**ile menu.
5. On the **F**ile menu, click Save **A**s.
6. In the Save As dialog box, type the name `Second Workbook` in the File **N**ame text box.
7. From the Save **I**n drop-down list, select the folder or file where you want to save the document.
8. Click **S**ave.
9. Close the `Second Workbook` document.
10. Close Excel.

4. Customizing the Microsoft Office Shortcut Bar

Now that you know more about Office and the Office applications, customize the Microsoft Office Shortcut bar so that the commands and programs you need most often will always be easily accessible.

To Customize the Microsoft Office Shortcut Bar

1. Start Windows, and open the Office Shortcut Bar.
2. See how it looks if you customize the Shortcut bar to use large buttons.
3. Change back to the small buttons.
4. Add the Programs toolbar to the Shortcut bar.
5. Remove the Programs toolbar from the Shortcut bar.
6. Add a space between Microsoft PowerPoint and Microsoft Binder buttons on the Shortcut bar.
7. Move the Microsoft PowerPoint button up so that it is displayed to the left of the Microsoft Access button.

5. Using the Office Assistant

When you have a question about a feature you are using in any Office application, you can get answers quickly by using the Office Assistant or another Help feature. In this exercise, you practice using the Office Assistant to get help.

To Use the Office Assistant

1. Start Microsoft Word using either the Programs menu or the Office Shortcut bar.
2. Click **H**elp on the menu bar.
3. Click Microsoft Word **H**elp on the **H**elp menu.
4. In the Office Assistant balloon, type `Save a document`.
5. Click **S**earch.
6. From the list of topics displayed in the Office Assistant balloon, click Save a Document.
7. Scroll down to the bottom of the Help window so you can see if there are any hypertext links.
8. In the last paragraph, click the word Internet that appears in green with a dotted underline.
9. Click any of the other hypertext links in the window that you want.
10. Close the Help window.
11. Close the Office Assistant.
12. Close Microsoft Word.

Challenge

The following challenges enable you to use your problem-solving skills. Take time to work through these exercises now.

1. Exploring the Business Documents Available in Office

You can use Microsoft Office to create many different types of business documents. In this study, you explore the built-in document templates that are available in Office.

To Explore the Business Documents Available in Office

1. Start Windows 95.
2. Open the New dialog box.
3. Use the page tabs to display the different document templates that are available in Office.
4. Preview at least one document on each page.
5. Make a note of the different types of documents you can create with each Office application.
6. When you are done, click Cancel to close the New dialog box without creating any documents.

2. Planning Microsoft Office Documents to Help Your Business

Once you are familiar with the types of documents available in Office, you can begin planning for your small business. For this study, use a pencil and paper to make of list of the types of Microsoft Office documents you believe you will need to run a small business effectively.

To Plan Microsoft Office Documents to Help Your Business

1. Think about the kind of Microsoft Office documents you need to create to help run a small business.
2. Make a list of all the types of documents you think you will use. Consider all the things you need to organize and communicate in writing to keep your business running smoothly.
3. Organize your list of documents according to the Microsoft Office application you will use to create them.
4. Note why you think that application is appropriate for creating that kind of document.

3. Creating and Saving Office Documents

Once you decide which documents you think will help you the most, use Office to create and save at least three of them.

To Create and Save Office Documents

1. Start Windows.
2. Create a new letter document using one of the Letter templates. Save the document with the name `Business Letter`.
3. Create a new marketing plan presentation. Save the document with the name `Marketing Presentation`.
4. Create a fax cover sheet document. Save the document with the name `Customer Fax`.
5. Close all open files and applications and then shut down Windows.

4. Opening and Saving Copies of Your Office Documents

Time is a valuable commodity in running a small business. You can save time by copying existing documents and then modifying the copies to create new documents. In this exercise, open the documents you created in the previous exercise and save them with new names.

To Open and Save Copies of Your Office Documents

1. Open the document `Business Letter` and save it with the name `Employee Letter`.
2. Open the document `Marketing Presentation` and save it with the name `Training Presentation`.
3. Open the document `Customer Fax` and save it with the name `Supplier Fax`.
4. Close all open documents.
5. Close all open applications.

5. Customizing Office to Suit Your Business

In this study, customize the Office Shortcut bar and the Office Assistant to reflect your small business. You can establish an identity by using colors and icons on-screen as well as in your documents. Also, you can insure that Office is set up to best suit the way your business works.

To Customize Office to Suit Your Business

1. Make sure the Office Shortcut bar displays buttons for all of the applications and features you plan to use most frequently. For example you may want to add the Windows Explorer in addition to the Microsoft Office applications.
2. Change the color of the Office Shortcut bar to one that you think reflects the attitude of your small business. For example, if your business is a garden shop, you may want to use yellow or even pink. If your business is an investment consulting service, you may want to use gray or deep blue.
3. Select the animated graphic image you want to use as the Office Assistant from the Office Assistant Gallery. (Hint: click the **O**ptions button in the Office Assistant balloon.) For example, if your business is a pet shop, you may want to use Scribble (the cat) or the Power Pup. If you run a book shop, you may want to use William Shakespeare.
4. Review the options set for the Office Assistant to make sure the ones you need are selected, and that the ones you don't need are not selected. For example, if you have a small office where people work close together, you may not want the Office Assistant to use sounds.
5. When you are done, close all open applications.

Project 2

Working with Word Documents

Editing a Letter

In this project, you learn how to:

- Open an Existing Document
- Move around in a Document
- Correct Text
- Insert New Text
- Print a Document

Why Would I Do This?

Now that you have become familiar with starting and exiting the Microsoft Office 97 applications, it's time to put the applications to work for you. One of the most useful functions available to personal computer users is word processing. Word 97 is the word processor portion of Microsoft Office 97.

Using the sample letter and instructions provided in this project, you work through the steps for opening an existing document and moving around in the document. You then make necessary corrections, save changes, and print the final result.

Lesson 1: Opening an Existing Document

Supplied for you is an existing letter containing basic information. You now want to make some corrections and changes.

Now try opening the existing letter.

To Open an Existing Document

1 If Word is not already running on your system, start the program as described in Project 1.

2 On the Standard toolbar in Word, click the Open tool.

The Open dialog box is displayed, as shown in Figure 2.1. (You can also open this dialog box by choosing **F**ile, **O**pen.)

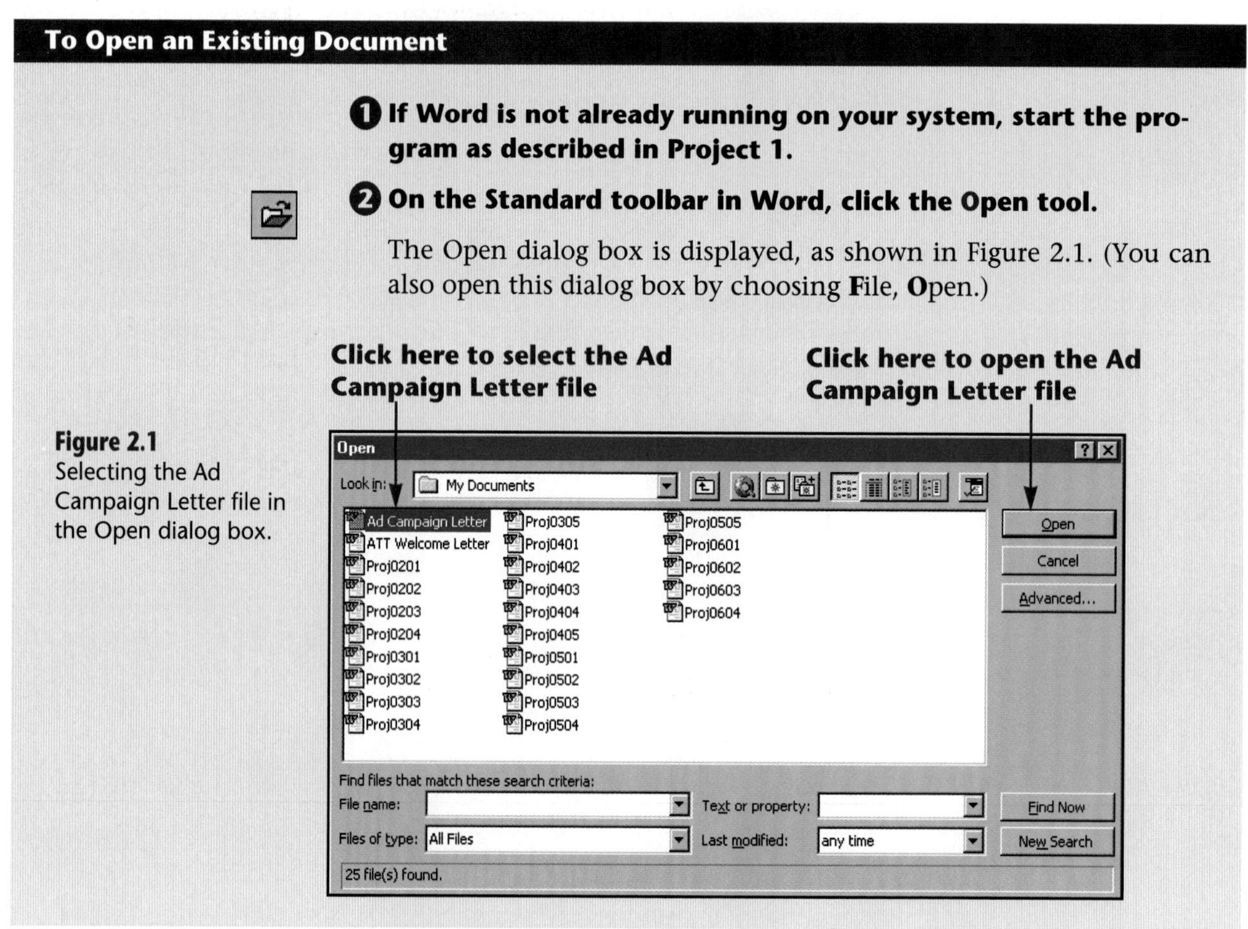

Figure 2.1
Selecting the Ad Campaign Letter file in the Open dialog box.

3 Click `Ad Campaign Letter` in the file list.

Clicking a file name selects it so that you can take action on it. In this case, the action you take is to open the file.

If you have problems...

If you don't see the file in the Open dialog box, try scrolling through the list. If you don't find the file, it's probably on another drive or in another folder. Make sure that you are looking at the correct drive and folder.

4 Choose Open.

Word places the letter in a document window with the file name, `Ad Campaign Letter`, displayed in the title bar (see Figure 2.2). Keep `Ad Campaign Letter` open because you continue to work with it for the rest of this project.

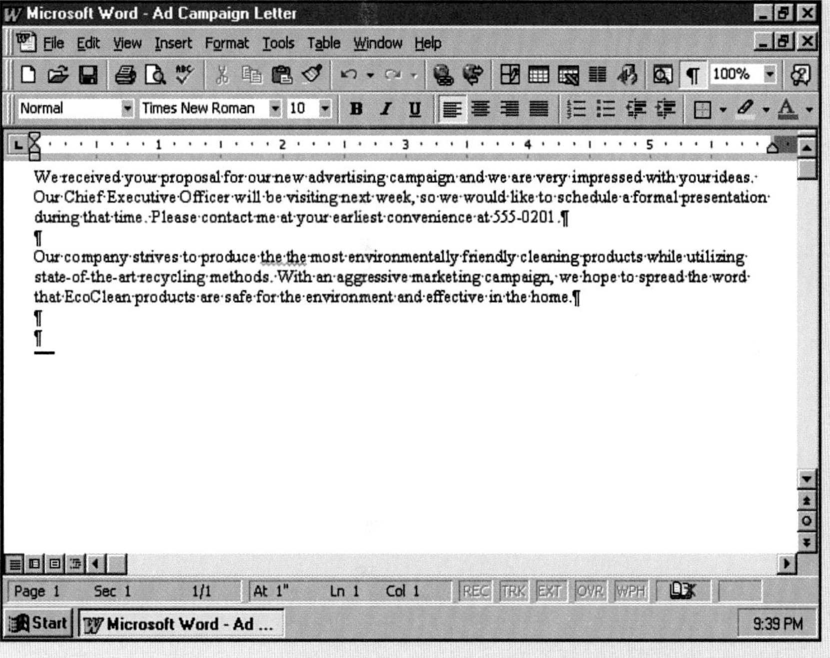

Figure 2.2
Your letter open in a document window.

In the Open dialog box, instead of selecting the name of the document and choosing **O**pen, you have another option to open a file. You can simply double-click the document icon in the list. You can use this technique to select items in most dialog boxes.

There are several alternatives for starting Word and opening an existing document. First, you can use Explorer (or My Computer) to locate the file you want to open. Double-click the file icon and Windows automatically starts the originating program (in this case, Word) and opens the document. Second, you can use the Open Office Document option on the Start menu. Here again, you have the opportunity to browse for the file. Double-click the file icon to start Word and open the document. Finally, you can choose from a list of recently opened files at the bottom of the **F**ile menu. Choosing a file from this list is much faster than browsing through your system to find it. Depending on how your system is set up, you can have from 4–9 files in the list.

Lesson 2: Moving around in a Document

To make changes and corrections quickly and easily, you need to learn the various ways of moving around in a document. For example, you can use either the mouse or the keyboard to move the insertion point in Word. Table 2.1 (following this lesson) shows useful keyboard shortcuts for moving around in a document.

The Ad Campaign Letter file should be open on your screen and ready to edit. Practice moving around in the letter by using both the mouse and the keyboard now.

To Move around in a Document

1 In `Ad Campaign Letter`, press Ctrl+End.

This action moves the insertion point to the end of the document (see Figure 2.3).

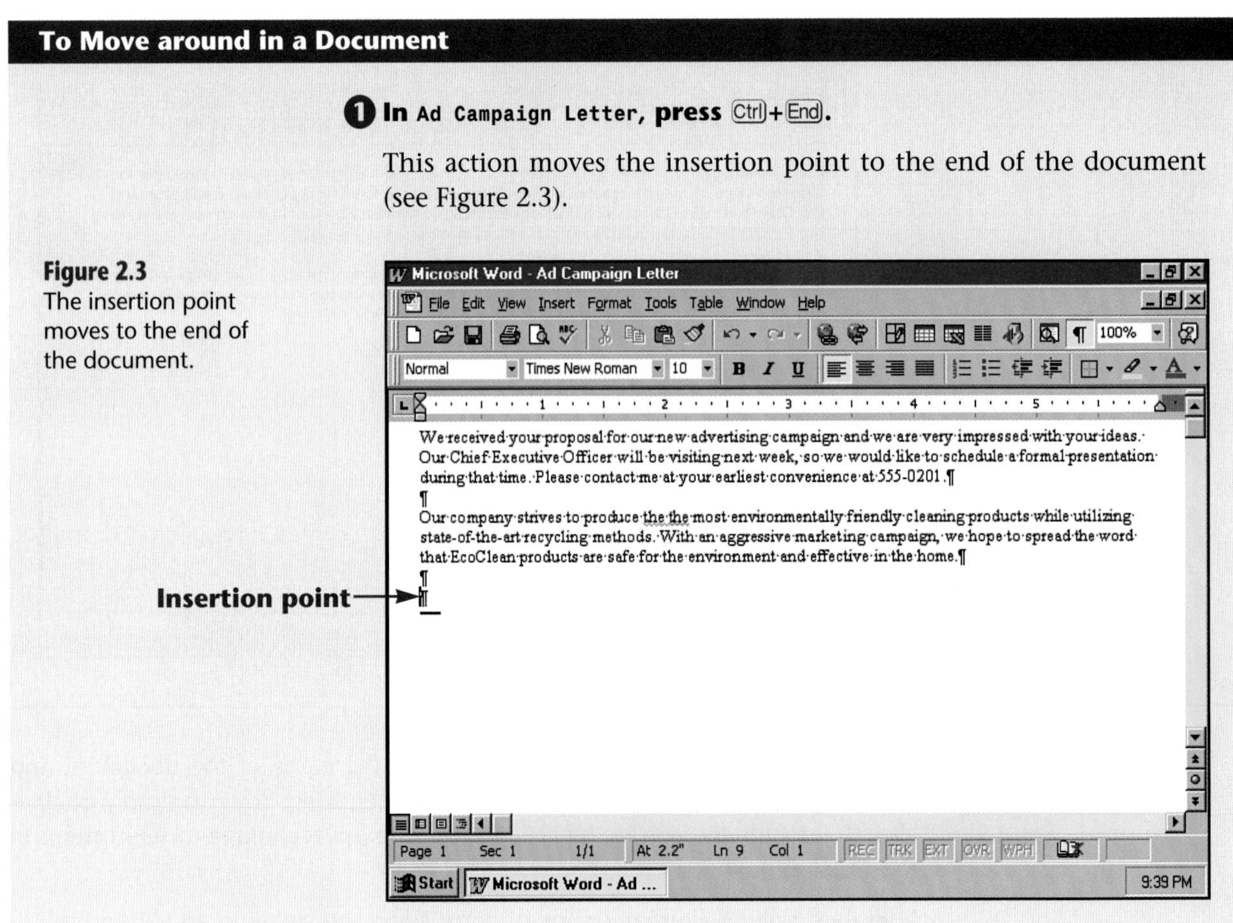

Figure 2.3
The insertion point moves to the end of the document.

2 Position the mouse pointer between the `2` and the `0` in the phone number `555-0201`, and then click the left mouse button.

When the mouse pointer is shaped like an I-beam, you can use it to place the insertion point anywhere in the document window. If you type any new text or make any changes, this is where they will go.

3 In the vertical scroll bar, click the area between the scroll box and the bottom scroll arrow.

This action scrolls the document down one screen at a time to the end of the document; you can scroll up or down in this way. You may be surprised to see that you have a virtually blank document window, but don't panic. You have simply moved to the very end of the document (see Figure 2.4). Keep in mind, however, that the insertion point has not moved. It remains in the phone number, where you last positioned it.

Figure 2.4
The end of the Ad Campaign Letter.

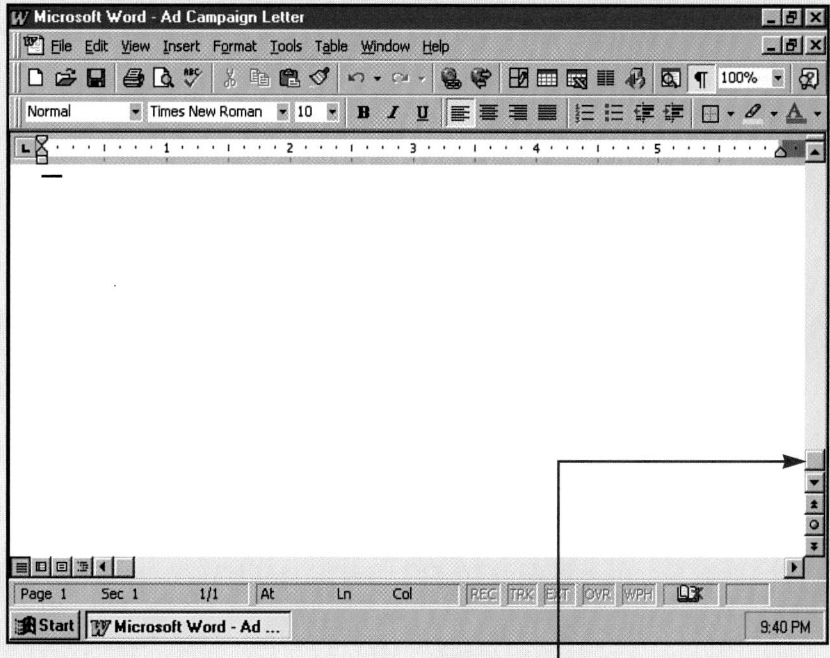

4 Click the scroll box and, while holding the mouse button down without letting go, drag the box up to the top of the scroll bar.

This action scrolls the document back into view. Now practice using the keyboard to move the insertion point. Again, notice that the insertion point has not moved; it's exactly where you left it earlier.

5 Press ↓ three times.

Pressing ↓ moves the insertion point down one line at a time, so the insertion point should now be in the second line of the second paragraph.

continues

To Move around in a Document (continued)

6 Press End.

Pressing End moves the insertion point to the end of the line. Compare your letter with the screen in Figure 2.5.

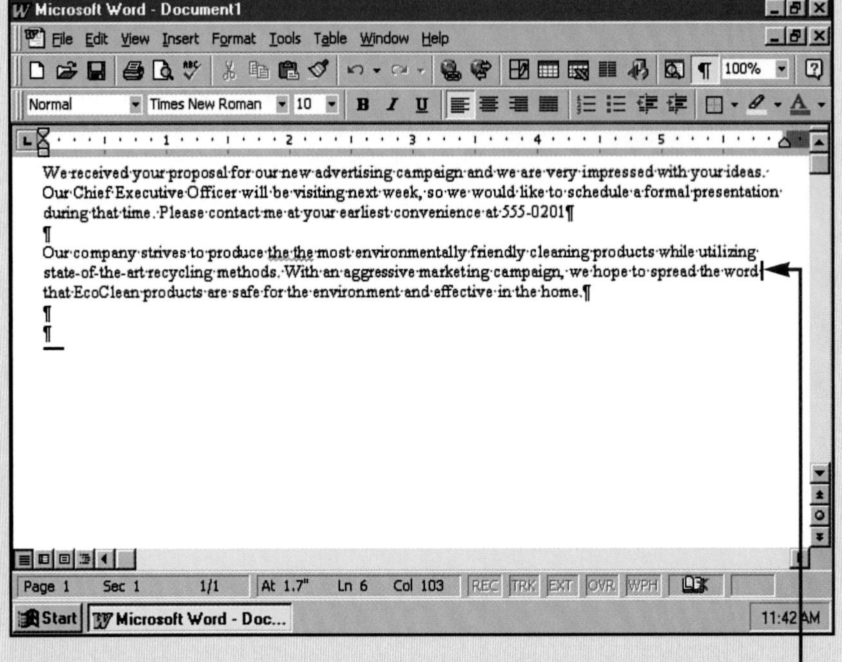

Figure 2.5
The insertion point is now at the end of the line.

7 Press Ctrl+Home

This action moves the insertion point to the beginning of the document. Take a minute now to try some of the other keyboard shortcuts listed in Table 2.1.

In most cases, you save your changes to the document before continuing to the next lesson. Because you just practiced moving around in the document (and you made no changes), you don't need to save the document now. In the next lesson, you learn how to correct your text.

Table 2.1 Keyboard Shortcuts for Moving around in a Document

Key(s)	Action
←	Moves the insertion point one character to the left.
→	Moves the insertion point one character to the right.
↑	Moves the insertion point up one line.
↓	Moves the insertion point down one line.
Home	Moves the insertion point to the beginning of the line.

Key(s)	Action
End	Moves the insertion point to the end of the line.
PgUp	Moves the insertion point up one window or page.
PgDn	Moves the insertion point down one window or page.
Ctrl+Home	Moves the insertion point to the beginning of the document.
Ctrl+End	Moves the insertion point to the end of the document.
Ctrl+←	Moves the insertion point one word to the left.
Ctrl+→	Moves the insertion point one word to the right.
Ctrl+↑	Moves the insertion point up one paragraph.
Ctrl+↓	Moves the insertion point down one paragraph.
Ctrl+PgUp	Moves the insertion point to the top of the previous page.
Ctrl+PgDn	Moves the insertion point to the top of the next page.

You can go directly to a specific location by using the **G**o To page of the Find and Replace box. The quickest way to access this page is to press Ctrl+G. If you want to use the mouse to open the Go To dialog box, double-click in the area of the status bar (where the current page number, section, and current page/last page are indicated).

By using the **G**o To options in this dialog box, you can move the insertion point to a specific page, section, line, bookmark, annotation, footnote, endnote, or other part of the document. Click the Go **T**o button when you have made your selection. See Figure 2.6 for an example.

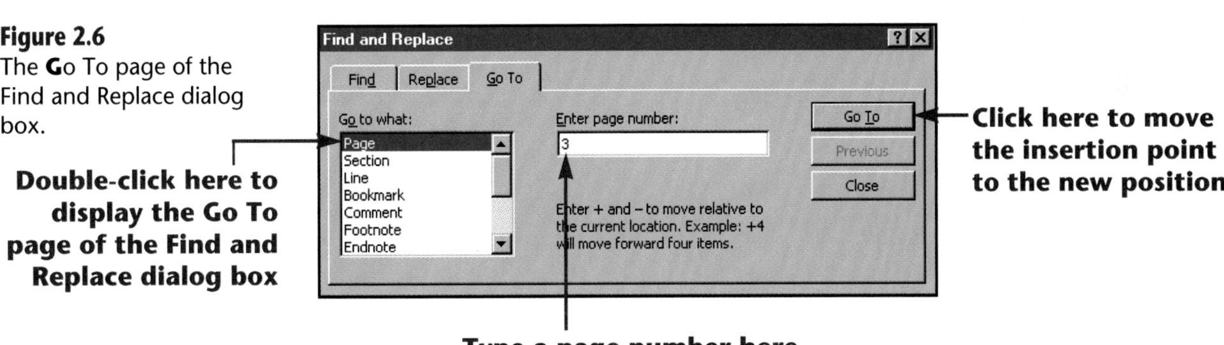

Figure 2.6
The **G**o To page of the Find and Replace dialog box.

Lesson 3: Correcting Text

After you read the first draft of your letter, you may decide that you don't like the way a particular sentence sounds, or you may find that you have simply entered the wrong information. Word enables you to delete text you don't want, enter new text, and correct existing text.

You can save a lot of time and effort by changing existing documents and saving them as new versions. For example, after you create a letter like this one, you can change the letter and use it again for a different advertising agency.

In this lesson, you learn how to make basic corrections to text in a document.

To Correct Text

1 In the `Ad Campaign Letter`, double-click the word `methods` in the second line of the second paragraph.

The word `methods` is *highlighted* (see Figure 2.7); that is, the word's letters now are white, and surrounded by a black box. This action is called *selecting* text for editing. When text is selected, anything you type replaces the selected text. Replace the word `methods` with **`techniques`** now. (Selecting text is covered in more detail in Project 3, "Editing Documents.")

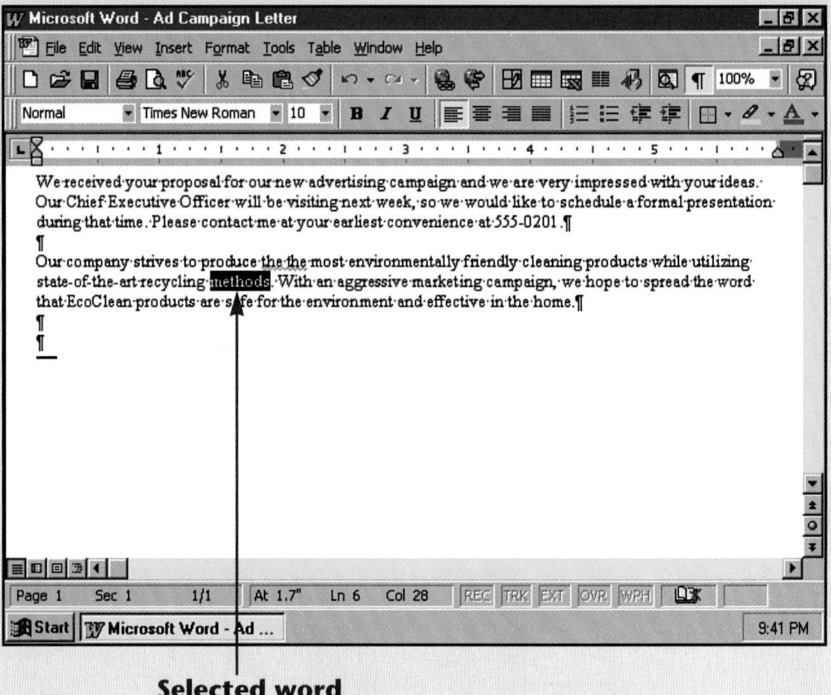

Figure 2.7
The word *`methods`* is selected.

2 Type `techniques`.

This action makes a slight change in the meaning of the sentence. Notice that the existing text moves to the right to make room for the new text you just entered, indicating that Word is in *Insert mode*. Insert mode enables you to enter new text without the new text replacing (or overwriting) the existing text.

3 Position the insertion point after the first `the` in the first line of the second paragraph.

This sentence has a duplicate word `the`. Delete the first `the` now.

4 Press Ctrl+Del once to erase the extra `the`.

Pressing Ctrl+Backspace erases the word and the extra space after the word.

5 Position the insertion point before the first `0` in the phone number.

This phone number is incorrect; you need to replace `0` with the correct number.

6 Double-click the OVR indicator on the status line.

Notice that the OVR indicator appears darker. You have now switched to *Overtype mode*. In this mode, Word overwrites (or erases) existing text as you type new text when you make a correction.

7 Type `0328` to insert the correct phone number.

Notice that the new number replaces the old number. Be careful not to type over the wrong text when correcting words in Overtype mode. Compare your letter with the one in Figure 2.8.

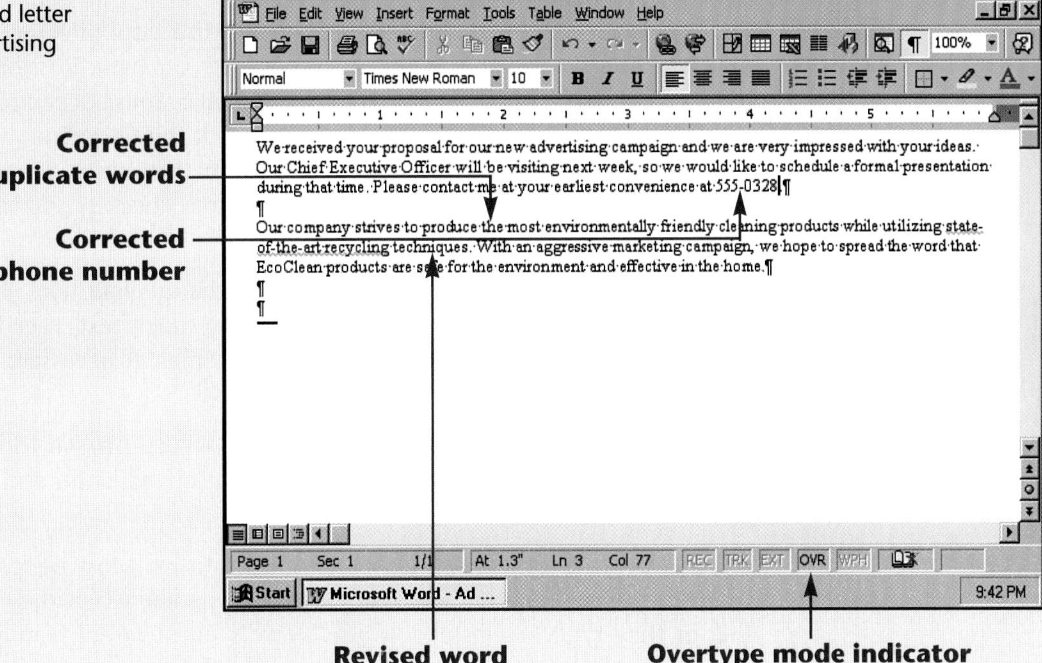

Figure 2.8
The corrected letter for the advertising campaign.

8 Double-click the OVR indicator again.

Double-clicking the OVR indicator again returns Word to Insert mode.

9 Click the Save button on the toolbar.

This action saves the changes you just made to `Ad Campaign Letter`. Don't close this document. You use it again in the next lesson, when you learn how to insert new text.

Jargon Watch

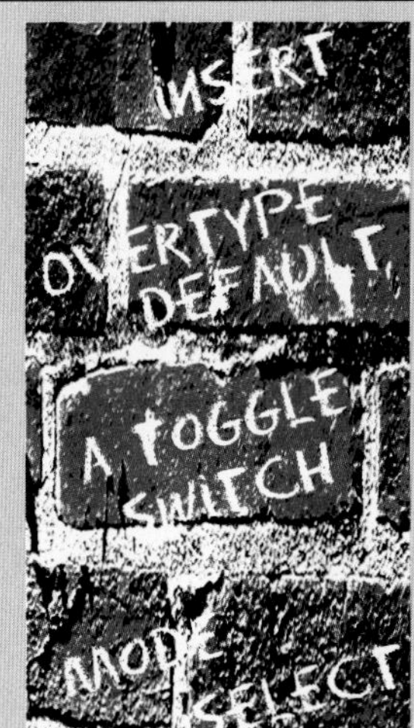

As you just learned, you can switch between **Insert** and **Overtype** mode by double-clicking the OVR indicator on the status bar. This action is sometimes called a **toggle switch** because it enables you to switch, or toggle, between two different states. When you start Word 97, Word uses Insert mode by **default**. A default setting is the way something is automatically done. A **mode** is simply a particular way of doing things. When you **select** text, you are marking it so that you can take action on it. For example, you select text, then underline it.

It may sound impressive to say that "Word 97 operates in Insert mode by default," but this just means that Word automatically moves text to the right when you type new text. If you want to type over existing text, just double-click the OVR indicator.

The Overwrite feature should be used with caution. It's easy to accidentally overwrite text that you wanted to preserve. A safer method is to select the text you want to replace, and then type the new text.

You may notice the wavy underlines beneath the duplicate `the` and the word `EcoClean`. Word spell-checks the document as you type. Possible misspellings are marked with a red wavy underline; potential grammatical errors are marked with a green wavy underline. You can right-click the underlined words to open a Spelling and Grammar pop-up menu. From this menu, you can choose a replacement word, run the Spelling and Grammar checker, add the word to the Word dictionary, or ignore the word.

If you make a mistake as you type, or want to change your text, you can use the Undo button. For example, if you type over too much text, click the Undo button on the toolbar (or press Ctrl+Z) as many times as necessary to go back to your original text.

To redo those same actions, click the Redo button on the toolbar (or press Ctrl+Y). Click the down arrow at the right side of the Undo and Redo buttons to select from a list of recent actions.

Word also has another way of preventing mistakes. Most people make errors when they type; for example, many people type **`adn`** when they mean to type **`and`**, or they type **`hte`** instead of **`the`**. Word's AutoCorrect feature detects and corrects these and similar errors automatically as you type. If you want to change the AutoCorrect settings, choose the **T**ools menu and then choose **A**utoCorrect. The AutoCorrect dialog box is displayed, with a place for you to add additional words you want corrected (see Figure 2.9).

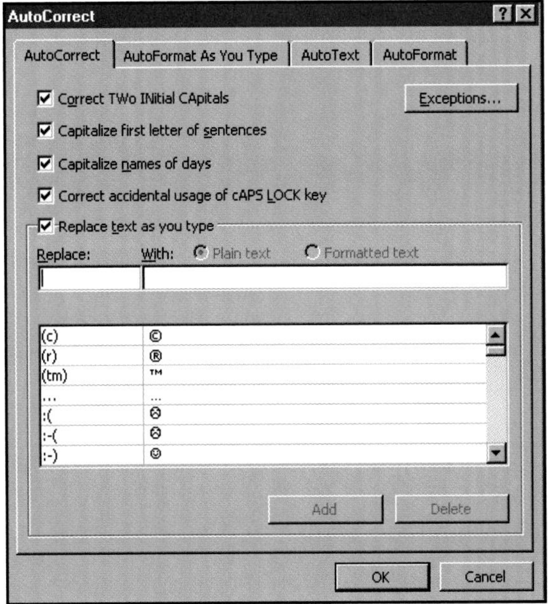

Figure 2.9
The AutoCorrect dialog box.

Lesson 4: Inserting New Text

One of the most attractive features of word processing software is that it enables you to add new information to an existing document. The letter you have created is not yet complete. You need to add a mailing address, greeting, and closing before you can mail the letter.

In this lesson, you edit the letter by inserting new text.

To Insert New Text

1 In `Ad Campaign Letter`, press Ctrl+Home.

This action moves the insertion point to the beginning of the first paragraph in the document (even if the first paragraph is just a blank line). This step is unnecessary if the insertion point is already there. This is where you want to insert today's date.

2 Choose Insert, Date and Time.

This opens the Date and Time dialog box (see Figure 2.10). This dialog box contains a list of today's date and time in different formats to suit virtually any type of document. A checkbox at the bottom of the dialog box lets you insert a date (or time) that is automatically updated each time you open the document. This type of date is frequently inserted into form documents, such as memos, fax cover sheets, and invoices.

To Insert New Text (continued)

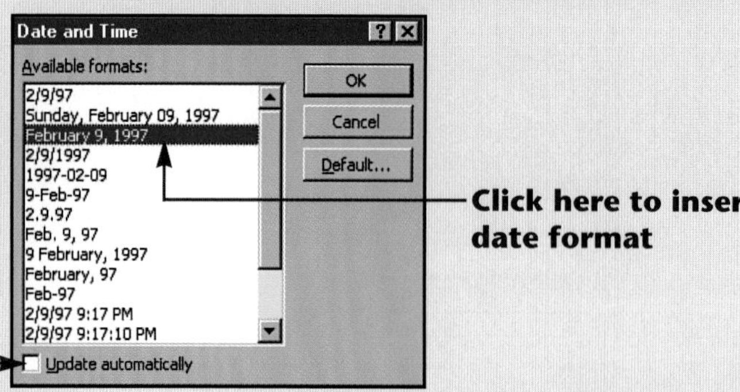

Figure 2.10
Use the Date and Time dialog box to insert the current date and time in a variety of different formats.

For this letter, choose the format that spells out the name of the month followed by the numeric day, followed by a four-digit year (for example, February 9, 1997).

3. **Double-click the date format (for example, February 9, 1997).**

You have just added the date for your sample letter. Now, add some space between the date and the mailing address.

4. **Press ↵Enter twice.**

5. **Type the following text:**

```
Ms. Rebecca Keeper
Keeper Advertising
1501 Red River
Suite 300
Boulder, CO  47802
```

Pressing ↵Enter at the end of each of these short lines tells Word to go to the next line. Word automatically moves the existing text down to make room for the new text you enter. Your letter should look like Figure 2.11.

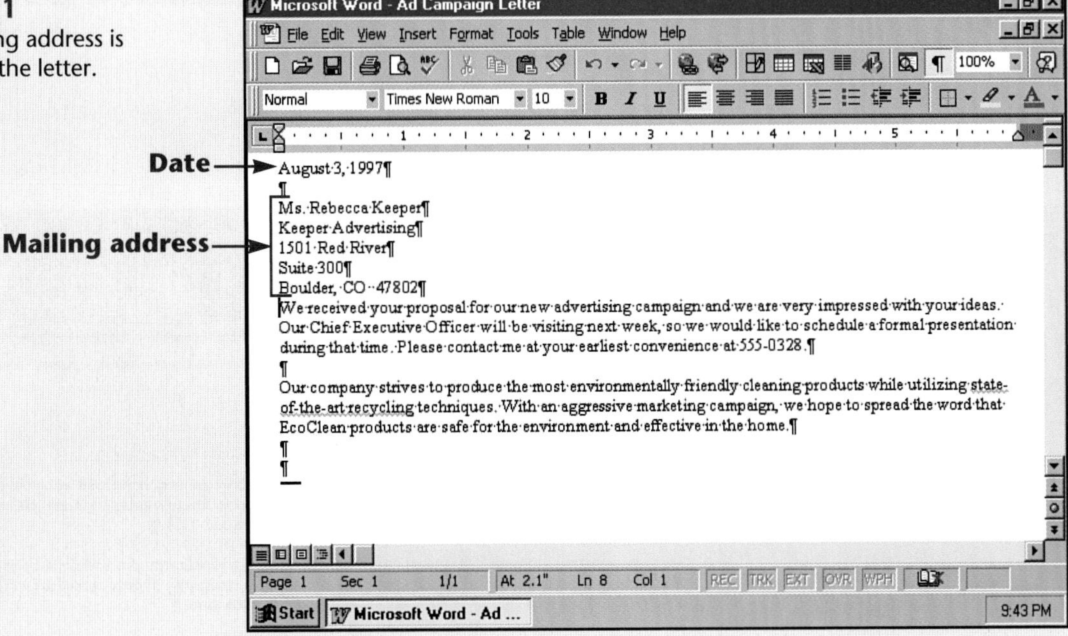

Figure 2.11
The mailing address is added to the letter.

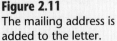

6 Press Enter again.

This action inserts a blank line after the mailing address.

7 Type the following text:

`Dear Ms. Keeper:`

8 Press Enter twice.

This action tells Word to go to the next line and leave a blank line between your greeting and the body of your letter. At this point, the Office Assistant may pop up and ask if you want help creating the letter. If you ask for more help, the Office Assistant starts the Letter Wizard, which helps you create letters and gives you a wide variety of formats from which to choose.

9 Press Ctrl+End.

Pressing Ctrl+End moves the insertion point to the end of the letter (on the blank line below the last line of text). If you like, you can also use the scroll box to move to the end of the document. Remember that after you have moved to the end of the document with the scroll box, you must click inside the document to move the insertion point.

10 Type `Sincerely,` and press Enter four times.

This step enters the closing of your letter and leaves enough room for you to sign your name after the word `Sincerely`.

continues

To Insert New Text (continued)

11 Type your name.

The letter is now complete. Compare your letter with the one in Figure 2.12.

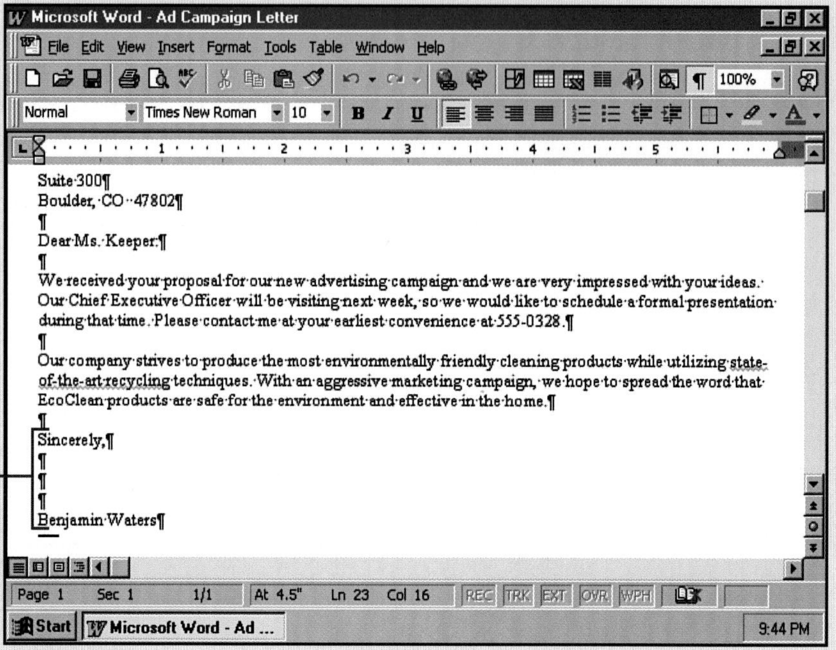

Figure 2.12
The letter with the closing information inserted.

Letter closing

12 Click the Save button.

Because this document already has a name and a place on the disk, Word saves the changes to the document with the existing name and location and does not prompt you for any further information. Leave this document open for use in the next lesson.

Lesson 5: Printing a Document

Now that you have completed your letter, you will want to print a paper copy to mail to the advertising agency. In addition, you may want to keep an extra paper copy for your files or for review away from the computer.

This lesson shows you how to print a basic document.

To Print a Document

1 Check the printer.

You can't print if the printer is off, doesn't have any paper, or is not online (connected to the computer). Printers often have a light that indicates whether the printer is online or receiving commands from the computer. You receive an error message on your computer screen if the printer is not online.

After the printer is ready to go, you need to check the document you are going to print. Use the Print Preview feature to display the whole page on your screen.

2 Click the Print Preview button.

Print Preview displays the entire page as it will look when printed. Your letter should now look like the one in Figure 2.13. This view of the letter enables you to see the text spacing and margins so that you have a better idea of how the letter looks on the page. Notice that the letter seems to be squeezed at the top of the page. Add some line spacing to improve the letter's appearance.

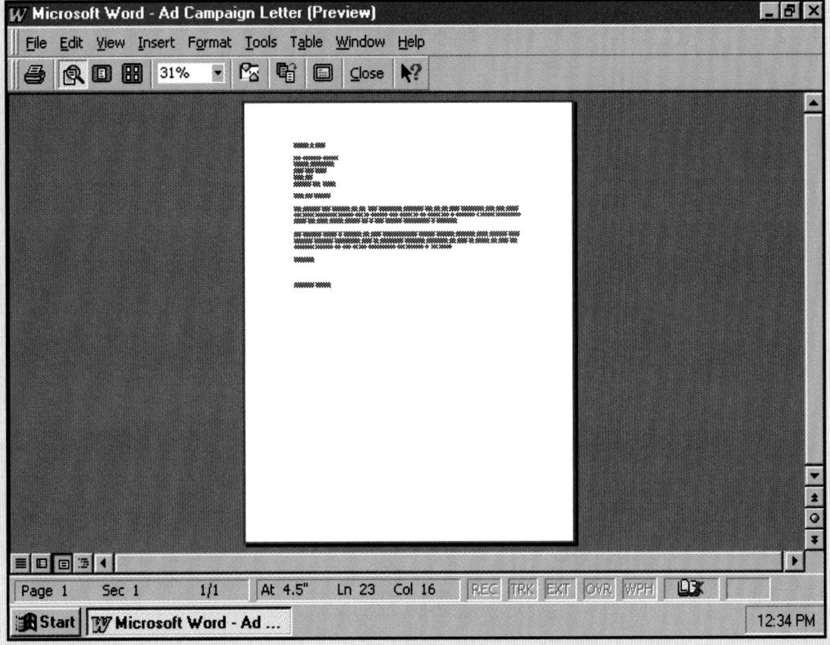

Figure 2.13
Print Preview enables you to view the entire page before you print.

3 Click the Close button to close Print Preview.

You must close Print Preview before you can make changes to the document.

4 Press Ctrl+Home.

This moves the insertion point to the top of the document, at the beginning of the date.

5 Press ↵Enter four times.

You have just added some space to the top of the letter.

6 Press ↓ one time; then press ↵Enter four times.

This moves the insertion point down one line to the blank line between the date and the first line of the address, and adds four blank lines there.

continues

To Print a Document (continued)

You have just added more line spacing to the letter so that it uses more of the printed page. Now use Print Preview to view your changes.

7 Click the Print Preview button.

Compare your letter with the one in Figure 2.14. Notice the improvement in the spacing on the page.

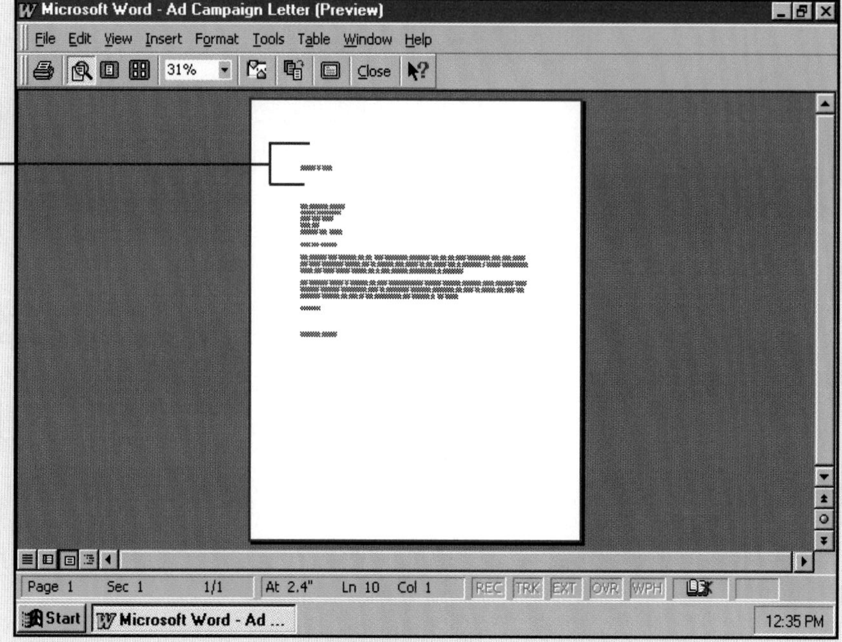

Figure 2.14
By adding space to the beginning and opening of the letter, you improve its appearance on the page.

8 Choose Close.

When you are satisfied with your document's appearance, you can print the document.

9 Choose File, Print.

This action opens the Print dialog box (see Figure 2.15). You can now choose to print all or part of your document. You can also select another printer, if necessary. By default, Word prints the full document; Word can even print multiple copies of your document.

Figure 2.15
The Print dialog box.

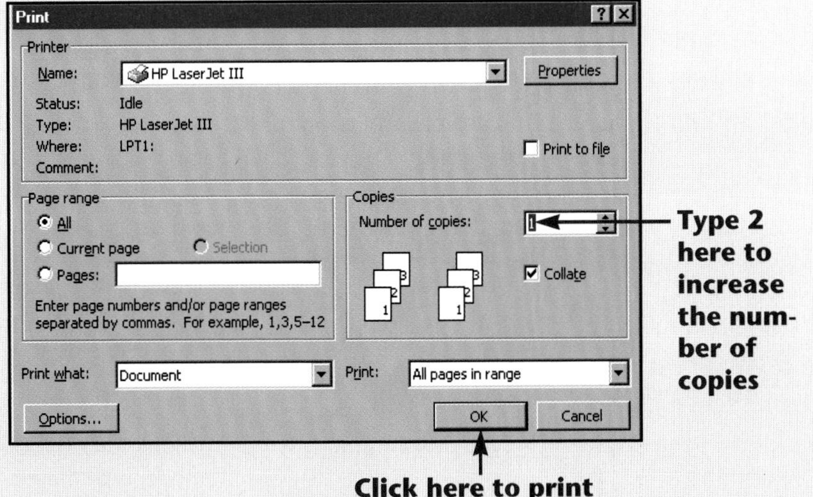

10 Type `2` in the Number of copies text box.

The number `1` in this text box is already selected, so the **2** that you type automatically replaces the `1`. Typing **2** tells Word to print two copies of your letter.

11 Choose OK to print the letter.

Word prints two copies of your letter. Printing multiple copies is helpful when you need more than one original.

Save your work and close `Ad Campaign Letter`. If you have completed your session on the computer, exit Word and shut down Windows before turning off the computer. Otherwise, continue with the next section, "Checking Your Skills."

To open the Print dialog box, quickly press Ctrl+P. You can bypass the Print dialog box completely by clicking the Print button, which by default, sends the entire document to the printer.

Project Summary

To	Do This
Open a document	Choose **F**ile, **O**pen or click the Open tool. Double-click the file in the list box, or select the file and then choose **O**pen.
Move to the top of the document	Press Ctrl+Home.
Move to the bottom of the document	Press Ctrl+End.
Move to the end of the line	Press End.

continues

To	Do This
Move the insertion point	Point to a place in the document and click the left mouse button.
Scroll down through the document	Click the down scroll arrow.
Scroll up through the document	Click the up scroll arrow.
Delete text	Press ←Backspace to delete the character immediately to the left. Press Del to delete the character immediately to the right.
Delete a word	Double-click the word and press Del.
Type over existing text	Double-click the OVR indicator to turn on Overtype mode, type the new text, and double-click the OVR indicator to turn off Overtype mode.
Reverse the last action on the document	Click the Undo button or press Ctrl+Z.
Redo the last Undo action performed	Click the Redo button or press Ctrl+Y.
Change AutoCorrect settings	Choose **T**ools, **A**utoCorrect.
Preview a document before printing	Click the Print Preview tool.
Close Print Preview	Choose **C**lose in the Print Preview window.
Print a document	Click the Print tool or choose **F**ile, **P**rint, OK.

Checking Your Skills

True/False

For each of the following, check *T* or *F* to indicate whether the statement is true or false.

__T __F **1.** Word automatically opens a document for you when you start the program.

__T __F **2.** AutoCorrect is used to correct common errors as you type.

__T __F **3.** Double-clicking the name of a document in the file list box opens it.

__T __F **4.** Insert mode enables you to overwrite existing text as you enter new text.

__T __F **5.** Ctrl+P opens the Print dialog box.

__T __F **6.** Clicking the scroll bar moves the insertion point in the document.

__T __F **7.** The name of an open document window displays in the Status bar.

__T __F **8.** You can use the Explorer program to open a Word document.

__T __F **9.** You can use the mouse or the keyboard to move the insertion point in Word.

__T __F **10.** You can make changes to a document in Print Preview mode.

Multiple Choice

Circle the letter of the correct answer for each of the following questions.

1. Where does the Go **T**o option enable you to move quickly?

a. A page

b. A file

c. A paragraph

d. A folder

2. The **P**rint command is found under which menu?

a. **F**ile

b. **E**dit

c. **V**iew

d. **P**rint

3. What does clicking the Print Preview button do?

a. It increases the size of the text when printed.

b. It opens an earlier version of the document.

c. It enables you to view full pages as they will appear when printed.

d. It prints the document.

4. Which of the following moves the insertion point to the beginning of a document?

a. Ctrl+Home

b. Clicking the Undo button.

c. Ctrl+G

d. Ctrl+End

5. Which keystroke(s) are/is used to move to the end of a document quickly?

a. End

b. PgDn

c. Insert

d. Ctrl+End

6. The Date and **T**ime command is found under which menu?

a. **I**nsert

b. **E**dit

c. **V**iew

d. F**o**rmat

7. How do you open an existing document?

a. Click the Open button on the status bar.

b. Choose **O**pen, **F**ile.

c. Choose **F**ile, **O**pen.

d. Choose **V**iew, **F**ile.

8. You can use the mouse pointer to place the insertion point anywhere in a document when it has what shape?

a. arrow

b. hand

c. I-beam

d. two-headed arrow

9. What combination of keys do you press to delete an entire word?

a. Ctrl+Del

b. Alt+Del

c. ⇧Shift+←Backspace

d. ⇧Shift+Alt+Del

10. What does double-clicking a word do?

a. It deletes the word.

b. It selects the word.

c. It moves the word to a new location.

d. It spell-checks the word.

Completion

In the blank provided, write the correct answer for each of the following statements.

1. The quickest way to restore the most recent change made to a document is to use the ____________ command.
2. You preview a document by choosing ____________ from the **F**ile menu.
3. Clicking the ____________ indicator switches to Overtype mode.
4. Pressing ↵Enter at the end of a line of text inserts a(n) ____________ return in the document.
5. New text is entered at the ____________ point, a blinking vertical bar in the document window.
6. To use the keyboard to move down one line in a document, press the ____________ key.
7. In ____________ mode, Word automatically moves text to the right when you type new text.
8. To reverse actions you have undone, click the ____________ button on the toolbar.
9. If you click the ____________ button, Word saves the document with the existing name and in the existing location.
10. When text is ____________, anything you type replaces this text.

Matching

In the blank next to each of the following terms or phrases, write the letter of the corresponding term or phrase. (Note that some letters may be used more than once.)

____**1.** Moves the insertion point one character to the left

____**2.** Moves the insertion point to the beginning of the line

____**3.** Deletes the character immediately to the left

____**4.** Reverses the last action on the document

____**5.** Moves the insertion point to the end of the line

____**6.** Moves the insertion point down one line

____**7.** Accesses the Go To page of the Find and Replace dialog box

____**8.** Adds a blank line

____**9.** Moves the insertion point to the end of the document

___**10.** Reverses the action you have undone

a. Undo button

b. ←

c. Redo button

d. Ctrl+G

e. End

f. ←Backspace

g. Ctrl+End

h. ↓

i. ↵Enter

j. Home

Screen ID

Identify each of the items shown in Figure 2.16.

Figure 2.16

1. ____________
2. ____________
3. ____________
4. ____________
5. ____________
6. ____________

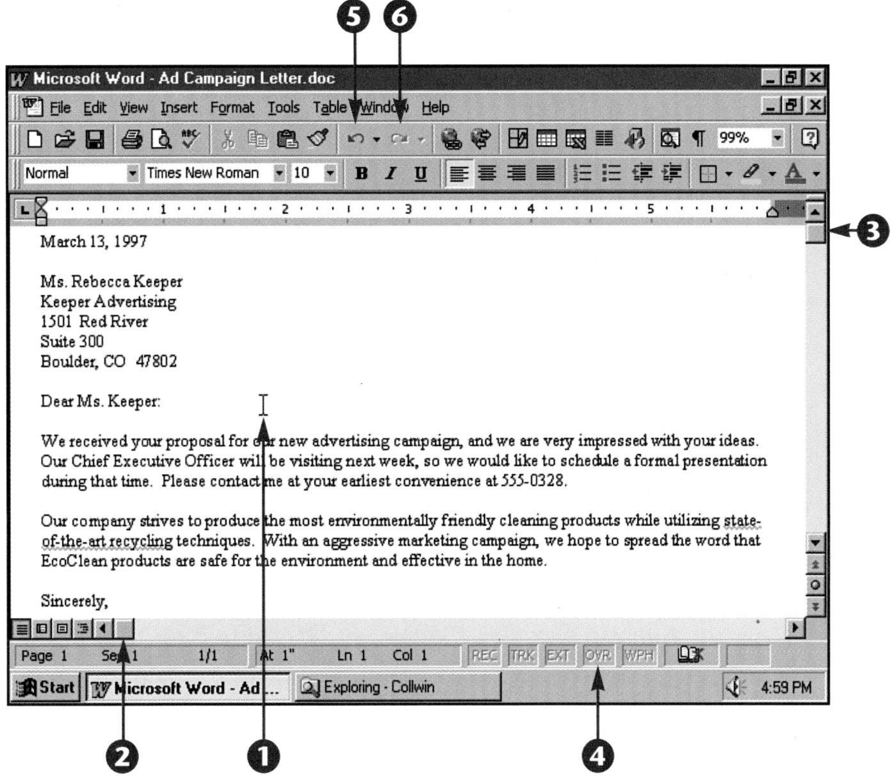

Applying Your Skills

Practice

The following exercises enable you to practice the skills you have learned in this project. Take a few minutes to work through these exercises now.

1. Editing Radio Ad Copy

To publicize a new business, you have created a radio advertisement that will air on a local radio station. Open a Word document containing the ad copy. Then improve the copy by inserting and deleting text.

To Edit Radio Ad Copy

1. Open the file named Proj0201.DOC and resave it as **`Ad Copy`**.
2. Insert title text at the top of the document. For example, type **`Copy for Radio Advertisement`**.
3. Delete the extra word `all` in the second sentence of the first paragraph.
4. Correct the misspelled word `wrtie` in the second paragraph.
5. Change the phone number at the bottom of the document to **`555-4431`**.

6. Add your name, title, and company name to the bottom of the document.
7. Save the document and, if requested by your instructor, print two copies. Close the document.

2. Editing a Memo

Edit a memo written to inform employees of a new parking rule.

To Edit a Memo

1. Open the file named Proj0202.DOC and resave it as `Parking Memo`.
2. Type the current date on the Date line.
3. Insert your name on the From line.
4. At the end of the document, delete the sentence `You must follow these rules or else!`
5. Finish the document by inserting this sentence at the end: `Please do your best to meet these guidelines.`
6. Preview the memo in Print Preview.
7. Close Print Preview, save the document, and then close it.

3. Editing an Article for the Company Newsletter

Edit an article about the company softball team for the company newsletter.

To Edit an Article

1. Open the file named Proj0203.DOC and resave it as `Softball Article`.
2. Insert this headline at the top of the document: `SOFTBALL TEAM BEGINS SEASON WITH A 12-TO-3 WIN.`
3. Change the line at the beginning of the article to your city and state.
4. Change the score in the second sentence to `12 to 3`.
5. Insert a blank line before the start of each new paragraph.
6. Change the day and time in the last sentence to `Thursday at 5:45`.
7. Save the document and, if requested by your instructor, print two copies. Then close the document.

4. Editing a Cover Letter

Edit a cover letter that you plan to send out with your résumé in search of a better job position.

To Edit a Cover Letter

1. From the Student Disk, open the file named Proj0204.DOC, and resave it as `Cover Letter`.
2. Insert a date at the top of the letter.
3. Replace the sample name and address with your name and address.
4. Correct the spelling of `advertisement` in the first sentence.
5. Delete the word `Yours` from the closing.

6. Insert four lines after the close and type **Karena Oshawa**.
7. Preview the document in Print Preview; then save the document. If requested by your instructor, print two copies. Then close the file.

5. Editing a Welcome Letter

Edit an existing welcome letter.

To Edit the Welcome Letter

1. Open the file named Proj0205.DOC, and save it as **Welcome Letter**.
2. Insert the current date at the top of the letter.
3. Type the following address and greeting several lines below the date:

    Ms. Cheryl Olson

    459 S. Sunny Ridge Drive

    Chicago, IL 60603

    Dear Cheryl:

4. Add the area code **(317)** in front of the telephone number in the second paragraph.
5. Change the last name Landow in the second paragraph to **Landers**.
6. Type your name at the end of the document.
7. Preview the document, and adjust the spacing if necessary.
8. Save the document and, if requested by your instructor, print one copy. Then close the document.

Challenge

The following challenges enable you to use your problem-solving skills. Take time to work through these exercises now.

1. Editing the CTC Cover Letter

You decide to edit the cover letter you typed earlier to be sent to those who request information. Open the file Proj0206.DOC and save it as **CTC Cover Letter 2**.

Insert the current date at the top of the letter. Add the following paragraph between the two existing paragraphs:

> **All of our instructors are experts in the software they teach. They also are experienced business people who can help you use the software to become productive immediately. I am sure you will be very pleased with the quality of our training.**

Add the text **state-of-the-art training** in front of the word facility in the first sentence of the last paragraph.

Preview the document, then adjust the line spacing as necessary. Print three copies of the letter, then save the file again. Close the file when you have finished.

2. Editing the Course Descriptions Document

You need to make some additional changes to the course descriptions you previously typed. Open the file PROJ0207.DOC on the Student Disk and save it as **Course Descriptions 2**.

Add the following three-line heading to the top of the document:

Computer Training Concepts
Course Descriptions
Fall, 1997

You continue formatting this heading in a later project.

Change the word intermediate in the description of Excel II to **advanced**.

At the end of the first line of the heading, type **(CTC)**.

Save the file again, then print two copies. Close the file when you have finished.

3. Creating a Menu for Main Street Deli

The owner of the Main Street Deli has asked you to print a sign to post in the restaurant window listing the daily specials. You decide to use Word to create this sign so that it can be easily formatted and updated. In a blank Word document, type the following text. Press Tab to indent the food items.

Main Street Deli

Daily Specials

Tuna Melt	**$4.95**
American Sub	**$3.50**
Minestrone Soup	**$2.50**

Come in and see how good freshness tastes!

Save the document as **Deli Sign** and print one copy. Close the document when you have finished.

4. Editing the Membership Renewal Letter

As the manager of a health spa, you need to send letters to clients reminding them to renew their memberships for the following year. You kept the letter on file from the previous year, and decide to reuse it, with some modifications. Open the Proj0208.DOC and save it as **Membership Renewal**. Make the following changes to the letter:

1. Insert the current date at the top of the letter.
2. Change all occurrences of 1996 to 1997.
3. Add HealthFirst to the spelling dictionary.
4. Read the letter, and correct any misspellings.
5. Add your name to the end of the letter.
6. Insert the following paragraph in front of the last paragraph:

    In addition to the benefits you have been enjoying, we are planning to make some improvements. These improvements include two additional racquetball courts, a new aerobic exercise room, and new weight-lifting equipment. We are also expanding the children's program to include swimming lessons.

7. Preview the letter to see how it will look on the page. Make any necessary adjustments to the line spacing.
8. Save the letter again, then print one copy. Close the file when you have finished.

5. Creating a Reunion Planning Letter

You are organizing a reunion for your family. To help in your planning, you decide to survey family members regarding the location and activities preferred. Open the Proj0209.DOC file and save it as **Reunion Planning**. Make the following changes:

1. Insert the current date at the top of the document.
2. Type your last name in the first sentence of the letter, in front of the word **family**.
3. Add **Myrtle Beach, South Carolina** to the location list. (Press Tab to indent the item.)
4. Add **shopping and local shows** to the activities list.
5. Add **August 15-19** to the dates.
6. Type your name at the bottom of the letter.
7. Read the letter and correct any misspellings.
8. Save the letter again, and close the document when you are finished.

Project 3

Editing Word Documents

Enhancing a Status Report

In this project, you learn how to:

- Select Text
- Enhance Text
- Move and Copy Text
- Use the Undo Feature
- Check a Document for Spelling and Grammatical Errors
- Use the Thesaurus

Why Would I Do This?

In the last project, you learned some of the most basic editing techniques in Word, such as inserting and deleting text, and moving around in the document. Now that you know some editing fundamentals, you are ready to learn more about editing in Word. In this project, you open a sample report so that you can proofread and correct the information in it. Because your correspondence is important, it should look professional, as well as convey your ideas clearly.

Lesson 1: Selecting Text

Select
To define a section of text so that you can take action on it, such as copying, moving, or formatting it.

After you have typed a document, you may want to go back and make changes to sections of the text. You use Word's text-selection options to define the area of text you want to edit. When you *select* text, it becomes highlighted (the letters turn white and the background turns black), indicating that any actions you take will affect only the selected text. By selecting text in a document, you can make any number of local changes to individual parts of the document—single paragraphs, sentences, lines, words, or even single characters.

Because you can use either the mouse or the keyboard to select text, you learn both techniques in this lesson.

A sample report has been provided for your use in this project, so the first step is to open the file for editing. In this and future lessons, you open existing documents supplied on your student data disk; you then save the documents using realistic file names. Saving a document under a different name lets you use the original, unchanged document at a later time. If you don't have a copy of the resource disk containing the supplied documents, ask your trainer to tell you which drive and folder contain these data files. You need these files so that you can work through the lessons in this book.

In this project, the sample status report is for the division managers at EcoClean. The report updates them on the status of a technology training conference.

To Select Text

1. **From the Student Disk, open the file Proj0301.**
2. **Choose File, Save As, type `Status Report`, and then choose Save.**

   This step saves the student file to a different file name so you can go back to the original file if necessary. You'll use these same steps to open each file from the disk.

Word places the report in a new document window (see Figure 3.1). You can now begin editing the sample report. Notice that this document was saved with the Show/Hide feature turned on. Recall from Project 1 that clicking the Show/Hide button turned the feature on and off. If you prefer a cleaner screen, you can turn off the Show/Hide feature.

Word has marked potential spelling and grammatical errors with wavy underlines. Ignore these for now; you'll take care of them in a later lesson.

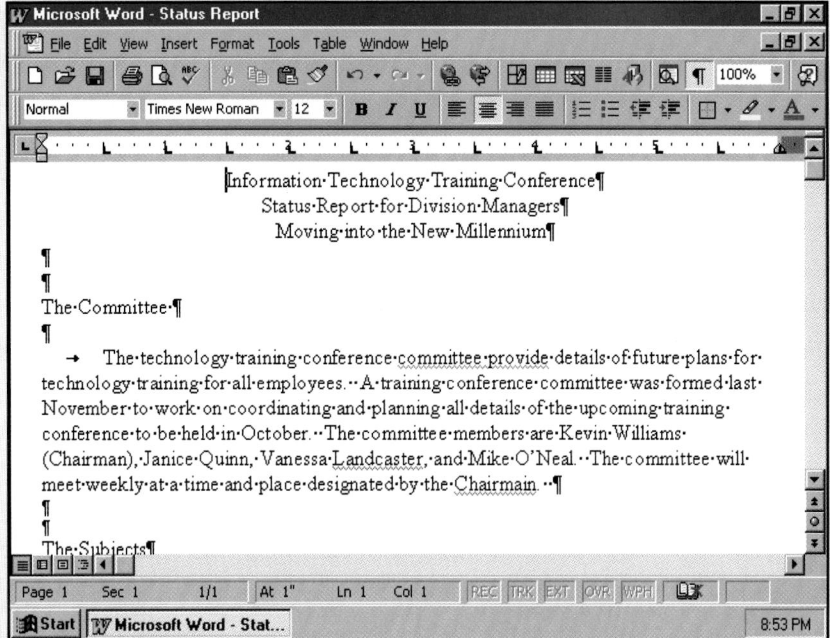

Figure 3.1
The sample report open in a document window.

3 Move the I-beam mouse pointer to the beginning of the title, located at the top of the report.

4 Click and hold down the mouse button while you drag the mouse down the page.

Selected text is displayed highlighted (white text on a black background), as shown in Figure 3.2. Make sure you continue holding down the mouse button for the next step.

continues

To Select Text (continued)

Figure 3.2
The report with selected text.

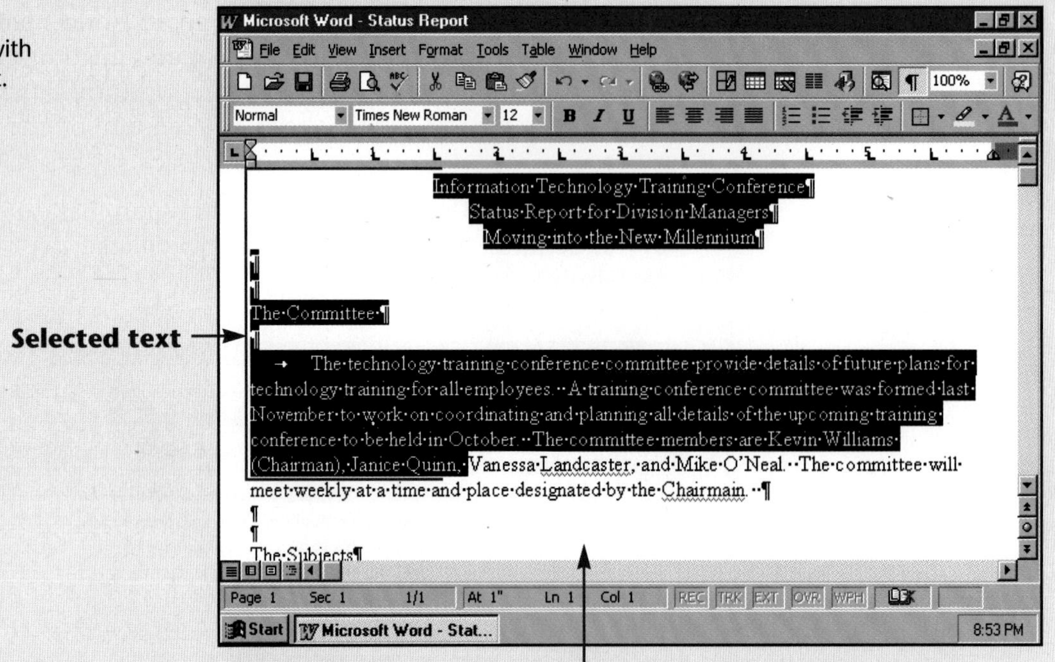

5 While holding down the mouse button, move the mouse pointer back up through the page.

This action deselects the text. You can use this method if you accidentally select too much text. If you start selecting in the wrong place, you need to cancel the selection and start over.

6 Click the mouse anywhere inside the document window.

This action cancels the current selection; all the highlighting disappears and the text returns to normal.

Clicking and dragging the mouse pointer through text is the fastest way to select large sections of text. At times, however, you may need to select small sections of text, such as a single word, or a sentence.

7 Double-click the word `November` in the first paragraph.

The word `November` is selected (highlighted), as shown in Figure 3.3.

Figure 3.3
The sample report with a selected word.

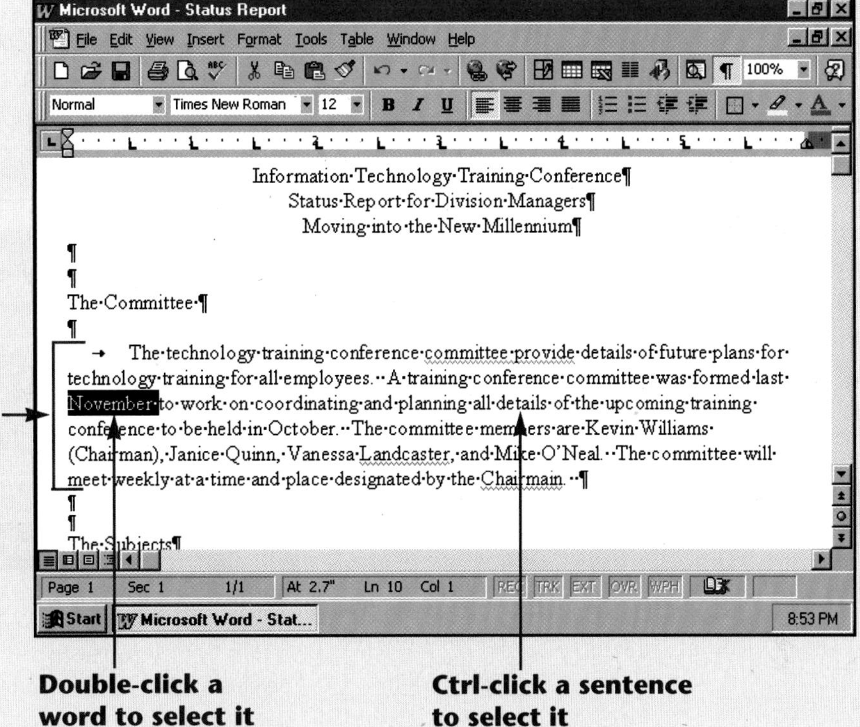

❽ **Press and hold down Ctrl; then click the second sentence of the same paragraph.**

This action selects the entire sentence, along with any additional blank spaces after the period. The entire sentence should appear highlighted.

❾ **Triple-click anywhere inside the paragraph.**

If you have problems...

If the paragraph isn't selected, make sure that you click the mouse three times in quick succession and that you don't move the mouse as you click.

❿ **Click inside the document window to cancel the selection.**

Because you haven't made any changes to the text, it isn't necessary to save the file now. Keep the Status Report document open to use in the next lesson, where you learn to add emphasis to the text.

You can also use the arrow keys on the keyboard to select text. You may find this method more convenient when selecting small sections of text or if you prefer to keep your hands on the keyboard. First, you position the insertion point where you want to start selecting text. Press Shift and then use the arrow keys to select text. Release Shift and press any arrow key to turn the selection off.

You can also use the left margin area to select text quickly. Move the mouse pointer into the left margin area; notice how the pointer changes to an arrow that points to the right (the normal mouse pointer points to the left). A single click selects the adjacent line; a double-click selects the adjacent paragraph.

When you select a paragraph, Word looks for a hard return (or paragraph mark) to signal the end of the paragraph. If you have several short lines (name and address information, for example) that end in a hard return, Word treats each line as a paragraph.

Table 3.1 Keyboard Shortcuts to Select Text

Shortcut	Function
Shift+an arrow key	Selects text.
Shift+Ctrl+←	Selects a word at a time moving to the left.
Shift+Ctrl+→	Selects a word at a time moving to the right.
Shift+Ctrl+↑	Selects text within a paragraph from the insertion point upward.
Shift+Ctrl+↓	Selects text within a paragraph from the insertion point downward.
Shift+Home	Selects from the insertion point to the beginning of the line.
Shift+End	Selects from the insertion point to the end of the line.
Shift+PgUp	Selects from the insertion point up to the top of the screen.
Shift+PgDn	Selects from the insertion point down to the bottom of the screen.
Shift+Ctrl+Home	Selects from the insertion point up to the top of the document.
Shift+Ctrl+End	Selects from the insertion point down to the bottom of the document.
Click, and then Shift+click	Selects from the first click down to the second click.

Lesson 2: Enhancing Text

Now that you have learned how to select sections of text, you can add some variety and emphasis to the report by enhancing sections of text with boldface and italic. Each of the headings should be bold for emphasis, and certain elements can be italicized for variety and readability.

To Enhance Text

1 In the `Status Report` document, select the three lines in the title at the top of the report.

Notice that the title information is centered between the left and right margins. You learn how to center text in Project 4, "Formatting Documents."

2 Click the Bold button in the Formatting toolbar.

The title is now displayed in bold, so it stands out from the rest of the text. Click inside the document window to deselect the title so that you can see how the boldface text differs from the regular typeface (see Figure 3.4).

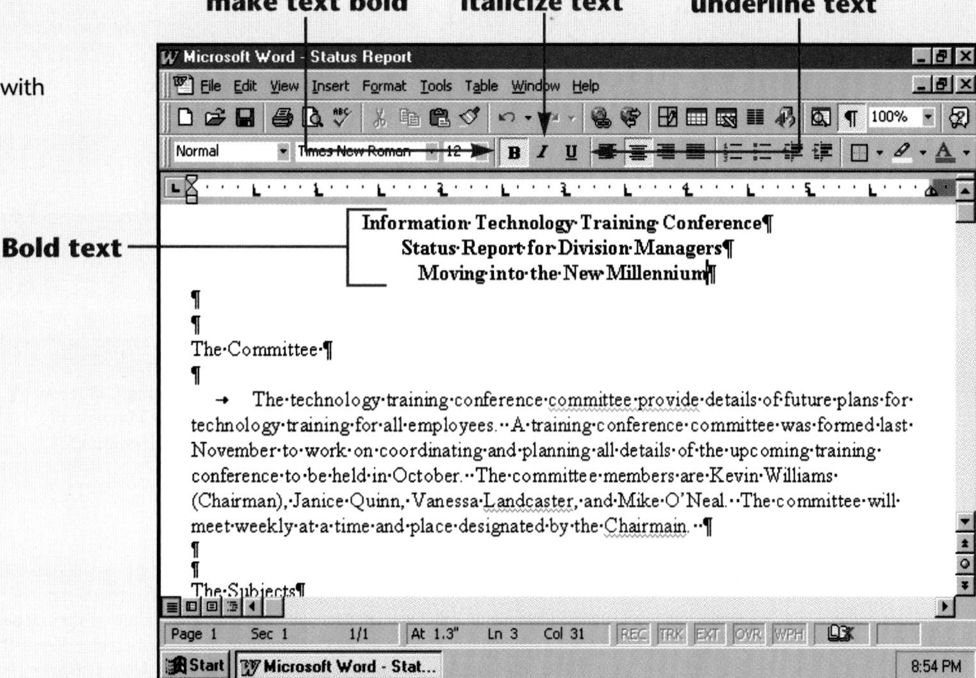

Figure 3.4
The sample report with the title in bold.

3 Select the list of names in the first paragraph.

The list of committee members needs to be emphasized so that the names stand out from the rest of the paragraph.

4 Click the Italic button.

The use of italicized type adds a more subtle form of emphasis than boldface and is easier to read than underlining.

5 Select the first heading, `The Committee`.

This time, use both bold and underline to make the headings stand out. When your headings are emphasized, you can easily scan a document to get an idea of the contents.

continues

To Enhance Text (continued)

6 Click the Bold button.

The heading is now bold. While the heading is still selected, you can add other enhancements such as underline or italic.

7 Click the Underline button.

Now select the other two headings and add bold and underline to the text.

8 Select the heading `The Subjects`, click the Bold button, and then click the Underline button.

9 Select the heading `The Goals`, click the Bold button, and then click the Underline button.

The headings now have a consistent appearance. Each one is bold and underlined.

10 Press Ctrl+Home.

Pressing Ctrl+Home moves the insertion point to the top of the document. The sample report should now look similar to Figure 3.5.

Figure 3.5
The sample report with enhancements added to the text.

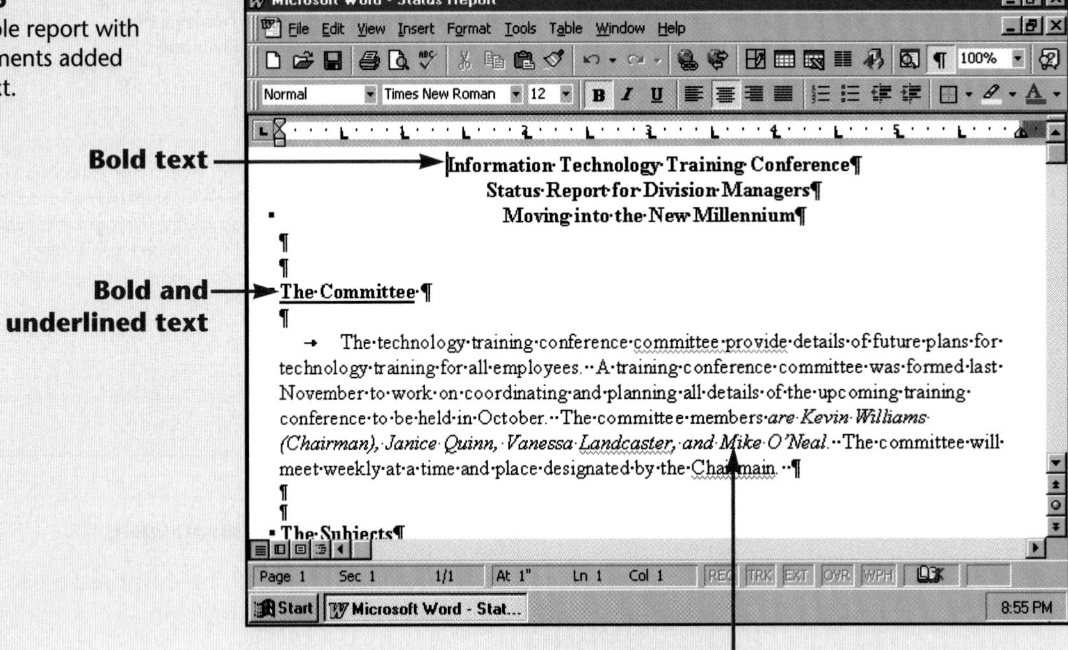

With only minimal effort, you have significantly improved the appearance of this report. Although plain text is neat and easy to read, you want your report to attract the reader's attention and create a polished appearance that the division managers will notice.

11 Click the Save button.

Clicking the Save button saves your changes. Keep the document open to use in the next lesson.

You might be interested to know the shortcut keys for the Bold, Italic, and Underline features. The shortcut keys are Ctrl+B for Bold, Ctrl+I for Italic, and Ctrl+U for Underline. To use the shortcuts, first select the text and then press the shortcut keys.

If you want to remove bold, italic, or underline, first select the text and then click the appropriate tool or use the appropriate shortcut key again. The tools and shortcut keys act as toggles for these formatting features, turning them on and off.

Word offers a wide variety of other text-enhancement features, including double-underline, strikethrough, small caps, and others. They are found in the Font dialog box, which is introduced in Project 4, "Formatting Documents."

Lesson 3: Moving and Copying Text

After you learn to enhance text, the most important skill you can learn is how to move and copy text. How many times have you written a paragraph and then decided you need to reorder the sentences? What about putting a phrase at the bottom of the page, only to wish you could move it to the top?

Now that you have improved the appearance of the report by adding bold, italic, and underline to the text, take a look at the content and organization to see whether you can make any improvements. In this lesson, you move `The Goals` section so it rests above `The Subjects` section; this move improves the document's organization.

To Move and Copy Text

1 Using any of the selection methods you learned earlier in this project, select the heading `The Goals`, the paragraph below it, and the blank lines below the paragraph, as shown in Figure 3.6.

If you have problems...

If you're having problems selecting this text, place the insertion point at the beginning of `The Goals`, and then press Ctrl+Shift+End.

You use the Select feature to tell Word what section of text you want to move, copy, enhance, or edit. In this case, you want to move the entire `The Goals` section.

continues

To Move and Copy Text (continued)

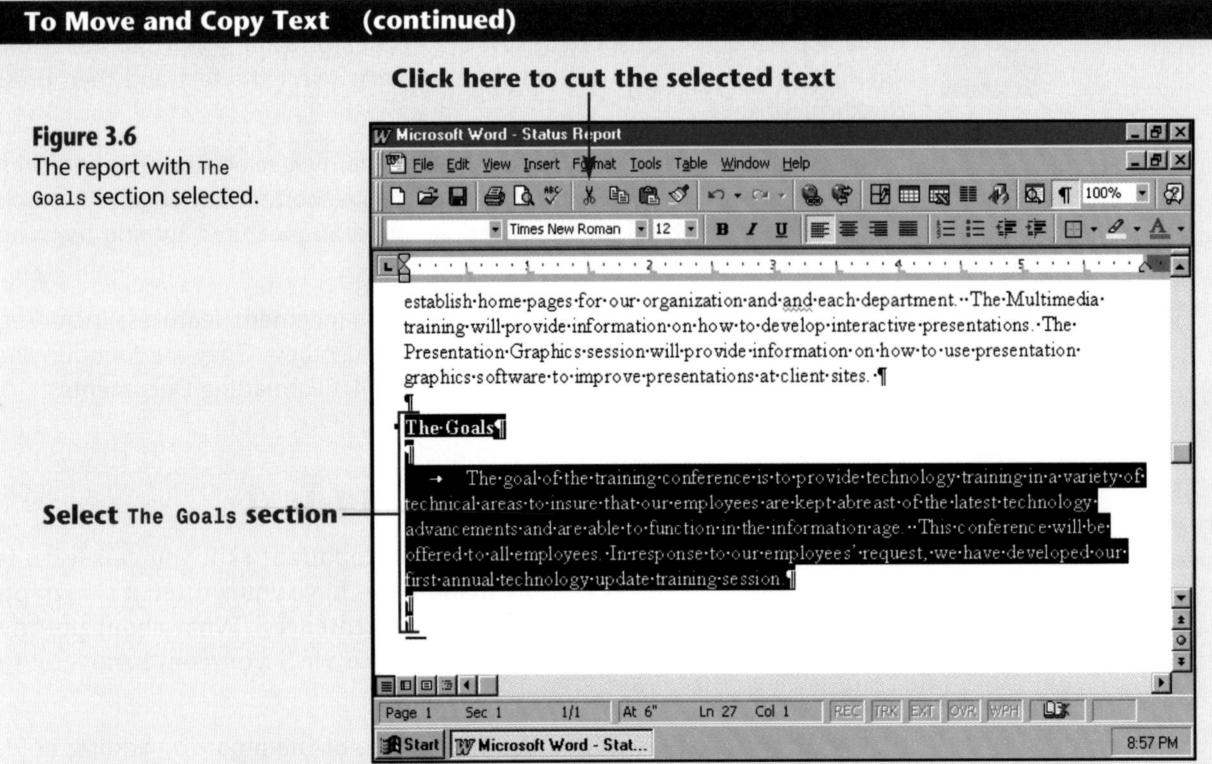
Click here to cut the selected text
Select The Goals section
Microsoft Word - Status Report
File Edit View Insert Format Tools Table Window Help
Times New Roman 12
100%
establish home pages for our organization and and each department. The Multimedia training will provide information on how to develop interactive presentations. The Presentation Graphics session will provide information on how to use presentation graphics software to improve presentations at client sites.
The Goals
The goal of the training conference is to provide technology training in a variety of technical areas to insure that our employees are kept abreast of the latest technology advancements and are able to function in the information age. This conference will be offered to all employees. In response to our employees' request, we have developed our first annual technology update training session.
Page 1 Sec 1 1/1 At 6" Ln 27 Col 1 REC TRK EXT OVR WPH
Start Microsoft Word - Stat...
8:57 PM

Figure 3.6
The report with `The Goals` section selected.

❷ **Click the Cut button.**

`The Goals` section disappears from the document, but it is not entirely gone. The text has been moved to the Windows Clipboard, which stores the text until you paste it back into the document. (Cutting, pasting, and the Clipboard are explained in more detail at the end of this lesson.)

❸ **Position the insertion point at the beginning of the heading `The Subjects`.**

You need to position the insertion point right where you want the new section to appear—in this case, before `The Subjects` section.

❹ **Click the Paste button.**

When you paste `The Goals` section into its new location, `The Subjects` section moves down to accommodate it (see Figure 3.7).

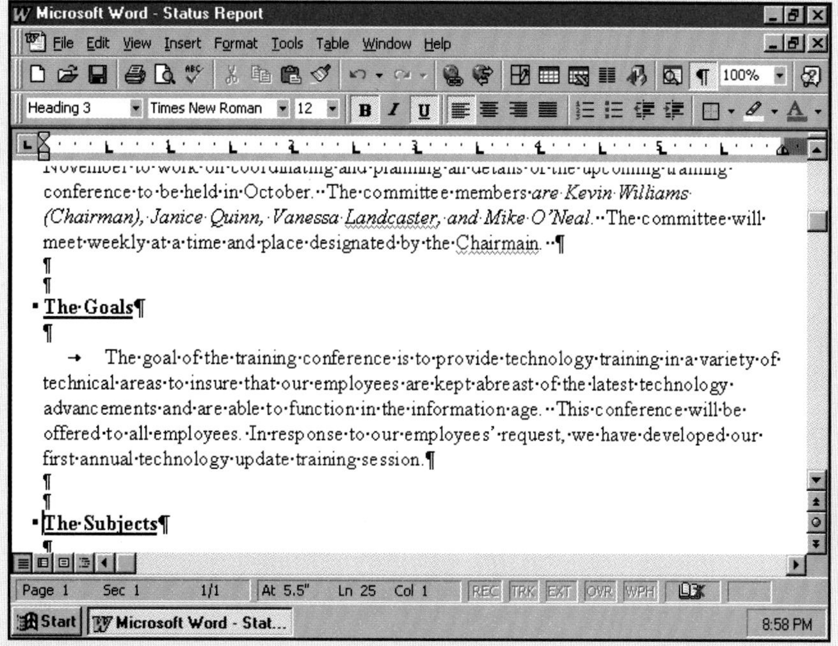

Figure 3.7
`The Goals` section now precedes `The Subjects` section.

❺ **Select the multimedia sentence in the paragraph under `The Subjects`.**

The sentence describing the multimedia training needs to be last so that the order of the sentences in the paragraph matches the order of the list of subjects (in the first sentence).

❻ **Press Ctrl+X.**

If you use the keyboard methods to select text, pressing the Ctrl+X shortcut is faster than reaching for the mouse to click the Cut button.

❼ **Position the insertion point at the end of the paragraph.**

Again, you want the multimedia sentence to be last, so you need to position the insertion point at the end of the paragraph before you paste the sentence.

❽ **Press Ctrl+V.**

Here again, the shortcut key may be faster than reaching for the mouse to click the Paste button. The new order of the sentences matches the list of subjects given in the first sentence. Depending on how you select a sentence, you may or may not select the blank space(s) before or after the sentence. The same thing can happen when you select words. Because of this, you should always double-check the spacing after you move or copy text.

In this case, you may need to add some spaces before the pasted sentences so that `The Subjects` section looks similar to Figure 3.8. Save your work and keep the `Status Report` file open to use in the next lesson, where you learn how to undo changes made.

continues

To Move and Copy Text (continued)

Figure 3.8
The sample report with the revised description for training subjects.

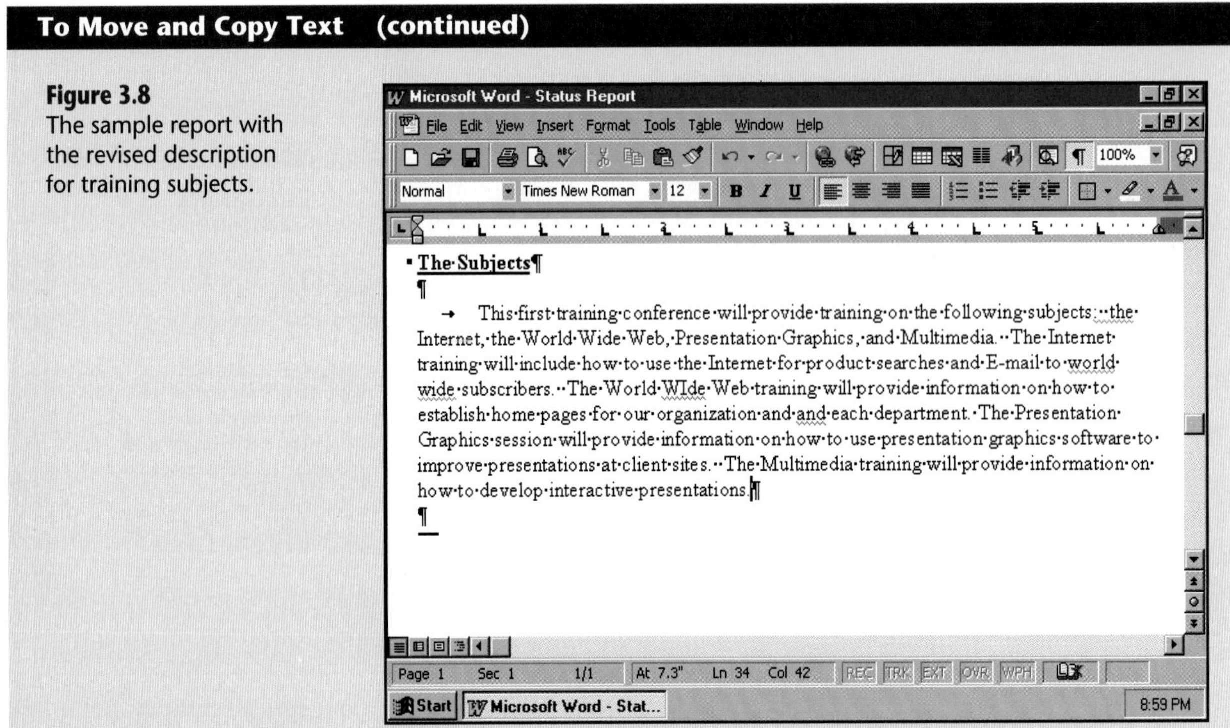

Microsoft Word - Status Report
File Edit View Insert Format Tools Table Window Help
Normal
Times New Roman
12
The Subjects
This first training conference will provide training on the following subjects: the Internet, the World Wide Web, Presentation Graphics, and Multimedia. The Internet training will include how to use the Internet for product searches and E-mail to world wide subscribers. The World WIde Web training will provide information on how to establish home pages for our organization and and each department. The Presentation Graphics session will provide information on how to use presentation graphics software to improve presentations at client sites. The Multimedia training will provide information on how to develop interactive presentations.
Page 1 Sec 1 1/1 At 7.3" Ln 34 Col 42
Start
Microsoft Word - Stat...
8:59 PM

Jargon Watch

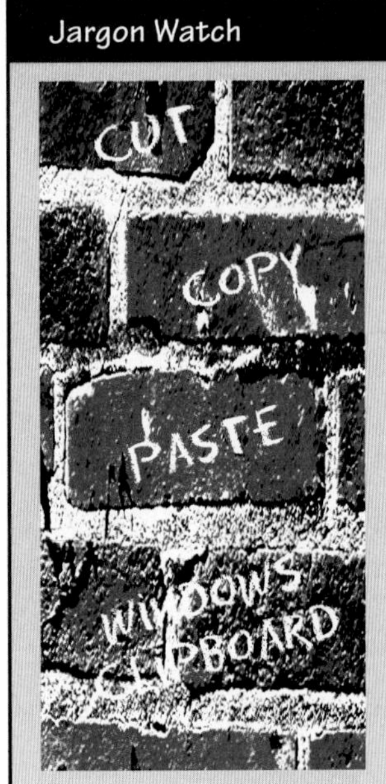

Word uses the terms *cut*, *copy*, and *paste* to describe moving and copying text. (You find each of these commands on the **E**dit menu.) When you **cut** text, you take the text out of its present location. When you **copy** text, you leave the text alone; that is, you just make a copy that you can put somewhere else. When you **paste** text, you insert the cut or copied text into a new location.

The **Windows Clipboard** is an area in memory reserved for text that you cut and copy. Because the Clipboard is a Windows feature, it is available to all Windows applications. This enables you to cut or copy text from one application (such as Word) and paste it into a document in another Windows application (such as Excel or your e-mail client).

When you cut or copy a section of text, the text stays in the Clipboard so that you can paste it into a new location. The text remains in the Clipboard until you copy or cut a new item, so you can paste it repeatedly to different locations. Because the Clipboard is shared by all Windows applications, make sure that you are finished with the first clipping before you cut or copy another one.

The steps for copying text are the same as for cutting text. The only difference is that you click the Copy button instead of the Cut button.

Word also offers several text-editing shortcuts. First, you can click to select text and—while holding down the mouse button—drag the text to a new location. If you click and drag, you move the selected text. If you hold down Ctrl while dragging, you copy the selected text. Of course, you can also use several keyboard shortcuts. Table 3.2 lists the shortcuts you can use to cut, copy, and paste text.

Finally, you can select text and then click the right mouse button (in the unselected area or in the window) to open a quick menu. The *shortcut menu* contains the Cu**t**, **C**opy, and **P**aste commands so that you can use them without leaving the mouse or having to move the mouse pointer to the menu items or toolbar.

Table 3.2 Keyboard Shortcuts to Cut, Copy, and Paste Text

Shortcut	Function
Shift+Del or Ctrl+X	Cuts text
Ctrl+Insert or Ctrl+C	Copies text
Shift+Insert or Ctrl+V	Pastes text

Lesson 4: Using the Undo Feature

The Undo feature reverses the actions that you take on a document. For example, if you accidentally rearrange the wrong paragraph or assign the wrong formatting command, the Undo feature lets you correct your mistake. Undo works for virtually every action you can take on a document—formatting, deleting, sorting, placing graphics, and so on.

For this lesson, you "accidentally" paste text into the middle of a paragraph. You then use the Undo feature to correct the error.

To Use the Undo Feature

1. **In the `Status Report` document, select `The Subjects` section, from the heading down through the paragraph.**

   You copy this section so that you can paste it into the wrong location.

2. **Click the Copy button.**

   The selected text doesn't change because this time you have copied text, not moved it. Word has made a copy of the text and saved it to the Clipboard so that you can paste the text somewhere else.

3. **Position the insertion point in the middle of `The Goals` section paragraph, as shown in Figure 3.9.**

continues

To Use the Undo Feature (continued)

Click the Paste button to insert the text

Click the Undo button to reverse the action

Position the insertion point here

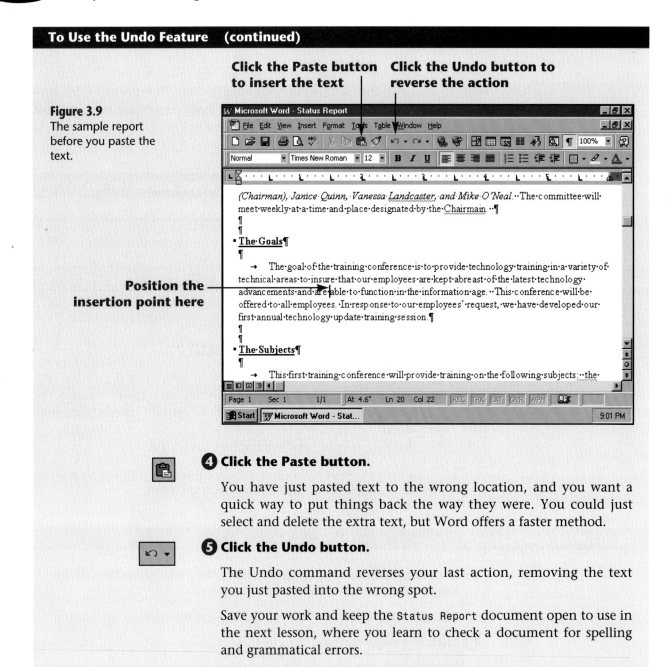

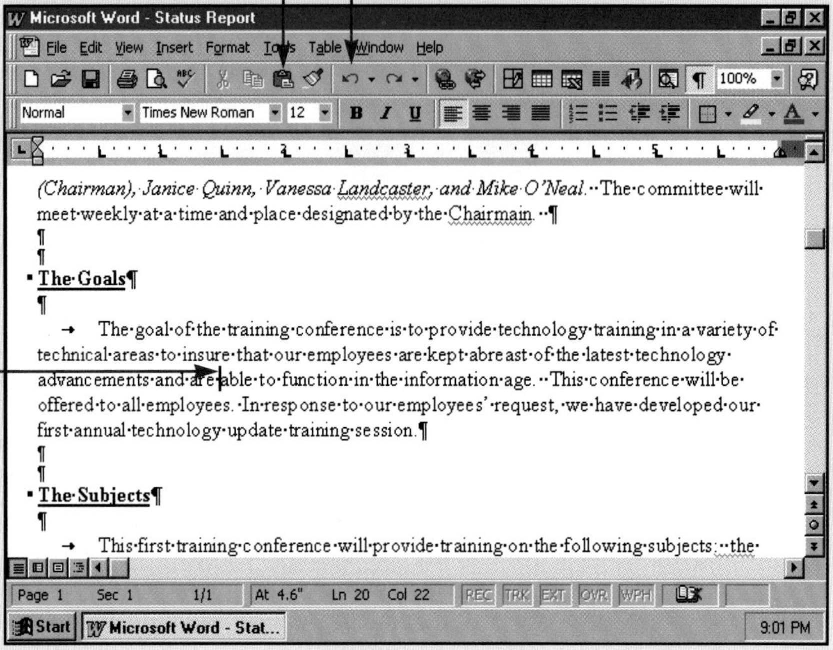

Figure 3.9
The sample report before you paste the text.

4 Click the Paste button.

You have just pasted text to the wrong location, and you want a quick way to put things back the way they were. You could just select and delete the extra text, but Word offers a faster method.

5 Click the Undo button.

The Undo command reverses your last action, removing the text you just pasted into the wrong spot.

Save your work and keep the `Status Report` document open to use in the next lesson, where you learn to check a document for spelling and grammatical errors.

If you have problems...

If Undo doesn't remove the pasted text, you probably performed another action on the document after you pasted the text. Any action, such as adding a space or deleting a word, is considered an action.

Clicking Undo reverses only the very last action taken, which may not be the one you intended to reverse. To undo a previous action, click the Undo button again. If you click the Undo button too many times, click the Redo button to reverse the undo actions.

You can undo a specific action by choosing the action from the Undo drop-down list. Simply click the Undo drop-down list arrow and select the action. Word reverses the actions up to and including that action.

The shortcut key for Undo is Ctrl+Z.

Lesson 5: Checking a Document for Spelling and Grammatical Errors

Even the best typists and spellers make mistakes now and then. With important documents, such as the status report, you don't want to make any mistakes. Word has a Spelling Checker program that you can use to check your documents for misspelled words, duplicate words, and irregular capitalization. The Grammar Checker proofs a document for problems with grammar, style, punctuation, and word usage. This program also offers advice for fixing potential problems. The two programs can be used together or separately, whichever you prefer. As you have already seen in earlier projects, they can both be turned on to mark potential problems (with a wavy underline) while you type.

Before you begin checking the status report, configure your system to check grammar with spelling and to show the readability statistics.

To Check a Document for Spelling and Grammatical Errors

1. **Choose Tools, Options.**

   The Options dialog box opens.

2. **Click the Spelling & Grammar tab.**

   This displays the Spelling & Grammar page of the Options dialog box, where you can customize the spelling and grammar checking. Make sure that the `Check spelling as you type`, `Check grammar with spelling` and `Show readability statistics` options are selected (they have check marks next to them).

3. **If the `Check spelling as you type` option does not have a check mark next to it, select it now.**

4. **If the `Check grammar with spelling` option does not have a check mark next to it, select it now.**

5. **If the `Show readability statistics` option does not have a check mark next to it, select it now.**

If you have problems...

If either of the two options are dimmed, it means that they are currently unavailable, so you need to install the Grammar Checker. Consult Microsoft Help, or ask your instructor for assistance.

continues

To Check a Document for Spelling and Grammatical Errors (continued)

6 Choose OK.

This closes the Options dialog box and saves your changes. Now, start the Spelling and Grammar checker.

7 In the `Status Report` file, press Ctrl+Home, and then click the Spelling and Grammar button.

The Spelling and Grammar dialog box opens, and Word starts checking the report. When Word finds a potential problem, it stops, highlights the word (or phrase) in the text, and makes suggestions on how you can correct it.

In this case, Word has stopped on the phrase `committee provide` (see Figure 3.10). The title of the top window identifies the problem as Subject-Verb Agreement, which is a grammatical error. The Suggestions window displays two suggestions that might correct the problem.

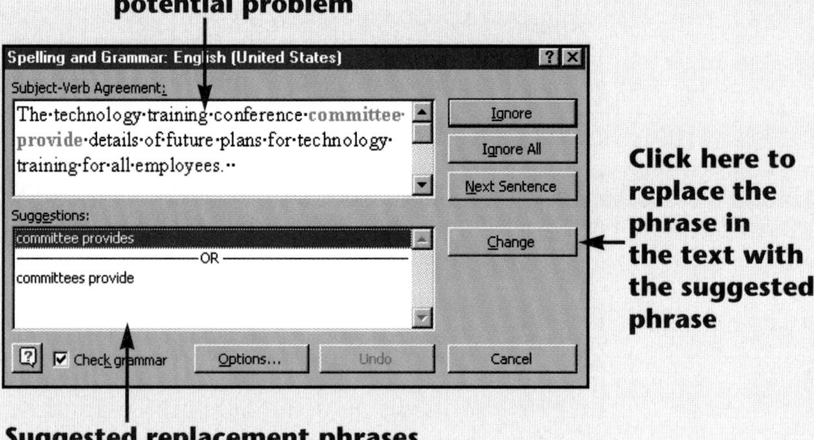

Figure 3.10 The Spelling and Grammar dialog box after a grammatical error has been detected.

If you have problems...

If you don't understand the grammatical error, click the Office Assistant button in the Spelling and Grammar dialog box. The Office Assistant displays explanatory messages that define the grammatical error and provide examples to help illustrate the concept. Click the button again to clear the messages.

8 Choose Change.

Because the phrase `committee provides` was already selected, choosing **C**hange replaces the phrase in the text with this phrase. Word continues checking the document and stops on the word `Landcaster` (see Figure 3.11). The program indicates that the word does not appear in the dictionary, and suggests a replacement word. This last name is misspelled; the correct spelling is *Lancaster*.

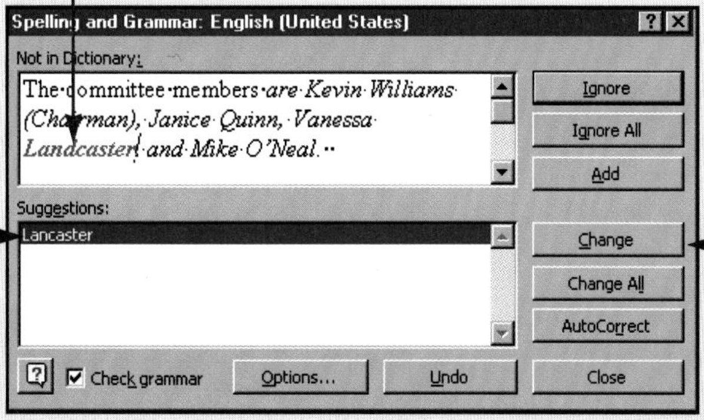

Misspelled word

Suggested replacement

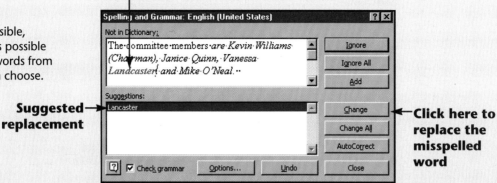

Click here to replace the misspelled word

Figure 3.11
Whenever possible, Word suggests possible replacement words from which you can choose.

9 Choose Change.

Word replaces the misspelled word with the correct spelling, `Lancaster`, and continues checking the document.

The Spelling Checker stops on another last name, `O'Neal`. This name isn't misspelled; it just isn't in the dictionary. Now you have a choice. You can ignore the word here (choose **I**gnore), or here and elsewhere in the document (choose I**g**nore All), or you can add the word to a custom dictionary. You will be using this name often in documents, so add the word to the dictionary.

10 Choose Add.

The next misspelled word is `Chairmain`. The suggested replacement word has the correct spelling, `Chairman`, so choose to replace it now.

11 Choose Change.

Word continues checking the document and stops on the phrase `:  the` because there is an extra space between words. While it is traditional to include two spaces after a colon, current writing styles use only one space. The suggestion is the same phrase with only one space.

12 Choose Change.

The next problem Word stops on is that of compound words. To get more information on this type of problem, open the Office Assistant.

13 Click the Office Assistant button in the Spelling and Grammar dialog box.

Clicking the Office Assistant button displays a message explaining the concept of compound words (see Figure 3.12). Read the information, then close the Office Assistant.

continues

To Check a Document for Spelling and Grammatical Errors (continued)

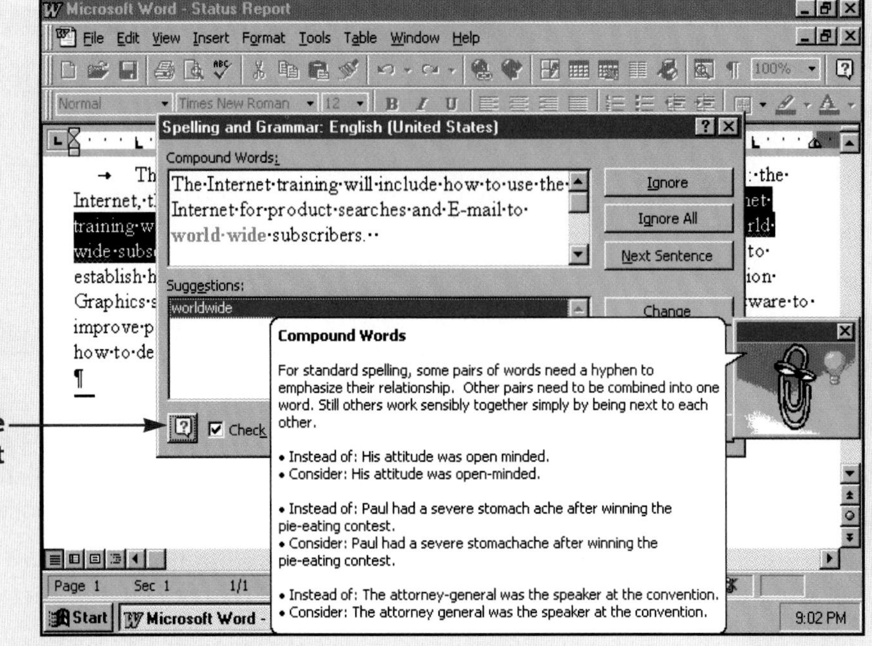

Figure 3.12
The Office Assistant offers more detailed information about grammatical errors.

14 Click the Office Assistant button.

This closes the Office Assistant and clears the message. Now, choose to change the phrase `world wide` with the correct one, `worldwide`.

15 Choose Change.

The next problem Word finds is with the word `WIde`, which contains irregular capitalization. The suggested replacement word has the correct capitalization, `Wide`, so choose to replace it now.

16 Choose Change.

The next error found is a duplicate word (`and and`). Read the phrase carefully before you choose to remove the duplicate word; in some cases, it is grammatically correct to have duplicate words. In this case, however, you want to delete the second occurrence of the word.

17 Choose Delete.

When the Spelling and Grammar checker finishes, the Readability Statistics dialog box is displayed with a list of word counts, averages, and readability scores for the document. These statistics help you determine if your document is meeting your needs (see Figure 3.13).

Figure 3.13
The Readability Statistics dialog box.

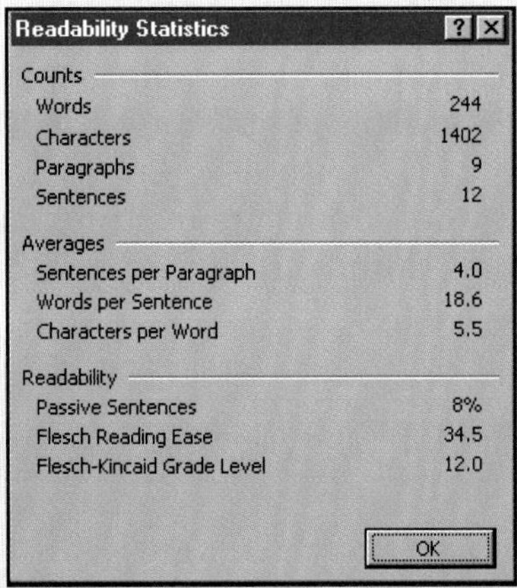

Readability Statistics
Counts
Words 244
Characters 1402
Paragraphs 9
Sentences 12
Averages
Sentences per Paragraph 4.0
Words per Sentence 18.6
Characters per Word 5.5
Readability
Passive Sentences 8%
Flesch Reading Ease 34.5
Flesch-Kincaid Grade Level 12.0
OK

If you have problems...

If the Readability Statistics dialog box doesn't appear, the Show **r**eadability statistics option in the Options dialog box isn't selected. Choose **T**ools, **O**ptions, click the Spelling & Grammar tab, and choose Show **r**eadability statistics; place a check mark in the checkbox to turn this feature on.

18 Choose OK.

Choosing OK clears the Readability Statistics dialog box. Save your work and keep the Status Report document open to use in the next lesson.

As a reminder, you can make corrections to a document as you type by right-clicking the words (or phrases) with the wavy underline. Right-clicking opens a Shortcut menu where you can choose an option. You can also correct the text manually. If the wavy underline disappears, the problem has been resolved.

In the preceding lesson, you chose to replace the misspelled last name `Landcaster` with `Lancaster`. If you often misspell this last name, consider adding it to the AutoCorrect list and let Word correct it for you. Simply choose AutoCorrect the next time Word stops on the word during a Spelling and Grammar check. Word adds the misspelled word and the selected replacement word to the AutoCorrect list. From now on, AutoCorrect makes the replacement for you as you type.

If you prefer, you can start the Spelling and Grammar checker by choosing **T**ools, **S**pelling and Grammar. Or you can just press F7.

When you start the Spelling and Grammar checker, the program checks the whole document by default, but you can change these settings. For example, if you have to edit a long document and you want to check only the area where you have made changes, you first select the text and then start the Spelling and Grammar checker. You can also check the spelling of a single word, which lets you verify the accuracy of the word without having to run the Spelling and Grammar checker on the whole document.

Lesson 6: Using the Thesaurus

When you need just the right word to describe something, Word has a Thesaurus program. This program also comes in handy if you discover that you have used the same word repeatedly in your document and you want to find a substitute. The Thesaurus program lists synonyms (words with similar meanings), antonyms (words with opposite meanings), and related words for a selected word.

To Use the Thesaurus

1 In the `Status Report` document, position the insertion point in the word `function` in the middle of the second paragraph.

This action selects the word you want to look up. You can also start Thesaurus from a blank screen.

2 Choose Tools, Language; then choose Thesaurus.

The Thesaurus dialog box opens with a list of synonyms and meanings for the word `function`, as shown in Figure 3.14.

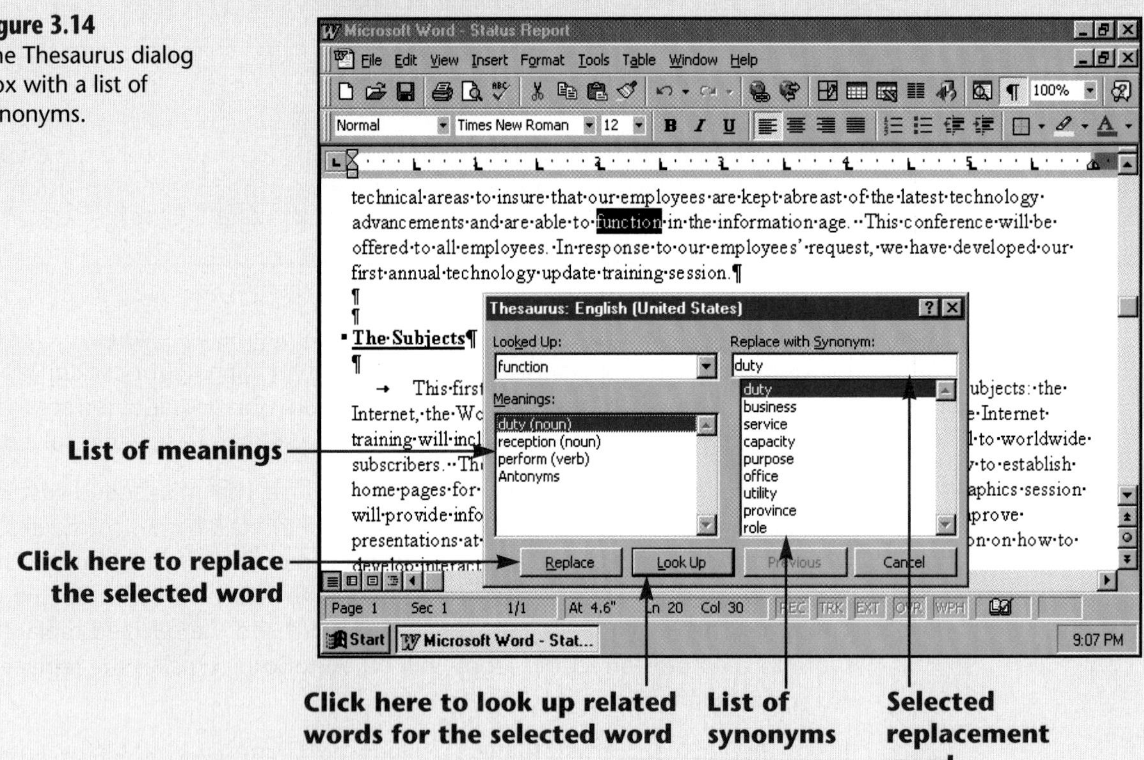

Figure 3.14
The Thesaurus dialog box with a list of synonyms.

3 Click the word `perform` in the Meanings list box.

This action places the word in the Replace with **S**ynonym text box and displays a list of meanings for the word `perform`. Suppose that you look through this new list and decide that the word `perform` fits the best. Because `perform` is already in the Replace with **S**ynonym text box, you can choose **R**eplace now.

4 Choose Replace.

With the help of the Thesaurus, you have improved the description in `The Goals` section.

Save your work and close `Status Report`. If you have completed your session on the computer, exit Word and shut down Windows before turning off the computer. Otherwise, continue with the next section, "Checking Your Skills."

If you prefer, you can open the Thesaurus by pressing Shift+F7.

You can look up synonyms by double-clicking a word in the Replace with **S**ynonym list box or by clicking a word in the **M**eanings list box. If the Thesaurus can't find any synonyms for a selected word, it displays a list of words with similar spellings in the **M**eanings list box. The **M**eanings list box may contain the terms `Antonyms` or `Related Words`. Click `Antonyms` to display a list of antonyms for the selected word; click `Related Words` to display a list of related words for the selected word.

Project Summary

To	Do This
Select text	Point to where you want to start selecting. Click and drag through the text, or hold down Shift and use the arrow keys and Ctrl, Home, End, PgUp, or PgDn to select text.
Deselect text	As long as you haven't released the mouse button as you select text, you can drag backward through the selected text to deselect text. If you're using Shift along with arrow keys, you can press the opposite arrow key to deselect text.
Cancel the selection	Click in the document window.
Select a word	Double-click the word.
Select a sentence	Hold down Ctrl and click the sentence.
Select a paragraph	Triple-click inside the paragraph or double-click once in the left margin area.
Bold text	Select the text and click the Bold button or press Ctrl+B.
Italicize text	Select the text and click the Italic button or press Ctrl+I.
Underline text	Select the text and click the Underline button or press Ctrl+U.
Move text	Select the text and click the Cut button or press Ctrl+X. Position the insertion point in the new location for the text, and then click the Paste button or press Ctrl+V.

continues

To	Do This
Copy text	Select the text and click the Copy button or press Ctrl+C. Position the insertion point in the new location for the text, and then click the Paste button or press Ctrl+V.
Reverse the last action	Click the Undo button or press Ctrl+Z.
Redo the last action	Click the Redo button or press Ctrl+Y.
Check a document for spelling and grammatical errors	Click the Spelling and Grammar button or press F7.
Look up a word in the Thesaurus	Position the insertion point within the word. Choose **T**ools, **L**anguage, **T**hesaurus; or press ⇧Shift+F7.

Checking Your Skills

True/False

For each of the following, check *T* or *F* to indicate whether the statement is true or false.

__T __F **1.** The Spelling and Grammar checker proofs your document for errors in word usage.

__T __F **2.** Moving a section of text is a two-step process: cut and paste.

__T __F **3.** A single mouse click on a word selects the word.

__T __F **4.** A green wavy underline indicates a possible grammatical error.

__T __F **5.** The Undo feature reverses the last action taken on a document.

__T __F **6.** If you press ⇧Shift+End, text is selected from the insertion point to the end of the document.

__T __F **7.** The formatting buttons and shortcut keys (bold, italic, and underline) work as toggles, turning formatting on and off.

__T __F **8.** You can undo a specific action by choosing the action from the **U**ndo drop-down list.

__T __F **9.** You cannot add more than one formatting feature (bold, underline, or italic) to selected text.

__T __F **10.** After you choose the **P**aste command, position the insertion point where you want the text located.

Multiple Choice

Circle the letter of the correct answer for each of the following questions.

1. What does the Spelling and Grammar checker look for?

- **a.** misspelled words
- **b.** duplicate words
- **c.** irregular capitalization
- **d.** All the above

2. How do you select an entire paragraph?

- **a.** By triple-clicking the paragraph
- **b.** By clicking the left margin area
- **c.** By double-clicking a sentence
- **d.** By holding down Ctrl and then clicking the sentence

3. Which menu contains the option to start the Thesaurus?

- **a.** Tools
- **b.** Edit
- **c.** Format
- **d.** Language

4. In the Spelling and Grammar dialog box, which choice ignores a single occurrence of a word?

- **a.** Change
- **b.** Ignore All
- **c.** Ignore
- **d.** Add

5. Ctrl+B is the shortcut for which feature?

- **a.** Italic
- **b.** Spelling Checker
- **c.** Bold
- **d.** Undo

6. If you want to copy a selection of text, click which button?

- **a.** Move
- **b.** Copy
- **c.** Duplicate
- **d.** Cut

7. What is the correct keyboard shortcut to cut selected text?

- **a.** Ctrl+X
- **b.** Ctrl+C
- **c.** Ctrl+T
- **d.** Ctrl+U

8. You can copy selected text by holding down which key and dragging the text to the new location?

- **a.** Alt
- **b.** Shift
- **c.** Ctrl
- **d.** Tab

9. If you click the Undo button three times, Word will undo which of the following?

- **a.** The most recent action three times
- **b.** Nothing after the last action is undone
- **c.** The three most recent actions
- **d.** Everything you have done since you saved the document

10. If you use a word often that is not in the dictionary, you should do what?

- **a.** Choose Ignore All to always ignore the word.
- **b.** Choose Ignore to ignore the word one time.
- **c.** Choose Skip to skip over this word.
- **d.** Add the word to the custom dictionary.

Completion

In the blank provided, write the correct answer for each of the following statements.

1. To move a section of text, you must ______________ the text first.
2. If you accidentally assign the wrong formatting to your document, use the ______________ feature to correct your mistake.
3. The Thesaurus displays lists of ______________ and ______________ for a word.
4. The **P**aste command ______________ text at the insertion point.
5. Right-clicking a word or phrase with a(n) ______________ opens a QuickMenu where you can choose from a list of suggested replacement words.
6. To select a sentence, hold down the ______________ key and click within the sentence.
7. When you cut or copy text, the text is placed on the Windows ______________.
8. The Cu**t**, **C**opy, and **P**aste commands are located on the ______________ menu.
9. If you often misspell the same word, you may want to add it to the ______________ list.
10. If you don't understand a grammatical error, click the ______________ ______________ button in the Spelling and Grammar dialog box.

Matching

In the blank next to each of the following terms or phrases, write the letter of the corresponding term or phrase. (Note that some letters may be used more than once.)

____**1.** Cancels current text selection

____**2.** Selects a word

____**3.** Selects text from insertion point to the beginning of the line

____**4.** Selects text from the insertion point up to the top of the document

____**5.** Italicizes selected text

____**6.** Duplicating text in multiple locations

____**7.** Removing text to be inserted in another location

____**8.** Skips all occurrences of a word not in spelling dictionary

____**9.** A word with a similar meaning to the word you are looking up

____**10.** A word that means the opposite of the word you are looking up

a. Shift+Ctrl+Home

b. antonym

c. cutting

d. Ctrl+I

e. synonym

f. clicking the mouse anywhere in the document window

g. copying

h. double-clicking a word

i. I**g**nore All

j. Shift+Home

Screen ID

Identify each of the items shown in Figure 3.15.

Figure 3.15

1. ____________
2. ____________
3. ____________
4. ____________
5. ____________
6. ____________
7. ____________

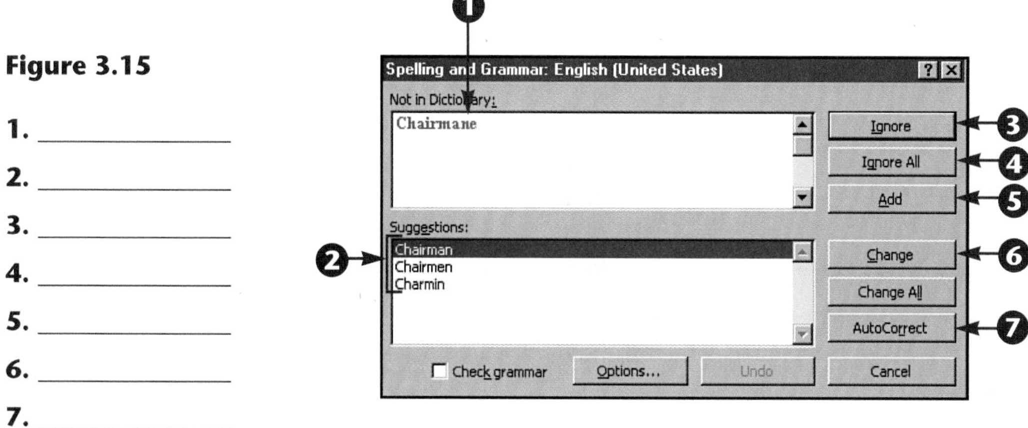

Applying Your Skills

Practice

The following exercises enable you to practice the skills you have learned in this project. Take a few minutes to work through these exercises now.

1. Preparing a Resume

To make a resume look more appealing, you can enhance certain text and rearrange existing text. Use the sample resume provided or substitute the sample text for your own personal information.

To Prepare a Resume

1. Open Proj0302 and save it as **Resume**.
2. Emphasize the name and address at the top of the resume with boldface. Make the heading **EXPERIENCE** bold. Add a heading to the section on education. Make sure that it matches the **EXPERIENCE** heading.
3. Underline every occurrence of the company name, CDs and Things, Inc., and change every occurrence of the subhead **Duties:** to italic.
4. Highlight your degrees by using bold, underline, or italic.
5. See how the resume will look if you move the **EDUCATION** section above the **EXPERIENCE** section.
6. Undo the move because it looks better the original way.
7. Check the spelling and grammar in the document.
8. Save the changes and, if requested by your instructor, print two copies. Then close the document.

2. Enhancing Radio Ad Copy

Enhance the radio ad copy you worked on in Project 2.

To Enhance Radio Ad Copy

1. Open the file Proj0303 and save it as `Enhanced Ad Copy`.
2. Emphasize the title with boldface.
3. Rearrange the sentences so that the information about where the store is located precedes the information on what the store sells. If necessary, edit the copy so that it makes sense.
4. Change every occurrence of the name of the store and of different types of music to italic.
5. Make the phrase `CD and tape exchange` bold and underline it.
6. Copy the name of the store, the address, and the phone number to the bottom of the document. Put each item on a separate line and make all three lines bold.
7. Check the spelling and grammar in the document.
8. Save the document and, if requested by your instructor, print two copies. Then close the document.

3. Organizing a Guest List

Organize a list of people you are thinking of inviting to a dinner party.

To Organize a Guest List

1. Open the file Proj0304 and save it as `Party List`.
2. Make the title bold and underline it.
3. You will invite only local people to the party, so delete all names and address of those not living in Indiana.
4. Highlight all names in boldface to make it easier to identify them.
5. You want to invite an even number of guests, so add Tracy Richardson's roommate, Steven McGee, to the list. Copy Tracy's address information for Steven.
6. Check the spelling in the list. Because the list includes many names you plan to use frequently, add the names that the Spelling and Grammar checker questions to the dictionary. Notice that, if you repeat the Spelling and Grammar check after adding the names to the dictionary, Word does not question them anymore.
7. Save the document and, if requested by your instructor, print two copies. Then close the document.

4. Enhancing the Parking Memo

Enhance the parking memo that you worked on in Project 2 to emphasize the information you feel is most important and to make a greater impression on the employees.

To Enhance the Parking Memo

1. Open the file Proj0305 and save it as `Enhanced Memo`.
2. Make the words `Date:`, `To:`, `From:`, and `Regarding:` bold.
3. Make the phrase `may have their parking privileges revoked` bold.

4. Switch the order of the last two sentences in the memo.
5. Add this line at the bottom: **I repeat, owners of cars that are found to be in violation of these regulations may have their parking privileges revoked.** To add this line, copy the existing line.
6. Use the Bullets button on the formatting toolbar to change the list of guidelines into a bulleted list. (*Hint:* Select the list and then click the button.)
7. Use italic to emphasize the first word in each item in the bulleted list.
8. Check the spelling and grammar in the document.
9. Save your changes. If requested by your instructor, print two copies. Then close the document.

5. Editing the Welcome Letter

Edit the welcome letter that you worked on in Project 2 to make it look more professional. There are also several spelling and grammatical errors that need to be fixed.

To Edit the Welcome Letter

1. Open the file named Proj0306.DOC, and save it as `Welcome Letter 2`.
2. Italicize **Association for Technical Trainers** in the first sentence.
3. Use the thesaurus to replace the word `special` in the first paragraph with a synonym.
4. Move the second paragraph above the first paragraph.
5. Spell check and grammar check the letter, making any necessary corrections. The name *Landers* is spelled correctly, so choose **I**gnore in the Spelling and Grammar dialog box.
6. Save the document and, if requested by your instructor, print two copies. Then close the document.

Challenge

The following challenges enable you to use your problem-solving skills. Take time to work through these exercises now.

1. Enhancing the Computer Training Cover Letter

You want to further enhance and edit the cover letter you worked on in Project 2 to be sent to those who request information from Computer Training Concepts. Open the file Proj0307.DOC and save it as `CTC Cover Letter 3`.

You want to emphasize the words **Computer Training Concepts (CTC)** and **excellent** in the first paragraph. Decide how to emphasize these words.

You decide to change the second occurrence of **facility** to a different word, so locate a synonym for this word.

Spell check and grammar check the letter, making any necessary corrections.

Print two copies of the letter, then save the file again. Close the file when you have finished.

2. Formatting the Course Descriptions Document

Now that you have learned to do some text formatting, you decide to improve the appearance of the Course Descriptions document you created in previous projects. Open the file Proj0308.DOC and save it as `Course Descriptions 3`.

Bold the three-line heading at the top of the document.

Italicize each course name in the document.

Move the descriptions of the Excel courses above the Word courses.

Cut the Word for Windows II course description. Undo this change, because this information was accidentally cut.

Save the file again, then print two copies. Close the file when you have finished.

3. Enhancing the Main Street Deli Menu

You decide to use some text formatting techniques to improve the appearance of the sign you created for the Main Street Deli. Open the Proj0309.DOC file and save it as `Deli Sign 2`.

You decide how to enhance the appearance of the sign, using bold, italic, and underlining.

Alphabetize the daily specials.

Save the document again and print one copy. Close the document when you have finished.

4. Enhancing the Membership Renewal Document

You need to edit the Membership Renewal document to enhance the text and make spelling and grammatical corrections. Open the Proj0310.DOC and save it as `Membership Renewal 2`.

Decide how to emphasize the text `HealthFirst Health Club` and `before` in the first paragraph. Emphasize the telephone number in the last paragraph.

Spell check and grammar check the letter.

Save the letter again, then print one copy. Close the file when you have finished.

5. Enhancing the Reunion Letter

To improve the appearance of the reunion letter you edited in Project 2, you decide to use some of the editing techniques you learned in this project. Open the Proj0311.DOC file and save it as `Reunion Planning 2`. Make the following changes:

Italicize each of the options in the question categories.

Bold the word `two` in the header sentence above each list of choices.

Move the date section above the location section of the letter.

Find an appropriate synonym for the word `new` in the locations section of the letter.

Save the letter again, then print three copies. Close the document when you are finished.

Project 4

Formatting Word Documents

Formatting an Annual Report

In this project, you learn how to:

- Change Margins
- Change Line Spacing
- Change Text Alignment
- Indent Text
- Insert Page Numbers
- Insert Page Breaks
- Change the Font and Font Size
- Insert a Header

Why Would I Do This?

Formatting
To arrange text and other page elements so the information is easier to read and appears polished.

Now that you have some experience creating and editing documents, you are ready to begin *formatting* your documents. Word has standard format settings already in place, enabling you to create many basic documents without changing any settings. To create a more professional-looking document, however, you can change the standard settings.

Simple formatting changes, such as using different margins and line spacing, can make a document easier to read. Page numbers, headers, and footers provide important information for the reader. One of the most popular enhancements—changing the font and font size—can improve the appearance of any document.

Lesson 1: Changing Margins

A document's margin settings determine how much white space there is around the text. You can specify left, right, top, and bottom margin settings for any document. Word has preset margins of 1" on the top and bottom, and 1.25" on the left and right sides. Because these are the standard margin widths for many kinds of business documents, you can create many documents without changing the margins.

In this lesson, you learn how to set different margin widths in a document. A section of an annual report has been provided for your use in this project, so you can open the file to begin formatting.

To Change Margins

1 From the Student Disk, open the Proj0401 file and save it as `Annual Report`.

Word opens the annual report in a new document window, as shown in Figure 4.1. You can now begin formatting the sample report.

2 Choose File, Page Setup.

The Page Setup dialog box is displayed, as shown in Figure 4.2. This dialog box has four different tabs. By default, the **M**argins tab is positioned in front of the other tabs. The dialog box features a sample document page (called the Preview area) so that you can preview your changes before you apply them to the document.

Figure 4.1
The annual report open in a document window.

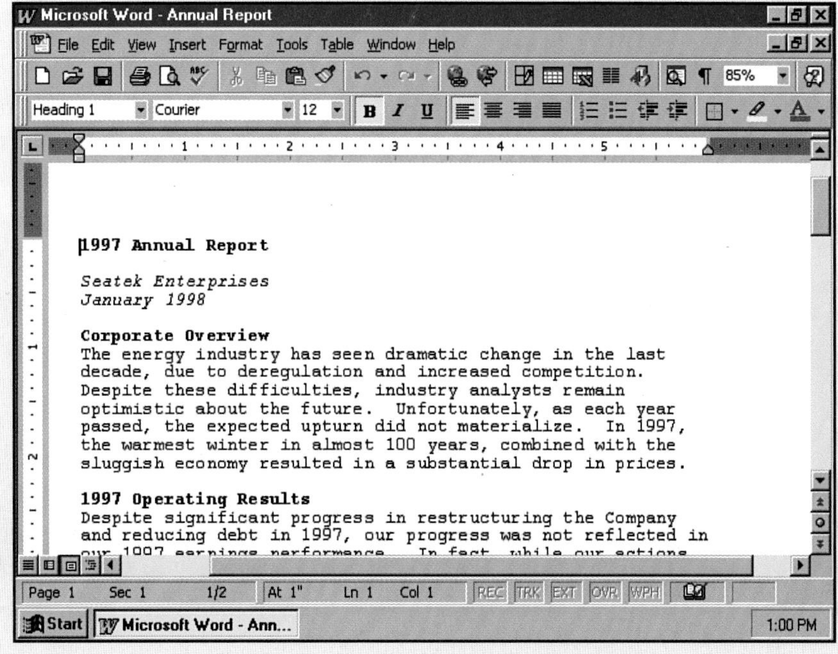

Figure 4.2
The **M**argins tab of the Page Setup dialog box.

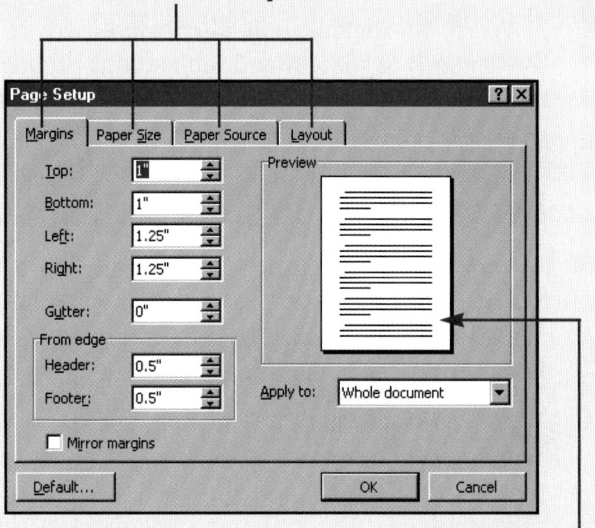

❸ Type `1.25` in the Top text box.

Because the **T**op text box is already selected when you open the Page Setup dialog box, you simply type the margin setting you want; your action replaces the old setting. Note that it isn't necessary to type the inch marks when you change a margin. If you prefer, you can click the up and down arrows (called *spinners*) at the right side of the **T**op text box to increase or decrease the setting.

continues

Change Margins (continued)

❹ **Press Tab and then type** `1.25`**.**

Pressing Tab moves you down to the **B**ottom text box and selects the current setting so that you can type a new setting in its place.

❺ **Press Tab again.**

Pressing Tab again moves you down to the Le**f**t text box and selects the contents. In this case, you simply want to move the insertion point, which updates the preview page. The preview page now shows you how the new top and bottom margins will look.

❻ **Choose OK.**

The new margins are applied to the document, and Word automatically repaginates the text accordingly.

❼ **Save your work and keep the** `Annual Report` **file open to use in the next lesson, where you learn to change the line spacing.**

You can also open the Page Setup dialog box (with the **M**argins tab showing) by double-clicking on the ruler, outside the margin settings.

In Word, the default unit of measurement is an inch, so you type measurements, such as margin and tab settings, in inches. You can change this unit of measure if you like. The other choices are centimeters, points, and picas.

Lesson 2: Changing Line Spacing

As you may have noticed when you worked on your letter in Project 2, Word uses single-spacing on all new documents. You can use the Line Spacing feature to change the amount of spacing between lines. For example, if you need to double-space a document, you change the line spacing to double.

You can set line spacing for the entire document, so you can have consistent settings for all paragraphs; you can also set line spacing for a single paragraph, so you can have special settings for different types of paragraphs. One of the many advantages of using styles is that you can use them to automate line spacing.

Try changing the line spacing for the report to double-spacing now.

To Change Line Spacing

1 In the `Annual Report` file, position the insertion point at the beginning of the heading `Corporate Overview`.

Before you can change the line spacing setting, you need to select the paragraphs that you want to change. In this case, you want to change the line spacing for the body of the document, but not the titles. Therefore, you need to select from the headings to the end of the document.

2 Press Ctrl+Shift+End.

Pressing all three keys at the same time selects text from the insertion point to the end of the document.

3 Choose Format, Paragraph.

The Paragraph dialog box is displayed, as shown in Figure 4.3. This dialog box has two tabs: the **I**ndents and Spacing tab and the Line and **P**age Breaks tab.

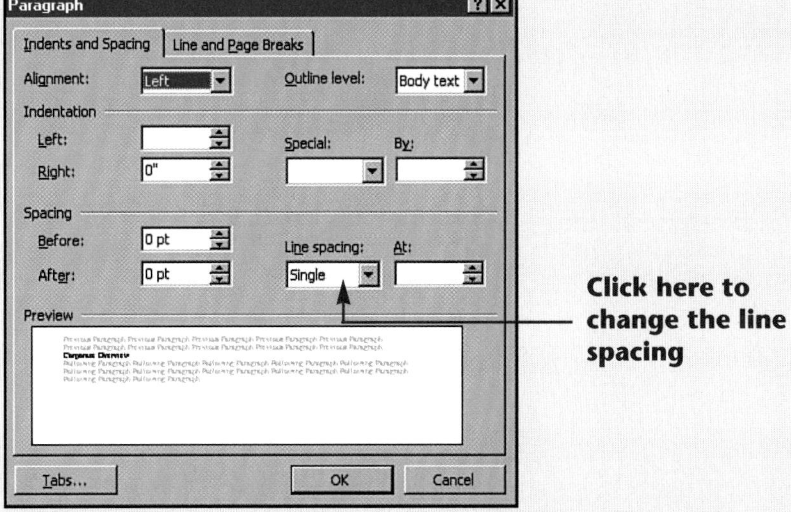

Figure 4.3
Use the Paragraph dialog box to set formatting for a selected paragraph or series of paragraphs.

4 Click the drop-down arrow next to the Line spacing box.
A drop-down list is displayed, listing the different line spacing options available. Table 4.1 lists the different line spacing options and their definitions.

5 Choose Double from the drop-down list, and then choose OK.

The Double option sets up double-spacing for the document. When you double-space your text, you have one blank line between lines in a paragraph and two blank lines between paragraphs.

continues

To Change Line Spacing (continued)

6 Press Ctrl+Home.

Pressing Ctrl+Home moves the insertion point to the top of the document and deselects the text. Now you need to add some spacing between the title and the two italicized lines.

7 Position the insertion point on the blank line below the title `1997 Annual Report`, and then press ↵Enter twice.

The report should now look like Figure 4.4.

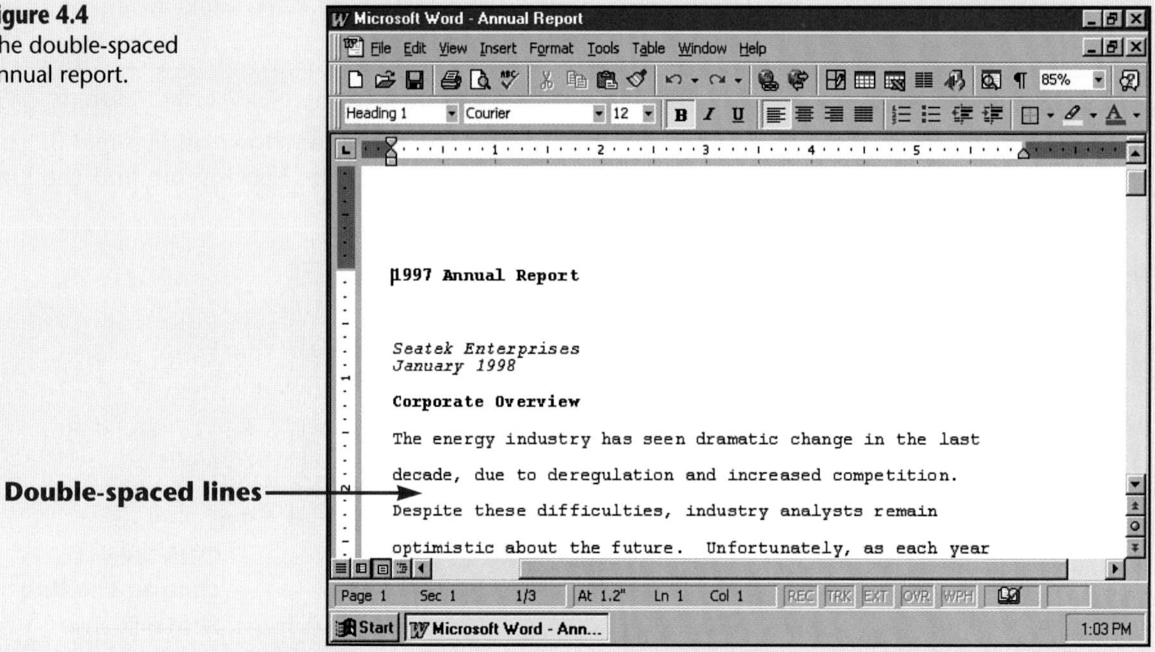

Figure 4.4
The double-spaced annual report.

Double-spaced lines

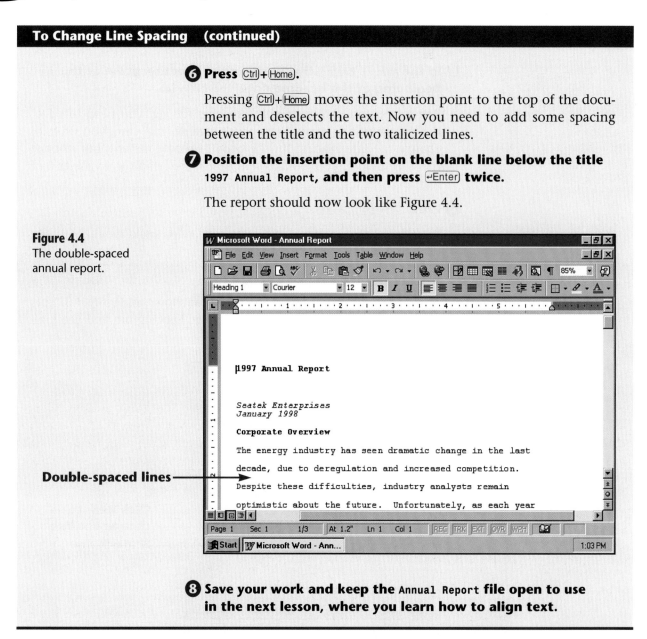

8 Save your work and keep the `Annual Report` file open to use in the next lesson, where you learn how to align text.

Table 4.1 Line Spacing Options

Spacing Option	Description
Single	A small amount of space is added between each line of text so the lines do not run together. The amount of space depends on the font used.
1.5 Lines	The line spacing is set to one and a half times that of single line spacing. The font used determines exactly how much space is used.
Double	The line spacing is set to two times that of single line spacing. The font used determines exactly how much space is used.

Spacing Option	Description
At Least	The minimum amount of spacing that Word can adjust to accommodate larger fonts or graphics that won't fit within the specified line spacing.
Exactly	The line spacing is fixed at the measurement that you specify. Word cannot adjust the line spacing to accommodate larger elements.
Multiple	You specify how much Word can adjust the line spacing (up or down) by specifying a percentage. For example, a setting of 1.25 increases the space by 25%; a setting of .75 decreases the space by 25%.

Word also provides keyboard shortcuts for changing the line spacing. Press Ctrl+1 for single-spacing, Ctrl+2 for double-spacing, and Ctrl+5 for 1.5 spacing.

You can also open the Paragraph dialog box by right-clicking any paragraph and choosing **P**aragraph from the shortcut menu.

Lesson 3: Changing Text Alignment

Alignment
The placement of text along the left margin, right margin, or both margins.

Alignment describes how text is placed between the left and right margins. Align Left (where text is aligned flush with the left margin, but not with the right) is the most commonly used setting; Word uses Left Justify as the default setting. Table 4.1 (following this lesson) provides a description of the four types of text alignment.

Now try changing the alignment of the text in the annual report.

To Change Alignment

1. **In the `Annual Report` file, choose Edit, Select All.**

   Because you want to change the alignment of the text for the entire annual report, you need to select all the text at once. Now that you have selected the text, you can choose the alignment option.

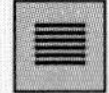

2. **In the Formatting toolbar, click the Justify button.**

   When you click the Justify button, Word inserts a small amount of space between the characters so that the text is placed against both the left and right margins. Fully justified text creates a more formal appearance.

3. **Click inside the document window to deselect the text.**

   The annual report text should now appear fully justified (with smooth left and right margins). Now center the report's title.

continues

To Change Alignment (continued)

4 Position the insertion point within the title, `1997 Annual Report`.

This is the text you want to center. If your title was more than one line (with hard returns separating the lines), you would have to select all the lines to center them.

5 In the Formatting toolbar, click the Center button.

The title is now centered between the left and right margins, as shown in Figure 4.5.

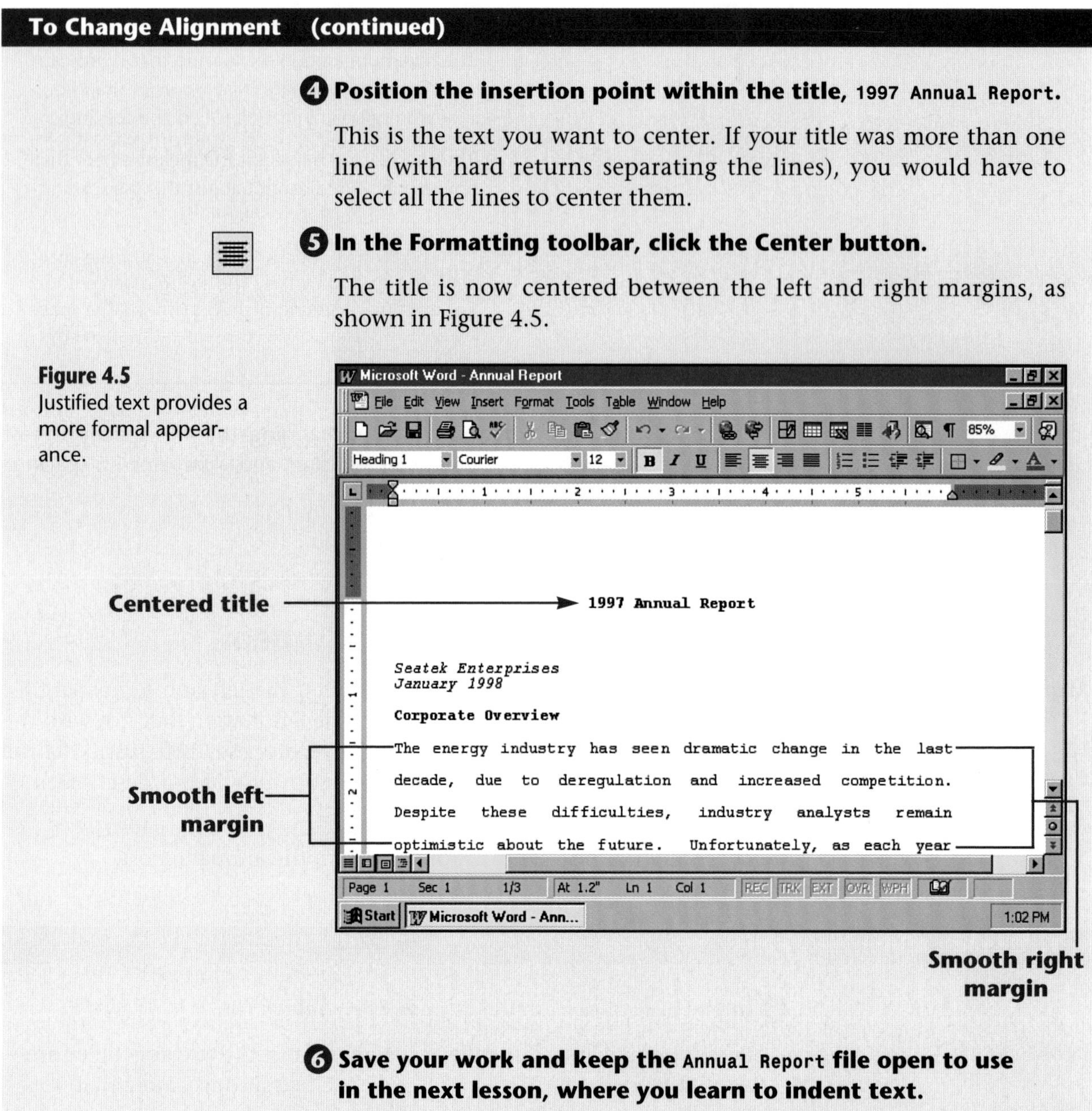
Microsoft Word - Annual Report
Centered title
1997 Annual Report
Seatek Enterprises
January 1998
Corporate Overview
The energy industry has seen dramatic change in the last
decade, due to deregulation and increased competition.
Despite these difficulties, industry analysts remain
optimistic about the future. Unfortunately, as each year
Smooth left margin
Smooth right margin

Figure 4.5
Justified text provides a more formal appearance.

6 Save your work and keep the `Annual Report` file open to use in the next lesson, where you learn to indent text.

Table 4.1 Justification Options

Button	Option	Effect on the Text
	Align Left	Aligns text along the left margin only; the left side appears smooth, and the right side appears ragged. Align Left is the default setting for all new documents.
	Center	Centers text between the left and right margins.

Button	Option	Effect on the Text
	Align Right	Aligns text along the right margin only; the right side appears smooth, and the left side appears ragged.
	Justify	Aligns text along the left and right margins so that both sides appear smooth.

If you prefer, you can use Ctrl+A to select all the text, instead of choosing **E**dit, Select A**l**l.

Lesson 4: Indenting Text

You can use Tab to indent (move to the right) the first line of a paragraph. People often use this style in formal reports, letters, and legal documents. If you need to indent all the lines in a paragraph, you can use the Indent feature.

Don't make the mistake of using Tab at the beginning of each line in a paragraph. The paragraph may look okay now, but if you change anything later that causes the text to reformat (such as adding or deleting text, or changing the margins), the tabs move around with the text and end up in the wrong places. You need to use Indent instead.

At the top of the third page of the annual report, you see a quotation from the Chief Financial Officer, Grant Keeper. The correct format for a quotation is to be indented along both the left and right sides (a double indent), with single-spaced lines within the quotation. Try making these adjustments to the quotation now.

To Indent Text

1 In the `Annual Report` file, position the insertion point at the beginning of the following quotation:

`1998 is the year we take the bull by the horns. Everyone at Seatek must pull together and work toward our mutual success. I'm counting on each and every employee to focus on our common goals.`

This quotation needs to be indented (see Figure 4.6). Because you are formatting only a single paragraph, you don't need to select the text first; just make sure that the insertion point is in the paragraph you want to format.

continues

To Indent Text (continued)

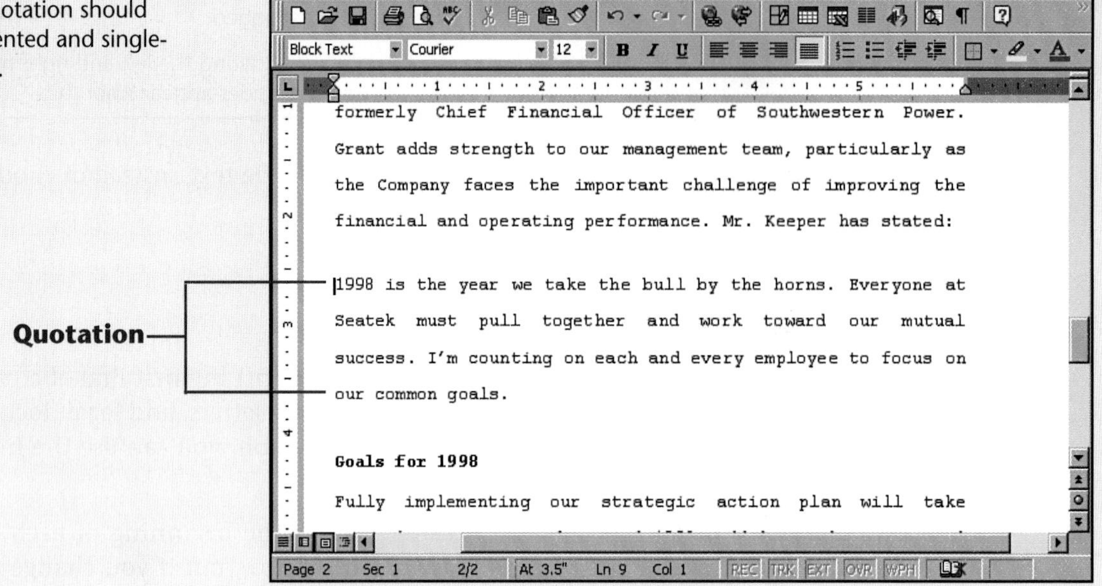

Quotation
File Edit View Insert Format Tools Table Window Help
Block Text
Courier
12
formerly Chief Financial Officer of Southwestern Power.
Grant adds strength to our management team, particularly as
the Company faces the important challenge of improving the
financial and operating performance. Mr. Keeper has stated:
1998 is the year we take the bull by the horns. Everyone at
Seatek must pull together and work toward our mutual
success. I'm counting on each and every employee to focus on
our common goals.
Goals for 1998
Fully implementing our strategic action plan will take
Page 2 Sec 1 2/2 At 3.5" Ln 9 Col 1 REC TRK EXT OVR WPH

Figure 4.6
This quotation should be indented and single-spaced.

2 Choose Format, Paragraph.

The Paragraph dialog box is displayed. You need to set the indent space in the Indentation section of the dialog box.

3 Press Tab twice.

Pressing Tab twice moves the insertion point down to the **L**eft spin box and selects the contents.

4 Type 1 in the Left text box and press Tab.

Typing 1 sets the Left indentation at one inch. Pressing Tab moves the insertion point to the **R**ight text box and selects the current setting.

5 Type 1 in the Right text box.

The quotation is indented by one inch on both sides. Next, you want to single-space the quotation.

6 Click the Line Spacing drop-down list arrow, choose Single; then choose OK.

The quotation appears indented on both sides and single-spaced. The report should now look like Figure 4.7.

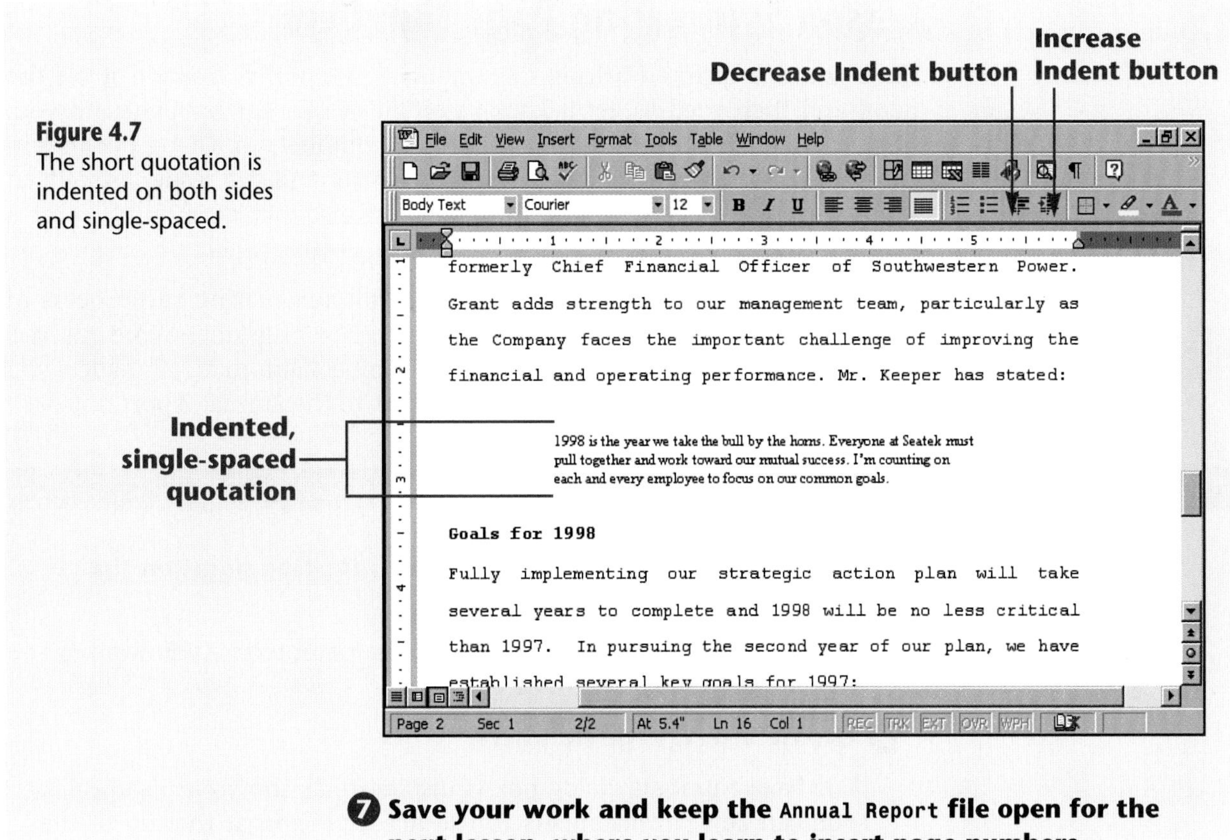
Increase Indent button
Decrease Indent button
Indented, single-spaced quotation
File Edit View Insert Format Tools Table Window Help
Body Text
Courier
12
formerly Chief Financial Officer of Southwestern Power.
Grant adds strength to our management team, particularly as
the Company faces the important challenge of improving the
financial and operating performance. Mr. Keeper has stated:
1998 is the year we take the bull by the horns. Everyone at Seatek must
pull together and work toward our mutual success. I'm counting on
each and every employee to focus on our common goals.
Goals for 1998
Fully implementing our strategic action plan will take
several years to complete and 1998 will be no less critical
than 1997. In pursuing the second year of our plan, we have
Page 2 Sec 1 2/2 At 5.4" Ln 16 Col 1 REC TRK EXT OVR WPH

Figure 4.7
The short quotation is indented on both sides and single-spaced.

7 Save your work and keep the `Annual Report` file open for the next lesson, where you learn to insert page numbers.

The Formatting toolbar has two Indent buttons (refer to Figure 4.7). The Increase Indent button indents the text (from the left side only) to the next tab setting. Each time you click this button, the text moves one tab setting to the right. The Decrease Indent button moves the text to the left by one tab setting.

There is another shortcut for indenting text from the left side only. Press Tab at the beginning of the first line in the paragraph. Move down to the beginning of any other line in the paragraph and press Tab. Each time you press Tab, Word indents the paragraph over one more tab setting.

You can create a hanging indent and a single-line indent by choosing one of the options from the **S**pecial drop-down list in the Paragraph dialog box. If you choose the First Line option, you specify how much you want the first line indented in the B**y** text box; if you choose the Hanging option, you specify how much you want the second and subsequent lines indented in the B**y** text box.

You can also set up indents on the ruler. Although it is not as quick and easy as the method described previously, the ruler gives you more control by allowing you to pick the exact space for the indent. For more information, refer to the Microsoft Help Topic, `Set left and right indents by using the ruler.`

Lesson 5: Inserting Page Numbers

Have you ever printed a long document, accidentally dropped it on the floor, and then tried to get it back in order? If this has happened to you, then you already know why you want page numbers in a long document. Page numbers offer a convenience for the writer and the reader as well. In some cases, such as long legal documents or transcripts, page numbers are a required element.

The Page Numbers feature saves you time by automating the process of including page numbers in your documents. Not only does Word insert a page number for you, but it updates the numbers automatically when you add or delete pages. Try adding page numbers to the annual report now.

To Insert Page Numbers

1 In the `Annual Report` file, position the insertion point on the first page of the document.

The first step is to position the insertion point where you want the page numbering to begin.

2 Choose Insert, Page Numbers.

The Page Numbers dialog box is displayed, as shown in Figure 4.8. You can add page numbers to the header region at the top of the page or to the footer region at the bottom of the page. By default, the **P**osition setting puts page numbers on the bottom right side of the page (the footer region).

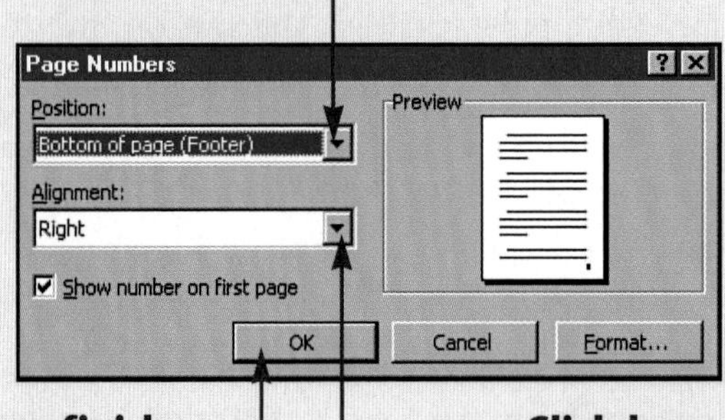

Figure 4.8
Use the Page Numbers dialog box to insert page numbers into a document.

3 Choose Center from the Alignment drop-down list and then choose OK.

This choice centers the numbers at the bottom of every page. Notice that Word has switched to the Page Layout view. In order to see the page numbers at the bottom of the page, you have to be in Page Layout view, so Word is anticipating your needs by automatically switching to this view. If you prefer, you can switch back to Normal view by choosing **V**iew, **N**ormal.

In many cases, you don't want the page number to appear on the first page. If not, click the **S**how Number on First Page check box to deselect the option (and suppress the page number on the first page only). For this report, however, you do want the page number printed on the first page, so you should leave this option selected.

To preview the page numbers without printing the document, you use the Print Preview feature.

4 Click the Print Preview button.

The Print Preview window is displayed, as shown in Figure 4.9. Notice the page numbers centered at the bottom of each page.

Figure 4.9
The annual report is displayed in the Print Preview window.

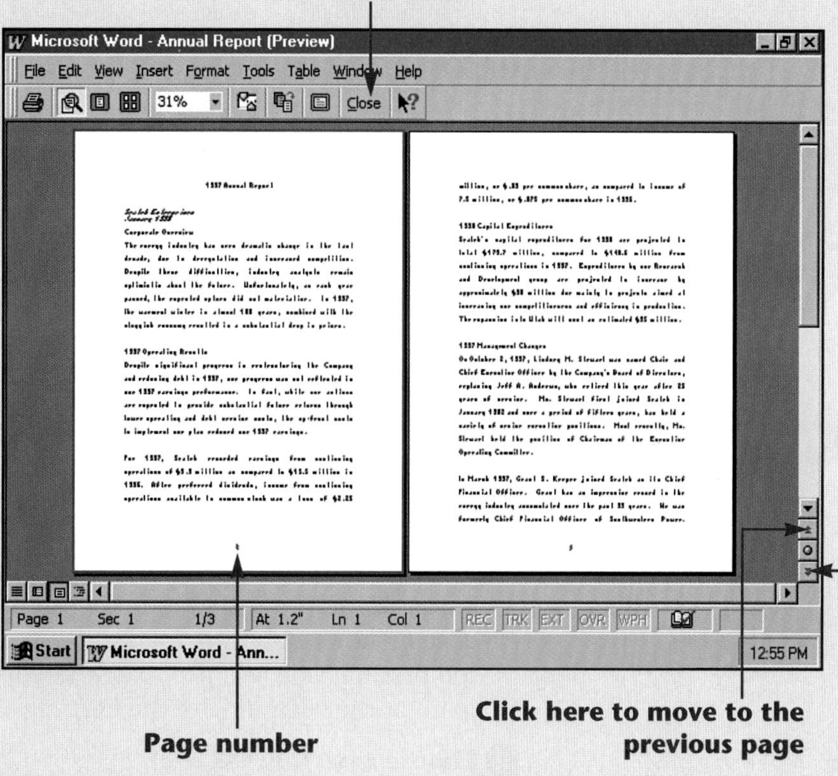

5 Click the Close button on the Print Preview toolbar.
Clicking the **C**lose button closes Print Preview and redisplays the report in the document window.

6 Save your work and keep the `Annual Report` file open to use in the next lesson, where you learn to insert page breaks.

You can insert page numbers in headers or footers; or on the left, center, or right side of the page. If you insert page numbers in these regions, you'll need to view the header or footer (choose **V**iew, **H**eader and Footer) to edit or format the page numbers. If you decide to insert the page number inside the text, you can click and drag the page number frame to position the page number exactly where you want it; then you can format the page number inside the frame.

Running-total page numbers (such as `Page x of y`) can be created in the header or footer regions of the page. You have your choice of numeric, alphabetic, or Roman Numeral page numbers, and because page numbers are inserted directly into the text, you can surround them with dashes or precede them with text (such as `Page 1`). You can restart page numbers at the beginning of each chapter or section and you can include the chapter numbers in the page numbering scheme if you like (such as `1-2`).

Lesson 6: Inserting Page Breaks

When you have typed enough text to fill the current page, Word automatically creates a new page for you, creating a *soft page break*. In certain documents, however, you may want to control where page breaks occur. In such cases, you can insert a page break, called a *hard page break*.

For example, you may decide that you want each heading to start on a new page. You can do this by inserting page breaks. In the sample annual report, insert page breaks so that each heading starts on a new page.

To Insert a Page Break

1 In the `Annual Report` file, position the insertion point at the beginning of the second heading, `1997 Operating Results`.

Make sure that you position the insertion point where you want the page break to occur. In this case, you want the heading to become the first item on the new page, so you need to place the insertion point at the beginning of the heading.

2 Choose Insert, Break.

The Break dialog box is displayed (see Figure 4.10). The **P**age Break option is already selected.

3 Choose OK.

Choosing OK inserts a page break at the point you indicated (see Figure 4.11). Depending on the view mode you are using (Page Layout or Normal), hard page breaks look different on-screen. In Normal View, a hard page break is indicated by a dotted line across the page with the words `Page Break` in the center of the line. Soft page breaks are indicated by a dotted line only. In Page Layout view, both types of page breaks are indicated by the bottom edge of the previous page and the top edge of the next page; a gray border separates the pages.

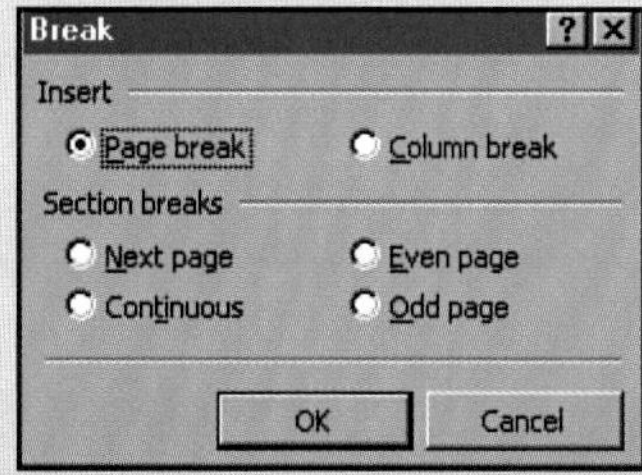

Figure 4.10
Use the Break dialog box to insert different types of breaks within a document.

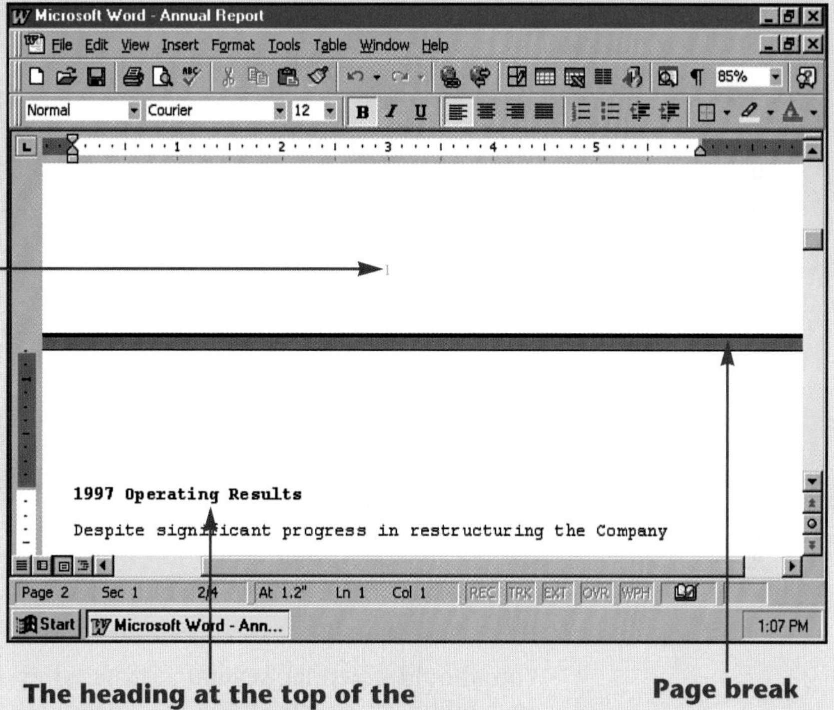

Figure 4.11
In Page Layout view, the bottom edge of the current page and top edge of the next page are shown with a gray border between them.

4. **Position the insertion point at the beginning of the next heading,** `1998 Capital Expenditures`**.**

5. **Press Ctrl+Enter.**

   Pressing Ctrl+Enter inserts a page break at the beginning of the heading so that it begins on a new page. Most people find this shortcut to be the fastest way to insert page breaks.

6. **Position the insertion point at the beginning of the next heading,** `1997 Management Changes`**.**

7. **Press Ctrl+Enter.**

8. **Position the insertion point at the beginning of the next heading,** `Goals for 1998`**.**

continues

To Insert a Page Break (continued)

9. **Press Ctrl+Enter.**

   Now each section of the report begins on a new page.

10. **Save your work and keep the `Annual Report` file open to use in the next lesson, where you learn to change the font and font size.**

Jargon Watch

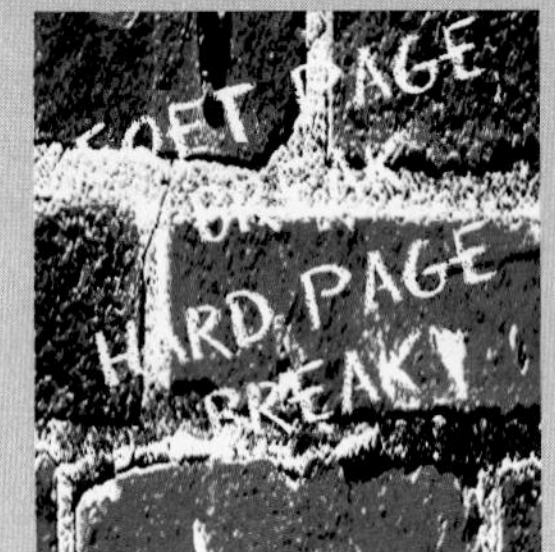

When Word automatically creates a new page for you, that page is called a **soft page break**. A soft page break operates much like a soft return, which Word inserts in the document at the end of each line in a paragraph. As with a soft return, you can't delete a soft page break.

As you recall from Project 2, when you press Enter you insert a hard return, which forces Word to move to a new line. If you want to force Word to move to a new page, you insert a **hard page break**. Because you insert hard returns and hard page breaks in the document, you can delete these items as needed.

Lesson 7: Changing the Font and Font Size

Font
The style, weight, and typeface of a set of characters.

Simply put, a *font* is the style of type used for your text. When typewriters were the primary source of printed pages, the choice of fonts was extremely limited. Now, in the age of word processing software and laser printers, you can choose from literally thousands of fonts. You can use one font for all the text in a document, or you can use different fonts for different parts of the document. For example, you may choose one font for headings, another for body text, and yet another for special notes or tables.

You should consider several factors when choosing a font, including its readability, its suitability to the document's subject, and its appeal to the reader.

Font size
The size of a font is actually the height of a character, which is measured in points. A 72-point font has characters that are roughly one inch high.

In Word, the default font is Times New Roman; the default *font size* is 10-point. Unless you change to another font or font size, your documents are created with this font. A 10-point or 12-point font is appropriate for most business documents.

In the annual report, all the text is formatted in 12-point Courier. Try changing the font and font size for the text, title, and headings in the annual report now.

To Change the Font and Font Size

1 In the `Annual Report` file, choose Edit, Select All.

For this example, you need to change the font for the entire document, so you need to select the document first.

2 Click the Font drop-down arrow on the Formatting toolbar.

The Font drop-down list displays the available fonts for the current printer (see Figure 4.12). You can scroll through the list to see all the font choices.

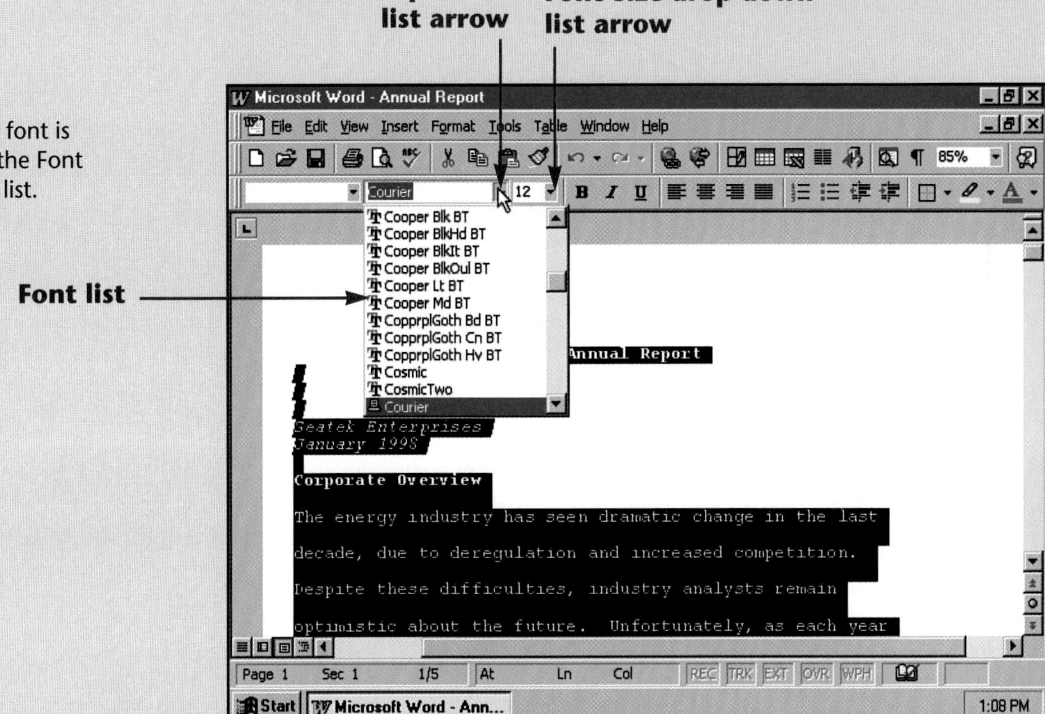

Figure 4.12 The current font is selected in the Font drop-down list.

3 Choose Times New Roman (scroll down through the list, if necessary).

The document is now displayed in the Times New Roman font, a font often used for body text (see Figure 4.13). Next, change the font and font size for the title.

continues

To Change the Font and Font Size (continued)

Figure 4.13
The sample report with the text in a new font.

Times New Roman font
Microsoft Word - Annual Report
1997 Annual Report
Seatek Enterprises
January 1998
Corporate Overview
The energy industry has seen dramatic change in the last decade, due to deregulation and
increased competition. Despite these difficulties, industry analysts remain optimistic about

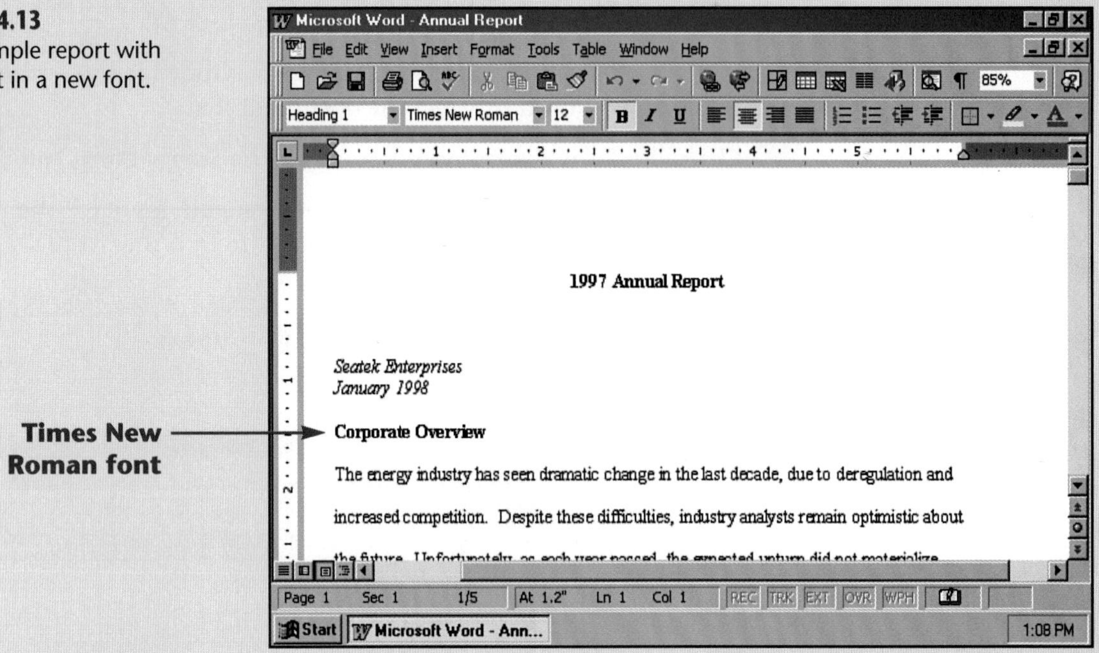

4. **Select the title `1997 Annual Report`.**
5. **Click the Font drop-down arrow.**
6. **Choose Arial.**

   Arial is a popular font and is often used for titles and headings to make them stand out from the rest of the text. While the title is still selected, increase the size of the font as well.

7. **Click the Font Size drop-down arrow.**

   The Font Size drop-down list displays a range of font sizes. You can scroll through the list if you don't see the size you want.

8. **Choose 16.**

   Clicking 16 changes the point size of the title to 16, which is 4 points larger than the body text of the report. You want the title to be large enough to set it apart from the rest of the report, but not so large that it distracts the reader.

9. **Click inside the document window to deselect the heading.**

   The report should look like Figure 4.14.

10. **Save your work and keep the `Annual Report` file open to use in the next lesson, where you learn to insert a header.**

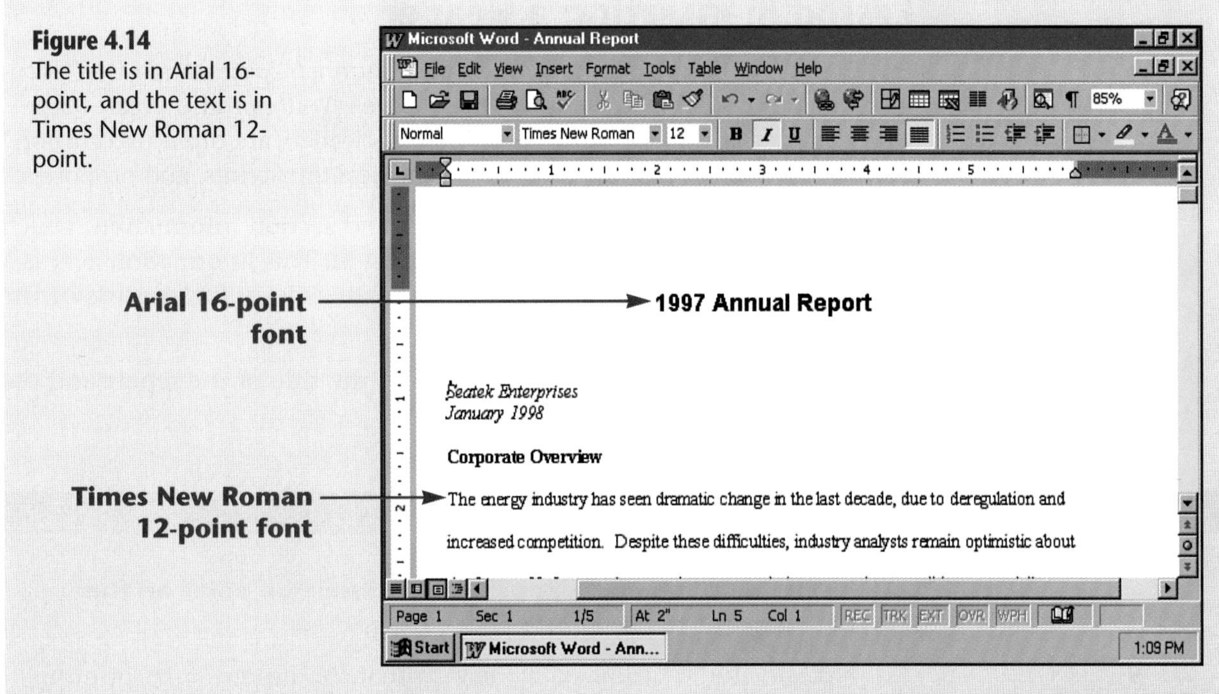

Figure 4.14
The title is in Arial 16-point, and the text is in Times New Roman 12-point.

Jargon Watch

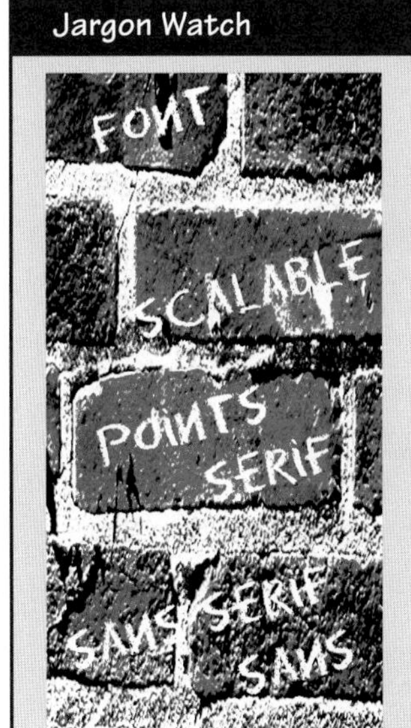

The term **Font** describes the size and style of the typeface used in your text. The Windows program includes a collection of scalable fonts that you can use with Word. **Scalable** fonts aren't restricted to a specific size; the font files contain all the information you need to create a character in any size. Non-scalable fonts are only available in one size because the font file contains the characters in that size only.

Font sizes are measured in **points**, a measurement of the font height. For example, a 12-point font is the standard size for most documents; a 72-point font is roughly one inch high.

The body text of the report in this project appears in the Times New Roman font, a **serif** font. A serif font has tiny flourishes on each character that help move the reader's eye across the line, making long passages of text easier to read. The title is in the Arial font, a **sans serif** font. **Sans** means "without," so a sans serif font doesn't have the flourishes. The sans serif font has a cleaner look, which makes it better suited to short blocks of text, such as titles and headings.

If you want to see a preview of a particular font, or if you want to see and change all the font options in one place, you can use the Font dialog box to make your changes. Choose F**o**rmat, **F**ont to access the Font dialog box. The Font and Font Size lists are also found in this dialog box, along with special font effects and color.

Lesson 8: Inserting a Header

Headers let you place document titles, page numbers, dates, and other document identification at the top of every page. (You can also create *footers*, which appear at the bottom of every page.) Headers are often used in long documents, such as reports, legal briefs, medical transcripts, and proposals.

A header may contain the current chapter and section information, which you can change for each new chapter or section. This information acts as a point of reference for readers so that they can quickly locate parts of the document.

In this lesson, you add a header containing the title of the report and the date the annual report was prepared.

To Insert a Header

1 In the `Annual Report` file, position the insertion point on the first page of the document.

Position the insertion point here so that the header starts printing on the first page.

2 Choose View, Header and Footer.

Word switches to Page Layout view. A Header and Footer toolbar is displayed in the middle of the screen. The header area on the page is outlined with a dotted line (see Figure 4.15).

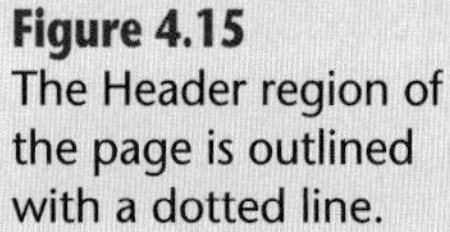

Figure 4.15
The Header region of the page is outlined with a dotted line.

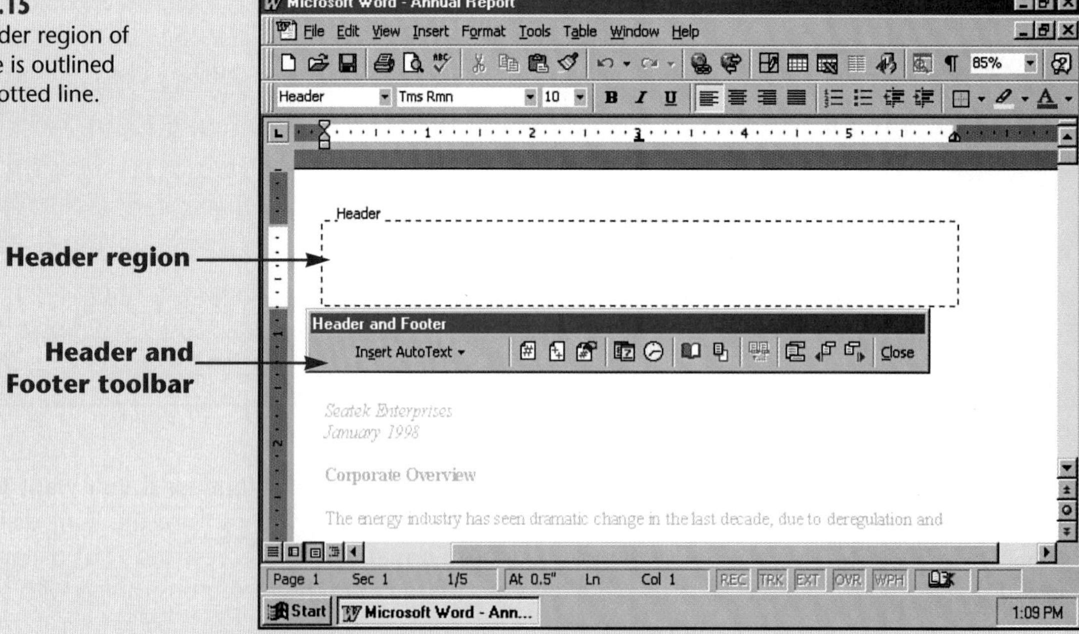

3 Type `1997 Annual Report`.
Look at the Formatting toolbar and notice that Word has already selected a 10-point font for the header text. This size ensures that the header does not distract the reader from the body text.

4 Press Tab twice.

In the Header region, pressing Tab once moves you to the center of the line; pressing Tab twice moves you to the right side of the header box (or flush right).

5 Type `January 1998.`

Your report should now look similar to Figure 4.16.

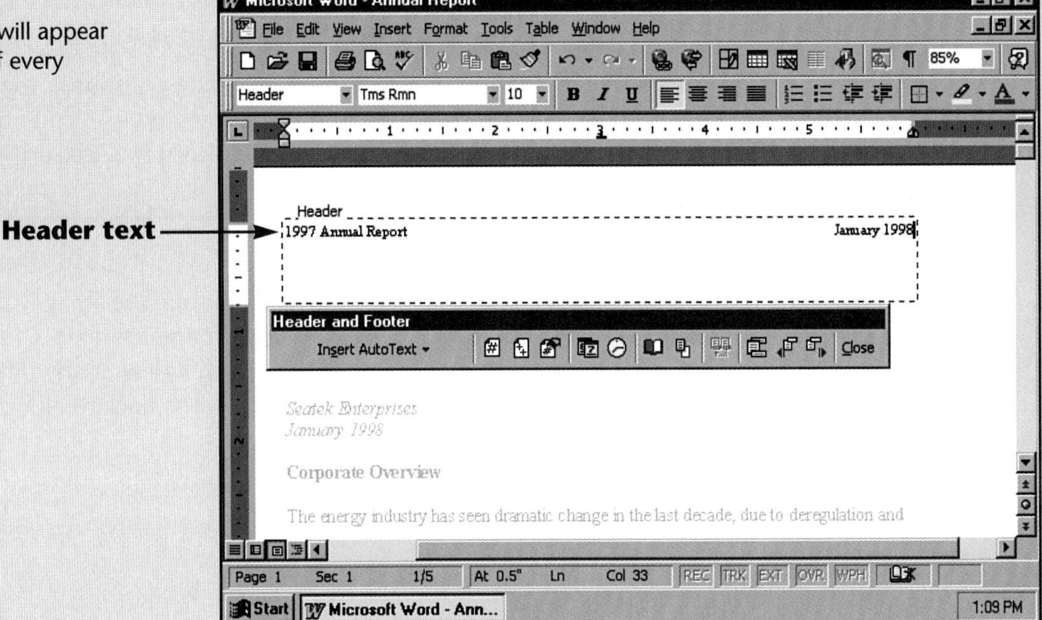

Figure 4.16 The header will appear at the top of every page.

The last step is to suppress the printing of the header on the first page of the report. Because this page contains the report title, the header text might look out of place.

6 Click the Page Setup button.

Clicking the Page Setup button opens the **L**ayout page of the Page Setup dialog box. In the Headers and Footers section, there is an option called Different **f**irst page. When you select this option, you can create a separate header for the first page only. For this document, you'll leave this header empty, so nothing will print in the header region of the first page.

7 Choose Different first page and then choose OK.

The Header region at the top of the first page is now clear with the title `First Page Header` above the dotted line. This should remain empty so nothing prints on the first page. The header text you typed earlier will appear on all the subsequent pages.

continues

To Insert a Header (continued)

8 Click the Close button on the Header and Footer toolbar.

Word clears the Header and Footer toolbar from the document window. If you like, you can use the Print Preview feature or switch to the Page Layout view (**V**iew, **P**age Layout) to see the header at the top of the pages.

9 Save your work and print a copy of `Annual Report` for your review. If requested by your instructor, print two copies. Close the `Annual Report` file after you print it.

If you have completed your session on the computer, exit Word for Windows and then shut down Windows before you turn off the computer. Otherwise, continue with the next section, "Checking Your Skills."

When you create a header or a footer, Word automatically switches you to the Page Layout view. This view shows you all the page elements (headers, footers, page numbers, and so on). You can switch to this view at any time by selecting **V**iew, **P**age Layout. Choose **V**iew, **N**ormal to switch back to Normal view.

Jargon Watch

A **header** is defined as text that appears at the top of every page, and a **footer** is defined as text that appears at the bottom of every page.

In most cases, you want the same header (or footer) to print on every page. If you want to use a different header or footer on odd and even pages, choose **F**ile, Page Set**u**p. Click the **L**ayout tab. In the Headers and Footers section, choose Different **o**dd and even (a check mark should appear in the checkbox). Choose OK.

Project Summary

To	Do This
Change the margins	Position the insertion point where you want to begin the margin change. Choose **F**ile, Page Set**u**p. If necessary, click the **M**argins tab to switch to the Margins page. In the **T**op, **B**ottom, Le**f**t, and Ri**g**ht text boxes, type the margins you want. Choose OK.
Change the line spacing	Position the insertion point in the paragraph, or select the series of paragraphs whose line spacing you want to change. Choose F**o**rmat, **P**aragraph. Choose a line spacing option from the Li**n**e Spacing drop-down list. Choose OK.

To	Do This
Change the justification	Select the text for which you want to change the justification. Click one of the four justification buttons on the Formatting toolbar.
Indent text	Position the insertion point in the paragraph, or select the series of paragraphs for which you want to change the indentation. Choose F**o**rmat, **P**aragraph. In the **L**eft text box, type the amount of indentation you want on the left side. In the **R**ight text box, type the amount of indentation you want on the right side. Choose OK.
Insert page numbers	Position the insertion point at the top of the page where you want the page numbers to start (usually on page 1). Choose **I**nsert, Page N**u**mbers. If necessary, choose a position from the **P**osition drop-down list. If necessary, choose where you want the page numbers printed from the **A**lignment drop-down list. Choose OK.
Insert a page break	Position the insertion point where you want the new page to appear. Choose **I**nsert, **B**reak, OK; or press Ctrl+↵Enter.
Change the font	Select the text in the font you want to change. Click the Font drop-down list arrow. Choose a font name from the list, scrolling through the list if necessary.
Change the font size	Select the text with the font size you want to change. Click the Font Size drop-down list arrow. Choose a font size from the list; scroll through the list, if necessary.
Insert a header	Position the insertion point on the page where you want to start printing the header. Choose **V**iew, **H**eader and Footer. Type the information you want to appear in the header. Choose **C**lose.

Checking Your Skills

True/False

For each of the following, check *T* or *F* to indicate whether the statement is true or false.

__T __F **1.** You should always select the text to be affected before making a formatting change.

__T __F **2.** The **P**aragraph option on the F**o**rmat menu opens the Page Setup dialog box.

__T __F **3.** The Line Spacing feature controls the amount of spacing between paragraphs.

__T __F **4.** The Indent feature moves the first line of a paragraph over by half an inch.

__T __F **5.** You can set page numbers to appear in the header or footer region on the page.

__T __F **6.** To indent all the lines of a paragraph, press Tab at the beginning of each line.

__T __F **7.** The formatting toolbar has two Indent buttons.

__T __F **8.** You cannot prevent a page number from displaying on the first page.

__T __F **9.** A 12-point or 18-point font is appropriate for most business documents.

__T __F **10.** Word's preset margin settings are 1[dp] on the top and bottom, and 1.25[dp] on the left and right sides.

Multiple Choice

Circle the letter of the correct answer for each of the following questions.

1. Which dialog box contains the Indent feature?

- **a.** Page Setup
- **b.** Paragraph
- **c.** AutoFormat
- **d.** Indent

2. What is the function of the Justification buttons on the toolbar?

- **a.** To display a drop-down list of justification options
- **b.** To display the four options for aligning text
- **c.** To open the Justification dialog box
- **d.** To center the current line

3. What is the function of the Page Numbering feature?

- **a.** To automatically insert a number in the center of the last line on a page
- **b.** To insert page numbers in one of several predefined locations
- **c.** To create a header with a page number
- **d.** To count the number of pages in the document

4. A page break is used to do what?

- **a.** Create a new page at the insertion point.
- **b.** Create a new page at the bottom of the document.
- **c.** Create a new page that cannot be deleted.
- **d.** Create a blank page at the top of the document.

5. Where does a header appear in a document?

- **a.** At the top of every page
- **b.** At the bottom of every page
- **c.** Only on the first page
- **d.** Only on the last page

6. The default for margin and tab settings is which unit of measurement?

- **a.** inch
- **b.** centimeter
- **c.** point
- **d.** pica

7. What is the first step in changing line spacing?

- **a.** To open the Format menu
- **b.** To click the Line Spacing button
- **c.** To select the paragraphs you want to change
- **d.** To open the Paragraph menu

8. What type of page break does Word automatically create when a page is filled?

- **a.** hard
- **b.** automatic
- **c.** formatting
- **d.** soft

9. A font size of how many points is approximately one inch in height?
   a. 72
   b. 36
   c. 48
   d. 18

10. The command to insert a header or footer is located on which menu?
   a. Edit
   b. View
   c. Format
   d. Insert

Completion

In the blank provided, write the correct answer for each of the following statements.

1. A(n) ______________ contains information to be inserted at the top of every page.
2. The Font drop-down list arrow displays a list of fonts for the current ______________.
3. The most commonly used justification setting is ______________.
4. Paragraph formatting can be assigned to a single paragraph or a series of ______________ paragraphs.
5. Word enables you to indent text from both the ___________and___________ sides equally.
6. To prevent Word from adjusting line spacing to accommodate larger fonts, choose the ______________ line spacing option.
7. To preview page numbers without printing the document, use the ______________ ______________ feature.
8. When you create a header or footer, Word automatically switches you to ______________ ______________ view.
9. If you want to align text along the left and right margins, click the ______________ button.
10. To indent text from both the left and right margins, use the ______________ dialog box.

Matching

In the blank next to each of the following terms or phrases, write the letter of the corresponding term or phrase. (Note that some letters may be used more than once.)

_____ **1.** Arranging text so the information is easy to read and has a polished appearance

_____ **2.** The height of a character, measured in points

_____ **3.** Changes line spacing to 1.5 spacing

_____ **4.** Indents left side of text to next tab setting

_____ **5.** Moves text to the left by one tab setting

_____ **6.** A page break inserted by the user

_____ **7.** The style, weight, and typeface of a set of characters

_____ **8.** Text that displays at the top of every page

_____ **9.** Text that displays at the bottom of every page

_____ **10.** Placement of text along the left and right margins

a. font
b. alignment
c. footer
d. Increase Indent
e. Ctrl+5
f. hard page break
g. formatting
h. font size
i. header
j. Decrease Indent

Screen ID

Identify each of the items shown in Figure 4.17.

Figure 4.17

1. ______________
2. ______________
3. ______________
4. ______________
5. ______________

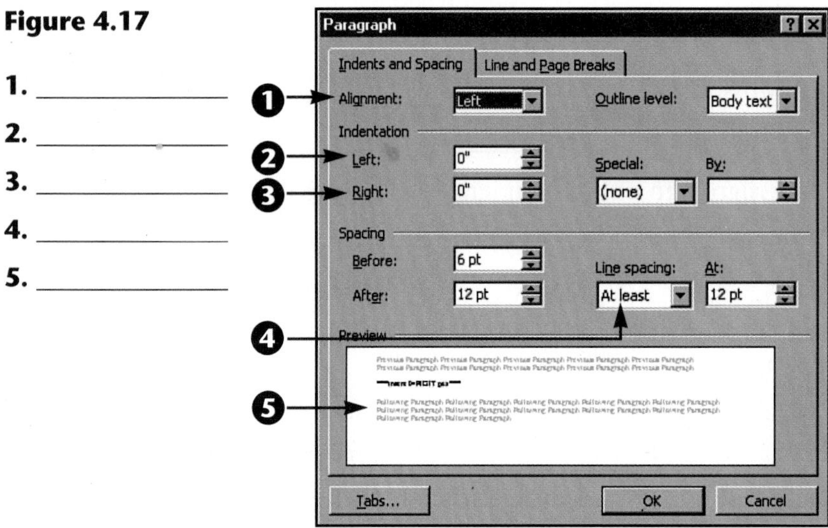

Applying Your Skills

Practice

The following exercises enable you to practice the skills you have learned in this project. Take a few minutes to work through these exercises now.

1. Formatting a Research Paper

Format a lengthy research paper for submission to a scholarly journal. Some of the techniques you can use to format the paper include justifying text, enhancing headings and subheadings, adjusting line spacing to improve readability, and adding a header and a footer.

To Format a Research Paper

1. In Word for Windows, open Proj0402 and save it as `Research Paper.`
2. Set the top and bottom margins to 1.25 inches.
3. Double-space the entire document.
4. Justify the entire document.

5. On page 2 of the document, format the quotation `It is abundantly clear that whatever information occurs first has disproportionate influence on the final outcome of interviews.` Indent the quotation one inch on both the left and the right sides. Single-space the quotation.
6. Increase the font size of the major headings to 14-point. Change the font to Arial.
7. Change the font for the secondary headings to Arial. Leave the point size at 12-point.
8. Insert a header with your name on the left and the current date on the right. Insert a footer with the page number centered. Start printing the header on page two.
9. Preview the document and insert page breaks, if necessary, to be sure that headings do not start at the bottom of a page.
10. Save the changes and, if requested by your instructor, print two copies. Then close the document.

2. Formatting a Loan Proposal

Format a small business loan proposal to submit to a local bank.

To Format a Loan Proposal

1. Open the file PROJ0403 and save it as **`Loan Proposal`**.
2. Create a title page using the two introductory paragraphs. Center the paragraphs on the title page and change the font to Garamond, 26-point. The two paragraphs should appear alone on the first page.
3. In the body of the document, change the top and bottom margins to 1.25 inches, double-space the lines, and justify the text. If you like, choose a different font that you think makes the proposal look more important.
4. Increase the size of the heading `Loan Proposal` and center it on the page.
5. Indent each of the three lists two inches from the left margin and change the lists to single-spacing. Highlight the total amount of anticipated expenses by increasing the font size and making the text bold. Do the same for the `Last Year` and `Next Year` headings.
6. On every page but the first, insert a header with the name of your proposal on the left and your name on the right. Insert a footer with the date on the left and the page number on the right. (*Hint:* Use the **L**ayout page in the Page Set**u**p dialog box.)
7. Preview the document and insert page breaks where necessary.
8. Save the document and, if requested by your instructor, print two copies. Then close the document.

3. Formatting a Letter to Attendees of an International Symposium

Format a letter to the attendees of an international symposium you are organizing.

To Format a Letter

1. Open the file Proj0404 and save it as **`Symposium`**.
2. Insert the date at the top of the letter; leave four blank lines between the date and the salutation.
3. Set the margins to 1.5 inches on all sides.

4. Format the paragraphs of the body of the letter to leave 6 points of space before and after each paragraph.
5. Add four blank lines to the end of the document and type your name and title.
6. Check the spelling and grammar in the letter.
7. Preview the document to see how the formatting looks. If necessary, adjust the margins and spacing so that the letter fits correctly on the page.
8. Save the document and, if requested by your instructor, print two copies. Then close the document.

4. Formatting an Invitation to a Dinner Party

Format an invitation to a dinner party at your home.

To Format an Invitation

1. Open the file Proj0405 and save it as `Invitation`.
2. Make the title bigger, bolder, and centered on the page. Because this is a fun invitation, try some different fonts, such as Braggadocio, Desdemona, or Wide Latin.
3. Pick another font for the body of the invitation. Try to find one that coordinates with the one you use for the title.
4. If you have access to a color printer, change the color of the text in the letter.
5. Insert 3 points of space before and after each paragraph.
6. Justify the first two paragraphs and center the rest of the invitation.
7. Preview the invitation to see how it looks on the page. If necessary, adjust the spacing between paragraphs to align the document better on the page.
8. Check the spelling, and then save the document. If requested by your instructor, print two copies. Then close the document.

5. Editing the Welcome Letter

You use several of the formatting techniques you learned in this project to improve the appearance of the Welcome Letter.

To Edit the Welcome Letter

1. Open the file named Proj0406.DOC, and save it as `Welcome Letter 3`.
2. Press ↵Enter four times after the date at the top of this letter. Type your name and address as the return address.
3. Select the return address, then right-align it by clicking the Align Right button on the formatting toolbar.
4. Because this is such a short letter, change the margins to space it more appropriately. Use the Page Setup dialog box to change the top and bottom margins to 2" and the left and right margins to 1.5".
5. Change the font size for the entire document to 12 points.
6. Save the document and, if requested by your instructor, print a copy. Then close the document.

Challenge

The following challenges enable you to use your problem-solving skills. Take time to work through these exercises now.

1. Improving the Appearance of the Computer Training Concepts Letter

You want to use the formatting techniques you have learned to improve the appearance of the letter to be sent to those who request information from Computer Training Concepts. Open the file Proj0407.DOC and save it as `CTC Cover Letter 4`.

Justify the entire document.

Change the top and bottom margins to 2".

Change the font to 12-point Arial.

Print two copies of the letter, then save the file again. Close the file when you have finished.

2. Formatting the Course Descriptions Document

Now that you have learned to do some document formatting, you decide to improve the appearance of the Course Descriptions document you created in previous projects. Open the file Proj0408.DOC and save it as `Course Descriptions 4`.

Center the three line heading at the top of the document.

Center the headings `Spreadsheet Courses` and `Word Processing Courses`.

Insert a page break above the `Word Processing Courses` heading so that this section appears on a separate page.

Insert page numbers at the bottom of the document, but do not display the page number on the first page.

Add a header to the second page. Type `Computer Training Concepts` on the left side of the header, and `Course Descriptions` along the right side.

Change the top and bottom margins to 2.5"and the left and right margins to 1.5".

Change the line spacing of the course description paragraphs to 1.5.

Save the file again, then print a copy. Close the file when you have finished.

3. Formatting the Main Street Deli Sign

You decide to use some formatting techniques to improve the appearance of the sign you created for the Main Street Deli. Open the Proj0409.DOC file and save it as `Deli Sign 3`.

Center the headings `Main Street Deli` and `Daily Specials`. Also center the last line, `Come in and see how good freshness tastes!`

Indent the food items 1.7". Add any tabs if necessary to line up the prices.

Double-space the entire document.

Change the font of the entire document to Arial.

Change the font size of the `Main Street Deli` heading to 20.

Change the font size of the rest of the sign to 14.

Save the document again and print one copy. Close the document when you have finished.

4. Formatting the Membership Renewal Document

You need to format the Membership Renewal document to improve its appearance. Open the Proj0410.DOC and save it as `Membership Renewal 3`.

Justify the entire letter.

Right-align the date and the closing in the letter.

Change the font and font size to a different one of your choice.

Adjust the margins to improve the alignment on the page. Use Print Preview to see how the margins look.

Save the letter again, then print one copy. Close the file when you have finished.

5. Formatting the Reunion Letter

To improve the appearance of the reunion letter you edited in the previous project, you decide to use some of the formatting techniques you learned in this chapter. Open the Proj0411.DOC file and save it as `Reunion Planning 3`. Make the following changes:

Change the line spacing of the lists of choices to 1.5.

Add a hard page break above the last list of choices, the activities.

Add a header to the second page that contains the date and the page number.

Choose a different font for the entire document.

Save the letter again, then print a copy. Close the document when you are finished.

Project 5

Using Tables and Graphics in Word

Completing a Newsletter

In this project, you learn how to:

- Create a Table
- Enter Text into a Table
- Format a Table
- Calculate Values in a Table
- Insert a Picture
- Move and Resize a Picture

Why Would I Do This?

Table
A series of rows and columns. The intersection of a row and column is called a cell, which is where you type text and numbers.

The Tables feature is one of the most versatile and easy-to-use features in Word. Although you can use the Tables feature in many ways, people most often use it to display information that needs to be formatted into columns. You can use the Columns feature to accomplish this task also, but the Tables feature is easier to use and has more options for formatting the information and the *table* itself. In fact, the Table AutoFormat tool lets you assign complex formatting with just a few mouse clicks. The Tables feature also has several built-in spreadsheet functions that perform basic mathematical operations.

Graphic
Graphic images come in all shapes and sizes. Typical graphics include clip art images, drawings, photographs, scanned images, signature files, and so on.

Clip art
A collection of graphic images.

You can also use *graphics* in your documents to illustrate a point, provide excitement, or add creative flair. You can add graphic images that you create in Word, as well as those created in other programs. Stock graphics called *clip art* are available through software stores, mail-order catalogs, and online services. In fact, Word includes a wide variety of clip art for use in both formal and informal documents.

In this project, you use tables and graphics to put the finishing touches on a company newsletter.

Lesson 1: Creating a Table

Spreadsheet
An accounting form that contains rows and columns. The intersection of a row and column is called a cell.

Word's tables are similar to *spreadsheets*, such as those in Microsoft Excel, in both operation and terminology. Spreadsheets and Word tables are made up of a grid of columns and rows. When you create a table, you need to estimate how many columns and how many rows (or lines) you will need.

To Create a Table

1 Open the file Proj0501 and save it as `June Newsletter`.

The sample newsletter has two columns under the title (or masthead), as shown in Figure 5.1. As discussed previously, Word has different views, or ways to display the document. Because Normal view is faster to work in, most of the figures in this book are shown in this view. The advantage of using Page Layout view is that it shows you what the document will look like when printed. Switch to Page Layout view now so you can see how the newsletter looks in both Page Layout and Normal view.

2 Choose View, Page Layout.

In the sample newsletter, the columns are shown side-by-side below the masthead. Because editing is faster and easier in Normal view, however, you need to change to that now.

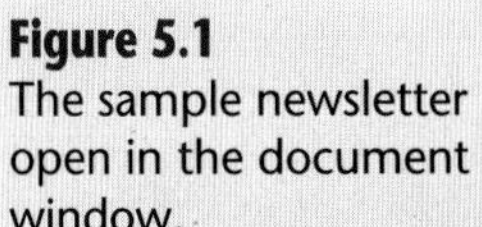

Figure 5.1
The sample newsletter open in the document window.

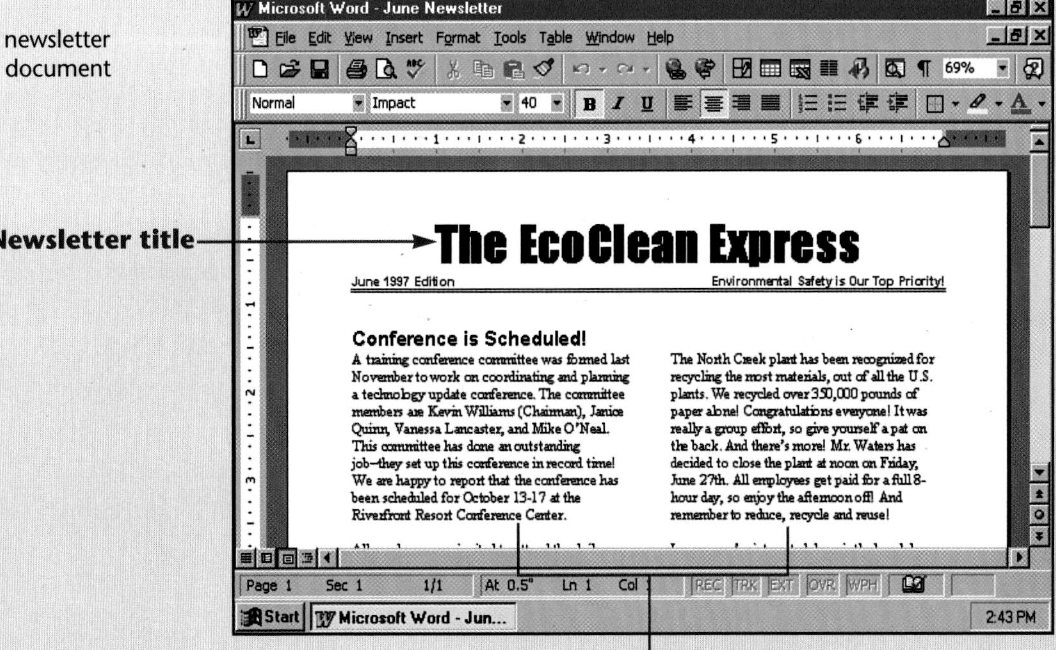

Newsletter text in columns

❸ Choose View, Normal.

In Normal view, the text is formatted into one single column on the left side of the screen. You can switch back and forth between the two views, so you can use the one that helps you the most, depending on which type of document you are working on.

In Normal view, you can see the *section break* that has been inserted below the masthead. Any document can have multiple sections, and each *section* can be formatted separately without affecting any of the other sections. In this case, the second section is formatted into two columns.

❹ Scroll through the document until you see the heading `Just a Reminder...`, and position the insertion point on the blank line above this heading.

You want to create the table that shows the training class schedule, and place it in this spot.

❺ Click the Insert Table button.

Word displays an empty grid. You have to click and drag the mouse in the grid in order to highlight the number of rows and columns you need. Drag the mouse slowly until you get the hang of it.

❻ Click and drag the mouse over and down until the bottom of the grid reads `6x2 Table`; then release the mouse button.

The number `6` represents the number of rows, and the number `2` represents the number of columns. Make sure that you have 2 columns and 6 rows selected.

continues

To Create a Table (continued)

If you have problems...

If you have problems clicking and dragging across this grid, you can create the table by using the Table menu. Before you use this method, drag the mouse back up to the top-left corner of the grid until the bottom reads `Cancel`. Then, from the Table menu, choose Insert Table. The Insert Table dialog box is displayed. Use the spinner arrows next to Number of Columns and Number of Rows to specify two columns and six rows. Choose OK to create the table.

If you have already inserted the table but chose the wrong dimensions, use the Undo command to remove the table. Then try again, either by clicking the Insert Table button or by choosing Insert Table from the Table menu.

Word creates the table at the insertion point. Notice that the table is created within the margins of the newsletter column and that both columns in the table have the same width. By default, Word creates evenly spaced columns between the available margin space. You can easily change the column widths, if necessary. Your newsletter should now look like Figure 5.2.

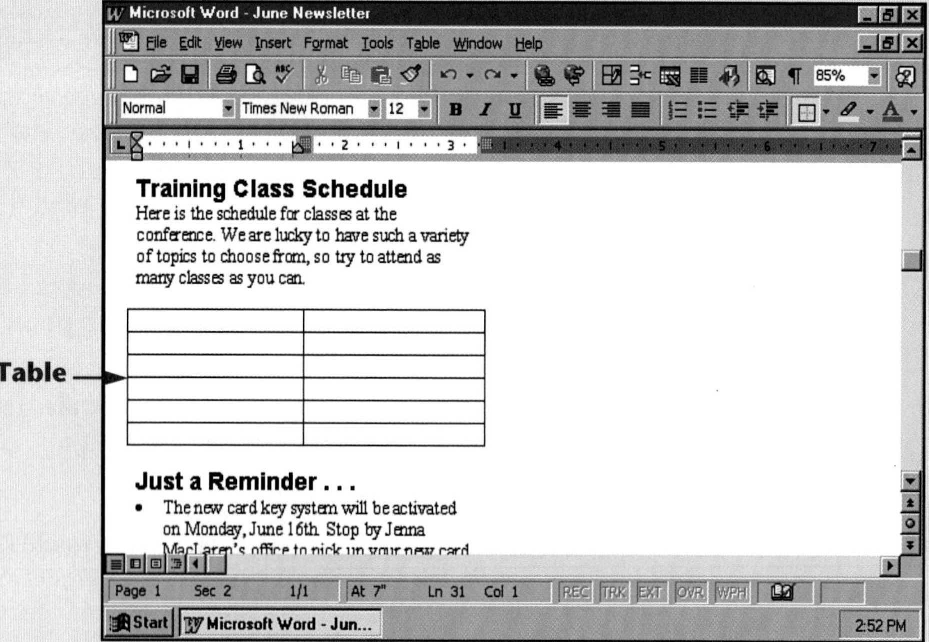

Figure 5.2
The newly created table in the company newsletter.

By default, tables are created with a single-line border that prints out with the rest of the table. You'll learn more about borders in Lesson 3, "Formatting a Table," later in this chapter. If you choose a different table format or remove some of the borders in your document, table gridlines appear on your screen to help you see the table structure.

Save your work and keep the June Newsletter file open to use in the next lesson, where you learn to enter text into a table.

Jargon Watch

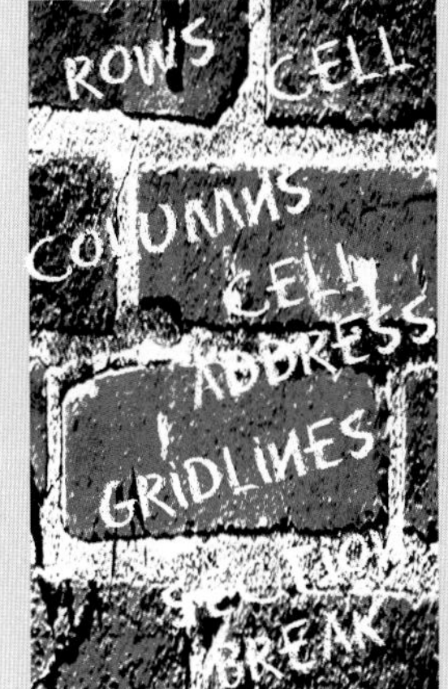

Tables are composed of **rows** and **columns**. The intersection of a row and a column is called a **cell**. Rows are numbered from top to bottom, and columns are labeled with letters from left to right. Each cell has a unique address, called a **cell address**, which is composed of the column letter followed by the row number. For example, the top-left cell is A1.

Gridlines, dotted lines in and around the table, help you see the size and position of the table cells. These lines don't print.

A **section break** divides a document into different sections, which you can format separately. For example, in the sample newsletter, a new section was created so the newsletter text could be formatted into columns. Any time you want to format a portion of a document separately, you insert a section break and format that section.

In this lesson, you learned how to create a table by clicking and dragging through the Insert Table grid to select the number of columns and rows. You also learned that you can use the **I**nsert Table option on the T**a**ble menu to create a table. There is another option, called Draw Ta**b**le, that is lots of fun to use. You use a drawing tool in the same way that you would use a pen to draw a table. You simply click and drag to draw the table itself; then you click and drag within the table to create rows and columns. You can quickly create a custom table with cells of varying widths and heights.

Lesson 2: Entering Text into a Table

Typing text into a table works the same way as typing text into the document window, with only a few differences. One difference is that you use Tab and Shift+Tab to move from one cell to another in a table. Tab moves you one cell to the right; Shift+Tab moves you one cell to the left. When you type information into a cell, the text wraps within the cell's margins so that you don't have to worry about the cell's size.

In the newsletter document, you need to type the column headings first; you then type the date in the first column and the class title in the second column.

The insertion point is already displayed in the first cell (Word puts it there when you create the table), so you can start typing the first entry right now.

To Enter Text into a Table

1 In the `June Newsletter` **file, type** `Date` **in the table's first cell (cell A1).**

This is the column heading for the first column, which will contain the dates for the classes. Column headings act as labels for the information listed in the column.

2 Press Tab.

Pressing Tab moves the insertion point one cell to the right (cell B1). You type the second column heading here.

3 Type `Class Title`**.**

Unless you change the alignment, Word aligns the text on the left side of the cell. You can also center text or right-align text in the cell.

4 Press Tab.

When you press Tab in the last cell of a row, the insertion point moves to the first cell in the next row (cell A2).

5 Type `Monday, October 13` **and press Tab.**

Now type the name of the class scheduled for Monday.

6 Type `Navigating on the Internet` **and press Tab.**

Notice how the cell expanded as the text wrapped down to the second line of the cell. Your insertion point should now be positioned in the first cell of the next row (cell A3).

7 Type the following information to complete the table:

```
Tuesday, October 14       Multimedia
Wednesday, October 15     Publishing Web Pages
Thursday, October 16      Presentation Graphics
Friday, October 17        Navigating on the Internet
```

Don't press Tab in the last cell; if you do, Word automatically creates a new row that you don't need. Your table should now look like Figure 5.3.

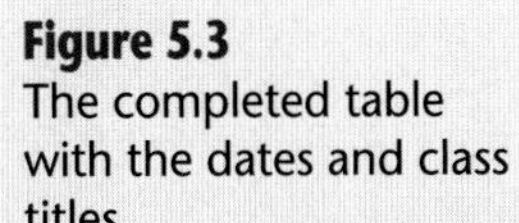

Figure 5.3
The completed table with the dates and class titles.

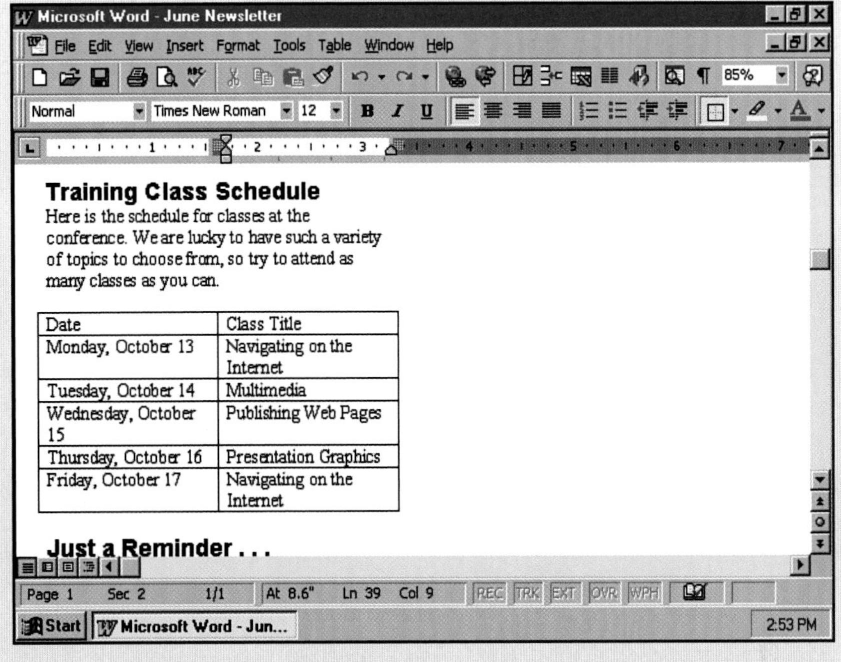

8 Save your work and keep the `June Newsletter` file open to use in the next lesson, where you learn to format a table.

You can also use the mouse to position the insertion point within a table. To move the insertion point to a specific cell, position the mouse pointer on the cell and click the left mouse button.

As mentioned earlier, you can align text in the center, on the right side, or on the left side of a cell. For a single cell, simply place the insertion point in the cell. For multiple cells, click and drag over the cells (just like you would to select text). Now, click the Align Left button, Center button, or Align Right button. If you click the Justify button, Word will justify the text within the cell so that the left and right margins are smooth.

Lesson 3: Formatting a Table

When you create a new table, Word uses a number of default format settings. As mentioned, single-line borders appear inside the table and form the outside border; the text is aligned on the left side of the cell, and the columns have equal widths. Word's Table AutoFormat feature enables you to adjust the format of your table by using preset templates.

You can also adjust individual format settings, such as column width. Try formatting the newsletter table now.

To Format a Table

1 In the `June Newsletter` file, position the mouse pointer on the vertical border between the first and second columns.

When you position the mouse pointer on this *vertical border*, the mouse pointer changes to a double vertical line with arrows on either side (see Figure 5.4). You use this *sizing pointer* to adjust the width of the columns.

You may have noticed that the row with `Wednesday, October 15` has the `15` on a second line by itself. Adjust the columns so that the `15` fits on the same line as `October`.

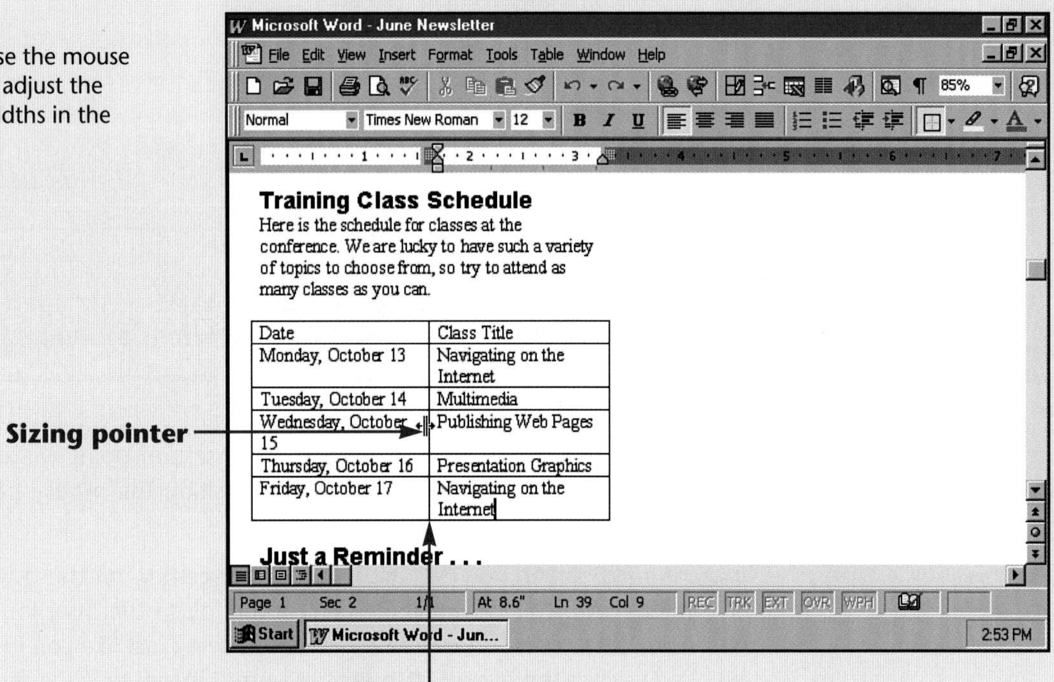

Figure 5.4
You can use the mouse pointer to adjust the column widths in the table.

2 Click and drag the border to the right, just enough to make room for the `15`.

When you click the vertical border with the sizing pointer, a dotted guide line is displayed, running from the ruler down to the status line. As you drag the mouse, this line helps you see the new column width. You need to increase the size of the left column so that all the dates fit on one line.

3 Release the mouse button.

Releasing the mouse button clears the guide line and adjusts the width of the columns. Your table should now look like Figure 5.5.

Figure 5.5
You can resize the left column to allow more room for the dates.

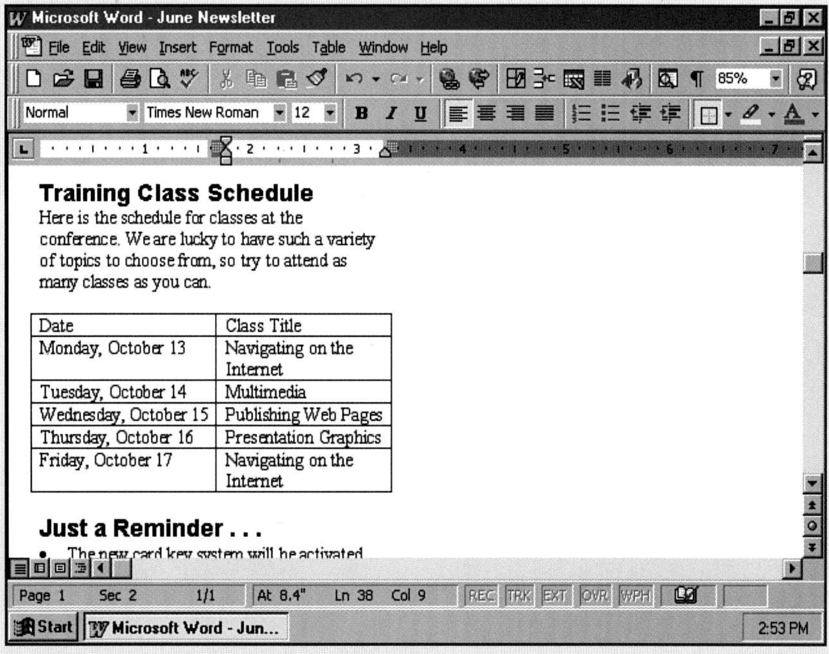

If you have problems...

If the date (`Wednesday, October 15`) still won't fit on one line in the table, click and drag the vertical border farther to the right. Be sure to wait until the sizing pointer is displayed before you click and drag the border.

4 Position the insertion point inside the first cell of the table.

5 Choose Table, Table AutoFormat.

The Table AutoFormat dialog box is displayed (see Figure 5.6). A list of available formats appears on the left side of the dialog box. When you choose a format, the sample table changes to show the new format.

Figure 5.6
The Table AutoFormat dialog box.

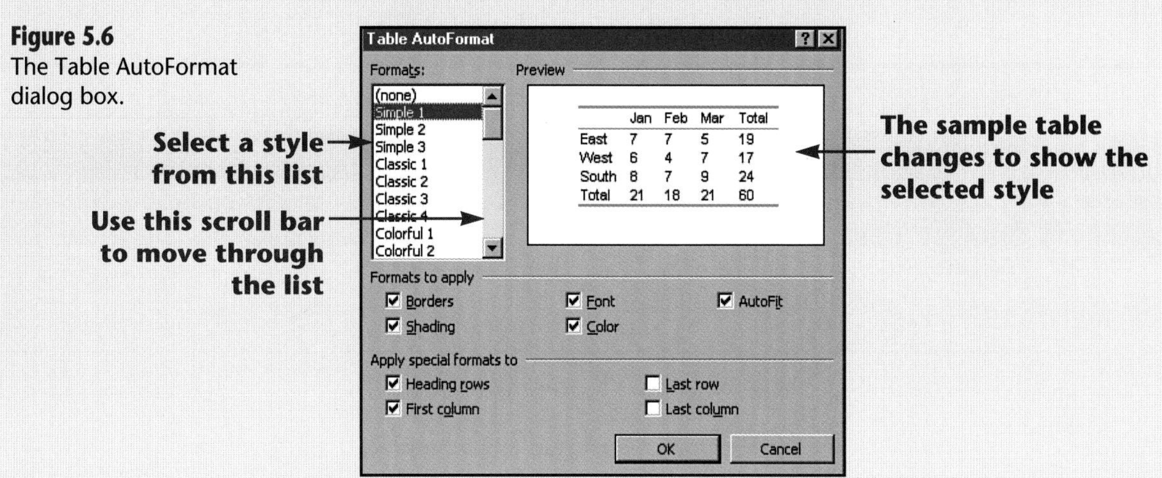

continues

To Format a Table (continued)

6 Press ↓ several times.

Take a minute and scroll through the list so that you can see the variety of styles available.

7 Select `Colorful 2` (by clicking it once) in the list of Formats; then choose OK.

The Colorful 2 style is applied to the table, making it look like Figure 5.7. The table has white text against red fill column headings, italicized column headings, an italicized left column, and a yellow background for the table content.

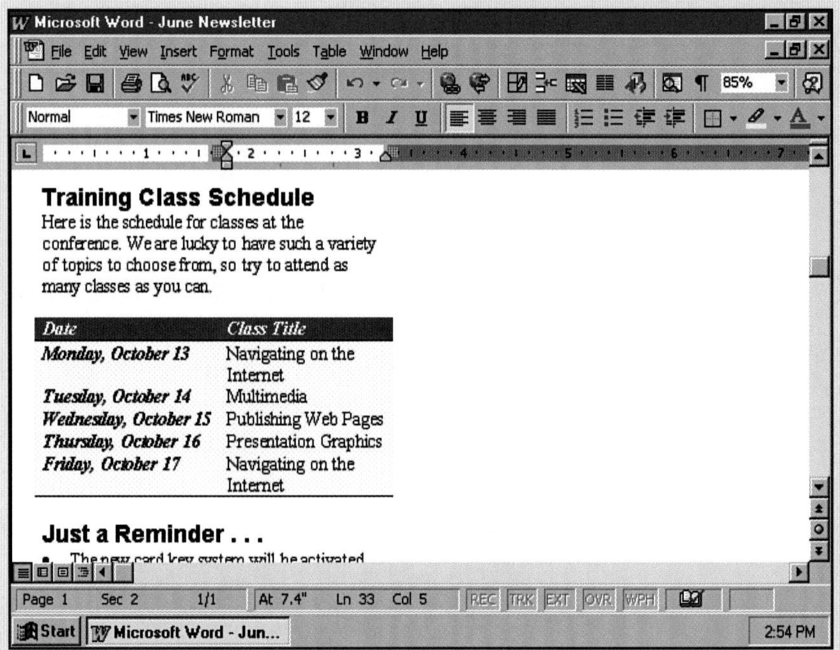

Figure 5.7
The table with the Colorful 2 style.

Save your work and keep the `June Newsletter` file open to use in the next lesson, where you learn to perform calculations in a table.

Jargon Watch

A **vertical border** separates two columns in a table. A **sizing pointer** is displayed when the mouse passes over a vertical border. When you see this pointer, you can click and drag the border to resize column widths in a table. You can also click and drag the outermost vertical borders to change the table margins.

In this lesson, you learned how to adjust the column widths by clicking and dragging the vertical border between columns. You can also adjust the height of a row by clicking and dragging the horizontal border between rows. Position the mouse pointer over a horizontal border and wait until the sizing pointer is displayed; then click and drag up or down to adjust the row height. (Clicking and dragging horizontal borders only works in Page Layout view.)

You can also use the Cell Height and Width dialog box to format rows and columns in a table. Choose T**a**ble, and then choose Cell Height and **W**idth to open the dialog box. The Row page enables you to move to each row in the table and set the options for that row. You can align table rows at the left margin, centered between margins, or at the right margin of the page. You can set an indent amount, and you can choose to allow the row to break across pages if necessary. You can also set a specific row height on the Row page.

Click the Column tab to switch to the Column page, which enables you to move across the columns in a table and specify a particular width (in inches) for each. This page has an **A**utoFit option that automatically adjusts the width of the column to accommodate the contents.

Spreadsheet functions
In spreadsheet programs, the most commonly performed numeric calculations (such as adding a column of numbers and averaging) are already set up for you to use.

Value
A numeric cell entry.

Lesson 4: Calculating Values in a Table

Word's Table feature includes built-in *spreadsheet functions* that you can use to perform mathematical calculations. The most common calculation, the SUM formula, adds *values* together to produce a total.

At the bottom of the newsletter, another table lists the amount of materials that were recycled in a year. The first column lists the material; the second column shows the number of pounds for each item. Try entering values and calculating a total in the table now.

To Calculate Values in a Table

1. **At the bottom of the `June Newsletter` file, position the insertion point in the second row of the second column in the second table (in the first blank cell).**

   This table has already been formatted with the Classic 2 style in the Table AutoFormat dialog box. The left column and the column headings are shaded (see Figure 5.8). In the left column, text is aligned on the left side of the cell. In the right column, the numeric cells have been formatted to align the values on the right side of the cell.

continues

To Calculate Values in a Table (continued)

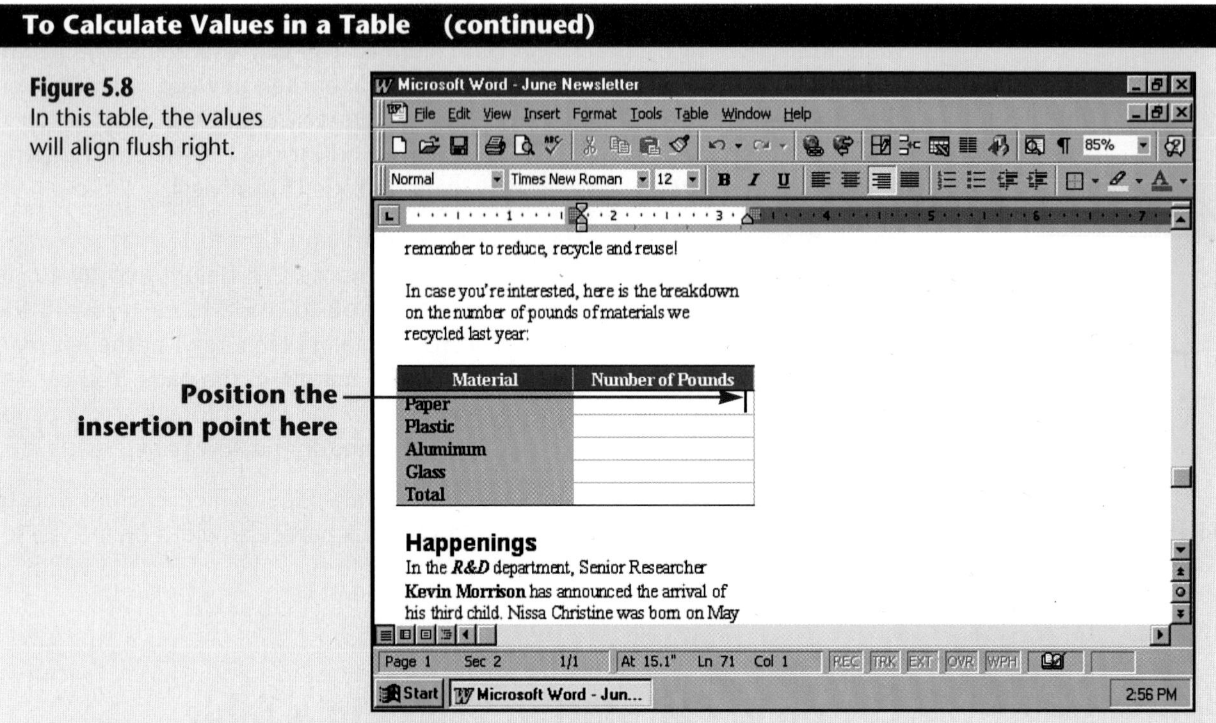

Figure 5.8
In this table, the values will align flush right.

2 Type `355,127` and press ↓.

This is the number of pounds of paper recycled last year. Pressing ↓ places the entry in the cell and moves you to the next row in the column. Make sure that you press ↓ to move down to the next cell. If you press Enter, Word inserts a blank line in the cell instead of moving you to the next cell.

3 Type `111,098` and press ↓.

This is the number of pounds of plastic that were recycled last year.

4 Type `75,842` and press ↓.

5 Type `73,951` and press ↓.

This completes the typing of the amounts for the recycled materials. Your table should now look like Figure 5.9.

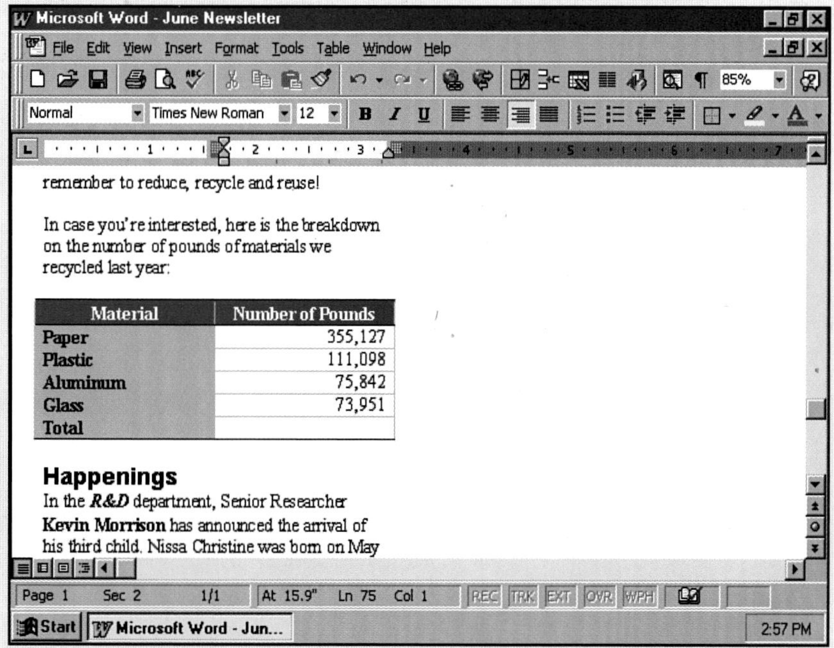

Figure 5.9
The table with the values entered.

The insertion point should be displayed in the last cell in the second column (cell B6). If it isn't, click in this cell to move the insertion point now. You need to insert a formula to calculate the total amount here.

6 Choose Table, Formula.

The Formula dialog box is displayed with the suggested formula (see Figure 5.10). Word assumes that you want to add the numbers in the column and place the total inside this cell. Because Word has assumed correctly in this case, you don't need to change the entry in the **F**ormula box. Next, you choose a format for the total amount.

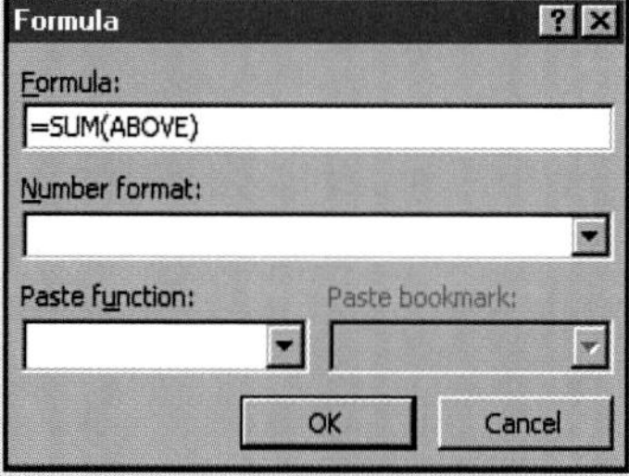

Figure 5.10
The Formula dialog box with the suggested formula.

7 Choose Number Format.

Choosing **N**umber Format opens a drop-down list of formats for the result of the calculation.

continues

To Calculate Values in a Table (continued)

8 Choose the first format in the list, `#,##0`.

This format inserts a comma if you have a number greater than or equal to 1,000. If the amount is zero, a zero will be shown.

9 Choose OK.

Choosing OK inserts the result of the `SUM` formula into the cell, using the chosen format. The table should now look like Figure 5.11.

Figure 5.11
The table with the total amount calculated.

Total amount

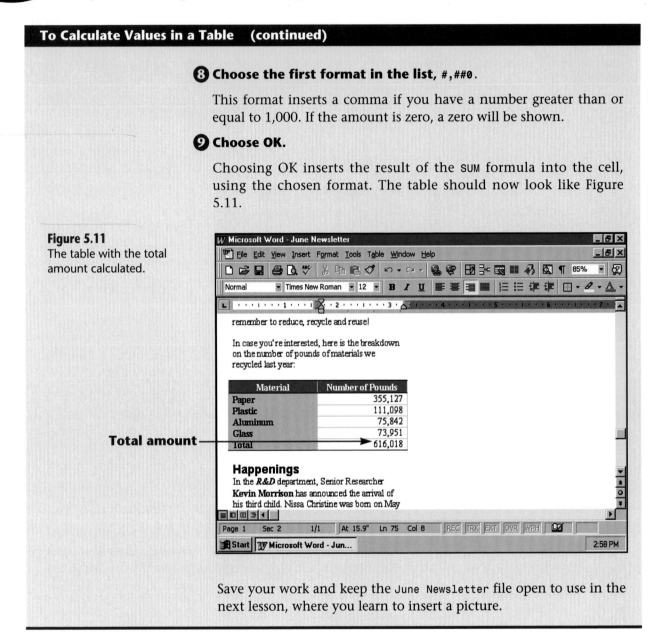

Save your work and keep the `June Newsletter` file open to use in the next lesson, where you learn to insert a picture.

If you change any of the values in cells that are included in a formula, or if you alter a formula, you need to recalculate the table. That's easy to do; just select the cell containing the total amount, and then press F9 to update the amount.

Lesson 5: Inserting a Picture

Word makes it easy for you to insert a wide variety of graphic images into your documents by either creating your own images or importing graphics files from other programs. Word accepts most popular graphic file formats, including WordPerfect Graphic Files, files found on most online services (GIF, JPEG), Windows Bitmap, and Windows Metafile. The Office 97 suite includes the Microsoft 3.0 Clip Gallery that contains a variety of clip art, pictures, sounds, and video clips. Try inserting a picture into the newsletter now.

To Insert a Picture

1 In the `June Newsletter` file, position the insertion point at the beginning of the paragraph under the heading `Recycling Effort Pays Off`.

This is where you want to insert an illustrative picture.

2 Choose Insert, Picture, Clip Art.

The Microsoft Clip Gallery 3.0 dialog box is displayed (see Figure 5.12). There are four tabs in this dialog box: **C**lip Art, **P**ictures, **S**ounds, and **V**ideos. The **C**lip Art page contains vector (or draw-type) images; the **P**ictures page contains scanned images, digital photographs, and other bitmaps; the **S**ounds page contains sound files; the **V**ideos page contains video clips and animations.

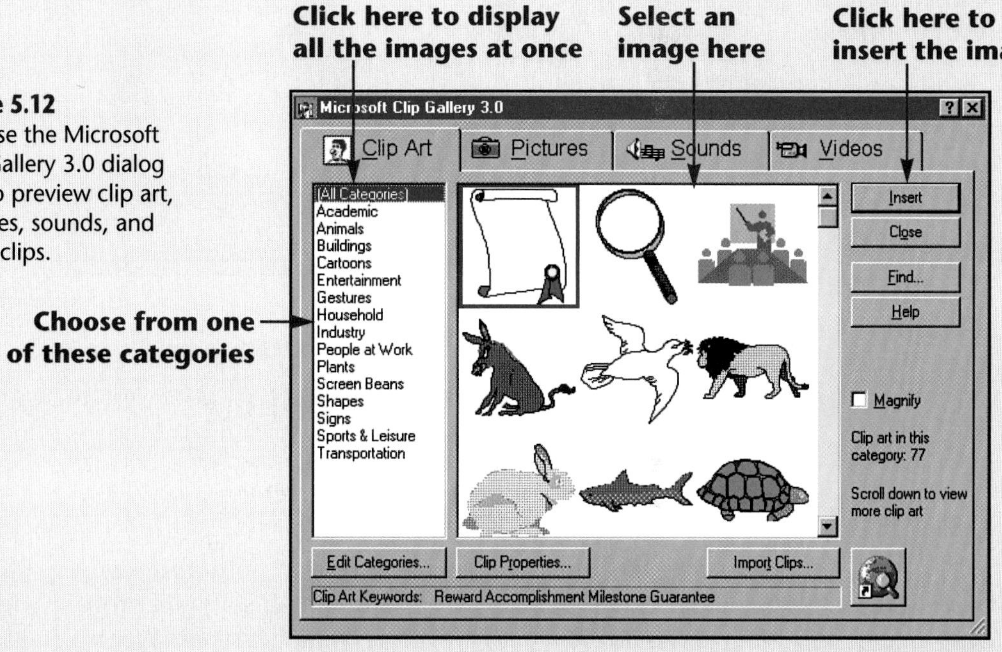

Click here to display all the images at once

Select an image here

Click here to insert the image

Choose from one of these categories

Figure 5.12
You use the Microsoft Clip Gallery 3.0 dialog box to preview clip art, pictures, sounds, and video clips.

If you have problems...

If your dialog box doesn't match the one shown in Figure 5.12, click the **C**lip Art tab to switch to the Clip Art page. Next, click the `(All Categories)` item at the top of the list of categories. If the images still don't match the ones shown in the figure, your system may have the additional images available on the MS Office 97 CD already installed in the Clip Gallery. Your system may also have images from other applications in the Clip Gallery.

continues

To Insert a Picture (continued)

3 In the list of categories, click `Shapes`.

When you choose a category, only those images in the category are displayed in the preview window (see Figure 5.13). In this case, you want to use one of the arrow-based shapes.

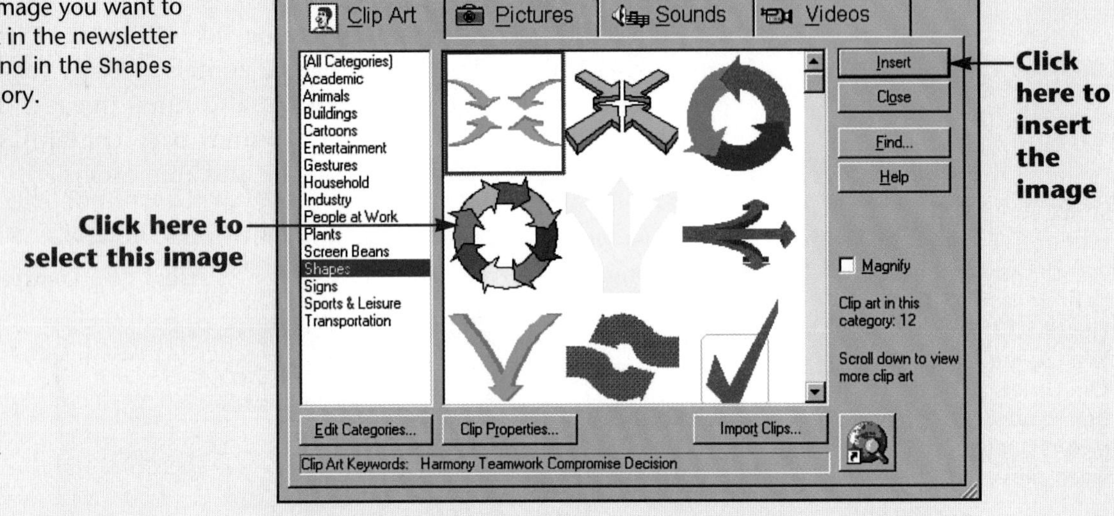

Figure 5.13
The image you want to insert in the newsletter is found in the `Shapes` category.

4 Click the image in the left corner of the second row.

If you have additional images installed on your system, you may have to scroll down through the list to find the image shown in Figure 5.13.

5 Choose Insert.

Word inserts the picture at the insertion point (see Figure 5.14). The original size of the clip art is maintained, so you'll probably need to resize the image to fit within the available space. When you insert a picture in a document, Word automatically switches to Page Layout view. This view enables you to see how objects will be positioned on the printed page, which is helpful when you are working with graphics.

Notice that when you insert a clip art image in the document, a border with eight small squares appears around the picture (see Figure 5.14). The squares—called sizing handles—enable you to increase and decrease the size of a picture.

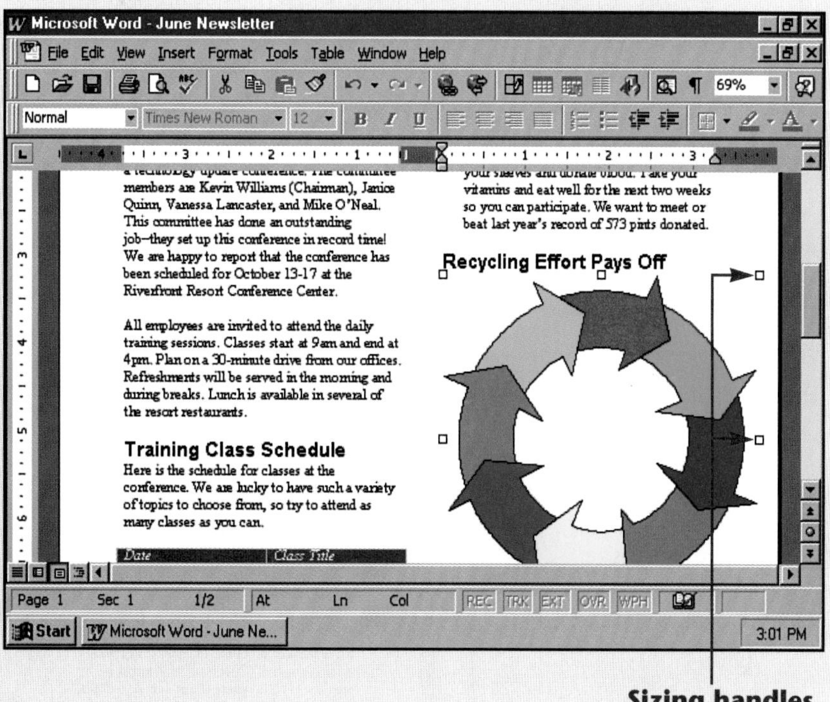

Figure 5.14
The clip art image is inserted into the document in its original size.

Save your work and keep the `June Newsletter` file open to use in the next lesson, where you learn how to move and resize a picture.

If you need to know the format of a selected image in the Clip Gallery, click the Clip Properties button to display a properties sheet. The Clip Properties dialog box details the name of the file, the file format, and its location on your system.

You must have the appropriate drivers installed on your computer to be able to play sound and video clips in the Clip Gallery (or in your documents). Some of the most commonly used drivers are installed automatically with Windows 95. If you still can't play a clip, check with the source of the clip for the necessary driver(s).

Lesson 6: Moving and Resizing a Picture

When you insert a picture into a document, Word maintains the original size of the image. You can easily resize the picture to suit your needs.

The easiest way to move and resize a picture is to use the mouse. When you click a picture, you select it. Sizing handles display on all four sides and at all four corners. The locations of the sizing handles indicate which way the graphic box will be resized. If you click and drag a sizing handle at the corner, you can resize the box in two directions at the same time. Moving a picture is easy; you just click and drag the picture to the new position.

In the company newsletter, you need to size the graphic box so that it takes up roughly one-third of the column width. In addition, you need to move the box into the paragraph so that the first two to three lines of text are above the picture and the rest of the lines wrap around it. Try moving and resizing the image now.

To Move and Resize a Picture

1 In the `June Newsletter` file, position the mouse pointer on the sizing handle at the lower-right corner of the picture.

The mouse pointer should change to a two-sided diagonal arrow (see Figure 5.15).

Figure 5.15
Click and drag a corner sizing handle to resize two sides at the same time.

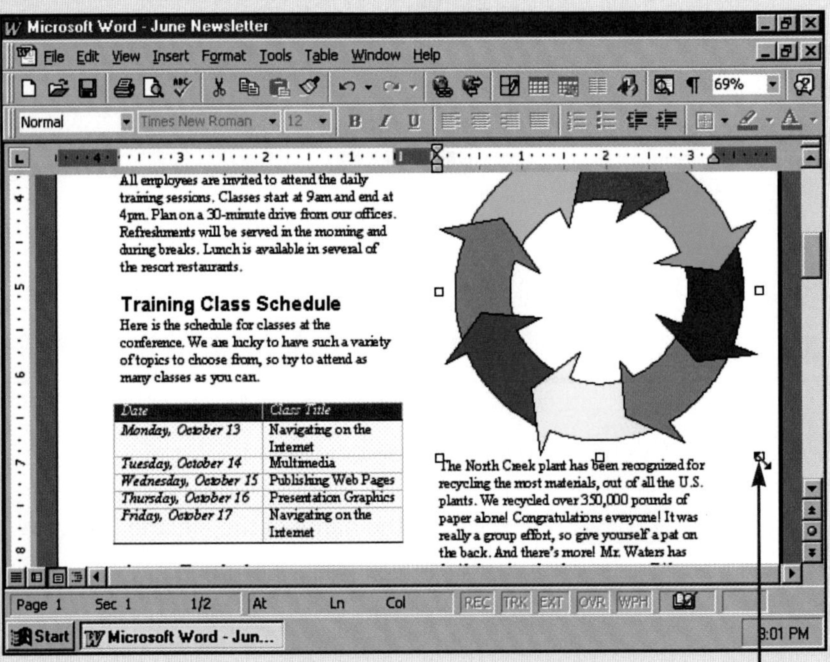

2 Click and drag the sizing handle upward and to the left.

Resize the picture until it becomes roughly one-third of the width of the column. When you drag a sizing handle, a dotted guide line is displayed to show you how big the graphic box will be when you release the mouse button (see Figure 5.16). Dragging a corner handle causes Word to maintain the original proportions of the picture. If the height changes, the width adjusts automatically, and vice versa.

Figure 5.16
The dotted line acts as a guide while you resize the box.

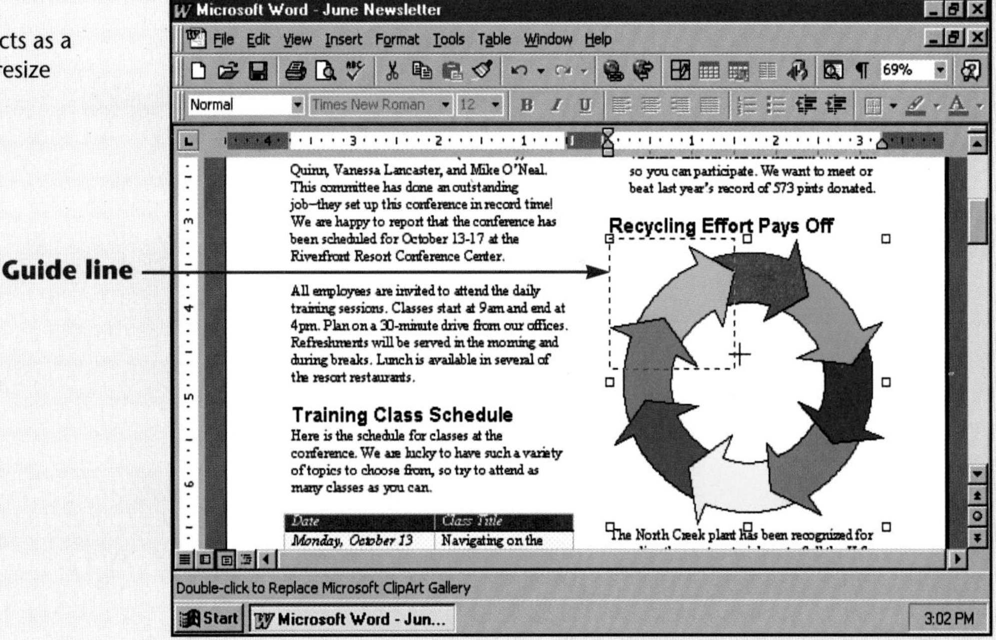

❸ **Release the mouse button.**

When you release the mouse button, Word resizes the picture to fit the new dimensions. Now, you want to move the picture down into the paragraph and have the text wrap around the picture. First, format the picture so the text wraps around the image.

❹ **Choose Format, Picture.**

The Format Picture dialog box is displayed. All of the formatting options for pictures have been consolidated into this single dialog box. You need to switch to the Wrapping page.

❺ **Click the Wrapping tab.**

The Wrapping page displays sample pages illustrating the differences in the Wrapping options (see Figure 5.17). To have the text wrap around the contours of the object itself, choose **T**ight. To have the text wrap around the objects bounding box (the border with the sizing handles), choose S**q**uare. In this case, you want the text to wrap around the object itself.

continues

To Move and Resize a Picture (continued)

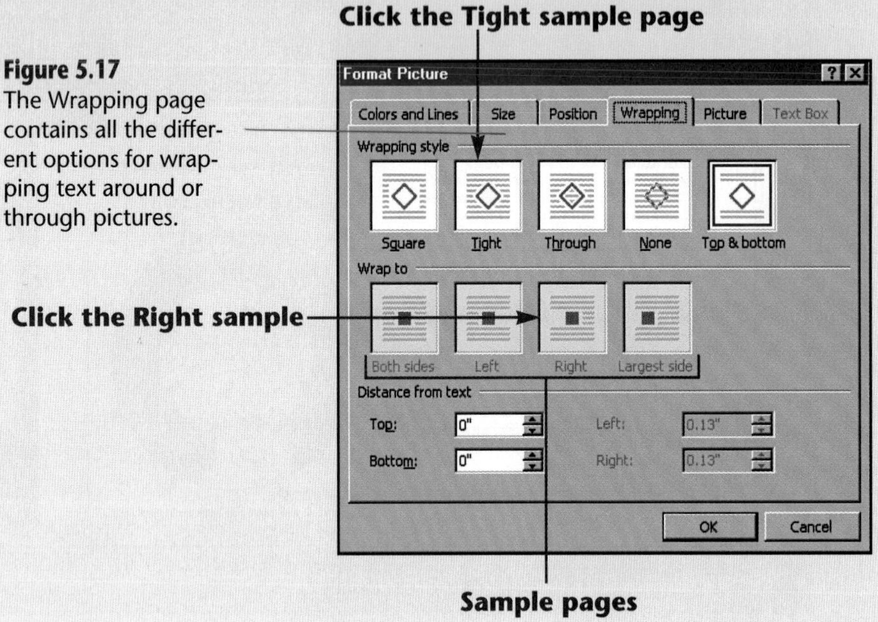

Click the Tight sample page

Figure 5.17
The Wrapping page contains all the different options for wrapping text around or through pictures.

Click the Right sample

Format Picture

Colors and Lines | Size | Position | Wrapping | Picture | Text Box

Wrapping style

Square Tight Through None Top & bottom

Wrap to

Both sides Left Right Largest side

Distance from text

Top: 0" Left: 0.13"

Bottom: 0" Right: 0.13"

OK Cancel

Sample pages

❻ **Choose Tight.**

When you choose **T**ight, the items in the Wrap section become available. In this example, you want the text to wrap on the right side of the picture. If you want to position the picture in the middle of a paragraph and have the text wrap around both sides, you need to choose **B**oth.

❼ **Choose Right, and then choose OK.**

Next, you want to drag the picture down into the paragraph so that the first three lines are above the picture and the other lines are below the picture.

❽ **Click and drag the picture into the middle of the paragraph.**

You may have to make small adjustments to move the picture to this position. When you finish, your newsletter should look similar to Figure 5.18. Notice how the text wraps around the contour of the arrows, not around the invisible *bounding box*.

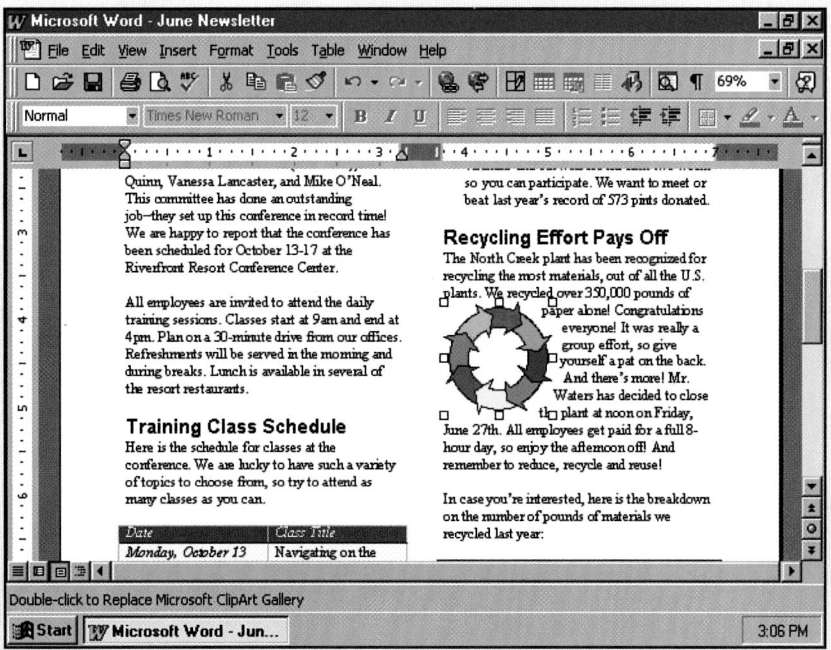

Figure 5.18
The text of the paragraph wraps around the graphic box.

9 Click inside the document window.

Clicking inside the document window deselects the picture. You have now completed the newsletter.

Save your work and print a copy of `June Newsletter`. If requested by your instructor, print two copies. Close `June Newsletter` after printing it. If you have completed your session on the computer, exit Word and shut down Windows before turning off the computer. Otherwise, continue with the next section, "Checking Your Skills."

Jargon Watch

Sizing handles are small squares on a picture border that you use to size a picture. A corner sizing handle sizes in two directions at the same time. The **bounding box** is an invisible box around a graphic file. By default, text wraps around the bounding box. If you choose to wrap text around the contour of the graphic, the text is placed next to the actual contours of the image, not the bounding box.

If you prefer, you can right-click a picture and choose Format Picture from the shortcut menu to open the Format Picture dialog box.

You can choose from a color palette for the *fill* (or background) to be used in the picture. There are also a variety of fill patterns, and you can choose a foreground and background color for them. You can also choose a line color and pattern if you decide you want a border around the picture.

continues

continued

Moving and sizing a picture with the mouse is fast and easy, but it can be difficult to be precise. Use the Size and Position pages of the Format Picture dialog box to type in exact measurements.

If necessary, you can crop a picture from any side and you can change the brightness and contrast settings in the Picture page of the Format Picture dialog box.

Project Summary

To	Do This
Change to Page Layout view	Choose **V**iew, **P**age Layout.
Change to Normal view	Choose **V**iew, **N**ormal.
Create a table	Click the Insert Table button. Click and drag the mouse to select the number of rows and columns you need. You can also choose T**a**ble, **I**nsert Table, and then specify the number of rows and columns in the Insert Table dialog box. Finally, you can choose Draw T**a**ble from the T**a**ble menu and use the pencil pointer to draw the table border, columns, and rows.
Type text in a table	Position the insertion point in the cell, and then type the text.
Move forward one cell	Press Tab.
Move backward one cell	Press Shift+Tab.
Move the insertion point to a cell	Click in the cell.
Select cells	Click and drag over the cells.
Adjust the width of a column	Position the mouse pointer over the vertical border between the columns. When the sizing pointer is displayed, click and drag the mouse to adjust the column width. Release the mouse button to resize the column.
Adjust the height of a row	Position the mouse pointer over the horizontal border between the rows. When the sizing pointer is displayed, click and drag the mouse to adjust the row height. Release the mouse button to resize the row.
Use the Table AutoFormat feature	Position the insertion point in the table. Choose T**a**ble, Table Auto**F**ormat. Select a style from the list of Forma**t**s, and choose OK.
Add a column of numbers	Position the insertion point in the cell below the column of numbers. Choose T**a**ble, F**o**rmula. The **F**ormula text box should contain `=SUM(ABOVE)`. Choose **N**umber Format, and pick a format for the total figure. Choose OK.

To	Do This
Insert a picture	Position the insertion point where you want the picture inserted. Choose **I**nsert, **P**icture, **C**lip Art. Click the Clip Art tab to switch to that page. Double-click a clip art image to insert it in the document.
Resize a picture	Click the picture. When the sizing handles are displayed, position the mouse pointer over a sizing handle. Click and drag the mouse to size the picture. Release the mouse button.
Move a picture	Click the picture. Move the mouse pointer into the picture. A four-headed arrow appears. Click and drag the mouse to move the picture. Release the mouse button to drop the picture.
Format a picture	Click the picture. Choose F**o**rmat, P**i**cture.
Set the wrap options	Click the picture. Choose F**o**rmat, P**i**cture, and then click the **W**rapping tab.

Checking Your Skills

True/False

For each of the following, check *T* or *F* to indicate whether the statement is true or false.

__T __F **1.** The Table AutoFormat feature has a series of styles that you can choose from to format a table.

__T __F **2.** Tables can be used to format text and numbers into columns.

__T __F **3.** The spreadsheet functions in Word are similar to those seen in powerful spreadsheet programs such as Excel.

__T __F **4.** You can wrap text around both sides of a picture.

__T __F **5.** A table formula is inserted as a field.

__T __F **6.** By default, tables are created with a single-line border.

__T __F **7.** Gridlines print automatically in a table.

__T __F **8.** Clicking and dragging horizontal borders works only in Page Layout view.

__T __F **9.** Tables display in a single column in Normal view.

__T __F **10.** If you type an entry that is too long for a table cell, Word displays an error message.

Multiple Choice

Circle the letter of the correct answer for each of the following questions.

1. You can place which of the following items in a document?
   a. video clips
   b. sound clips
   c. clip art files
   d. all the above
2. What is the most commonly used calculation in the Table feature?
   a. Average
   b. Minimum Value
   c. Maximum Value
   d. SUM
3. You must choose which option to allow text to wrap around the picture?
   a. Contour Wrap
   b. Wrapping
   c. Text Placement
   d. Position
4. Pressing Shift+Tab moves you where within a table?
   a. One cell to the right
   b. One cell to the left
   c. To the top cell of a table
   d. To the bottom cell of a table
5. Clicking and dragging which type of border adjusts the row height?
   a. vertical
   b. sizing
   c. horizontal
   d. bounding
6. If you choose 6 × 2 in the grid after you click the Insert Table button, what size table is created?
   a. 6 columns and 2 rows
   b. 6 inches tall by 2 inches wide
   c. 6 centimeters tall by 2 centimeters wide
   d. 6 rows by 2 columns
7. What happens if you press Tab in the last cell of a table?
   a. Word moves into the document.
   b. A new row is automatically created.
   c. A new column is automatically created.
   d. You receive an error message.
8. How do you recalculate a table?
   a. Press F9.
   b. Choose T**a**ble, **R**ecalculate.
   c. Click the Recalculate button on the Standard toolbar.
   d. Click the Recalculate button in the Tables dialog box.
9. How do you size a picture to exact measurements?
   a. By using the mouse
   b. By using the Size and Position pages of the Format Picture dialog box
   c. By using the drop-down list that displays when you click the Size Picture button
   d. By using the ruler to accurately measure the picture
10. How do you position the insertion point into a specific table cell?
    a. Click in the cell.
    b. Press Tab or Shift+Tab to move to the cell you want.
    c. Use the **E**dit, **F**ind command to locate the cell you want.
    d. a or b

Completion

In the blank provided, write the correct answer for each of the following statements.

1. A(n) _____________ formula adds together a series of numbers.
2. The Microsoft _____________ contains clip art, pictures, sounds, and video clips that you can include in your documents.
3. A table _____________ is the intersection of a row and a column.
4. The cell address is composed of the column _____________ and the row _____________.
5. You can resize a picture by clicking and dragging the sizing _____________.
6. A _____________ border separates two columns in a table.
7. When you insert a picture in a document, Word automatically switches to _____________ _____________ view.
8. The _____________ box is an invisible box around a graphic file.
9. When you are moving a picture, the mouse pointer displays as a _____________-__________ arrow.
10. To have text wrap around the contours of an object, choose the _____________ wrapping option.

Matching

In the blank next to each of the following terms or phrases, write the letter of the corresponding term or phrase. (Note that some letters may be used more than once.)

____**1.** Numeric cell entry

____**2.** The view that shows how the document looks when printed

____**3.** The view in which editing is faster

____**4.** Used to identify rows

____**5.** Used to identify columns

____**6.** Use this dialog box to format rows and columns

____**7.** Automatically adjusts the width of a column to accommodate its contents

____**8.** A collection of graphic images

____**9.** A series of rows and columns

___**10.** An accounting form that contains rows and columns

a. Cell Height and Width

b. spreadsheet

c. letters

d. numbers

e. Normal

f. clip art

g. AutoFit

h. value

i. table

j. Page Layout

Screen ID

Identify each of the items shown in Figure 5.19.

Figure 5.19

1. ____________
2. ____________
3. ____________
4. ____________
5. ____________
6. ____________

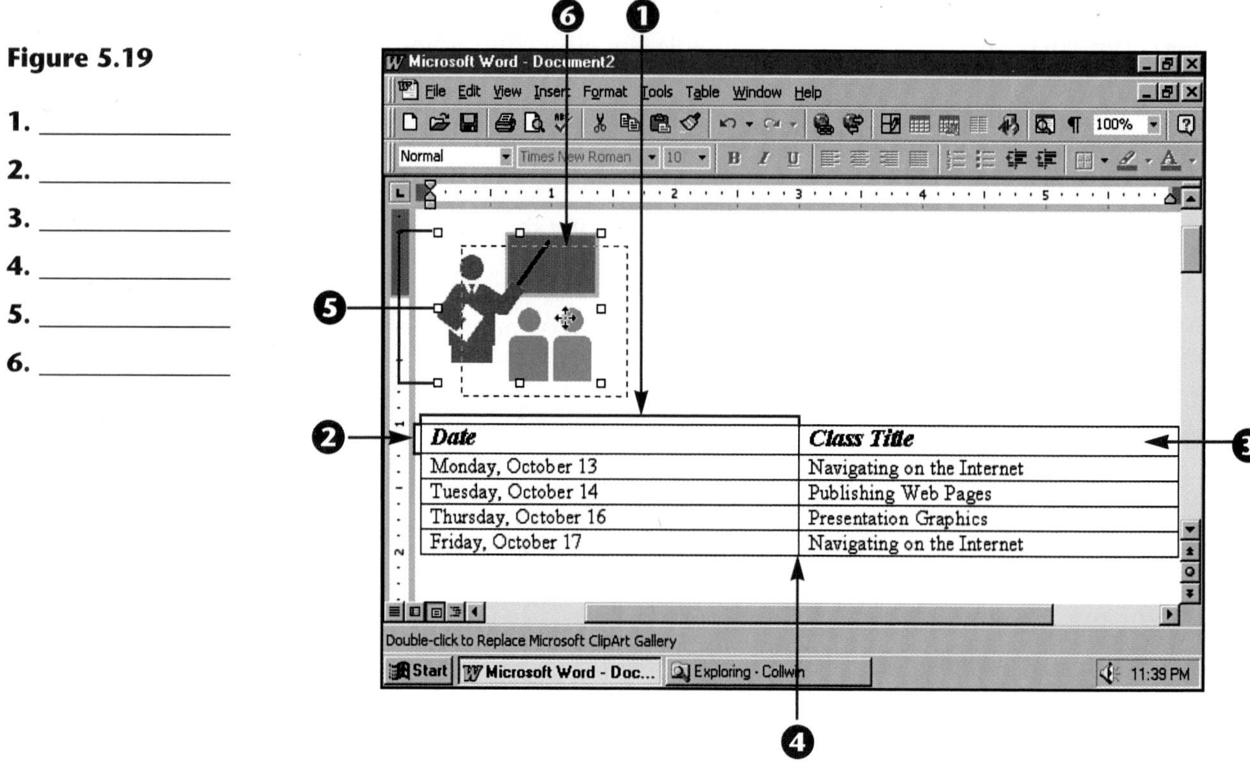

Applying Your Skills

Practice

The following exercises enable you to practice the skills you have learned in this project. Take a few minutes to work through these exercises now.

1. Adding Clip Art to an Invitation

Insert a picture into your invitation document.

To Add a Picture to the Invitation

1. In Word for Windows, open Proj0502 and save it as `Better Invitation`.
2. Change to Page Layout view.
3. Insert a blank line at the top of the document so that you have a place to insert the picture.
4. Open the Clip Art folder and choose an appropriate picture. For example, insert a picture of champagne popping.
5. Preview the invitation to see how it fits on the page.
6. If necessary, adjust the size and position of the picture to complement the invitation text.
7. Save the document and, if requested by your instructor, print two copies. Then close the document.

2. Adding Tables to a Loan Proposal

Add tables to the loan proposal you formatted in Project 4. You can create tables that automatically calculate the total amount that you anticipate is needed for renovations, as well as show your net profits.

To Format the Loan Proposal

1. Open the file Proj0503 and save it as **`Enhanced Proposal`**.
2. Between the second and third paragraphs, insert a table that is two columns wide by five rows high.
3. In the first cell of the first row, enter the title **`Anticipated Expenses`**.
4. In the remaining cells, enter the following data:

Demolition	**$10,000.00**
Construction	**$10,000.00**
Decorating	**$ 2,500.00**
Total	

5. In the last cell of the second column, create a formula to calculate the total anticipated expenses.
6. Using the AutoFormat feature, format the table with the Professional Format. Make sure the AutoFit option is selected.
7. Between the third and fourth paragraphs, insert a table to accommodate the following data (six rows by three columns):

	This Year	**Next Year**
Quarter 1	**$20,000.00**	**$25,000.00**
Quarter 2	**$22,000.00**	**$26,000.00**
Quarter 3	**$23,000.00**	**$27,000.00**
Quarter 4	**$24,000.00**	**$28,000.00**
Totals		

8. Create formulas to calculate the total for each year.
9. Format the table to match the other table.
10. Save the document and, if requested by your instructor, print two copies. Then close the document.

3. Creating a Schedule of Activities

Create a schedule of activities for the symposium.

To Create a Schedule

1. Open the file Proj0504 and save it as **`Activities Schedule`**.
2. Insert a table to accommodate the following data:

Time	Monday	Tuesday	Wednesday	Thursday	Friday
7:30 - 8:00	Breakfast	Breakfast	Breakfast	Breakfast	Breakfast
8:00 - 9:00	Round Table	Panel	Lecture	Panel	Round Table
9:00 - 12:00	Panel	Round Table	Panel	Round Table	Panel
12:00- 1:30	Lunch	Lunch	Lunch	Lunch	Lunch
1:30 - 3:00	Seminar	Seminar	Seminar	Seminar	Seminar
3:00 - 5:30	Free	Free	Free	Free	Free
5:30 - 7:00	Reception	Free	Free	Free	Reception
7:00 -	Free	Free	Free	Free	Dinner

3. Enter the data in the table.
4. Format the table so that it looks good on the page and is easy to read.
5. Insert a picture at the bottom of the document (below the table) to enhance the appearance of the schedule. Use a picture that captures the spirit of the symposium, such as shaking hands.
6. Save the document and, if requested by your instructor, print two copies. Then close the document.

4. Creating an Invoice

Create an invoice and set it up as a table. Use a calculating field to find the total due. You can insert a picture to customize the invoice.

To Create an Invoice

1. Open the file Proj0505 and save it as **Invoice**.
2. Insert a table to accommodate the following data:

Date	Description	Amount
5/1/97	Word 8 Intro	$200.00
6/1/97	Excel 8 Intro	$200.00
7/1/97	MS Outlook	$200.00
8/1/97	Internet Explorer	$200.00
Total		

3. Create a calculating field to total the amount due.
4. Format the table to look like an invoice when printed.
5. Insert a picture at the top of the document to enhance the invoice. Choose a picture that has something to do with the type of business.
6. Preview the invoice and make adjustments, if necessary.
7. Save the document and, if requested by your instructor, print two copies. Then close the document.

5. Editing the Welcome Letter

Insert a picture into the Welcome Letter to enhance its appearance.

To Edit the Welcome Letter

1. From the Student Disk, open the file named Proj0506.DOC, and save it as `Welcome Letter 4`.
2. Insert a Clip Art picture at the top of the page. Choose one of the pictures in the People at Work category.
3. Resize the picture so that it is approximately 1 ½ inches by 1 ½ inches.
4. Center the picture horizontally on the page.
5. Save the document and, if requested by your instructor, print a copy. Then close the document.

Challenge

The following challenges enable you to use your problem-solving skills. Take time to work through these exercises now.

1. Adding a Table to the Computer Training Concepts Letter

You want to use the formatting techniques you have learned to improve the appearance of the letter to be sent to those who request information from Computer Training Concepts. Open the file Proj0507.DOC and save it as `CTC Cover Letter 5`.

Add a table to the second page of the letter, listing the course descriptions. The following information should be included in the table.

Excel I	This course teaches you the basics of creating spreadsheets, including using functions, creating simple graphs, and using database features.
Excel II	In this advanced level course, you will learn to automate your work by using macros, linking worksheets and creating summary reports, and using the Scenario Manager.
Word for Windows I	You will learn the basics of word processing, including creating, formatting, and editing documents. In this class you will also be creating mail merge documents.
Word for Windows II	In this course, you will learn more advanced Word features including working with styles, creating tables, and using macros.

Use the Table AutoFormat command to format the table appropriately. You need to remove the checkmark from the Heading rows checkbox in the Table AutoFormat dialog box because this table does not have a heading row.

Print two copies of the letter, then save the file again. Close the file when you have finished.

2. Adding a Graphic to the Main Street Deli Sign

You decide to insert a picture to improve the appearance of the sign you created for the Main Street Deli. Open the Proj0508.DOC file and save it as `Deli Sign 4`.

Insert the traffic light picture that is in the Transportation clip art category. You decide how to size and locate the picture.

Save the document again and print one copy. Close the document when you have finished.

3. Adding a Table and a Graphic to the Membership Renewal Document

You decide to add a table to the Membership Renewal document to explain the annual membership fees. You also insert a picture to enhance the appearance of the document. Open the Proj0509.DOC and save it as `Membership Renewal 3`.

Add the following sentence to the end of the first paragraph:

`See the enclosed table explaining our membership rates.`

Type the following information into a table on the second page of the document:

Type of Membership	Annual Dues	Annual Dues Less 10% Discount
Basic	$600	$540
Basic Plus	$800	$720
Extended	$1000	$900
Premier	$1200	$1080

Use the Table AutoFormat command to format the table.

Insert an appropriate sports picture at the top of the document. You may need to change the page margins so that the letter fits on the first page, and the table on the second page.

Save the letter again, then print one copy. Close the file when you have finished.

4. Adding Tables to the Reunion Planning Letter

To improve the appearance of the reunion letter you edited in the previous project, you decide to add tables to the lists of options. Open the Proj0510.DOC file and save it as `Reunion Planning 4`.

Change the format of each list of options so that it displays in a table. The first column should contain the option text, while the second column should be blank so that the recipient can check the appropriate options.

Adjust the width of the second column. Select each table, and center the table between the left and right margins.

Adjust the page margins so that the letter fits on one page.

Save the letter again, then print a copy. Close the document when you are finished.

5. Adding a Table and a Graphic to the Computer Training Concepts Price List

A price list is needed to send with proposals for the courses Computer Training Concepts (CTC) offers. Type the following text into a table:

Course	Fee
Excel I	$225
Excel II	$250
Word for Windows I	$230
Word for Windows II	$255
Package Price	

For the package price, create a formula to calculate the total for all the classes. Use Table AutoFormat to format the table.

At the bottom of the document, add the following text:

Discounts are offered for three or more students from the same company.

Add the following heading to the top of the document:

Computer Training Concepts

Current Fees

Format the heading.

Insert a picture at the top of the document that would be appropriate for a computer training company.

Adjust the margins so that the document looks good on the page.

Save the document as **CTC Price List** and print a copy. Close the document when you are finished.

Project 6

Building a Spreadsheet

Creating an Office Expense Budget

In this project, you learn how to:

- Open an Existing Worksheet
- Select Worksheet Items
- Use AutoFill
- Add and Remove Rows and Columns
- Undo and Redo Actions
- Copy Information
- Move Information

Why Would I Do This?

Data
The information that you work with in a spreadsheet, in cluding text, numbers, and graphic images.

Worksheet
One page of your work in an Excel 97 workbook.

Now that you are familiar with using Word 97 and the basics of entering *data* and saving files, it's time to work with the spreadsheet application in Office 97, Excel 97. In this project, you learn to use Excel to create a budget *worksheet* that includes office expense information for several months.

Using the sample budget information, you learn how to control the structure of a worksheet by adding and deleting columns and rows. You also learn how to use Excel's editing features to make your work faster and easier.

Lesson 1: Opening an Existing Worksheet

Workbook
An Excel file that contains one or more worksheets.

After you create a *workbook* and save it to your hard disk or floppy disk, you can reopen the workbook and resume working with its data. With Excel, you can open a new workbook file, open an existing workbook file, or work with the default workbook. The default worksheet appears on-screen whenever you start Excel, or when you create a new file using the General Workbook file template.

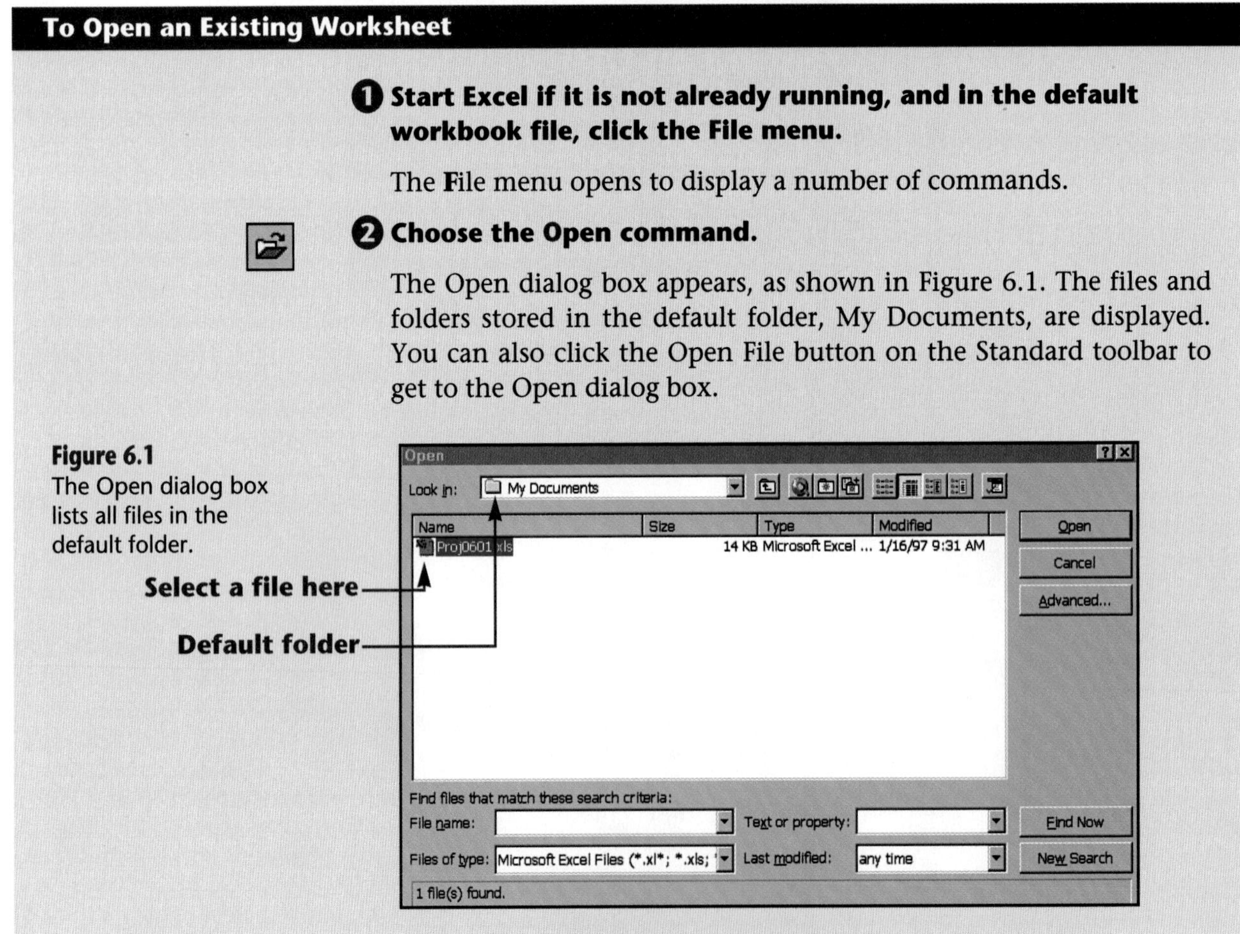

To Open an Existing Worksheet

1 Start Excel if it is not already running, and in the default workbook file, click the File menu.

The **F**ile menu opens to display a number of commands.

2 Choose the Open command.

The Open dialog box appears, as shown in Figure 6.1. The files and folders stored in the default folder, My Documents, are displayed. You can also click the Open File button on the Standard toolbar to get to the Open dialog box.

Figure 6.1
The Open dialog box lists all files in the default folder.

3 In the list of files and folders, click the `Proj0601` file icon to select it.

This file may already be selected. If you don't see `Proj0601` in the list, try opening another folder from the Look **i**n drop-down list, or try looking on another drive. The file may be stored in a different location on your system. If you can't find the file on your computer, ask your instructor for the location of the data files you will use with this book.

If you have problems...

If, when you click the file to select it, the characters in the file name become highlighted instead of the entire file name, it means you changed to Rename mode. In Rename mode, you can change the name of an existing file or folder. To select the file, make sure you click its icon.

4 Choose Open.

The office budget sample worksheet (`Proj0601`) appears on-screen, as shown in Figure 6.2. Now use the Save **A**s command to save a copy of this sample file under a more descriptive file name. The original data file will be stored intact.

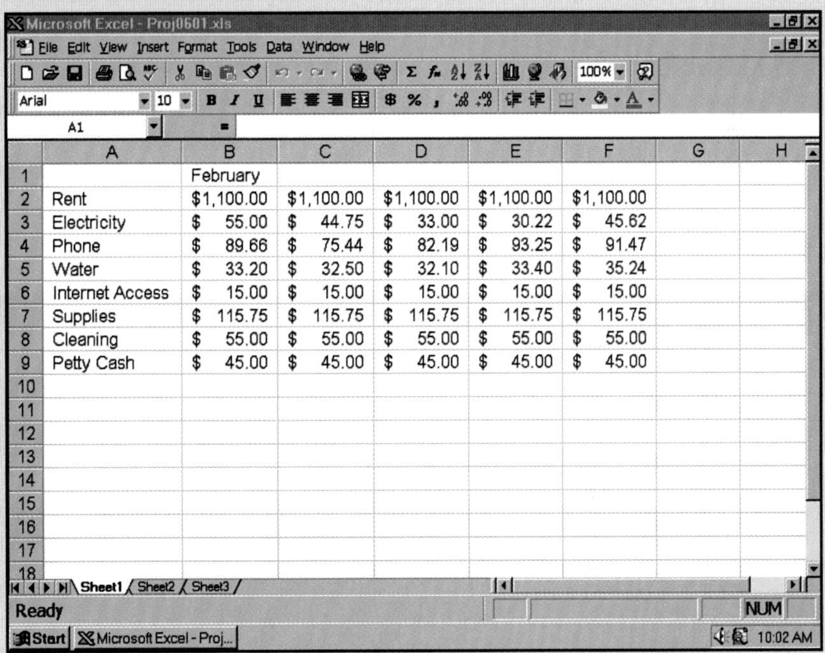

Figure 6.2
Save the sample file `Proj0601` as **`Budget`** to use in this project.

5 Choose the File menu again, then choose the Save As command.

The Save As dialog box appears.

continues

To Open an Existing Worksheet (continued)

❻ **In the File name text box, type `Budget` to replace Proj0601.**

`Budget` is the workbook file name that is used throughout this project.

❼ **From the Save in drop-down list, select the appropriate drive and folder for saving the new file.**

If necessary, ask your instructor where you should save the new workbook file.

❽ **Choose Save.**

Excel saves the workbook as `Budget` and automatically closes the original data file. Keep the `Budget` workbook open to use in the next lesson.

To open a file quickly from the Open dialog box, double-click the file icon in the list of files. If you double-click the file name, however, you may end up in Rename mode.

Lesson 2: Selecting Worksheet Items

Selecting
Designating an item on-screen so you can do something with it. Also called *highlighting*.

In order to build a worksheet, you must learn how to *select* items in the worksheet. When you select an item, you highlight that item so you can make changes to it. You select a cell, for example, so you can copy the cell's content into another cell. You must select a column so that you can change the column's width.

In this lesson, you learn how to select items in the `Budget` worksheet.

To Select Worksheet Items

❶ **Click cell B1 in the `Budget` worksheet.**

You have selected cell B1 by clicking in it. Once you select a cell, the cell's border is highlighted in bold, the cell address appears in the name box of the formula bar, and the cell's content appears in the contents area of the formula bar. In addition, the letter heading of the column and the number heading of the row in which the cell is located appear in bold.

❷ **Click cell A2, press and hold down the left mouse button, then drag the mouse pointer to cell G2. Release the left mouse button when the mouse pointer is in cell G2.**

Range
A cell or a rectangular group of adjacent cells.

Several adjacent cells—called a *range*—are now selected (see Figure 6.3). As you drag the mouse, the name box on the formula bar shows you how many rows and columns you are selecting. Dragging the mouse is an easy way to select a range of cells. After you finish selecting the range, the entire range of selected cells is highlighted, but only the address of the first cell—in this case, A2—appears in the name box, and only the content of the first cell appears in the Formula bar. That's because only the first cell is the active cell.

Now practice selecting an entire column of the worksheet.

Figure 6.3
The first cell in the selected range is active while the rest of the selected cells are highlighted.

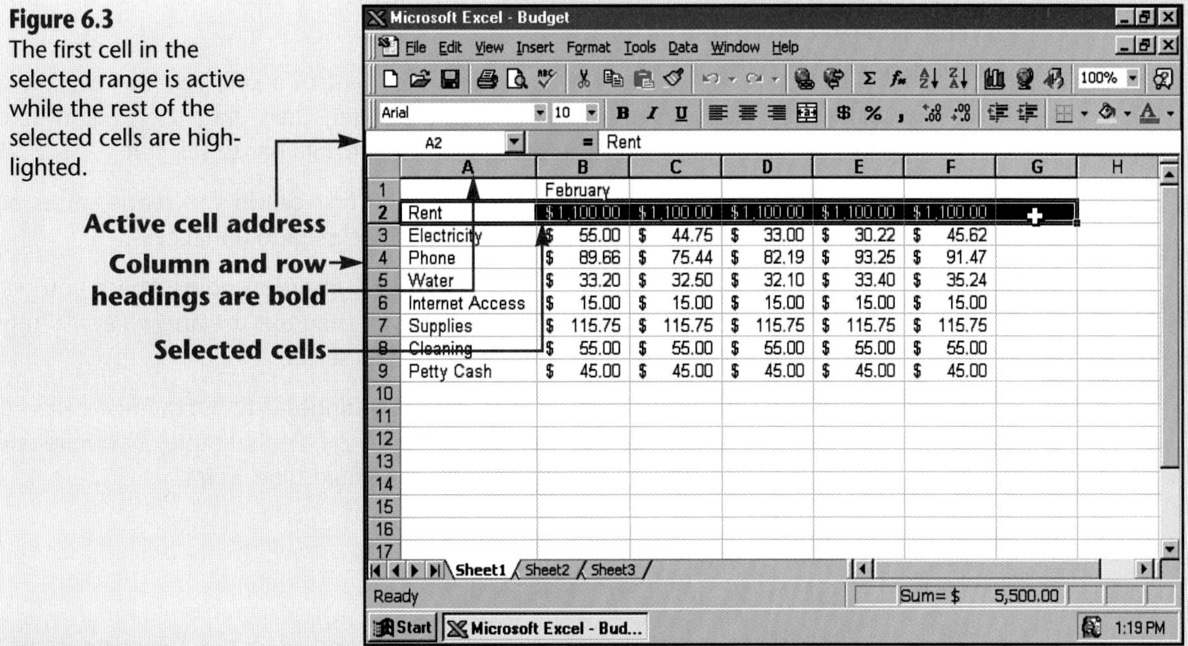

Worksheet frame
The horizontal bar containing the column letters and the vertical bar containing the row numbers, located in the worksheet area.

3 Click column heading B in the *worksheet frame.*

This selects the entire worksheet column B, as shown in Figure 6.4. Keep the `Budget` worksheet open to use in the next lesson.

Figure 6.4
You can quickly select a column or row by clicking the column or row heading in the worksheet frame.

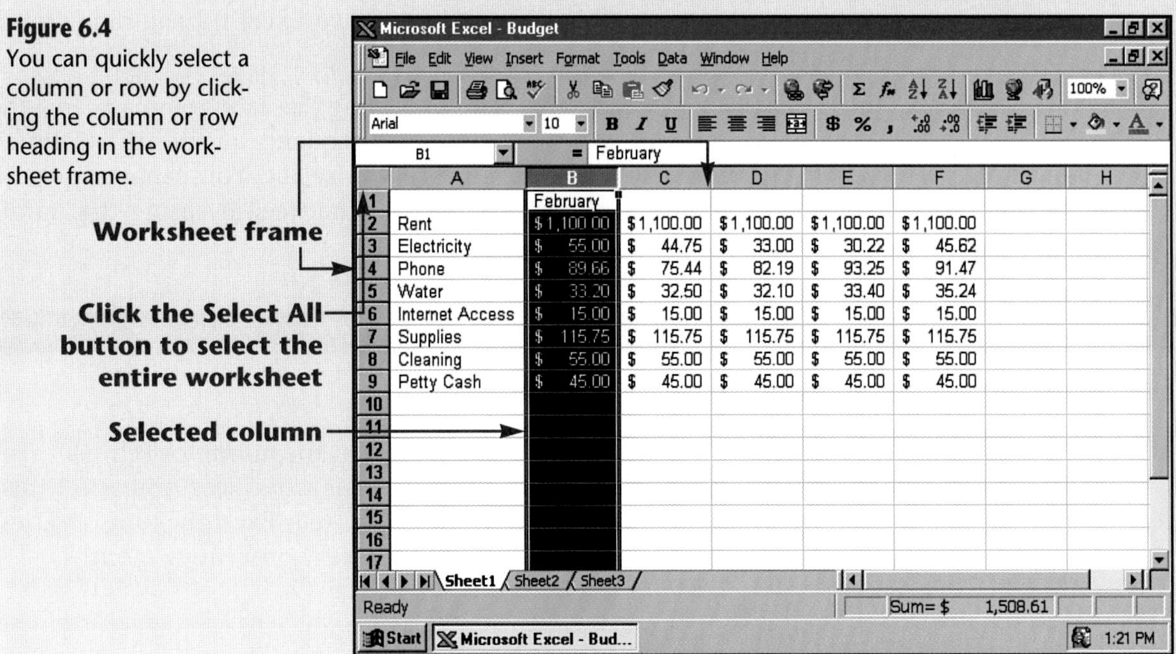

You can select two or more rows, columns, or cells by pressing and holding down Ctrl while you click the individual elements. This way, you don't have to select rows, columns, or cells in succession.

To select the entire worksheet, click the Select All button, the rectangle in the top-left corner of the worksheet frame.

To select non-adjacent cells, click the first cell, then press and hold Ctrl and click additional cells. The last cell that you click is the active cell, but the others remain selected.

To select just the content or part of the content of a cell, you can click in the active cell to display the I-beam mouse pointer, then drag the I-beam across any part of the text or data in the cell or the formula bar to select it.

To select cells with the keyboard, select the first cell in the range, press and hold down Shift, then use the arrow keys to select additional cells.

To select data with the keyboard, position the insertion point where you want to start selecting, press and hold down Shift, then use the arrow keys to move the insertion point to the last item you want to select.

In Excel, the standard notation for identifying ranges is to list the first cell in the range, then a colon, then the last cell in the range. For example, if you are referring to the range of cells from A1 to F9, you would type **A1:F9**.

Lesson 3: Using AutoFill

You have now opened the Budget worksheet and practiced selecting items in the worksheet. The Budget worksheet contains information on various expenses over several months, but before the worksheet is complete, a few items need to be changed.

As you can see, row 1 of the Budget worksheet should have column headings for each month of expenses you track. Using the AutoFill command, you can easily select a range of cells to have Excel fill the range with a sequence of information.

In this case, by selecting the cell containing the label February and then selecting a range of cells, you can add a sequence of months (February, March, April, and so on) to the range you select. You can also set up a sequence of numbers, letters, and days of the week by using the AutoFill command.

To Use AutoFill

1 Click cell B1 in the Budget worksheet.

Cell B1 contains the column heading for the month of February. To build column headings for the rest of the worksheet, you select this cell as the starting value for the fill. This tells Excel the type of series you want to create—in this case, a series of consecutive months.

2 Move the mouse pointer to the *fill handle* (the small, black box in the lower right corner of cell B1) until the pointer changes to a thin, black plus sign.

When the mouse pointer changes to a black plus sign, Excel is ready to select a range of cells to be filled (see Figure 6.5).

3 Press the left mouse button and drag right to cell F1, then release the mouse button.

This action selects the range B1 through F1. As you drag, notice that ScreenTips indicate the data that Excel will use to fill each cell. When you release the mouse button, Excel fills the range with months (starting with February and increasing by one month for each cell in the range), and selects it, as shown in Figure 6.6.

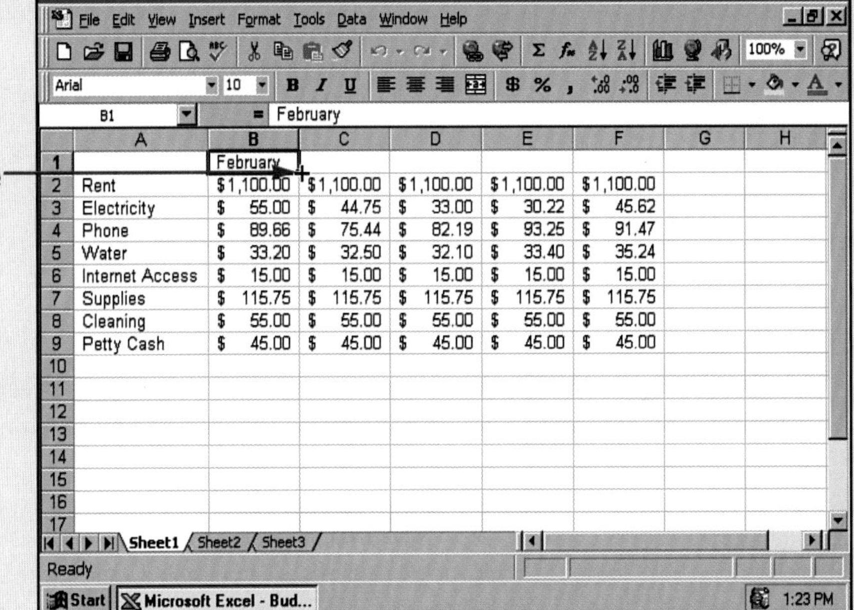

	A	B	C	D	E	F	G	H
1		February						
2	Rent	$1,100.00	$1,100.00	$1,100.00	$1,100.00	$1,100.00		
3	Electricity	$ 55.00	$ 44.75	$ 33.00	$ 30.22	$ 45.62		
4	Phone	$ 89.66	$ 75.44	$ 82.19	$ 93.25	$ 91.47		
5	Water	$ 33.20	$ 32.50	$ 32.10	$ 33.40	$ 35.24		
6	Internet Access	$ 15.00	$ 15.00	$ 15.00	$ 15.00	$ 15.00		
7	Supplies	$ 115.75	$ 115.75	$ 115.75	$ 115.75	$ 115.75		
8	Cleaning	$ 55.00	$ 55.00	$ 55.00	$ 55.00	$ 55.00		
9	Petty Cash	$ 45.00	$ 45.00	$ 45.00	$ 45.00	$ 45.00		

Figure 6.5
The fill handle is a thin black plus sign.

continues

To Use AutoFill (continued)

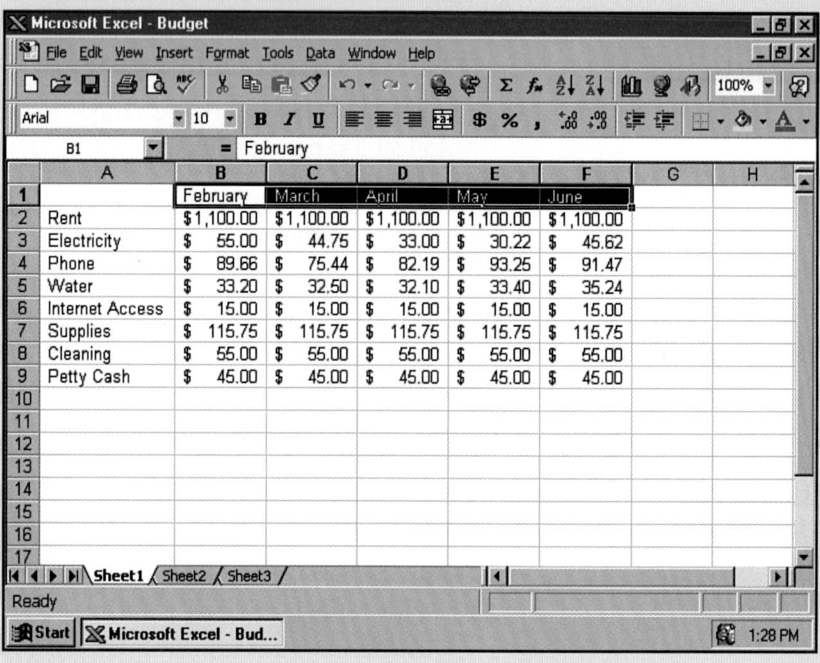

	A	B	C	D	E	F	G	H
1		February	March	April	May	June		
2	Rent	$1,100.00	$1,100.00	$1,100.00	$1,100.00	$1,100.00		
3	Electricity	$ 55.00	$ 44.75	$ 33.00	$ 30.22	$ 45.62		
4	Phone	$ 89.66	$ 75.44	$ 82.19	$ 93.25	$ 91.47		
5	Water	$ 33.20	$ 32.50	$ 32.10	$ 33.40	$ 35.24		
6	Internet Access	$ 15.00	$ 15.00	$ 15.00	$ 15.00	$ 15.00		
7	Supplies	$ 115.75	$ 115.75	$ 115.75	$ 115.75	$ 115.75		
8	Cleaning	$ 55.00	$ 55.00	$ 55.00	$ 55.00	$ 55.00		
9	Petty Cash	$ 45.00	$ 45.00	$ 45.00	$ 45.00	$ 45.00		

Figure 6.6
The AutoFill command is used here to create a series of months.

4 Click any cell.

This deselects the range. From here you can take the next step to build your `Budget` worksheet: adding and deleting columns and rows.

Save your changes and keep the worksheet open for the next lesson.

If you have problems...

When using AutoFill, if you select cells that already contain data, Excel overwrites the data in the cells. You can reverse this action by choosing **E**dit, **U**ndo before performing any other action.

You can fill columns as well as rows. Simply use the fill handle to drag down or up the column the same way you drag left or right to fill a row.

If you want to create a sequence of consecutive increments to fill by example (1, 2, 3, and so on), you enter the first two items in the sequence and select those cells. If you want to create a sequence of values in increments other than 1 (5, 10, 15), you enter the data in two cells and select those cells before filling the range.

You may already have noticed that sometimes Excel seems to anticipate what you are going to enter into a cell. For example, you may start typing a column label, and Excel automatically completes the word you have begun—sometimes correctly, sometimes incorrectly. This is a feature called AutoComplete.

With AutoComplete, as you enter new data, Excel considers data you have recently entered to see if they seem to match. If so, Excel automatically enters the same data you entered previously. For example, if you enter the label `Winter` in a cell and then start typing `Wi` into another cell, Excel assumes you are entering `Winter` again. If Excel is correct, this saves you some typing. If not, you can edit the entry.

To disable AutoComplete, choose **T**ools, **O**ptions, click the Edit tab, and deselect the Enable Auto**C**omplete for Cell Values check box. Then choose OK.

Lesson 4: Adding and Removing Rows and Columns

If you decide to add more information to your worksheet, Excel enables you to add rows and columns. You may, for example, want to add expense information for the month of January to your worksheet. Also, the cost of insurance, a common expense, is not listed in your worksheet. If you no longer want to include certain information, you can also remove columns and rows.

In this lesson, you learn how to add and remove rows and columns in a worksheet.

To Add and Remove Rows and Columns

1. **In the `Budget` worksheet frame, click the row heading for row 8.**

   The entire row 8, Cleaning, is highlighted to show that it has been selected.

2. **Choose Insert, Rows.**

   The content of row 8 and all rows below it move down one row. A new, blank row is inserted as the new row 8 (see Figure 6.7). Notice that all the rows beneath the new row 8 are automatically renumbered. Excel always inserts the new row above the row you select.

continues

To Add and Remove Rows and Columns (continued)

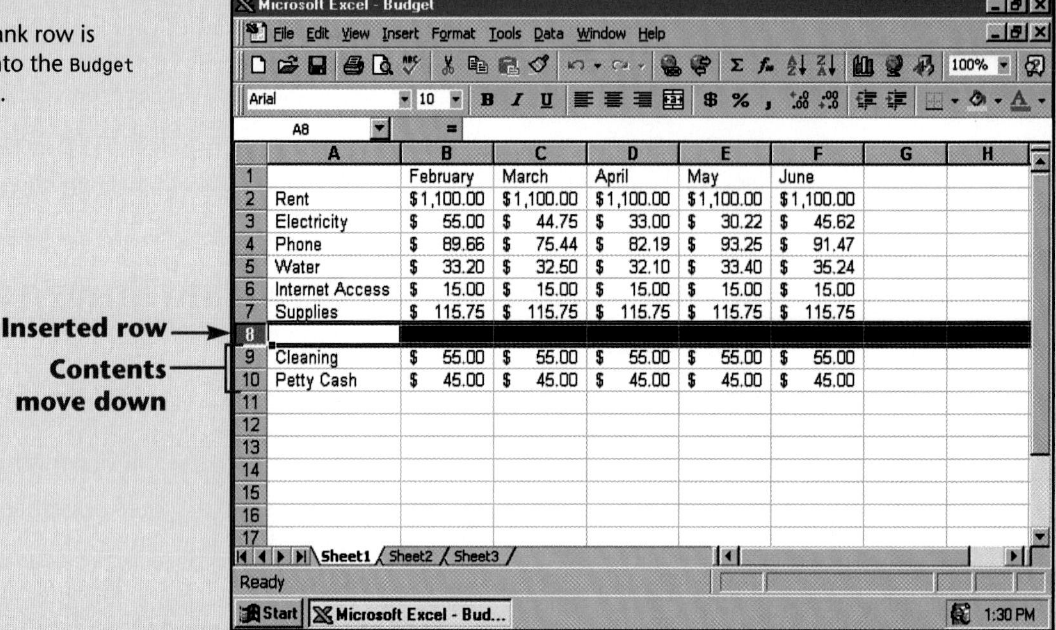

Figure 6.7
A new, blank row is inserted into the `Budget` worksheet.

❸ **Click cell A8 and type `Insurance`, then press Enter.**

You have inserted and labeled a new row for insurance expenses. Now insert a new column for January's expenses.

❹ **In the `Budget` worksheet frame, click the column heading for column B.**

The entire column B, February, is highlighted to show that it has been selected.

❺ **Choose Insert Columns.**

The content of column B and all columns to the right of column B, move to the right and have new letters assigned to them. A new, blank column B is added to the worksheet. Excel always inserts a new column to the *left* of the column you select.

❻ **Click cell B1 and type `January`, then press Enter.**

You have inserted and labeled a new row for January expenses. Finally, you decide that you don't want to include petty cash expenses in your worksheet. Delete the entire row 10 to remove Petty Cash data.

❼ **In the worksheet frame, click the row heading for row 10.**

The entire row 10, Petty Cash, is highlighted.

❽ **Choose Edit, Delete.**

Row 10 is now deleted. When you delete a selected column or row, you also delete any content in that column or row. Your worksheet should now look similar to Figure 6.8.

Figure 6.8
Use the **E**dit, **D**elete command to remove unwanted columns or rows.

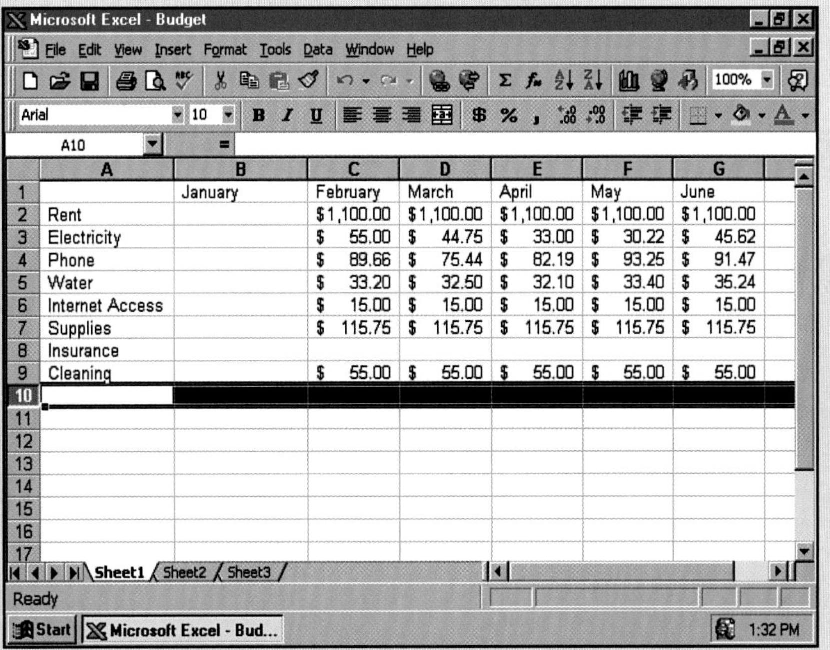

	A	B	C	D	E	F	G
1		January	February	March	April	May	June
2	Rent		$1,100.00	$1,100.00	$1,100.00	$1,100.00	$1,100.00
3	Electricity		$ 55.00	$ 44.75	$ 33.00	$ 30.22	$ 45.62
4	Phone		$ 89.66	$ 75.44	$ 82.19	$ 93.25	$ 91.47
5	Water		$ 33.20	$ 32.50	$ 32.10	$ 33.40	$ 35.24
6	Internet Access		$ 15.00	$ 15.00	$ 15.00	$ 15.00	$ 15.00
7	Supplies		$ 115.75	$ 115.75	$ 115.75	$ 115.75	$ 115.75
8	Insurance						
9	Cleaning		$ 55.00	$ 55.00	$ 55.00	$ 55.00	$ 55.00
10							
11							
12							
13							
14							
15							
16							
17							

Save your changes and leave the `Budget` worksheet open to use in the next lesson.

If you want to insert more than one row or column at a time, select as many adjacent rows or columns as you need blank rows or columns, then choose **I**nsert, **R**ows or **I**nsert, **C**olumns. For example, if you want to insert five new rows beginning at row 4, select rows 4 through 8 and then choose **I**nsert, **R**ows. The same is true for deleting rows and columns. To delete five columns, select the five columns you want to delete and then choose **E**dit, **D**elete.

You can also delete only the contents of selected cells. Select the cells and press Del, or choose **E**dit, Cle**a**r, Co**n**tents.

You can use shortcut menus to insert or delete columns, rows, and cell contents. Select the item you want to insert or delete, move the mouse pointer to it, and click the right mouse button. Choose the appropriate command from the shortcut menu that appears.

If you change your mind about what you added or deleted, choose **E**dit, **U**ndo. Undo reverses the last action you performed.

If you have problems...

If the Delete dialog box appears when you choose **E**dit, **D**elete, it means that you didn't select the entire row or column before choosing the command. You can either cancel the dialog box and try selecting the row again, or select Entire **R**ow or Entire **C**olumn in the dialog box, and choose OK to complete the deletion. The same is true for inserting and deleting rows and columns.

Lesson 5: Undoing and Redoing Actions

By inserting and deleting rows and columns, you have changed the structure of your worksheet. However, when you use insert and delete commands, you can see that it is possible to accidentally make changes you didn't want to make. Luckily, Excel is very forgiving: You can use the Undo command to quickly reverse the last action and the Redo command to quickly reverse the Undo command.

Excel even lets you undo or redo a series of actions; if you don't realize you made a mistake right away, you can still recover the data you need. In this lesson, you practice undoing and redoing actions in your `Budget` worksheet.

To Undo and Redo Actions

1 In the worksheet frame, click the heading for row 9, then choose Edit, Delete.

This selects, then deletes row 9.

2 Choose Edit, Undo Delete.

Excel reverses the last action you performed, which was the deletion of row 9. The row and all of its contents are put back in the worksheet. Notice that the Undo command includes a description of the last action. The command changes according to the action that will be reversed.

3 Choose Edit, Redo Delete.

Excel reverses the last action of the Undo command. In this case, Excel deletes row 9 again. Like Undo, the Redo command also includes a description of the last action.

4 Click in cell A11, type `Miscellaneous` and press Enter.

The text is entered in cell A11. At this point, you realize you really need row 9 back in the worksheet. However, the last action you performed was typing text into cell A11. You must use multiple undo to reverse more than one action.

5 Click the Undo drop-down arrow on the Standard toolbar.

A list of the actions that can be reversed is displayed, as shown in Figure 6.9. The most recently performed action is at the top of the list. You can chose to undo as many or as few of these actions as you want.

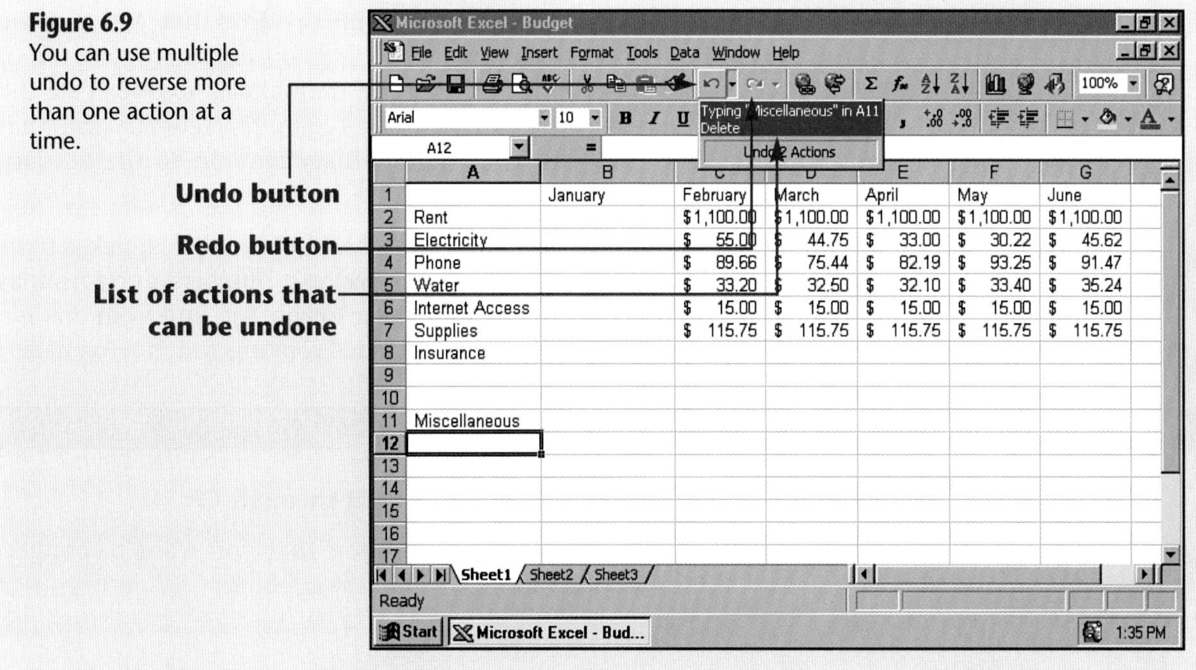

Figure 6.9
You can use multiple undo to reverse more than one action at a time.

6 Click the word `Delete` in the Undo drop-down list.

Excel reverses the action, as well as any actions above it in the list. The text Miscellaneous is deleted from cell A11, and row 9 is placed back in the worksheet.

Save your changes and leave the `Budget` worksheet open to use in the next lesson.

You can use multiple level Redo to redo more than one action. Click the Redo drop-down arrow on the Standard toolbar to display the Redo list, then click the last action you want to redo. All of the actions above the selected action are reinstated.

To quickly undo the most recent action, click the Undo button on the Standard toolbar, or press Ctrl+Z.

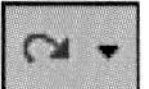

To quickly redo the most recent action, click the Redo button on the Standard toolbar, or press Ctrl+Y.

If an action cannot be undone, the Undo command and Undo button are dimmed. If an action cannot be redone, the Redo command and Redo button are dimmed.

Lesson 6: Copying Information

By adding and removing columns and rows, you have made some important changes to your `Budget` worksheet. You still need to insert expense information, however, in the new row for Insurance and the new column for January.

Because you don't have the exact information for your office insurance bills or for your January expenses in this example, assume that you can use information from other parts of your worksheet to estimate these parts of your budget. You might assume, for example, that January expenses are the same as your February expenses. Instead of retyping the February information, you can copy the cells from the February column to the January column.

Copying information from one column to another is much quicker than typing it a second time. You can copy or move text, numbers, and formulas from one cell to another, from one worksheet to another, and from one file to another. Use the `Budget` worksheet to practice copying and moving data.

To Copy Information

1 In the `Budget` worksheet, select cells C2 through C9.

This highlights the expense information that you want to copy from the February column into the January column.

2 Choose Edit, Copy.

A copy of the selected cells' contents is placed in the Windows *Clipboard*. The Clipboard stores information or formulas that you want to move (copy) to another location. (See the Jargon Watch at the end of this lesson for more about the Clipboard.) A flashing dotted line appears around the copied cells.

3 Click cell B2.

This selects the location where you want the copied information to appear. You do not have to select a range that is the same size as the range you are copying; Excel automatically fills in the data starting with the one cell you select. Notice that the flashing dotted line still appears around the copied cells, even though the cells are no longer selected. This helps you remember which cells are currently stored on the Clipboard.

4 Choose Edit, Paste.

The copied cells' content appears in cells B2 through B9, as shown in Figure 6.10. As indicated by the commands you have chosen, this process is called *copying and pasting*, and is a very common procedure in Windows applications. The flashing dotted line still appears around cells C2 through C9 because they are still stored on the Clipboard.

Note that the expense information in the January column is exactly the same as the information in the February column. To estimate your office insurance expense, assume for now that your monthly insurance bill is the same as your monthly office rent payment.

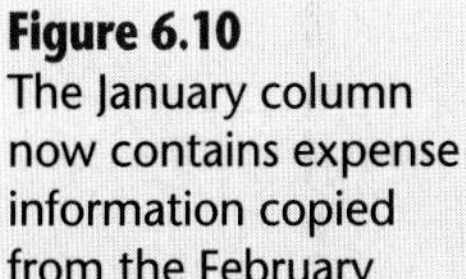

Figure 6.10
The January column now contains expense information copied from the February column.

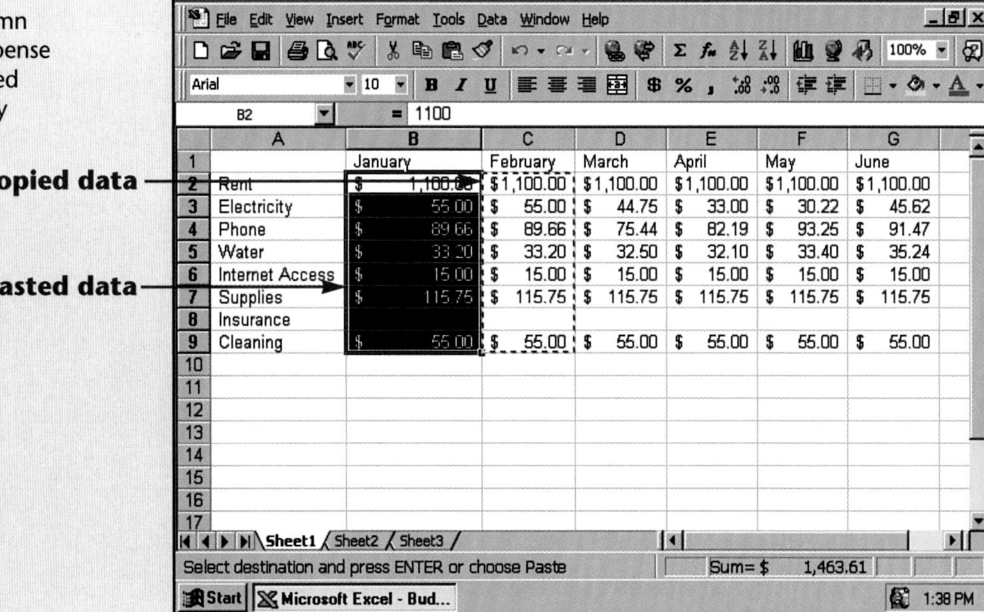

5 Select cells B2 through G2.

To estimate your insurance expenses, copy the rent expense information that you just selected to the Insurance row.

6 Click the Copy button on the Standard toolbar.

This copies the selected cells the same way as when you use the **E**dit, **C**opy command. The cells' contents are stored in the Clipboard, ready to be pasted. Now, the flashing dotted line appears around cells B2 through G2.

7 Click cell B8.

This selects the new location for the copied information.

8 Click the Paste button on the Standard toolbar.

The contents of the copied cells are pasted into the new location. Again, notice that the Insurance expense information is exactly the same as the Rent information in row 2. In Project 9, "Improving the Appearance of a Worksheet," you use formulas to change the amount you just copied. Save your most recent changes and keep the `Budget` worksheet open to use in the next lesson.

Jargon Watch

When you **copy** or **cut** information in Excel, it moves to the Windows **Clipboard**—a part of memory set aside for storing data that you want to move or copy to another location. The cut or copied information stays in the Clipboard until you cut or copy something else. Remember that the Clipboard can hold only one item, although that

continues

Continued

item can be quite large. Whenever you cut or copy a new piece of information and place it in the Clipboard, it overwrites any information that is already there. Because information that you cut or copy is stored in the Clipboard, you can **paste** the item many times and in many different places.

One thing to keep in mind while you are working in Excel is the difference between the Edit menu commands **Cut**, **Clear**, and **Delete**. Edit, Cut removes an item from the worksheet and moves it to the Clipboard where it is stored for later use. Edit, Clear removes the selected information completely. You can choose Clear, Contents to clear cell contents, Clear, Formats to clear cell formatting, or Clear, All to clear both the formatting and the contents. Edit, Delete removes not only the selected information but the cells containing it as well. If you choose the wrong command by mistake, press Ctrl+Z to undo the command, click the Undo button on the Standard toolbar, or choose Edit, Undo.

Lesson 7: Moving Information

Your `Budget` worksheet now has expense information in every cell, but what if you want to look at a certain type of expense separately? For example, perhaps you want to see how your utility expenses compare to the rest of your expenses.

You can use Excel's Cut and Insert Cells commands to remove cells from one location in a worksheet and place them in another location. You can use these commands to move cells so that you don't have to go to each cell, enter the same information, and then erase the information in the old location.

In this lesson, you move the rows containing utility expenses to another part of the worksheet.

To Move Information

1. **Select rows 3 through 5 in the `Budget` worksheet frame.**

   This highlights the rows of your worksheet that contain utility expenses. These are the rows you will move to another part of the worksheet.

2. **Choose Edit, Cut.**

   The information in rows 3 through 5 moves to the Clipboard (although you can still see it in the worksheet), and a dotted outline appears around the cut text, as shown in Figure 6.11. You can also click the Cut button on the Standard toolbar.

Figure 6.11
Cut cells appear in the worksheet surrounded by a flashing dotted line until you move them to a new location.

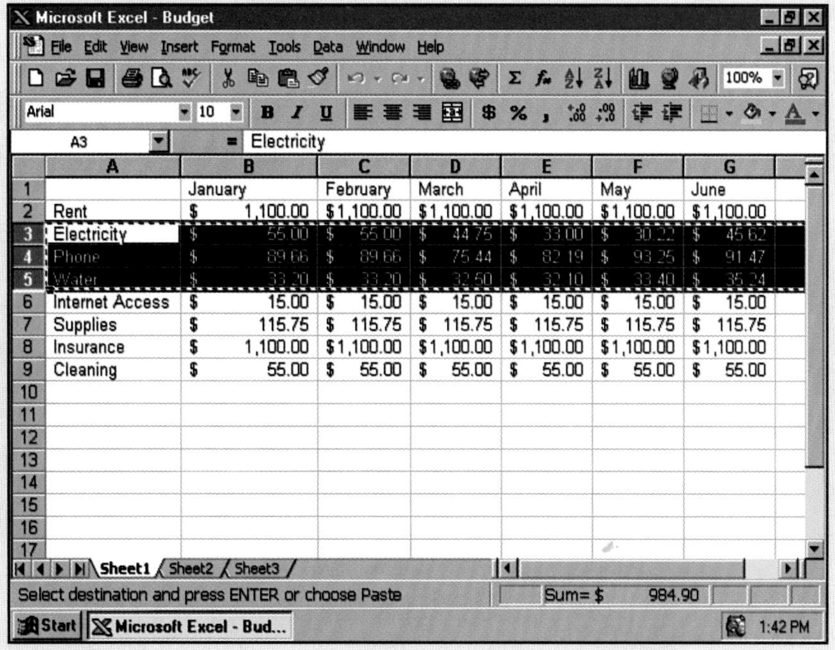

❸ **Click cell A11 to select it and then choose Insert, Cut Cells.**

The rows containing the utility expense information are cut from their original location in the worksheet and are inserted in the new location. The information now appears in rows 8, 9, and 10 (see Figure 6.12).

Figure 6.12
The cut cells are moved to a new location in the worksheet.

Microsoft Excel - Budget

A8 = Electricity

	A	B	C	D	E	F	G
1		January	February	March	April	May	June
2	Rent	$ 1,100.00	$1,100.00	$1,100.00	$1,100.00	$1,100.00	$1,100.00
3	Internet Access	$ 15.00	$ 15.00	$ 15.00	$ 15.00	$ 15.00	$ 15.00
4	Supplies	$ 115.75	$ 115.75	$ 115.75	$ 115.75	$ 115.75	$ 115.75
5	Insurance	$ 1,100.00	$1,100.00	$1,100.00	$1,100.00	$1,100.00	$1,100.00
6	Cleaning	$ 55.00	$ 55.00	$ 55.00	$ 55.00	$ 55.00	$ 55.00
7							
8	Electricity	$ 55.00	$ 55.00	$ 44.75	$ 33.00	$ 30.22	$ 45.62
9	Phone	$ 89.66	$ 89.66	$ 75.44	$ 82.19	$ 93.25	$ 91.47
10	Water	$ 33.20	$ 33.20	$ 32.50	$ 32.10	$ 33.40	$ 35.24

Ready Sum= $ 984.90

continues

To Move Information (continued)

Table 6.1 shows some shortcuts for the commonly used Cu**t**, **C**opy, and **P**aste commands.

You have now completed the changes to the `Budget` worksheet.

4 Save your changes to the `Budget` worksheet and print two copies, if requested by your instructor. Then close the `Budget` file.

You have now completed the lesson on building a spreadsheet. Save the changes you have made to the `Budget` worksheet. If requested by your instructor, print two copies, then close the `Budget` file. If you have completed your session on the computer, exit Excel and Windows 95. Otherwise, continue with the "Checking Your Skills" section at the end of this project.

You can use Excel's shortcut menus to perform many common commands, including Cut, Copy, Paste, and Insert Cut Cells. To open a shortcut menu, move the mouse pointer to the cell or area you want to affect, then press the right mouse button. To select a command, click its name in the shortcut menu. Make sure that you move the mouse pointer to the correct cell before you click the shortcut menu command. Shortcut menu commands happen at the location of the mouse pointer, not necessarily in the current cell.

You can also use Excel's Cut and Paste commands to remove information from one cell and place it in another cell. Select the cell or cells you want to move and choose **E**dit, Cu**t**. Select the cell where you want to place the information and choose **E**dit, **P**aste. Excel moves the information, but leaves the cells where the information had been intact in the worksheet. You can insert new data, or delete the cells.

A handy way of quickly moving one or more cells of data is to select the cells and position the mouse pointer on any border of the cells so that the cell pointer changes to a white arrow. Click and drag the white arrow to the new location. An outline of the cells that you are moving appears as you drag, and a ScreenTip shows you the current active cell where the information will appear when you release the mouse button. If the new location already contains information, a dialog box appears, asking whether you want to replace the current information.

You can also copy data by pressing Ctrl and dragging the cells to the new location.

Table 6.1 Copying, Cutting, and Pasting

Command	Tool	Shortcut Key
Edit, Cu**t**		Ctrl+X
Edit, **C**opy		Ctrl+C
Edit, **P**aste		Ctrl+V

Project Summary

To	Do This
Open an existing file	Choose **F**ile, **O**pen, select the file name in the Open dialog box, then choose **O**pen.
Save a file with a new name	Choose **F**ile, Save **A**s, type a new name in the File **n**ame text box, then choose **S**ave.
Select a cell	Click the cell you want to select, or use the arrow keys to move to it.
Select a range of cells	Drag from the first cell to the last cell in the range, or use Shift and the arrow keys to highlight cells using the keyboard.
AutoFill a range of cells	Select the cell containing the first entry in the series, then drag across the range you want to fill.
Insert rows or columns	Select the rows or columns, then choose **I**nsert, **R**ows or **I**nsert, **C**olumns.
Delete rows or columns	Select the rows or columns, then choose **E**dit, **D**elete.
Reverse the last action	Choose **E**dit, **U**ndo.
Reverse a series of actions	Click the Undo drop-down arrow, then select the last action you want to reverse.
Redo the last undone action	Choose **E**dit, **R**edo.
Redo a series of undone actions	Click the Redo drop-down arrow, then select the last action you want to redo.
Copy cells	Select the cells to copy, then click the Copy button on the Standard toolbar. Select the first cell in the new location, then click the Paste button on the toolbar.
Move cells	Select the cells to move, then click the Cut button on the Standard toolbar. Select the first cell in the new location, then choose **I**nsert, Cut C**e**lls.
Paste cells	Copy or cut the cells, select the new location, then click the Paste button on the Standard toolbar.

Checking Your Skills

True/False

For each of the following, check *T* or *F* to indicate whether the statement is true or false.

__T __F **1.** You use the **F**ile, **O**pen command to retrieve a file that has been previously saved.

__T __F **2.** Select the entire worksheet by clicking the sheet tab.

__T __F **3.** To insert two rows, select two rows and then choose the **E**dit, **I**nsert command.

__T __F **4.** Use AutoFill to fill the selected cells with a shade of gray.

__T __F **5.** Pressing F9 is a shortcut for deleting selected rows.

__T __F **6.** To save a file using a different file name, use the **S**ave command on the **F**ile menu.

__T __F **7.** You can automatically enter a sequence of days of the week using the AutoFill command.

__T __F **8.** Excel automatically inserts a new column to the right of the column you select.

__T __F **9.** To open a file quickly from the Open dialog box, double-click the file's icon.

__T __F **10.** If you select cells that already contain data when using AutoFill, Excel overwrites the data in the cells.

Multiple Choice

Circle the letter of the correct answer for each of the following questions.

1. What does the mouse pointer look like when Excel is ready to use AutoFill?

a. An arrow

b. A hand

c. A thin, black plus sign

d. A thick, white plus sign

2. What appears around cells that have been copied or cut to the Clipboard?

a. A flashing dotted line

b. A solid double line

c. A thick red border

d. A red dotted double line

3. Which of the following cannot be pasted?

a. Data that has been cut

b. Data that has been cleared

c. Data that has been copied

d. Data you just pasted

4. What command do you use to save an existing file with a new name?

a. **F**ile, **S**ave

b. **F**ile, **O**pen

c. **F**ile, **N**ew

d. **F**ile, Save **A**s

5. What do you click to quickly select an entire row?

a. The row number

b. The column letter

c. The Select All button

d. The name box

6. To select non-adjacent cells, you hold down which Key(s) while you click the cells that you want?

a. Alt

b. Ctrl

c. Shift

d. Shift + Ctrl

7. To identify the range of cells from A1 to Z100, type which of the following?
   a. A1:Z100
   b. A1;Z100
   c. A1-Z100
   d. A1,Z100
8. Which Excel feature anticipates what you are going to enter and enters the data automatically?
   a. AutoFill
   b. Automatic Entry
   c. AutoComplete
   d. QuickComplete
9. To use the keyboard to select a range of cells, hold down which of the following keys while pressing the arrow keys?
   a. Alt
   b. Ctrl
   c. Shift
   d. Shift + Ctrl
10. How do you display a shortcut menu?
   a. Double-click any menu option
   b. Double-click within a range of selected cells
   c. Choose **E**dit, **S**hortcut
   d. Click the right mouse button

Completion

In the blank provided, write the correct answer for each of the following statements.

1. To retrieve a file that has already been saved, you open the **F**ile menu and choose the ______________ command.
2. To select a range of cells, you ______________ the mouse over the cells.
3. When using AutoFill, the next item in sequence after April is ______________.
4. Use the ______________ command to reverse the last action.
5. Select or ______________ a cell when you want to cut or copy the cell content.
6. The command to clear the contents of select cells is located on the ______________ menu.
7. The Clipboard can hold ______________ item(s).
8. If an action cannot be undone, the **U**ndo command and Undo button are ______________.
9. To move entire cells (the cells and their contents) to another location, use the ______________ ______________ command.
10. The Copy and Paste buttons are located on the ______________ toolbar.

Matching

In the blank next to each of the following terms or phrases, write the letter of the corresponding term or phrase.

_____ 1. Moves an item from the worksheet to the Clipboard

_____ 2. Removes the selected information from the worksheet, but not the cells

_____ 3. Removes the selected cells and the information they contain

_____ 4. Places a duplicate of the information on the Clipboard

_____ 5. A cell or rectangular group of adjacent cells

_____ 6. The shortcut for the **E**dit, Cu**t** command

_____ **7.** The shortcut for the **E**dit, **C**opy command

_____ **8.** The mouse pointer that displays as a black plus sign

_____ **9.** This command reverses the last action you performed

_____ **10.** A part of the computer's memory that stores information or formulas you want to copy or move to another location

a. Clipboard

b. range

c. **E**dit, **C**opy

d. Ctrl + X

e. **E**dit, Clea**r**

f. fill handle

g. Undo

h. Ctrl + C

i. **E**dit, Cu**t**

j. **E**dit, **D**elete

Screen ID

Label each element of the Excel screen shown in Figure 6.13.

Figure 6.13

1. ______________

2. ______________

3. ______________

4. ______________

5. ______________

6. ______________

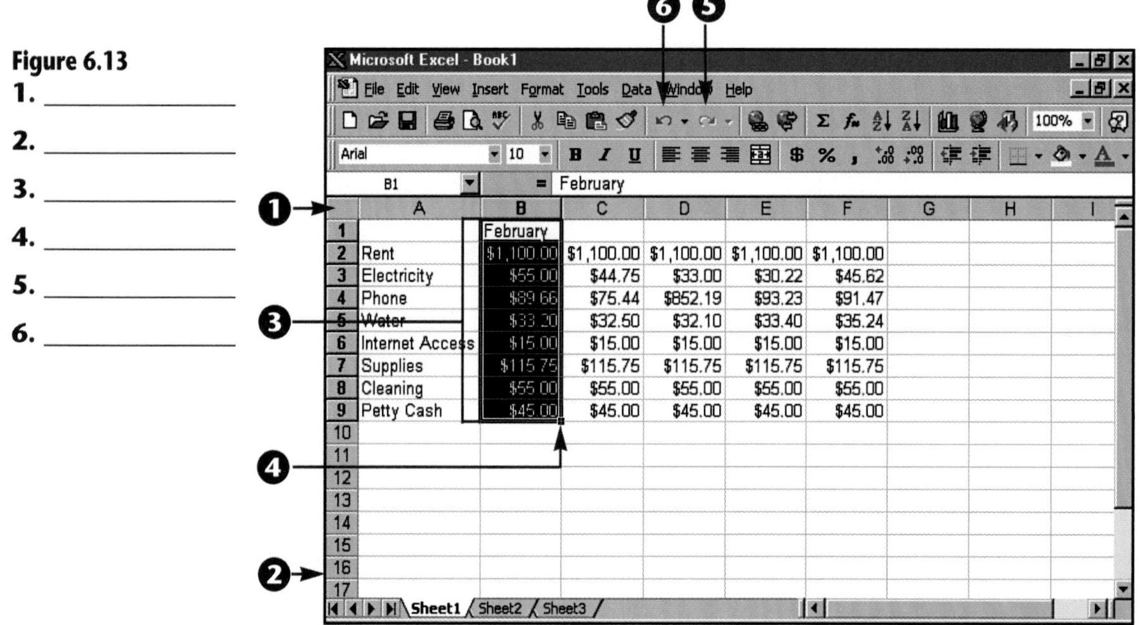

Applying Your Skills

Practice

The following exercises enable you to practice the skills you have learned in this project. Take a few minutes to work through these exercises now.

1. Reworking the Job List

In this exercise, follow the steps below to rework the `Job List` worksheet supplied to you. To make the worksheet suitable as a list of job positions rather than a list of employees, you want to add a new job position and delete the information about specific employees.

To Rework the Job List

1. Open the file Proj0602 and save it as **`Job List2`**.
2. Insert a new row 3 and label it **`Buyer`**.
3. Delete columns D, E, and F.
4. Save the changes.
5. If requested by your instructor, print two copies of the file, then close it.

2. Completing a Schedule of Events

In this exercise, follow the steps below to complete a schedule of monthly coffee tastings that you will hold in your coffee shop.

To Complete a Schedule of Events

1. Open the file Proj0603 and save it as **`Tastings`**.
2. Insert a new row 1 and enter the title **`Coffee Tastings`** in cell A1.
3. Use AutoFill to complete the list of months from cell A3 down to cell A8.
4. Copy the data from cells C3:C8 into cells D3:D8.
5. Save the file, print two copies, then close it.

3. Organizing the Inventory Worksheet

In this exercise, follow the steps below to organize the `Inventory` worksheet supplied to you.

To Organize the Inventory Worksheet

1. Open the file Proj0604 and save it as **`Inventory2`**.
2. Insert a new row 1 and enter the title **`Inventory`** in cell A1.
3. Rearrange the columns so the data for French Roast is between the data for Arabica and Kona.
4. Save the changes, print two copies of the worksheet, then close it.

4. Expanding the Paper Costs Worksheet

In this exercise, follow the steps to expand the `Paper Costs` worksheet supplied to you.

To Expand the Paper Costs Worksheet

1. Open the file Proj0605 and save it as **`Paper Costs2`**.
2. Insert a new row 6 and label it for fax paper.
3. In cell B6, enter **`500`** as the amount you spent on fax paper.
4. Rearrange the rows so that the cost of mailing labels and the cost of envelopes are at the top of the worksheet.
5. Label column B **`Cost`**.
6. Save the worksheet. If requested by your instructor, print two copies, then close it.

5. Opening a Workbook and Selecting Worksheet Items

In this project, you learned how to open an existing workbook and how to use various methods to select worksheet items. In this exercise, you practice completing these tasks.

To Open a Workbook and Select Worksheet Items

1. Choose **F**ile, **O**pen to display the Open dialog box.
2. Select your floppy disk drive in the Look in drop-down list box.
3. From the list of files, select Proj0606.
4. Click the **O**pen button to open the file.
5. Save the file under a new name by choosing **F**ile, Save **A**s. The Save As dialog box displays on your screen.
6. In the File **n**ame text box, type `Medical Expenses 2`.
7. Click the Save button to save the file.
8. Select the range of cells from B4:D9 by clicking cell B4, holding down the mouse button, and dragging the mouse down to cell D9.
9. Select row 8 of the worksheet by clicking the row number 8 in the worksheet frame.
10. Select column D by clicking column heading D in the worksheet frame.
11. Leave the workbook open for the following Challenge exercise.

Challenge

The following challenges enable you to use your problem-solving skills. Take time to work through these exercises now.

1. Adding and Removing Rows and Columns in the Medical Expenses Workbook

You have decided to add and remove some rows and columns in the `Medical Expenses 2` workbook. Insert two columns to the left of column C and then enter the following information:

1. In cell C3, type `Illness`.

2. In cells C4:C9, type the following descriptions of illnesses:

```
bronchitis
ear infection
check up
check up
eye infection
check up
```

You decide that you no longer need column D, so delete it. Insert a blank row above row 6 and enter the following information:

```
Joe    28-Feb    follow-up    Dr. visit    45
```

Save your changes to the workbook and leave it open for the following exercise.

2. Undoing and Redoing Actions in the Medical Expenses Workbook

You know how easy it is to make mistakes while editing a worksheet so you decide to practice undoing and redoing actions in the `Medical Expenses 2` workbook. Delete column D and then undo the action. Change the first number in column E to `55`, the next number to `60`, and the third number to `65`. You realize that all three of these changes are incorrect, so use the Undo button on the Standard toolbar to undo the changes. Change the name in cell A4 to `Mark` and then undo the change. Redo the action by using the Redo button on the Standard toolbar. Save and print the workbook before closing it.

3. Using the AutoFill Command

Because you are short on time, you decide to use the AutoFill command when creating a worksheet. In a new, blank workbook, use the AutoFill command to enter the days of the week in cells A1 to G1. In cells A4 to A15, use the AutoFill command to enter the numbers `1-12`. In cells B4 to B15, enter the numbers 5 to 60 in increments of 5. In cells C4 to C15 enter the word `Category` using the AutoFill command. Save the workbook as `AutoFill` Practice and leave it open for the next exercise.

4. Copying and Moving the AutoFill Practice Workbook

Because you often need to change the location of information in a worksheet, you decide to practice copying and moving information to different locations in the `AutoFill Practice` workbook. Copy the days of the week in cells A1:G1 to cells A18:G18 and cells A20:G20. Move the data in cells A4:A15 to cells E4:E15; then move that data to cells C4:C15. Save and print the file before closing it.

5. Balancing Your Checkbook Using Excel

Now that you are familiar with various editing techniques, you decide to balance your checkbook using an Excel worksheet. Open Proj0607 and save it as `Checking Account 2`. Use the AutoFill command to enter the sequence of check numbers, starting with 500, in column A. Insert a blank row above row 12. Add an entry for a $500 deposit on April 26th. Delete column B and then undo the deletion. Save and print the worksheet before closing it.

Project 7

Creating Formulas

Expanding the Office Expense Budget Worksheet

In this project, you learn how to:

- Create Formulas Using Mathematical Operators
- Create Formulas by Selecting Cells
- Copy Formulas
- Use Absolute Cell References

Why Would I Do This?

Formula
A calculation that Excel performs on data entered in a worksheet.

Function
A built-in formula that automatically performs calculations.

Formula Palette
A feature that enables you to view the result of a formula before you actually enter it.

AutoSum Button
A feature that quickly finds the total of a row or column of data.

A *formula* is a calculation that Excel performs on data entered in a worksheet. You can use formulas to add, subtract, multiply, and divide data with basic mathematical operators. You can also use Excel's built-in *functions* to simplify the number of characters required in a formula. Formulas are the most valuable part of spreadsheet software such as Microsoft Excel. A worksheet full of data would be of little use without built-in ways to perform calculations on the data.

Once you write a formula using cell addresses, you can change the information in one or more of the cells referenced in the formula, and the formula automatically recalculates the result. You can also copy the formula from one location to another in the worksheet, so you do not have to re-enter the formula to perform the same calculation on different data.

In this project, you learn how to create basic formulas in your budget worksheet using mathematical operators. You also learn how to use some of Excel's features for automating formulas—including the *Formula palette*, which enables you to view the result of a formula before you actually enter it in a cell, and the *AutoSum button*, which quickly finds the total of a row or column of data. Finally, you learn the difference between relative and absolute cell references, and how to copy formulas from one location in a worksheet to another.

Lesson 1: Creating Formulas Using Mathematical Operators

You can easily create a basic formula to find the total of a list of expenses by typing an equation into a cell. To create the formula, type the actual values you want to use in the calculation or the addresses of the cells that contain the values you want to use, separated by the mathematical operators that specify the type of calculation (a plus sign for addition or a minus sign for subtraction, for example). Table 7.1 lists some common mathematical operators.

In this lesson, you open a version of the budget worksheet you created in Project 6, "Building a Spreadsheet," and create some basic formulas.

Table 7.1 Common Mathematical Operators

Description	Operator
Addition	+ (plus sign)
Subtraction	– (minus sign)
Multiplication	* (asterisk)
Division	/ (forward slash)
Exponents	^ (caret)

To Create Formulas Using Mathematical Operators

1 Open the file Proj0701 and save it as `Budget2`.

This is an expanded version of the office budget worksheet you created in Project 6.

2 Select cell B5 in the `Budget2` worksheet.

Cell B5 is now the current (active) cell, and it is where you want to create your first formula in this example. After looking at the expense worksheet again, you might decide that estimating insurance expenses to be the same as rent is too high. To change the insurance bill estimate, divide the amount of rent in half using a formula.

3 In cell B5, type the formula `=b2/2`.

This formula tells Excel to divide the contents of cell B2 by 2. The equal sign (=) tells Excel that you are about to enter a formula. If you do not type an equal sign, Excel enters the values as text data in the cell. `B2` is the cell address of the January rent expense: $1,100. The slash (/) is the operator that tells Excel which mathematical operation you want to perform—in this case, division.

4 Click the Enter button (the green check mark) on the formula bar.

This tells Excel to enter the formula in the cell and calculate the formula. The result of the formula appears in cell B5, as shown in Figure 7.1. Notice that the formula `=B2/2` appears in the formula bar. The formula is entered in cell B5, but Excel displays the result of the formula—not the formula itself. Now try using the Formula palette to create a formula for the February insurance bill.

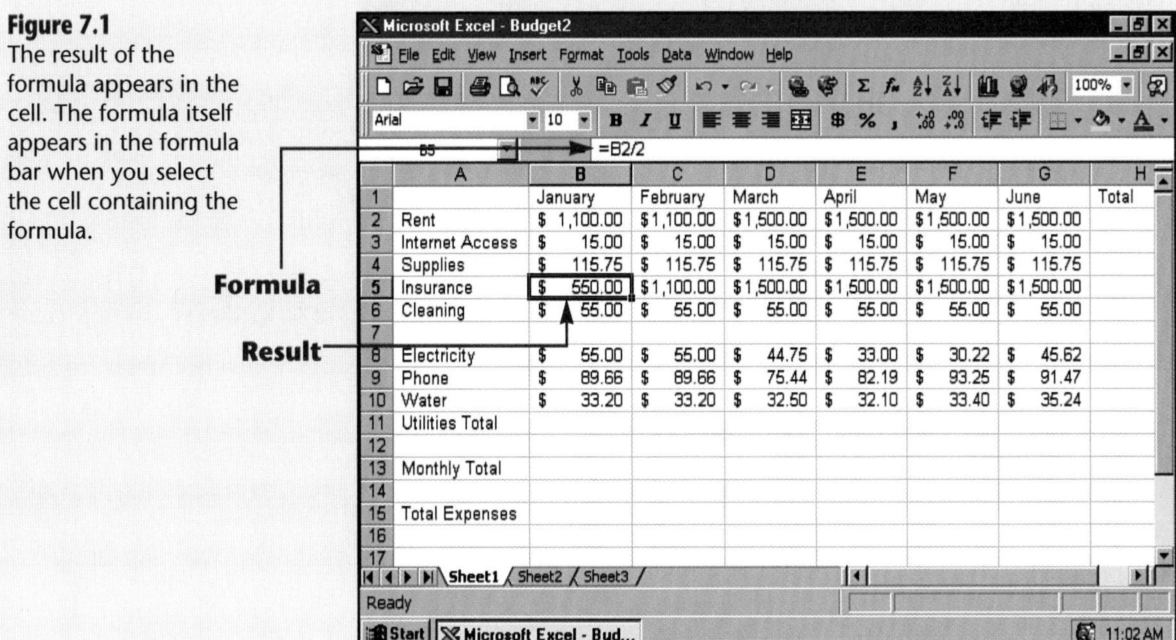

	A	B	C	D	E	F	G	H
1		January	February	March	April	May	June	Total
2	Rent	$ 1,100.00	$1,100.00	$1,500.00	$1,500.00	$1,500.00	$1,500.00	
3	Internet Access	$ 15.00	$ 15.00	$ 15.00	$ 15.00	$ 15.00	$ 15.00	
4	Supplies	$ 115.75	$ 115.75	$ 115.75	$ 115.75	$ 115.75	$ 115.75	
5	Insurance	$ 550.00	$1,100.00	$1,500.00	$1,500.00	$1,500.00	$1,500.00	
6	Cleaning	$ 55.00	$ 55.00	$ 55.00	$ 55.00	$ 55.00	$ 55.00	
7								
8	Electricity	$ 55.00	$ 55.00	$ 44.75	$ 33.00	$ 30.22	$ 45.62	
9	Phone	$ 89.66	$ 89.66	$ 75.44	$ 82.19	$ 93.25	$ 91.47	
10	Water	$ 33.20	$ 33.20	$ 32.50	$ 32.10	$ 33.40	$ 35.24	
11	Utilities Total							
12								
13	Monthly Total							
14								
15	Total Expenses							
16								
17								

Figure 7.1
The result of the formula appears in the cell. The formula itself appears in the formula bar when you select the cell containing the formula.

continues

To Create Formulas Using Mathematical Operators (continued)

If you have problems...

If your formula results in #NAME? instead of a value, it means you made a mistake entering the formula. You may have typed a cell address that doesn't exist, one of the cells in the formula may have an error, the operator you are using may be incorrect—for example, back slash (\) instead of slash (/)—or you may be trying to perform an impossible calculation. Check your formula carefully, correct any mistakes, and try again.

5 Select cell C5 and press Del.

This deletes the contents of cell C5. To enter a new formula with the Formula palette, the active cell must be empty.

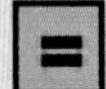

6 Click the Edit Formula button on the formula bar.

Excel inserts an equal sign into the formula bar and opens the Formula palette (see Figure 7.2). With the Formula palette, you can see the result of the formula as you create it. You can also select functions to include in the formula, as you learn in Project 4, "Calculating with Functions."

7 Type c2.

The cell address appears in the formula bar and in the active cell. In the Formula palette, you can see the result of the formula so far, which is simply the value of cell C2: $1,100 (see Figure 7.2).

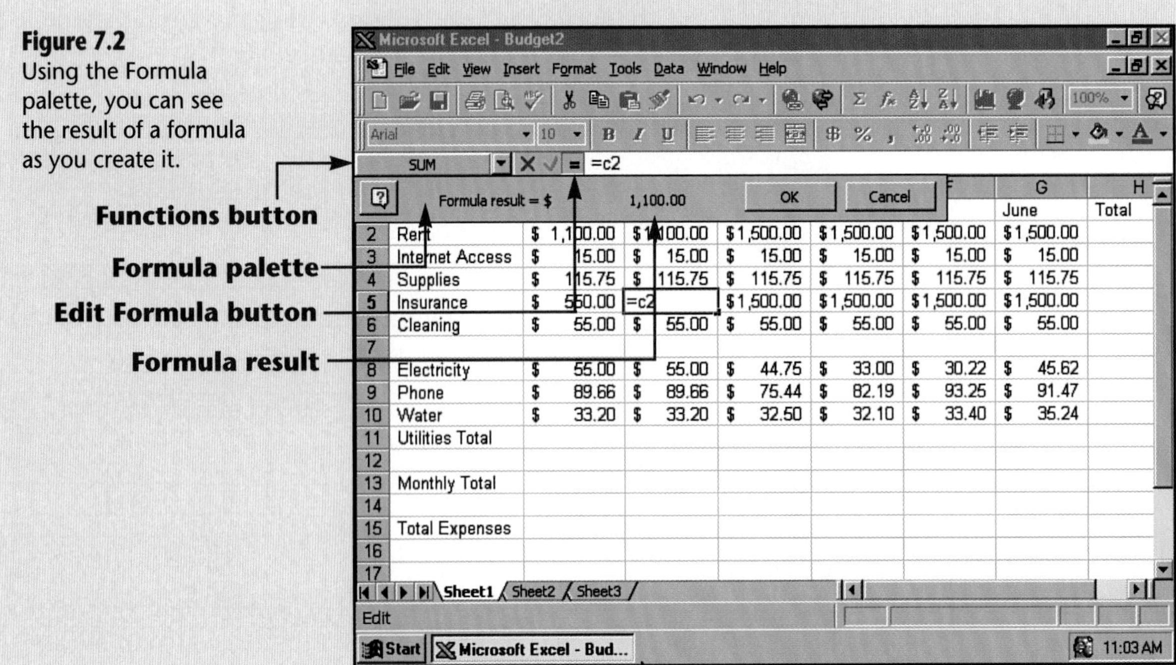

Figure 7.2
Using the Formula palette, you can see the result of a formula as you create it.

8 Type `*.5`.

This completes the formula for multiplying the value of cell C2 by one-half (0.5). The asterisk (*) is the operator for multiplication. (Press Shift+8 to enter the asterisk.) Notice that Excel updates the result of the formula in the Formula palette.

9 Click OK in the Formula palette.

Excel closes the palette, enters the formula in cell C5, and displays the result. You can click the Enter button or press Enter instead of clicking OK. Save the changes you have made to the `Budget2` worksheet and keep it open. In the next lesson, you learn how to create formulas by selecting cells.

The parentheses in a formula tell Excel which order to use when performing calculations. For example, if you want to add two numbers and then divide them by 2, you use the formula **`=(A12+B12)/2`**. The part of the formula in parentheses takes precedence over the other parts of the formula.

If you don't use parentheses in a formula, Excel sets precedence in the following way: exponential calculations first, multiplication and division second, and addition and subtraction third. Therefore, with such a formula as `=B12+C12/A10`, Excel first divides C12 by A10, then adds the resulting number to B12. If you want to add the first two cells and then divide, use the formula **`=(B12+C12)/A10`**.

You can use Excel's AutoCalculate feature to find out the result of a calculation without actually entering a formula. Simply select the cell or range of cells you want to total, and look at the AutoCalculate button on the status bar. By default, Excel uses the SUM function. To select a different function, right-click the AutoCalculate button and choose the function you want to use.

Lesson 2: Creating Formulas by Selecting Cells

You can also enter cell addresses into formulas by selecting the cell or range of cells in the worksheet. This simplifies the process of creating a formula, and also helps to ensure that you enter the correct cell address that you want to use.

In this lesson, you create a formula for totaling the monthly utility expenses by selecting the cells you want to include. You then create a formula that includes a function and a selected range of cells.

To Create Formulas by Selecting Cells

1 In the `Budget2` worksheet, select cell B11 and click the Edit Formula button.

You want the result of the formula displayed in cell B11. To calculate the total, add the values in cells B8, B9, and B10.

continues

To Create Formulas by Selecting Cells (continued)

2 Click cell B8.

Excel enters `B8` into the formula. A flashing dotted line appears around the cell to remind you that it is the cell you selected for the formula. Also, the value of cell B8 appears in the Formula palette.

3 Press + and click cell B9, then press + again and click cell B10.

The formula appears in the formula bar and in cell B11. You can see the result of the formula in the Formula palette (see Figure 7.3).

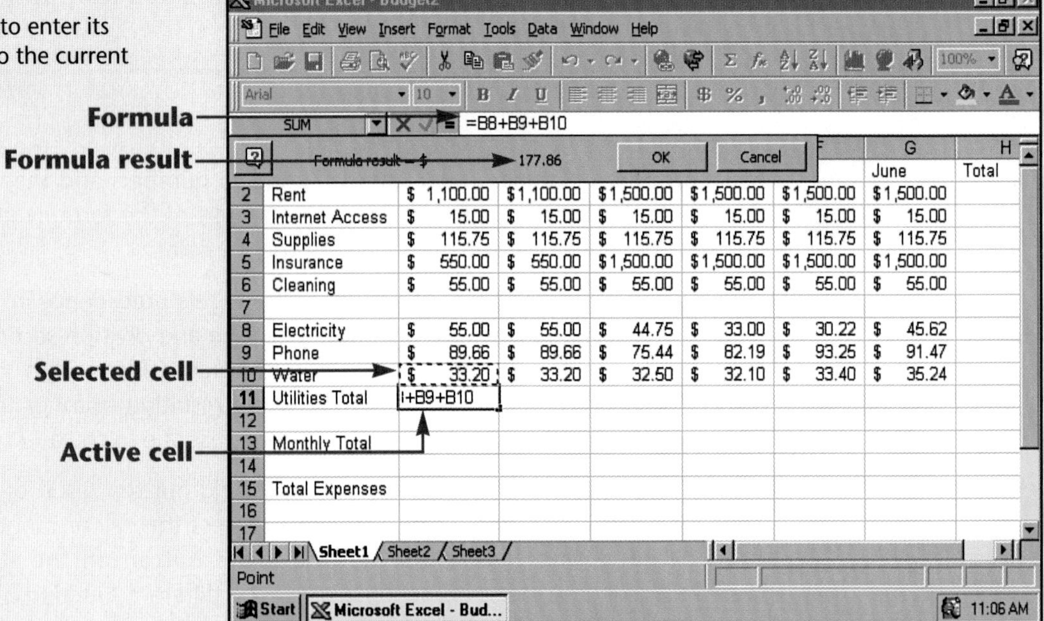

Figure 7.3
Click a cell to enter its address into the current formula.

4 Click OK in the Formula palette.

Excel enters the formula in cell B11 and displays the results in that cell. Now, try creating a formula to calculate the total of January's expenses by clicking the AutoSum button and selecting a range of cells.

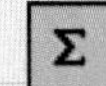

5 Select cell B13 and click the AutoSum button on the Standard toolbar.

Clicking the AutoSum button automatically enters a formula that uses the `SUM` function to calculate the total of the cells above or to the left of the active cell. In this case, the formula `=SUM(B8:B12)` appears in cell B13 and in the formula bar. `SUM` is the function; the address of the range to be added appears selected within the parentheses (see Figure 7.4). However, to correctly calculate January's expenses, you must add the values in cells B2:B10. Before you enter the formula into the active cell, change the range in the formula so that it includes cells B2:B10.

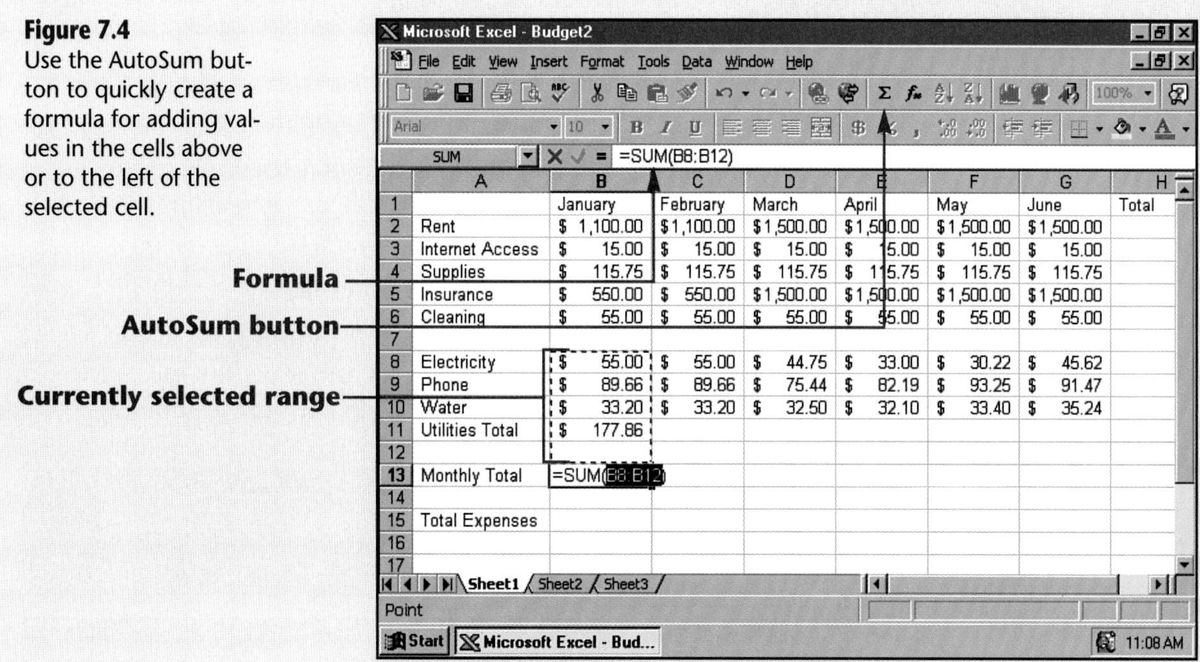

Figure 7.4
Use the AutoSum button to quickly create a formula for adding values in the cells above or to the left of the selected cell.

6 Click cell B2 and drag down to cell B10, then release the mouse button.

Dragging across the cells selects them; they replace the range previously entered in the formula.

7 Click the Enter button on the formula bar.

The values in cells B2 to B10 are totaled, and the result, `$2,013.61`, appears in cell B13 (see Figure 7.5). Now use AutoSum to enter a formula totaling all the rent expenses in the worksheet.

Figure 7.5
You can quickly build a formula by selecting a range of cells.

Formula — B13 =SUM(B2:B10)

	A	B	C	D	E	F	G	H
1		January	February	March	April	May	June	Total
2	Rent	$ 1,100.00	$1,100.00	$1,500.00	$1,500.00	$1,500.00	$1,500.00	
3	Internet Access	$ 15.00	$ 15.00	$ 15.00	$ 15.00	$ 15.00	$ 15.00	
4	Supplies	$ 115.75	$ 115.75	$ 115.75	$ 115.75	$ 115.75	$ 115.75	
5	Insurance	$ 550.00	$ 550.00	$1,500.00	$1,500.00	$1,500.00	$1,500.00	
6	Cleaning	$ 55.00	$ 55.00	$ 55.00	$ 55.00	$ 55.00	$ 55.00	
7								
8	Electricity	$ 55.00	$ 55.00	$ 44.75	$ 33.00	$ 30.22	$ 45.62	
9	Phone	$ 89.66	$ 89.66	$ 75.44	$ 82.19	$ 93.25	$ 91.47	
10	Water	$ 33.20	$ 33.20	$ 32.50	$ 32.10	$ 33.40	$ 35.24	
11	Utilities Total	$ 177.86						
12								
13	Monthly Total	$ 2,013.61						
14								
15	Total Expenses							
16								
17								

Result

Ready

continues

To Create Formulas by Selecting Cells (continued)

Σ

8 Select cell H2 and click the AutoSum button on the Standard toolbar.

This time, clicking the AutoSum button totals the cells to the left of the cell you selected. The formula `=SUM(B2:G2)` appears in the formula bar. This formula is correct for totaling all rent expenses.

✓

9 Click the Enter button on the formula bar.

Excel enters the formula and displays the result `$8,200` in cell H2, as shown in Figure 3.6. Save your changes and leave the `Budget2` worksheet open. You learn to copy formulas in the next lesson.

Figure 7.6
The result of the formula in the Formula bar appears in cell H2.

Formula → H2 =SUM(B2:G2)

Result → H2 $ 8,200.00

	B	C	D	E	F	G	H	I
1	January	February	March	April	May	June	Total	
2	$ 1,100.00	$1,100.00	$1,500.00	$1,500.00	$1,500.00	$1,500.00	$ 8,200.00	
3	$ 15.00	$ 15.00	$ 15.00	$ 15.00	$ 15.00	$ 15.00		
4	$ 115.75	$ 115.75	$ 115.75	$ 115.75	$ 115.75	$ 115.75		
5	$ 550.00	$ 550.00	$1,500.00	$1,500.00	$1,500.00	$1,500.00		
6	$ 55.00	$ 55.00	$ 55.00	$ 55.00	$ 55.00	$ 55.00		
7								
8	$ 55.00	$ 55.00	$ 44.75	$ 33.00	$ 30.22	$ 45.62		
9	$ 89.66	$ 89.66	$ 75.44	$ 82.19	$ 93.25	$ 91.47		
10	$ 33.20	$ 33.20	$ 32.50	$ 32.10	$ 33.40	$ 35.24		
11	$ 177.86							
12								
13	$ 2,013.61							

Range Finder
A feature of Excel that helps you locate cells referenced in a formula by color coding them. The range in the formula is highlighted in the same color as the range in the worksheet.

You can change the cell addresses in a formula in a few different ways. You can simply click in the Formula bar to position the insertion point where you want to make a change, then delete the incorrect characters and type the correct ones.

When you click in the formula bar to edit a formula, Excel starts the *Range Finder*. You can use the Range Finder to replace cell addresses in the formula. When the Range Finder is active, Excel displays each cell address or range in the formula in a different color, and highlights the actual cells in the worksheet in corresponding colors.

To change an address in the formula, drag the corresponding colored cell border to the correct address in the worksheet. To add or remove cells from a range, drag the handle on the lower-right corner of the colored border to include more or fewer cells. When you finish making changes, click the Enter button on the formula bar. You can also start the Range Finder by double-clicking the cell that contains the formula you want to change.

Lesson 3: Copying Formulas

After you create a formula, you can copy it to other cells or worksheets to help speed up your work. You copy formulas in Excel using the same techniques you used in Project 6 to copy cells and data.

Relative cell reference
A reference to the contents of a cell that is adjusted by the program when you copy the formula to another cell or range of cells.

When you copy a formula from one cell to another, Excel automatically changes the formula so that it is *relative* to its new location. That means that it changes the cell addresses in the formula, thus making it correct in a new location. For example, if you copy a formula that adds the contents of cells A1:A9 from cell A10 to cell B10, Excel automatically changes the formula to add the contents of cells B1:B9.

Now copy formulas in the `Budget2` worksheet.

To Copy Formulas

1. **Select cell C5 in the `Budget2` worksheet.**

   Cell C5 contains the formula `=C2*0.5`, which is the formula you want to copy to the rest of the cells in the Insurance row.

2. **With the mouse pointer in cell C5, click the right mouse button.**

   A shortcut menu appears, which you can use to copy the formula.

3. **Click the Copy command on the shortcut menu.**

   The shortcut menu disappears, and the formula is copied to the Clipboard. Remember, you are copying the formula, not the value in the cell.

4. **Select cells D5 through G5.**

   This is the range where you want to paste the copied formula.

5. **Move the mouse pointer to the active cell (D5), right-click to open the shortcut menu, then choose the Paste command.**

   Excel pastes the copied formula into the selected cells, as shown in Figure 7.7. Again, make sure that you move the mouse pointer to the active cell before you issue the **P**aste command. Notice that the formulas copied into each cell are *relative* to the new cells. For example, the formula in D5, `=D2*0.5`, refers to rent information for the month of March rather than the month of February. Because there was an increase in rent in March, there is also an increase in the insurance expense for March. The results of the new formulas are displayed in each cell.

continues

To Copy Formulas (continued)

Figure 7.7
The formula calculates the Insurance amount and enters the result in the correct cells.

Pasted formula becomes relative to the new location

Active cell

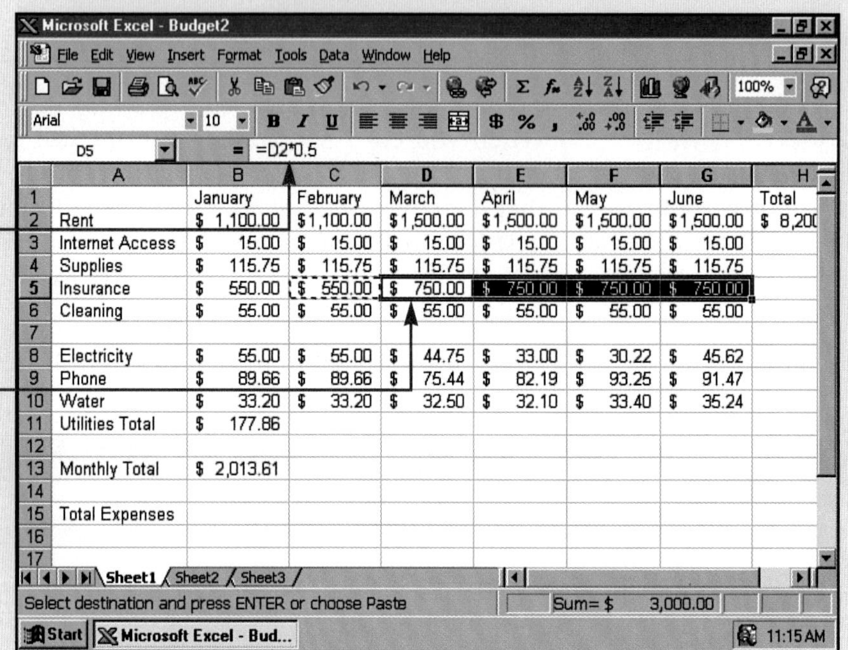

	A	B	C	D	E	F	G	H
1		January	February	March	April	May	June	Total
2	Rent	$ 1,100.00	$1,100.00	$1,500.00	$1,500.00	$1,500.00	$1,500.00	$ 8,20
3	Internet Access	$ 15.00	$ 15.00	$ 15.00	$ 15.00	$ 15.00	$ 15.00	
4	Supplies	$ 115.75	$ 115.75	$ 115.75	$ 115.75	$ 115.75	$ 115.75	
5	Insurance	$ 550.00	$ 550.00	$ 750.00	$ 750.00	$ 750.00	$ 750.00	
6	Cleaning	$ 55.00	$ 55.00	$ 55.00	$ 55.00	$ 55.00	$ 55.00	
7								
8	Electricity	$ 55.00	$ 55.00	$ 44.75	$ 33.00	$ 30.22	$ 45.62	
9	Phone	$ 89.66	$ 89.66	$ 75.44	$ 82.19	$ 93.25	$ 91.47	
10	Water	$ 33.20	$ 33.20	$ 32.50	$ 32.10	$ 33.40	$ 35.24	
11	Utilities Total	$ 177.86						
12								
13	Monthly Total	$ 2,013.61						
14								
15	Total Expenses							
16								
17								

Now copy the formula for the Utilities total for the rest of the months using buttons on the Standard toolbar.

If you have problems...

The flashing dotted line remains around the cell you copied to the Clipboard until you copy or cut another selection. You can continue working as usual, but if you find the flashing dotted line distracting, simply press Esc to cancel it.

6 Select cell B11 and click the Copy button on the Standard toolbar.

You can use the toolbar buttons or menu commands to copy and paste formulas the same way you copy text or numbers.

7 Select cells C11 through G11.

You want to paste the formula into these cells.

8 Click the Paste button on the toolbar.

Excel copies the formula to add the Utilities total in each month to the cells you selected. Again, notice that the cell references in the formulas refer to the appropriate month in each case.

Now use the fill handle to copy the formula, calculating the totals for each expense category.

9 Select cell H2 and move the mouse pointer to the lower-right corner of the cell so that the pointer changes to a thin black plus sign.

You can use the fill handle to copy the contents of a cell to other cells, just as you used it to fill a range with a series of data in Project 2. You may have to scroll the worksheet to see all of column H.

10 Click the left mouse button and drag down to select cells H3 to H11.

This selects the range you want to fill. When you release the mouse button in cell H11, Excel fills the range with the formula and displays the results of the formula in each cell. Again, the formulas are relative to their locations. Finally, copy and paste the formula to calculate the monthly totals.

11 Select cell B13, then drag the fill handle right to cell H13.

Excel copies the formula from cell B13 to the other cells in the row. The results appear, as shown in Figure 7.8. Because you don't need the formula in cell H7, delete it now.

12 Click cell H7 to make it active, press Del, then press ↵Enter.

Excel deletes the contents of the cell. Save your changes. In the next lesson, you learn how to use absolute cell references in a formula.

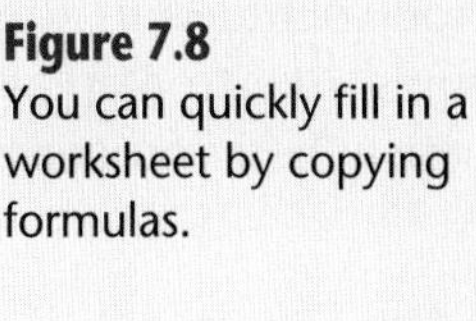

Figure 7.8
You can quickly fill in a worksheet by copying formulas.

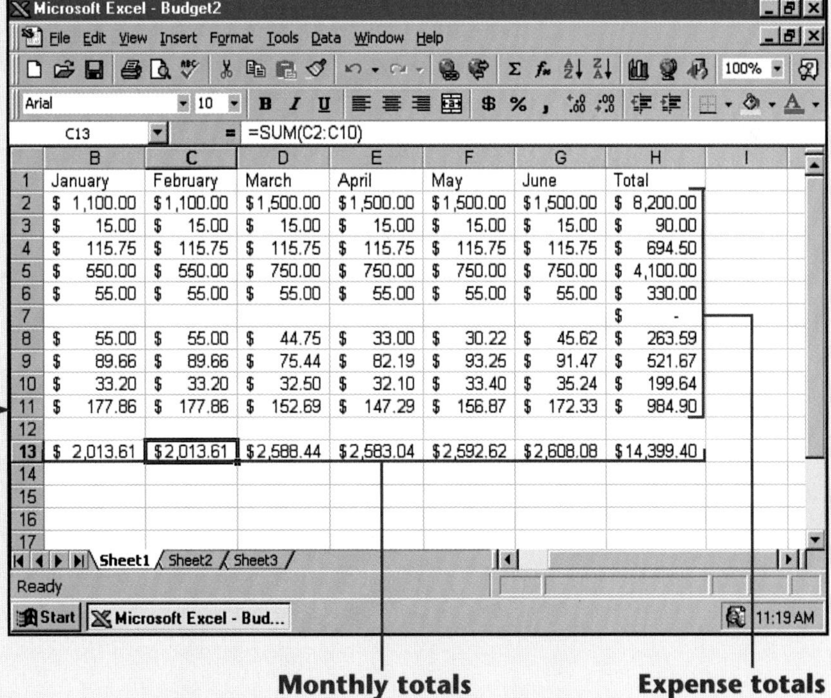

	B	C	D	E	F	G	H
1	January	February	March	April	May	June	Total
2	$ 1,100.00	$1,100.00	$1,500.00	$1,500.00	$1,500.00	$1,500.00	$ 8,200.00
3	$ 15.00	$ 15.00	$ 15.00	$ 15.00	$ 15.00	$ 15.00	$ 90.00
4	$ 115.75	$ 115.75	$ 115.75	$ 115.75	$ 115.75	$ 115.75	$ 694.50
5	$ 550.00	$ 550.00	$ 750.00	$ 750.00	$ 750.00	$ 750.00	$ 4,100.00
6	$ 55.00	$ 55.00	$ 55.00	$ 55.00	$ 55.00	$ 55.00	$ 330.00
7							$ -
8	$ 55.00	$ 55.00	$ 44.75	$ 33.00	$ 30.22	$ 45.62	$ 263.59
9	$ 89.66	$ 89.66	$ 75.44	$ 82.19	$ 93.25	$ 91.47	$ 521.67
10	$ 33.20	$ 33.20	$ 32.50	$ 32.10	$ 33.40	$ 35.24	$ 199.64
11	$ 177.86	$ 177.86	$ 152.69	$ 147.29	$ 156.87	$ 172.33	$ 984.90
12							
13	$ 2,013.61	$2,013.61	$2,588.44	$2,583.04	$2,592.62	$2,608.08	$14,399.40

Lesson 4: Using Absolute Cell References

As you learned in Lesson 3, when you copy a formula, Excel assumes that the formula is relative. If, for example, you copy the formula `=SUM(A2:A9)` from cell A10 to cell B10, the formula automatically changes to `=SUM(B2:B9)`. No matter where you copy the formula, it updates to reflect the cells that are relative to it.

Absolute cell reference
A cell reference that always refers to cells in a specific location.

However, if you want to copy a formula to another cell and have it return exactly the same result as in the original location, you must specify *absolute* cell references. To do so, add a dollar sign ($) before the values specifying the cell address. In other words, you insert a dollar sign before each column and row indicator in the formula. For example, to copy `=SUM(A2:A9)` and make sure that the resulting value is the same no matter where in the worksheet the formula is pasted, change the formula to **`=SUM($A$2:$A$9)`**.

In this lesson, you create a formula that uses absolute cell references, so you can copy the formula to a different location in the worksheet and obtain the same result.

To Use Absolute Cell References

1 In the `Budget2` worksheet, click cell H13 then click the Copy button on the Standard toolbar.

This copies the formula in H13 to the Clipboard. This formula calculates the total expenses for the six-month period included in the worksheet by adding each expense total. You would like to display this total in cell B15 as well. First, see what happens when you copy and paste the relative formula.

2 Click cell B15, then click the Paste button on the Standard toolbar.

Excel pastes the formula into cell B15 and displays the results, as shown in Figure 7.9. Notice that the result is not the same as in cell H13 because Excel has automatically changed the cell references in the formula so they are relative to the new location.

Figure 7.9
When you copy and paste a relative formula, the result may not be the value you want.

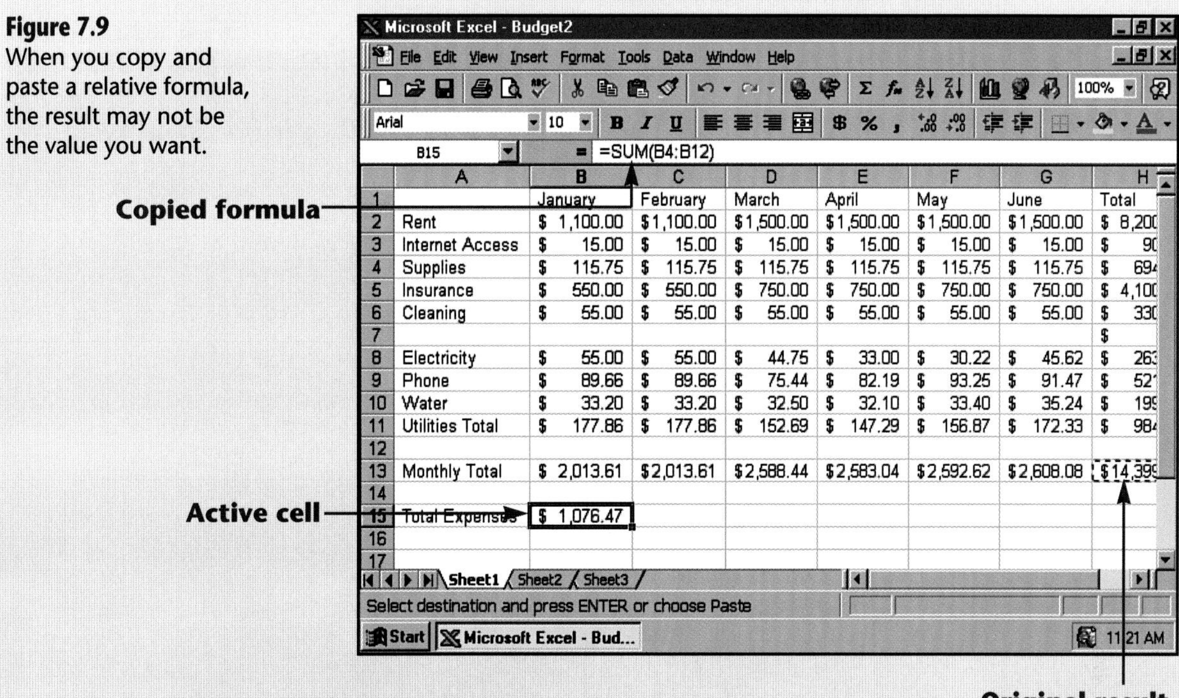

	A	B	C	D	E	F	G	H
1		January	February	March	April	May	June	Total
2	Rent	$ 1,100.00	$1,100.00	$1,500.00	$1,500.00	$1,500.00	$1,500.00	$ 8,20
3	Internet Access	$ 15.00	$ 15.00	$ 15.00	$ 15.00	$ 15.00	$ 15.00	$ 9
4	Supplies	$ 115.75	$ 115.75	$ 115.75	$ 115.75	$ 115.75	$ 115.75	$ 69
5	Insurance	$ 550.00	$ 550.00	$ 750.00	$ 750.00	$ 750.00	$ 750.00	$ 4,10
6	Cleaning	$ 55.00	$ 55.00	$ 55.00	$ 55.00	$ 55.00	$ 55.00	$ 33
7								$
8	Electricity	$ 55.00	$ 55.00	$ 44.75	$ 33.00	$ 30.22	$ 45.62	$ 26
9	Phone	$ 89.66	$ 89.66	$ 75.44	$ 82.19	$ 93.25	$ 91.47	$ 52
10	Water	$ 33.20	$ 33.20	$ 32.50	$ 32.10	$ 33.40	$ 35.24	$ 19
11	Utilities Total	$ 177.86	$ 177.86	$ 152.69	$ 147.29	$ 156.87	$ 172.33	$ 98
12								
13	Monthly Total	$ 2,013.61	$2,013.61	$2,588.44	$2,583.04	$2,592.62	$2,608.08	$14,39
14								
15	Total Expenses	$ 1,076.47						
16								
17								

3 Press Del to delete the formula from cell B15, and select cell H13 again.

To be sure that Excel returns the actual total of all expenses, you must make the cell references in the formula absolute.

4 Click in the formula bar, and position the insertion point between the open parentheses and the first column letter H.

This places the insertion point in the formula where you want to make a change. You want to insert a $ in front of each column and row reference in the formula. When you click in the Formula bar, Excel assumes you want to change the cell addresses in the formula, so it activates the Range Finder. You can ignore the Range Finder; Excel will close it automatically.

5 Type $ and press →; type $ and press → twice; type $ and press →; type $.

You should now have a dollar sign in front of each column and row reference in the formula, as shown in Figure 7.10.

continues

To Use Absolute Cell References (continued)

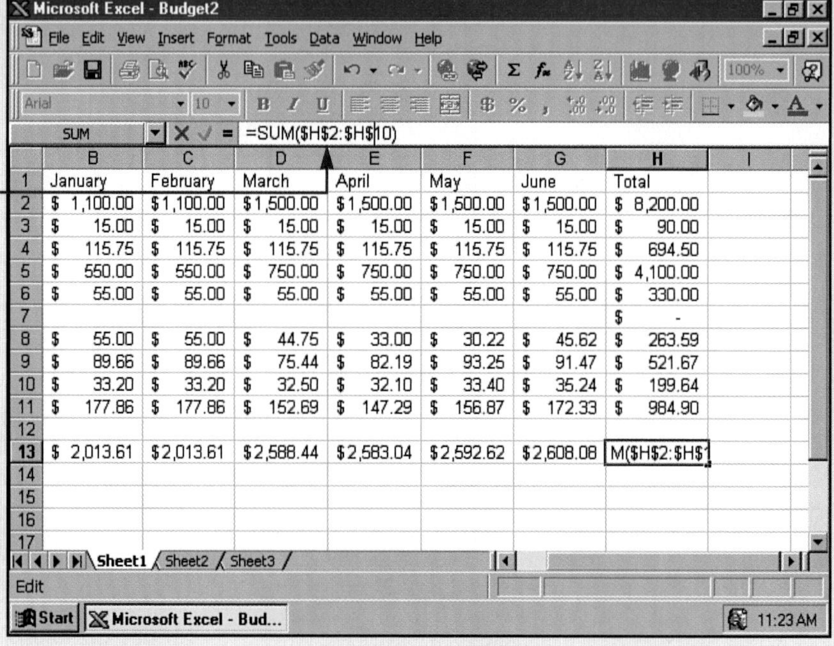

	B	C	D	E	F	G	H	I
1	January	February	March	April	May	June	Total	
2	$ 1,100.00	$1,100.00	$1,500.00	$1,500.00	$1,500.00	$1,500.00	$ 8,200.00	
3	$ 15.00	$ 15.00	$ 15.00	$ 15.00	$ 15.00	$ 15.00	$ 90.00	
4	$ 115.75	$ 115.75	$ 115.75	$ 115.75	$ 115.75	$ 115.75	$ 694.50	
5	$ 550.00	$ 550.00	$ 750.00	$ 750.00	$ 750.00	$ 750.00	$ 4,100.00	
6	$ 55.00	$ 55.00	$ 55.00	$ 55.00	$ 55.00	$ 55.00	$ 330.00	
7							$ -	
8	$ 55.00	$ 55.00	$ 44.75	$ 33.00	$ 30.22	$ 45.62	$ 263.59	
9	$ 89.66	$ 89.66	$ 75.44	$ 82.19	$ 93.25	$ 91.47	$ 521.67	
10	$ 33.20	$ 33.20	$ 32.50	$ 32.10	$ 33.40	$ 35.24	$ 199.64	
11	$ 177.86	$ 177.86	$ 152.69	$ 147.29	$ 156.87	$ 172.33	$ 984.90	
12								
13	$ 2,013.61	$2,013.61	$2,588.44	$2,583.04	$2,592.62	$2,608.08	M($H$2:$H$1	
14								
15								
16								
17								

Figure 7.10
Dollar signs in a formula tell Excel to use absolute cell references.

6 Click the Enter button on the formula bar.

Excel enters the new formula in cell H13. The result of the formula is the same. Now see what happens when you copy and paste the formula with absolute cell references.

7 With cell H13 still selected, click the Copy button on the Standard toolbar, select cell B15, then click the Paste button on the Standard toolbar.

Excel copies the formula exactly as it appears in cell H13 into cell B15 and displays the result, as shown in Figure 7.11.

You have now completed the lessons on creating basic formulas. Save the changes you have made to the `Budget2` worksheet. If requested by your instructor, print two copies, then close the `Budget2` file. If you have completed your session on the computer, exit Excel and Windows 95. Otherwise, continue with the "Checking Your Skills" section at the end of this project.

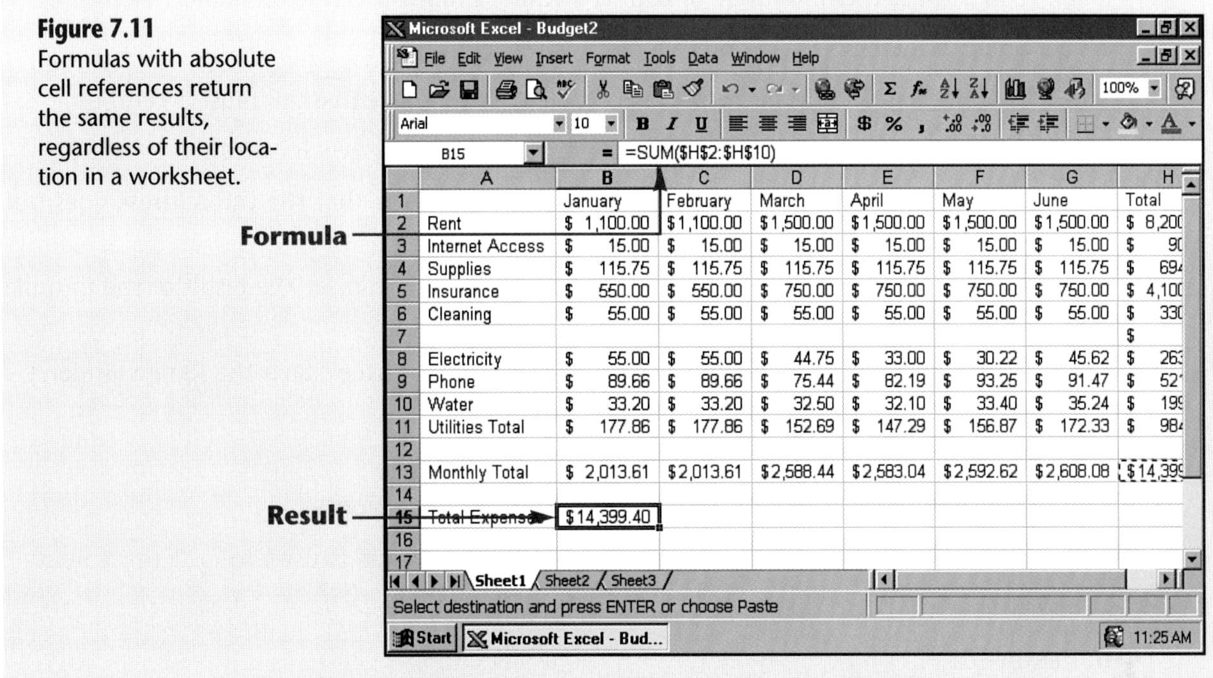

Figure 7.11
Formulas with absolute cell references return the same results, regardless of their location in a worksheet.

Project Summary

To	Do This
Enter a formula	Type an equal sign (=), then type the formula.
Open the Formula palette	Click the Edit Formula button on the Formula palette.
Automatically total a row or column of cells	Click the AutoSum button on the Standard toolbar.
Copy a formula	Select the cell containing the formula, click the Copy button, select the cell where you want to paste the formula, and click the Paste button.
Use absolute cell reference	Type a dollar sign ($) in front of the row number and column letter in the cell address in the formula.

Checking Your Skills

True/False

For each of the following, check *T* or *F* to indicate whether the statement is true or false.

__T __F **1.** Excel can use only mathematical operators for addition and subtraction.

__T __F **2.** Excel automatically updates the result of a formula when you change a value referenced in the formula.

__T __F **3.** To make a cell address absolute, you must type a dollar sign before each row and column reference in the formula.

__T __F **4.** You can use the fill handle to copy a formula from one cell to an adjacent cell.

__T __F **5.** You can reference only one cell address in each formula.

__T __F **6.** To enter a new formula with the Formula palette, the active cell must be empty.

__T __F **7.** By default, when you copy a formula it is relative to its new location.

__T __F **8.** If a formula is relative to its new location, this means that the cell address does not change when you copy it to a new location.

__T __F **9.** An advantage to using the Formula palette is that you can see the result of the formula as you create it.

__T __F **10.** When you click in the formula bar to edit a formula, Excel starts the Range Finder.

Multiple Choice

Circle the letter of the correct answer for each of the following questions.

1. Which of the following is a valid formula?

- **a.** B3+B4+B5
- **b.** (B3+B4+B5)
- **c.** =B3+B4+B5
- **d.** $B$3+$B$4+$B$5

2. Which of the following cannot be used to copy a formula?

- **a.** the Copy button on the Standard toolbar
- **b.** the **E**dit, **C**opy command
- **c.** the fill handle
- **d.** the Range Finder

3. Which of the following is a valid mathematical operator?

- **a.** ^ (caret)
- **b.** @ (*at* sign)
- **c.** $ (dollar sign)
- **d.** ? (question mark)

4. What appears in the active cell where you enter a formula?

- **a.** the formula
- **b.** the result of the formula
- **c.** the cell address
- **d.** an equal sign

5. What function is used to add the values in a range of cells?

- **a.** ADD
- **b.** PLUS
- **c.** SUM
- **d.** TOTAL

6. If you do not use parenthesis in a formula, which type of calculation takes precedence?

- **a.** exponential calculations
- **b.** multiplication
- **c.** division
- **d.** addition

7. What is the operator for multiplication?

- **a.** caret (^)
- **b.** asterisk (*)
- **c.** forward slash (/)
- **d.** back slash (\)

8. In the formula =(A12+B12)*C2^2/7, which calculation is performed first?

- **a.** adding A12 + B12
- **b.** multiplying B12 by C2
- **c.** squaring C2
- **d.** dividing the square of C2 by 7

9. What is the resulting function when you copy the function =SUM(C2:C10) from cell C12 to cell E12?

   a. =SUM(C2:C10)

   b. =SUM(D2:D10)

   c. =SUM(E2:E10)

   d. =SUM(E4:E12)

10. When you copy the formula =$C$2+$C$3 from cell C4 to cell D4, what is the resulting formula?

    a. =$D$1+$D$2

    b. =$D$2+$D$3

    c. =$C$1+$C$2

    d. =$C$2+$C$3

Completion

In the blank provided, write the correct answer for each of the following statements.

1. Type a dollar sign in front of a cell address to make the reference _____________.
2. Click the Edit Formula button on the formula bar to open the ________________.
3. Every formula must start with a(n) _____________ sign.
4. To quickly create a formula to total a row or column of numbers, click the _____________ button.
5. To make sure Excel performs one calculation before another in a formula, enclose the first calculation in _________________.
6. To find out the result of a calculation without actually entering a formula, use the _____________ feature.
7. Clicking the _____________ button automatically enters a formula that uses the SUM function to calculate the total of the cells above or to the left of the active cell.
8. To remove the flashing dotted line around the cell you copied to the Clipboard, press _____________.
9. When you click the Edit Formula button, Excel inserts a(n) ______________ into the formula bar and opens the Formula palette.
10. You can start the Range Finder by _____________ the cell that contains the formula you want to change.

Matching

In the blank next to each of the following terms or phrases, write the letter of the corresponding term or phrase.

_____ **1.** A built-in formula that automatically performs calculations

_____ **2.** A calculation that Excel performs on data entered in a worksheet

_____ **3.** The mathematical operator for division

_____ **4.** The mathematical operator for exponents

_____ **5.** Helps you locate cells referenced in a formula by color coding them

_____ **6.** A formula that is updated to reflect its new location

_____ **7.** A formula that remains exactly the same, no matter where it is copied in the worksheet

_____ **8.** The first calculation performed in a formula

_____ **9.** The second calculation performed in a formula

_____ **10.** The third calculation performed in a formula

a. relative

b. Range Finder

c. addition and subtraction

d. absolute

e. formula

f. multiplication and division

g. ^ (caret)

h. exponential calculations

i. function

j. / (forward slash)

Screen ID

Label each element of the Excel screen shown in Figure 7.12.

Figure 7.12

1. ______________

2. ______________

3. ______________

4. ______________

5. ______________

6. ______________

7. ______________

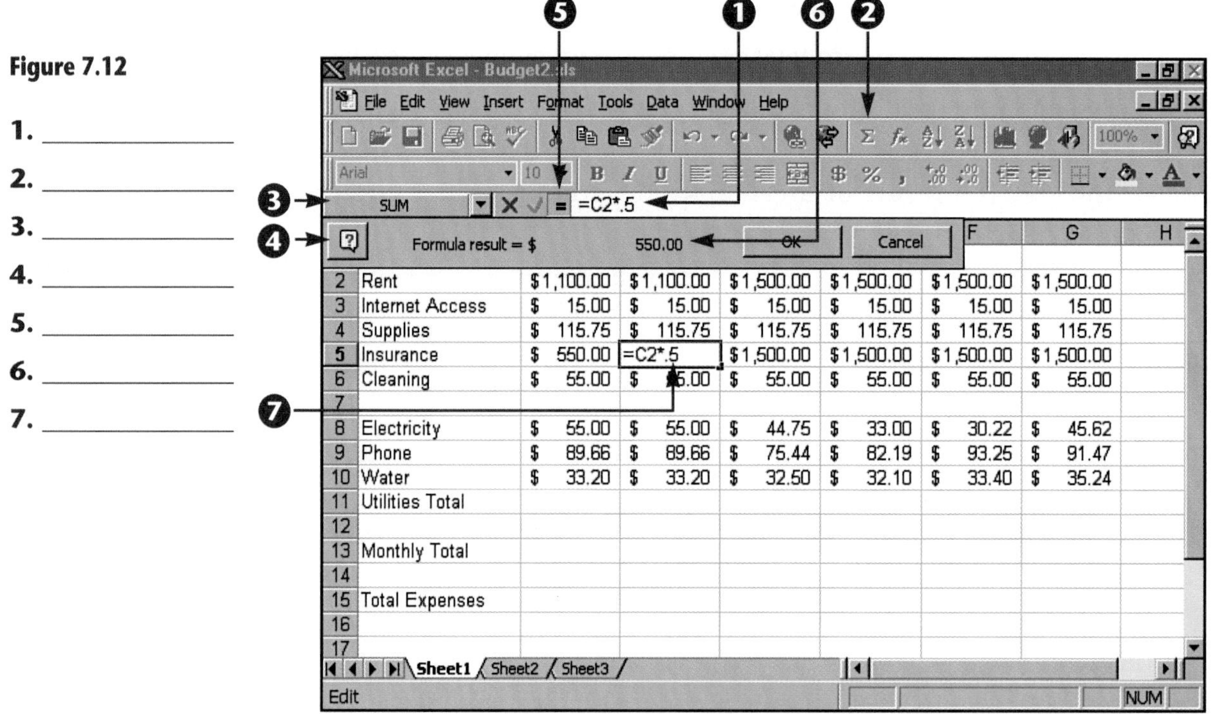

Applying Your Skills

Practice

The following exercises enable you to practice the skills you have learned in this project. Take a few minutes to work through these exercises now.

1. Estimating Attendance

Now that you are familiar with Excel formulas, you can make use of them to estimate how many people will attend the monthly coffee tastings you hold at the shop.

To Estimate Attendance

1. Open the file Proj0702 and save it as `Attendance`.
2. Assuming that ¾ of the number of invitees will actually attend a tasting, enter a formula in cell D3 to calculate the estimated number of attendees.
3. Copy the formula from cell D3 to cells D4:D8.
4. Use AutoSum to enter a formula calculating the total number of invitees and the total number of attendees.
5. Change the number of guests invited in October to 15 and in November to 20.
6. Save the changes to the worksheet. If requested by your instructor, print two copies of the worksheet, then close it.

2. Calculating Costs

Calculate the costs of ordering inventory for your coffee shop. Using the sample file Proj0703, complete the worksheet by creating formulas.

To Calculate Costs

1. Open the file Proj0703 and save it as `March Orders`.
2. In cell B7, create a formula that calculates the cost of ordering Arabica in March by multiplying the price per pound by the amount ordered.
3. Copy the formula to cells C7 and D7 to find the cost of ordering French Roast and Kona, respectively.
4. In cell B8, create a formula that calculates the total cost of ordering coffee in March.
5. Save your work. If requested by your instructor, print two copies. Close the `March Orders` file.

3. Calculating Salaries

Use the information provided to complete a worksheet calculating the new salaries for your coffee shop employees.

To Calculate Salaries

1. Open the file Proj0704 and save it as `Salary`.
2. In cell D4, enter a formula that calculates the new salary for the buyer by multiplying the old salary by the percent of increase, then adding that total to the old salary.
3. Copy the formula from cell D4 to cells D5:D8.
4. In cell B10, use AutoSum to enter a formula to calculate the total of the old salaries.
5. Copy the formula from cell B10 into cell B11, then edit the range in the formula so it calculates the total of the new salaries. (*Hint:* You can type the new range, select the new range, or use the Range Finder to change the range.)
6. In cell B13, enter a formula to calculate the increase in salary.
7. Save the changes to the worksheet. If requested by your instructor, print two copies of the worksheet, then close it.

4. Calculating Advertising Costs

Use the worksheet provided to calculate the costs of advertising your coffee shop and to determine which type of advertisement generates the most effect in terms of revenue and which generates the most profit.

To Calculate Advertising Costs

1. Open the file Proj0705 and save it as `Ad Costs`.
2. In cell F3, enter a formula to calculate the profit generated by the print ad by subtracting the cost from the effect.
3. Copy the formula from cell F3 to cells F4 and F5.
4. In cell B7, create a formula for totaling the cost of the three ads.
5. In cell B8, create a formula for totaling the effect of the three ads.
6. In cell B9, create a formula for totaling the profits generated by the three ads.
7. In cell G3, create a formula to calculate the print ad's percentage of the total effect.
8. Copy the formula from cell G3 to cells G4 and G5. Notice that Excel returns a result of `0` in both cells G4 and G5 because it changes the copied formula to keep it relative to the new locations.
9. Edit the formula in G3 so it always references cell B8, then copy it again to cells G4 and G5.
10. In cell H3, create a formula to calculate the print ad's percentage of the total profit using an absolute cell reference for cell B9, then copy the formula from cell H3 to cells H4 and H5.
11. Save the changes to the worksheet. If requested by your instructor, print two copies of the worksheet, then close it.

5. Creating a Formula Using Mathematical Operators

In this project, you learned to perform calculations using formulas with mathematical operators. In this exercise, you calculate the co-payment amount for each medical expense in the Medical Expenses worksheet.

To Create a Formula

1. Open Proj0706 and save it as `Medical Expenses 3`. Notice that this is the same file you used in the previous project, with a column added for the co-payment amount.
2. Your co-payment is 20% of the charge. You need to enter a formula to calculate this amount. Activate cell F4.
3. Enter the formula `=E4*.2` into this cell. This calculates 20% of the amount in cell E4 and enters it into the cell.
4. Select cell F4 again, and copy it to the other cells by positioning the mouse pointer on the fill handle.
5. Hold down the left mouse button, and drag the mouse pointer down to cell F10. Release the mouse button, and the formula is copied to the remaining cells.
6. Save the file, and leave it open for the following challenge exercise.

Challenge

The following challenges enable you to use your problem-solving skills. Take time to work through these exercises now.

1. Totaling Medical Expenses

To total all of your medical expenses for the year, enter the SUM function into the `Medical Expenses 3` worksheet. Total the co-payments for the year and enter the word `TOTAL` in cell D12. Save and print two copies of the workbook before closing it.

2. Calculating Sales Commissions

As sales manager for your company, you want to calculate sales commission and gross profit for the year. You do so by using a formula. Open the file Proj0707 and save it as `Profit Loss Stmt`. In cell B7, enter the formula `=B5*.025` to calculate sales commissions of 2.5% of the total sales. Enter the formula `=B5-B6-B7` into cell B9 to calculate the gross profit (sales minus expenses minus sales commissions). Save the workbook and leave it open for the following exercise.

3. Calculating Yearly Taxes

You now need to calculate taxes due for the year by multiplying the tax rate by the gross profit. To do so, you enter a formula into the `Profit Loss Stmt` workbook. Because you will be copying this formula to other cells, the reference to the cell containing the tax rate (cell B17) needs to be absolute.

In cell B11, enter the formula `=B9*$B$17`. Make sure you include the dollar signs in the cell address for the tax rate. Enter the formula `=B9-B11` into cell B13 to calculate the net profit by subtracting the taxes from the gross profit. Save the workbook again, and leave it open for the following exercise.

4. Copying Formulas from the Profit Loss Stmt Workbook

Now that you have the formulas entered into the `Profit Loss Stmt` workbook, you need to copy them to the columns for May and June.

Copy the sales commission formula (cell B7) to cells C7:D7. Copy the formula in cell B9 to cells C9:D9. Copy the remaining formulas using AutoFill. Select cells B11:B13. Notice that all of these formulas are copied with relative cell addresses, except the formula for the taxes. The cell address remained B17 when you copied it to the other cells, because you entered the cell address as an absolute address. Save the workbook and, if requested by your instructor, print two copies before closing it.

5. Balancing Your Checkbook Using Formulas

To keep a running balance of the total in your checkbook, you decide to use formulas. Open Proj0708 file and save it as **`Checking Account 3`**. Add a formula to cell F6 to calculate the total in the checking account after making the mortgage payment. Because you will be copying this formula to other cells, be sure to add any amounts in the Deposit column, and subtract any amounts in the Check Amount column. Copy this formula down the column. Save the workbook and, if requested by your instructor, print two copies before closing it.

Project 8

Calculating with Functions

Projecting Office Expenses

In this project, you learn how to:

- Name Ranges
- Use Named Ranges
- Use Functions
- Build Formulas with Functions
- Use Conditional Statements

Why Would I Do This?

In Project 7, "Creating Formulas," you learned to devise formulas to calculate values in your worksheet and use cell addresses to refer to specific cells. You also learned how to use simple functions to help speed up your work with formulas. In this project, you expand your knowledge of formulas and functions so that you can easily perform more complex calculations. You learn to automate data input using such functions as TODAY (which inserts the current date in a worksheet). You also learn how to use conditional functions, such as IF, to provide different answers depending on the results of your calculations.

Another useful feature of Excel that can help you simplify the process of creating formulas is the range name. You can assign a descriptive name to a value or a formula in a single cell or a range of cells, then use the assigned name rather than the cell addresses when specifying cells that you want to use.

In this project, you use range names and functions to project the costs of rent, paper, and other supplies for your office for the coming months.

Lesson 1: Naming Ranges

When you create a worksheet and plan to use a cell or range of cells many times, you may want to name the range. For example, you can name the range containing the total income to make the income range easy to use in formulas. Rather than look up the address of the range, simply name the range *income*, and use the range name in the formula in place of the range address. You can also use range names in other Excel commands and to move around the worksheet.

Range names can be up to 255 characters long, but you should keep them short so that you can easily remember them and have more room to enter the formula. Range names of up to 15 characters can be displayed in most scrolling list boxes. Additionally, observe the following rules when naming ranges:

- Both upper- and lowercase letters can be used.
- Range names cannot contain spaces.
- Range names must begin with a letter or underscore.
- Any characters except math operators and hyphens can be used.
- Range names can contain numbers, but cannot start with a number.

Avoid combinations of letters and numbers that look like a cell address (such as a34) because that can be confusing. Choose names that describe the contents or the use of the range, such as *expenses*, *income*, and *average*.

Try naming ranges using the sample office expenses worksheet supplied for this project.

To Name Ranges

1 Open the file Proj0801 and save it as `Office`.

2 Click cell B3 and drag to cell C4 to select the range B3:C4.

This is the first range you want to name. (You learned the different methods for selecting cells and ranges in Project 6, "Building a Spreadsheet.")

3 Open the Insert menu, move the mouse pointer to the Name command, then choose Define from the submenu that appears.

The Define Name dialog box appears (see Figure 8.1). By default, Excel assumes that the label text from the row in which the active cell is located will be the range name, and enters it in the Names in workbook text box. The selected range address is entered in the Refers to text box, including the current worksheet name, `Sheet1`, and absolute references.

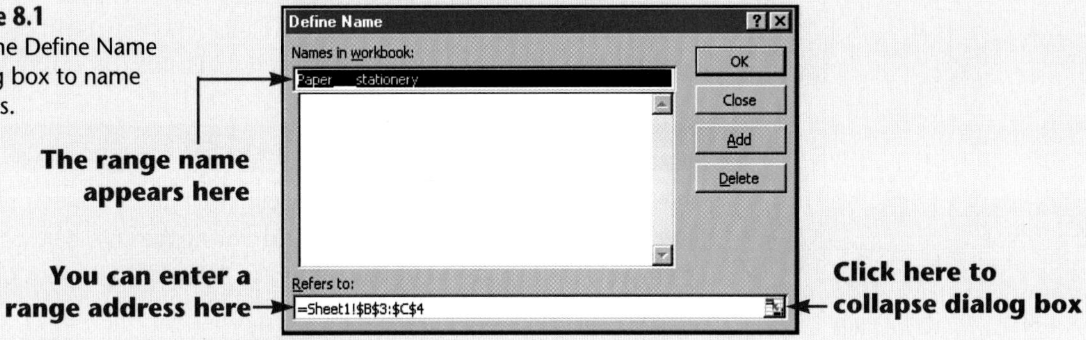

Figure 8.1
Use the Define Name dialog box to name ranges.

4 Replace the default name `Paper_stationery` (in the Names in workbook text box) with `paper97`.

This name describes the cells in the range, which includes all your paper expenses for 1997.

5 Click OK.

The dialog box closes, and the selected range is now named `paper97`. Notice that the range name appears in the Name box in the Formula bar because the range is still selected. Now name another range.

6 Select cells F3 through G4 in the worksheet.

This selects the next range you want to name.

7 Open the Insert menu, move the mouse pointer to the Name command, then choose Define from the submenu that appears.

This opens the Define Name dialog box again. Notice that the `paper97` range name now appears in the Names in workbook list.

continues

To Name Ranges (continued)

8 In the Names in Workbook text box, type `paper98`**, then click the Add button.**

The new range name appears in the Names in **w**orkbook list. Now try naming a range without closing the Define Names dialog box.

9 In the Define Name dialog box, click the collapse button at the right end of the Refers to text box (refer to Figure 8.1).

This collapses the dialog box so that you can select the range you want to name in the worksheet. Only the **R**efers to text box is still visible on the screen with the absolute reference to the current range entered: `$F$3:$G$4`. Now, select the new range you want to name.

10 Select cells B5 through C6 in the worksheet.

A flashing dotted line appears around the selected cells, and the **R**efers to text box displays the new range address, as shown in Figure 8.2. The flashing dotted line indicates the cells that you have selected to include in the named range. Cells F3:G4 are still selected and highlighted in the worksheet, and cell F3 is still the active cell.

If you have problems...

If the collapsed dialog box covers the cells you want to select, simply drag it out of the way. To drag it, point at the title bar, press and hold the left mouse button, and drag. Release the mouse button when the box is where you want it.

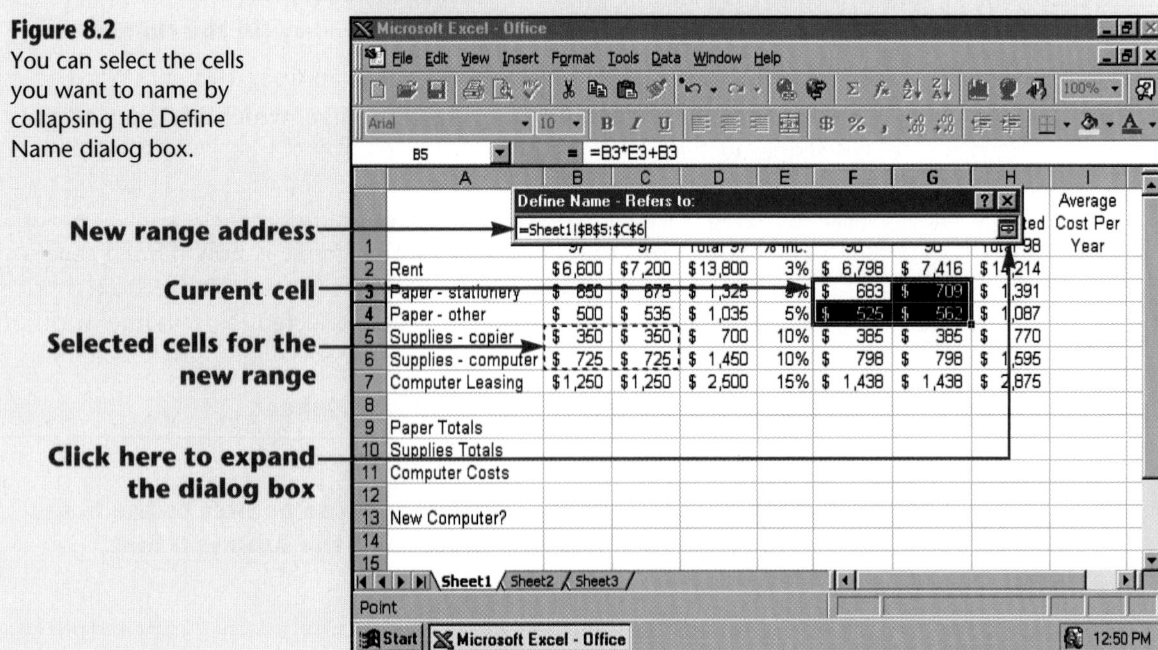

Figure 8.2
You can select the cells you want to name by collapsing the Define Name dialog box.

⑪ **Click the expand button at the right end of the Refers to text box.**

Excel expands the Define Name dialog box. The new range now appears in the **R**efers to text box, but you must still enter a name for the new range.

⑫ **In the Names in workbook text box, replace `paper98` with `supplies97`, and then click Add.**

The `supplies97` range includes all your expenses for supplies for 1997. Now name one more range.

⑬ **Click the button to collapse the Define Name dialog box, then select cells F5 through G6 in the worksheet.**

⑭ **Click the button to expand the Define Name dialog box, name the new range `supplies98`, then click Add.**

You have now named four ranges that you can use later to build formulas and move around the worksheet. All four are listed in the Define Name dialog box.

⑮ **Click OK to close the dialog box.**

Click anywhere outside the selected cells to better see your worksheet. Save your work and keep the Office worksheet open to use in the next lesson.

To quickly name a range, select the range, type the name in the Name box on the Formula bar, and press Enter. If you add or delete cells, rows, or columns to a named range, you may have to redefine the range to be sure it includes all of the cells you want.

You can delete the name of a range by choosing **I**nsert, **N**ame, **D**efine to open the Define Name dialog box. Select the name in the Names in **w**orkbook list, and click **D**elete. Click OK to close the dialog box. If you delete the definition of a named range in a cell with a formula that uses it, then `#NAME?` appears in the cell. You must edit the formula to include the correct range, cell, or value so that the formula can compute the result. Alternatively, delete the formula.

Lesson 2: Using Named Ranges

You can use a named range in any formula to quickly and easily refer to a specific cell or range of cells. You can also use the Name box in the formula bar to quickly move to and select a named range. Now practice using named ranges to move around the `Office` worksheet.

To Use Named Ranges

1 In the `Office` worksheet, click the drop-down arrow to the right of the Name box in the formula bar (see Figure 8.3).

This displays a list of the named ranges that you created for this worksheet, as shown in Figure 8.3.

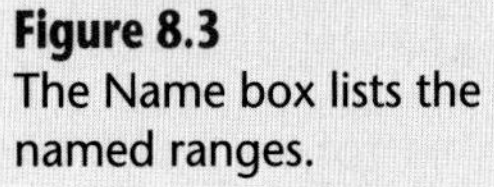

Figure 8.3
The Name box lists the named ranges.

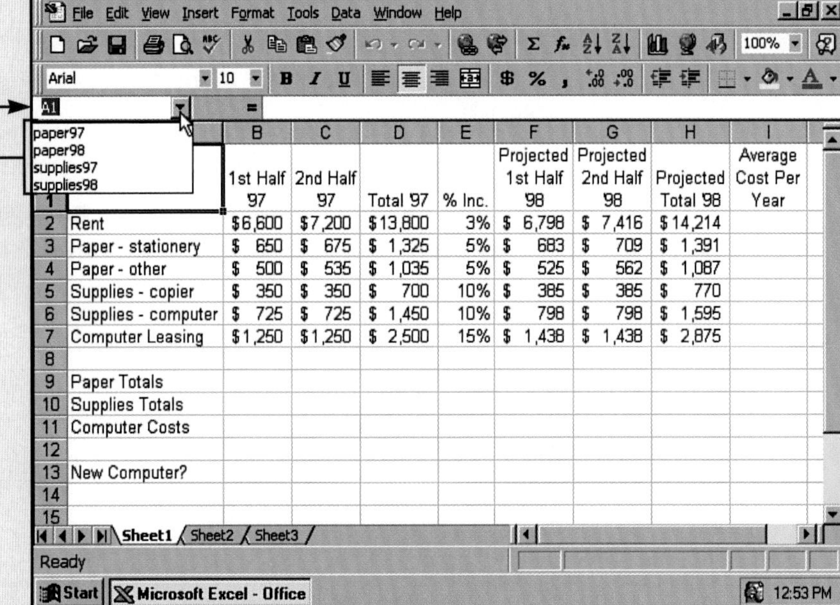

	A	B	C	D	E	F	G	H	I
1		1st Half 97	2nd Half 97	Total 97	% Inc.	Projected 1st Half 98	Projected 2nd Half 98	Projected Total 98	Average Cost Per Year
2	Rent	$6,600	$7,200	$13,800	3%	$ 6,798	$ 7,416	$14,214	
3	Paper - stationery	$ 650	$ 675	$ 1,325	5%	$ 683	$ 709	$ 1,391	
4	Paper - other	$ 500	$ 535	$ 1,035	5%	$ 525	$ 562	$ 1,087	
5	Supplies - copier	$ 350	$ 350	$ 700	10%	$ 385	$ 385	$ 770	
6	Supplies - computer	$ 725	$ 725	$ 1,450	10%	$ 798	$ 798	$ 1,595	
7	Computer Leasing	$1,250	$1,250	$ 2,500	15%	$ 1,438	$ 1,438	$ 2,875	
8									
9	Paper Totals								
10	Supplies Totals								
11	Computer Costs								
12									
13	New Computer?								
14									
15									

2 From the Name box drop-down list, select `paper98`.

This selects the range `paper98`, as shown in Figure 8.4. You can now edit, copy, move, or otherwise modify the named range. This shortcut for moving to named ranges is especially useful when you create workbooks that contain multiple worksheets. Now try moving to another named range.

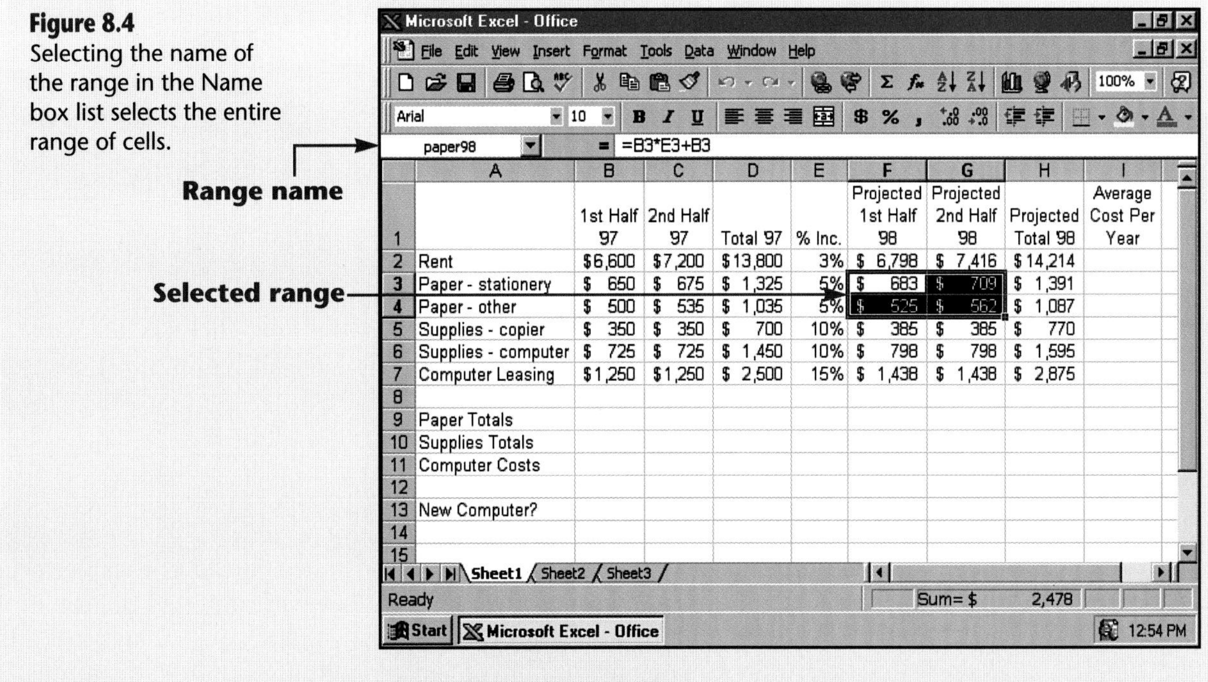

Figure 8.4
Selecting the name of the range in the Name box list selects the entire range of cells.

❸ Click the Name box drop-down arrow, and select `supplies97`.

The `supplies97` range is now selected in the worksheet. Notice that the name of the range appears in the Name box. Save your work and keep the `Office` worksheet open. You use range names and functions to continue creating the worksheet in the next lesson.

To use a range in a formula, simply type the name in the formula in place of the range address. You learn more about using range names in formulas in Lesson 7.

In Excel, you can also name your worksheets and reference them in formulas. At the bottom of each worksheet is a sheet tab with the default sheet name on it. The first sheet is called `Sheet1`, the second sheet is called `Sheet2`, and so on. To view a different sheet, click the sheet tab. To change a sheet name, double-click the sheet tab, and type the new name.

To reference a worksheet, type the worksheet name followed by an exclamation point and the cell address, range address, or range name. For example, if you have a workbook for a five-year forecast with each year's data on a different worksheet, you can reference the different worksheets to create formulas to total, average, or in other ways work with the data from each worksheet. You saw an example of this in the **R**efers to text box in the Define Name dialog box while you were naming ranges in Lesson 5.

If you have problems...

If you use a range name in a formula before you assign the name, Excel returns the error message #NAME?. Name the range first, and then you can use it in a formula.

If you receive an error message dialog box when using the named range in a formula, check for spaces, math operators, or numbers at the beginning of the name. If the name contains any of these, then remove the offending characters and try your formula again. Before you can make changes, you must first respond to the dialog box: click OK to make changes to your name, or choose **H**elp to get online help from Excel.

Lesson 3: Using Functions

As you learned in Project 7, *functions* are shortened formulas that perform specific operations on a group of values. You have already used the SUM function to total columns and rows of numbers, so you know that SUM is the function to automatically add entries in a range. Excel provides hundreds of functions that fit into 10 categories to help you with tasks, such as determining loan payments and calculating interest on your savings. Table 8.1 describes some common functions used in Excel.

Table 8.1 Common Functions

Function	Category	Description
AVERAGE	Statistical	Displays the average of a list of values.
AVERAGEA	Statistical	Displays the average of a list of arguments, including numbers, text, and logical values.
CELL	Information	Returns information about a cell or its contents.
DATE	Date & Time	Lists the date according to the computer's clock.
ERROR.TYPE	Information	Displays a number corresponding to one of Excel's error values. Used to debug macros and worksheets.
EVEN	Math & Trig	Rounds a value up to the nearest even integer.
MAX	Statistical	Finds the largest value in a list of numbers.
MAXA	Statistical	Finds the largest value in a list of arguments, including text, numbers, and logical values.
MIN	Statistical	Finds the smallest value in a list of numbers.
MINA	Statistical	Finds the smallest value in a list of arguments, including text, numbers, and logical values.
NOW	Date & Time	Calculates the current date and time on the computer's clock.
ODD	Math & Trig	Rounds a value up to the nearest odd integer.
PMT	Financial	Calculates the periodic payment amount needed to repay a loan.

Function	Category	Description
PRODUCT	Math & Trig	Calculates the product of a list of values by multiplying each value in turn.
ROUND	Math & Trig	Rounds a value to a specific number of decimal places.
SUM	Math & Trig	Adds a list of values.
TIME	Date & Time	Lists the time according to the computer's clock.
TODAY	Date & Time	Calculates the serial number for the current date and displays it in date format. It is used for date and time calculations.

You can enter functions into Excel formulas in many ways. If you know the name of the function you want to use, you can type it into the cell where you want the result to appear, or you can type it into the Formula bar. You can also use the Formula palette or the Paste Function dialog box to select from a list of functions.

In this lesson, you learn to include functions in formulas using the different methods described previously. You also learn how to include range names in formulas and how to use the TODAY function, which displays the current system date. Try using functions to build the `Office` worksheet now.

To Use Functions

1 Click cell D2 in the `Office` worksheet.

Cell D2 already contains a formula that uses the SUM function to calculate the total rent for 1997. You can see the formula in the formula bar and the result of the formula in cell D2. Now, try using the TODAY function to enter today's date in a cell in the worksheet.

2 Select cell A1 in the `Office` worksheet.

This is where you want the result of the formula—today's date—to appear. To create a formula using a function, you can type the formula in the cell or the Formula bar.

3 Type `=today()` and click the Enter button (the green check mark) on the Formula bar.

Arguments
The values on which the function performs its calculations. An argument can be a single cell, a range of cells, or any value you enter.

This is the formula that uses the TODAY function to calculate today's date. Excel enters the system date in cell A1. Like all formulas, functions begin with an equal sign. You then type the function name in uppercase or lowercase letters without leaving any spaces. The function name is followed by the function *arguments*, which are enclosed in parentheses and separated by commas. With the TODAY function, you do not need to include any arguments. Now use the Formula palette to enter a function to find the total amount you will spend on paper in 1997.

continues

To Use Functions (continued)

4 Select cell D9 and click the Edit Formula button on the Formula bar.

Excel opens the Formula palette. With the Formula palette, you can select a function and enter the arguments you want to use.

5 Click the drop-down arrow to the right of the Function button.

A list of functions appears, as shown in Figure 8.5. The most recently used functions appear at the top of the list. You can click More Functions to open the Paste Function dialog box and display additional functions.

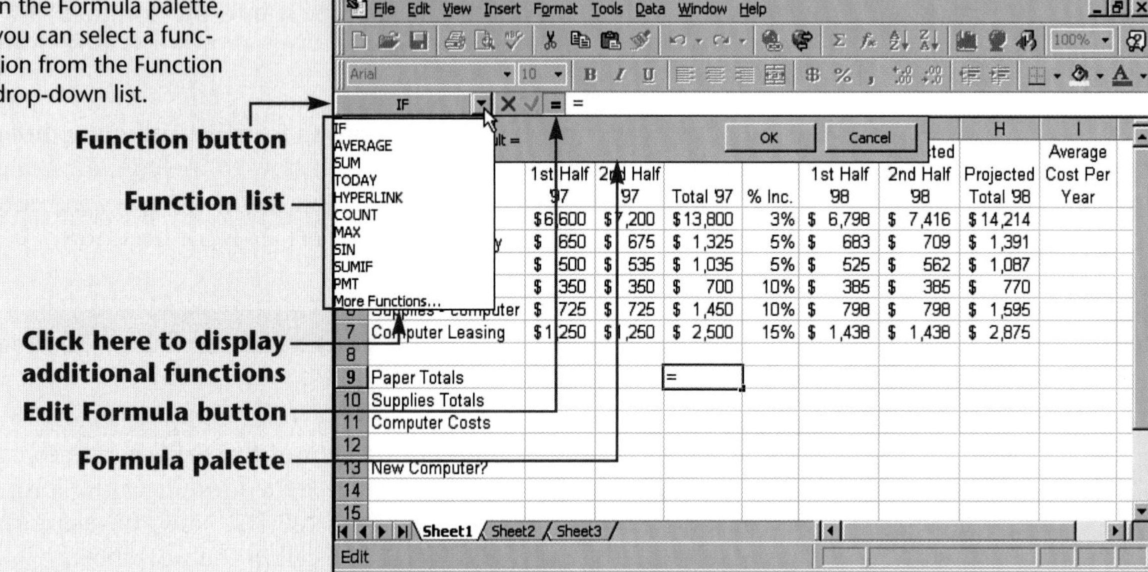

Figure 8.5
In the Formula palette, you can select a function from the Function drop-down list.

6 Select SUM.

Excel inserts the SUM function into the formula and expands the Formula palette, as shown in Figure 8.6. In the expanded palette, you can enter arguments, read a description of the function, and preview the result of the formula. Excel guesses which cells you want to total and displays the range address in the Number 1 text box. In this case, however, it guesses wrong. To correct the formula, you must enter the correct arguments or range of cells that you want to total.

If you have problems...

If the SUM function does not appear in the drop-down list of functions, select More Functions to open the Paste Function dialog box. In the Function **C**ategory list, select All, then scroll down in the Function **N**ame list, and select SUM. Choose OK to enter the SUM function in the formula.

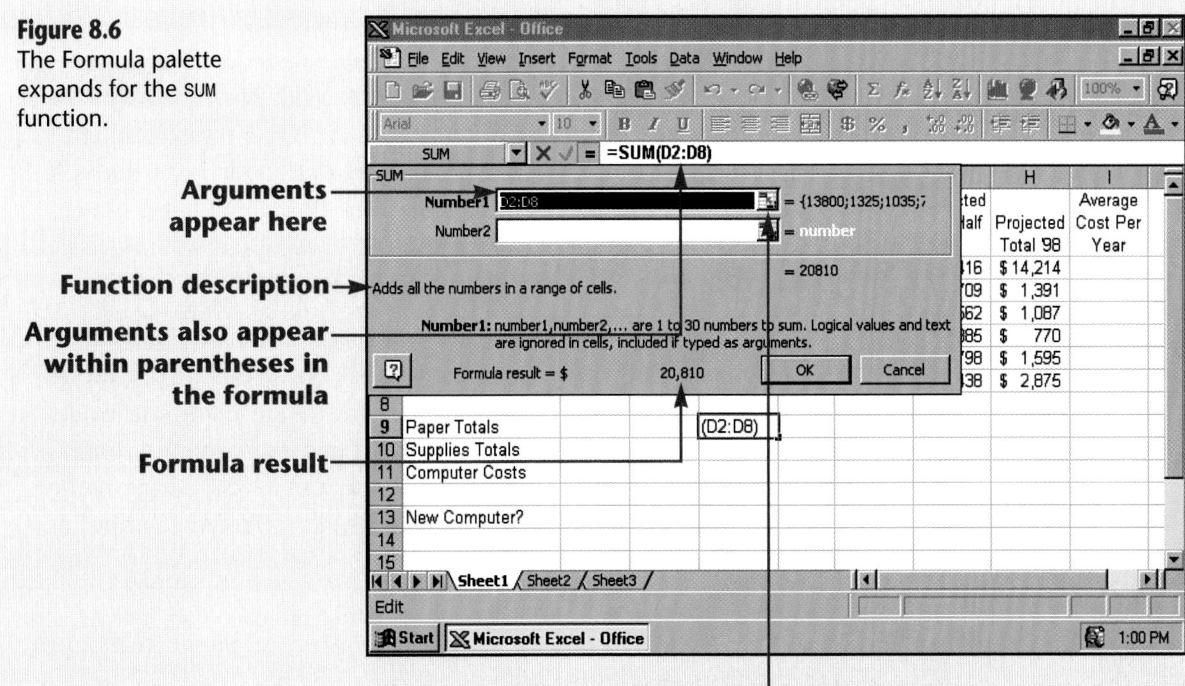

Figure 8.6
The Formula palette expands for the SUM function.

7 In the Number 1 text box, type `paper97` and then click OK.

This enters the named range `paper97` into the formula as the argument and tells Excel to calculate the total. The amount spent for paper in 1997 now appears in cell D9 (see Figure 8.7).

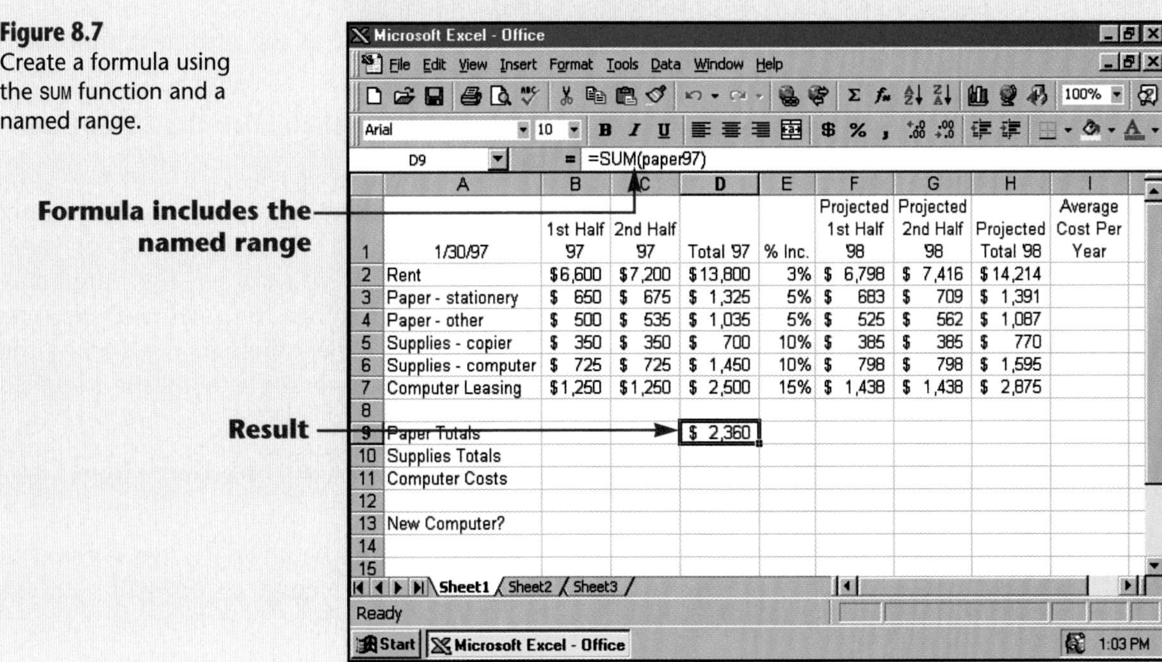

Figure 8.7
Create a formula using the SUM function and a named range.

continues

To Use Functions (continued)

If you have problems...

If you enter a function with a mistake in it, Excel displays an error message in the cell, such as #NAME? or #VALUE?. If Excel thinks it knows the problem, it displays a message box asking if it is okay to go ahead and correct it. Choose **Y**es to have Excel automatically correct the formula, or **N**o to try to fix it on your own.

When troubleshooting formulas, first make sure that you used an existing named range and then check for typos in the range name. Study the formula and check the range name for invalid characters, such as punctuation marks and mathematical operators. The error message #NAME? will appear if your range name contains any of these symbols. Remove the offending symbol or number and try again.

Now enter functions to total the rest of your paper and supply expenses for 1997 and 1998.

8 In cell D10, type `=sum(supplies97)`, and then press Enter.

The sum showing the total spent for supplies in 1997 appears in the cell. You could also click the Enter button on the Formula bar instead of pressing Enter.

Σ

9 Select cell H9, then click the AutoSum button on the Standard toolbar.

The SUM function with the *incorrect* range as the argument appears in cell H9.

✓

10 In the worksheet, select cells F3:G4, then click the Enter button on the Formula bar.

This replaces the incorrect range in the formula with the correct range—paper98—and enters the formula. The projected total paper expenses for 1998 appears in cell H9. As you can see, there are many ways to enter functions and arguments into formulas in Excel. You can decide for yourself which is the easiest method or which is the most appropriate. Enter one more formula for totaling the expenses for supplies for 1998.

11 Select cell H10, click the Edit Formula button, then choose SUM from the Function drop-down list.

Excel opens the Formula palette with the wrong range entered as the argument. Try selecting the correct range to insert it into the formula.

⓬ Click the collapse button at the right end of the Number 1 text box (refer to Figure 8.6).

Excel collapses the Formula palette so you can select the cells you want to use in the worksheet. Only the Number 1 text box appears on-screen.

⓭ Select cells F5:G6 to enter the `supplies98` range, then click the expand button at the right end of the Number 1 text box.

Excel expands the Formula palette with the correct range entered in the formula.

If you have problems...

If the collapsed palette covers the column or row labels, you should still be able to select the correct range by counting the rows and columns or by referring to the numbers and letters that are visible. If the palette covers the range that you want to select, you must move it out of the way while it is full-size. To move it, expand it, point anywhere within the palette area, then click and drag to move it out of the way. When it is out of the way, try collapsing it and selecting the cells again.

⓮ Click OK in the Formula palette.

The projected total expense for supplies in 1998 appears in cell H10. Your worksheet should now look similar to the one shown in Figure 8.8. Save your work and keep the `Office` worksheet open for the next lesson, in which you create more complex formulas with functions.

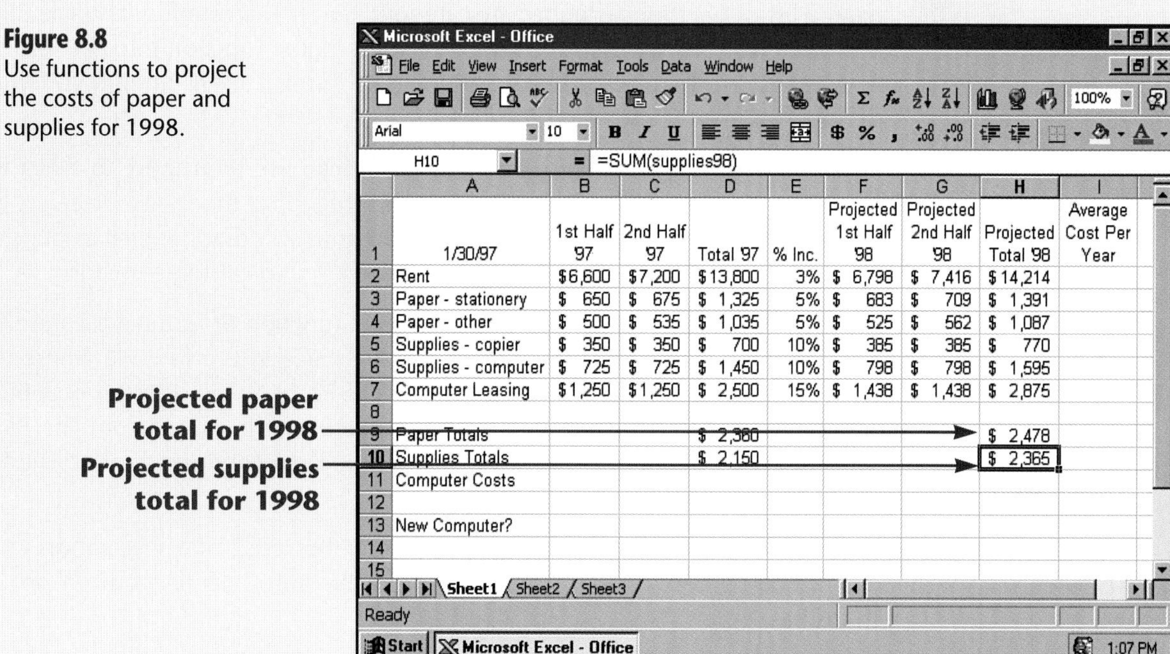

Figure 8.8
Use functions to project the costs of paper and supplies for 1998.

If you have problems...

If you think a function that uses a range is not returning the correct answer, make sure that the range is entered correctly. Ensure that all cells you need are included and that no extra cells containing data are included.

Jargon Watch

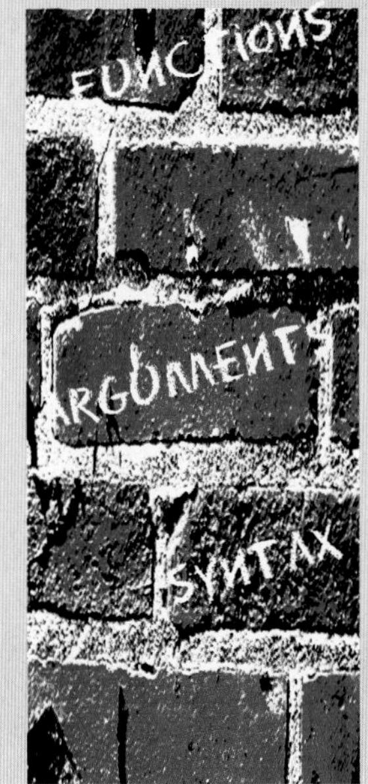

Several differences exist between regular formulas and **functions**. One difference is that you can customize regular formulas more to your liking. You use functions as shortcuts to tell Excel how to calculate values.

As demonstrated in Project 3, entering a function, such as **=SUM(B2:B9)**, is quicker and easier than entering its corresponding formula: **=B2+B3+B4+B5+B6+B7+B8+B9**. In a regular formula, you must specify every operation to be performed. That's why there are so many plus signs in the preceding formula. In a function, however, the operations are programmed in, so you need only supply the necessary information in the form of **arguments**. In the function =SUM(B2:B9), B2:B9 is the argument. Functions can include multiple arguments, as you learn in Lesson 4.

When you add arguments to a function, you must use the proper **syntax**, which is simply the exact and correct way to type commands and functions. In general, computer programs are inflexible about even one wrong keystroke, such as a missing comma.

If your formula returns an error message, use the Excel Help feature to find out more about the syntax for the specific function you are trying to use.

You can also use the Paste Function dialog box to select a function. Click the Paste Function button on the Standard toolbar to open the dialog box. It displays a list of functions grouped by category. Select the category and the function you want to use, then click OK. Excel inserts the function into the formula and opens the Formula palette, so you can enter the arguments you want to use.

Instead of typing a range into a function, you can use the mouse to select the range. For example, you can type **=SUM(** and then drag the mouse to select the range. Excel enters the range in the formula bar as you drag, as well as the closing parenthesis. End the function by pressing ↵Enter to calculate the formula.

Another way to enter the name of a range in a function or formula is to use the Paste Name dialog box. When you reach the place in the formula where you want to insert the named range, press F3. The Paste Name dialog box appears with a list of named ranges. Choose the name of the range from the Paste **N**ame list box. Click OK to close the dialog box, then continue creating the formula.

Also, don't forget that you can quickly check the result of a calculation without actually entering the formula by using the AutoCalculate button on the status bar.

Lesson 4: Building Formulas with Functions

Nest
To place one function within another.

Functions are easy to use in building complex formulas. For example, you can add two SUM functions together (as you do in this lesson using the `Office` worksheet). You can also *nest* functions by using them as arguments for other functions.

This lesson shows you how to create complex formulas by combining and nesting functions.

To Build Formulas with Functions

1 In cell I2 of the `Office` worksheet, enter the formula `=average(b2+c2,f2+g2)`.

This enters the formula and calculates the average cost of rent per year. When you use two arguments in a function, you separate them with a comma. Don't forget to click the Enter button on the Formula bar.

Note that you can get the same result from the simple formula `=average(d2,h2)`. In general, it's best to use the simplest formula possible in your worksheets. You are asked to build more complex formulas in this lesson to learn how functions can be used together.

If you have problems...

If the average doesn't appear to be correct, make sure that the ranges you used don't include any extra cells with values or labels. When using the AVERAGE function, be sure to use only the specific cells with the contents you want to average.

2 Select cell I2 again, click the right mouse button to open the shortcut menu, then choose Copy.

This copies the formula in cell I2 to the Windows Clipboard.

3 Select cells I3 through I7, open the shortcut menu, then choose Paste.

This copies the formula to cells I3 through I7 where the results are displayed, as shown in Figure 8.9. Because no decimal places are displayed, Excel rounds the totals to the nearest whole number; however, the actual value is used in all calculations. The formulas in the cells are relative. In Project 7, you learned that *relative* means that the formula conforms to its current address, no matter where it was first entered. In this example, the formula is always relative to the numbers in the cells to the left of the formula's current cell address.

continues

To Build Formulas with Functions (continued)

	A	B	C	D	E	F	G	H	I
1	1/30/97	1st Half '97	2nd Half '97	Total '97	% Inc.	Projected 1st Half '98	Projected 2nd Half '98	Projected Total '98	Average Cost Per Year
2	Rent	$6,600	$7,200	$13,800	3%	$ 6,798	$ 7,416	$ 14,214	$14,007
3	Paper - stationery	$ 650	$ 675	$ 1,325	5%	$ 683	$ 709	$ 1,3	$ 1,358
4	Paper - other	$ 500	$ 535	$ 1,035	5%	$ 525	$ 562	$ 1,087	$ 1,061
5	Supplies - copier	$ 350	$ 350	$ 700	10%	$ 385	$ 385	$ 770	$ 735
6	Supplies - computer	$ 725	$ 725	$ 1,450	10%	$ 798	$ 798	$ 1,595	$ 1,523
7	Computer Leasing	$1,250	$1,250	$ 2,500	15%	$ 1,438	$ 1,438	$ 2,875	$ 2,688
8									
9	Paper Totals			$ 2,360				$ 2,478	
10	Supplies Totals			$ 2,150				$ 2,365	
11	Computer Costs								
12									
13	New Computer?								
14									
15									

Figure 8.9
The function averages the values relative to its current cell address.

4 In cell D11, enter the formula `=sum(b6:c6)+sum(b7:c7)`.

This calculates the total computer costs for 1997 by adding the total costs of computer supplies and the total costs of computer leasing. You built the formula by combining two functions with the plus sign operator.

Once again, you are using more complex formulas than are necessary, so you can learn the different methods of entering functions. You can get the same result with the simple formula `=D6+D7`, which adds the total computer supplies and computer leasing expenses for the year.

Now use the Formula palette to enter a formula to calculate the total computer costs for 1998.

5 Select cell H11, click the Edit Formula button, and choose the SUM function.

Instead of combining two SUM functions to complete the formula, try using two arguments within one function.

6 In the Number 1 text box, type the range `f6:g6`, and press Tab. Then, in the Number 2 text box, type the range `f7:g7`, and click OK.

Excel sets up the formula by enclosing the arguments in parentheses and separating them with a comma. The projected total computer cost for 1998 appears in cell H11, as shown in Figure 8.10.

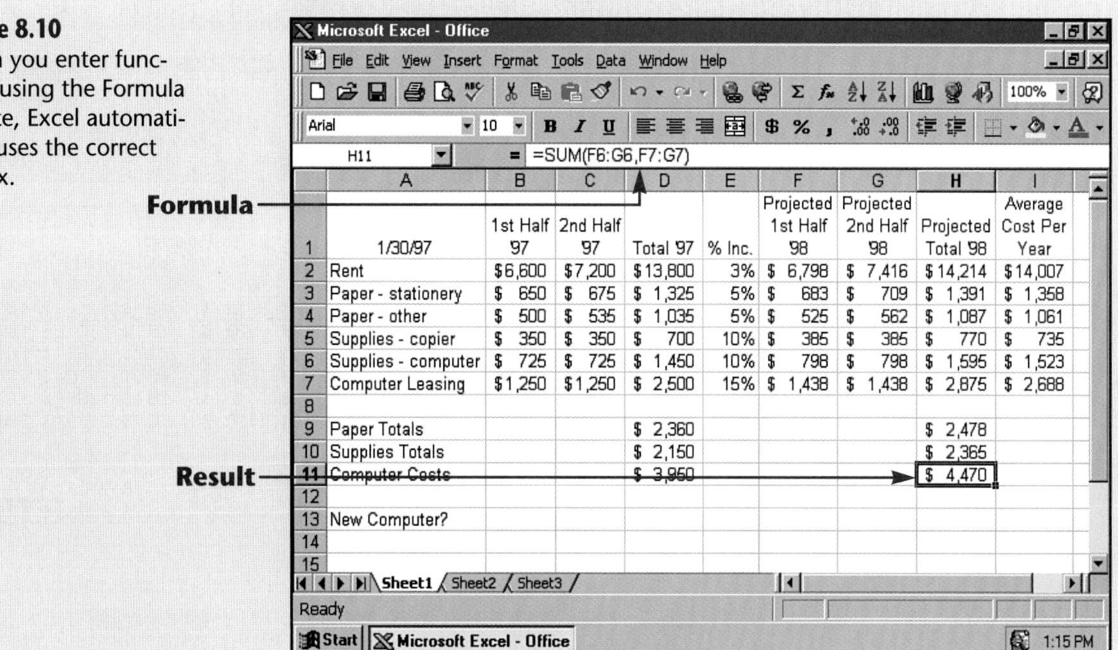

	A	B	C	D	E	F	G	H	I
1	1/30/97	1st Half '97	2nd Half '97	Total '97	% Inc.	Projected 1st Half '98	Projected 2nd Half '98	Projected Total '98	Average Cost Per Year
2	Rent	$6,600	$7,200	$13,800	3%	$ 6,798	$ 7,416	$14,214	$14,007
3	Paper - stationery	$ 650	$ 675	$ 1,325	5%	$ 683	$ 709	$ 1,391	$ 1,358
4	Paper - other	$ 500	$ 535	$ 1,035	5%	$ 525	$ 562	$ 1,087	$ 1,061
5	Supplies - copier	$ 350	$ 350	$ 700	10%	$ 385	$ 385	$ 770	$ 735
6	Supplies - computer	$ 725	$ 725	$ 1,450	10%	$ 798	$ 798	$ 1,595	$ 1,523
7	Computer Leasing	$1,250	$1,250	$ 2,500	15%	$ 1,438	$ 1,438	$ 2,875	$ 2,688
8									
9	Paper Totals			$ 2,360				$ 2,478	
10	Supplies Totals			$ 2,150				$ 2,365	
11	Computer Costs			$ 3,950				$ 4,470	
12									
13	New Computer?								
14									
15									

Figure 8.10
When you enter functions using the Formula palette, Excel automatically uses the correct syntax.

Now create a complex formula to calculate the average total computer cost per year. Use your choice of methods to enter the formula.

7 In cell I11, enter the formula `=average(sum(b6:c7),sum(f6:g7))`.

In this formula, the `SUM` functions are nested as arguments for the `AVERAGE` function. Excel calculates the sum of `B6:C7` and the sum of `F6:G7`, then finds the average of the two resulting values. By combining several functions, you have created a formula that calculates the average total computer cost per year, as shown in Figure 8.11. Note the placement of the parentheses, which specify the arguments that are used for each function.

Again, note that you can also achieve the same result with the simpler formula **`=AVERAGE(D11,H11)`**, which adds the total costs for 1997 and 1998, then finds the average of the two. Note also that D11 equals `SUM(D6:D7)` and that H11 equals `SUM(H6:H7)`. In creating the more complex formula, you have simply replaced the `SUM` functions for cells D11 and H11.

continues

To Build Formulas with Functions (continued)

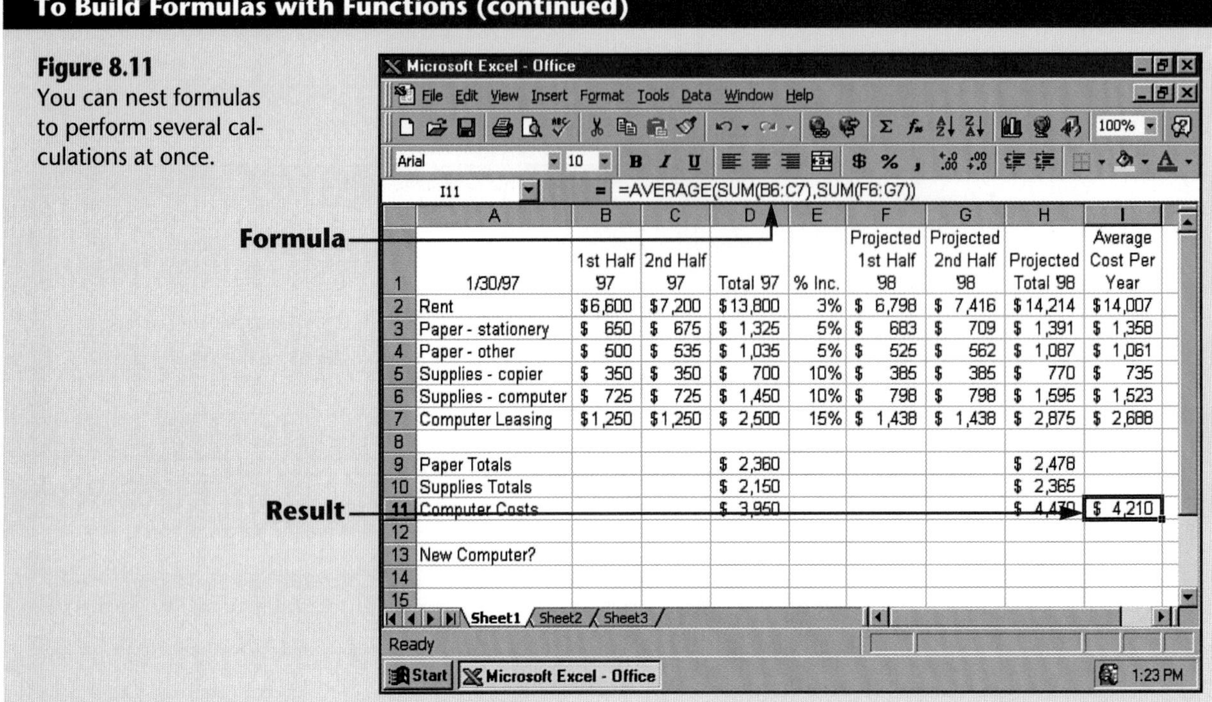

	A	B	C	D	E	F	G	H	I
1	1/30/97	1st Half 97	2nd Half 97	Total 97	% Inc.	Projected 1st Half 98	Projected 2nd Half 98	Projected Total 98	Average Cost Per Year
2	Rent	$6,600	$7,200	$13,800	3%	$ 6,798	$ 7,416	$14,214	$14,007
3	Paper - stationery	$ 650	$ 675	$ 1,325	5%	$ 683	$ 709	$ 1,391	$ 1,358
4	Paper - other	$ 500	$ 535	$ 1,035	5%	$ 525	$ 562	$ 1,087	$ 1,061
5	Supplies - copier	$ 350	$ 350	$ 700	10%	$ 385	$ 385	$ 770	$ 735
6	Supplies - computer	$ 725	$ 725	$ 1,450	10%	$ 798	$ 798	$ 1,595	$ 1,523
7	Computer Leasing	$1,250	$1,250	$ 2,500	15%	$ 1,438	$ 1,438	$ 2,875	$ 2,688
8									
9	Paper Totals			$ 2,360				$ 2,478	
10	Supplies Totals			$ 2,150				$ 2,365	
11	Computer Costs			$ 3,950				$ 4,47[illegible]	$ 4,210
12									
13	New Computer?								
14									
15									

Figure 8.11
You can nest formulas to perform several calculations at once.

You have now created formulas to calculate all the information you need to track your office expenses. Save your work and keep the `Office` worksheet open for the next lesson, where you use a function to tell you whether you would save money by purchasing a personal computer instead of leasing it.

If you have problems...

A common mistake in complex functions involves parentheses. Be sure that for every open parenthesis, there is a corresponding close parenthesis. All parentheses must be placed in the correct location to avoid a syntax error.

Another fairly common mistake is substituting a plus sign for the colon in a `SUM` formula. The formula `=SUM(D10:I10)` is much different than `=SUM(D10+I10)`. In the latter formula, only the first and last cells are added, whereas in the first formula, all cells from D10 to I10, including D10 and I10, are added.

If Excel responds with the error message `#NAME?`, don't worry. Simply check your formula carefully to make sure that all parentheses are present and all addresses are correct. If you still can't find the problem, check the values and formulas in the referenced cells for typos. One typographical error can affect formulas in many parts of the worksheet if the formulas refer to the cell containing the error.

A colon between the cell addresses in a range argument (such as `F6:G7`) is simply the standard method that Excel uses to show the range. A comma is used to separate arguments in a function.

To nest one function within another using the Formula palette, simply make sure the insertion point is in the location where you want the nested function to appear in the formula, then select the function from the Function drop-down list. The insertion point can be in an argument text box in the Formula palette or in the Formula bar. Excel will open the Formula palette for the nested function. When you have entered all of the arguments for the nested function, click in the Formula bar to display the Formula palette for the original function.

Remember, when you paste a formula from one cell into another, each cell reference in the original formula is converted to a relative reference.

Lesson 5: Using Conditional Statements

Your `Office` worksheet now contains information and formulas that you need to track the cost of running an office over two years. Now look at how you can have the worksheet calculate whether you should purchase computer equipment instead of continuing to lease it.

Conditional statement
A function that returns different results depending on whether a specified condition is true or false.

Using *conditional statements,* you can implement different actions, depending on whether a condition is true or false. The simplest conditional function in Excel is the `IF` function: If the condition is true, then Excel displays one result; if the condition is false, then Excel displays a different result.

Try using the `IF` function to see whether your computer costs are sufficiently high to warrant purchasing a personal computer.

To Use Conditional Statements

1. **Select cell B13 of the `Office` worksheet.**
2. **Click the Paste Function button on the Standard toolbar.**

   The Paste Function dialog box opens.
3. **Choose Logical in the Function Category list, and then choose `IF` in the Function Name list.**

   Excel displays the function syntax—`=IF(logical_test,value_if_true,value_if_false)`—at the bottom of the dialog box, along with a description of the function (see Figure 8.12).

continues

To Use Conditional Statements (continued)

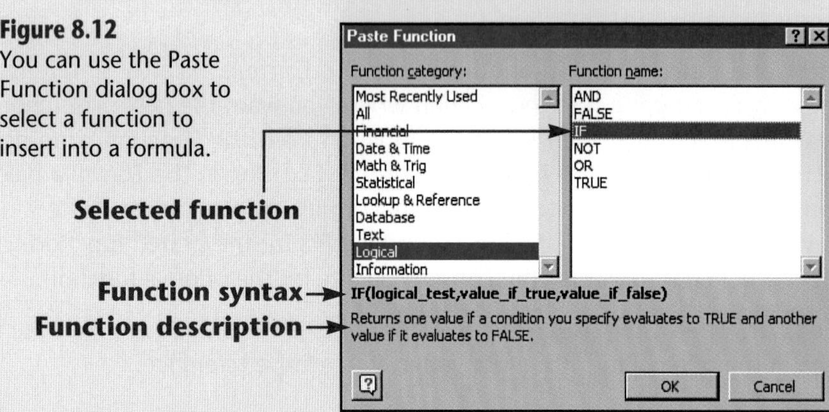

Figure 8.12
You can use the Paste Function dialog box to select a function to insert into a formula.

Selected function

Function syntax

Function description

For this example, the logical test is whether or not your yearly computer costs are greater than $4,000. *If* they are, *then* it makes sense to purchase a computer. *If* they are not, *then* it makes sense to continue leasing.

4 Click OK.

Excel pastes the selected function into the formula and opens the Formula palette, so you can enter the arguments (see Figure 8.13).

Figure 8.13
The Formula palette can be used for creating a conditional formula with the IF function.

Logical test argument

Value if true argument

Value if false argument

You can preview the formula result here

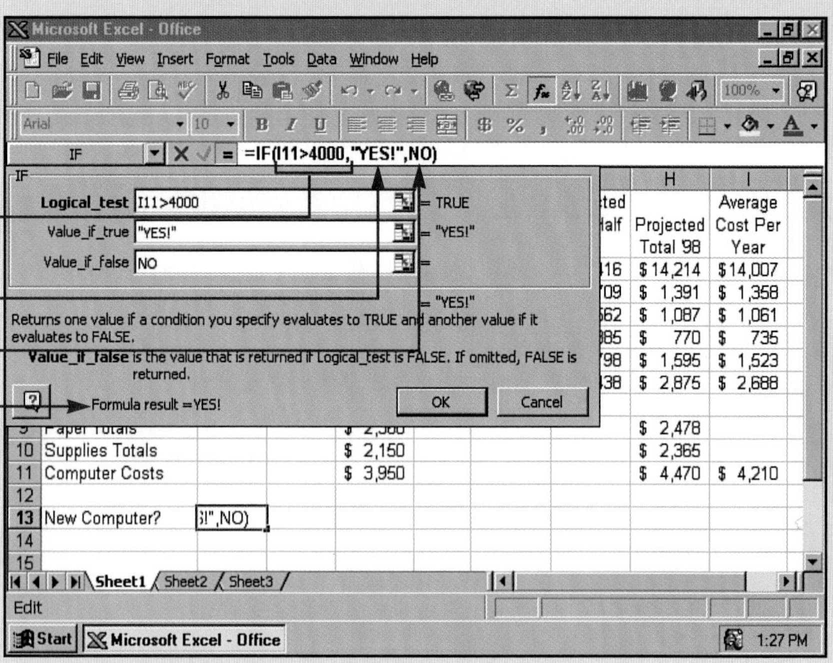

5 In the Logical_Test text box, type `I11>4000` and press Tab.

This enters the logical test argument, and moves the insertion point to the next text box. `I11` refers to the cell where the average total computer costs are calculated, the > sign is the mathematical operator that means *greater than,* and `4000` is the value you want to use for comparison.

6 In the Value_if_true text box, type `YES!`, including the exclamation mark, and press Tab.

This enters the `value_if_true` argument of the function. It tells Excel what value to display in the cell if the condition is true. In other words, if the total average cost per year is greater than $4,000, Excel will enter `YES!` in the current cell.

7 In the Value_if_false box, type `NO`.

This enters the `value_if_false` argument. It tells Excel the value to display if the condition is false—that is, if the value in cell I11 is less than $4,000. The Formula palette should now look like the one in Figure 8.13.

8 Click OK.

Excel performs the calculation, and the word `YES!` should now appear in cell B13, as shown in Figure 8.14. When you use the `IF` function, Excel tells you that you should purchase the computer based on the information currently in the worksheet. If the projected expenses were to decrease so that the average total was less than $4,000, Excel would return `NO` as the response.

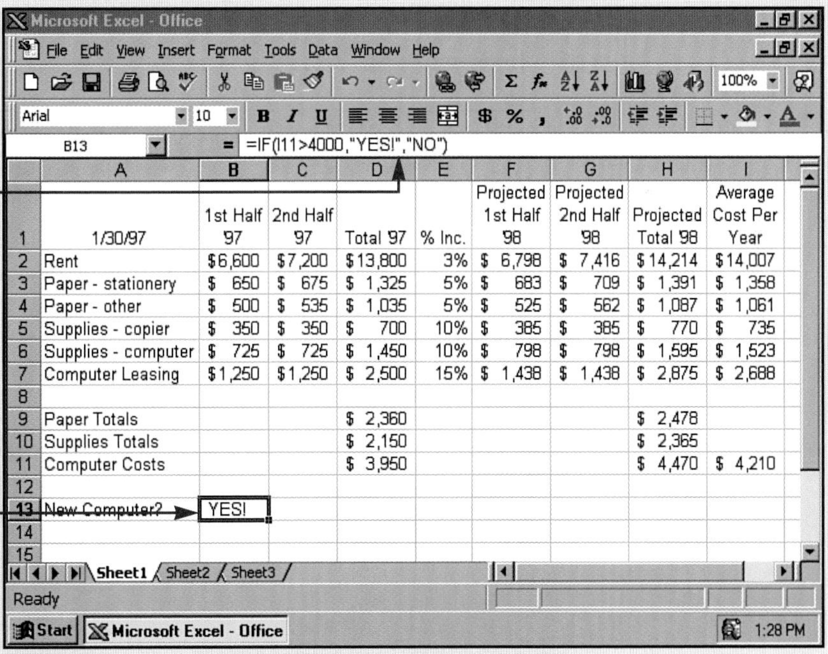

Figure 8.14
The result of the conditional statement is `Yes!`

Microsoft Excel - Office

File Edit View Insert Format Tools Data Window Help

B13 = =IF(I11>4000,"YES!","NO")

Conditional statement formula

	A	B	C	D	E	F	G	H	I
1	1/30/97	1st Half '97	2nd Half '97	Total '97	% Inc.	Projected 1st Half '98	Projected 2nd Half '98	Projected Total '98	Average Cost Per Year
2	Rent	$6,600	$7,200	$13,800	3%	$ 6,798	$ 7,416	$14,214	$14,007
3	Paper - stationery	$ 650	$ 675	$ 1,325	5%	$ 683	$ 709	$ 1,391	$ 1,358
4	Paper - other	$ 500	$ 535	$ 1,035	5%	$ 525	$ 562	$ 1,087	$ 1,061
5	Supplies - copier	$ 350	$ 350	$ 700	10%	$ 385	$ 385	$ 770	$ 735
6	Supplies - computer	$ 725	$ 725	$ 1,450	10%	$ 798	$ 798	$ 1,595	$ 1,523
7	Computer Leasing	$1,250	$1,250	$ 2,500	15%	$ 1,438	$ 1,438	$ 2,875	$ 2,688
8									
9	Paper Totals			$ 2,360				$ 2,478	
10	Supplies Totals			$ 2,150				$ 2,365	
11	Computer Costs			$ 3,950				$ 4,470	$ 4,210
12									
13	New Computer?	YES!							
14									
15									

Result

Sheet1 / Sheet2 / Sheet3

Ready

Start | Microsoft Excel - Office | 1:28 PM

Save your work. If requested by your instructor, print two copies, then close the worksheet. If you have completed your session on the computer, exit Excel and Windows 95 before turning off the computer. Otherwise, continue with the "Checking Your Skills" section at the end of this project.

Jargon Watch

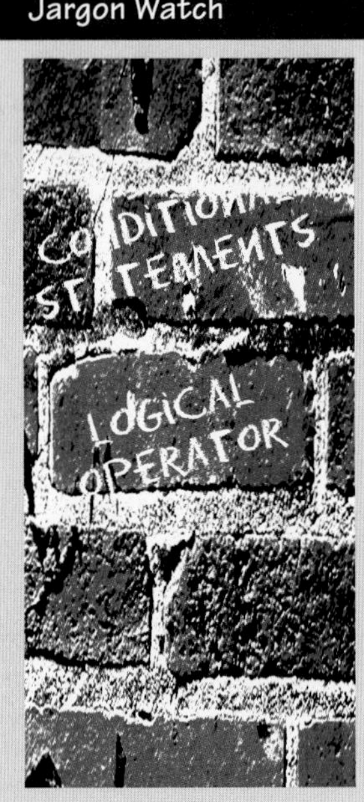

Conditional statements use many mathematical terms that can be confusing. In most cases, however, a conditional statement takes the form of a simple if/then sentence: *if* this happens, *then* that happens.

Conditional statements or arguments, such as the one in this lesson, typically use a **logical operator**. Logical operators include the following:

Operator	Meaning
=	Equal
<	Less than
>	Greater than
<=	Less than or equal to
>=	Greater than or equal to

Think of these operators simply as replacements for the words in the "Meaning" column above.

Project Summary

To	Do This
Name a range	Select the range, choose **I**nsert, **N**ame, **D**efine, type a name in the Names in **w**orkbook text box, and click OK.
Select a named range	Click the drop-down arrow in the Name box in the Formula bar, and choose the range name.
Enter a function in a formula	Type an equal sign followed by the function name and the arguments enclosed in parentheses (separated by commas). Or, click the Paste Function button on the Standard toolbar, select the function, then click OK. Or, open the Formula palette, and select the function from the Function drop-down list. Complete the formula and then click OK.
Perform *what-if* analyses on data	Use the logical IF function.

Checking Your Skills

True/False

For each of the following, check *T* or *F* to indicate whether the statement is true or false.

__T __F **1.** You can name a range, but not an individual cell.

__T __F **2.** Range names can consist of up to 255 characters.

__T __F **3.** If Excel displays the error message #NAME? when using a named range in a formula, check to make sure you have the equal sign in the name.

__T __F **4.** An IF function includes a condition and two arguments.

__T __F **5.** Use the CALENDAR function to display the current system date.

__T __F **6.** You can use both upper- and lowercase letters in a range name.

__T __F **7.** Range names must begin with a letter, underscore, or number.

__T __F **8.** To display a list of named ranges in the worksheet, right-click the Formula bar.

__T __F **9.** You cannot use spaces in a function name.

__T __F **10.** You cannot delete the name of a defined range.

Multiple Choice

Circle the letter of the correct answer for each of the following questions.

1. Which of the following is a collection of cells that you can use in a formula?

- **a.** B2...B2
- **b.** B2:G2
- **c.** B2:G2,B6
- **d.** B4+C4,C6

2. Which of the following is a valid formula?

- **a.** =AVERAGE(B2;C2;D4;G4)
- **b.** SUM(B2:B8)-AVG(D2:D4)
- **c.** =SUM(AVG(C3;C4),(AVG F6:F9
- **d.** =SUM:AVG(SUM,(C3:C9,SUM,(D3:D9))

3. Which of the following is a valid range name?

- **a.** tuitionandfees96
- **b.** tuition 1996
- **c.** tuition+fees
- **d.** 96tuitionandfees

4. What can you do when using the IF conditional statement?

- **a.** Set a condition and get one answer if the condition is true and a second answer if the condition is false
- **b.** Set one condition and one argument to analyze a formula
- **c.** Enter a condition that performs a calculation on a formula
- **d.** List between two and six arguments that apply to the IF condition

5. Which of the following could cause the error message #NAME? to be returned as a result?

- **a.** Using too many functions
- **b.** Using a nonexistent range name
- **c.** Using too many parentheses
- **d.** Using the wrong symbols for operators

6. The command used to name a range is located on which menu?
   a. Edit
   b. Insert
   c. Format
   d. Tools
7. To quickly name a range, you select the range and then type the name in the Name box in which location?
   a. Formula bar
   b. Formatting toolbar
   c. Standard toolbar
   d. Status bar
8. To calculate a loan payment, you use which function?
   a. SUM
   b. MAX
   c. MIN
   d. PMT
9. Which cells are totaled in the function =SUM(D10:I10)?
   a. Cell D10 and cell I10
   b. All cells from D10 through I10
   c. All the cells between D10 and I10
   d. None of the above
10. An argument in a function can be which of the following?
    a. A single cell
    b. A range of cells
    c. Any entered value
    d. All the above

Completion

In the blank provided, write the correct answer for each of the following statements.

1. The ______________ in the formula bar lists named ranges.
2. When you use a named range in a formula before you assign the name, Excel returns a(n) ______________ in the cell.
3. You can combine or ______________ functions within a formula so that you can perform complex calculations at one time.
4. The ______________ is always placed within parentheses to indicate which data the function will use to perform its calculation.
5. Click the ______________ button on the Standard toolbar to select a function.
6. Functions must begin with a(n) ______________.
7. You can use the ______________ ______________ dialog box to select a function.
8. When you use two arguments in a function, separate them with a(n) ______________.
9. To change the name of a worksheet, ______________ the sheet tab, then type the new name.
10. To use the Paste Name dialog box to insert the name of a range in a function or formula, press ______________.

Matching

In the blank next to each of the following terms or phrases, write the letter of the corresponding term or phrase. (Note that some letters may be used more than once.)

_____ **1.** The exact and correct way to type commands and functions.

_____ **2.** The values on which the function performs its calculations.

_____ **3.** To place one function within another.

_____ **4.** A function that returns different results depending on whether a specified condition is true or false.

_____ **5.** Greater than or equal to.

_____ **6.** Less than or equal to.

_____ **7.** A name given to a cell or range of cells.

_____ **8.** Function arguments are enclosed in these.

_____ **9.** Function that finds the largest value in a list of numbers.

_____ **10.** Function that finds the smallest value in a list of numbers.

a. >=

b. range name

c. MIN

d. conditional statement

e. parentheses

f. <=

g. MAX

h. nest

i. arguments

j. syntax

Screen ID

Label each element of the Excel screen shown in Figure 8.15.

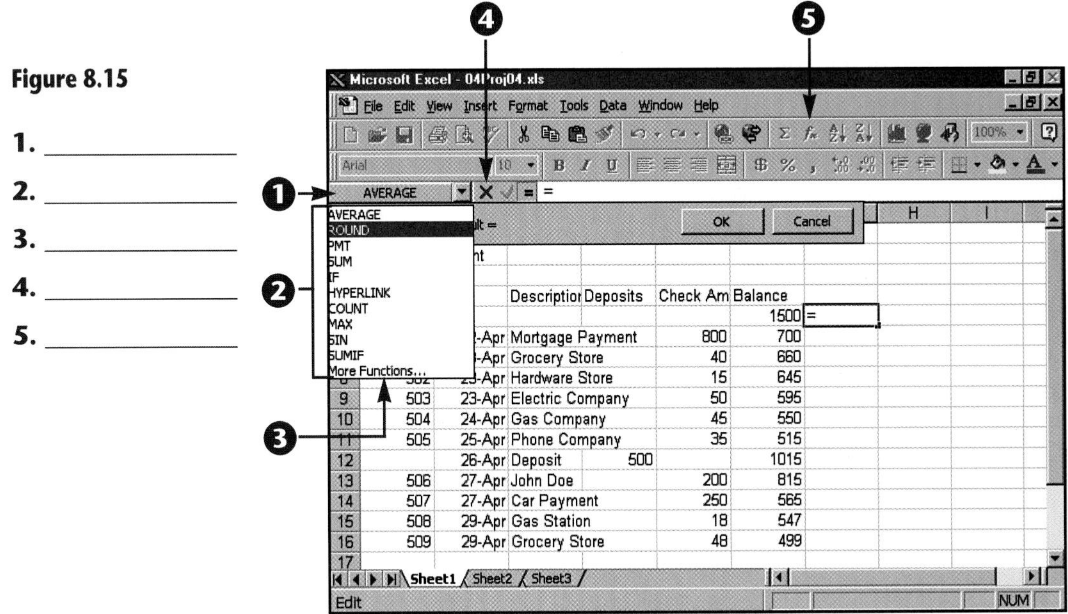

Figure 8.15

Applying Your Skills

Practice

The following exercises enable you to practice the skills you have learned in this project. Take a few minutes to work through these exercises now.

1. Checking Sales Figures

As the owner and business manager of a small coffee shop, you need to evaluate the performance of the merchandise you stock in your store. You want to know if you are buying the right mix of coffees to satisfy your customers.

To find out if you are buying the right coffee, use the sample sales figures provided in `Proj0402` to calculate total sales for the first quarter for each type of coffee. Devise a formula using conditional statements that will alert you if sales of any type fall below a certain level. If necessary, use the Excel Help feature to find out more about the function you use.

To Check Sales Figures

1. Open the file Proj0802 and save it as `Sales Figures`.
2. In the Total column, create a formula to calculate the total sales for January, February, and March for each type of coffee. Have the formula round the totals to whole numbers (no decimal places). (*Hint:* Use more than one function.)
3. In the Check column, use functions to return a message that either warns of sales below a minimum level of $500 or reports that sales are OK. Include this check for each type of coffee you sell.
4. Save your work. If requested by your instructor, print two copies of the completed worksheet, then close it.

2. Calculating Future Salary Requirements

You can use functions and formulas to determine whether your business can support increasing salaries. Use the data provided to calculate the amount of money spent on current salaries and to forecast projected salaries.

To Calculate Future Salary Requirements

1. Open the file Proj0803 and save it as **`Salary Forecast`**.
2. Calculate the projected salaries for each employee.
3. Calculate the average current salary in cell C8 and the average projected salary in cell E8.
4. Calculate the total amount of all current salaries in cell C10 and of all projected salaries in cell E10.
5. In cell B12, use a conditional statement to determine whether you will be able to increase salaries as proposed. To make the decision, assume that if the average projected salary is less that $21,500, you can afford increases.
6. Change all of the increase percentages to five percent to see how the conditional statement is affected.
7. Save your work. If requested by your instructor, print two copies before closing the document.

3. Creating a Worksheet to Calculate the Benefits of Advertising

Create a worksheet that calculates the average amount you spend on each type of advertising each month and how much revenue the advertising generates. Use a conditional statement that will tell you which ad campaigns are worth continuing and which you should cancel.

To Create the Advertising Worksheet

1. Open the file Proj0804 and save it as `Ad Revenues`.
2. In column F, calculate the revenues derived from each type of advertising.
3. In cell B8, calculate the average cost of advertising, rounded to two decimal places. (*Hint:* Nest the AVERAGE function within the ROUND function.)
4. In cell B9, calculate the average ad revenue, rounded to two decimal places.
5. In cell G4, create a conditional statement that tells you whether you should continue to use print advertising. For this study, assume that if you generate more revenue than the ad costs, you should continue.
6. Copy the formula to cells G5 and G6.
7. Save the worksheet. If requested by your instructor, print two copies, then close it.

4. Calculating Utility Expenses

Create a worksheet to calculate the utility expenses for the coffee shop and to see if you can afford air conditioning for the shop.

To Calculate Utility Expenses

1. Open the file Proj0805 and save it as `Utility Expenses`.
2. In column I, calculate the average cost per month of each of the three utilities.
3. In row 7, calculate the average total cost of all utilities for each month.
4. In cell B9, use a conditional statement to determine whether or not you can afford air conditioning. For this example, the average monthly cost of electricity must be less than $40, or the average monthly phone bill must be less than $30 for you to be able to afford air conditioning. (*Hint:* Nest an OR function within an IF function.)
5. Save the worksheet. If requested by your instructor, print two copies before closing it.

5. Naming Ranges in a Worksheet

In this project, you learned to use named ranges to make it easier to use ranges in formulas and to quickly access certain areas of the worksheet. In this exercise, you name ranges in the Profit Loss worksheet.

To Name Ranges in a Worksheet

1. Open Proj0806 file and save it as `Profit Loss 2`.
2. Select the range of cells B5:B13.
3. Choose Insert, Name, Define to display the Define Name dialog box.
4. Make sure April displays in the Names in workbook text box, then click OK. The range B5:B13 is now named April.
5. Now name the columns for May and June.
6. Save the workbook again and leave it open for the following Challenge.

Challenge

The following challenges enable you to use your problem-solving skills. Take time to work through these exercises now.

1. Using Named Ranges in Formulas

Now that you have named ranges, you can use them in formulas or to quickly select a named range. Select the April range that you named in the Profit Loss 2 worksheet and then copy the range to the Sheet2 worksheet. Select the May range and copy it to Sheet3. Save the workbook and leave it open for the next exercise.

2. Using the AutoSum and Average Functions to Calculate Profits

Your boss has asked that you calculate quarterly profits in the Profit Loss 2 workbook. Because functions make it much easier to perform various calculations in Excel, you decide to use them.

In cell F4, type **`Quarterly Profit`**. Move to cell F5 and click the AutoSum button on the Standard toolbar. When the range for the argument displays, drag across cells B13:D13. Click the Enter button on the Formula bar. The net profit for April, May, and June is calculated and entered into this cell.

Move to cell G4 and type **`Quarterly Average`**. Activate cell G5 and click the Edit Formula button on the Formula bar. Use the AVERAGE function to average the net profit for this quarter.

Save and print one copy of all the worksheets in the workbook. Close the workbook when you have finished.

3. Using Conditional Statements

As manager of a hardware store, you need to use conditional statements to determine if a customer has earned a discount by paying a bill promptly. If a customer pays their bill within 10 days of the billing date, they receive a 2% discount. To calculate whether the customer receives a discount, you must determine if the payment was received in 10 days or less. If it was, the customer receives a 2% discount. If not, the customer does not receive a discount.

Open Proj0807 and save it as **`Billing`**. Activate cell E4 and enter the following function:

```
=IF(D4-A4<=10,-C4*.02,0)
```

Copy this function down the column. Next, you need to calculate the amount due. Activate cell F4 and enter the formula **`=C4+E4`**. Copy this formula down the column. Save the workbook and leave it open for the following exercise.

4. Using Conditional Statements to Determine Discounts and Penalties

You now want to determine if customers are entitled to a discount or if they owe a penalty for paying a bill past 30 days.

Select cell E4 in the Billings worksheet and double-click the cell to edit the function so that it reads as follows:

```
=IF(D4-A4<=10,-C4*.02,IF(D4-A4>30,C4*.015,0))
```

This complex formula now determines if the bill was paid within 10 days, the company gets a 2% discount, if the bill was paid in more than 30 days, the company is charged 1.5%, if the payment does not meet either condition, a 0 is entered into the cell.

Copy the formula down the column.

Next, you need to determine the balance owed for each company. In cell H4, enter the formula `=F4-G4`. Copy this formula down the column. Save the file again and print a copy. Close the workbook when you have finished.

5. Using a Function to Determine Minumum Balance

You have decided that you no longer want to pay your bank service fees. You use an Excel function to identify when your checking account goes below the minimum balance.

Open Proj0808 and save it as **Checking Account 4**. In cell G4, type **Below Min?** Add a function to cell G5 to determine if the balance is below the minimum of $500. If the balance is below $500, you want to enter **Yes** into the cell. If it is not below $500, **No** should be entered into the cell. Copy the function down the column. Save the file again and print two copies. Close the file when you have finished.

Project 9

Improving the Appearance of a Worksheet

Formatting a Budget

In this project, you learn how to:

- Use Fonts and Their Attributes
- Change Column Width
- Align Text and Numbers
- Format Numbers
- Add Borders and Shading
- Use Conditional Formatting
- Use the AutoFormat Feature
- Use the Spelling Checker

Why Would I Do This?

Having completed the first three projects of the Excel portion of Micorosoft Office Professional 97, you now know how to build your own Excel worksheet. The budget worksheets you have created contain formulas and functions that provide you with useful information about your expenses.

Formatting
Applying attributes to text and data to change the appearance of a worksheet or to call attention to certain information.

After you create a basic worksheet, however, you may want to improve its appearance by *formatting* it so that it is more readable and attractive. In this project, you learn how to improve the appearance of worksheets by using many of Excel's formatting features. You also learn how to check for spelling errors in a worksheet.

Lesson 1: Using Fonts and Their Attributes

Font
The typeface, type size, and type attributes of text or numbers.

You can dramatically improve the appearance of your worksheet by using different fonts. A *font* is the typeface, type size, and type attributes that you apply to text and numbers. Office 97 and Windows 95 supply a variety of typefaces and sizes that you can use.

In this lesson, you use toolbar buttons and the Font dialog box to format with fonts and font attributes. Toolbar buttons let you quickly apply a single formatting characteristic, such as a different font, while the dialog box enables you to preview and apply many formatting characteristics at one time. Try using some different fonts and type attributes in a worksheet now.

To Use Fonts and Font Attributes

1. **Open the Proj0901 worksheet and save it as Expenses.**

2. **Select cells B3 through H3 in the Expenses worksheet.**

   This selects the column headings in the Expenses worksheet—the first text you want to change. In Excel, you can change the formatting of a single selected cell or a range of selected cells.

3. **Choose Format, Cells.**

   Excel displays the Format Cells dialog box, in which you can change a number of formatting settings for the selected cells.

4. **Click the Font tab.**

   The Font options appear, as shown in Figure 9.1.

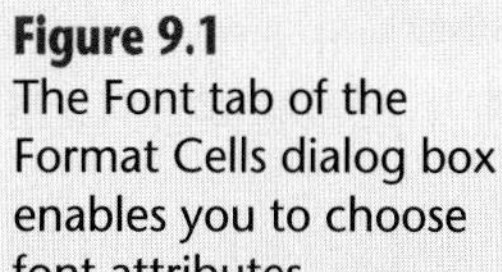

Figure 9.1
The Font tab of the Format Cells dialog box enables you to choose font attributes.

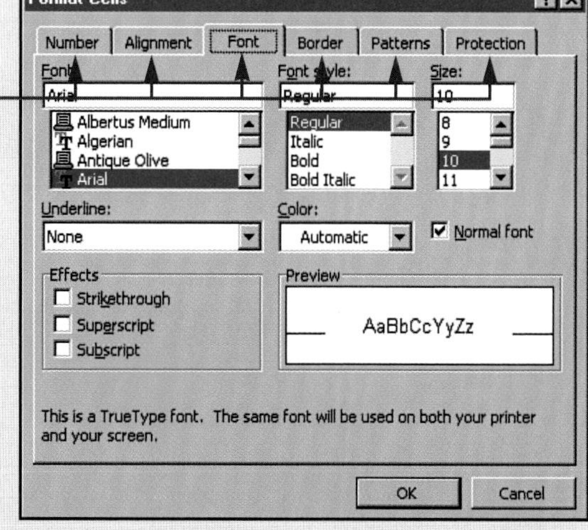

Click a tab to display other formatting options.

❺ In the Font list box, select Times New Roman.

This selects the typeface you want to apply to the selected cells in this example. You may have to use the scroll arrows to scroll down through the list of fonts to get to Times New Roman. Excel displays a sample of the typeface in the Preview box.

❻ In the Size list box, select 12.

Point
A unit of measurement used in printing and publishing to designate the height of type. There are roughly 72 points in an inch.

Again, you may need to scroll down the list to find 12. The numbers in the Size list refer to *point* size, which is the unit of measurement of font characters. The default type size is 10 points, so changing the size to 12 increases the size of the type. Excel shows how the new type will look in the Preview box.

❼ In the Font style box, select Bold.

The text in the Preview box now appears bold.

❽ Choose OK.

The dialog box closes, and all the formatting changes are applied to the selected cells. All the month headings now appear in the new font and font attributes. Deselect the cells to get a better look at the formatting, as shown in Figure 9.2. Notice that the row height automatically adjusts to accommodate the new type size, although the column widths do not.

Next, format the worksheet's title—Expenses—so that it is obviously the main title. In the following steps, you use the Formatting toolbar's buttons to apply fonts and their attributes.

continues

To Use Fonts and Font Attributes (continued)

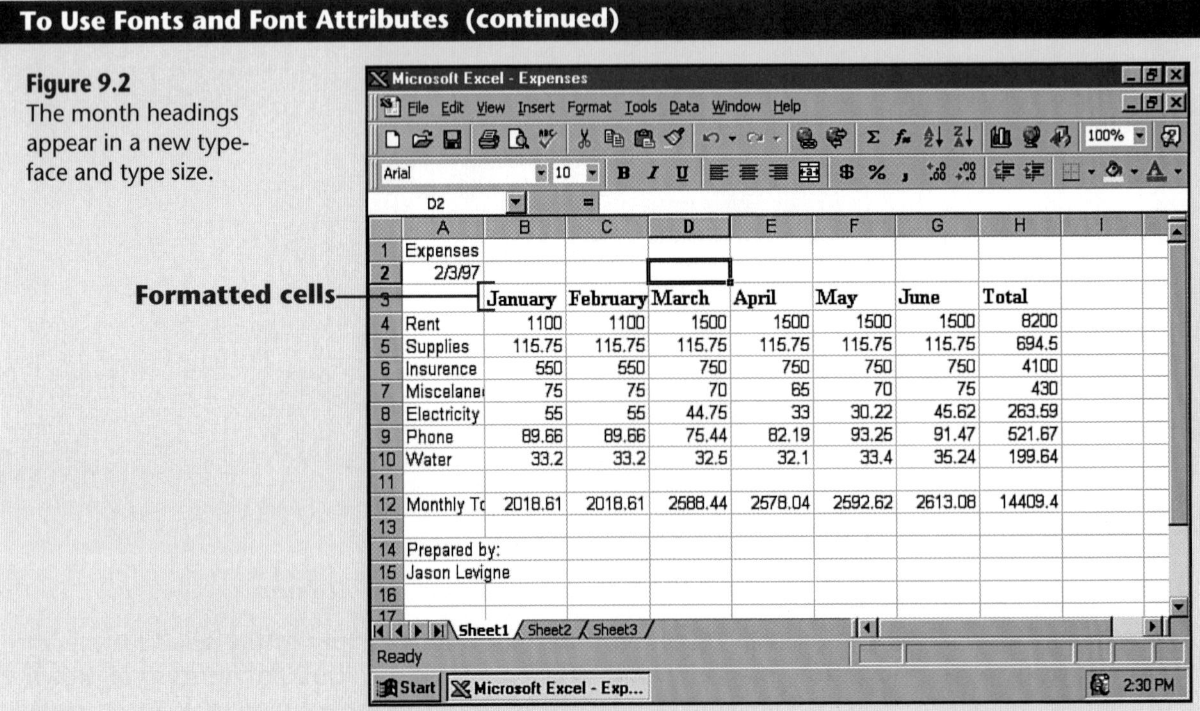

Figure 9.2
The month headings appear in a new typeface and type size.

9 Select cell A1, then click the Font drop-down arrow on the Formatting toolbar.

A list of fonts appears, as shown in Figure 9.3.

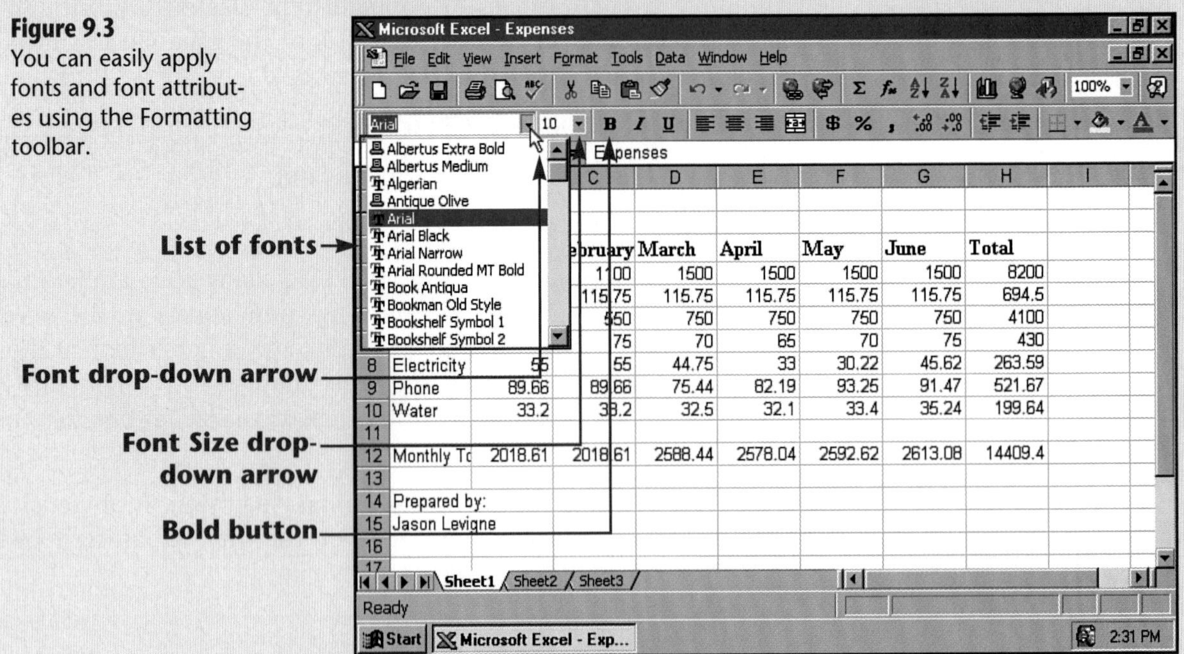

Figure 9.3
You can easily apply fonts and font attributes using the Formatting toolbar.

10 Select Times New Roman from the list.

Excel changes the font in the selected cell.

11 Click the Font size drop-down arrow on the Formatting toolbar and select 18.

Excel increases the font size in the selected cell.

B

12 Click the Bold button on the Formatting toolbar.

Excel applies the bold attribute to the selected cell.

When you have formatted a cell the way you like, you can use the Format Painter button to copy that formatting to one or more other cells. This tool is extremely handy because it enables you to format cells quickly without opening dialog boxes or making multiple selections from toolbars. Next, use the Format Painter button to copy the type style used for the column headings to the expense labels in column A.

13 Select cell B3, then click the Format Painter button on the Standard toolbar.

A flashing dotted line appears around cell B3, and the Format Painter button appears pressed in. Note that you only need to select one cell to copy formatting. Just choose one of the cells that already contains the desired formatting, then click the Format Painter.

14 Select cells A4 to A12, then release the mouse button.

When you release the mouse button, the formatting from cell B3 is applied to the range you selected. When you deselect the range, your worksheet should look similar to the one shown in Figure 9.4.

Microsoft Excel - Expenses

File Edit View Insert Format Tools Data Window Help

Arial 10 B I U 100%

C2 =

	A	B	C	D	E	F	G	H	I
1	Expenses								
2	2/3/97								
3		January	February	March	April	May	June	Total	
4	Rent	1100	1100	1500	1500	1500	1500	8200	
5	Supplies	115.75	115.75	115.75	115.75	115.75	115.75	694.5	
6	Insurenc	550	550	750	750	750	750	4100	
7	Miscelan	75	75	70	65	70	75	430	
8	Electricit	55	55	44.75	33	30.22	45.62	263.59	
9	Phone	89.66	89.66	75.44	82.19	93.25	91.47	521.67	
10	Water	33.2	33.2	32.5	32.1	33.4	35.24	199.64	
11									
12	Monthly	2018.61	2018.61	2588.44	2578.04	2592.62	2613.08	14409.4	
13									
14	Prepared by:								

Sheet1 / Sheet2 / Sheet3 /

Ready

Start Microsoft Excel - Exp... 2:33 PM

Figure 9.4
Fonts and their attributes can be applied to a range of cells, using the Format Painter button.

Save your work and leave the Expenses workbook open for the next lesson, where you learn how to change the widths of columns in your worksheet.

In Excel, you can use the buttons on the Formatting toolbar to italicize and underline characters as well as apply boldface. To change attributes, simply select the cells that you want to format, then click the relevant button on the formatting toolbar, or use the following keyboard shortcuts: Bold is Ctrl+B, italic is Ctrl+I, and underline is Ctrl+U. To remove an attribute, click its button again.

To quickly open the Format Cells dialog box, press Ctrl+1, or right-click the active cell and choose Format Cells from the shortcut menu.

To quickly scroll through the Font drop-down list, start typing the name of the font you want to apply. Excel locates the fonts alphabetically.

Lesson 2: Changing Column Width

As you may have noticed, several of the column and row labels of the Expenses worksheet don't fit in the default column width. Although row heights adjust automatically when you change fonts, column widths do not. As a result, data entered in one column may be hidden by the data in the column to its right. To make your information fit, you can increase or decrease column widths; you can also change row height, if necessary.

To Change Column Width

1 In the Expenses worksheet frame, move the mouse pointer to the line to the right of column letter A.

The mouse pointer changes to a double-headed black arrow, as shown in Figure 9.5. Column A is the first column you want to change. Notice that several of the expense labels in column A are covered by information in column B. Notice also that when there is no data in column B, Excel simply extends the data in column A across the cell border.

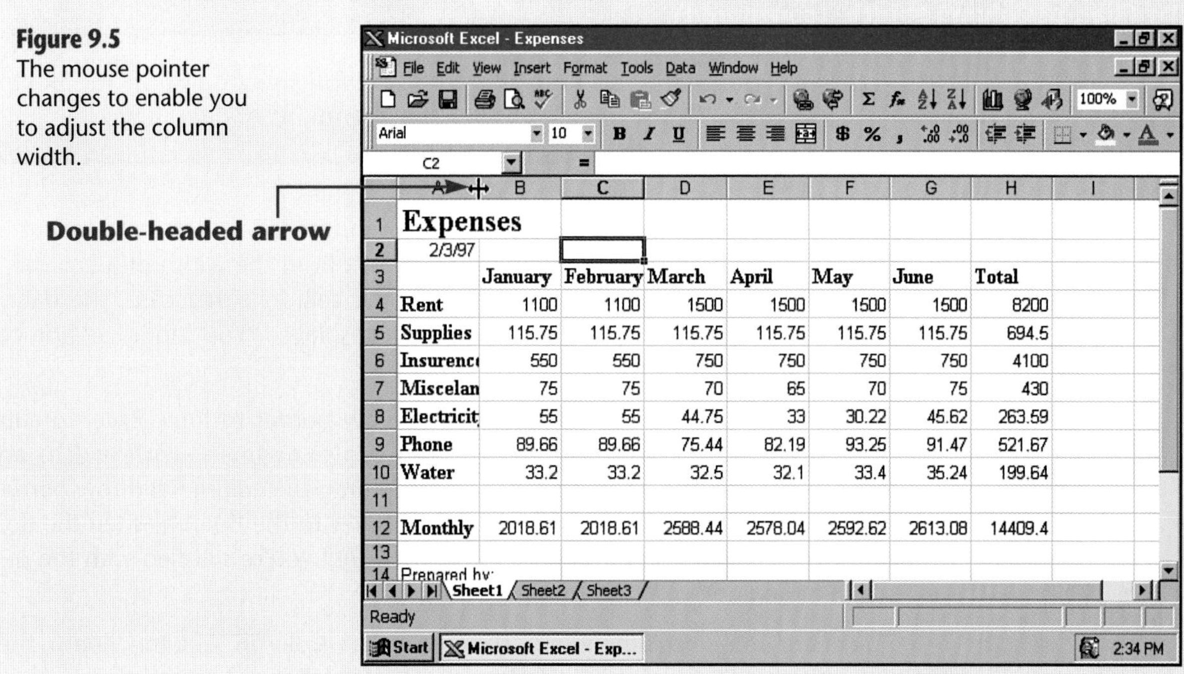

	A	B	C	D	E	F	G	H
1	Expenses							
2	2/3/97							
3		January	February	March	April	May	June	Total
4	Rent	1100	1100	1500	1500	1500	1500	8200
5	Supplies	115.75	115.75	115.75	115.75	115.75	115.75	694.5
6	Insurenc	550	550	750	750	750	750	4100
7	Miscelan	75	75	70	65	70	75	430
8	Electricit	55	55	44.75	33	30.22	45.62	263.59
9	Phone	89.66	89.66	75.44	82.19	93.25	91.47	521.67
10	Water	33.2	33.2	32.5	32.1	33.4	35.24	199.64
11								
12	Monthly	2018.61	2018.61	2588.44	2578.04	2592.62	2613.08	14409.4
13								
14	Prepared by:							

Figure 9.5 The mouse pointer changes to enable you to adjust the column width.

2 Double-click the left mouse button.

When you double-click the column border between column letters A and B, the width of column A automatically adjusts to fit the longest entry. Now adjust the widths of columns B and C.

3 Double-click the column border to the right of column B, then double-click the column border to the right of column C.

These actions adjust the widths of columns B and C to fit the longest entry. Your worksheet should now look like Figure 9.6.

Figure 9.6 The adjusted column width fits the longest entry in the column.

	A	B	C	D	E	F	G	H
1	Expenses							
2	2/3/97							
3		January	February	March	April	May	June	Total
4	Rent	1100	1100	1500	1500	1500	1500	8200
5	Supplies	115.75	115.75	115.75	115.75	115.75	115.75	694.5
6	Insurence	550	550	750	750	750	750	4100
7	Miscelaneous	75	75	70	65	70	75	430
8	Electricity	55	55	44.75	33	30.22	45.62	263.59
9	Phone	89.66	89.66	75.44	82.19	93.25	91.47	521.67
10	Water	33.2	33.2	32.5	32.1	33.4	35.24	199.64
11								
12	Monthly Total	2018.61	2018.61	2588.44	2578.04	2592.62	2613.08	14409.4
13								
14	Prepared by:							

continues

To Change Column Width (continued)

Save your work and keep the Expenses worksheet open. In the next lesson, you learn how to change the alignment of data in a cell.

When text doesn't fit in the width of a column, the label appears to be cut off or hidden by the next cell. If a number doesn't fit in the width of a column, a series of pound signs (######) appears in the cell. In either case, the data is stored in the worksheet; it just might not be displayed. You can adjust the column width to display the entire cell contents.

Rather than double-clicking the column or row border to force Excel to automatically reset the width or height, you can experiment with widths and heights by using the double-arrow pointer to drag the column and row borders in the worksheet frame. Move the mouse pointer to the border; when the double arrow appears, click and drag the border until you're satisfied with the new width or height.

To enter a precise column width, choose F**o**rmat, **C**olumn, Column **W**idth, then enter the width (in number of characters) in the **C**olumn Width text box and choose OK. To enter a precise row height, choose F**o**rmat, **R**ow, Row H**e**ight, then enter the height (in points) in the Row Height text box and choose OK. The default row height is 12.75 points.

If you want to reset the column width to the original setting, choose F**o**rmat, **C**olumn, **S**tandard Width; make sure that **8.43** is entered in the Standard Column Width box, and then choose OK.

To undo the most recent formatting changes, click the Undo button, or choose **E**dit, **U**ndo.

You can select several cells, columns, or rows simultaneously to apply any formatting changes to all the selected parts of the worksheet.

Lesson 3: Aligning Text and Numbers

When you enter information into a cell, text aligns with the left side of the cell, and numbers, dates, and times automatically align with the right side of the cell. You can change the alignment of information at any time. For instance, you may want to fine-tune the appearance of column headings by centering all the information in the column. You can also align data across several columns in one step, wrap data onto multiple lines, and rotate text within the cell.

To Align Text and Numbers

1 Select cells A1 through H1 in the Expenses worksheet.

You want this title centered over the width of the worksheet.

2 Click the Merge and Center button on the Formatting toolbar.

Excel merges the selected cells into one cell, and centers the text across the width of the worksheet. Even though the worksheet title is centered across the worksheet, it is still located in cell A1. If you want to select the text for further formatting or editing, you must select cell A1. Now, try aligning the column labels.

3 Select cells B3 through H3.

This selects all the cells you want to align. Notice that the column labels are left-aligned. You can improve the appearance of the worksheet by centering the data in the selected cells.

4 Click the Center button on the Formatting toolbar.

Excel centers the data in each cell, as shown in Figure 9.7. However, the column labels might look even better if the text appeared vertical or at an angle in the cells. Try rotating the text now.

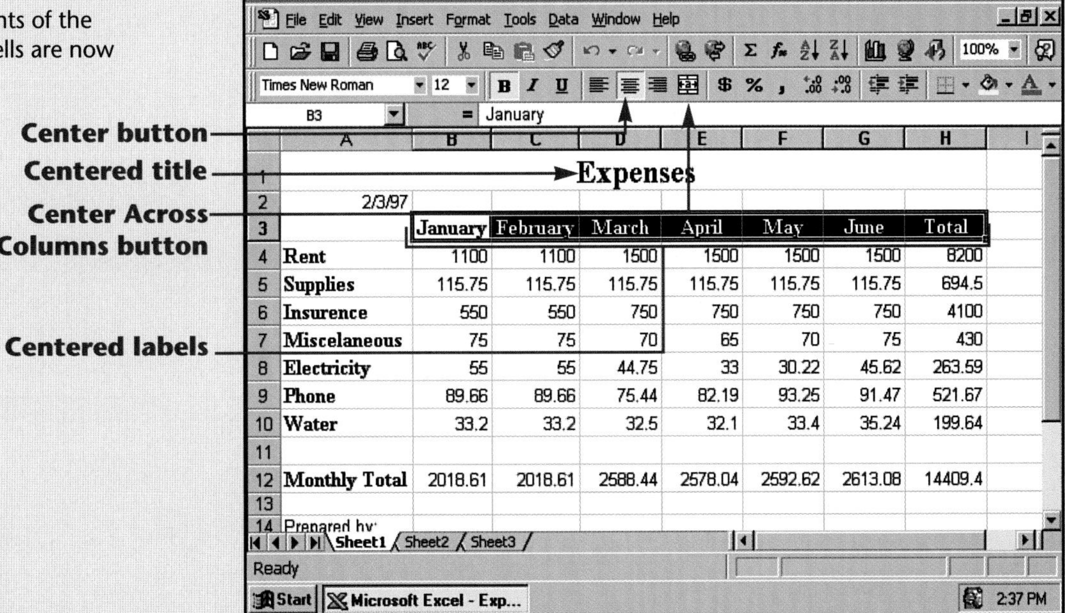

Figure 9.7
The contents of the selected cells are now centered.

5 Right-click anywhere along the selected range of cells, and choose Format Cells from the shortcut menu.

The Format Cells dialog box is displayed.

6 Click the Alignment tab.

The Alignment options are displayed, as shown in Figure 9.8.

continues

To Align Text and Numbers (continued)

Figure 9.8
The Alignment tab of the Format Cells dialog box enables you to choose from a variety of text-alignment options.

Click here to rotate the text vertically

Enter the degrees of rotation here

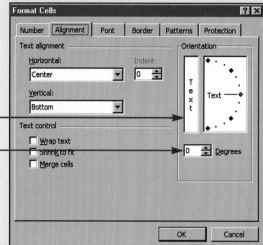

❼ **In the Orientation area, type** `45` **in the Degrees text box.**

This tells Excel to rotate the text in the selected cells 45 degrees up. To rotate the text down, enter a negative number.

❽ **Choose OK.**

Excel rotates the text. Deselect the cells so you can see the formatting clearly. Your worksheet should look similar to the one in Figure 9.9.

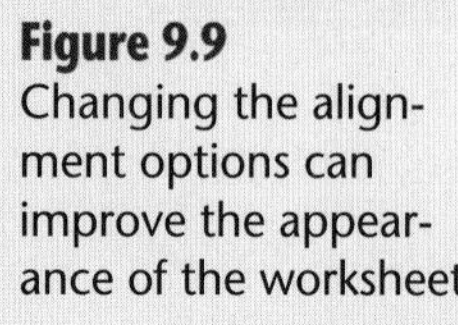

Figure 9.9
Changing the alignment options can improve the appearance of the worksheet.

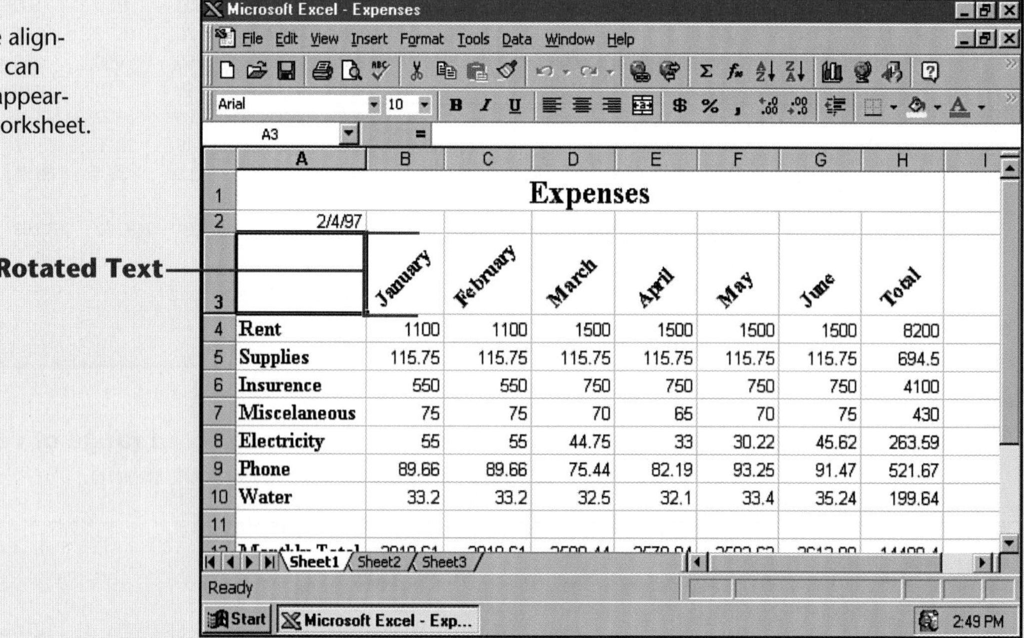

	A	B	C	D	E	F	G	H
3		January	February	March	April	May	June	Total
4	Rent	1100	1100	1500	1500	1500	1500	8200
5	Supplies	115.75	115.75	115.75	115.75	115.75	115.75	694.5
6	Insurence	550	550	750	750	750	750	4100
7	Miscelaneous	75	75	70	65	70	75	430
8	Electricity	55	55	44.75	33	30.22	45.62	263.59
9	Phone	89.66	89.66	75.44	82.19	93.25	91.47	521.67
10	Water	33.2	33.2	32.5	32.1	33.4	35.24	199.64

Save your work and keep `Expenses` open for the next lesson, where you learn how to apply different number formats to cells.

If you want text to appear vertically—one character above the next—click the Vertical orientation box on the Alignment page of the Format Cells dialog box.

On the Alignment page of the Format Cells dialog box, you can also select a **W**rap Text option, a Shrin**k** to Fit option, and a Merge cells options. Choose **W**rap Text when you want to enter more than one line of text within a cell. As you type, the text automatically wraps to the next line in the cell. Choose Shrin**k** to Fit when you want to reduce the appearance of the data so it fits within the displayed column width. Choose **M**erge Cells when you want to combine two or more selected adjacent cells into one larger cell.

If you want to indent characters from the left edge of the cell, select Left alignment, then enter an increment in the **I**ndent text box on the Alignment page of the Format Cells dialog box. Each increment you enter in the text box is equal to the width of one character.

Lesson 4: Formatting Numbers

When you enter a number or a formula into a cell, the entry may not appear as you hoped it would. You might type `5`, for example, but want it to look like `$5.00`. You could type the dollar sign, decimal point, and zeros, or you can have Excel automatically format the number for you. When you want to apply a standard format to a number, you format the cell in which the number is displayed.

In Excel, you can format numbers in many ways. You will usually format numbers as currency, percentages, dates, or times of day. Remember that when you apply any kind of formatting, you apply it to the worksheet cell, not to the information itself. This means that if you change the information, the formatting still applies. You can even format empty cells so that when data is entered, it automatically appears with the correct format.

To Format Numbers

1. **Select cells B4 through H12 in the `Expenses` worksheet.**

   You want to format these cells as currency.

2. **Click the Currency Style button on the Formatting toolbar.**

   $

   This changes the selected cells to display the default currency format, as shown in Figure 9.10. Note that the blank cells within the selection are formatted as well, even though the formatting doesn't show; if you enter data in those cells, it will appear in the currency style.

continues

To Format Numbers (continued)

Figure 9.10
You can quickly select a format for the cells by using the Formatting toolbar's buttons.

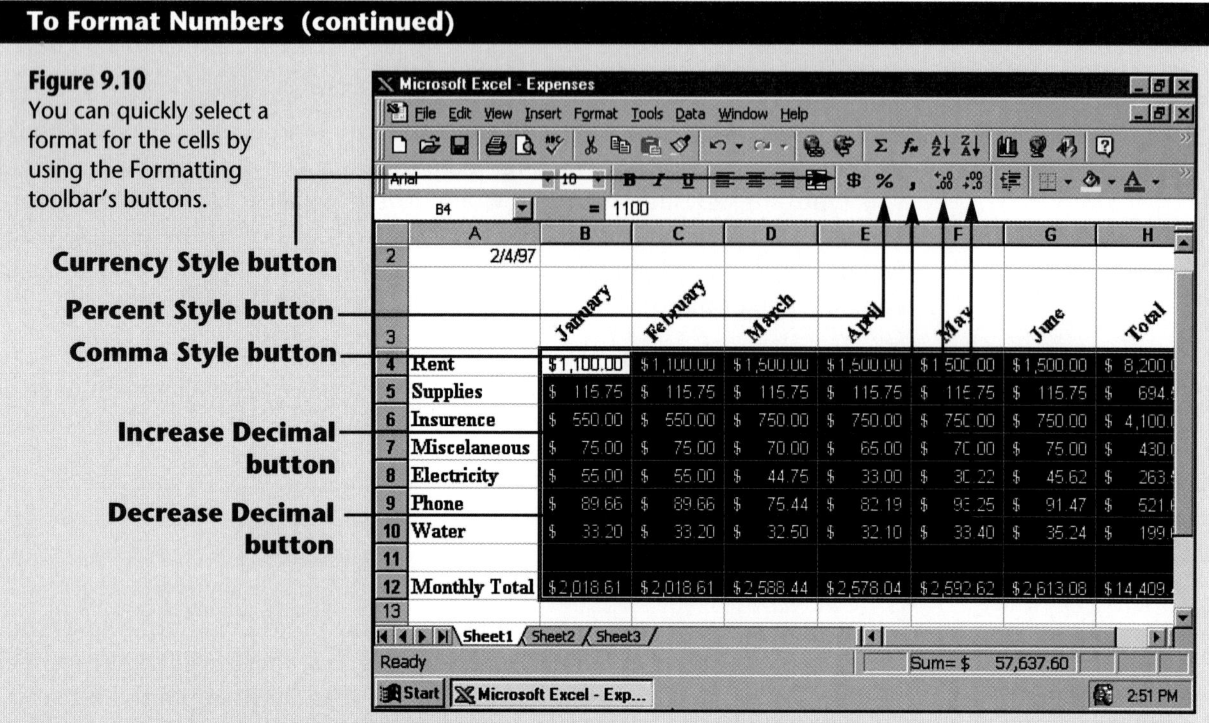

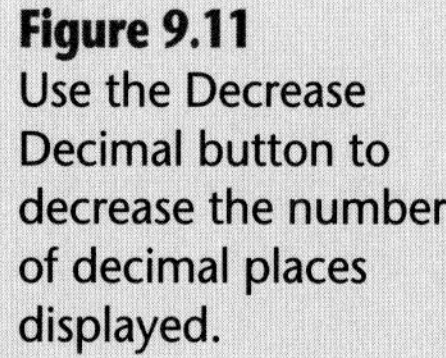

❸ With cells B4:H12 still selected, click the Decrease Decimal button twice.

Each time you click the button, Excel removes one decimal place. Because no decimal places are displayed, Excel rounds the values that are displayed to fit this format. However, the actual values will be used in any calculations. You can adjust column widths again to fit the worksheet within the document window (see Figure 9.11).

Now, change the way the date is displayed in the worksheet.

Figure 9.11
Use the Decrease Decimal button to decrease the number of decimal places displayed.

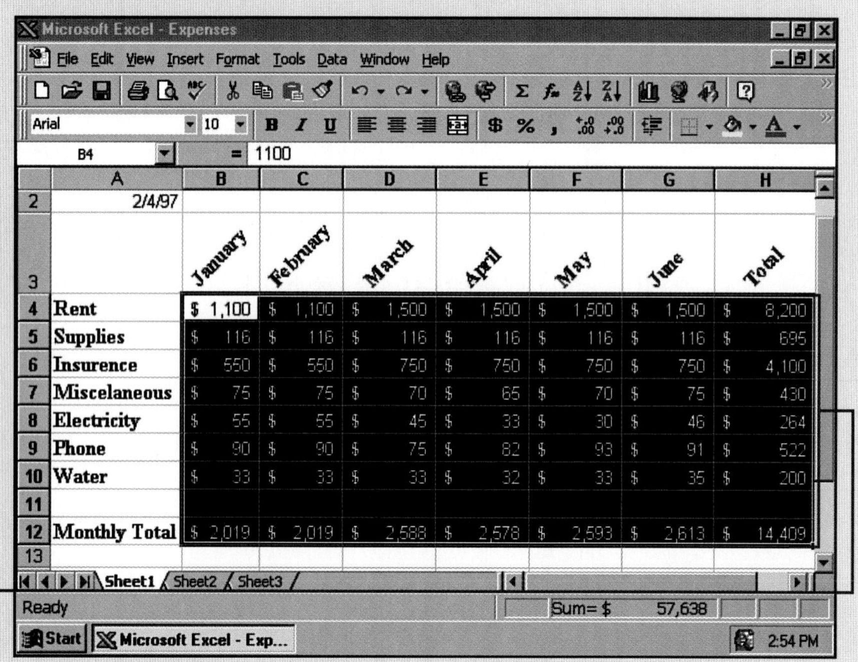

Rounded numbers with zero decimal places

4 Move the mouse pointer to cell A2, click the right mouse button, and choose Format Cells from the shortcut menu.

Excel opens the Format Cells dialog box.

5 Click the Number tab in the Format Cells dialog box.

Excel displays the Number options (see Figure 9.12). Since the selected cell contains a date, the Date category is already selected. You can choose the general type of formatting you want from the **C**ategory list, then select the specific format from the **T**ype list.

6 Select the 4-Mar-97 format from the Type list box.

Notice that the Sample line shows the date in cell A2 in the format you selected.

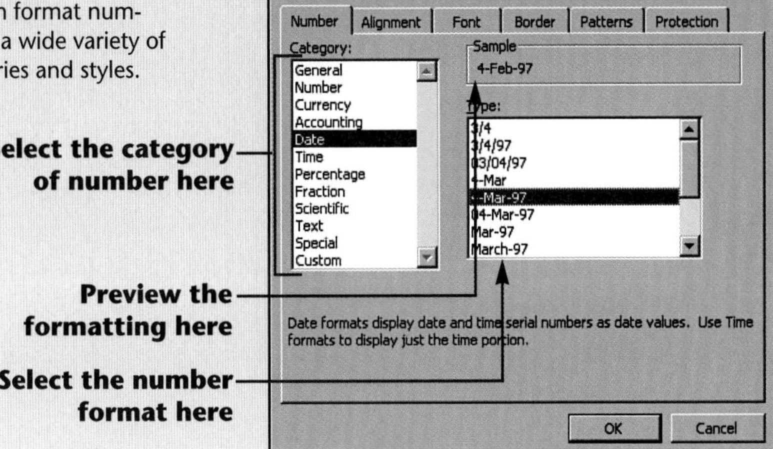

Figure 9.12
You can format numbers in a wide variety of categories and styles.

7 Choose OK.

Excel displays the date in the new format. Save your changes to the Expenses worksheet and leave it open to use in the next lesson.

Lesson 5: Adding Borders and Patterns

To call attention to specific cells in a worksheet, you can enhance them with formatting. You can make them stand out by changing the font or font attributes of the numbers, as you learned in Lesson 1, or you can change the appearance of the cell itself.

You can add patterns to a cell or range of cells to emphasize important information. For example, you may want to call attention to the highest sales for a month and the grand total. In addition, when you print a worksheet, the grid between columns and rows does not appear. If you want to include lines between cells, you must add borders.

To Add Borders and Patterns

1 Select cell G12 in the Expenses worksheet.

The monthly expenses for June are the highest in the worksheet. In this example, you decide to emphasize this cell with a pattern and a border.

2 Choose Format, Cells, then click the Patterns tab in the Format cells dialog box.

Excel displays the Patterns options in the Format Cells dialog box, as shown in Figure 9.13.

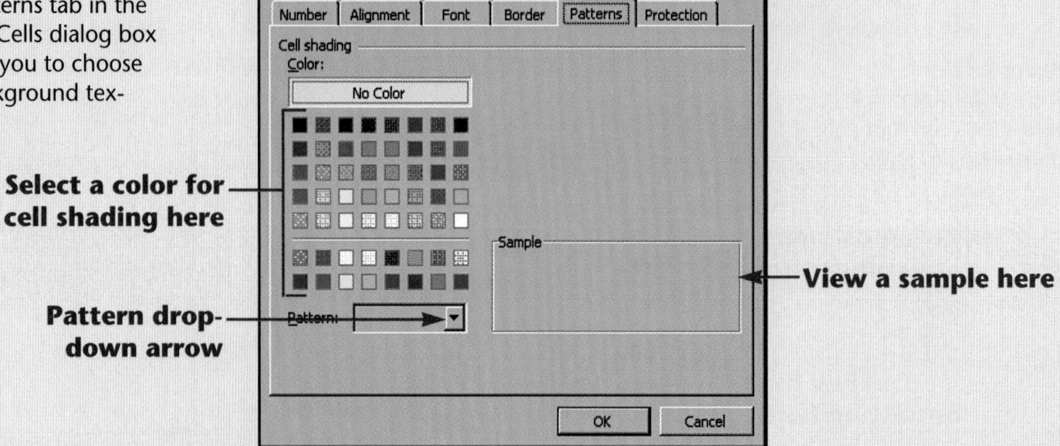

Figure 9.13
The Patterns tab in the Format Cells dialog box enables you to choose cell background textures.

3 Click the Pattern drop-down arrow.

A palette of shading patterns appears, as shown in Figure 9.14. You can choose a color or a geometric pattern, then preview a sample in the Format Cells dialog box.

Figure 9.14
The Pattern palette in the Format Cells dialog box offers a wide variety of patterns and colors.

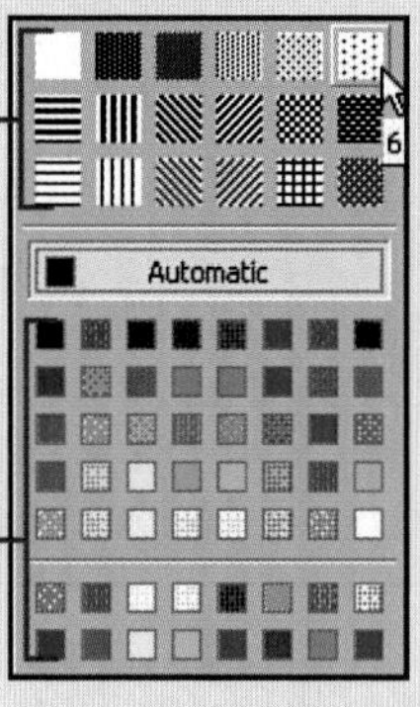

Automatic

Choose a pattern here

Choose a color here

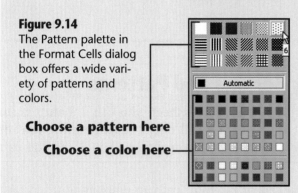

4 Click the 6.25% Gray pattern at the far right in the first row of the palette.

This selects a light, dotted pattern, which is displayed in the sample box. This simple pattern will not obscure data entered in the formatted cell.

5 Choose OK.

This confirms the change. You see the shading in cell G12 on-screen (see Figure 9.15). Next, add a border to outline the cell.

6 Click the Borders drop-down arrow on the Formatting toolbar.

A palette of border options is displayed, as shown in Figure 9.15.

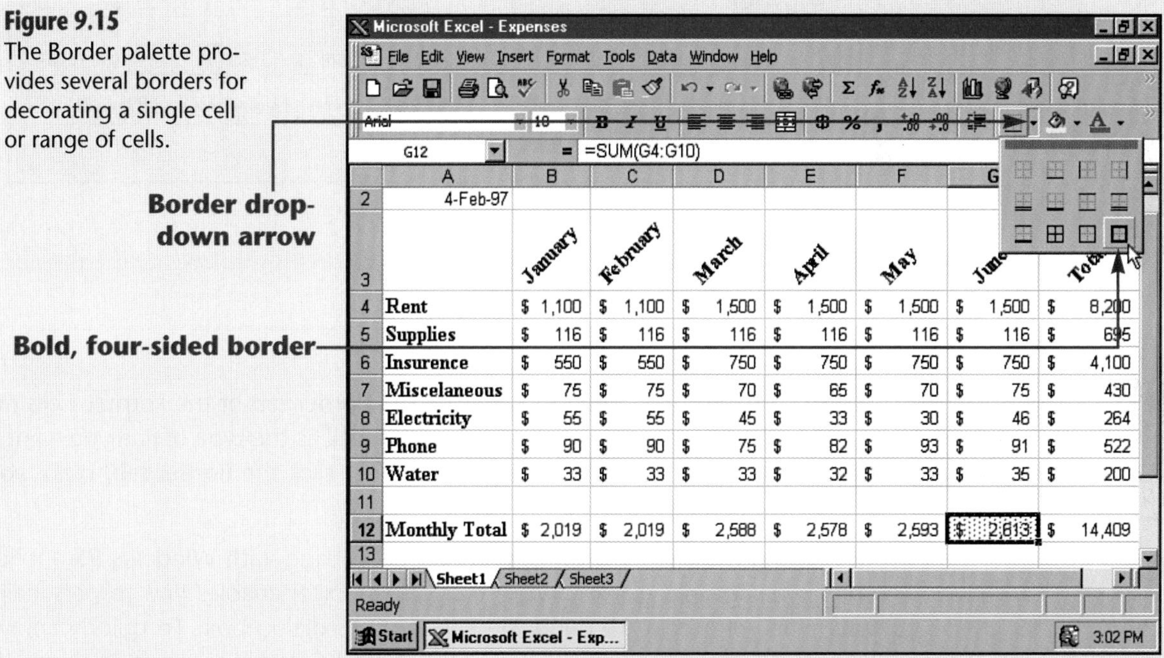

Figure 9.15
The Border palette provides several borders for decorating a single cell or range of cells.

7 Click the bold, four-sided border on the bottom row.

Excel applies the border to the selected cell. Deselect the cell to get a good look at the formatting. Your worksheet should now look like the one shown in Figure 9.16.

continues

To Add Borders and Patterns (continued)

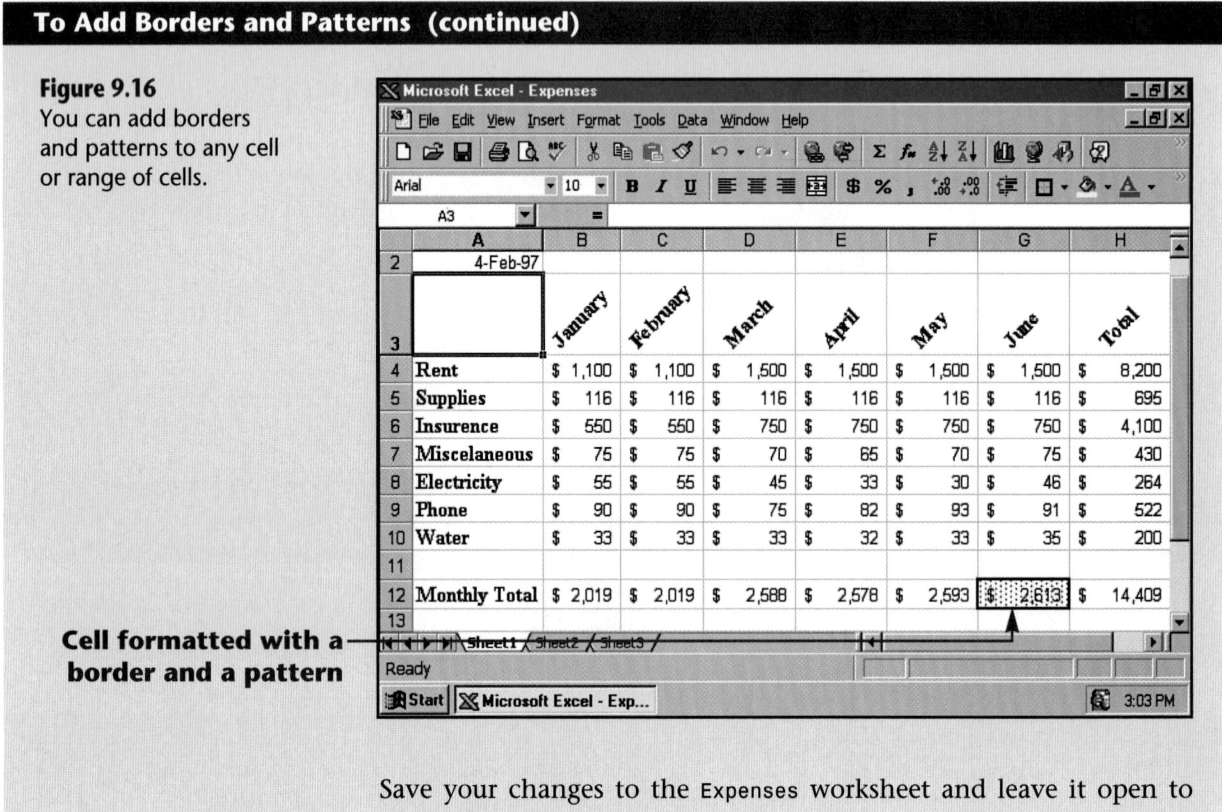

	A	B	C	D	E	F	G	H
2	4-Feb-97							
3		January	February	March	April	May	June	Total
4	Rent	$ 1,100	$ 1,100	$ 1,500	$ 1,500	$ 1,500	$ 1,500	$ 8,200
5	Supplies	$ 116	$ 116	$ 116	$ 116	$ 116	$ 116	$ 695
6	Insurence	$ 550	$ 550	$ 750	$ 750	$ 750	$ 750	$ 4,100
7	Miscelaneous	$ 75	$ 75	$ 70	$ 65	$ 70	$ 75	$ 430
8	Electricity	$ 55	$ 55	$ 45	$ 33	$ 30	$ 46	$ 264
9	Phone	$ 90	$ 90	$ 75	$ 82	$ 93	$ 91	$ 522
10	Water	$ 33	$ 33	$ 33	$ 32	$ 33	$ 35	$ 200
11								
12	Monthly Total	$ 2,019	$ 2,019	$ 2,588	$ 2,578	$ 2,593	$ 2,613	$ 14,409
13								

Figure 9.16
You can add borders and patterns to any cell or range of cells.

Save your changes to the Expenses worksheet and leave it open to use in the next lesson.

You can customize borders and lines on the Border tab of the Format Cells dialog box. You can select border placement as well as the type of line you want to use. Simply open the Format Cells dialog box, click the Border tab, make your selections, then choose OK.

One of the most entertaining things about working with Windows 95 applications is being able to use a variety of colors. Excel enables you to personalize your work with color through the Format Cells dialog box. To quickly apply a color to fill a selected cell or range, click the Fill Color drop-down arrow on the Formatting toolbar, and select a color from the palette. To quickly apply a color to the data in a selected cell or range, click the Font color drop-down arrow on the Formatting toolbar, and select a color from the palette.

Unfortunately, colored letters on a colored background may be clear and attractive on-screen, but hard to read in printed form. Keep in mind that you need to be connected to a color printer to be able to print color worksheets. Without a color printer, colors may turn out to be muddy gray on paper, and all but the simplest patterns can make information on the worksheet hard to read.

Have fun experimenting with the colors and patterns in the Format Cells dialog box, but keep the formatting simple on worksheets that you need to print.

Lesson 6: Using Conditional Formatting

Using formats to emphasize cells in a worksheet can call attention to specific data. When you format a cell, however, the formatting remains in effect even if the data changes. If you want to accent a cell depending on the value of the cell, you can use *conditional formatting.*

Like the conditional statements you used in formulas in Project 8, "Calculating with Functions," conditional formats return a result based on whether or not the value in the cell meets a specified criteria. For example, in a worksheet tracking monthly sales, you may want to accent a monthly total only if it is less than the previous month's total or if it is greater than the target sales figure you have set.

To Use Conditional Formatting

1 In the Expenses worksheet, select cells B9 to G9.

This selects the row containing phone expenses. For this example, you want to emphasize any monthly phone expenses that exceed $90.

2 Choose Format, Conditional Formatting.

The Conditional Formatting dialog box appears, as shown in Figure 9.17.

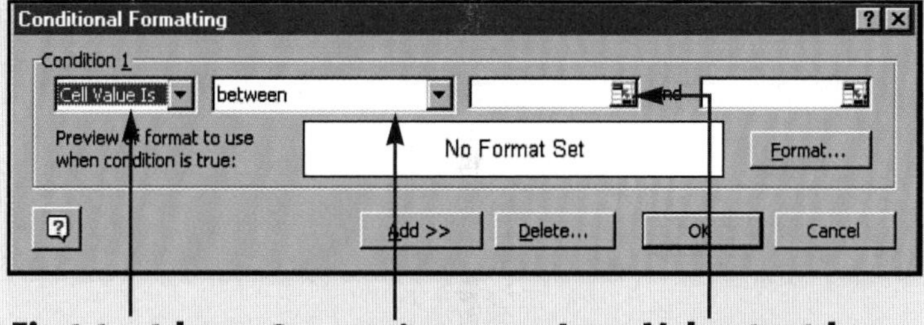

Figure 9.17
The Conditional Formatting dialog box enables you to format a cell based on the value in the cell.

If you have problems...

If the Office Assistant opens, click the No, Don't Provide Help Now button to close it and continue.

3 Make sure Cell Value appears in the first text box, then press Tab.

This tells Excel that the condition you are going to specify depends on the constant value entered in the selected cells, then moves the insertion point to the comparison text box. You can also choose to use the value of the formula in the selected cells.

continues

To Use Conditional Formatting (continued)

4 From the comparison drop-down list (the second drop-down list in the dialog box), select greater than, then press Tab.

This identifies the type of comparison you want to use, and moves the insertion point to the value text box.

5 In the value text box, type 90.

The conditional statement now tells Excel that if the cell value is greater then 90, it should apply the specified formatting. Now, set the formatting.

6 Click the Format button.

The Format Cells dialog box is displayed. You can set font style, color, underline, and strikethrough on the Font page, and you can choose border and patterns formatting as well.

7 Click Bold in the Font style list, click the Color drop-down arrow, click the red square in the color palette, then choose OK.

This tells Excel to format the data in the cell in red bold type if the condition is met. In this case, if the monthly phone expense is more than $90, it appears in red. In the Conditional Formatting dialog box, you see a sample of the formatting, as shown in Figure 9.18.

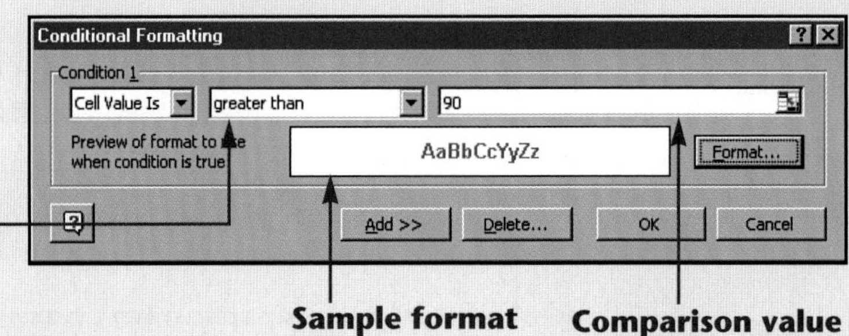

Figure 9.18
The conditional statement determines whether a cell is formatted or not.

8 Choose OK.

Excel applies the formatting to any of the selected cells that meet the specified criteria, in this case, cells F9 and G9. Deselect the cells so you can get a better look at the result. Your worksheet should look similar to the one in Figure 9.19.

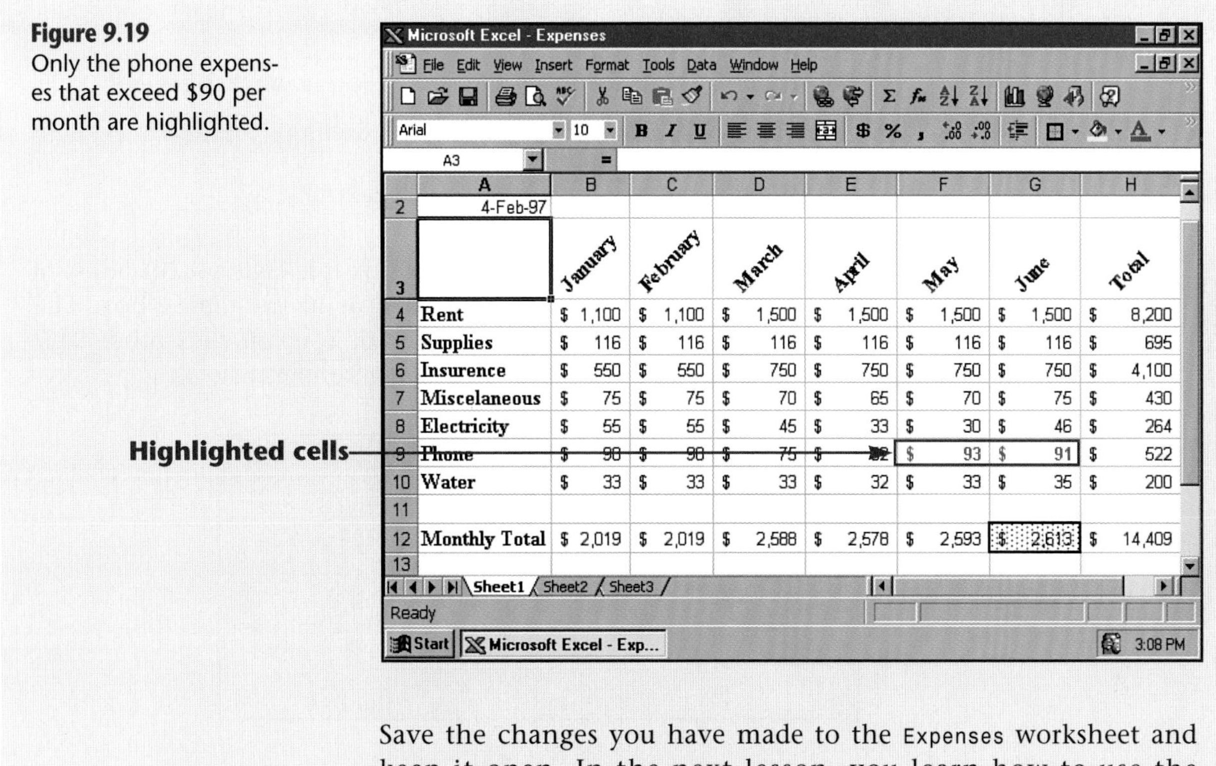

	A	B	C	D	E	F	G	H
2	4-Feb-97							
3		January	February	March	April	May	June	Total
4	Rent	$ 1,100	$ 1,100	$ 1,500	$ 1,500	$ 1,500	$ 1,500	$ 8,200
5	Supplies	$ 116	$ 116	$ 116	$ 116	$ 116	$ 116	$ 695
6	Insurence	$ 550	$ 550	$ 750	$ 750	$ 750	$ 750	$ 4,100
7	Miscelaneous	$ 75	$ 75	$ 70	$ 65	$ 70	$ 75	$ 430
8	Electricity	$ 55	$ 55	$ 45	$ 33	$ 30	$ 46	$ 264
9	Phone	$ 98	$ 98	$ 75	$ [illegible]	$ 93	$ 91	$ 522
10	Water	$ 33	$ 33	$ 33	$ 32	$ 33	$ 35	$ 200
11								
12	Monthly Total	$ 2,019	$ 2,019	$ 2,588	$ 2,578	$ 2,593	$ 2,613	$ 14,409

Figure 9.19
Only the phone expenses that exceed $90 per month are highlighted.

Save the changes you have made to the Expenses worksheet and keep it open. In the next lesson, you learn how to use the AutoFormat feature.

You can set up to three conditions that must be met in order for the formatting to be applied. Simply click **A**dd in the Conditional Formatting dialog box to display another set of Condition text boxes. Use the **D**elete button to remove one or more conditions.

Lesson 7: Using AutoFormat

If you don't want to spend a lot of time formatting a worksheet, or if you want to rely on someone else's flair for design, you can use Excel's AutoFormat feature. The AutoFormat feature contains several pre-defined table formats that you can apply to selected cells in your worksheet.

Each format contains various alignment, number format, color, and pattern settings to help you create professional-looking worksheets. Generally, you apply one format at a time to a selected cell or range of cells. With a table format, however, you can apply a collection of formats supplied by Excel all at once.

To Use AutoFormat

1 Select cells A1 through H15 in the Expenses **worksheet.**

This highlights the entire worksheet. Now apply a new format to this range.

2 Choose Format, AutoFormat.

Excel displays the AutoFormat dialog box (see Figure 9.20). A list of table formats and a Sample area appear in the dialog box. The Simple table format is currently selected. You can click other table formats to see what they look like in the Sample area.

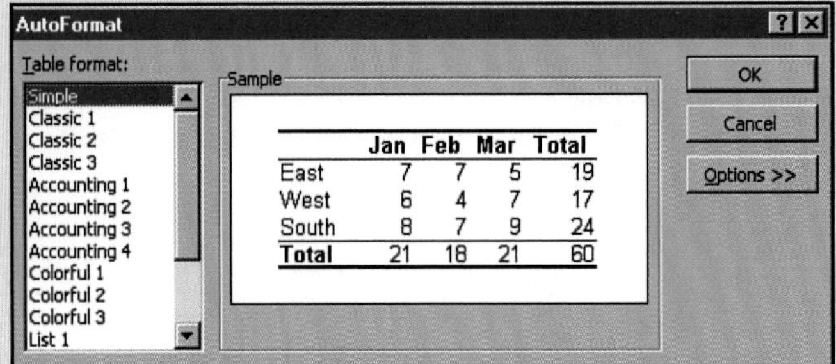

Figure 9.20
The AutoFormat dialog box enables you to format a range of cells by choosing from a list of standard table styles.

3 Scroll down the Table format list box and select the 3D Effects 1 format.

This selects the 3D Effects 1 table format and displays the formatting in the sample area.

4 Choose OK.

Excel changes the selected cells to the new format. Click any cell to deselect the range so that you can see the formatting clearly, as shown in Figure 9.21. Notice that the previous formatting in the Expenses worksheet has been replaced by the new format. Only the conditional formatting is still in effect. If you plan to use the AutoFormat feature, apply AutoFormat before adding other formatting.

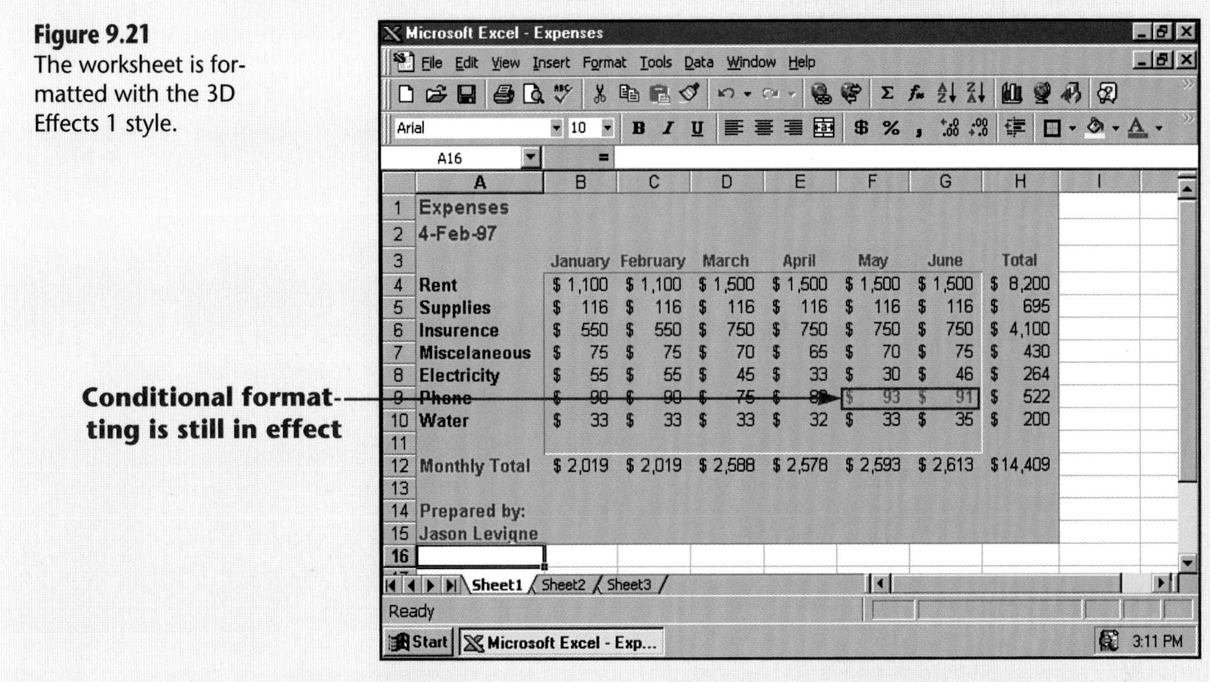

Figure 9.21
The worksheet is formatted with the 3D Effects 1 style.

Save your changes to the `Expenses` worksheet and leave it open for the next lesson, where you learn how to check for spelling errors.

If you have problems...

The table formats in the AutoFormat dialog box can drastically change the appearance of your worksheet. If you don't like the results after closing the AutoFormat dialog box, choose the **E**dit, **U**ndo command before you take any other action. Alternatively, you can continue making formatting changes to the worksheet.

Lesson 8: Checking the Spelling in a Worksheet

When presenting a worksheet, you should make sure that no misspelled words are in the document. You can use the Excel spelling checker feature to rapidly find and highlight any misspelled words in a worksheet.

The spelling checker highlights words that it doesn't recognize—which, in addition to misspelled words, may be proper nouns, abbreviations, technical terms, and so on—that actually are spelled correctly, but aren't in Excel's spelling dictionary. You have the option of correcting or bypassing words that the spelling checker highlights. To personalize the program, you can add proper names, cities, and technical terms to a spelling dictionary file called `CUSTOM.DIC`.

The spelling checker won't alert you to a word that is spelled correctly, but used incorrectly, such as *principle* when you mean *principal.* You still need to be watchful when creating a document, and not rely on the spelling checker to catch every possible mistake.

Table 9.1 describes the common options used in the Spelling dialog box.

Table 9.1 Spelling Button Options

Option	Description
Change **A**ll	Substitutes all occurrences of the questionable word with the word in the Change To text box.
Change	Substitutes only one occurrence of the questionable word with the word in the Change To text box.
I**g**nore All	Ignores all occurrences of the questionable word in a worksheet.
Ignore	Ignores only one occurrence of the questionable word.
Add	Adds the word to the dictionary (`CUSTOM.DIC` file).

To Check the Spelling in a Worksheet

1. **Select cell A1.**

   This makes A1 the current cell so that Excel will begin checking the spelling at the top of the worksheet.

2. **Choose Tools, Spelling.**

   Excel starts to search the worksheet for spelling errors. When it finds a word it doesn't recognize, it stops, highlights the word in the text, and opens the Spelling dialog box in which it offers suggestions for correcting the word.

   In this example, Excel stops on the word `Insurence` and displays the Spelling dialog box. "Insurence" is misspelled, so it does not appear in the spelling dictionary. Excel makes a guess as to what word you really meant to type, and suggests a list of alternative spellings. The correct spelling—`Insurance`—is highlighted at the top of the list. You can select a different alternative, or, if the correct spelling isn't listed, you can type it in the Change **t**o text box.

3 Choose Change.

Excel replaces the incorrect spelling with the correct spelling and continues to check the spelling of the rest of the worksheet. The spelling checker stops at `Miscelaneous`, which is also misspelled, and offers a list of alternatives. The correct spelling is highlighted.

4 Choose Change.

Excel replaces the word and continues checking the spelling. It stops at `Levigne`, which is a proper noun that is not in the main spelling dictionary, but it is spelled correctly. If you think you will include the name in many workbooks, you should add it to the custom dictionary. Then if you use the word in the future, Excel won't stop and highlight it if it is spelled correctly, and will suggest a correction if it is misspelled.

5 Choose Add.

Excel adds the name to the `CUSTOM.DIC` dictionary and moves on. Excel doesn't find any more misspelled words, so it displays the message `The spell check is complete for the entire sheet.`

6 Choose OK.

This confirms that the spelling check is complete. The words `Insurance` and `Miscellaneous` are now spelled correctly in the `Expenses` worksheet, and the name `Levigne` has been added to the `CUSTOM.DIC` dictionary.

Save your work and close the worksheet. If you have completed your session on the computer, exit Excel and Windows 95 before turning off the computer. Otherwise, continue with the "Checking Your Skills" section at the end of this project.

If you have problems...

If the Spelling dialog box doesn't suggest alternatives to a misspelled word, you need to select the Alwa**y**s suggest check box in the Spelling dialog box. Conversely, if you don't want it to suggest alternatives, make sure the Alwa**y**s suggest check box is not selected.

To quickly start the spelling checker, click the Spelling button on the Standard toolbar or press F7.

If you start the spelling checker in the middle of the worksheet, when Excel reaches the end of the worksheet, it asks if you want to continue checking from the beginning. Choose **Y**es to check the spelling from the beginning of the worksheet. Choose **N**o to close the spelling checker.

Excel comes with an AutoCorrect feature that automatically corrects common spelling errors. For example, if you type **adn**, Excel will automatically replace it with `and`. To see the list of words that Excel automatically corrects, choose **T**ools, **A**utoCorrect. To add your own spelling bugaboos to AutoCorrect, enter the incorrect spelling in the **R**eplace text box and the correct spelling in the **W**ith text box, choose **A**dd, then choose OK. Alternatively, when the spelling checker stops on a misspelled word, you can choose AutoCo**r**rect in the Spelling dialog box to add it to the AutoCorrect spelling list.

Project Summary

To	Do This
Change fonts, font sizes, or font attributes	Select the cells to format, and choose F**o**rmat, C**e**lls. Click the Font tab, make selections, and choose OK.
Align data	Select the cells and click the appropriate alignment button on the toolbar or open the Format Cells dialog box. Click the Alignment tab, make selections, and choose OK.
Change column width	Drag the column border to the desired width.
Automatically adjust column width	Double-click the border between columns.
Format numbers as currency	Select the cells and click the Currency button on the toolbar.
Change the format of numbers	Select the cells and choose F**o**rmat, C**e**lls. Click the Numbers tab, select the number type, select the number format, and choose OK.
Add borders to cells	Select the cells and choose F**o**rmat, C**e**lls. Click the Borders tab, select the border location, select the border style, and choose OK.
Add patterns or shading to cells	Select the cells and choose F**o**rmat, C**e**lls. Click the Patterns tab, choose the pattern or shading options, and choose OK.
Apply conditional formatting	Select the cell and choose F**o**rmat, Con**d**itional Formatting. Select the type of comparison, enter the value to compare, click Format, select the formatting, choose OK, then choose OK again.
Automatically format a range	Select the cells and choose F**o**rmat, **A**utoFormat. Select the table format and choose OK.
Check spelling in a worksheet	Click the Spelling Checker button on the toolbar, and follow the prompts.
Copy formatting	Select the formatted cell, click the Format Painter button, and select the cells to format.

Checking Your Skills

True/False

For each of the following, check *T* or *F* to indicate whether the statement is true or false.

__T __F **1.** You can quickly adjust the column width to fit the column contents by right-clicking the line between two columns.

__T __F **2.** AutoFormat overrides conditional formatting already in the worksheet.

__T __F **3.** By default, numbers are right-aligned in a cell.

__T __F **4.** You can add a border to one cell or to a group of cells, but you cannot add shading to more than one cell at a time.

__T __F **5.** You can add the name of the city you live in to the spelling Checker dictionary so that it doesn't question you every time it comes across that name.

__T __F **6.** When you use the Merge and Center button to center a heading, the heading text remains in cell A1.

__T __F **7.** The column width adjusts automatically when you change the type size.

__T __F **8.** When text doesn't fit in the width of the column, a series of pound signs (######) appears in the cell.

__T __F **9.** When you apply formatting, it applies to the worksheet cell, not to the number itself.

__T __F **10.** You should use a lot of different colors for the letters and the background to improve the appearance of your spreadsheets.

Multiple Choice

Circle the letter of the correct answer for each of the following questions.

1. Which of the following options lets you skip a word that Excel identifies as misspelled?

- **a.** **I**gnore
- **b.** **C**hange
- **c.** **A**dd
- **d.** A**l**ternatives

2. Which of the following is *not* a method of adjusting column width?

- **a.** F**o**rmat, **C**olumn, Width command
- **b.** **E**dit, **C**olumn, Width command
- **c.** double-clicking the right column border on the worksheet frame
- **d.** dragging the column border on the worksheet frame

3. Which of the following *cannot* be formatted using the Formatting toolbar?

- **a.** Fonts
- **b.** Type size
- **c.** Column width
- **d.** Numerical formatting

4. How many conditions can you apply to each conditional format?

- **a.** One
- **b.** Two
- **c.** Three
- **d.** Four

5. If pound signs (######) fill a cell, it means which of the following?
   a. The cell is not active.
   b. The formula is impossible.
   c. The column is not wide enough.
   d. You must recalculate the formula.
6. To copy formatting from one cell to another, you use which of the following?
   a. Formatting toolbar
   b. Font dialog box
   c. Format Painter button
   d. shortcut menu
7. What is the keyboard shortcut to bold selected text?
   a. Ctrl + B
   b. Ctrl + O
   c. Ctrl + L
   d. Ctrl + 1
8. When you enter the column width in the Column Width text box, you enter the width in which of the following?
   a. points
   b. number of characters
   c. inches
   d. centimeters
9. To rotate text 90 degrees down, you enter what in the Degrees text box?
   a. 90 d
   b. 90
   c. 90 down
   d. -90
10. You can set up to how many conditions that must be met for formatting to be applied?
    a. three
    b. four
    c. two
    d. five

Completion

In the blank provided, write the correct answer for each of the following statements.

1. ________________ the left mouse button to quickly adjust column width to fit the longest entry.
2. To customize the spelling checker, add words to the ____________.
3. When formatting a number as currency, you can use the ______________ ______________ tool to add decimal places.
4. ______________ height adjusts automatically to accommodate changes in font size.
5. When aligning data in a cell, use __________ numbers to rotate text down.
6. The numbers in the Font Size list box refer to the _____________ size.
7. To enter more than one line of text within a cell, choose the ______________ ______________ option on the Alignment page of the Format Cells dialog box.
8. To accent a cell depending on the value of the cell, use _____________ _____________.
9. To quickly start the spelling check, press the _____________ function key.
10. The _____________ feature automatically corrects common spelling errors.

Matching

In the blank next to each of the following terms or phrases, write the letter of the corresponding term or phrase. (Note that some letters may be used more than once.)

_____ **1.** The typeface, type size, and type attributes of text or numbers

_____ **2.** A unit of measurement used to designate the height of type

_____ **3.** Keyboard shortcut to italicize text

_____ **4.** Keyboard shortcut to underline text

_____ **5.** To set a precise column width, use an option on this menu

_____ **6.** Aligns with the left side of a cell

_____ **7.** Aligns with the right side of a cell

_____ **8.** Centers text across columns

_____ **9.** Centers text in a cell

_____ **10.** You can add words to this spelling dictionary

a. Ctrl+I

b. Center button

c. Format

d. Merge and Center button

e. numbers

f. custom

g. font

h. Ctrl+U

i. point

j. text

Screen ID

Label each element of the Excel screen shown in Figure 9.22.

Figure 9.22

1. _______________

2. _______________

3. _______________

4. _______________

5. _______________

6. _______________

7. _______________

8. _______________

9. _______________

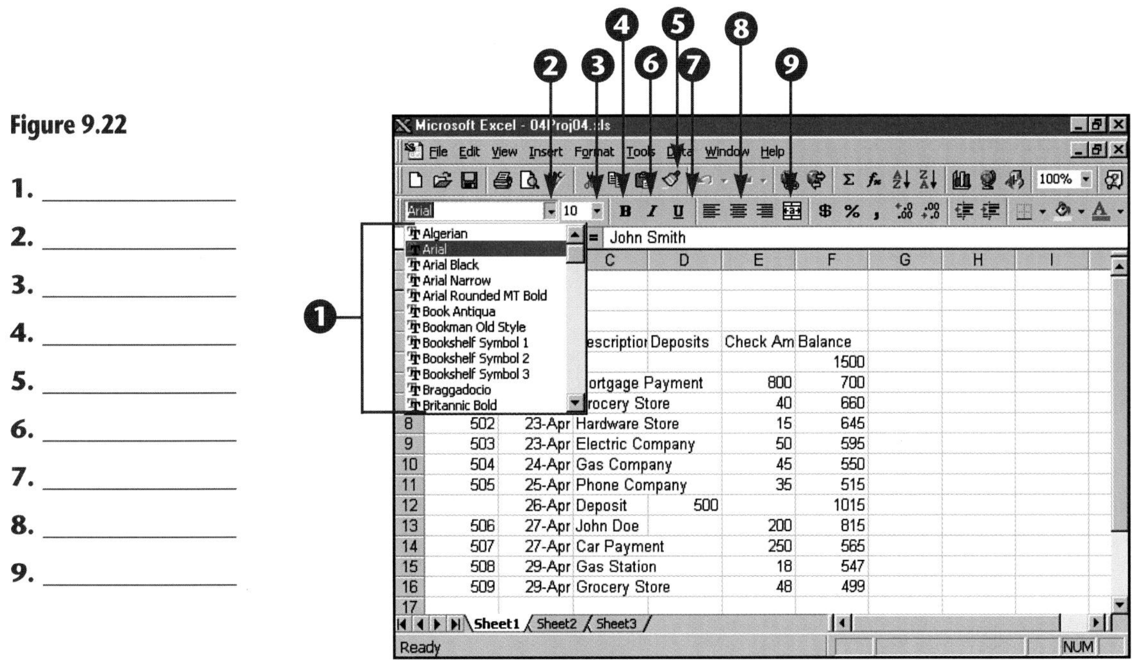

Applying Your Skills

Practice

The following exercises enable you to practice the skills you have learned in this project. Take a few minutes to work through these exercises now.

1. Formatting the Sales Worksheet

Practice using different formatting techniques to improve the appearance of the worksheet detailing monthly sales figures. Center the title, change the font and font size of the headings, adjust column widths, add borders or patterns, and check the spelling in the worksheet.

To Format the Sales Worksheet

1. Open the file Proj0902 and save it as `Sales 2`.
2. Center the title across the worksheet.
3. Make the column headings stand out by changing the font, font size, and other attributes.
4. Copy the formatting from the column headings to the row headings.
5. Adjust column widths to fit all the data.
6. Format all dollar values as currency with two decimal places.
7. Add borders or patterns to highlight the monthly totals.
8. Check and correct the spelling, and add proper names to your personal dictionary if you want.
9. Save the worksheet. If requested by your instructor, print two copies, then close the file.

2. Formatting the Ad Revenues Analysis

Format the Ad Revenues worksheet to improve its appearance. Use conditional formatting to draw attention to the most profitable ad campaign. Use AutoFormat to quickly apply formatting.

To Format the Ad Revenues Analysis

1. Open the file Proj0903 and save it as `Ad Revenues 2`.
2. Change the number formatting so that dollar values appear as currency with zero decimal places.
3. Change the date formatting to 9/27/97.
4. Set up conditional formatting to highlight ad revenues that fall between $200 and $300.
5. Use the AutoFormat feature to apply an appropriate table format.
6. Check the spelling.
7. Save the worksheet. If requested by your instructor, print two copies, then close it.

3. Formatting the Salary Forecast

Format the salary forecast worksheet using conditional formatting, number formatting, and alignment.

To Format the Salary Forecast

1. Open the file Proj0904 and save it as `Salary 2`.
2. Adjust the column widths.
3. Increase the font size of the title to 14 points, then center the title across the worksheet.
4. Use number formats to display all dollar values as currency with zero decimal places, and to display the percent increase values as percentages with percent signs.
5. Use conditional formatting to highlight projected salaries that exceed $20,000.
6. Rotate the text in the column headings 45 degrees.
7. Save the worksheet. If requested by your instructor, print two copies, then close it.

4. Formatting the Utility Expense Worksheet

Practice formatting techniques to improve the appearance of the utility expense worksheet. Apply the proper number format where needed, make the headings stand out, and change the text font to add interest. Adjust column widths. You can also add borders and shading to emphasize important cells. Use conditional formatting and change alignment within cells. If you want, use AutoFormat to quickly format the worksheet, then fine-tune it manually. Don't forget to check your spelling.

To Format the Utility Expense Worksheet

1. Open the file Proj0905 and save it as `Utilities 2`.
2. Make formatting changes as suggested. Be creative, but also try to keep the formatting clean and simple so that the worksheet will look professional.
3. Check the spelling in the worksheet.
4. Save your changes. If requested by your instructor, print two copies, then close it.

5. Using Fonts and Their Attributes

You have learned to change the font and the appearance of text in your worksheets. In this exercise, you improve the appearance of the Profit Loss workbook by changing fonts and font attributes.

To Use Fonts and Their Attributes

1. Open the file Proj0906 and save it as `Profit Loss 3`.
2. Select cells A1:A2 and choose Format, Cells.
3. Click the Font tab.
4. Change the font style to bold and the font size to 14.
5. Click OK to return to the worksheet.
6. Select cells B4:D4.
7. Click the Bold button on the Formatting toolbar to boldface these cells.
8. Save the file again, then leave it open for the following Challenge exercise.

Challenge

The following challenges enable you to use your problem-solving skills. Take time to work through these exercises now.

1. Formatting the Profit Loss 3 Workbook

Your boss has asked you to format your department's profit and loss statement. Make sure that the Profit Loss 3 workbook is open and then change the width of column A to 18. Widen column F so that the longest entry fits in the cell. Merge and center the first heading across the width of the worksheet. Center the headings in cells B4:D4. Save the file and leave it open for the next exercise.

2. Formatting the Profit Loss 3 Workbook Further

Your boss has now decided that he would like you to format the profit and loss workbook further. Make sure that the Profit Loss 3 workbook is open. Change the format of the numbers in cells B5:G13 to include a 1000 separator (,) and two decimal places. Add a light gray shading to the monthly numbers (cells B4:D13). Save and print two copies of the worksheet before closing it.

3. Using Conditional Formatting and AutoFormat

You have been asked by your demanding boss to quickly identify those customers who owe your company money and those who have overpaid the company. He would also like you to format the information before you present it. He wants you to have the information ready for him within the hour. You decide to use Conditional formatting and the AutoFormat feature to accomplish these tasks quickly.

Open Proj0907 and save it as `Billing 2`. Select cells H4:H9 and set up condition 1 so that if the cell value is greater than 0, the value displays in red. Set up condition 2 so that if the cell value is less than 0, the value displays in blue.

Merge and center the headings in cells A1:H1. Use the AutoFormat feature to change to List 3 format. Make sure the columns are wide enough for the data to fit. Save the workbook and leave it open for the following exercise.

4. Using the Spelling Checker on the Billing to Worksheet

You decide to use the Spelling Checker before you present the worksheet to your boss. Make sure the Billing worksheet is open and then check the spelling in the entire worksheet. Correct any misspelled words. Save and print two copies of the worksheet before closing it.

5. Improving the Appearance of the Checking Account Worksheet

You have decided that you are ready to practice your formatting techniques to improve the appearance of your checking account worksheet.

Open Proj0908 and save it as `Checking Account 5`. Center the headings in the top two rows across the worksheet columns, and boldface the text. Increase the font size of these headings. Format the numbers in columns D, E, and F so that they use commas as the thousands separator and display with two decimal places. Boldface the headings in row 4. Adjust the column widths so that they are wide enough to fit all the entries. Use Conditional Formatting so that if the balance goes below 500, the amount displays in red. Spell check the worksheet before saving the file and print two copies. Close the file when you have finished.

Project 10

Using Charts and Maps

Objectives

In this project, you learn how to:

- Create a Chart
- Format Text in a Chart
- Change the Chart Type
- Enhance a Chart
- Print a Chart
- Create a Map

Why Would I Do This?

After you create a worksheet, you may want to show the information to someone else. You can simply print the worksheet if you need only numerical detail, or you can transform the information in the worksheet into a chart. With Excel, you can also chart geographical information with maps. Charts and maps are great for visually representing relationships between numerical values while improving the appearance of a presentation.

This project shows you how to use sample data to create and enhance various types of charts. You also learn how to add a map to a worksheet.

Lesson 1: Creating a Chart

Embedded chart
A graphical representation of worksheet data created within the worksheet rather than as a separate worksheet.

In Excel, you can create an embedded chart directly on the worksheet. An *embedded chart* is a graphic object—a picture of the data—that appears on the worksheet along with your worksheet data. You can also add a chart of the data on a separate worksheet.

To create a chart, you select the data you want to use in the chart; then choose **I**nsert, C**h**art or click the Chart Wizard button on the Standard toolbar. The Chart Wizard provides step-by-step assistance through a series of dialog boxes to choose a chart type and specify chart options; then automatically creates the chart from the selected data and places it in a box (frame). You can then change or enhance the chart. Now try creating a chart to help you analyze your monthly office expenses.

To Create a Chart

1. **Open the file Proj1001 and save it as Expenses2.**

   This is the workbook file you use in this project.

2. **Select cells A2 through G7.**

   This is the data you will use to create the chart. You can create a chart using any of the information in the worksheet. The range you selected here lets you see how your expense costs change over the course of six months.

3. **Click the Chart Wizard button on the Standard toolbar.**

   Excel displays the Chart Wizard - Step 1 of 4 - Chart Type dialog box, as shown in Figure 10.1. This dialog box contains two tabs, Standard Types and Custom Types, which contain chart types from which to make your selection.

Figure 10.1
The Chart Wizard - Step 1 of 4 - Chart Type dialog box enables you to choose a chart type and sub-type.

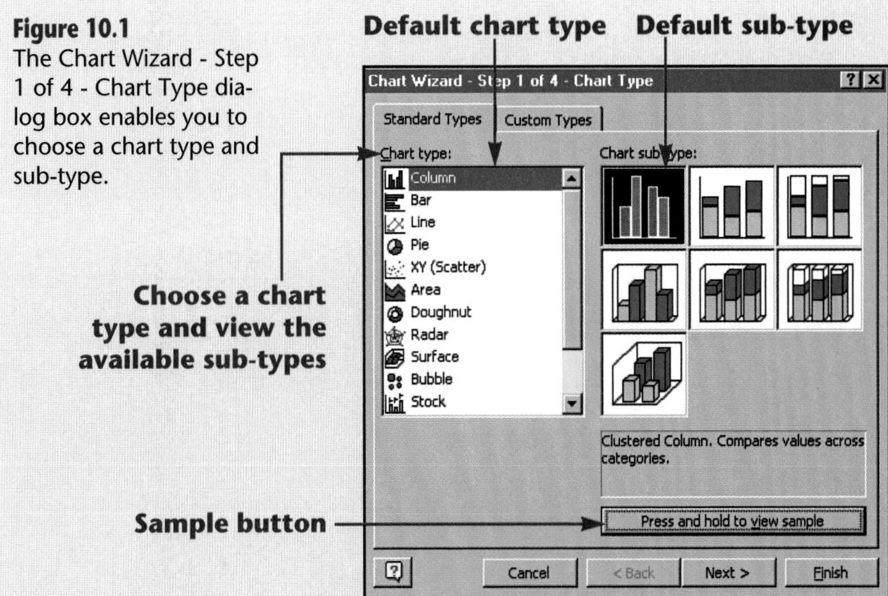

❹ **In the Chart Type list, click Column, if it is not already selected.**

For this example, the default chart type, Column, is acceptable. Otherwise, you could select a different chart type. Now you can choose a chart sub-type. In this case, you will use the default clustered column sub-type for the column chart.

❺ **Make sure the Clustered Column sub-type from the Chart Sub-Type list is selected.**

❻ **Point to the Press and hold to View sample button; then click and hold down the left mouse button.**

A sample of your chart is displayed in the Sample box.

❼ **Release the mouse button; then click the Next button.**

The chart type and sub-type are accepted and the Chart Wizard - Step 2 of 4 - Chart Source Data dialog box appears, as shown in Figure 10.2. A sample of the chart you are creating is displayed in the Data Range tab of the dialog box. If necessary, you can change the way the *data series* is displayed from rows to columns, but for this example the default settings are fine. The Series tab enables you to add or remove a series or change the ranges being used for the names and values of each chart series.

continues

To Create a Chart (continued)

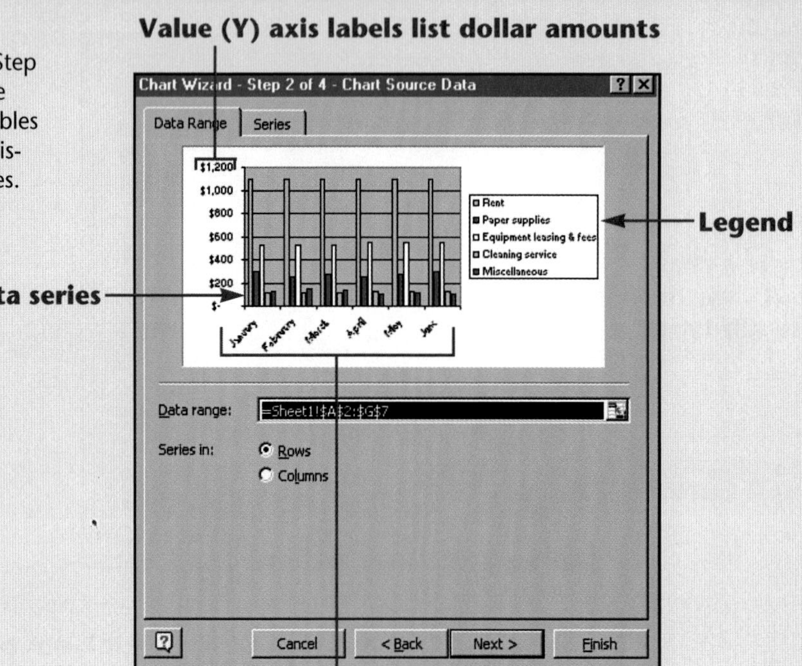

Figure 10.2
The Chart Wizard - Step 2 of 4 - Chart Source Data dialog box enables you to change the display of the data series.

8 Click the Next button.

The defaults are accepted and the Chart Wizard - Step 3 of 4 - Chart Options dialog box appears. Here, the tabs are displayed so that you can choose to add chart *titles*, label the *axes*, add *gridlines*, hide or change the placement of the *legend*, add *data labels*, or show the *Data table*.

9 Click the Titles tab; then click the Chart title text box. Type `Office Expenses` and then press Tab.

Excel adds the title to the chart and moves the insertion point to the Category (X) Axis text box.

10 Type `Months` in the Category (X) axis text box, press Tab, and then type `Dollars` in the Value (Y) axis text box.

Excel labels the axes on the chart. The Chart Wizard - Step 3 of 4 - Chart Options dialog box should now look like the one shown in Figure 10.3.

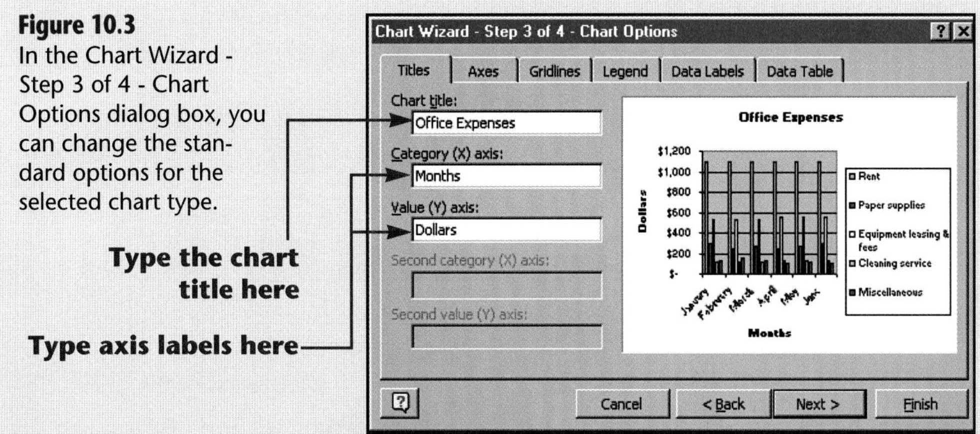

Figure 10.3
In the Chart Wizard - Step 3 of 4 - Chart Options dialog box, you can change the standard options for the selected chart type.

11 Click the Next button.

The Chart Wizard - Step 4 of 4 - Chart Location dialog box appears, as shown in Figure 10.4. If you want to see the chart displayed next to its source data, you can embed it as an object on the worksheet. If you prefer to work with the chart separately, place it on its own sheet and Excel will automatically size it to fill an entire page.

Figure 10.4
The Chart Wizard - Step 4 of 4 - Chart Location dialog box enables you to specify the location of your chart.

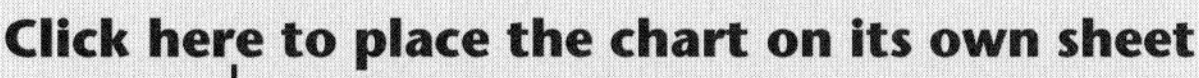

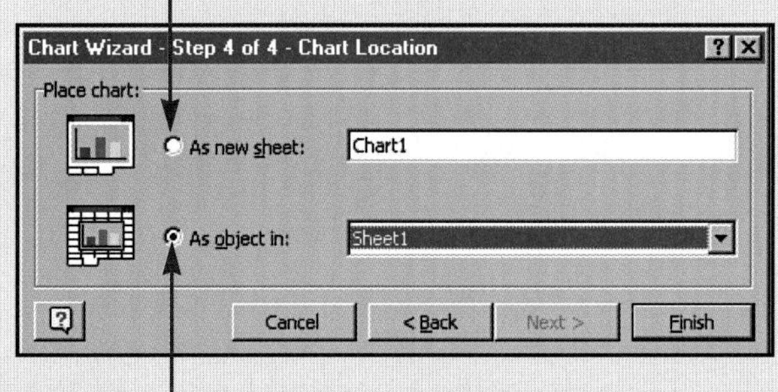

Click here to embed the chart on the worksheet of your choice

12 Click Finish.

Handles
Black squares that display around the perimeter of a chart, enabling you to drag the chart to a new position in a worksheet.

Excel creates the chart and displays it with eight black squares called *handles* surrounding the box, as shown in Figure 10.5. The Chart toolbar, which you can use to edit the chart, should automatically appear. If it does not, choose **V**iew, **T**oolbars, Chart to display it.

With the chart selected, selection handles are displayed, and you can drag the chart to a new position below the worksheet.

continues

To Create a Chart (continued)

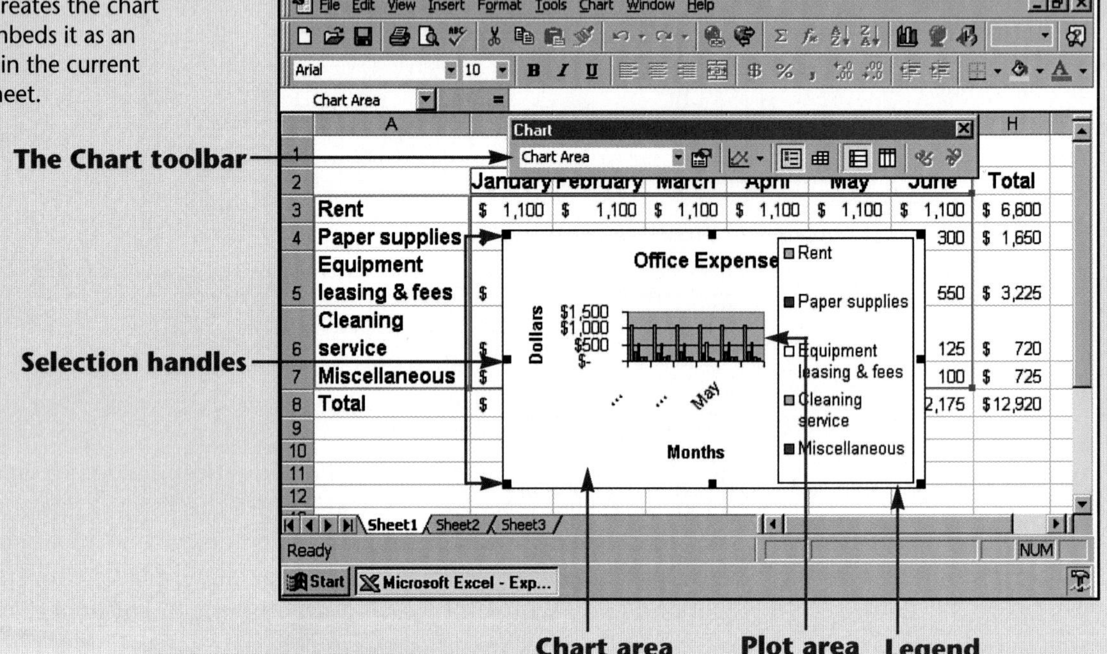

Figure 10.5 Excel creates the chart and embeds it as an object in the current worksheet.

13 Click inside the chart area (in any blank area) and drag the chart so that the upper-left corner is positioned in cell A10.

As you drag the chart, the pointer changes to a four-headed arrow. The chart is repositioned, but it needs resizing. It is important to resize the chart before you format it. If you do not resize first, the formatting and added enhancements will be out of proportion with the chart.

14 Point to the selection handle in the lower-right corner of the chart.

The pointer changes to a two-headed diagonal arrow.

15 Drag this selection handle down and to the right until the chart expands through cell G25.

The chart now fills cells A10:G25.

Save your work and keep the `Expenses` worksheet open for the next lesson, where you learn how to format and enhance the appearance of the chart.

Jargon Watch

Charts and maps are considered to be **objects** in Excel. An object is an item that has its own frame or box and that can be selected, moved, copied, sized, and formatted independently of the worksheet cells behind it. Other objects in Excel include text boxes and clip art.

Charts consist of a number of elements, most of which you can modify or delete. A chart's **title**, for example, is simply the chart's name.

Charts can also include other text such as a **legend**, **notes**, and **data labels**. A legend tells what each color or symbol in the chart's data series represents. Notes are brief descriptions or explanations of the data in the chart. Data labels are names such as "Months" or "Dollars" that appear along the vertical and horizontal **axes** to describe the data in the chart. The **data series** is a range of values in a worksheet, such as the expense information you used to create the chart in Lesson 1.

The axes provide the scale used to measure the data in the chart. The **Value axis** (Y-axis) is the vertical line of the chart and the **Category axis** (X-axis) is the horizontal line. On a 3-D chart, a second **Value axis** (Z-axis) is included.

You can move a selected chart or its elements (such as the legend and titles) on the chart by dragging them to a new location. You can also resize a selected chart or element by positioning the mouse pointer over any one of the chart box handles until the pointer changes to a two-headed arrow. Drag the handle away from the center of the chart box to enlarge the box and toward the center of the box to reduce it.

When you drag a handle on the middle of one side of the box, you change the size horizontally or vertically. When you drag a corner handle, you change the vertical and horizontal dimensions at the same time. If you hold down Shift while dragging a corner handle, you maintain the original proportions of the chart.

Be careful when increasing the size of a chart, as data series proportions can be misleading. For example, if you stretch the height of a chart without maintaining the original proportions, you visually exaggerate the numerical differences in the data, which can change the impact of the information.

If you want to delete a chart, simply select the chart and press Del.

You can create a chart on its own sheet in the default (2-D column) chart type by selecting the data and pressing F11 or the Alt + F1 key combination. You can then modify the chart by using the chart commands.

Lesson 2: Formatting Text in a Chart

After you create a chart, you can format chart text to enhance the chart's title, axes labels, or legend. You can even change the emphasis of the chart's details. You can change text in a chart simply by clicking the text area you want to modify and then making the change, or by formatting the text in the entire chart area at the same time.

You change the format of the text in Excel charts using the same methods you use to format text in worksheet cells. Now try formatting text in the chart you created in Lesson 1.

To Format Text in a Chart

1 In the `Expenses` worksheet, scroll up until you can see the top of the chart. If the handles are not displayed, click anywhere in the chart area.

The selected chart can be edited and formatted. The Chart Objects text box in the Chart toolbar shows that the chart area is selected.

If you cannot see the Chart toolbar on your screen, choose **V**iew, **T**oolbars, and then click the Chart option.

2 Click the Format Chart Area button on the Chart toolbar.

The Format Chart Area dialog box is displayed.

3 Click the Font tab.

This displays the Font options used to change the appearance of text in a chart, as shown in Figure 10.6.

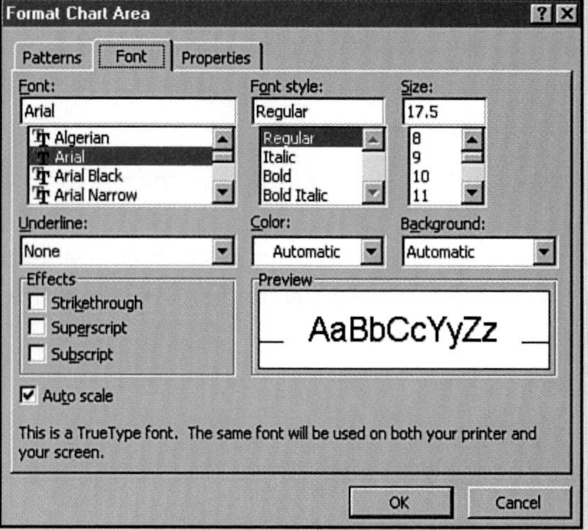

Figure 10.6
The Font tab of the Format Chart Area dialog box enables you to change the appearance of the chart text.

4 In the Font list, select Times New Roman. In the Font Style list, select Bold. In the Size list, select 8. Then click OK.

This changes all of the text in the chart to the Times New Roman font with bold style, and reduces the font size to 8 points.

5 Double-click the chart title.

A selection box appears around the chart's title and the Format Chart Title dialog box appears.

6 Click the Font tab if it is not displayed.

7 In the Size list box, select 24; then click OK.

This increases the size of the chart's title to 24 points and closes the dialog box.

8 Scroll down the worksheet until the bottom of the chart appears; then double-click a Category (X) axis label.

The Format Axis dialog box appears. Now you will change the orientation (direction) of the text for the Category (X) axis. From the Chart toolbar, you can rotate text up or down 45 degrees; however, if you want the text to be rotated 90 degrees, you need to use the Alignment tab in this dialog box.

9 Click the Alignment tab of the Format Axis dialog box.

The alignment options are displayed, as shown in Figure 10.7.

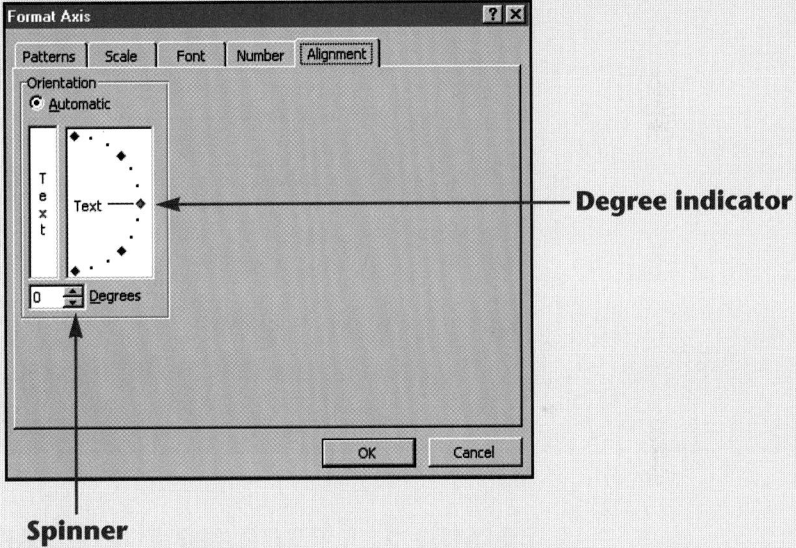

Figure 10.7
The orientation of the text for the chart's titles, except for the legend, can be rotated upward or downward.

10 Drag the degree indicator up until 90 degrees is displayed; then click OK.

The Format Axis dialog box closes. Now view the completed chart in its own window. This eliminates scrolling through the worksheet to view a chart, and chart editing can be done while the chart is open in the window.

11 Choose View, Chart Window.

The entire chart appears in a chart window that is the same size as the chart on your worksheet, as shown in Figure 10.8.

continues

To Format Text in a Chart (continued)

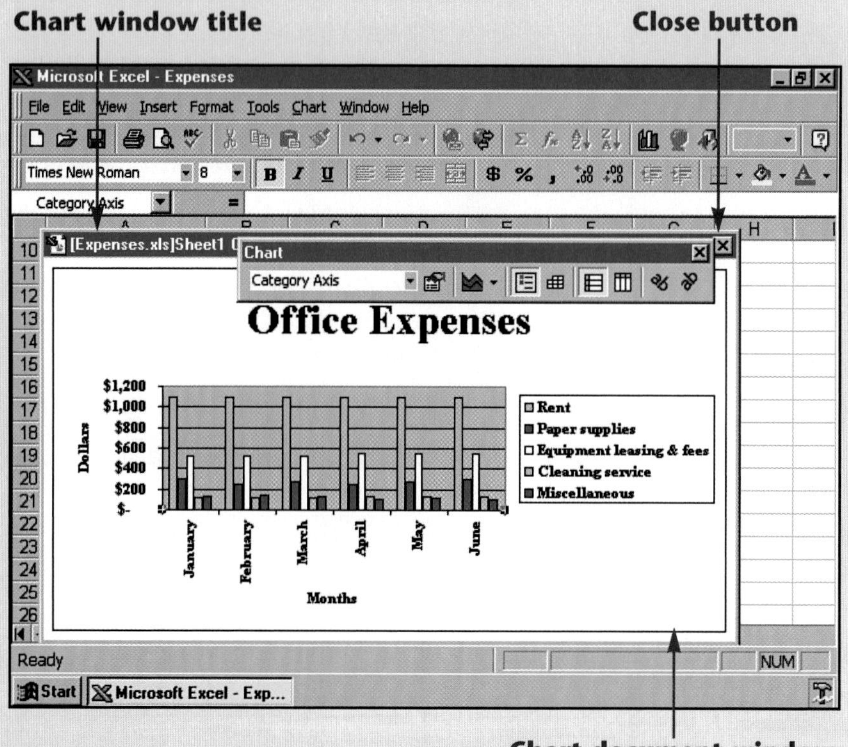

Figure 10.8
The chart title now appears in 24-point Times New Roman. The legend, Value (Y) axis, and Category (X) axis appear in 8-point Times New Roman. The Category axis is rotated 90 degrees.

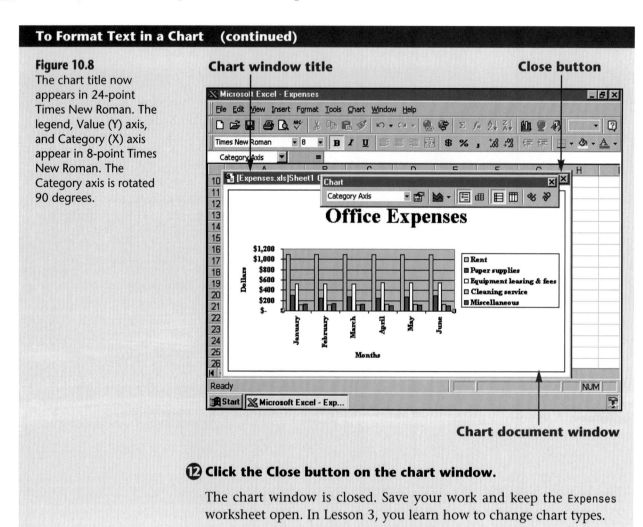

⓬ **Click the Close button on the chart window.**

The chart window is closed. Save your work and keep the Expenses worksheet open. In Lesson 3, you learn how to change chart types.

Lesson 3: Changing the Chart Type

After you create a chart, you may decide that you do not like the type of chart you have selected. Because Excel has a wide variety of chart types, you can display information in a way that best conveys its meaning.

Certain chart types are best for certain situations. It is important to select a chart type that can help you display the information in the most dramatic, appropriate, and meaningful manner possible. For example, you can usually spot trends more easily with a line chart, while a pie chart is best for showing parts of a whole.

Now try changing the Expenses chart to a different type of chart.

To Change the Chart Type

1 In the `Expenses` **worksheet, make sure the chart is selected and the Chart toolbar is displayed.**

Eight selection handles appear on the chart box frame to show that the chart is selected, as shown in Figure 10.9. When you select the chart, the Chart toolbar automatically appears so that the tools associated with charting are available for your use.

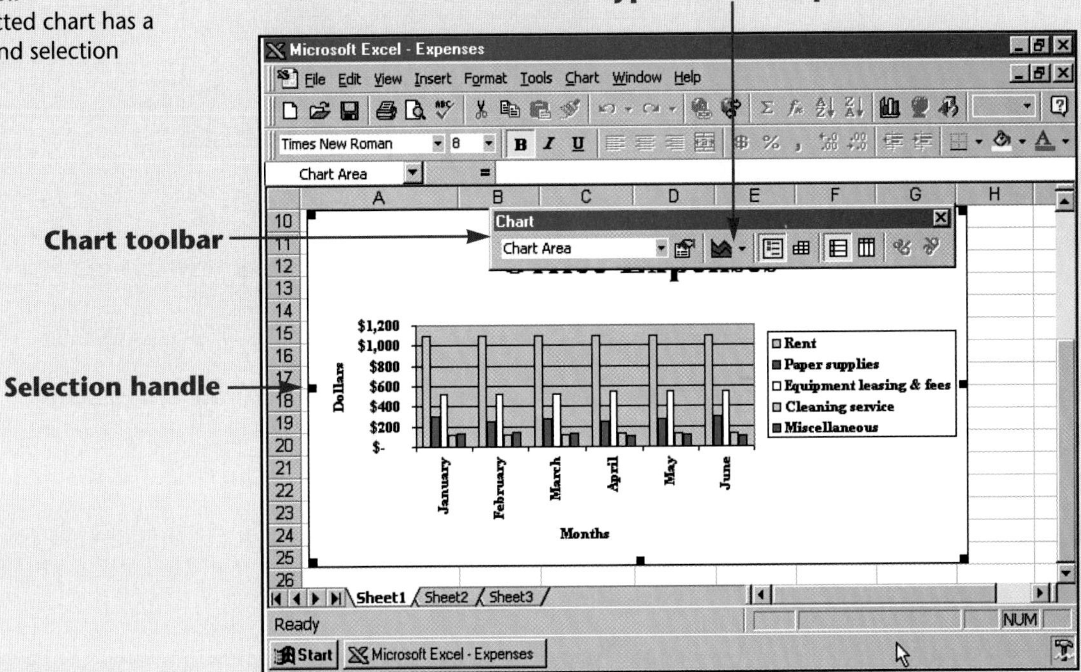

Figure 10.9
The selected chart has a border and selection handles.

2 Click the drop-down arrow next to the Chart Type button on the Chart toolbar.

The various chart types are displayed in a three-column, drop-down list, as shown in Figure 10.10. If you cannot see the Chart toolbar on your screen, choose **V**iew, **T**oolbars, and then click the Chart option.

continues

To Change the Chart Type (continued)

Figure 10.10
Select a chart type from the drop-down list.

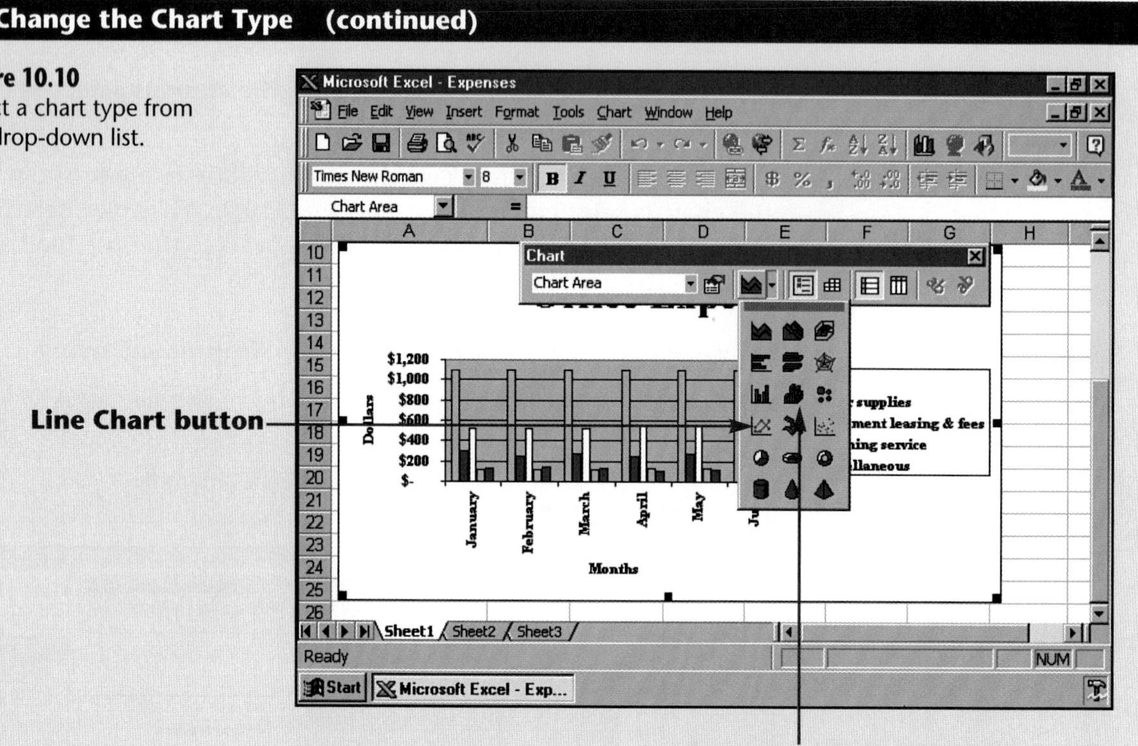

3 Click the 3-D Column Chart button (the third button down in the second column).

Excel changes the chart type to the 3-D column format, as shown in Figure 10.11.

Figure 10.11
The Expenses data appears as a 3-D column chart.

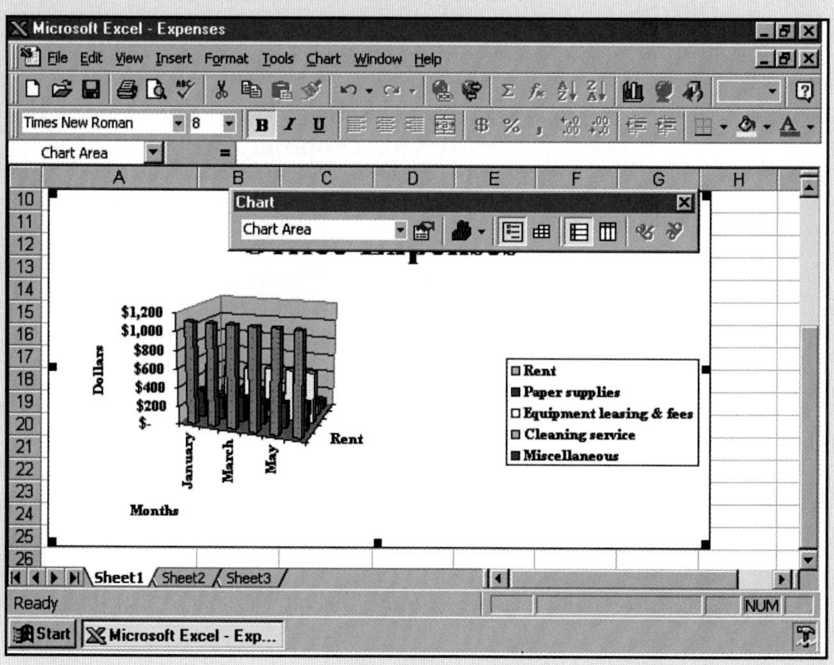

The 3-D column chart does not provide a very good representation of your data. If you want to examine the trends of the source of your income over time, there may be better chart types to use. Consult Table 10.1 to learn more about the different chart types and how they represent your data. Now you will select another type of chart that can more clearly illustrate the trend.

4 In the Chart Type drop-down list, click the Line Chart button (the fourth button down in the first column).

The chart type changes to a line chart, as shown in Figure 10.12.

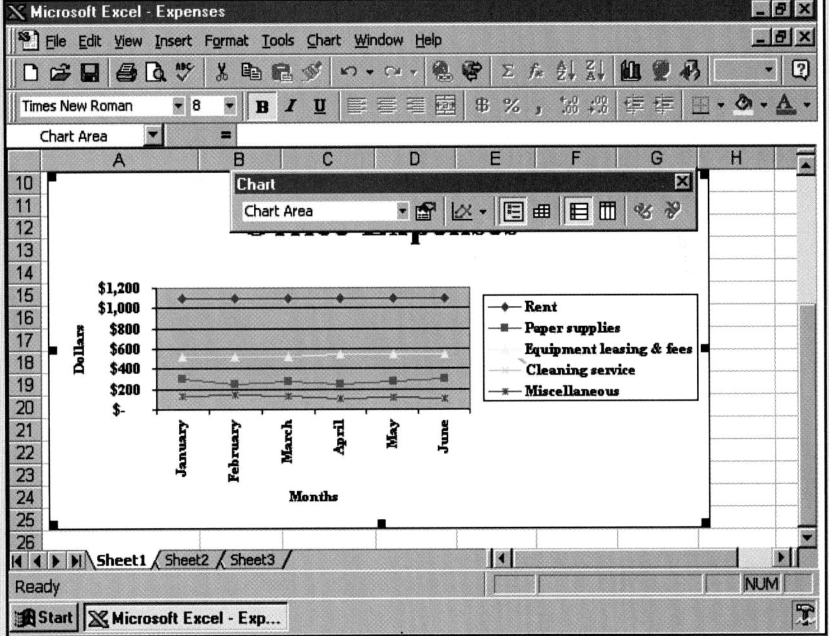

Figure 10.12
In a line chart, you can easily examine trends over time.

Save your work and keep the `Expenses` worksheet open. In Lesson 4, you learn how to enhance your chart's appearance.

If you have problems...

If you are not sure which chart type to select for a specific job, select one chart type and study the results. Check to see whether the data is accurately represented and conveys the appropriate meaning. Try various chart types until you find the one that best suits your needs.

Table 10.1 describes the various chart types available in Excel.

Table 10.1 Common Chart Types

Chart Type	Description
Area	A line chart that shows the area below the line filled with a color or pattern. Use an area chart to compare several sets of data.
Bar or Column	A chart that represents data by the height of the vertical columns or length of the horizontal bars. Use a bar chart to compare one item to another or to compare different items over a period of time.
Line	A chart consisting of a series of data at various points along the axis. The points are connected by a line. Use a line chart to indicate a trend over a period of time.
Pie	A circular chart in which each piece (wedge) shows a data segment and its relationship to the whole. Use a pie chart to sort data and compare parts of the whole.
Doughnut	A circular ring-shaped chart that compares the sizes of pieces in a whole. It is similar to a pie chart but can include multiple data series, appearing in concentric rings.
Radar	A line or area chart enclosed around a central point. Use a radar chart to show the uniformity of data.
XY or Bubble (Scatter)	A chart in which data points are placed along the Value (Y) axis and a numeric X-axis, similar to a line chart. Use an XY chart to compare trends over uneven time or measurement intervals (scientific data). Use a Bubble chart to plot two variables against the Category (X) and Value (Y) axis, similar to the XY chart, adding a third variable represented by the size of the bubble.
Combination	A chart that combines parts from a line, bar, or area chart so that you can plot data in two forms on the same chart. Use a combination chart to show a correlation between two data series.
Surface	A chart that represents optimum combinations between two sets of data. Patterns and colors are added to indicate sections that are in the same range of values.
Stock	A chart to plot stock prices; the data must be organized in the correct order. It can also be used for scientific data.
3-D (Area, Bar, Line, Pie)	A chart that represents data in the same way as its two-dimensional counterpart. Besides displaying height and width, however, a 3-D chart adds depth to the appearance of the chart.
Cone, Cylinder, Pyramid	A chart that enhances the data markers on 3-D column and bar charts.

Lesson 4: Enhancing a Chart

After you have decided which type of chart best conveys the information in your worksheet, you can enhance the chart's appearance in several ways. The most common enhancements include changing chart colors, adding a grid, and formatting the chart labels.

The easiest way to change any part of a chart is to select the chart, move the mouse pointer over the part you want to change, click the right mouse button, and then choose a command from the shortcut menu.

Now try using this easy method to enhance the `Expenses` chart.

To Enhance a Chart

1. **In the Expenses worksheet, make sure that the chart is selected.**

   With the chart selected, the selection handles are displayed and individual elements of the chart can be edited.

2. **Right-click one of the points of the line representing Rent in the chart.**

   A shortcut menu appears and the Rent line is selected, as shown in Figure 10.13.

Figure 10.13
Each element of a chart has its own shortcut menu for editing.

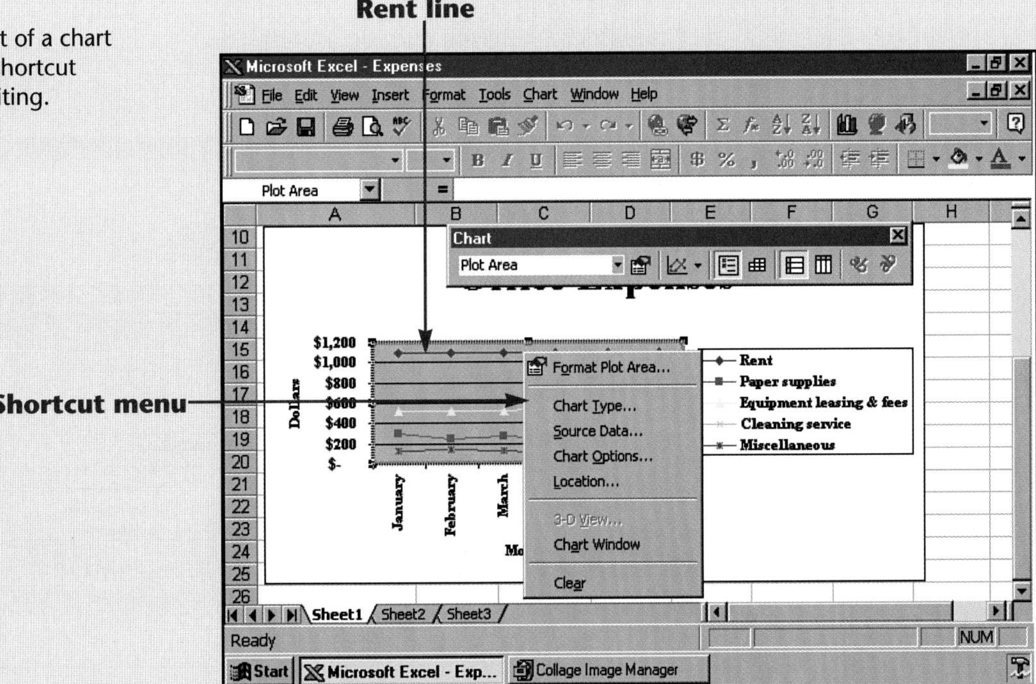

3. **Choose Chart Type from the shortcut menu.**

   The Chart Type dialog box appears, as shown in Figure 10.14.

continues

To Enhance a Chart (continued)

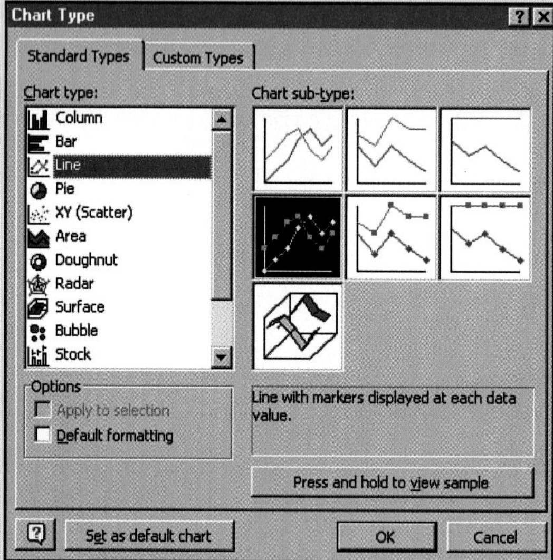

Figure 10.14
The Chart Type dialog box enables you to change the chart type and subtype.

4 Click Area in the Chart type list; then click the first chart (Area) in the Chart sub-type list and click OK.

The chart is now a combination area and line chart, as shown in Figure 10.15. Rent, the element you selected to edit, is represented by the large area from $- to the straight black line at $1100 on the Value (Y) axis, while the rest of the chart remains unchanged. Now change the color of the total area.

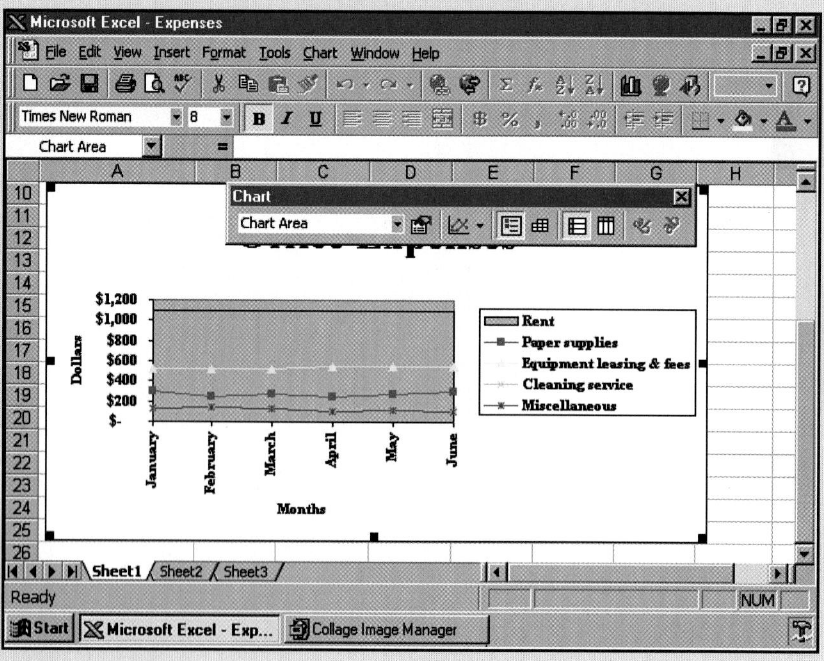

Figure 10.15
This is an example of a combination area and line chart.

5 Right-click the Rent area and choose Format Data Series from the shortcut menu.

The Format Data Series dialog box opens with the Patterns tab selected. In the Area section of the dialog box, a palette of colors is displayed. The current color for the Rent area is shown in the Sample box in the lower-left corner.

6 Select gray, the third color down in the last column.

The new color appears in the Sample box, as shown in Figure 10.16.

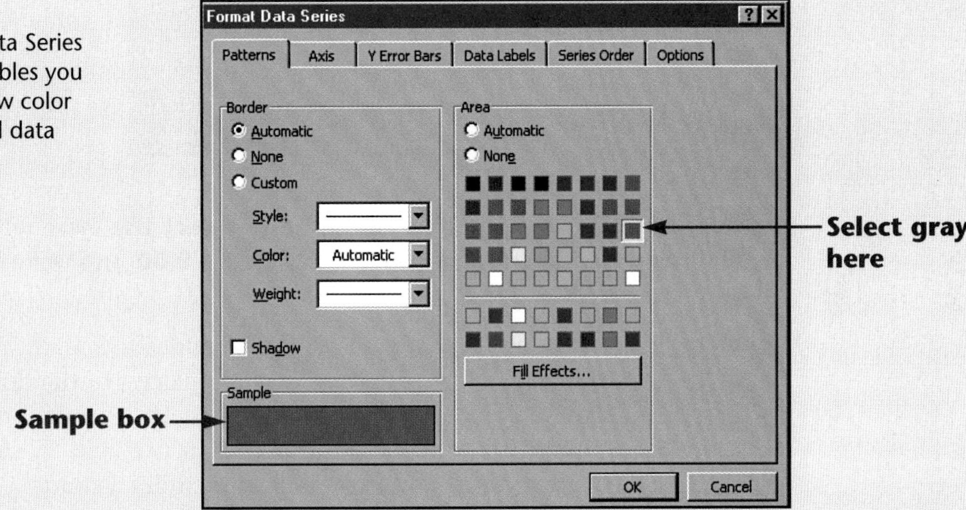

Figure 10.16
The Format Data Series dialog box enables you to choose a new color for the selected data series.

7 Click OK.

The dialog box closes and the new color appears in the chart. Now you will change the number format of the labels on the Value (Y) axis to show dollars with two decimal places.

8 Right-click any of the dollar amounts on the Value (Y) axis of the chart and choose Format Axis from the shortcut menu.

The Format Axis dialog box appears.

9 Select the Number tab.

The Number tab and its options appear with the Custom category selected, as shown in Figure 10.17.

continues

To Enhance a Chart (continued)

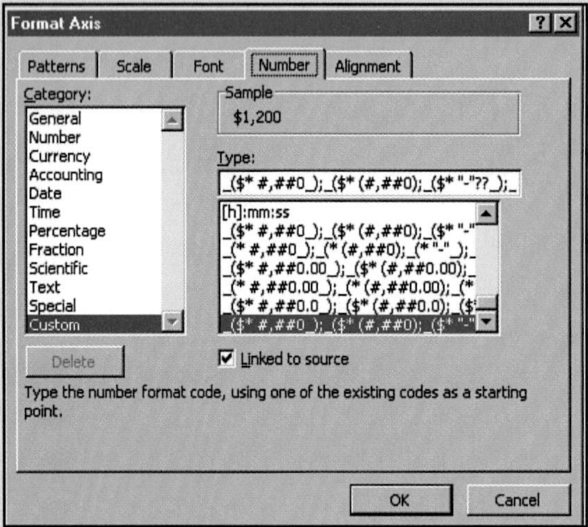

Figure 10.17
On the Number tab of the Format Axis dialog box, you can specify a different number format.

10 Scroll through the Type list and select the type with a dollar sign and two decimal places, $*#,##0.00_);($*#,##0.00); then click OK.

Excel applies this format, which includes a $ sign, a comma as a thousands separator, and two decimal places, to the dollar values on the Value (Y) axis, as shown in Figure 10.18. Save your work and keep the `Expenses` workbook open. You use it in the next lesson to learn how to print a worksheet that includes a chart.

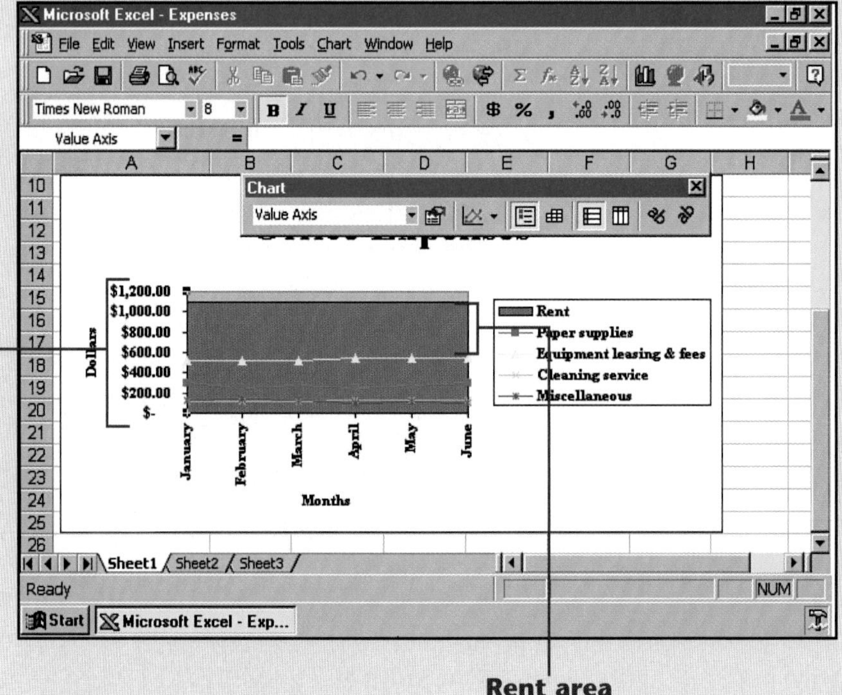

Figure 10.18
The enhanced chart is easier to read.

Lesson 5: Printing a Chart

Unless you want to carry around a laptop computer to show your work on-screen, you need to be able to print your worksheets.

Printing lets you view the worksheets you have created, even when you are away from your computer. A printed copy of a chart combined with the worksheet data makes a very effective presentation. Now try printing the entire `Expenses` workbook file, including the chart.

To Print a Chart

1 In the Expenses worksheet, click anywhere outside the chart.

This makes sure that no range in the worksheet is selected, not even the chart. The Chart toolbar is removed from the screen.

2 Choose File, Page Setup.

The Page Setup dialog box appears, as shown in Figure 10.19. Use this dialog box to adjust the page setup before you print your worksheet. This dialog box provides a wide range of options from which you can choose to customize your printed worksheet. For this example, you will change the margins, header, and footer for the printed worksheet.

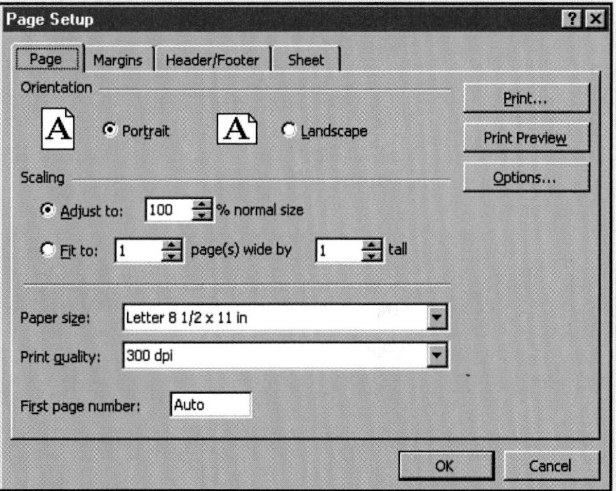

Figure 10.19 The Page Setup dialog box.

3 In the Page Setup dialog box, click the Header/Footer tab.

The Header and Footer options let you specify information to print in the header and footer area of each page. You can choose from predefined headers and footers, or you can create your own.

4 Click the drop-down arrow next to the Header text box, scroll up, and select (none).

This removes the default header text, and nothing will print in the header area.

continues

To Print a Chart (continued)

5 Click the drop-down arrow next to the Footer text box and select Expenses.

This footer prints the current file name in the center of the footer area.

6 Click the Margins tab in the Page Setup dialog box.

This displays the Margins options.

7 In the Top text box, click the up arrow twice.

This changes the top margin from 1 to 1.5.

8 In the Bottom text box, click the down arrow once.

This changes the bottom margin from 1 to 0.75. You have now finished setting up the worksheet page for printing. Now preview the page to make sure it is the way you want it to print.

9 Click the Print Preview button in the Page Setup dialog box.

Excel closes the Page Setup dialog box, makes the changes you requested to the page setup, and displays the Print Preview window, as shown in Figure 10.20. In Print Preview, you can see the worksheet as it will look when you print it. (You can also open the Print Preview window by clicking the Print Preview button on the Standard toolbar when the Page Setup dialog box is not open.) Everything looks right, so you are ready to print.

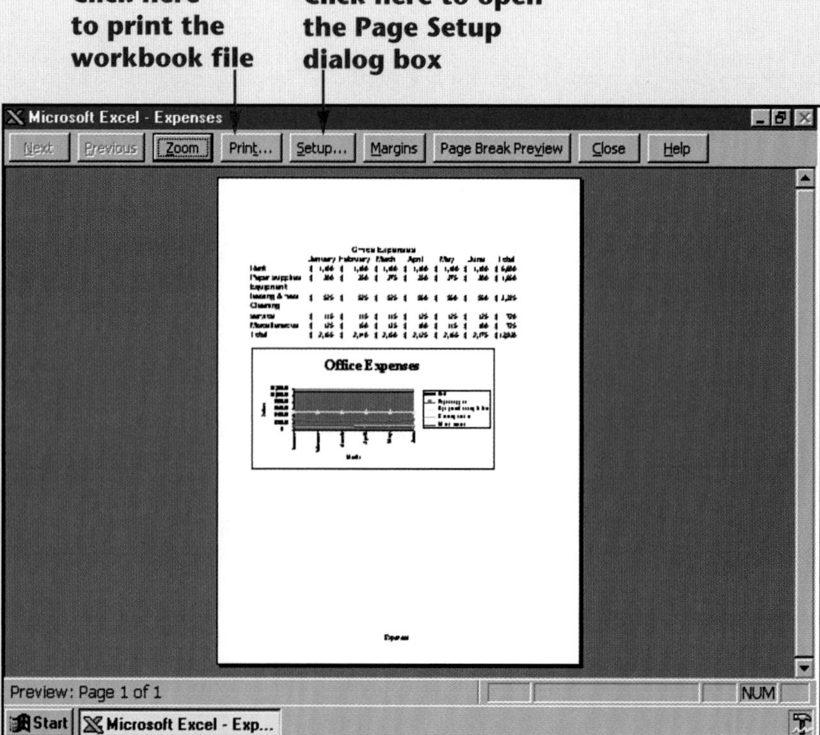

Figure 10.20
Print Preview shows you the page as it will print, including the chart.

⑩ **Click the Print button on the Print Preview toolbar.**

The Print Preview window closes and the Print dialog box appears.

⑪ **In the Number of Copies text box, change the number of copies to 2 and then click OK.**

Excel prints two copies of the worksheet, including the chart. When you are done printing, save and close the Expenses workbook. In Lesson 7, you learn how to create a map by using data in a different workbook file.

You can print just a chart in Excel without printing the entire worksheet. Select the chart; then choose **F**ile, **P**rint to open the Print dialog box. Click the Selected Chart option button in the Print What area, and then click OK.

If you want to leave additional space between the chart and the worksheet data, simply select the chart and drag it down a few rows. Remember to deselect the chart before printing.

Lesson 6: Creating a Map

Maps are useful for charting information that is defined by state, country, or province. Maps are not one of Excel's built-in chart types; rather, they are a separate feature of Excel. Maps can help you visualize your worksheet information geographically. In this lesson, you compare how many company offices are located in different states in the U.S. By creating a map, you can see where most of the offices are located.

Try creating a map now, using the sample worksheet provided.

To Create a Map

❶ **Open the file Proj1002 and save it as SiteMap.**

❷ **Select cell A3. Hold down Shift and press Ctrl+End.**

This selects all the data in the worksheet so that the information can be used to create your map.

❸ **Click the Map button on the Standard toolbar.**

The mouse pointer changes to a crosshair, which you can use to specify where in the worksheet Excel should create the map.

continues

To Create a Map (continued)

4 Click cell A21 and hold down the left mouse button; then drag the mouse to cell G35.

When you release the mouse button, Excel begins creating the map in the range A21:G35. This may take a few seconds. Excel looks to see which map the data belongs in, based on the geographical data included in the selected data range. If the data could fit in more than one map (which is the case in this example), the Multiple Maps Available dialog box appears, as shown in Figure 10.21.

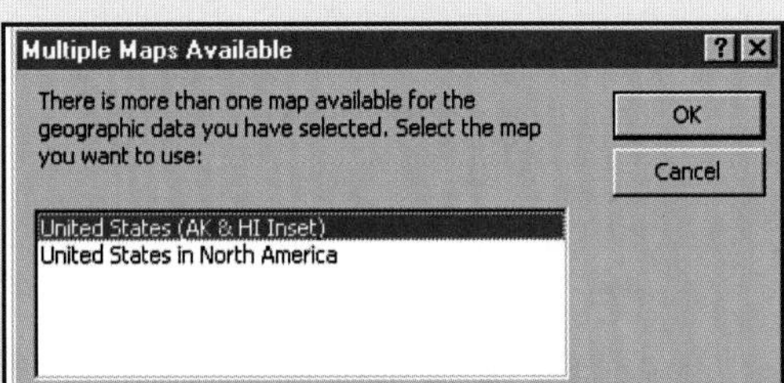

Figure 10.21
The Multiple Maps Available dialog box.

5 Select United States in North America; then click OK.

You may have to wait for several seconds while Excel composes the map. The map appears in the selected cells along with the Microsoft Map Control dialog box, as shown in Figure 10.22. The map is inserted into a frame, which you can use to resize and move the map. You can use the Microsoft Map Control dialog box to change some formatting characteristics of the map. Currently, the # of Offices column is displayed in the map. Because the shading values in the map are not easy to discern, try changing the colors of the map now.

Show/Hide Microsoft Map Control
Microsoft Map Control dialog box
Frame
Column buttons
Format buttons

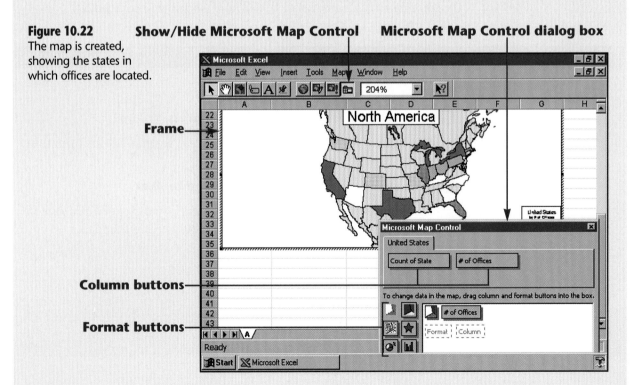

Figure 10.22
The map is created, showing the states in which offices are located.

If you have problems...

If the Microsoft Map Control dialog box is covering the map so you cannot see it, simply drag the dialog box out of the way. You can open and close the dialog box by using the Show/Hide Microsoft Map Control button on the toolbar.

6 In the Microsoft Map Control dialog box, drag the Category Shading button onto the # of Offices button, as shown in Figure 10.23.

Figure 10.23
Use the Microsoft Map Control dialog box to change the format of the map.

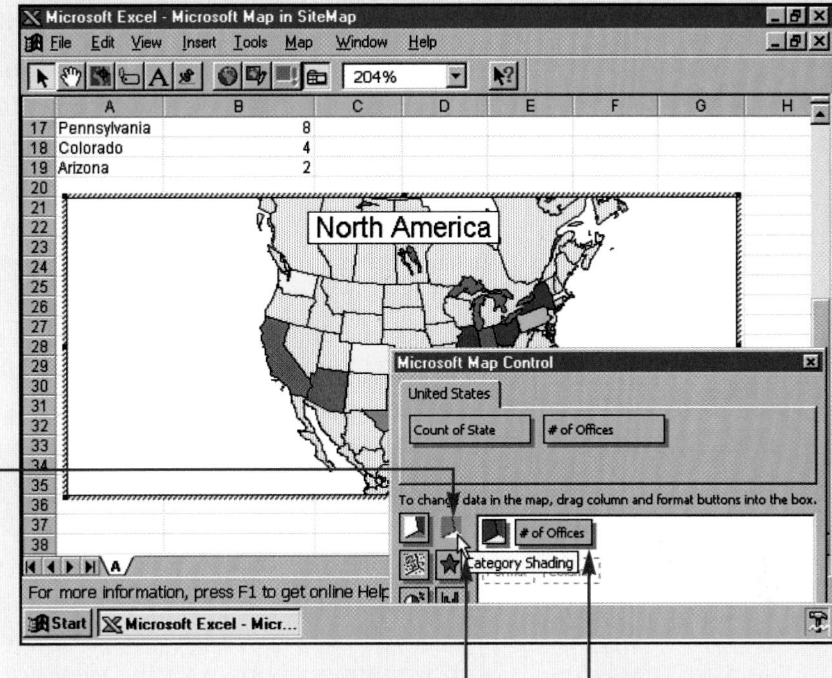

When you release the mouse button, Excel redraws the map, adding color to indicate the number of offices in each state.

7 Close the Microsoft Map Control dialog box.

The map is complete, as shown in Figure 10.24. The location of offices is now clearly indicated by different colors. The expanded legend is partially hidden in the map frame and is difficult to read.

continues

To Create a Map (continued)

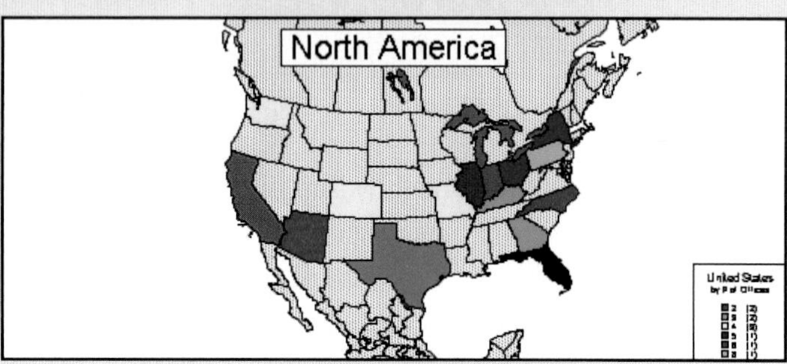

Figure 10.24
The map with an expanded legend.

❽ **Drag the legend up to display the entire box.**

❾ **Drag the upper-left corner of the legend box up and to the left (approximately even with row 24); then click inside the map to deselect the box.**

You can now see the colors and the numbers in the legend to identify which part of the country has the greatest number of offices (the number identifies the number of offices in each state by color; the number in parentheses identifies how many states have that number of offices). Decide to focus your research on the states surrounding Ohio. Try zooming in on the map now.

400%

❿ **Click the Zoom Percentage of Map drop-down arrow; then select 400%.**

Excel redraws the map, increasing its magnification. Now change the title of the map.

If you have problems...

If you are unhappy with the view, use the Zoom Percentage of Map button to change the view percentage. You can return to the previous view by opening the **V**iew menu and choosing **P**revious. To view the entire map, choose **V**iew, **E**ntire Map.

⓫ **Double-click the Map title.**

This selects the map's title and positions an insertion point in the text so that you can enter and edit the title text. You can change the text as well as the text attributes, including font, font size, and font style.

⓬ **Change the text to `Office Locations`; then press Enter.**

This changes the map's title. You can drag it to a new location on the map or resize it so that it does not cover any of the target states.

⓭ **Drag the map title to the upper-left corner of the map.**

The map title is moved. You can also reposition the map within its frame.

14 Click the Grabber button on the Microsoft Map toolbar; then click the map and drag it around in the frame until it is positioned to the left of the legend.

Click anywhere outside the map frame to deselect it. The map is complete, as shown in Figure 10.25. Save your work. If requested by your instructor, print two copies of the worksheet with the map. Then close the workbook.

If you have completed your session on the computer, exit Excel and Windows 95 before turning off your computer. Otherwise, continue with "Checking Your Skills" at the end of this project.

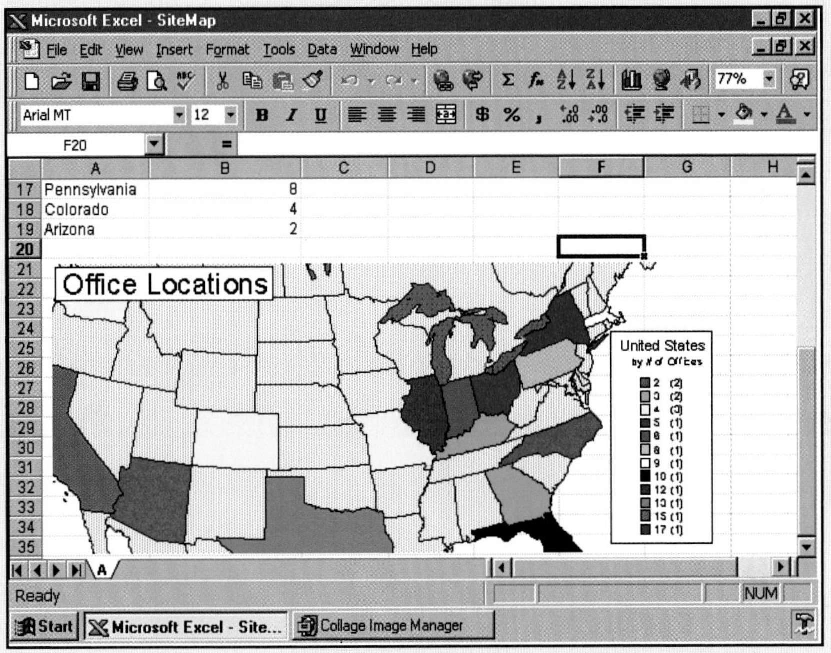

Figure 10.25
The completed map appears below the worksheet data.

When creating a map, you need to have two columns of data. The first column contains the name of the region, state, or country. You can use abbreviations—such as WV, TN, NC, and so on—or you can use the state's full name. The second column contains the worksheet information. The data in the second column is represented on the map by colors and/or patterns.

As with the elements in a chart, you can right-click elements in a map to open a shortcut menu. You can use the commands on the shortcut menus to quickly edit or enhance the parts of the map.

To print the worksheet with the map, choose **F**ile, **P**rint, select the options you want in the Print dialog box, and then click OK. To print the map without printing the entire worksheet, select the worksheet cells surrounding the map, click the Selectio**n** option button in the Print dialog box, and then click OK. You can change options such as the header, footer, and margins by using the Page Setup dialog box, just as you do for all worksheets.

Project Summary

To	Do This
Start the Chart Wizard	Select the range to be charted; then click the Chart Wizard button on the Standard toolbar or choose **I**nsert, C**h**art.
Select a chart	Click the chart.
Format a chart element	Click the chart element and click the right mouse button. From the shortcut menu, choose the F**o**rmat option.
Change a chart type	Select the chart; then choose a chart type from the Chart Type drop-down list on the Chart toolbar.
Print a chart	Select the chart; then click the Print button on the Standard toolbar.
Create a map	Select the range to be mapped; then click the Map button on the Standard toolbar and click in the worksheet where you want the upper-left corner of the map to appear.

Checking Your Skills

True/False

For each of the following, check *T* or *F* to indicate whether the statement is true or false.

__T __F **1.** A chart can only be placed on the worksheet with the data.

__T __F **2.** Charts and maps are objects on the worksheet.

__T __F **3.** An embedded chart must be viewed in a chart window before the elements can be selected, moved, copied, sized, or formatted.

__T __F **4.** The Category (X) axis provides the scale used to measure the data in the chart.

__T __F **5.** After a chart is created, you can choose another chart type if you are not satisfied with the representation of your data.

__T __F **6.** An object has its own frame.

__T __F **7.** When creating a map, the first column of data should contain the names of regions, states, or countries.

__T __F **8.** Three ways to create a chart from selected data in Excel are by pressing F11, pressing Alt+F1, and using the Chart Wizard.

__T __F **9.** Excel cannot create three-dimensional charts.

__T __F **10.** You should resize a chart before formatting it.

Multiple Choice

Circle the letter of the correct answer for each of the following questions.

1. Which type of chart usually helps you spot trends easily?

a. area

b. column

c. line

d. pie

2. Which type of chart is best for showing parts of a whole?

a. area

b. column

c. line

d. pie

3. What is the element of a chart that identifies colors or patterns assigned to a data series or chart categories?

a. chart area

b. chart title

c. legend

d. value (Y) axis

4. What are some common enhancements that are often made to a chart to improve its appearance?

a. add a grid

b. change colors

c. format the chart labels

d. all of the above

5. How many columns of data are needed in your worksheet to create a map?

a. one

b. two

c. three

d. as many as you want

6. What is the default chart type in Excel?

a. column

b. bar

c. pie

d. line

7. The mouse pointer changes to which of the following when you drag a chart?

a. 2-headed arrow

b. 4-headed arrow

c. hand

d. pointing finger

8. What is the third axis called in three-dimensional charts?

a. x

b. y

c. z

d. d

9. Which of the following is used to identify the data in a chart?

a. legend

b. gallery

c. Chart Wizard

d. none of the above

10. Use which type of chart to show a correlation between two data series?

a. column

b. combination

c. pie

d. line

Completion

In the blank provided, write the correct answer for each of the following statements.

1. The ______________ button on the Standard toolbar assists you in creating a chart.
2. Excel creates a chart from a ______________ you specify on the worksheet.
3. Click the ______________ mouse button on a chart or chart element to display a shortcut menu.
4. Select a chart or chart element; then drag a ______________ to resize it.
5. Create a ______________ to chart information that is defined by state, country, or province.
6. A(n) ______________ is a range of values in a worksheet.
7. The labels along the bottom of a chart are the ______________ labels.
8. The labels along the left side of a chart are the ______________-axis labels.
9. To delete an embedded chart, click it to select it, and press ______________.
10. The mouse pointer should be shaped like a(n) ______________ on the worksheet cell where you want the upper-left corner of a map to start.

Matching

In the blank next to each of the following terms or phrases, write the letter of the corresponding term or phrase. (Note that some letters may be used more than once.)

____**1.** A range of values in a worksheet

____**2.** Identifies data series

____**3.** Black squares surrounding a chart

____**4.** Vertical axis of a chart

____**5.** Horizontal axis of a chart

____**6.** A chart that appears on the worksheet along with the worksheet data

____**7.** Brief descriptions of the data in a chart

____**8.** A chart type in which each segment shows a data segment and its relationship to the whole

____**9.** A chart type consisting of a series of data at various points along the axis

___**10.** An item that has its own frame or box Screen ID

a. category axis

b. data series

c. embedded

d. handles

e. legend

f. line

g. notes

h. object

i. pie

j. value axis

Screen ID

Label each element of the Excel screen shown in Figure 10.25.

Figure 10.25

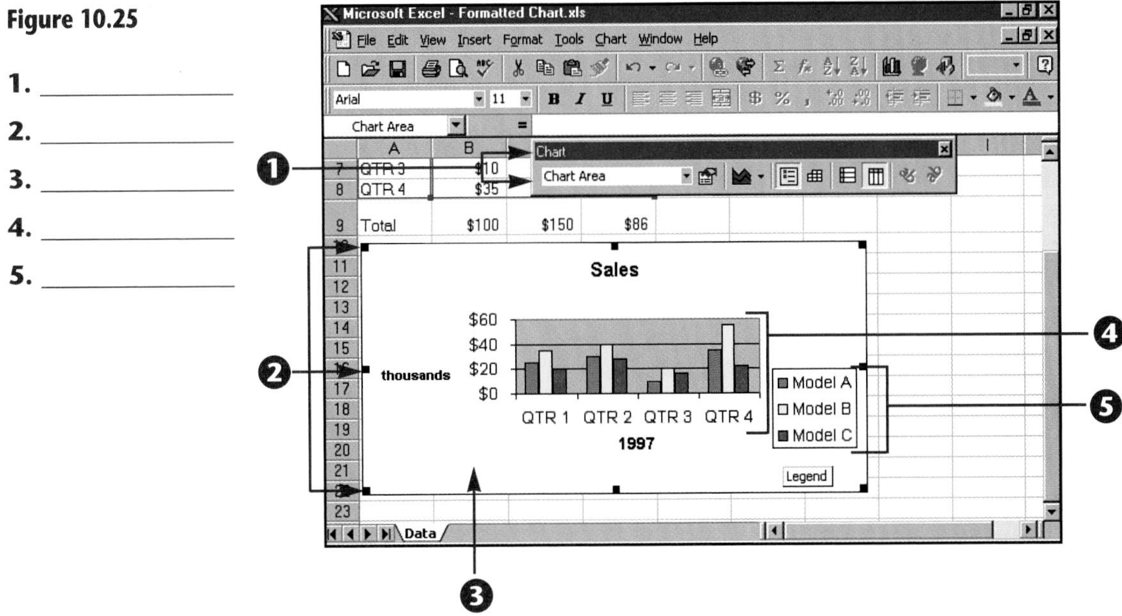

1. ______________
2. ______________
3. ______________
4. ______________
5. ______________

Applying Your Skills

Practice

The following exercises enable you to practice the skills you have learned in this project. Take a few minutes to work through these exercises now.

1. Creating a Chart and Map Showing Mail Order Sales

In the past six months, you have tried to expand your business by adding a mail order catalog that you send to potential customers in the western United States. Create a chart and a map to show the sales for a mail order catalog business in the first quarter of 1997.

To Create a Chart and Map Showing Mail Order Sales

1. Open the file Proj1003 and save it as `MOSChart`.
2. Select the data for both columns and create a chart embedded in the worksheet. Think about which type of chart will best show a comparison of the states in the mail order channel. Do not forget to add a title to the chart.
3. Move the chart below the worksheet, starting in cell A20. Increase the size of the chart so that it fills the range A20:G35.
4. Format the Chart Area, changing the font to a 10-point size.
5. Select the data for both columns and create a map, starting in cell A37 through cell G50 of the worksheet.
6. Experiment with some of the map features to enhance the map. For example, change the colors on the map. Change the zoom percentage to draw attention to the states where the sales are concentrated. Move the legend so that it is displayed inside the map frame.

7. Change the map title to **`Mail Order Sales`**. Try editing the font and font size in the title text.
8. Save your work. If requested by your instructor, print two copies of the worksheet with the chart and map before closing the file.

2. Comparing Expenses Using a Chart

Using Proj1004, create a pie chart that compares how much you spend on various types of school expenses. Your tuition each semester is determined by the university, but you can try to manage other costs. Use the chart to see how changes in how much you spend on the Books—Additional category affects the makeup of the total amount.

To Compare Expenses Using a Chart

1. Open the file Proj1004 and save it as **`Charting Expenses`**.
2. Create a pie chart, using the expense data for only the Spring 1997 semester for the following expense headings:

   `Books – Main subjects`

   `Books – Additional`

   `Supplies – General`

   `Supplies – Lab`

   `Lab Fees`

   Move the chart below the worksheet data.
3. Now change the chart type so that you can compare how the various types of expenses contribute to your total expenses for the semester. (*Tip:* Refer to Table 10.1.) Resize the chart and reduce the size of the font for the chart area to make sure that the Category (X) axis displays all the expense labels.
4. What happens to the worksheet and the chart when you decrease the amount in the worksheet for Books—Additional from $85 to $25?
5. What happens to the worksheet and the chart when you drastically increase the amount in the worksheet for Books—Additional to $475?
6. Save your work and print two copies of the worksheet with the increased expense for Books—Additional.

3. Creating a Map of the Home States of Rollerblading Club Members

In an effort to show prospective club members how diverse the rollerblading club is, you decide to create a map showing the home states of all current members.

To Create the Map

1. Open Proj1005 and save it as **`Membership Map`**.
2. Use the data provided to create a map.
3. Zoom in on the target area.
4. Format the map to clearly show from which states most club members come. For example, make use of the legend, show the states in color, and use titles and text.
5. Save the worksheet. If requested by your instructor, print two copies. Then close the worksheet.

4. Creating an Embedded Area Chart

In this exercise, you create an area chart for the first quarter sales expenses of Midwestern Enterprises.

To Create an Embedded Area Chart

1. Open Proj1006 and save it as `Quarterly Expenses`.
2. Create an embedded area chart using the data range of A4:D9.
3. Position the chart below the data area (rows 13 through 24).
4. Use the Chart, Chart Options command to insert a chart title, an x-axis title, and an y-axis title. The chart title is 1st Quarter Expenses. The x-axis title is Office Expenses, and the y-axis title is in dollars.
5. Adjust the size of the chart so that the category x labels are displayed.
6. Print two copies of the worksheet and chart—one to keep and one to turn in to your instructor.
7. Save and then close the workbook.

5. Creating a Line Chart on a Chart Sheet

In this exercise, you have the opportunity to create a chart on a separate chart sheet, then change the chart type and add titles.

To Create a Line Chart on a Chart Sheet

1. Open Proj1007 and save it as `Beverages`.
2. Select the data range of A4:D7, then press F11 to create a chart on its own sheet.
3. When the chart sheet appears, right-click to display a chart shortcut menu.
4. Select the Chart Type command to change the column chart to a line chart.
5. Right-click to display a chart shortcut menu, then select the Chart Options command to insert a chart title and an x-axis title. The chart title is 1st Quarter Sales. The x-axis title is Beverage Sales.
6. Print two copies of the worksheet and chart—one to keep and one to turn in to your instructor.
7. Save and then close the workbook.

Challenge

The following challenges enable you to use your problem-solving skills. Take time to work through these exercises now.

1. Creating an Embedded Pie Chart

To show your employees the sales results for July, you create an embedded pie chart. Open Proj1008 and save it as `July Sales`. Use the data range A5:B11 to create the chart. Position the chart in rows 14 through 25 below the data area. Insert the chart title `July Sales`. Print two copies of the worksheet and chart—one to keep and one to turn in to your instructor. Save and then close the workbook.

2. Formatting a Columnar Sales Chart

Your boss has asked you to format a columnar sales chart that he will be using in a meeting. Open Proj1009 and save it as `Formatted Chart`. Position the chart below the data area (rows 10 through 22). Insert the chart title Sales. Label the x-axis as `1997` and the y-axis title as `in thousands`. Change the Model B data series to the color yellow. Change the Model C data series to red. Change the chart type to bar. Print two copies of the worksheet and chart—one to keep and one to turn in to your instructor. Save and then close the workbook.

3. Creating a Map

Open Proj1010 and save it as `Company Agents`. Create a map using the State and Agents data columns. Add the map title, `Agents by State`. Apply Category Shading to the Count of State column. Finally, save and print two copies of the worksheet and map—one to keep and one to turn in to your instructor.

4. Creating a Column Chart

Open the Proj1011 and save it as `Garnet & Gold`. Create a column chart using the data in columns A and B. Move the chart to the range A15:E30. Add a chart title, `Garnet & Gold Industries`. Adjust the size of the chart so that all x-axis labels display. Also, delete the legend by selecting it and pressing Del. Print two copies of this chart. Change the chart type to a clustered column with a 3-D visual effect. Print two copies of the worksheet; save and then close the workbook.

5. Creating Embedded Column Charts

Open Proj1012 and save the workbook with the name `Motor Pool`. Create six embedded column charts, one for each car in the motor pool. Include appropriate chart titles. Print two copies of the worksheet. Save and then close the workbook.

Project 11

Using Excel with Other Programs

Integrating Applications

In this project, you learn how to:

- Switch among Applications
- Copy Data between Applications
- Link Data between Applications
- Work with Embedded Data
- Share Data across Applications

Why Would I Do This?

While at your desk, you probably do several things in rapid succession: work on a paper, talk on the phone, punch numbers into your calculator, and so on. Similarly, when you work on your computer, you may work for a few minutes on a document in a word processor, take a moment to update a worksheet, then look up a phone number in an electronic phone book.

Multitasking
The execution of more than one program at a time on a computer system.

One of the advantages of using software that runs under Windows 95 is that you have the capability to exchange data among various applications. In Windows 95, you can have more than one application running at once—called *multitasking*—so you can switch among applications as you need to work on different tasks. You can display several applications' documents at the same time, if necessary, and you can exchange data among those documents.

Integration
Using two or more software applications together to create a single document.

In addition, with Excel 97, you can easily open and work with documents that were created in different applications, such as Lotus 1-2-3. You can also save documents in different file formats so that people using other applications can open and work with worksheets created with Excel. This feature of Windows software is called *integration,* and it makes working with the computer easier and more intuitive.

Lesson 1: Switching among Applications

You can use the taskbar to switch among open applications and to start additional programs. The number of applications that you can have open at one time is largely determined by the amount of available memory in your computer.

To Switch among Applications

1 In Excel, open the file Proj1101 and save it as `Office Expenses`.

The worksheet is a version of the office expenses worksheet you have used in earlier projects of this book.

2 On the taskbar, click the Start button, then move the mouse pointer to the Programs command.

A submenu appears, similar to the one shown in Figure 11.1, listing all the programs installed on your computer.

Figure 11.1
In Windows 95, you can start programs by using the **P**rograms menu.

Programs command

Microsoft Word command

Click here to start

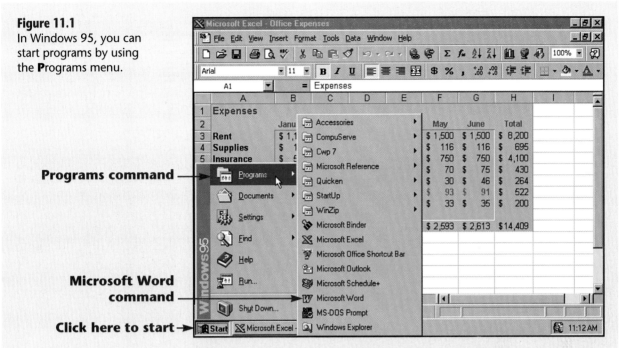

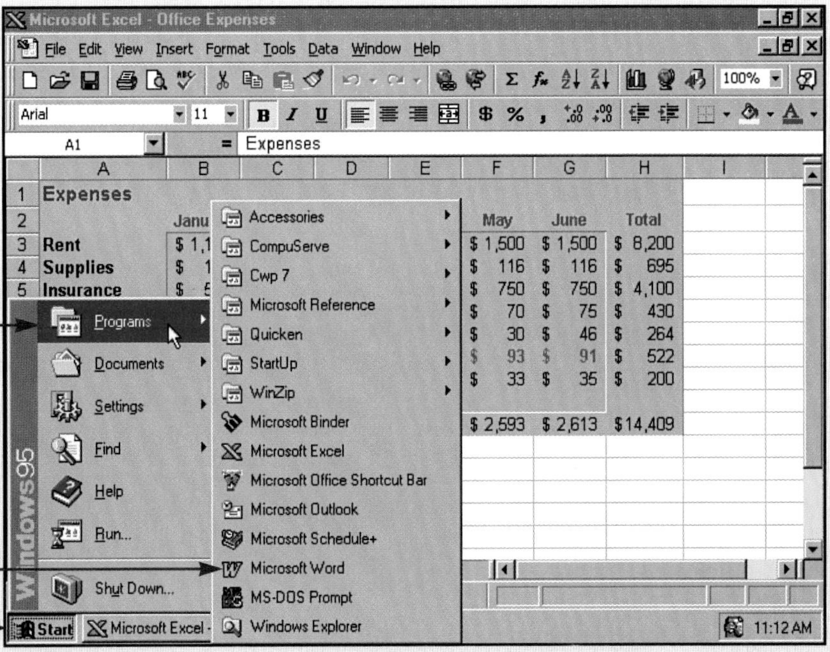

If you have problems...

If the taskbar does not appear at the bottom of your screen, it may have been moved to a different edge of your screen, or it may be hidden. If you see it in a different location, you can leave it there or drag it back to the bottom. If it doesn't appear at all, simply slide the mouse pointer down to the bottom of the screen to see if it appears. If you want the taskbar to be visible all the time, you can change the taskbar properties in Windows 95.

continues

To Switch among Applications (continued)

3 Click Microsoft Word on the Programs submenu.

Microsoft Word opens, as shown in Figure 11.2; Excel remains open and moves to the background. Notice that a button for Microsoft Word has been added to the taskbar. Microsoft Word is often used in conjunction with Excel.

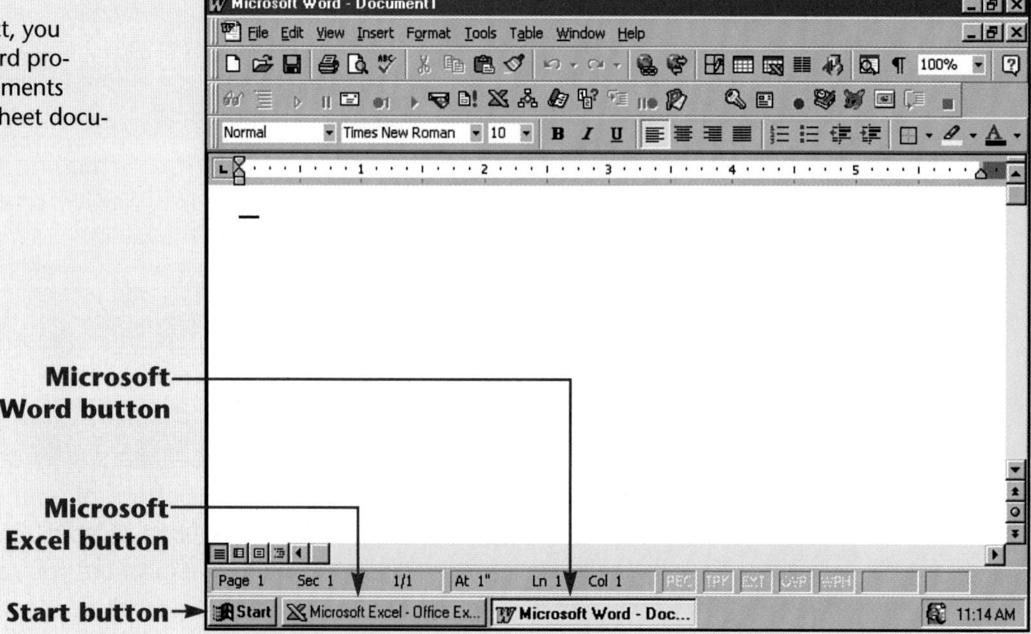

Figure 11.2
In this project, you integrate word processing documents with spreadsheet documents.

4 In Word, open the file Proj1102 and save it as `Memo`.

You will use the `Memo` document with the Excel `Office Expenses` document throughout this project (see Figure 11.3).

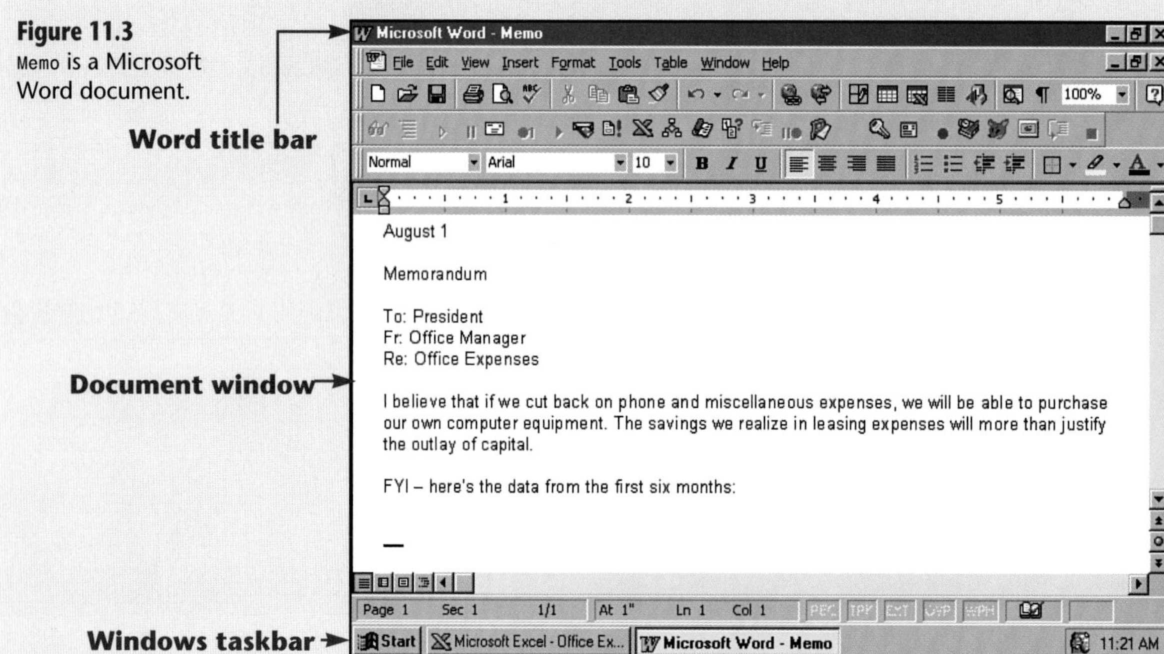

Figure 11.3
`Memo` is a Microsoft Word document.

5 Click the Microsoft Excel button on the taskbar.

This switches you back to Excel. Word remains open, running in the background. Keep all these documents and applications open. In Lesson 2, you learn how to copy data from one application to another.

Another quick way to switch among open applications is to press and hold down Alt as you press Tab. Each time you press Tab, the name of the next open application appears. When you see the name of the application you want to use, release both keys.

If you are distracted by an open application that is visible on the desktop behind the active application, maximize the active application to fill the desktop. If you want to switch to the application in the background, use the taskbar or press Alt+Tab.

Because you are using Microsoft Office, you can use the shortcut bar included with the suite to switch among programs. The shortcut bar usually appears in the title bar of the active applications, and it displays one button for each application in the suite. Click the application button to open or to switch to a different application.

If you have problems...

If you find that your system is slow or locking up, you may have unintentionally launched a program twice instead of simply switching to it. (You can launch a program again from the **P**rograms menu, even if it is already running, but not from the taskbar.) To avoid this problem, just check the taskbar before opening a new program to make sure that the program is not already running. If two buttons for the same program appear, right-click one of them and choose Close from the shortcut menu.

Lesson 2: Copying Data between Applications

It's easy to copy information from one application to another, and it saves you from having to re-enter data. For example, suppose that you want to include data from a worksheet in a letter to your company's president. You can perform this task easily by using the Windows Clipboard and task-switching capabilities.

To Copy Data between Applications

1. **In Excel, select cells A6:H9 in the `Office Expenses` worksheet.**

   This is the data you want to copy to the memo document.

2. **Click the Copy button on the Standard toolbar.**

   The data is copied to the Windows Clipboard. You can use the menu commands or the toolbar buttons to copy, cut, and paste data among applications. In short, you can use the Clipboard to copy or move data from one Windows application to another, just as you can copy or move data within a single document. For a refresher on using the Clipboard, refer to Project 6, "Building a Spreadsheet."

3. **Click the Microsoft Word button on the taskbar.**

   The `Memo` file that you opened earlier in this project should now be on your screen.

4. **Press Ctrl+End to move the insertion point to the blank line at the end of the memo.**

   This is where you want to insert the data you just copied from Excel.

5. **Click the Paste button on the Standard toolbar.**

   The data is pasted from the Clipboard into the letter at the insertion point's location (see Figure 11.4). The data is inserted in Word as a table, and retains most of the formatting from Excel. The table is in no way connected to the original data in Excel. Because you know how to use Word, you can edit and format the data using the T**a**ble menu features. The changes will have no effect on the worksheet data in Excel. Likewise, if you edit the Excel worksheet, the changes do not effect the table in Word.

   To prepare for the next lesson in this project, undo the paste action now to remove the Excel data from the Word document.

Figure 11.4
Selected data from the Excel worksheet now appears in the Word document.

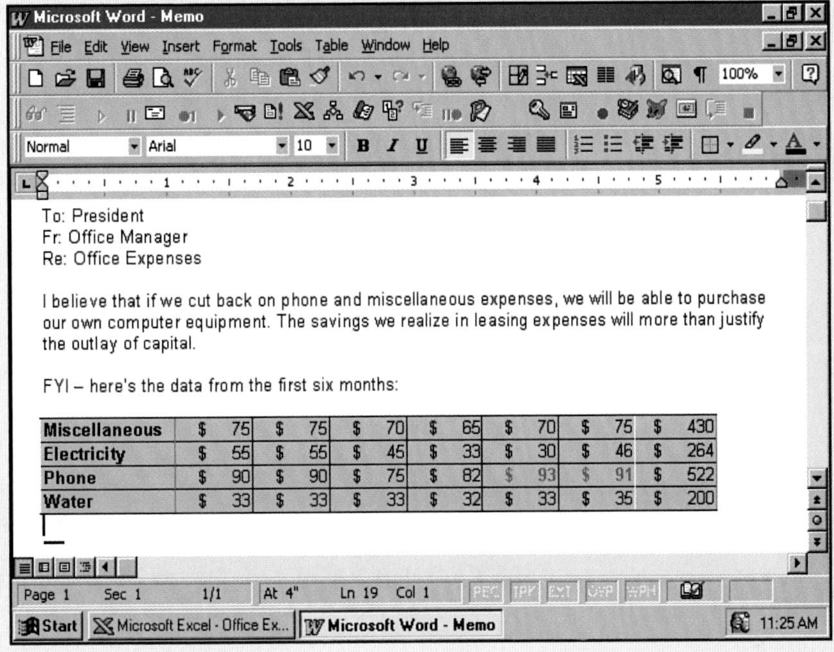

6 In the `Memo` **document, click the Undo button, or press** Ctrl+Z.

Word reverses the paste action, and the Excel data is removed from the `Memo` document.

Save your work, and keep all the current files and applications open. In the next lesson, you learn how to link data between Excel and Word.

To move data from one application to another, use the **Cu**t command or its toolbar button rather than the **C**opy command. If you are concerned about losing data, you can use the **C**opy command, then after you paste the data in the new location, return and delete it from the original location. You can also display both worksheets on-screen at the same time, then select and drag the data you want to move from one worksheet to the other.

Lesson 3: Linking Data between Applications

The next level of sophistication in using Excel with other applications is to *link* data from Excel to a document in another program. For example, you can link a range of cells from the expense worksheet to the memo in Word. Then, if you change any values in the worksheet, the information in the Word document is updated automatically. Keep in mind, however, that you cannot edit the linked data in the Word document. (Look for the Jargon Watch at the end of this lesson for more information about the terminology of sharing information between applications.)

You can link Excel data to many applications, including Word; presentation programs, such as PowerPoint; and database programs, such as Access. You can even link Excel data to programs that are not part of the Microsoft Office suite, as long as they support linking.

Another benefit of linking Excel data to other applications is that you can double-click the Excel data in the other document to quickly switch to the Excel worksheet where you originally created the data. Also, unlike the copy you made of the chart in the previous lesson, linking the chart updates the document.

You create a link so that you don't have to remember to update the same information in two places: the original worksheet and its representation in the letter.

To Link Data between Applications

1 Click the Excel button on the taskbar to switch to Excel, then select cells A1 through H11 in the `Office Expenses` worksheet.

This time, you want to link all of the worksheet data to your letter.

2 Click the Copy button.

This copies the selected range to the Windows Clipboard.

3 Click the Microsoft Word button on the taskbar to switch to Word.

Word is once again on-screen with `Memo` open.

4 Press Ctrl+End to move the insertion point to the blank line at the end of the document.

This is where you want to insert the linked data from Excel.

5 Choose Edit, Paste Special.

The Paste Special dialog box appears, as shown in Figure 11.5.

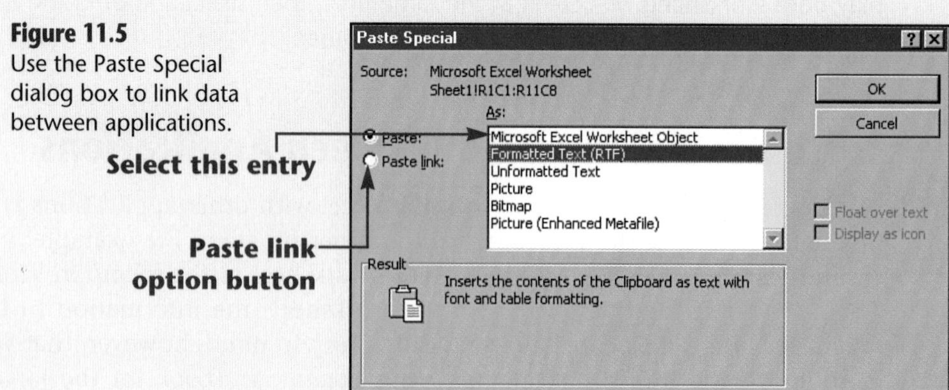

Figure 11.5
Use the Paste Special dialog box to link data between applications.

6 Click the Paste link option button.

This tells Word that you want to link the Excel data to the Word document.

7 Select Microsoft Excel Worksheet Object from the As data type list.

This tells Word that you want to paste the data as an actual Excel worksheet that will be updated any time changes are made in the `Office Expenses` worksheet. Notice that a description of the results of your selections appears in the Result area of the dialog box.

8 Choose OK.

The Excel data is pasted into the memo as an actual Excel worksheet object, as shown in Figure 11.6. Notice that Word changes the display view on the screen so that it can show the object in the document. The white boxes around the edges of the worksheet are called *selection handles*. You can drag a handle to change the size of the worksheet in the document.

Now try changing a cell in the Excel worksheet to see how the linked data changes automatically.

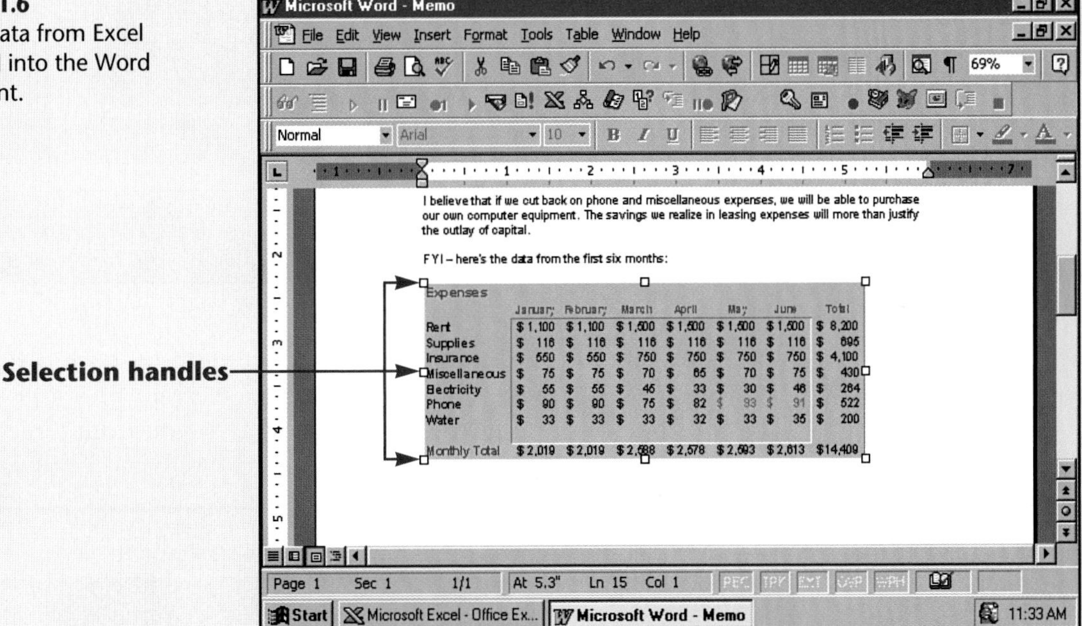

Figure 11.6 Linked data from Excel is pasted into the Word document.

9 Double-click anywhere within the Excel data in the Word document.

This switches back to Excel with the `Office Expenses` worksheet open. If necessary, maximize the worksheet.

10 Change cell F8 in the worksheet to `$80.00`.

This shows a decrease in the amount spent on phone expenses in May. Make sure that you press Tab or End to update the change to the cell. Notice that Excel automatically updates the conditional formatting, as well as the totals that depend on the data in cell F8.

continues

To Link Data between Applications (continued)

11 Click the Microsoft Word button on the taskbar.

Word appears, displaying the `Memo` document. Notice that the linked worksheet has been automatically updated to reflect the changes made in Excel, as shown in Figure 11.7. The May phone expenses, the totals, and the conditional formatting have all changed.

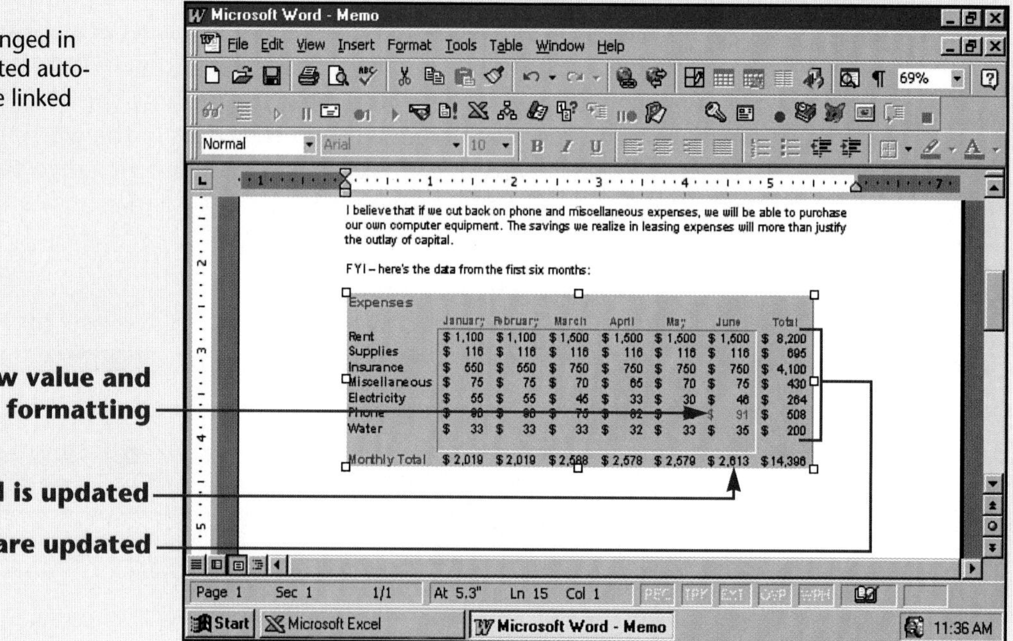

Figure 11.7
The values changed in Excel are updated automatically in the linked data in Word.

Save your work in both the Word document, `Memo`, and the Excel worksheet, `Office Expenses`. Keep all the current files and applications open for the next lesson. In Lesson 4, you work directly with the Excel object embedded in Word.

If you have problems...

If the data does not update in Word, you may have just pasted instead of pasting a link. Go back to Excel and copy the spreadsheet again, then switch to Word and make sure you choose **E**dit, Paste **S**pecial.

Also, if you change the location of either the source or the target document, the link between the two is broken. (See the following Jargon Watch for definitions of these terms.) For example, if you move the target document to a different folder or disk and then change the data in the source, Excel cannot automatically update the link. You must repeat the link procedure. If you plan to change the location of either document, you should consider simply copying the data from one to the other or embedding the data, as described in Lesson 4.

Jargon Watch

These days, **integration** is a hot buzz word in computing. For example, the Microsoft Office **suite** of applications are referred to as *integrated* because they share many features and standard commands, and because it is easy to integrate data from one program into another.

The common Windows platform enables many Windows applications to easily share data. This feature goes by the catchy names **OLE**, which stands for **object linking and embedding**, and **DDE**, which stands for **dynamic data exchange**.

DDE uses **linking** to set up communication between two files so that when you update the **source** file, the **target** file in the link is automatically updated. `Office Expenses` is the source file in Lesson 3, while `Memo` is the target file.

OLE uses **embedding** to create an **object** in the client file. You use embedding in Lesson 4 to make changes in an Excel object that resides in Word. With embedding, the object is not linked in any way to the source file; you can edit the worksheet data using Excel functions, but the changes do not affect the original data.

Lesson 4: Working with Embedded Data

In Lesson 3, you linked an Excel worksheet object into the Word document `Memo`. This is useful for keeping both the source and target documents current. However, there may be times when you want to keep the two separate—perhaps to experiment with the effects of possible changes in data or when you may not have access to the source file once the target file has been created. In cases such as these, you can embed the Excel worksheet object into the Word document instead of linking it.

Embedding the data enables you to edit the worksheet in the Word document without switching back to Excel. For example, if you want to take a quick look at the effect of decreased leasing costs on your expenses, double-click the embedded Excel worksheet object and make changes directly to the worksheet—without ever leaving the memo you are writing. The original source file, `Office Expenses`, is not affected by the change.

To Work with Embedded Data

1 In the Word file `Memo`, click the Excel data and press Del.

This selects the data, then deletes it, severing the link between the two applications. Now try embedding an Excel worksheet object into the Word document.

2 Click the Microsoft Excel button on the taskbar.

This switches you back to the `Office Expenses` worksheet.

continues

To Work with Embedded Data (continued)

3 Select cells A1 through H11, and click the Copy button on the Standard toolbar.

This copies the data you want to embed in the Word document onto the Windows Clipboard.

4 Click the Microsoft Word button on the taskbar.

This switches you back to Word.

5 Press Ctrl+End to position the insertion point on the blank line at the end of the memo, then open the Edit menu and choose Paste Special.

The Paste Special dialog box opens.

6 Choose Microsoft Excel Worksheet Object in the As list box, then choose OK.

Excel embeds the worksheet object at the insertion-point location. Do not choose the Paste **L**ink option button in the Paste Special dialog box. To embed the object, leave the **P**aste option button selected. Now try editing the worksheet.

7 Double-click the Excel worksheet object in the Word document.

The worksheet appears in its own Excel window within Word, as shown in Figure 11.8. Although the title bar tells you that you are still in Word, notice that the menu bar and toolbars have changed to include Excel commands and options. The formula bar even appears in your Word window now. Next, see what effect removing miscellaneous costs would have on your worksheet.

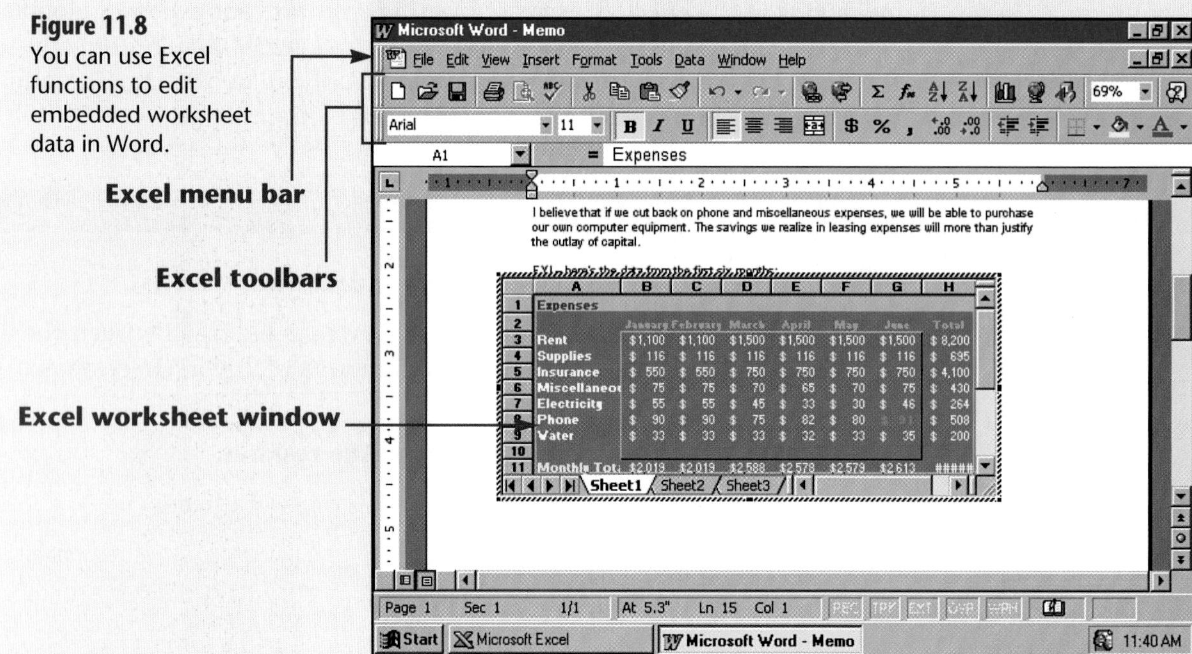

Figure 11.8
You can use Excel functions to edit embedded worksheet data in Word.

8 In the worksheet window, click the row 6 number in the worksheet frame, then choose Edit, Delete.

This selects then removes row 6 from the embedded worksheet. Notice that the total cells change automatically to reflect that miscellaneous expenses are no longer included.

9 Click anywhere in the Word document outside the worksheet window.

This closes the Excel worksheet, and Word returns to its normal state. Notice that the change you made in the data appears in the Word worksheet object, as shown in Figure 11.9. Save the Word document, then switch back to see how the changes affected the original worksheet document.

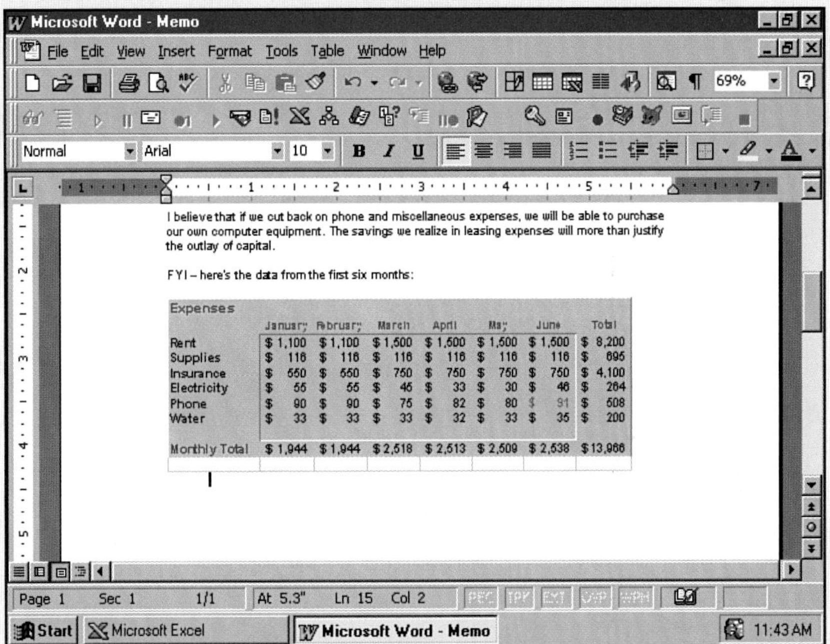

I believe that if we cut back on phone and miscellaneous expenses, we will be able to purchase our own computer equipment. The savings we realize in leasing expenses will more than justify the outlay of capital.

FYI – here's the data from the first six months:

Expenses	January	February	March	April	May	June	Total
Rent	$ 1,100	$ 1,100	$ 1,500	$ 1,500	$ 1,500	$ 1,500	$ 8,200
Supplies	$ 116	$ 116	$ 116	$ 116	$ 116	$ 116	$ 695
Insurance	$ 550	$ 550	$ 750	$ 750	$ 750	$ 750	$ 4,100
Electricity	$ 55	$ 55	$ 45	$ 33	$ 30	$ 46	$ 264
Phone	$ 90	$ 90	$ 75	$ 82	$ 80	$ 91	$ 508
Water	$ 33	$ 33	$ 33	$ 32	$ 33	$ 35	$ 200
Monthly Total	$ 1,944	$ 1,944	$ 2,518	$ 2,513	$ 2,509	$ 2,538	$ 13,966

Figure 11.9
The changes appear in the embedded worksheet, but not in the original Excel file.

10 In Word, choose File, Close, then click Yes to save the changes to the Word document `Memo`. Close Word.

When Word closes, Excel remains open on your screen. In Excel, you can see that no changes have been made to the original data.

Save your Excel work. In the next lesson, you learn how to share data across different applications.

Lesson 5: Sharing Data across Different Applications

Sometimes you may need to open files that have been created in a different application. Likewise, you may want to be able to open an Excel file using a different application. For example, you may use Excel at work but have Lotus 1-2-3 at home, or a coworker or client may use a different application.

Excel 97 is able to open and save files in a wide variety of file formats. When you open a file created in a different file format, Excel simply converts the data to the Excel format, so you can easily use all Excel commands and options. When you save the file, you have the option of saving it in its original format or in Excel 97 format. When you save a file in a different file format, Excel converts the file so that you can open it and edit it in the other application. In this lesson, you save the `Office Expenses` workbook file in a different file format.

To Share Data across Different Applications

1 In the `Office Expenses` worksheet, choose File, Save As.

The Save As dialog box is displayed. The default file type is Microsoft Excel Workbook. However, you want to save the file so that you can open it with Lotus 1-2-3.

2 Click the Save as type drop-down arrow.

A list of file formats that you can use to save the file opens, as shown in Figure 11.10.

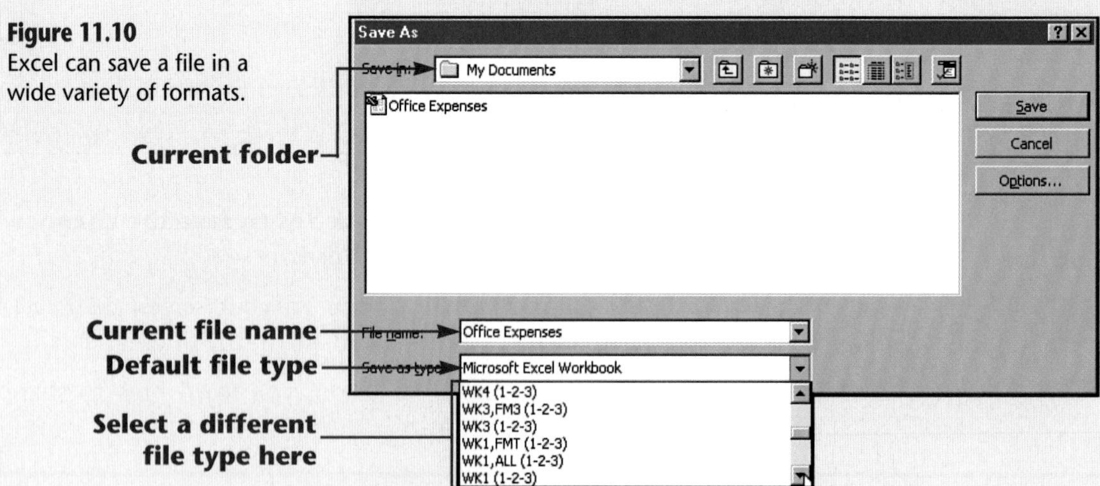

Figure 11.10
Excel can save a file in a wide variety of formats.

3 Scroll down the list and choose `WK4 (1-2-3)`.

This tells Excel you want to save the file in Lotus 1-2-3 Release 4 format.

❹ In the File name text box, type `Expenses123`**.**

This changes the file name to make it easier to identify which file is the Excel file and which is the Lotus 1-2-3 file. If necessary, select the folder or disk where you want to save the file from the Save **in** drop-down list.

❺ Choose Save.

Excel saves the file in 1-2-3 format and keeps it open on the screen, as shown in Figure 11.11. The Excel `Office Expenses` worksheet is saved in its original format and closed. All of the data in the `Expenses123` file appears as it did in the Excel format file; however, some of the formatting is changed to conform to the 1-2-3 standard. For example, notice that the dollar signs are no longer left-aligned in the cells formatted as currency. Also, notice that the conditional formatting is no longer in effect and that merged cells are split.

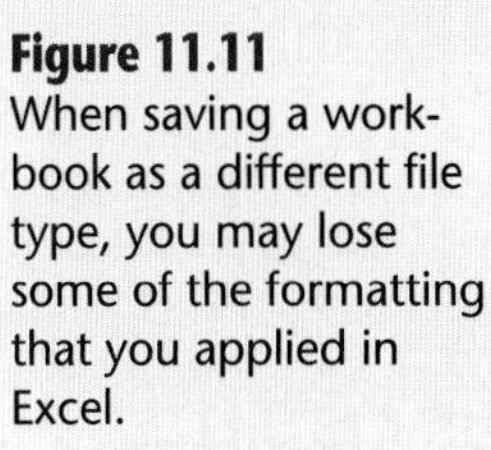

Figure 11.11
When saving a workbook as a different file type, you may lose some of the formatting that you applied in Excel.

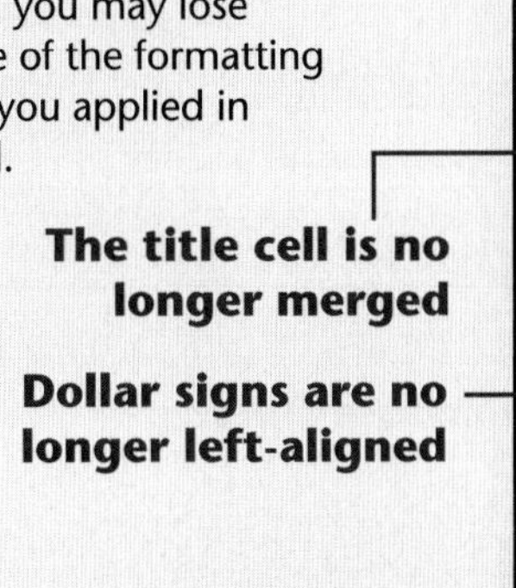

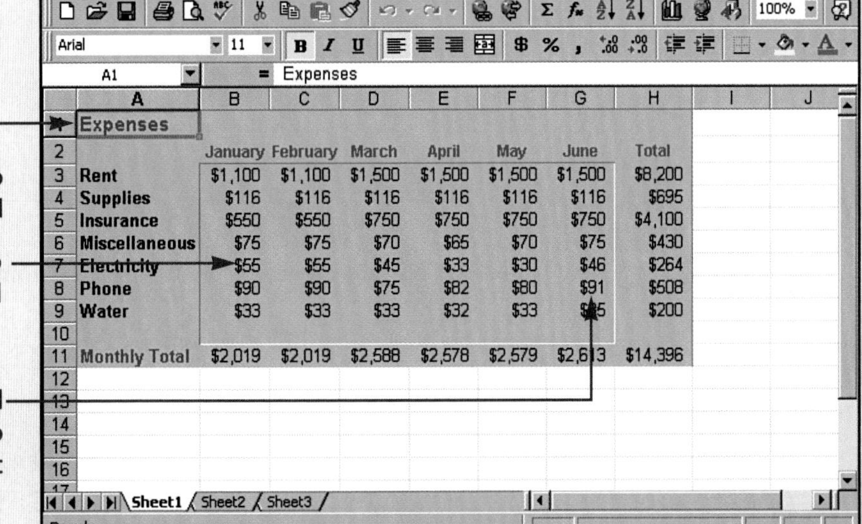

❻ Choose File, Close.

The first time you close a file saved in a different file format, Excel displays a message box asking if you want to convert the file back to Excel format before you close it.

❼ Choose No.

Excel saves the file in 1-2-3 Release 4 format and closes it. Now, try opening a file saved in a different file format.

continues

To Share Data across Different Applications (continued)

8 In Excel, choose File, Open.

The Open dialog box is displayed. Notice that only Excel files are listed.

9 From the Files of type drop down list, choose Lotus 1-2-3 Files.

This tells Excel to list files saved in the Lotus 1-2-3 format. In the Open dialog box, you see the `Expenses123` file name (see Figure 11.12).

Figure 11.12
You can use Excel to open files saved in other file formats.

File name

Files of type text box

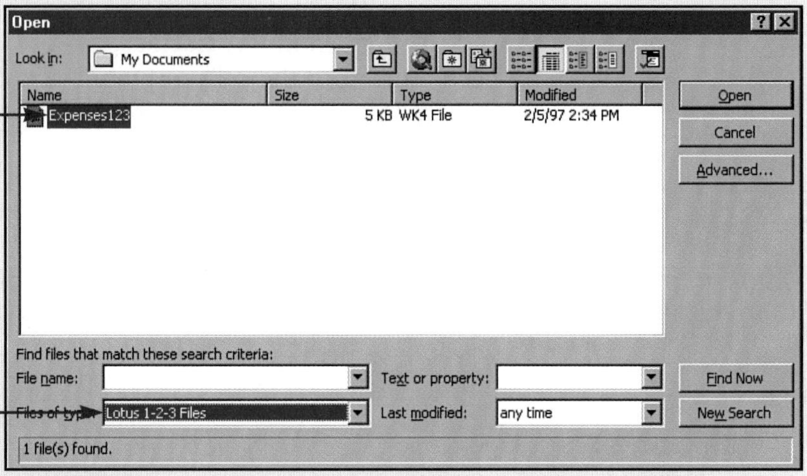

10 Select the `Expenses123` file name, then choose Open.

Excel opens the file.

11 Close the `Expenses123` file.

You have now completed the lessons in this project. If you have completed your session on the computer, exit all open applications and Windows 95 before turning off the computer. Otherwise, continue with the "Checking Your Skills" section.

With Excel 97, you can save data in the HTML format, which is used to store files on the Word Wide Web. To save data in HTML format, choose **F**ile, Save as **H**TML to start the Internet Assistant Wizard, then follow the instructions that the wizard displays on your screen.

In the Open dialog box, you can display all files stored in the current folder—regardless of file type—by choosing All Files from the Files of **t**ype drop down list.

Project Summary

To	Do This
Switch applications	On the Windows 95 taskbar, click the button for the application you want to make active, or press Alt+Tab.
Copy data between applications	Select the data to copy and click the Copy button on the Standard toolbar. Change to the target document, position the insertion point, and click the Paste button on the Standard toolbar.
Move data between applications	Select the data to move and click the Cut button on the Standard toolbar. Change to the target document, position the insertion point, and click the Paste button on the Standard toolbar.
Link data between applications	Select the data to link and click the Copy button on the Standard toolbar. Change to the target document, position the insertion point, and choose **E**dit, Paste **S**pecial. Click the Paste **L**ink option button, select the object type, and choose OK.
Edit linked data	Double-click the data to open the source document. Make changes, then close the source document.
Embed data	Select the data to embed and click the Copy button on the Standard toolbar. Change to the target document, position the insertion point, and choose **E**dit, Paste **S**pecial. Select the object type, and choose OK.
Edit embedded data	Double-click the data to open an editing window. Edit the document, then close the editing window.
Save a file in a different format	Choose **F**ile, Save **A**s. Select the file format from the Save as **t**ype drop-down list, then choose **S**ave.
Open a file in a different format	Choose **F**ile, **O**pen. Select the file type from the Files of **t**ype drop-down list, select the file you want to open, then choose **O**pen.

Checking Your Skills

True/False

For each of the following, check *T* or *F* to indicate whether the statement is true or false.

__T __F **1.** You can use the Windows taskbar to switch among programs, but not to open them.

__T __F **2.** On the taskbar, you click the Start button to start Microsoft Word.

__T __F **3.** You cannot use the keyboard shortcuts for copying, cutting, and pasting when you are integrating applications.

__T __F **4.** If your system slows down, it could be because you have two copies of the same program open.

__T __F **5.** Use the **E**dit, Paste **S**pecial command to link or embed data between applications.

__T __F **6.** If two documents are visible on your screen, you can drag data from one document to another.

__T __F **7.** Excel 97 is capable of opening and saving files in different formats, such as Lotus 1-2-3.

__T __F **8.** If you use the Copy and Paste commands to copy data from a worksheet to a word processing file, the data will be automatically updated when you make changes to one of the files.

__T __F **9.** You cannot link data between programs that are not part of the Microsoft Office suite.

__T __F **10.** The number of applications you can have open at one time is largely determined by the amount of your computer's memory.

Multiple Choice

Circle the letter of the correct answer for each of the following questions.

1. Which of the following is an easy way to switch among applications?

- **a.** Press Ctrl+Del.
- **b.** Press Alt+Ctrl.
- **c.** Click the application's button on the Windows taskbar.
- **d.** Click the application's Start box.

2. Which of the following can be passed over a link between applications?

- **a.** numbers
- **b.** charts
- **c.** ranges of cells
- **d.** all the above

3. One application opens within the other application when you do what between two applications?

- **a.** copy
- **b.** link
- **c.** move
- **d.** embed

4. Embedding and linking are part of a Windows feature called what?

- **a.** OLE
- **b.** LEO
- **c.** ELO
- **d.** LLE

5. You can make a change in the source, and the destination automatically updates when you do what?

- **a.** link
- **b.** embed
- **c.** copy
- **d.** paste

6. The changes you make in the target document do not affect the source when you do what to the data?

- **a.** link
- **b.** embed
- **c.** copy
- **d.** paste

7. Which of the following formats is used to store Excel files on the World Wide Web?

- **a.** WWW
- **b.** WK4
- **c.** HTML
- **d.** INT

8. What occurs when you double-click a linked object?

- **a.** The object is deleted from the document.
- **b.** You are switched back to the originating program.
- **c.** An error message displays.
- **d.** You can edit the document in the target file.

9. To embed data into a file, you use which dialog box to paste it into the target document?

- **a.** Paste Special
- **b.** Paste Object
- **c.** Embed Object
- **d.** Embed Data

10. To paste a link into a document, you choose which option button in the Paste Special dialog box?

- **a.** **P**aste
- **b.** **L**ink
- **c.** Link **d**ocument
- **d.** Paste **l**ink

Completion

In the blanks provided, write the correct answer for each of the following statements.

1. A link is a _____________-way connection between the source worksheet and the client file.
2. If your system slows when embedding, you may want to consider sharing your data by _____________ instead.
3. The taskbar displays buttons for all ____________ applications.
4. When pasting data into another program, the data appears at the _____________ point.
5. The _____________ application is the one in which the original object was created.
6. To switch to an application in the background, use the taskbar or press ____________+ _____________.
7. You can use the _____________ to copy or move data from one application to another.
8. If the taskbar does not appear at the bottom of the screen, it may have been moved or it may be _____________.
9. To move data from one application to another, use the _____________ command.
10. If you change the location of the source or target document, the link between the two is _____________.

Matching

In the blank next to each of the following terms or phrases, write the letter of the corresponding term or phrase.

____ **1.** White boxes around the edges of a worksheet object

____ **2.** The file in which linked data originates

____ **3.** The file in which linked data is pasted

____ **4.** Executing more than one program at a time

____ **5.** Using two or more software applications together to create a single document

____ **6.** Embedding is used to create this in a file

____ **7.** Uses linking to set up communication between two files

____ **8.** Used to switch among open applications and to start additional programs

____ **9.** Use this command to paste information from the Clipboard to another application

____ **10.** Use this command to paste a link or embed data into a document

a. taskbar
b. Paste
c. Paste **S**pecial
d. object
e. selection handles
f. multitasking
g. target file
h. integration
i. dynamic data exchange (DDE)
j. source file

Screen ID

Label each element of the Excel screen shown in Figure 11.13.

Figure 11.13

1. ____________
2. ____________
3. ____________
4. ____________
5. ____________
6. ____________
7. ____________

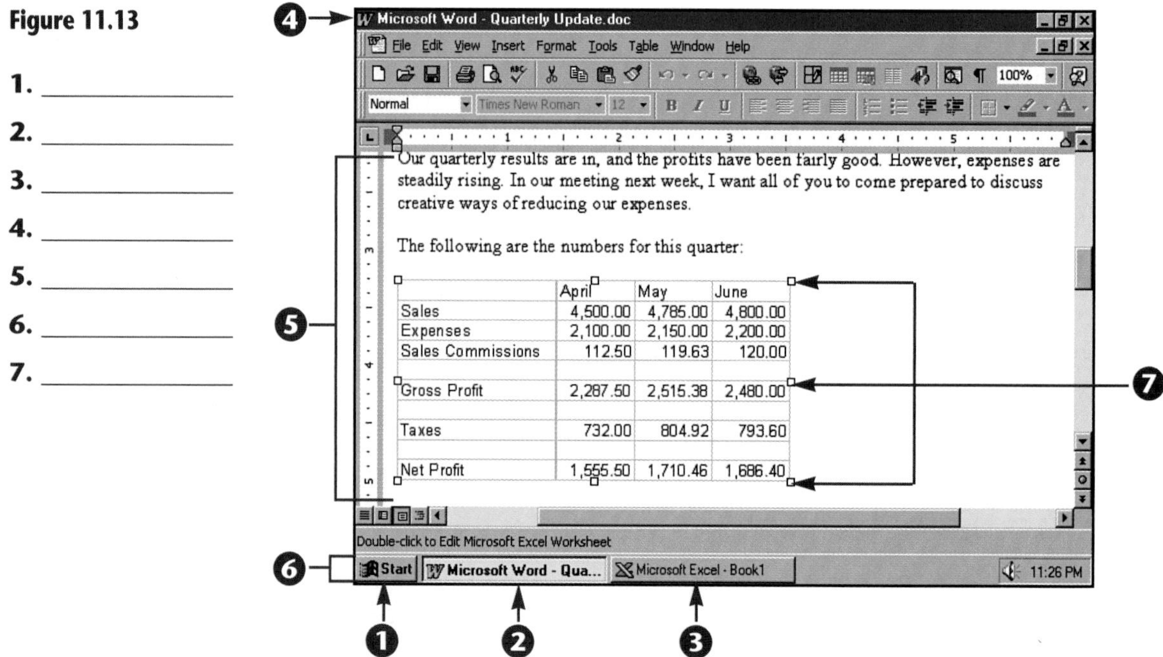

Applying Your Skills

Practice

The following exercises enable you to practice the skills you have learned in this project. Take a few minutes to work through these exercises now.

1. Switching among Applications

In this project, you learned how easy it is to open additional applications and to switch among these applications. In this exercise, you practice switching among applications.

To Switch among Applications

1. In Excel, open the file Proj1103 and save it as `Profit Loss 4`.
2. Start the Word application using the Start button on the taskbar. If Word is not on your computer, ask your instructor which application to use.

3. Open one more application located in the Accessories submenu. You choose which of these applications to open. Notice that a button for each of these applications displays on the taskbar.
4. Click the Microsoft Excel button to switch to this application.
5. Click the Microsoft Word button to switch to this application.
6. Hold down the Alt key and press Tab until the name of the Accessories application that you opened appears in the screen. Release both keys to access this application.
7. Close the Accessories application and Microsoft Word. Leave Excel open for the following exercise.

2. Creating a Letter

A friend of yours is thinking about relocating to a new state, and has asked you where your company has offices so she can contact them about employment opportunities. You agree to provide a list of the states where your company has offices. Because you already have a list of sites stored in an Excel worksheet, you simply copy the data into a word processing document to send to her.

To Create a Letter

1. In Excel, open the file Proj1103a and save it as `Relocate`.
2. In Word, open the file Proj1104 and save it as `Site Letter`.
3. Copy the entire list of offices and locations in the worksheet to the Clipboard.
4. Move to the end of `Site Letter` in Word, then paste the worksheet data.
5. Save the letter. If requested by your instructor, print two copies before closing both files.

3. Adding Names to Your Phone List

The company president sends you a file of a memo with the names of four new contacts who he thinks might be interested in your product. You want to add the names to the phone list that you already created in Excel. Instead of retyping the names and phone numbers, copy the data from the word processing document into Excel.

To Add Names to Your Phone List

1. Open the file Proj1105 in Excel, and save it as `Contacts`.
2. Open the file Proj1106 in Word, and save it as `New Names`.
3. Select the table in the Word document, then copy it to the Windows Clipboard.
4. Switch to Excel, and paste the data from the Clipboard to the end of the list.
5. Save the worksheet. If requested by your instructor, print two copies before closing both files.

4. Creating a Presentation for Potential Investors

Heading into your second year in business, you want to make a presentation to potential investors that will convince them to provide capital so you can open a second coffee shop. To do this effectively, you need to create a report in Word that includes narrative, as well as a worksheet showing strong sales for the current year. Link data from an Excel worksheet to the presentation document in Word, then make some last-minute changes in the Excel worksheet that will be updated in the linked chart.

To Create a Presentation for Potential Investors

1. In Excel, open the file Proj1107 and save it as `Coffee Sales`.
2. In Word, open the file Proj1108 and save it as `Presentation`.
3. In the `Coffee Sales` worksheet, select the entire worksheet (cells A1:E12) and copy it to the Clipboard.
4. Switch to Word and link the chart to the end of the `Presentation` document.
5. Switch back to the worksheet and make the following changes: in the January Mocha sales, change the value to `$300`; in the February Espresso sales, change the value to `$250`. Save the worksheet.
6. Switch back to the Word document to view the changes in the chart. Save the `Presentation` document. If requested by your instructor, print two copies of each file, then save and close all open documents.

5. Comparing Regional Sales Figures

The New England regional sales manager has submitted sales figures on a disk in Lotus 1-2-3 file format. You want to be able to compare the figures with other regional figures that you have already entered into Excel and then give the comparison back to the sales manager for review. Open the 1-2-3 file, copy the data into the Excel worksheet, then save the Excel worksheet as a new 1-2-3 file.

To Compare Regional Sales Figures

1. Open the file Proj1109 in Excel and save it as `Sales Comparison`.
2. Open the Lotus 1-2-3 file Proj1110 in Excel and save it in 1-2-3 format as `NE Sales123`.
3. Copy the sales data from the `NE Sales123` file into cells D2 through E12 in the `Sales Comparison` Excel workbook file.
4. Adjust the column width so you can read the data, then save the Excel file.
5. Save the `Sales Comparison` file in 1-2-3 file format with the name `Comparison123`.
6. If requested by your instructor, print two copies or each file, then close them.

Challenge

The following challenges enable you to use your problem-solving skills. Take time to work through these exercises now.

1. Copying Data from One Application to Another

Your boss has asked you to create a document containing data from an Excel worksheet. To save having to reenter the information, you decide to copy the data from one application to another. Open the Word file Proj1111 and save it as `Quarterly Update`. In the `Profit Loss 4` Excel worksheet (created in the previous exercise), copy the data in cells A4:D13 to the Clipboard. Switch back to the Word document and paste the data at the end of the Word document. Save the Word file and keep both Word and Excel open for the next exercise.

2. Linking Data

Now that you have copied the data, you realize that you could have linked the data. Then, if you have to make changes to the data in the original application, the target document is automatically changed.

Switch to the Word document, `Quarterly Update`. Select the information that you copied in the previous exercise, and then delete it. Switch back to the Excel document, `Profit Loss 4`. Copy the cells A4:D13 to the Clipboard and switch back to the Word document. Use the Paste Special dialog box to link the Excel worksheet object. In the Excel worksheet, change the April sales number in cell B5 to **`4,700`**. Switch back to Word to see the change in the `Quarterly Update` document. Save `Quarterly Update` and leave it open for the following exercise. Switch to Excel and save the `Profit Loss 4` workbook. Leave it open for the following exercise.

3. Embedding Data

Because you now want to make some changes in the Word document but don't want to affect the original Excel worksheet, you decide to embed the data instead of linking it.

Switch to the Word `Quarterly Update` document, and delete the data you linked from the Excel worksheet. Switch back to Excel. Copy the data in cells A4:D13 and use the Paste Special dialog box to embed the data at the end of the Word document. Double-click the Excel worksheet object in the Word document to display the worksheet in its own Excel window within Word. Change the number in cell B5 to **`4,500`**. Save the Word document before closing it. Switch to Excel. Notice that the value in cell B5 has not changed. Save the Excel workbook and leave it open for the following exercise.

4. Sharing Data across Applications

One of your co-workers needs to access some data in one of your Excel worksheets. The only problem is that he doesn't have Excel on his system; only Lotus 1-2-3. You decide to save the Excel file as a Lotus 1-2-3 file so that he can access the information.

In the `Profit Loss 4` workbook, choose **F**ile, Save **A**s to display the Save As dialog box. In the Save as **t**ype drop-down list, select WK3 (1-2-3). Choose **S**ave to save the file with the same name, but in the different format. Choose **F**ile, **C**lose. Excel displays a message box asking if you want to convert the file back to Excel format. Choose **N**o. The file is saved in the 1-2-3 format. Choose **F**ile, **O**pen. Because only Excel files display in the dialog box, click the Files of **t**ype drop down list. Choose Lotus 1-2-3 files. Select the `Profit Loss 4` file, then choose Open. The file is opened in the Lotus 1-2-3 format. Close the `Profit Loss 4` file.

5. Opening Files Created in a Different Application

Your checking account file was originally saved in Lotus 1-2-3 format. Now you have upgraded to the latest version of Excel, and you want to be able to use this file without having to reenter any information. You open the 1-2-3 file, then save it as an Excel file.

Open Proj1112.wk1. (Hint: You need to display Lotus 1-2-3 files to locate this file.) Save the file as `Checking Account 8` in Microsoft Excel 97 & 5.0/95 Workbook format. Close the file and reopen the `Checking Account 8` file, which is now in Excel format. When you have finished, close the `Checking Account 8` file.

Project 12

Creating a Database

Objectives

In this project, you learn how to:

- Create a New Database
- Create a New Table
- Save a Table and Create a Primary Key
- Add Fields
- Edit Fields
- Change Views and Move Fields
- Delete Fields

Why Would I Do This?

With Access, you can set up databases for a wide variety of purposes. For example, you may want a database (like the one you create in this project) to keep track of staff training for your company. You can set up various databases to store different sets of related information, and you can create as many databases as you need.

Think of the database as the shell that holds together all the other related objects. Within the shell, you can create other objects. The fundamental type of object in an Access database is a table. You use tables to store data and organize the information into a usable structure. You can also create other objects, such as forms and queries. You learn about these other database objects later in this book.

In this project, you learn how to create a database and table from scratch. You also learn how to edit the structure of the table.

Lesson 1: Creating a New Database

Remember that the table is the object in which you actually store and define the structure for your data and the database is the shell that houses all of the related tables and other objects.

It's tempting to create one big database that includes many tables to meet many different needs, but it's a better idea to create smaller databases, each of which is dedicated to a particular function. Doing so makes managing and using each database much easier. You can relate these smaller databases to one another later if necessary.

In this lesson, you create a new database to keep track of the personal computer software training received by your staff.

To Create a New Database

1 Launch Access.

The Microsoft Access dialog box is displayed (see Figure 12.1).

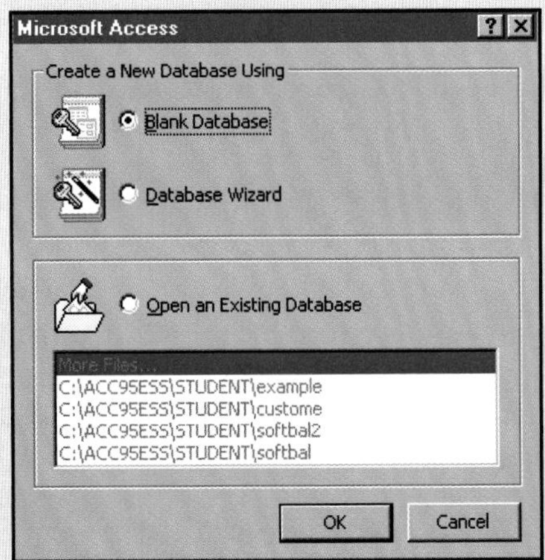

Figure 12.1
The Microsoft Access dialog box enables you to open an existing database or create a new one.

2 Click the Blank Database option, and then click OK.

Access displays the File New Database dialog box (see Figure 12.2). Access suggests a default name (db1) for the new database; however, you can assign a more descriptive name here, and you can also tell Access where you want to store the database.

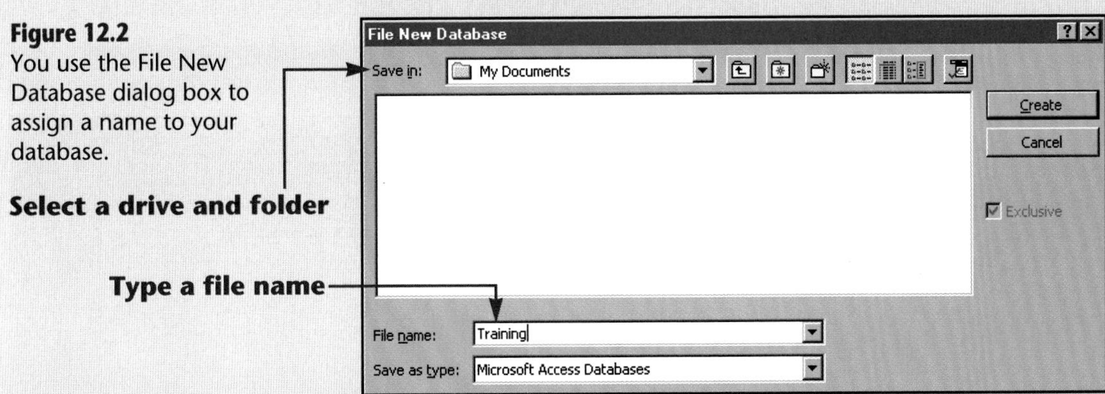

Figure 12.2
You use the File New Database dialog box to assign a name to your database.

3 In the File name text box, type `Training`.

This is the name you want to use for the new database. After you name the database the first time, you won't have to do it again. As you add or edit records, Access updates the database automatically. As you add new objects, however, you have to save each of them. When you add a table, for example, you must save it. Access then updates the database to incorporate this new table name.

continues

To Create a New Database (continued)

4 If you want to store the database in a different location, change to that drive or folder.

Access suggests a default drive and folder for saving the new database. Your instructor may want you to store the database on another drive or folder; check with your instructor for specific instructions. You can change folders by finding the folder you want in the list displayed in the Save **i**n box. To change the location where the database will be stored, click the drop-down list arrow at the right of the Save in box.

5 Click the Create button.

Access displays the database window for your new database. The name of the database is displayed in the title bar of the database window, as shown in Figure 12.3. Notice that the window is blank because you have not created any database objects (tables, queries, and so on). Keep the Training database open to use in Lesson 3. In that lesson, you learn how to add a new table to the database.

Database name

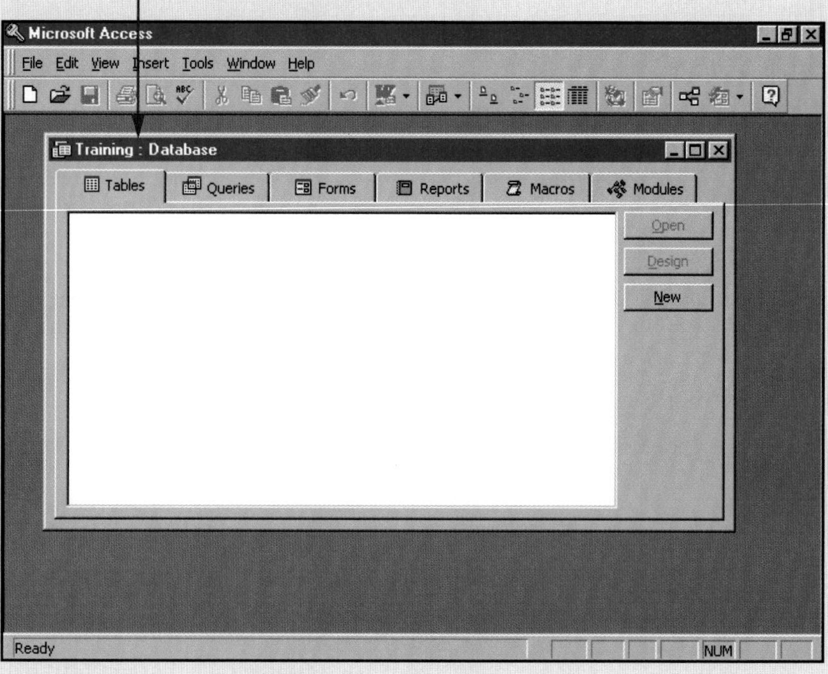

Figure 12.3
The name you assign to your database is displayed in the title bar of the database window.

There is usually more than one way to perform each function in Access. For example, to create a new database, you can press Ctrl+N, select **N**ew Database from the **F**ile menu, or click the New Database button on the toolbar.

Lesson 2: Creating a New Table

Field
One piece of information in a database or the location where a piece of information is entered. In Access, fields are stored in columns of a table.

After you create your database, you can add tables to it to store your information. A database is built on one or more tables, each of which holds a distinct set of information. The table defines the structure of the data—what pieces of data you enter and in what order. You should spend some time planning the structure of your database. How many *fields* do you need? What are their data types? If necessary, you can add fields later if you need them, but it is very important to map out the fundamental structure of the table before you get started.

Building a database without a plan is like building a house without a blueprint. The more work you invest in the initial design, the less you will spend in patchwork repairs later. Design your table structures first so that you can immediately put the database to work with confidence.

Record
One set of information in a database. In Access, records are stored in rows of a table.

When you create a new table, you can add any fields you want. Remember that the table consists of records (one set of information—such as the name, address, and phone number for one person) and fields. Fields are the individual pieces of information that together make up a record; for example, an address is a field. To add a field, you type a field name and then select a data type. Table 12.1 explains the various data types you can use. You can also type a description for the field and set field properties.

Table 12.1 Data Types and What They Mean

Data Type	Explanation
Text	The default data type. You can enter up to 255 numbers or letters.
Memo	You can include up to 1.2G (G stands for gigabyte; 1G = 1,073,741,824 characters). This type of field is not limited by size. This type of field is useful when you want to include sentences or paragraphs in the field—for example, a long product description.
Number	You can enter only numbers.
Date/Time	You can enter only dates or times.
Currency	You can enter numbers. Access formats the entry as currency. If you type `12.5`, for example, Access displays it as `$12.50`.
Counter	Access enters a value that is incremented automatically with each new record added to a table.
Yes/No	You can enter only `Yes` or `No` (or `True` or `False`). For example, you may have a Sent Christmas Card field in your address database that would work best as a Yes/No field.
OLE Object	You can insert OLE objects, graphics, or other data.

Object Linking and Embedding (OLE)
A set of standards that enables you to insert objects, such as pictures or spreadsheets, from one document created with one application into documents created with another application.

In this lesson, you create a table containing fields for first names, last names, and department names.

To Create a New Table

❶ **Click the Tables tab in the Training database window.**

❷ **Click the New button.**

Access displays the New Table dialog box (see Figure 12.4). You can choose between two views of a blank database, or you can launch one of three wizards to create a new table.

Figure 12.4
The New Table dialog box offers five choices for creating a database.

Design view
The view of the table you use when you are creating or changing fields. You see columns for the field name, data type, and description.

❸ **Select Design view and click OK.**

You see the table in *Design view* with the default name of Table1 (see Figure 12.5). The new table, as you can see, contains no fields. To add fields to the table, you must first enter the field names, data types, and descriptions. The blinking insertion point is displayed in the first row of the Field Name column. Here you type the first field name.

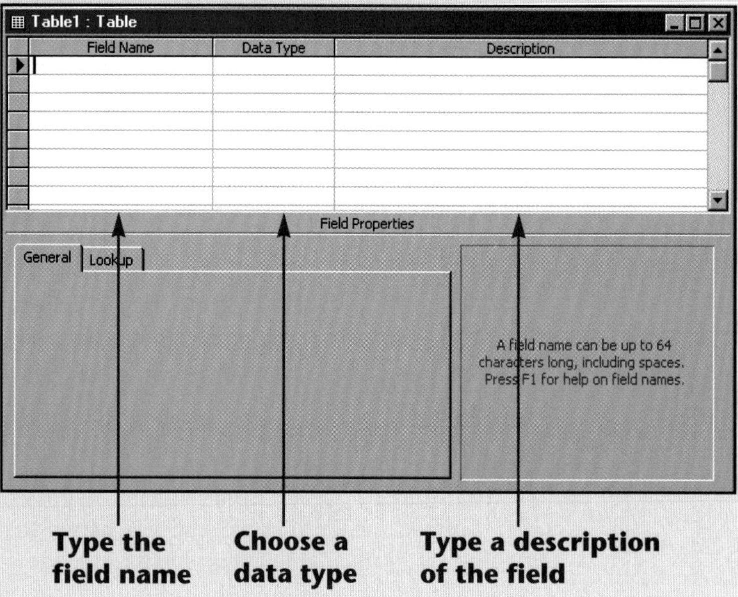

Figure 12.5
The blank table in Design view.

❹ **Type `First Name` and press Enter.**

Access enters the field name for the first field. In the lower half of the window, Access displays the field properties you can set. Access moves the insertion point to the Data Type column so that you can choose the type of data you want the field to contain. The most common data type is Text, which is the default. You can click the down arrow (which is displayed when you move to the Data Type column) to display a drop-down list of data types. For First Name, leave the data type as the default, which is Text.

5 Press ↵Enter.

Datasheet view
The view of the table you use when you enter or edit records. The field names you enter appear in the first row, followed by any records you have entered in the table.

Text is accepted as the data type, and Access moves the insertion point to the Description column.

6 Type `First name of staff member` and press ↵Enter.

Access enters the field description and moves the insertion point to the next row (see Figure 12.6). The description column comes in handy when you are in *Datasheet view* and enter a value in the First Name field. The field description will be displayed in the status bar. You are now ready to enter the next field name.

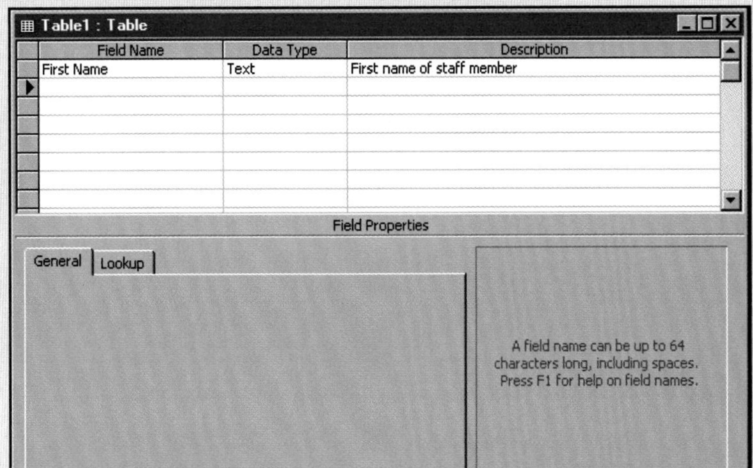

Figure 12.6
The first field of the Table1 table.

7 Type `Last Name` and press ↵Enter twice.

This enters the name for the field, accepts the default Text as the field type, and moves the insertion point to the Description column.

8 Type `Last name of staff member` and press ↵Enter.

As before, Access enters the field description for this second field and moves the insertion point to the next row so that you can add another field. Adding a field description is optional. If you do include a description, however, it is displayed in the status bar whenever you are in Datasheet view or Form view and place the insertion point in that field. Then the information in the status bar provides a more complete description of the purpose of the field to someone entering data.

continues

To Create a New Table (continued)

9 Type `Department` and press Enter twice.

Again, this step enters the field name, accepts Text as the data type, and moves the insertion point to the Description column.

10 Type `Staff member's department` and press Enter.

This is the description for the third field of your table, as shown in Figure 12.7. By adding these fields to the database table, you have taken the first steps toward creating a database to track staff training. Keep both this table and the Training database open. You learn how to save the table in the next lesson.

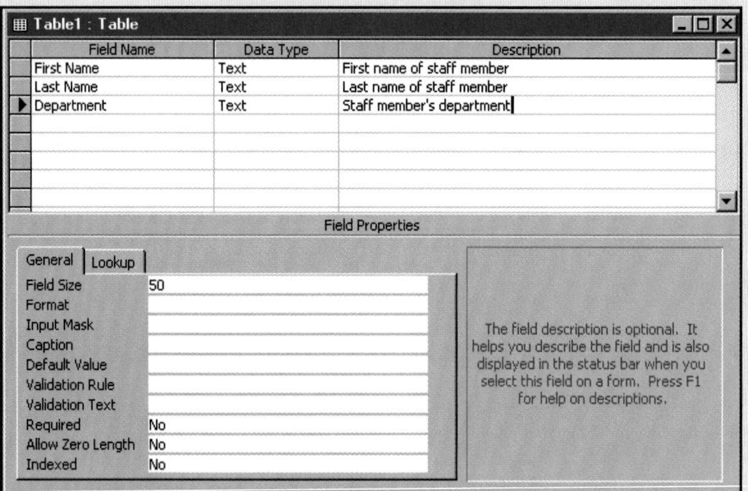

Figure 12.7
The Design view of a database table containing three fields.

You can create a field name using up to 64 characters. Try to use names that are short but meaningful (long names make the system work harder). You can use any combination of letters, numbers, spaces, and characters, with a few exceptions: periods (.), exclamation points (!), single quotation marks (‘), and brackets ([ ]) cannot appear anywhere in the name. Spaces are allowed, but not as the first character of the field name.

You can also use the Tab key in place of the Enter key when adding fields, choosing field types, and entering descriptions in the table Design view.

Lesson 3: Saving a Table and Creating a Primary Key

When you create a database table for the first time, you should save it as you work on it. The first time you save the table, you are prompted to assign a name. After you save and name the table the first time, it takes only a moment to save it as often as necessary. If you add new fields to the table, for example, you should save the table again.

If you have problems...

If you try to close the table without saving it, Access reminds you to save your work. Click the Yes button to save; click the Cancel button to return to the table in Design view without saving.

Primary key field
A field that contains a unique value for each record in the table.

In addition to saving new tables, you should assign or create *a primary key field* for each table in your database. Each record's primary key is a value that uniquely identifies it; no two records can have the same value as their primary key. You can use this feature to your advantage when you need to establish a relationship between one table and another. Assigning a primary key also ensures that you won't enter the same information for the primary key field more than once in a table (because it won't accept a duplicate entry). Because Access automatically builds an index for primary keys, it can easily search for information and sort tables based on the primary key field.

If you have a unique field, such as an ID number in your table, you can use that as the primary key field. Or you can have Access create a simple counter field. In this lesson, you have Access create a counter field to use as the primary key field because you cannot ensure that fields such as First Name, Last Name, and Department will contain unique information.

To Save a Table and Create a Primary Key

1 In the Training database, with Table1 open, click the Save button on the toolbar.

You could also open the **F**ile menu and choose the **S**ave command. You see the Save As dialog box, which prompts you to type a name for the table (see Figure 12.8). As you can see, the default name that Access provides doesn't tell you much, so you want to provide a more descriptive name.

Figure 12.8
You must give the table a name the first time you save it.

Type the table name

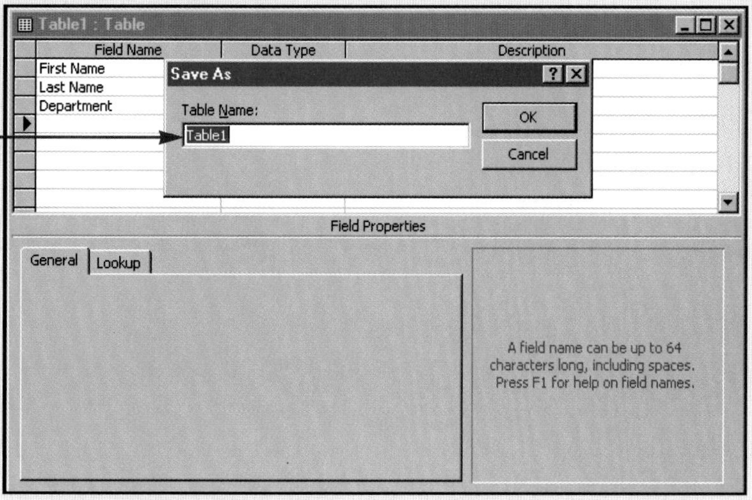

continues

To Save a Table and Create a Primary Key (continued)

2 Type `P C Software` and click OK.

This is the name you want to assign to the table for this example. The next time you see the list of tables in the database window, this name will be displayed. The size of a table name isn't limited to eight characters. You can use up to 64 characters, including spaces.

Access displays a reminder that no primary key has been defined (see Figure 12.9). You are not required to use a primary key, but it is a good idea to include one. An easy way to create a primary key field is to have Access create a counter field that automatically assigns a different number to each record in your table.

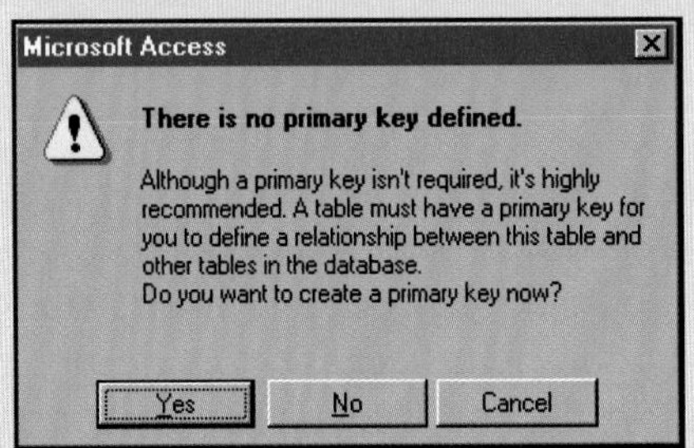

Figure 12.9
A dialog box warns you that you haven't defined a primary key.

3 Click the Yes button.

Access saves the table and adds a counter field named ID with an AutoNumber data type. This is now the primary key field. Access will automatically place sequential numbers in this field as you add new records. Your table should look like the one shown in Figure 12.10. Notice the key symbol in the *row selector* for the ID field. The key indicates that the ID field is the primary key field for this table.

Row selector
The gray area to the left of a field in Design view. Clicking a box in this area selects the entire row.

Keep the P C Software table of the Training database open. In the next lesson, you learn how to add new fields to the table.

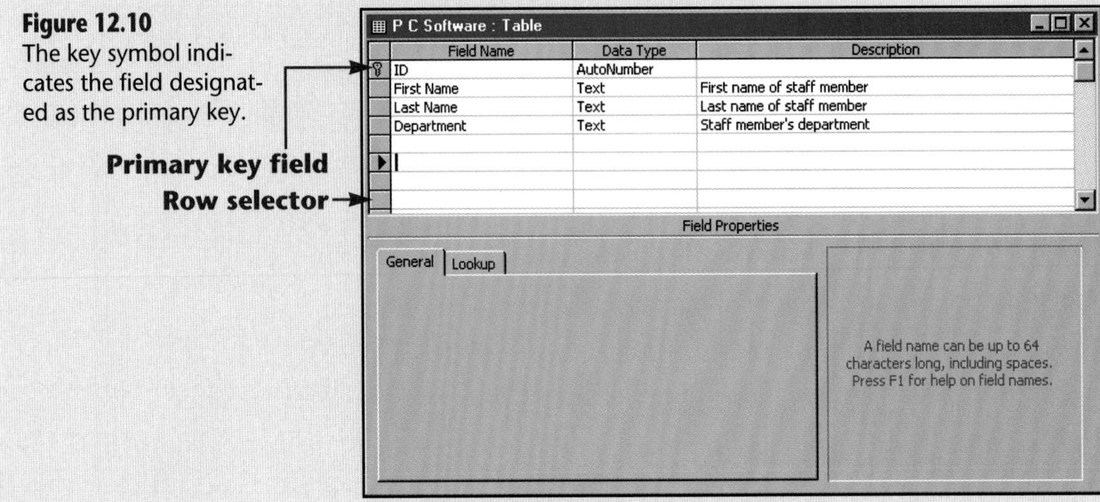

Figure 12.10
The key symbol indicates the field designated as the primary key.

To make another field in the database the primary key, click the row selector for the field you want. Then click the Primary Key button on the toolbar. You can also open the **E**dit menu and choose the Primary **K**ey command. The primary key field is indicated by the key symbol in the row selector.

To save a table quickly, press Ctrl+S.

Lesson 4: Adding Fields

What happens if you decide you want to track more information than you included in your original P C Software table? With Access, you can easily add new fields to track this additional data. Keep in mind, however, that if you already have added records to the table, any new fields in those existing records will be empty until you type information into them.

In this lesson, you add seven new fields to your P C Software table—one for training expense, one for employee number, one for employee's supervisor, and one each for four of the Microsoft Office software applications. Try adding these fields now.

To Add Fields

1 With the P C Software table of the Training database still displayed in Design view, position the insertion point in the next blank row of the P C Software table.

This is the row in which you want to enter the new field name. The black arrow should be displayed next to this row, as shown in Figure 12.11.

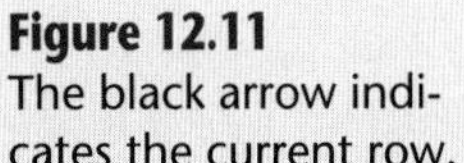

Figure 12.11
The black arrow indicates the current row.

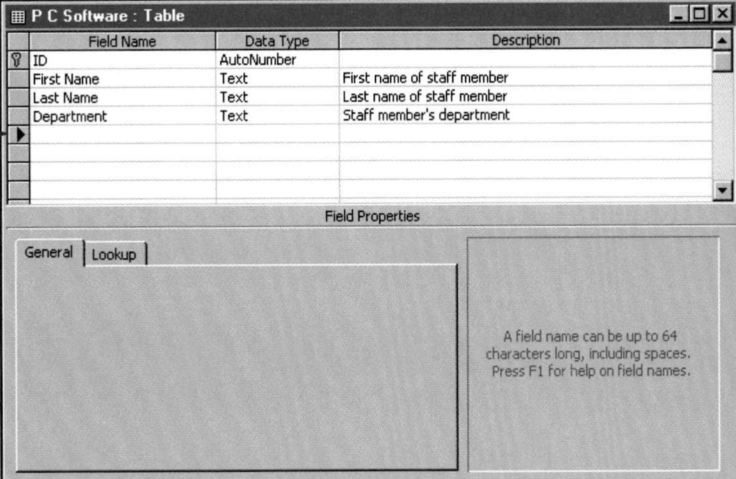

2 Type `Cost` and press Enter twice.

This enters the name of the field, accepts Text as the data type, and moves to the Description column.

continues

To Add Fields (continued)

3 Type `Cost of training` and press ↵Enter.

This is the description for the new field. When you press ↵Enter, Access moves the insertion point to the next row.

4 Type `Employee Number` and press ↵Enter three times.

By pressing ↵Enter three times you enter a name for this field, accept Text as the data type, and skip the Description column. Again, the insertion point is in position to add a new field to the table.

5 Type `Supervisor` and press ↵Enter three times.

Once again, you have added another new field to the table, accepting Text as the data type, skipping the description, and moving to the next row.

6 Type `Word` and press ↵Enter three times.

7 Type `Excel` and press ↵Enter three times.

8 Type `PowerPoint` and press ↵Enter three times.

9 Type `Access` and press ↵Enter three times.

You have now added seven additional fields to the table. Your table should look similar to the one in Figure 12.12, although you may have to scroll down to see the last couple of fields if you have a small monitor.

10 Save your work and leave both the P C Software table and the Training database open.

In the next lesson, you learn another way to alter the structure of your P C Software table.

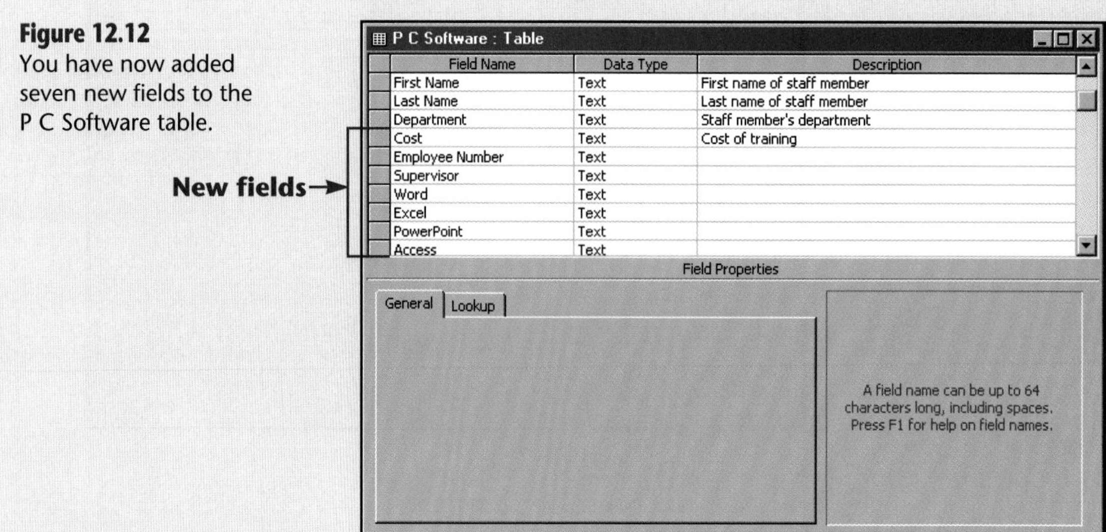

Figure 12.12
You have now added seven new fields to the P C Software table.

Lesson 5: Editing Fields

As you create your database, you may want to tinker with the structure. For example, you may want to change field names, choose a different data type, or edit the description. You make these changes in Design view.

Changing the field name or description does not have any effect on the data you already have entered in the table. Changing the field name may have an unintended effect, however; if any forms, queries, or reports refer to the field name, you must manually change the reference to reflect the new name. Otherwise, these database objects will no longer work as they did before.

Changing the field type may have an effect on the data in your table. For example, if you type text into a field and then change that field to a Yes/No field, you may encounter problems. Access prompts you to let you know when changes in the field type are made and when they might result in a loss of data. Be sure that you want to make the change before you confirm it.

In this lesson, you will edit the name of a field, add a description, and change the field type.

To Edit Fields

1 In the Design view of the P C Software, position the insertion point on the word Cost (the fourth field name) and double-click the mouse.

This selects the word you want to change. When you select the word, it is displayed in reverse video, as shown in Figure 12.13.

Figure 12.13
To change a field name, you first select it.

Selected text

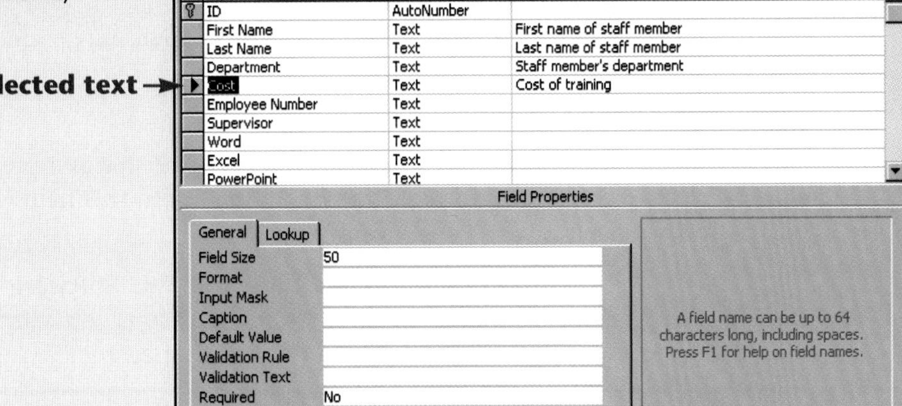

2 Type `Training Expense`.

The existing highlighted text is replaced with the new text.

continues

To Edit Fields (continued)

3 Click in the Description column for the Supervisor field.

After moving the insertion point to this field, you can add a description.

4 Type `Reporting Supervisor`.

The description that you enter provides information about what will be stored in this field. Now try changing the data type for one of the fields in the table.

5 Click in the Data Type column for the Training Expense field.

This is the field you want to change. Notice that a down arrow is displayed, which indicates a drop-down list of data type options.

6 Click the down arrow.

You see a drop-down list of choices, as shown in Figure 12.14.

Figure 12.14
When you click the down arrow in the Data Type column, a list of data types is displayed.

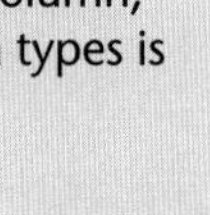

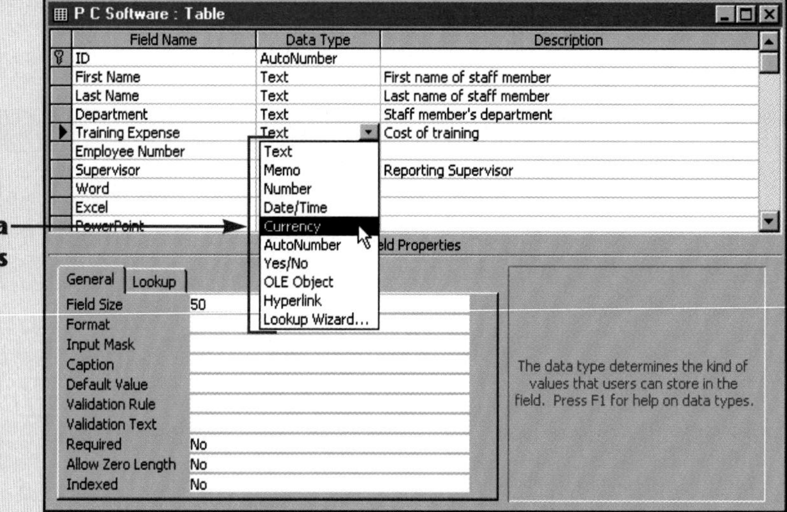

List of data types

7 From the list, click Currency.

You have changed the data type to a type that is more closely related to the information in this field. All data in this field will now be displayed in a currency format.

Save your work and leave both the P C Software table and the Training database open. In the next lesson, you learn how to move fields from one part of the table to another.

If you know the name of the data type you want to enter in the Data Type column, you don't have to use the mouse to open the drop-down list. Instead, with the insertion point in the Data Type column, you can type the first letter or two of the data type you want. Access fills in the rest of the characters for you. By typing the letters `Cu`, for example, Access fills in `Currency`.

Lesson 6: Changing Views and Moving Fields

In addition to changing the name and data type, you can change the order in which fields are displayed in your database. When you enter records, you may want the fields in a different order. In the P C Software table, for example, you may find it easier to enter the employee's number after you enter the employee's name. You may also want to move the ID or counter field to the end because you never have to enter anything in this field.

In this lesson, you first look at the table in Datasheet view—the view you use to enter records. You then change back to Design view to rearrange the fields.

To Change Views and Move Fields

1 Change from the current Design view to the Datasheet view by clicking the View button on the toolbar.

This changes your view of the database to Datasheet view (see Figure 12.15). Datasheet view is the view you use to enter, sort, and edit the records in the database.

The datasheet you see is blank, except for the field names, because the table doesn't contain records yet. You learn how to work with records in Project 3. In Datasheet view, you cannot make any changes to the structure of the table.

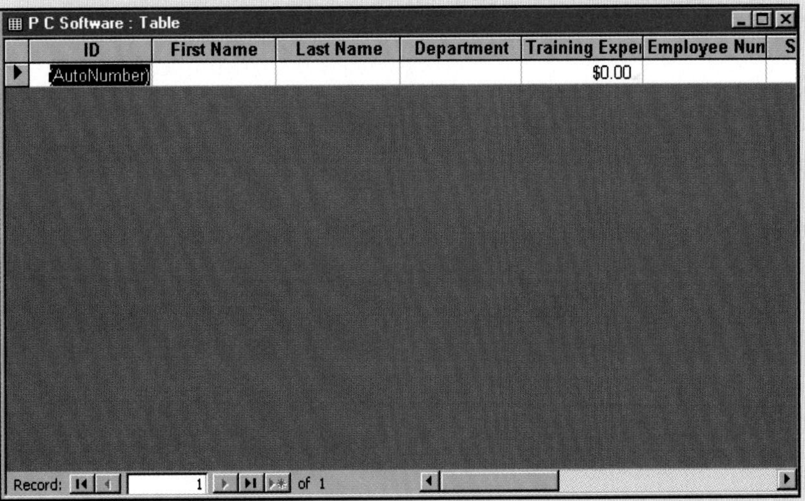

Figure 12.15 Viewing the P C Software table in Datasheet view.

2 Click the View button on the toolbar.

Notice that the View button looks different in the Datasheet view than it did in the Design view. This step returns you to Design view so that you can make changes.

continues

To Change Views and Move Fields (continued)

3 Click the row selector for the Employee Number field.

This step selects the field you want to move. Notice that the entire row is highlighted (see Figure 12.16). You will move this field so that it immediately follows the Last Name field.

Figure 12.16
You click the row selector to select the row you want to move.

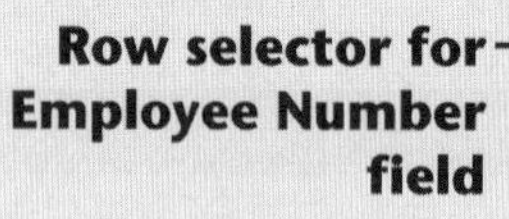

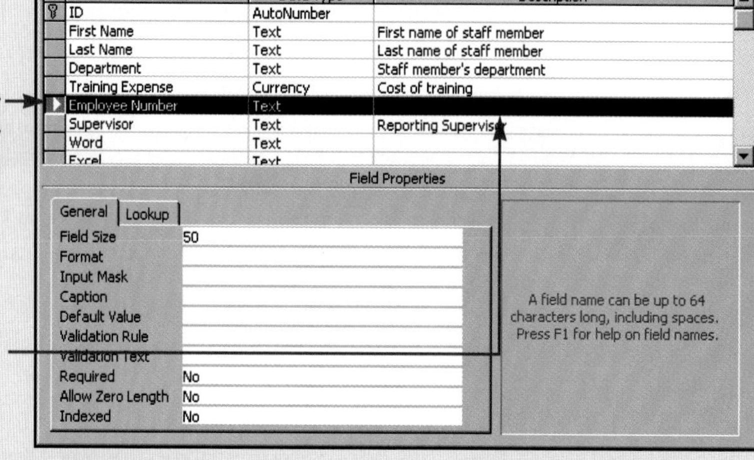

4 Drag the row to its new position under Last Name and release the mouse button.

As you drag, a small gray box is displayed under the mouse pointer, along with a horizontal line showing where the row will be placed. When you release the mouse button, Access places the row in its new spot (see Figure 12.17).

Figure 12.17
The Employee Number field in its new location.

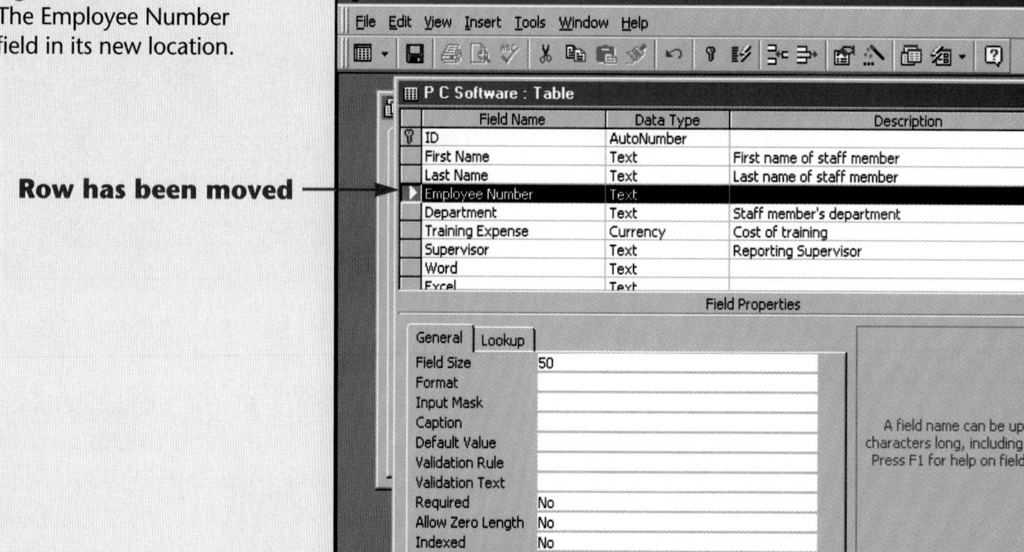

If you have problems...

If the field that you move is displayed in the wrong place after you drag and drop it, don't worry. Just move the field again.

If you see a double-headed arrow as you try to position the mouse, the mouse pointer isn't in the correct spot. If the double-headed arrow is displayed, Access thinks that you want to resize the row height or the design window.

If, when you drag, you accidentally resize rather than move your row, click the Undo button (or open the **E**dit menu and choose the **U**ndo command). The **U**ndo command reverses your most recent action, such as moving a row. Only the most recent change can be undone.

If your window is too small to see all of the rows, maximize the window by clicking on the Maximize button in the upper-right-hand corner of the table window.

5. **Select the ID row and drag it down to the first empty row of the table.**

This step moves the ID or counter field to the last position in the table. Next, try undoing the move.

6. **Click the Undo button.**

With Access, you can undo some of the changes you make to the database. In this example, however, you decide that you really do want the ID field at the end of the table.

7. **Select the ID row again and drag it back to the end of the table.**

This moves the ID field back to the end of the table. Save your work and keep both the P C Software table and the Training database open in the Design view. In the next lesson, you learn how to delete fields from your table structure.

Lesson 7: Deleting Fields

Another significant change that you can make to the structure of your P C Software table is to remove fields you no longer need. Suppose that you decide you don't really need a field for the supervisor. Instead of having it take up space in the table design, you can delete the field.

Keep in mind that deleting a field from your table also deletes all the data in that field. Because this may not be what you intended, Access displays a warning that asks you to confirm the change. Read the warning carefully and be sure that you want to delete all the data before you delete the field.

To Delete a Field

❶ In the P C Software table of the Training database, click the row selector for the Supervisor field.

Access highlights the entire Supervisor row, showing that the Supervisor field is selected. This is the field you want to delete.

❷ Click the Delete Rows button to delete the row from your table.

Access removes the field from the database table and deletes any data that was in that field. If you had entered any data into this field in the Datasheet view, Access would warn you that the data would be lost.

❸ Save your changes.

❹ Close the P C Software table by clicking the Close button in the upper-right corner of the table window.

❺ Close the Training database by clicking the Close button in the upper-right corner of the database window.

If you are finished with your session at the computer, click the Close button in the upper-right corner of the Access window. Otherwise, continue with the section "Checking Your Skills" in this project.

If you delete a row by mistake, immediately click the Undo button, or open the **E**dit menu and choose **U**ndo, or press Ctrl+Z to undo the deletion. When you undo the deletion of a field, you will also recover all of the data in that field in each of the records.

Project Summary

To	Do This
Create a new database	Start Windows and launch Access. Click **B**lank Database and then click OK. Type a file name and select the drive or folder location for the file. Click the **C**reate button.
Create a new table	In the database window, select the Tables tab. Click the **N**ew button, choose Design View, and click OK. Enter the field name, choose the data type, and enter a description for the field.
Save a table	Click the **S**ave button. Type a name for the table (on the first Save only). Click OK.
Create a primary key	Use the counter field by clicking Yes when prompted by the save sequence; or use the row selector to select a field and then click the Primary Key button.

To	Do This
Add fields	Work in Design view. Go to the next blank row and insert the new field name, data type, and description for each field to be added.
Edit fields	Work in Design view. Go to the field name, data type, or description you want to edit. Select the information you want to change, and type the new information. Use the drop-down box in the Data Type column to change the type of data allowed for that field.
Move fields	Work in Design view. Use the row selector to select the row you want to move. Click and drag the row to a new location and then release the mouse button.
Delete fields	Work in Design view. Use the row selector to select the row you want to delete. Click the Delete Row button.

Checking Your Skills

True/False

For each of the following, check *T* or *F* to indicate whether the statement is true or false.

__T __F **1.** You can include only eight characters in a database name in Access.

__T __F **2.** You can include only eight characters in a table name.

__T __F **3.** The most common data type is Text, the default.

__T __F **4.** You must have a Primary Key field.

__T __F **5.** You can enter only numbers in a Number field.

__T __F **6.** After you save your table structure, you cannot edit or change it.

__T __F **7.** A Yes/No field type limits your data to one of four values: Yes, No, True, or False.

__T __F **8.** To find the name of the database you have open, you must select **F**ile, **O**pen Database or use the **O**pen Database button.

__T __F **9.** It is best to build one large database with everything in one table.

__T __F **10.** If you add a new field to a database that already has information in it, the new field will be empty until you enter the information.

Multiple Choice

Circle the letter of the correct answer for each of the following questions.

1. Which of the following is not one of the ways you can create a new database?

a. Click the **O**pen menu and choose the New Database command.

b. Open the **F**ile menu and choose the New Database command.

c. Click the New Database button on the toolbar.

d. Press Ctrl+N.

2. Which of the following is not a valid data type?

a. Currency

b. Yes/No

c. Text

d. Text & Numbers

3. How do you select a row in Design view?

a. Drag across the entire row.

b. Click the row selector next to the row.

c. Click the Select Row button.

d. Press Ctrl+R.

4. If you let the program create a primary key for you, what field name does it use?

a. counter

b. ID

c. MDB

d. Primary

5. How do you select a data type?

a. Open the **E**dit menu and choose the type you want.

b. Click the Data Type button on the tool bar.

c. Press Ctrl+D.

d. Select the data type from the drop-down list.

6. In table Design view, a black arrow appears on the row selector of which of the following?

a. A row that has an error in the data

b. The primary key

c. A duplicate field definition

d. The row you are editing

7. In Design view, how can you tell that a field is the primary key?

a. The status bar displays text when you have the field selected.

b. There is no way to tell in Design view.

c. The field name is underlined.

d. The key symbol appears on the row selector button.

8. Why is the Description entry in table Design view handy?

a. It appears in the status bar when you enter the field in Datasheet view.

b. It appears as a pop-up label when you place the mouse pointer on the field in Datasheet view.

c. Access uses it to automatically test the data you enter into the field.

d. It serves no purpose at all.

9. To change the order of fields in a table in Design view, you select the field and then do which of the following?

a. Press Ctrl+O, entering the destination in the dialog box that appears.

b. Drag the field to the new location.

c. Press Alt as you select the new location.

d. Press Ctrl as you select the new location and then select S**w**ap from the shortcut menu.

10. Field names are limited to how many characters?

a. 255

b. 50

c. 64

d. 8

Completion

In the blank provided, write the correct answer for each of the following statements.

1. A(n) ______________ is a field that contains a unique value for each record in the table.
2. A(n) ______________ data type field is useful when you want to include sentences or paragraphs in the field.
3. Use ______________ view to enter records in a table.
4. Use ______________ view to change the table structure.
5. To select a row in Design view, click the ______________.
6. Table names are limited to ______________ characters.
7. To add a field in table Design view, type the field name in the ______________ box and press Enter.
8. Changing a field name or description has no effect on the ______________.
9. To save an object quickly in Access, press the shortcut ______________.
10. The ______________ data type can hold up to 255 digits or characters.

Matching

In the blank next to each of the following terms or phrases, write the letter of the corresponding term or phrase. (Note that some letters may be used more than once.)

_____ 1. A set of standards for inserting objects

_____ 2. Appears on the status bar in Datasheet view

_____ 3. A field that doesn't contain duplicate values

_____ 4. Changes on the toolbar depending on the current view

_____ 5. Highlights the entire row

_____ 6. Used to reverse the last action some of the time

_____ 7. An automatically incremented field

_____ 8. Used to resize a border

_____ 9. The default data type

_____ 10. Characters you cannot use in field names

a. View button
b. double-headed arrow
c. counter
d. OLE
e. square brackets, []
f. Text
g. row selector
h. field description
i. Primary key
j. Undo button

Screen ID

Identify each of the items shown in Figure 12.18.

Figure 12.18

1.________

2.________

3.________

4.________

5.________

6.________

7.________

8.________

9.________

10.________

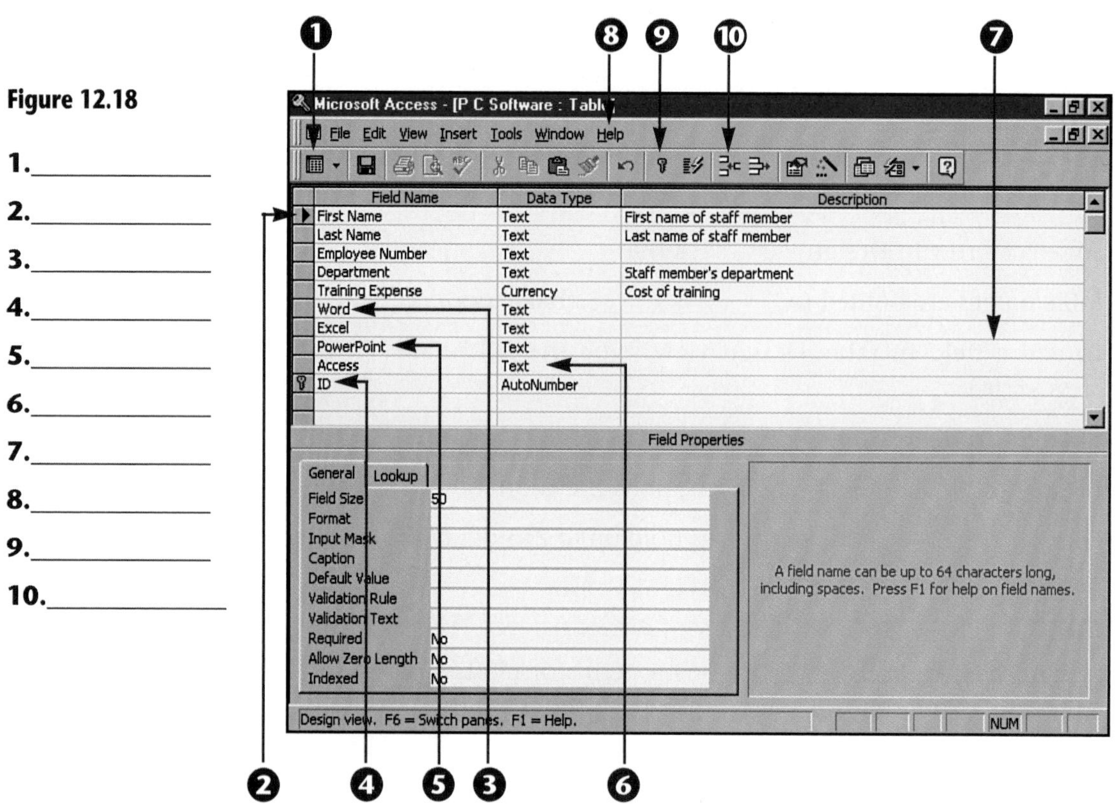

Applying Your Skills

Practice

The following exercises enable you to practice the skills you have learned in this project. Take a few minutes to work through these exercises now.

1. Keeping Track of Your Books

Suppose you want to set up a database to keep track of your books; build a database and table for your personal library that enables you to keep track of the author, title, type of book (reference, mystery, biography, and so on); and track the publication date of each book.

To Create a Books Database

1. Create a new database named `Library`.
2. Create a database table. Include fields for the author's last name, author's first name, book title, type of book, and year of publication. (Use a text field for the publication year; you usually don't have the day and month necessary for a date field.)
3. Set the book title field as the primary key field.
4. Save the database table and name it `Books`.

2. Creating a Music Store Database

As the owner and business manager of Sound Byte Music, one of your most important tasks in setting up the business is building a comprehensive database for your store. Create a new database for your business in which you can store all the tables, queries, and forms that you need for managing Sound Byte Music. Start building the database by creating a table to keep track of the record companies you deal with, including company names, addresses, phone numbers, and contacts.

To Create the Music Store Database

1. Create a new database and name it **SBMusic**.
2. Create a new table and add the following fields. All the fields can be text fields:

   Record Company

   Contact Name

   Address

   City

   State

   ZIP

   Phone

3. Set the Record Company field as the Primary Key field.
4. Save the table and name it **Suppliers**.

3. Planning a Database to Inventory Personal Computers

Whenever a company wants to upgrade its software, it must determine whether its computers are capable of running and storing the new, more demanding version. Having a list of equipment is useful in helping you determine which machines may need to be upgraded as well.

To Plan the Database

1. Create a new database named **PC**.
2. Create a table named **PC Hardware** and include the fields that you may want to track, such as type of processor, amount of RAM, size of hard drive, presence of 3 ½" disk drive, sound card, vendor, inventory code number, and date of purchase.
3. Choose a key field, such as inventory code number.
4. Create a table named **Vendor** and include the fields that contain important vendor information, such as name, address, city, state, zip code, and phone number. Feel free to add fields you think would be important.
5. Choose a key field, such as the vendor's name.

4. Getting a Helping Hand

Because software is constantly changing, you need a way to learn new software programs and where to get help. This exercise takes you to the appropriate help topics for the material covered in this project.

To Get Help on Topics in This Project

1. With the Office Assistant closed, choose **H**elp from the menu bar. A menu listing several items is displayed.
2. From the **H**elp menu, choose the **C**ontents and Index menu item. A dialog box with three tabs is displayed.
3. Select the leftmost tab, Contents, if it is not already selected. A list of books, or topic groups, is displayed on the tab.
4. Select the topic group `Creating, Importing, and Linking Tables`. The book icon opens with a list of subordinate topics and topic groups.
5. Select `Adding Fields and Choosing Data types`. The list is further expanded.
6. Select the first entry, `Add a field to a table in Design view`. The help window opens, and the topic of the same name is displayed.
7. Maximize the help window. You can now read how to add fields to a table. Try selecting the underlined words `Design view` and `data type`. These will show you a graphic and a definition, respectively. This topic has some good information for beginning database builders.

5. Exploring the World of Alaska

Now that you have an idea of how to add fields to a database, you decide to add two fields to a database called "Alaska." These fields are to help you keep track of photographs that you've received or scanned into your computer.

Adding Fields to the Alaska Database

1. Open the database named Proj1201 as a copy.
2. Open the Geography table in Design view.
3. Select the ID field and move it to the first unused field name space.
4. Place the insertion point in the ID field name box.
5. Click the Insert Row button on the toolbar. If you do not have the Insert Row button on your toolbar, you can choose **I**nsert, **R**ows. A blank row appears before the ID field.
6. Enter the field name **`Picture`** in the field name box and press Tab twice.
7. Enter the field description **`File name of picture`** in the field description box and press Tab.
8. Add a new row below the Picture field.
9. In the new field location, enter the field name **`Source`** and the description **`Where the picture came from or who took it.`**
10. Exit the table and save your changes.

Challenge

The following challenges enable you to use your problem-solving skills. Take time to work through these exercises now.

1. Creating a List of Club Members

Create a database to track information about members of an organization or club. Pick a name for the database that describes it. Create a table that includes fields such as Name, Donations, Street, City, State, ZIP, and Phone. Do not enter club member information at this time. Save the database and its table, using meaningful names. You use this database in similar exercises throughout this text.

2. Doing Customer Research

You have viewed the database started by the previous employee and noticed that two of the questions are not reflected in the table. You noticed also that two of the data types should be changed.

Adding Fields and Changing Data Types

1. Open the Proj1202 database as a copy named `Customer Research`.
2. Open the Questionnaire table in Design view.
3. Select the Data Type box for the Adults field.
4. Using the down arrow that appears in the box, change the data type to Number.
5. Change the data type in the Children field to Number.
6. Move the ID field to the end of the list.
7. Add fields, with descriptions, for the two missing questions on the questionnaire.
8. Close the table, saving your changes.

3. Owning a Vending Company

You have listed the information that you think should be included in each of three categories: suppliers, locations, and machines. Then you decide that you need three tables—one table for each category.

Create a new database called `Vending`. In that database, create three tables named `Suppliers`, `Locations`, and `Machines`.

In the Suppliers table, add fields for `Name`, `Address`, and `Phone`.

In the Locations table, add fields for `Site`, `Owner`, and `Machine Type`.

In the Machines table, add fields for `Machine Type`, `Supplier`, and `Cost`.

The only table that needs a primary key is the Locations table. If you answer yes to creating a primary key, Access creates an AutoNumber field called ID and adds it to your table.

4. Managing a Video Store

Now that you have had a chance to work in the store for a few days, you begin to see the complexity of the database you will need. Create a database for your store, incorporating information you would need to include in a database to control inventory. Give it a descriptive name. Create a table in the database that will include the video name and any other information you feel is necessary. Be sure that the database includes not only the information that the owners have in their spreadsheet, but also whether the video is currently rented (a Yes/No data type might work well here) and who the current renter is.

5. Taking a Home Inventory

Create the database for your home inventory, incorporating information you think is necessary for keeping track of your possessions. Add a table that includes the name of the item, the cost, the purchase date, and the insurance carrier with which you have the item insured. Include other fields that you think are essential to tracking your possessions. Be sure to consider major items, such as a car or boat, that are not in the home.

Project 13

Entering and Editing Data

Objectives

In this project, you learn how to:

- Add Records
- Move among Records
- Edit Records
- Insert and Delete Records
- Adjust Column Widths and Hide Columns
- Find a Record
- Sort Records

Why Would I Do This?

After you create a database and table, you want to be able to put them to work. For your database to be useful, you must enter data into the table. For example, you can use the Training database you created in Project 12 to keep track of training that your staff receives by entering information about the employees and the training they have received into the P C Software table. As you learned in Project 12, the set of information you enter for each row in a table is called a *record*.

One reason databases are so useful is that you can work with and modify the records after you enter them. With a paper filing system, you have to cross out, erase, or redo a record when the information changes. With database software, however, you can easily change a record in the table to correct a mistake or to update the information. You can delete records you no longer need, search for a particular record, and sort the records—all quickly and with little effort on your part.

In this project, you learn how to add records to your table, move around in the records within the table, and edit and delete records. You also learn how to search for a particular record and sort your records according to a system that you determine.

Lesson 1: Adding Records

As you recall from Project 12, you worked in Design view when you set up your table structure. In the Design view, you can make changes to the fields in the table—change a field name, add a field, change the data type, and so on. Then, when you want to work with the data in the table, you switch to the Datasheet view. In this view, you can add records or edit them.

In this lesson, you open a database, Training2, which matches your database and your P C Software table from Project 12. You switch to Datasheet view, then add records to the database.

To Add Records

1. **Make a copy of Proj1301 and name the copy `Training2`.**

   Return to Access and open the Training2 database.

2. **Click the Open button to open the P C Software table in the Datasheet view.**

   In this project, you use the Training database you created in Project 12. (Training2 is a completed version of your work from Project 12. You may use this file or open the Training database that you created.) You should see the P C Software table on-screen in the Datasheet view. Each of the field names appears along the top of the window. At this point, the table consists of only one row, and it is blank. The insertion point is in the first field, and you see a small, black arrow next to the first field. This arrow indicates the current record (see Figure 13.1).

Figure 13.1
A blank database table in the Datasheet view.

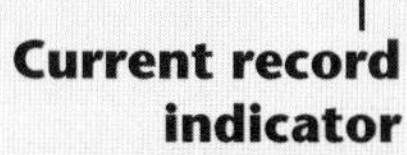

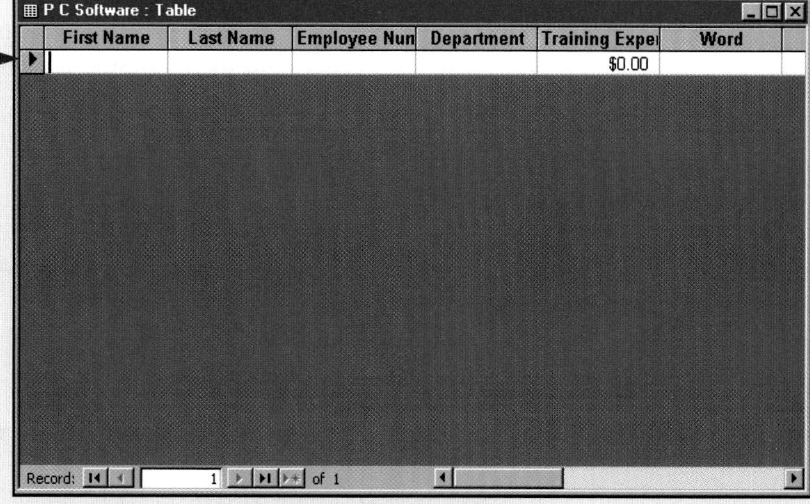

Record selector
The gray area to the left of a field in Datasheet view. Clicking in this area selects the entire record.

3 Type `Chantele` and press ↵Enter.

As you type, Access displays a pencil icon in the *record selector*. You can also use the Tab key in place of the ↵Enter key when adding data to the table.

4 Type `Auterman` and press ↵Enter.

The staff member's name is entered, and you move to the Employee Number field.

5 Type `77171` and press ↵Enter.

The employee number is entered, and you move to the Department field.

6 Type `Accounting` and press ↵Enter.

The department is entered, and you move to the Training Expense field.

7 Type `300.00` and press ↵Enter.

The expense for training this employee is entered, and you move to the four fields for specific software training. Notice that Access formats the entry as Currency because in Project 12 you set the data type to Currency after you created this field. Do not enter the dollar sign ($) into a currency field. If the dollar amount is a whole number, the program will also add the .00 automatically, even if you don't type that in.

continues

To Add Records (continued)

8 Type 3 and press ↵Enter, 1 and press ↵Enter, 0 and press ↵Enter, and finally 1 and press ↵Enter.

The level of classes taken are recorded in the four application fields. When you press ↵Enter the last time, Access moves to the counter field, which has a value that was automatically entered when you started entering data in the first field.

9 Press ↵Enter.

When you press ↵Enter, Access saves the record and moves to the next row so that you can add another record (see Figure 13.2).

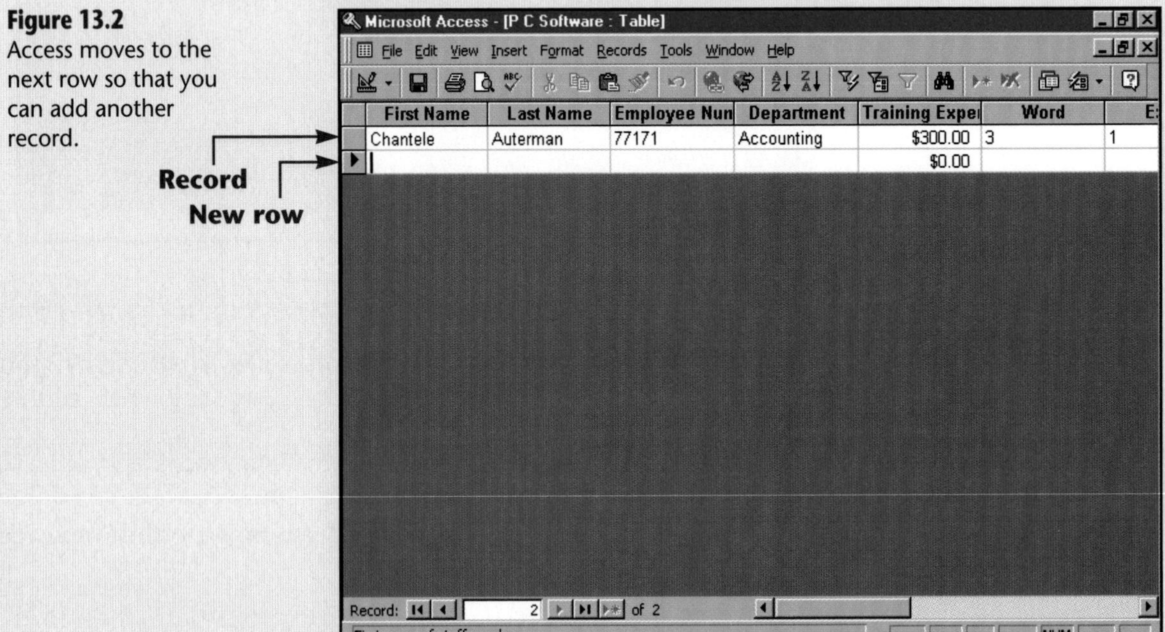

Figure 13.2
Access moves to the next row so that you can add another record.

10 Use the following list of data to add more records to the database table. (Because of the number of fields in each record, the items are separated by commas. Do not type in the commas.)

```
Chang,Sun,66242,Human Resources,0,0,0,0,0

Jane,Boxer,66264,Purchasing,450,1,2,1,3

Robert,Bauer,66395,Purchasing,0,0,0,0,0

Peter,Bullard,66556,Marketing,250,1,1,3,0

James,Baird,66567,Accounting,300,0,3,1,1

Wayne,Wheaton,66564,Human Resources,150,1,0,2,0

Chris,Hart,77909,Marketing,250,1,0,3,1
```

Access adds these records to the database table. You don't have to worry about saving the records because Access does that each time you press ↵Enter and move to the next row to add a new record.

Keep the P C Software table and the Training2 database open. In the next lesson, you learn how to move among the records in your table.

In the beginning of this lesson, you were asked to make a copy of a file (`Proj1301`) and rename it. In Windows 95, the right mouse button can be used to open a short list of helpful menu options. For example, you can copy, paste, and rename files within the Access program without using the Explorer. To do this, you start with the **F**ile, **O**pen Database command and locate the source file. If you point to the name of the source file (in this case, Proj1301) and click the right mouse button, a menu of options appears. Choose **C**opy, then click the right mouse button on an open area and choose **P**aste. The new file will be called `Copy of Proj1301`. Click on this new file with the right mouse button, choose Rena**m**e, and rename the file.

Lesson 2: Moving among Records

Earlier, you noticed that Access displays an arrow next to the current row. When you want to do something with a record, such as edit a field to change or update its information, you first must move to the row containing the record that you want to change. You can tell what row you have moved to because the current record indicator is displayed next to the current row.

You can move among the records by using one of several methods. If you can see the record you want on the screen, you can simply click it to select it. If you have numerous records in your table, however, you may have to scroll through the records until you can get to the one you want.

To move to a particular record, you can use the vertical scroll bar, the navigation buttons displayed along the bottom of the window, or the arrow keys on the keyboard. Table 13.1 explains how these navigation buttons and keys work.

Table 13.1 Moving among Records with the Navigation Buttons and Keys

To Move To	Buttons	Keyboard
First record in table	⏮	
Previous record in table	◀	↑
Next record in table	▶	↓
Last record in table	⏭	
New record at end of table	▶*	

In this lesson, you move among the records in your table by using each of these navigational methods.

To Move among Records

1 With the P C Software table of the Training2 database open, move the mouse pointer to the record selector at the left of the Wayne Wheaton record and click.

This selects the record.

2 Press Ctrl+Home.

Access moves you to the first record in the database table. Notice the current record indicator arrow next to the active record (see Figure 13.3).

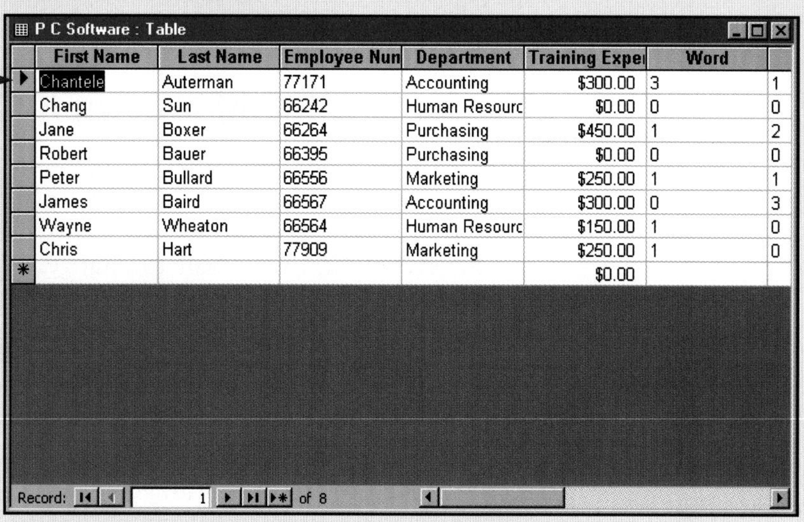

P C Software : Table

First Name	Last Name	Employee Nun	Department	Training Expe	Word	
Chantele	Auterman	77171	Accounting	$300.00	3	1
Chang	Sun	66242	Human Resourc	$0.00	0	0
Jane	Boxer	66264	Purchasing	$450.00	1	2
Robert	Bauer	66395	Purchasing	$0.00	0	0
Peter	Bullard	66556	Marketing	$250.00	1	1
James	Baird	66567	Accounting	$300.00	0	3
Wayne	Wheaton	66564	Human Resourc	$150.00	1	0
Chris	Hart	77909	Marketing	$250.00	1	0
				$0.00		

Record: 1 of 8

Current record indicator

Figure 13.3 Pressing Ctrl+Home moves you to the first record.

3 Press ↓.

Access moves you to the next record in the table.

4 Click the Last Record button.

Access moves you to the last record in the table.

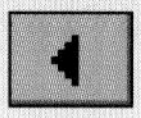

5 Click the Previous Record button.

Access moves you to the previous record in the table.

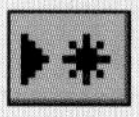

6 Click the New Record button.

The pointer moves to the next empty record.

Now that you know how to move among the records in your table, the next lesson shows you how to make changes to the records. Keep Training2 database and the the P C Software table open as you continue with Lesson 3.

Lesson 3: Editing Records

As you work with the data in the database table, you will find that you need to make changes from time to time. In your P C Software table, for example, you might want to correct a typing mistake or change other information. You can easily update or correct the records in your table.

The first step in making any change is to move to the record that you want to change. Next, you have to move to the field that you want to edit. To move among fields using the mouse, click in the field to which you want to move. When you click, Access places the insertion point in the field and does not select the text in that field.

You can also use the keys listed in Table 13.2 to move among fields. When you use these keys, Access moves to the specified field and selects all the text in that field.

Table 13.2 Moving among Fields with the Keyboard

To Move To	Press
Next field	Tab or →
Previous field	Shift+Tab or ←
First field in record	Home
Last field in record	End

After you are in a field, you can add to the current entry, edit the current entry, or delete the current entry. Try moving among the fields and making changes now.

To Edit Records

1. **With the P C Software table of the Training2 database open, move to the record for Peter Bullard.**

   You can click in that record, use the arrow keys, or use the navigation buttons to move to this record. You should see the current record indicator to the left of the first field in this record.

2. **In the record for Peter Bullard, click after the word `Marketing` in the Department column.**

   The insertion point is placed where you are going to add new text in the field.

3. **Type a comma (,), press Spacebar, and type `Corporate`.**

   As you start typing, notice that Access displays a pencil icon in the record selector next to the record. This icon reminds you that you are editing the record and that the change has not yet been saved (see Figure 13.4).

continues

To Edit Records (continued)

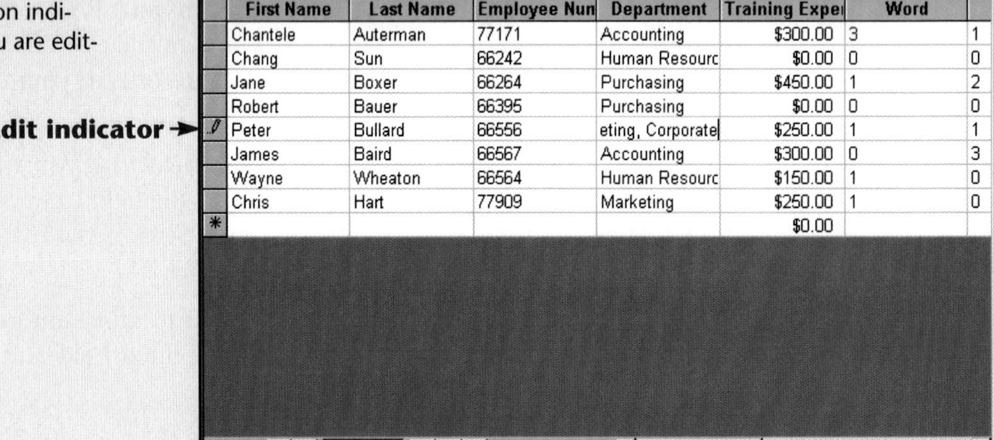

P C Software : Table

	First Name	Last Name	Employee Nun	Department	Training Expe	Word	
	Chantele	Auterman	77171	Accounting	$300.00	3	1
	Chang	Sun	66242	Human Resourc	$0.00	0	0
	Jane	Boxer	66264	Purchasing	$450.00	1	2
	Robert	Bauer	66395	Purchasing	$0.00	0	0
	Peter	Bullard	66556	eting, Corporate	$250.00	1	1
	James	Baird	66567	Accounting	$300.00	0	3
	Wayne	Wheaton	66564	Human Resourc	$150.00	1	0
	Chris	Hart	77909	Marketing	$250.00	1	0
*					$0.00		

Record: 5 of 8

Figure 13.4
The pencil icon indicates that you are editing a field.

❹ **Press ↑ twice.**

This moves you to the record for Jane Boxer. When you move to another record, Access updates the record you just changed.

❺ **Press ↵Enter to move to the Department field.**

The text in that field is selected, as shown in Figure 13.5. Anything you type replaces the selected text.

P C Software : Table

	First Name	Last Name	Employee Nun	Department	Training Expe	Word	
	Chantele	Auterman	77171	Accounting	$300.00	3	1
	Chang	Sun	66242	Human Resourc	$0.00	0	0
▶	Jane	Boxer	66264	Purchasing	$450.00	1	2
	Robert	Bauer	66395	Purchasing	$0.00	0	0
	Peter	Bullard	66556	Marketing, Corp	$250.00	1	1
	James	Baird	66567	Accounting	$300.00	0	3
	Wayne	Wheaton	66564	Human Resourc	$150.00	1	0
	Chris	Hart	77909	Marketing	$250.00	1	0
*					$0.00		

Record: 3 of 8

Selected field

Figure 13.5
Typing replaces the selected text.

❻ **Type** `Accounting`.

This employee transferred to a new department.

❼ **Press ↓.**

Access updates the record you just edited and moves to the next record.

Keep the P C Software table and the Training2 database open. In Lesson 4, you learn how to insert new records and delete records you no longer need.

If you have problems...

If you make a change by mistake, you can undo it by immediately clicking the Undo button, or by opening the **E**dit menu and choosing the **U**ndo command.

Lesson 4: Inserting and Deleting Records

When you first create your database table, you can't always predict exactly what information you want to include in it. As you use your database, you most likely will want to insert new records or delete outdated records.

With Access, you don't have to add all your records at one time. You can add a new record to the end of the table at any time. If you want to enter several records containing similar data, you can enter the data for one record, copy that record, paste the new record into your table, and then edit the data in that second record.

You can delete a record by removing the row from the database table. In this lesson, you learn how to insert new records and delete a record you no longer need.

To Insert and Delete Records

1 With the P C Software table of the Training2 database open, click in the First Name field of the row marked by an asterisk (see Figure 13.6).

Access moves to the last row in the table, where you can type the data for your new record.

continues

To Insert and Delete Records (continued)

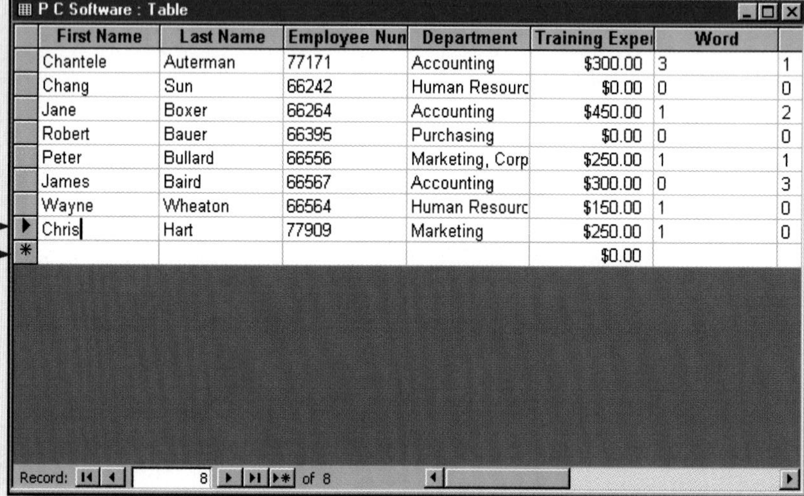

First Name	Last Name	Employee Nun	Department	Training Expe	Word	
Chantele	Auterman	77171	Accounting	$300.00	3	1
Chang	Sun	66242	Human Resourc	$0.00	0	0
Jane	Boxer	66264	Accounting	$450.00	1	2
Robert	Bauer	66395	Purchasing	$0.00	0	0
Peter	Bullard	66556	Marketing, Corp	$250.00	1	1
James	Baird	66567	Accounting	$300.00	0	3
Wayne	Wheaton	66564	Human Resourc	$150.00	1	0
Chris	Hart	77909	Marketing	$250.00	1	0
				$0.00		

Figure 13.6
To insert a new row, click the row with the asterisk.

❷ **Type the following data for your new record, pressing ↵Enter after each entry. After the last entry, press ↵Enter twice.**

```
William

Evich

77517

Accounting

300

0

3

0

2
```

Access adds the new employee record to your table. You can also copy a record and add the copy so that you have two versions of the same record. You may want to do this if you have two or more similar records. This might be appropriate for an inventory database of computer hardware. To practice this skill, you can copy the record you just added.

Clipboard
A temporary storage area in Windows that stores copied data and from which you can paste that data.

❸ **To copy this record, click in the record selector to select the entire row.**

Access highlights the entire row.

❹ **Click the Copy button.**

On-screen, you won't notice anything different after you copy the record. At this point, you have just placed a copy of the selected record onto the *Clipboard*. Next, you paste the copy of the record into your table.

5 Click the record selector to highlight the empty record at the end of the table, then click the Paste button.

Access adds, or appends, the record to the end of the database table only. Now that you have the basic data in place, you can make any changes necessary for this particular record. Rather than edit this duplicate record just now, you are going to use it to practice deleting a record.

6 Click in the record selector next to the new record you just inserted.

The record you just pasted is selected. You can also select the record by opening the **E**dit menu and choosing Se**l**ect Record when the insertion point is anywhere in the record.

7 Click the Delete Record button.

Access wants to be sure that you intended to delete the record, so you are prompted to confirm the deletion (see Figure 13.7). You cannot undo record deletions, so be absolutely sure that you want to delete the record before you confirm the deletion.

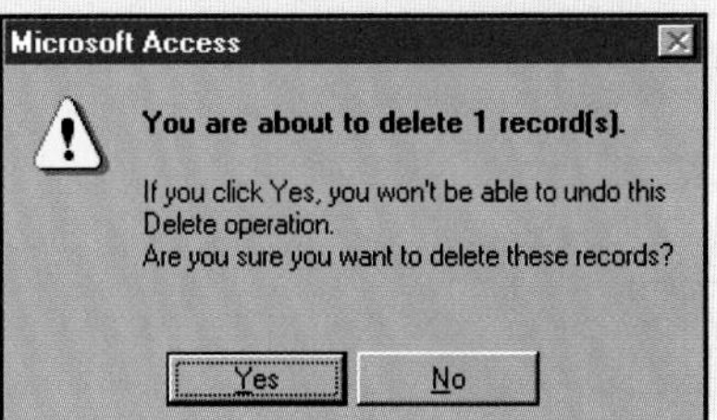

Figure 13.7
Access prompts you to confirm the deletion.

8 Click the Yes button.

Access deletes the record and saves the database table.

Keep the P C Software table open. In Lesson 5, you learn how to change the width of the columns in your table and how to hide and unhide columns.

In addition to copying entire records, you can also copy an entry from one field to another. If you want to enter another record for someone from the Marketing Department, for example, you can copy `Marketing` from the Department column to the new record.

To copy an entry, move to the appropriate field and select the text you want to copy by dragging across it. Then click the Copy button. Move to the location where you want to place the copied text and click the Paste button. Access pastes the selected text.

You can also use shortcut keys: Ctrl+C for Copy and Ctrl+V for Paste.

To delete a record, you can select the record and press Del. You can also click the New Record button on the toolbar to add a new record.

Lesson 5: Adjusting Column Widths and Hiding Columns

By default, Access displays all the columns in your table with the same width. You can change the column width, making some columns wider so that you can see the entire entry, and making other columns narrower so that they don't take up as much space. The easiest way to adjust the column width is to use the mouse.

In addition to changing the column width, you can also hide columns that you don't want displayed.

To Adjust Column Widths and Hide Columns

1 With the P C Software table of the Training2 database open, place the mouse pointer between the First Name and Last Name column headings.

The mouse pointer changes to a thick vertical bar with arrows on either side, as shown in Figure 13.8. This pointer indicates that you can now move the column borders.

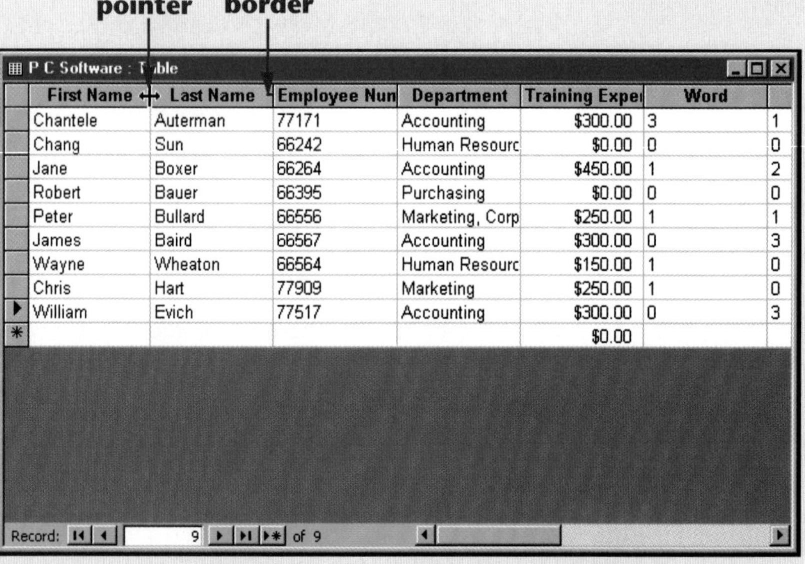

First Name	Last Name	Employee Nun	Department	Training Expe	Word	
Chantele	Auterman	77171	Accounting	$300.00	3	1
Chang	Sun	66242	Human Resourc	$0.00	0	0
Jane	Boxer	66264	Accounting	$450.00	1	2
Robert	Bauer	66395	Purchasing	$0.00	0	0
Peter	Bullard	66556	Marketing, Corp	$250.00	1	1
James	Baird	66567	Accounting	$300.00	0	3
Wayne	Wheaton	66564	Human Resourc	$150.00	1	0
Chris	Hart	77909	Marketing	$250.00	1	0
William	Evich	77517	Accounting	$300.00	0	3
				$0.00		

Figure 13.8
The appearance of the mouse pointer changes when you are preparing to resize a column.

2 Press and hold down the mouse button and drag to the left.

As you drag to the left, you make the column narrower. Notice that you can see the border of the column move as you drag. When you think the column is narrow enough and you can still see all the entries in the column, release the mouse button. The new width is set. You can shrink the size of the column far enough to cover up part of the field name.

If you have problems...

If you don't see the thick bar with the arrows, you don't have the pointer in the correct spot. Be sure that you are within the gray area of the column headings and that your pointer is sitting directly on the border separating the two columns.

3 Move the mouse pointer to the border between the Department and Training Expense columns and then double-click the mouse button.

Double-clicking is a shortcut method that automatically adjusts the column to fit the longest entry currently displayed on-screen in that column. This often creates a problem when you use long field names, because double-clicking will widen the column to show the whole field name if it is the longest entry in the column.

4 Drag across the column headings for the Training Expense, Word, Excel, PowerPoint, Access, and ID fields.

When you drag across the headings, you select all six columns (see Figure 13.9). You can then adjust the width of the six columns at one time.

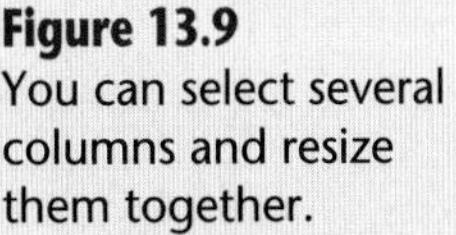
Figure 13.9
You can select several columns and resize them together.

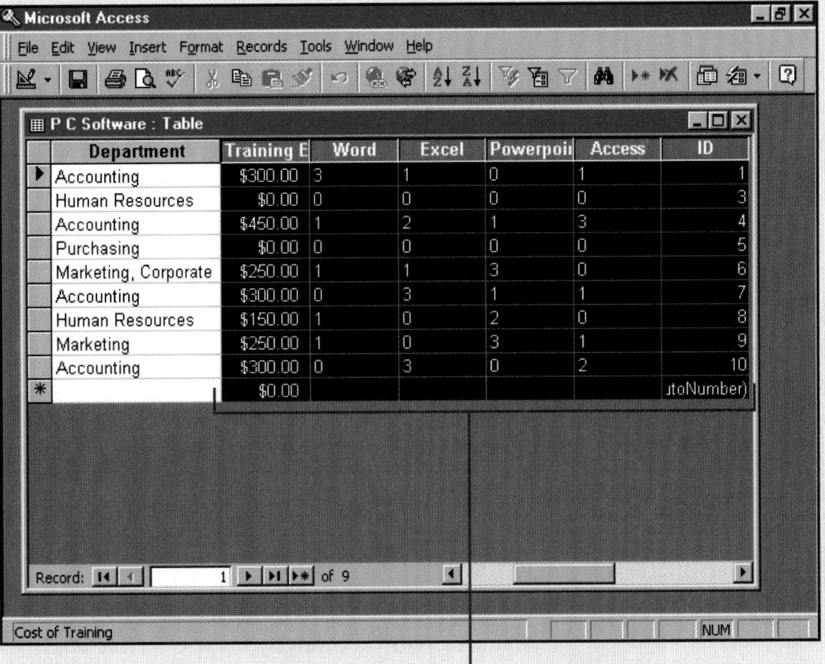

Department	Training E	Word	Excel	Powerpoi	Access	ID
Accounting	$300.00	3	1	0	1	1
Human Resources	$0.00	0	0	0	0	3
Accounting	$450.00	1	2	1	3	4
Purchasing	$0.00	0	0	0	0	5
Marketing, Corporate	$250.00	1	1	3	0	6
Accounting	$300.00	0	3	1	1	7
Human Resources	$150.00	1	0	2	0	8
Marketing	$250.00	1	0	3	1	9
Accounting	$300.00	0	3	0	2	10
	$0.00					ıtoNumber)

5 Drag a border from one of the six columns so that the columns are just big enough to hold the longest entry.

Dragging one of the borders resizes all six columns.

continues

To Adjust Column Widths and Hide Columns (continued)

6 Click anywhere in the table to deselect the columns.

7 Click in the column heading of the Employee Number field.

Now that you have selected this column, you can practice hiding it.

8 Open the Format menu and choose the Hide Columns command.

Access hides the column you had selected.

9 To unhide the column, open the Format menu and choose the Unhide Columns command.

Access displays the Unhide Columns dialog box, as shown in Figure 13.10. If the column has a check mark next to its name, the column is displayed. If there is no check mark, the column is hidden.

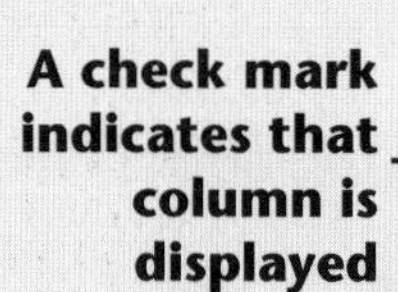

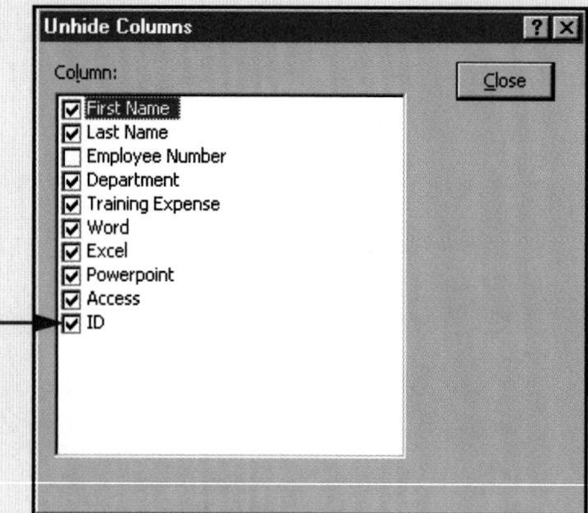

Figure 13.10 Use the Unhide Columns dialog box to unhide a column.

10 Click the Employee Number checkbox.

11 Click the Close button.

Access closes the Unhide Columns dialog box. The Employee Number column reappears on the screen.

Save your work and keep the P C Software table open. In Lesson 6, you learn how to search for particular records in your database.

You can also use the menus to adjust the column width. Move the pointer to the column you want to adjust. Then open the F**o**rmat menu and choose the **C**olumn Width command. Type a new value (the width of the column in points) and click the OK button.

You can also hide multiple columns by first selecting them and then selecting the **H**ide Columns command from the F**o**rmat menu. In addition, you can use the **U**nhide Columns dialog box to hide columns. In the list displayed in the dialog box, click on the checkbox next to a column to deselect it. This will hide the column.

Lesson 6: Finding Records

In a table with many records and many fields, it may be time-consuming to scroll through the records and fields to find a particular record. Instead, you can search for a specific field entry in order to find and move quickly to a record.

For example, if you want to find the Wayne Wheaton record, you can search for *Wheaton*. It's sometimes easier to select the column you want to use for your search and then search just that column, but you can also search for text in any column in the table. In this lesson, you find a record by first searching a single column and then by searching all columns.

To Find a Record

1 With the P C Software table of the Training2 database open, click in the Last Name field.

It doesn't matter what row you click in. Clicking anywhere in the field tells Access that you want to search for a particular record using the Last Name field only.

2 Click the Find button.

Access displays the Find dialog box (see Figure 13.11). Here you tell Access what you want to find and where you want to look.

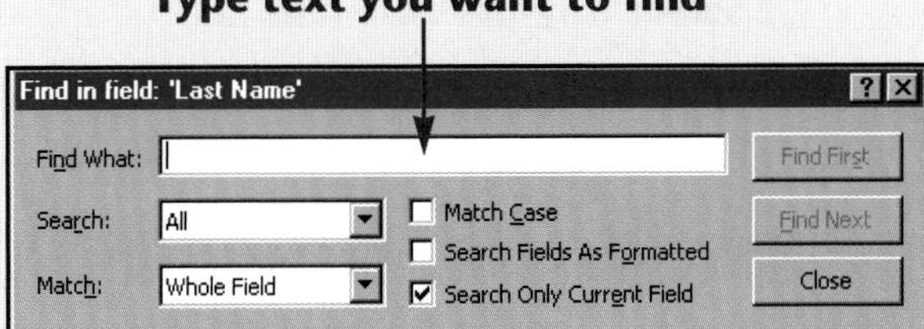

Figure 13.11
You use the Find dialog box to prepare for your search.

3 Type `Wheaton`.

This is the entry you want to find.

4 Click the Find First button.

Access moves to the first match, and the dialog box remains open. You can continue to search by clicking the **F**ind Next button until you find the record you want.

If you can't see the match because the dialog box is in the way, move the dialog box by dragging its title bar.

5 Drag across the text in the Find What text box to select it; then type `Resources`.

This is the next entry you want to find.

continues

To Find a Record (continued)

6 Deselect the Search Only Current Field option.

Instead of restricting the search to just the current column, you are now telling Access to look in all columns.

7 Click the drop-down list button next to the Match box.

The drop-down list box gives you three choices (see Figure 13.12).

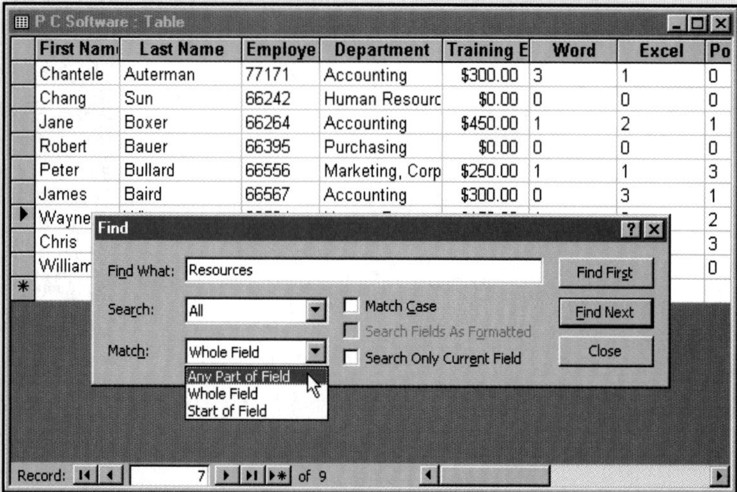

Figure 13.12
There are three choices in the Match drop-down box.

8 Select Any Part of Field.

The text you want to find (*Resources*) won't be the entire entry; it will be only part of the field. For this reason, you have to tell Access to match any part of the field. Figure 13.13 shows the options you have requested for this search.

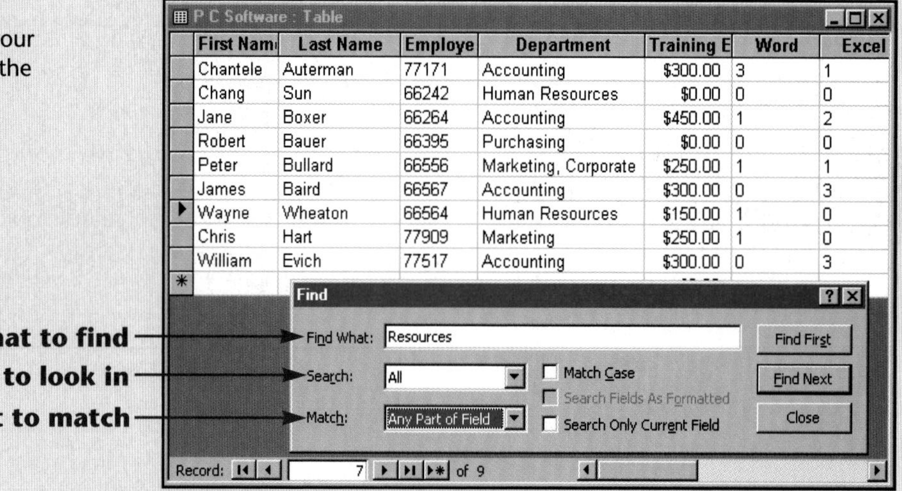

P C Software : Table
First Nam | Last Name | Employe | Department | Training E | Word | Excel
Chantele | Auterman | 77171 | Accounting | $300.00 | 3 | 1
Chang | Sun | 66242 | Human Resources | $0.00 | 0 | 0
Jane | Boxer | 66264 | Accounting | $450.00 | 1 | 2
Robert | Bauer | 66395 | Purchasing | $0.00 | 0 | 0
Peter | Bullard | 66556 | Marketing, Corporate | $250.00 | 1 | 1
James | Baird | 66567 | Accounting | $300.00 | 0 | 3
Wayne | Wheaton | 66564 | Human Resources | $150.00 | 1 | 0
Chris | Hart | 77909 | Marketing | $250.00 | 1 | 0
William | Evich | 77517 | Accounting | $300.00 | 0 | 3
Find
What to find
Find What: Resources
What fields to look in
Search: All
What to match
Match: Any Part of Field
Match Case
Search Fields As Formatted
Search Only Current Field
Find First
Find Next
Close
Record: 7 of 9

Figure 13.13
You can change your search options in the Find dialog box.

9 Click the Find First button.

Access moves to the first occurrence and highlights `Resources` in the Department column in the record for Chang Sun.

10 Click the Find Next button.

Access moves to the next occurrence and highlights `Resources` in the Department column in the record for Wayne Wheaton.

11 Click the Close button.

This step closes the Find dialog box.

Save your work and keep the P C Software table open. In Lesson 7, you learn how to sort the records in your table.

If you have problems...

If you see a message telling you that Access has reached the end of the records and asking whether you want to start searching from the beginning, click the Yes button. By default, Access searches from the current record down through the database. The record you want may be located before the current one.

If you see another message telling you that Access reached the end of the records, Access did not find a match. Try the search again. Be sure that you typed the entry correctly. You may need to change some of the options.

Lesson 7: Sorting Records

Access displays the records in your table in an order determined by the primary key. You learned how to create a primary key in Project 12. If your table has no primary key, Access displays the records in the order in which they were entered.

If you use a primary key, Access sorts the entries alphabetically or numerically based on the entries in that field. (If a counter field is your primary key, your records will be displayed in the order in which they were entered.) Fortunately, however, you aren't restricted to displaying your data only in the order determined by your primary key. With Access, you can sort the records by using any of the fields in the database table.

In this lesson, you first sort your data on the Last Name field. You will then use the toolbar to sort on the Employee Number field.

To Sort Records

1 With the P C Software table of the Training2 database open, click in the Last Name field.

Clicking in this field tells Access that you want to base your sort on the Last Name field.

continues

To Sort Records (continued)

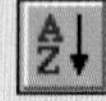

2 Click the Sort Ascending button.

Access sorts the records in ascending alphabetical order (*a* to *z*) based on the entries in the Last Name field (see Figure 13.14).

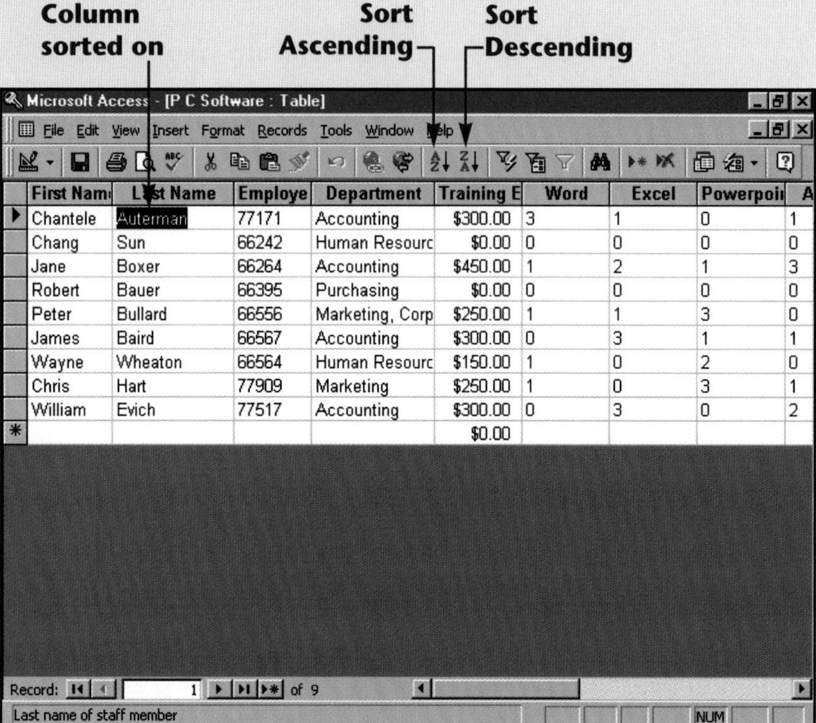

Figure 13.14
The result of an ascending sort based on the Last Name field.

3 Click in the Employee Number field.

Clicking in this field tells Access that you now want to base your sort on the Employee Number field.

4 Click the Sort Ascending button on the toolbar.

Access sorts the table by using the entries in the Employee Number field. Keep in mind that the sort order displayed on-screen in the datasheet does not affect the order in which the records are actually stored.

Close the P C Software table and save the changes. Close the Training2 database. In Project 14, you will use your P C Software table to learn about queries.

If you have completed your session on the computer, exit Access and Windows before turning off the computer. Otherwise, continue with the "Checking Your Skills" section in this project.

Project Summary

To	Do This
Add records	Open the table in Datasheet view. Type the appropriate information in each field. Move from field to field with ↵Enter. At the end of the information for one record, press ↵Enter. This moves you to the next row and saves the record just entered.
Go to first record in table	Click the First Record button.
Go to previous record	Click the Previous Record button.
Go to next record	Click the Next Record button.
Go to last record in table	Click the Last Record button.
Insert a record	Click the New Record button.
Edit records	Move to the record and field you want to edit. Click in the field and add, delete, or change the entry as needed. Press ↵Enter to complete the entry.
Delete a record	Click the record selector of the row to be deleted. Click the Delete Record button, then click Yes to confirm.
Adjust column widths	Place the mouse pointer between columns until it changes to a thick vertical bar with arrows on either side. Click and drag the line between the column to the right or left to adjust the column width. Select several columns at once and double-click one of the bars between the selected columns for automatic adjustment of all selected columns.
Hide columns	Click in the column heading. Open the F**o**rmat menu and choose the **H**ide Columns command. In the F**o**rmat menu, use **U**nhide Columns to display the column again.
Find a record	Click the Find button. In the dialog box, type what you want to find. You can search in the current field or all fields. You can also search in Any Part of Field. Click the Find Fi**r**st button to begin the search.
Sort records	Click the field you want to sort on. Click either the Sort Ascending or Sort Descending button.

Checking Your Skills

True/False

For each of the following, check *T* or *F* to indicate whether the statement is true or false.

__T __F **1.** You can edit records in Design view.

__T __F **2.** When the pencil icon appears in the record selector, it reminds you that the record has not been saved.

__T __F **3.** When you change the column width, you also change the field size.

__T __F **4.** You can add a record only to the end of a table.

__T __F **5.** You can undo record deletions.

__T __F **6.** The only way to delete a record is to use the Delete Record button.

__T __F **7.** You can hide a column so that it cannot be viewed.

__T __F **8.** The default search is in the field where the insertion point is located.

__T __F **9.** You can hide only one column at a time.

__T __F **10.** Records sorted on the screen do not affect the order in which they are stored.

Multiple Choice

Circle the letter of the correct answer for each of the following questions.

1. Which of the following will take you quickly to the first record in a table?

a. Ctrl+End

b. Home

c. Alt+Home

d. The First Record button

2. Which command do you use to paste an entire record?

a. Paste **R**ecord

b. Paste Appen**d**

c. **P**aste

d. Paste **A**ll

3. Which of the following is *not* a way to adjust the column width?

a. Double-click the column border.

b. Drag the column border.

c. Open the F**o**rmat menu and choose the Column **S**ize command.

d. Open the F**o**rmat menu and choose the **C**olumn Width command.

4. If you want Access to search all fields in the table, which option do you select in the Find dialog box?

a. Curr**e**nt Field

b. Match **C**ase

c. Search Fields As F**o**rmatted

d. All

5. Which of the following is *not* a way to sort the records in a table?

a. Click the Sort Descending button.

b. Click the Sort Ascending button.

c. Open the **R**ecords menu and choose the **S**ort command.

d. Open the **R**ecords menu and choose the **Q**uick Sort command.

6. Which of the following is *not* a way to delete a record?

   a. Highlight the record and press Del.

   b. Place the insertion point anywhere in the record and press Ctrl+D.

   c. Place the insertion point anywhere in the record and click the Delete Record button.

   d. Place the insertion point anywhere in the record and choose Delete **R**ecord from the **E**dit menu.

7. Access automatically saves the data you enter to disk when you do which of the following?

   a. Click the Save button on the toolbar.

   b. Leave the field in which you entered the data.

   c. Choose **S**ave from the **F**ile menu.

   d. All the above

8. To hide a column, you should do which of the following?

   a. Select the column and press Alt+H.

   b. Select the column and double-click the right column separator on the border.

   c. Place the insertion point in the column and select **H**ide Columns from the F**o**rmat menu.

   d. Place the insertion point in the column and select Auto**H**ide from the F**o**rmat menu.

9. Access identifies the record you are editing by which of the following?

   a. The arrow on the record selector

   b. The asterisk on the record selector

   c. The key symbol on the record selector

   d. The pencil icon on the record selector

10. What does the New Record button look like?

    a. An arrow pointing to an asterisk

    b. A folder with an arrow on it

    c. A folder with a star on it

    d. An arrow pointing to a line

Completion

In the blank provided, write the correct answer for each of the following statements.

1. To add a new record, click the _____________ button.
2. The _____________ field determines the default order of the records.
3. To hide a column, open the F**o**rmat menu and choose the _____________ command.
4. Press _____________ to move to the first field in the record.
5. Press _____________ to move to the last field in the record.
6. The _____________ is the gray box to the left of a record in Datasheet view.
7. To locate a record based on a specific entry, use the _____________ button on the toolbar.
8. When you enter a number in a(n) _____________ field, Access automatically adds the dollar sign and decimals to it.
9. You can change the arrangement of the records in Datasheet view by using the _____________ button.
10. You can _____________ to resize a column when the mouse pointer becomes a thick line with arrows on either side.

Matching

In the blank next to each of the following terms or phrases, write the letter of the corresponding term or phrase. (Note that some letters may be used more than once.)

_____ **1.** Used to move among records

_____ **2.** Moves you to the first field in a record

_____ **3.** Indicates the record you are editing

_____ **4.** Where pasted information comes from

_____ **5.** Arranges records by the chosen field starting with the letter closest to *A*

_____ **6.** The same as ⇤

_____ **7.** Arranges records in reverse alphabetical order

_____ **8.** Holds a temporary copy of the item you copy

_____ **9.** A field that is not visible

_____ **10.** Last row of the datasheet

a. Sort Ascending

b. Hidden Column

c. Clipboard

d. New Record location

e. Home

f. navigation buttons

g. Find button

h. ⇧Shift+Tab

i. Sort Descending

j. pencil icon

Screen ID

Identify each of the items shown in Figure 13.15.

Figure 13.15

1._______________

2._______________

3._______________

4._______________

5._______________

6._______________

7._______________

8._______________

9._______________

10._______________

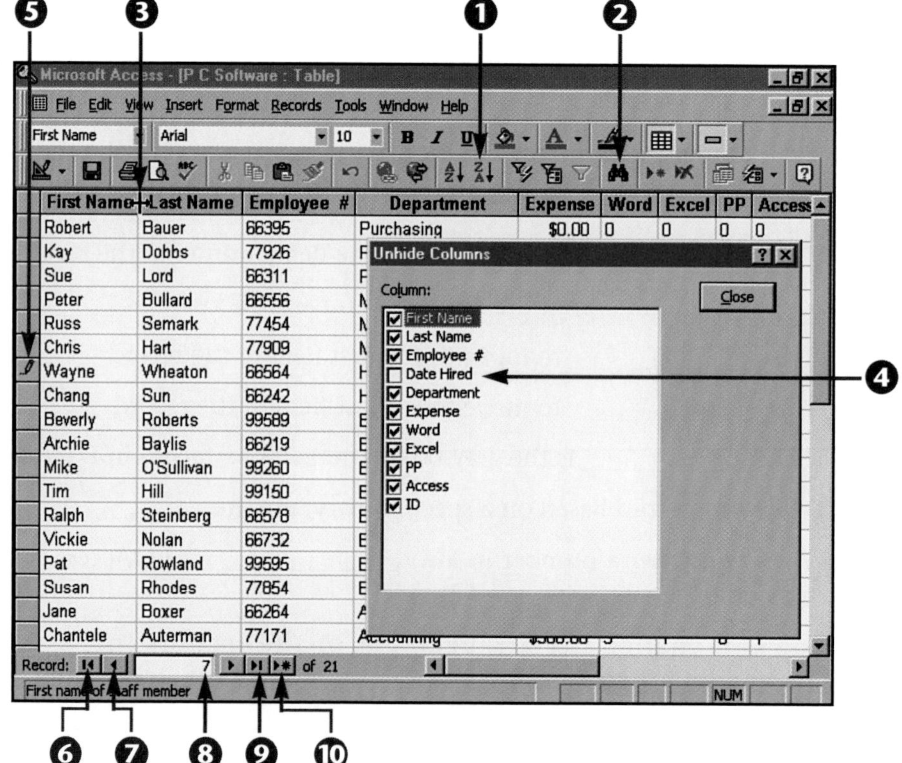

Applying Your Skills

Practice

The following exercises enable you to practice the skills you have learned in this project. Take a few minutes to work through these exercises now.

1. Cataloging Your Books

In "Applying Your Skills" in Project 12, you created a Library database with a table for your books. Now you can enter actual information about your book collection into this database table. Because you may not have access to your personal book collection while working through this project, some book information is provided for you.

To Enter Book Information

1. Copy the Proj1302 database file and name it `Library2`. Then open the Books table.
2. In Datasheet view, enter the author's last name, first name, book title, type of book, and year of publication for each book. Type the following information into the Books table:

Last Name	First Name	Book Title	Type of Book	Year of Publication
O'Rourke	P.J.	All the Trouble in the world	Nonfiction	1994
Gibbons	Kaye	Ellen Foster	Fiction	1990
Sandford	John	Silent Prey	Mystery	1992
Hiaasen	Carl	Skin Tight	Fiction	1989
Connelly	Michael	The Black Echo	Mystery	1992
Markoe	Merrill	What the Dogs Have Taught Me	Humor	1992

3. Adjust each column of the table so that you can see the longest entry in each field. If the column is much wider than the entry, make the column narrower.
4. Sort the records by author's last name.
5. Save your work and close the table and database.

2. Entering Record Company Information

In "Applying Your Skills" in Project 12, you created a database for your Sound Byte Music Store to help you keep track of data. You set up the database and also created a table for supplier information—that is, the names and addresses of the record companies you deal with. Now that you have the Suppliers table set up, you add records to it in this exercise.

To Enter Record Company Information

1. Copy the Proj1303 database files and name it **SBMusic2**. Then open the Suppliers table.
2. Enter the following records in Datasheet view:

Record Company	Contact Name	Address	City	State	ZIP	Phone
MCA Records	Shannon Kelly	554 S. Recording Lane	University City	CA	91608	(800)555-0122
Warner Bros. Records	Xavier Hurrle	3300 Warner Blvd.	Burbank	CA	91505	(800)555-9022
Atlantic Recording	Brendan O'Brien	75 Rockefeller Plaza	New York	NY	10019	(800)555-0917
Epic	Conner Denney	666 Fifth Avenue	New York	NY	10101	(800)555-7732

3. Adjust the column widths so that you can see the longest entry in each field.
4. Save your work.

3. Creating a Database to Track Personal Computer Hardware

You may find it difficult to keep track of the many different combinations of computer hardware that may exist in an organization. A database can help.

To Create the Database

1. Copy Proj1304 and rename it **PC2**. Open the database PC2.
2. Open the PC Hardware table and enter the following records. (Because of the number of fields in each record, the items are separated by commas.)

386,4,120,Yes,Yes,VGA,None,Yes,No,General Comp,1234, 2/5/92

386,8,40,No,Yes,VGA,None,No,No,General Comp,1235, 6/3/93

386,4,120,Yes,Yes,VGA,None,Yes,No,General Comp,1236, 6/1/94

486,8,500,Yes,No,SVGA,2X,Yes,Yes,Acme Computer,1237, 8/4/94

486,16,800,Yes,No,SVGA,2X,Yes,Yes,Acme Computer,1238, 8/4/95

Pentium,32,1250,Yes,No,SVGA,4X,Yes,Yes,Wilson Electric,1239, 10/9/96

3. Open the Vendors table and enter the following vendor information:

Name of Vendor	Street Address	City	State	ZIP Code	Phone Number
General Comp	123 Main	Ann Arbor	MI	48105	313-665-2345
Acme Computer	234 Cross	Ypsilanti	MI	48197	313-482-3456
Wilson Electric	122 Sill	Ypsilanti	MI	48197	313-487-1161

4. Close both tables and the database.

4. Getting a Helping Hand

Many useful Help utilities are available. One of the easiest to use is the What's **T**his? pointer. This feature can help you find out how to accomplish tasks and what certain parts of the window mean.

To Get Help on Topics in This Project

1. With a table in Datasheet view, choose the **H**elp menu.
2. Select the What's **T**his? menu item. The mouse pointer has a question mark appended to it.
3. Point to and click the record selector of any of the records. A window appears that explains the record selector and any of four conditions you will see.
4. Choose **H**elp and What's **T**his? again.
5. Point to and click any of the column headings. Notice that Access gives you hints on selecting and resizing the columns.
6. Choose **H**elp and What's **T**his? one last time.
7. Select the gray square at the intersection of the row and column selectors. Notice that you can use this button to select the entire datasheet.

5. Exploring the World of Alaska

You can use the sort buttons to answer questions in a database. Alaska has the northernmost, westernmost, and easternmost geographic points in the United States. You want to demonstrate this by using the limited Alaskan database.

To Use Sort in the Alaska Database

1. Open the Proj1305 database as a copy.
2. Open the Geography table in Datasheet view.
3. Maximize the window, if necessary.
4. Select the Latitude column. Latitude is the angle, in degrees, of a particular point from the equator. The north geographic pole is 90 degrees from the equator. As such, the northernmost geographic site in the database will have the highest latitude.
5. Click the Sort Descending button on the toolbar. Admiralty Bay becomes the second record displayed, and it is the northernmost point listed in this database. (The actual northernmost point on the landmass is Point Barrow, also on the Northern Slope.)

The westernmost and easternmost points can be found in a similar way. Longitude starts at zero degrees in Greenwich, England, and is measured east and west from there. The opposite side of the earth, in the Pacific Ocean, is 180 degrees longitude.

6. Select the Longitude column.
7. Click the Sort Descending button on the toolbar. Adak Strait has the highest west longitude and is therefore the westernmost point listed in the database. Aga Cove, also in the Aleutian Island chain, has the largest east longitude and is therefore the easternmost point in the database—more east than Maine (geographically).

Challenge

The following challenges enable you to use your problem-solving skills. Take time to work through these exercises now.

1. Creating a List of Club Members

Open the database that you created in Challenge exercise 1 in Project 12 to track information about members of an organization. Enter sample information for 10 club members. Save the database and its table.

2. Doing Customer Research

You changed the database structure to reflect all the questions and have received a few responses. Three more responses have arrived.

To Enter Customer Responses in the Database

1. Open the file Proj1306 as a copy.
2. Enter the following three responses:

`Adults`	`2`	`2`	`3`
`Children`	`4`	`2`	`0`
`Hours`	`1`	`3`	`5`
`No 1`	`DISNEY`	`DISCOVERY`	`CNN`
`No 2`	`TNT`	`DISNEY`	
`No 3`	`DISCOVERY`	`CNN`	
`Doing`	`Good`	`Okay`	`Okay`

As you begin to enter the first comment (provided in the next step), you notice that the comment will not fit in the space reserved. To get the data to fit, you must either increase the size of the text field or change the field type.

3. Change the type for the Improve field to **Memo** and continue to enter the data.

   Improvement comment for the first household: **`You're doing all right, but we sure would like to see more channels for the children. More educational channels.`**

   Comment for the second household: **`Don't see anything.`**

   The third household had no comments.
4. Sort the records to see which channel is rated number one for the most households.

3. Owning a Vending Company

You have gathered more information from the binders and will need to put it in the database you generated in the previous project. If you have not generated the database, you can use the file Proj1307.

To Enter Information in the Tables

1. Open the file Proj1307 as a copy.
2. Enter the following data in the Locations table:

Site	Owner	Machine Type
National Airport	Biggy Jones, Inc	6 Head Candy
International Airport	Biggy Jones, Inc	6 Head Candy
Jakes Hardware	Paul Jakes	Rotary Sandwich
Carter's Gifts	Don Carter	Card Maker

3. Enter the following information in the Suppliers table:

Name	Address	Phone
Cardstock Vending	Grover's Mills	(619) 342-9823
Food Venders, Inc	Placid Lake	(722) 871-9943
Bulk Foodstuffs	Carrinton	(433) 762-1925

4. Enter the following information in the Machines table:

Machine Type	Supplier	Cost
6 Head Candy	Food Venders, Inc	1,500
Rotary Sandwich	Food Venders, Inc	2,200
Card Maker	Cardstock Vending	4,750

5. Adjust the column widths so that all data can be seen in each table.
6. Hide the Machine Cost field.

4. Managing a Video Store

Open your video store database you created in the previous project and open the primary table that contains the list of videos. Enter at least ten videos in the database, inventing the information.

Hide the current renter field so that prying eyes can't view the data.

Sort the primary table based on the title of the video and then on the age of the video.

5. Taking a Home Inventory

In the home inventory database you created in the previous project, open the table that includes the item field and add at least ten records with varying item costs.

Sort the datasheet based on cost and then hide the cost field.

As you enter your data, be sure to include at least three different insurance companies; one for auto, one for home, and one for personal articles and furniture.

Sort the datasheet based on the insurance carrier to see the types of articles identified for each carrier.

Project 14

Querying Your Database

Objectives

In this project, you learn how to:

- Create a New Query
- Choose Fields for a Query
- Save a Query
- Edit a Query
- Sort a Query
- Match Criteria
- Save a Query with a New Name and Open Multiple Queries

Why Would I Do This?

Query
A question posed to the database that determines what information is retrieved.

Dynaset
A subset of records created as a result of a query.

The primary reason you spend time entering all your data into a database is so that you can easily find and work with the information. In your address database, for example, you may want to display all of your contacts in Florida. To do so, you would create a query. A *query* asks a question of the database, such as, "Which records have *FL* as the state?" and then pulls those records from the database into a subset of records. If the query simply selects or sorts data, the subset has the special name *dynaset*. You can then work with (or print) just those records selected by your query.

You can also create queries that display all of the records but only show selected fields. For example, you can display only the Last Name and Employee Number fields in the Training database. Or you can create a query that searches for values in one field, such as the Florida example just given, but displays only selected fields in the result. You can also create more complex queries. For example, you can query your Training database to display all staff members who have received training in either Microsoft Excel or PowerPoint. Queries are created and saved so they can be used over and over.

In this project, you learn how to create, save, and use a query.

Lesson 1: Creating a New Query

A table is the most common type of object you can include in a database, but you can also create other types of objects. A query is one of the other objects you can create in a database.

You may remember that when you open the database, you see the database window that lists the tables contained in the database and also includes tabs for queries, forms, reports, and so on. If you want to add a query to the table, you can start from this window.

In this lesson, you work with the data in the P C Software table of your Training database. The P C Software table on disk that you will copy and use in this project includes the records you entered in Project 13, as well as some additional records. The headings in the revised table have been modified slightly to adjust the size of each column, allowing more information to appear on the screen. You start by creating a query, and then you add the table you want to work with.

To Create a New Query

1. **Copy the Proj1401 database file to `Training3`. Then open the Training3 database in Access.**

   In this project, you use the Training database you worked with in Projects 12 and 13, but additional records have been added to it and the headings have been modified to shrink the width of some of the columns. You should see the database window, listing the P C Software table.

2 Click the Queries tab.

The Queries list is blank because you haven't created and saved any queries yet (see Figure 14.1).

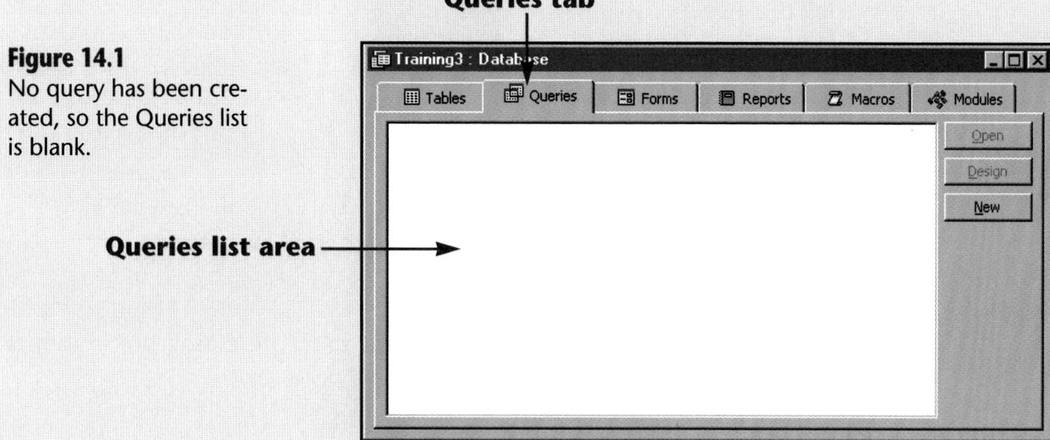

Figure 14.1
No query has been created, so the Queries list is blank.

3 Click the New button.

You see the New Query dialog box (see Figure 14.2). You can use one of the Query Wizards to create a query. This method works best for specific kinds of queries such as finding duplicate records. None of the wizards are appropriate for the query you want to create for this example, so you will use the more general method, Design view.

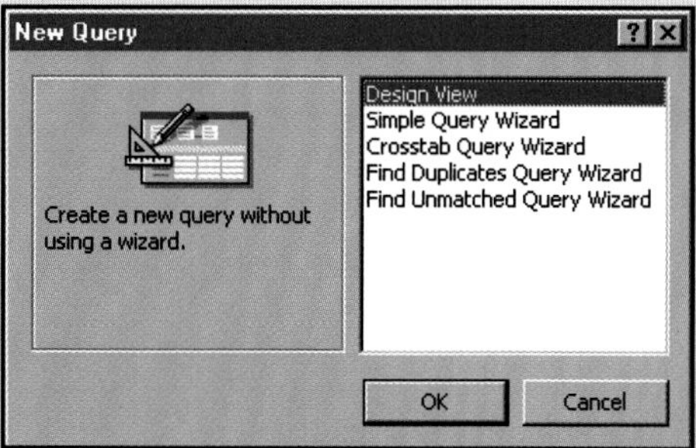

Figure 4.2
Choose the method you want to use to create a new query.

4 Click Design View and then click OK.

You see the Show Table dialog box (see Figure 14.3). Here you select the table(s) you want to use in your query. For complex queries, you can pull information from more than one table. For this example, you use just one table—the P C Software table.

continues

To Create a New Query (continued)

Figure 4.3
Select the table you want to use from the dialog box.

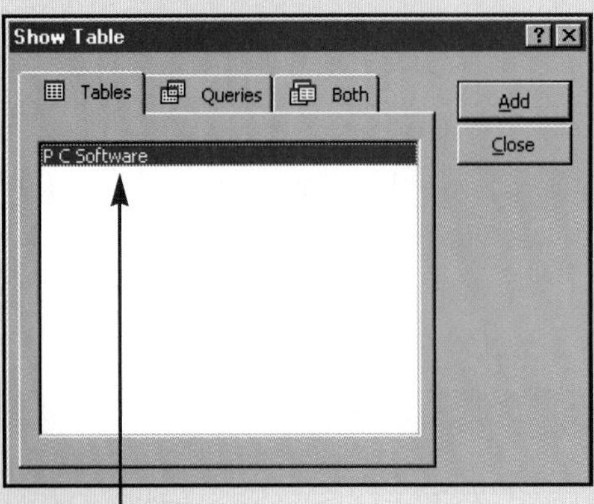

5 Click the P C Software table to select it, if necessary.

6 Click the Add button.

This step selects the table you want to use. The dialog box remains open so that you can add other tables if necessary.

7 Click the Close button.

Access closes the Show Table dialog box and displays the Select Query window (see Figure 14.4). You learn about Select Query in the next lesson. For now, leave the Select Query window open and continue with Lesson 2.

Figure 14.4
Use the query window to create a new query.

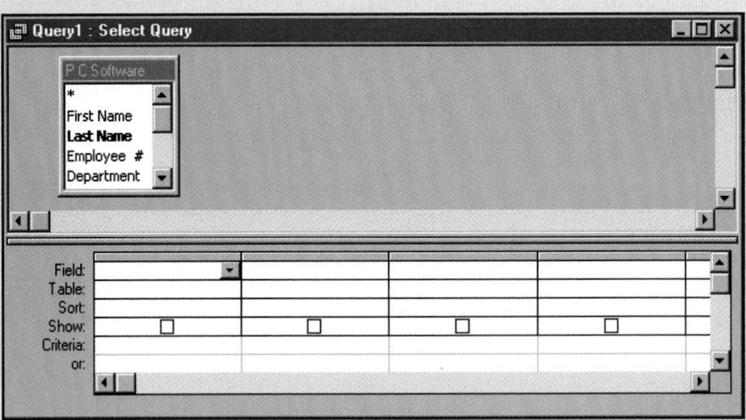

Lesson 2: Choosing Fields for a Query

After you open a new query and select a table, you see a window divided into two parts. The top half of the query window displays a scroll box containing a list of the fields from the table you selected. Notice that the primary key field appears in bold type. (In this version of the database, the Last Name field has been designated as the primary key.) You can use this field list to select the fields you want to include in your query.

Query By Example (QBE)
The QBE grid is used to define the parameters of a query. You can specify fields, sort order, and criteria to be used to search your database.

In the lower half of the query window, you see the *Query By Example (QBE)* grid with rows for Field, Table, Sort, Show, Criteria, and Or. All the columns are blank. The QBE grid controls which fields are included in your query.

You can create a query that displays just the Last Name and Department fields from your P C Software table. You add the fields you want to include in the query to the Field row in the QBE grid. You can include as many fields as you want in the query, but you must include at least one field.

In this lesson, you create a query that contains only the Last Name and Department from your P C Software table. This list might be handy if you need to know who has received training in each department. You don't really need any other information from your P C Software table.

You can use one of several methods to add fields to your query. Try adding fields using these different methods now.

To Choose Fields for a Query

1 In the field list in the top half of the Select Query window, click the Last Name field.

The query window should still be open from the preceding lesson. This step selects the field you want to add to the QBE grid.

2 Drag the selected field from the field list to the first column in the Field row of the QBE grid.

As you drag, a little field box is displayed. When you release the mouse button, Access displays the field name in the Field row, and the table name in the Table row (see Figure 14.5). The Show row in this column then displays a check mark in the checkbox, indicating that this field will be displayed in the query. (There are occasions when you may want to use a field but not display its contents. In that case, you would click on the Show box to deselect it.) Next, you add a second field to the query.

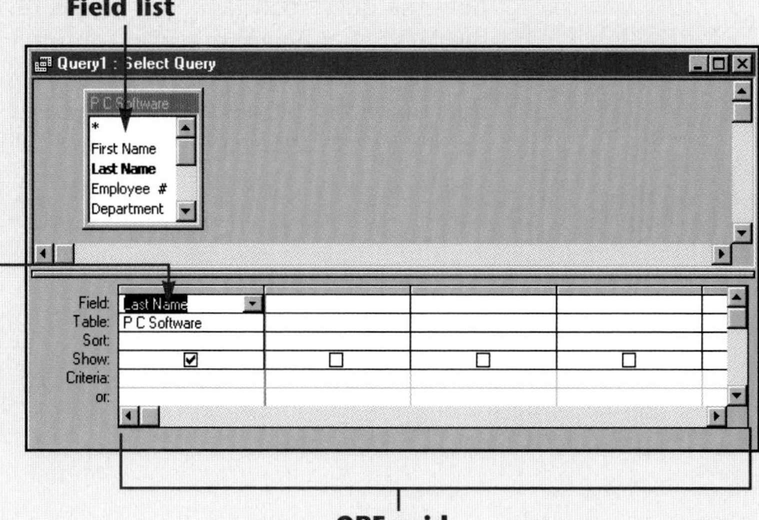

Figure 14.5
Choose the first field for the query by dragging it into place.

continues

To Choose Fields for a Query (continued)

3 Click in the second column of the Field row in the QBE grid.

You see a down arrow; clicking this arrow displays a drop-down list of fields from which you can choose the field you want to include in the query.

4 Click the down arrow.

Access displays the drop-down list of fields (see Figure 14.6).

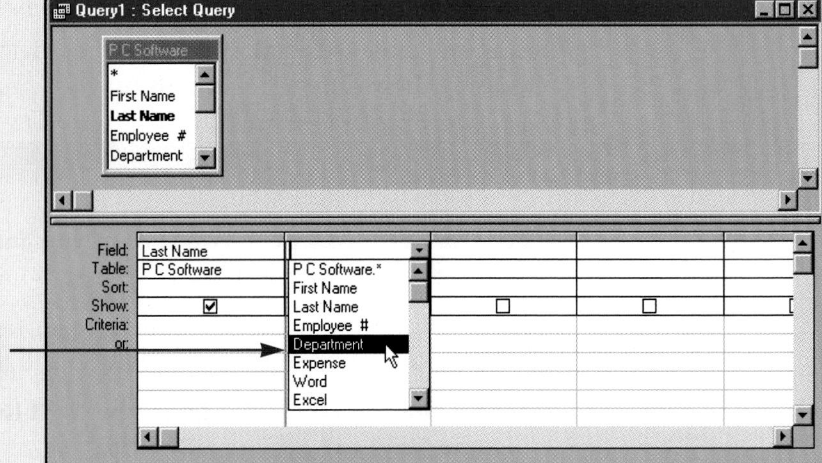

Figure 14.6
Use the drop-down list to select a field to add to the query.

5 Click Department in the list.

This selects the field to add to the query. This action has the same effect as dragging the field from the field list.

6 Click the View button on the toolbar.

This displays the records in Datasheet view, using the fields you selected in the query. Using this command, you can check to see how the query will look (see Figure 14.7). Notice that the title bar displays Select Query to remind you that you are viewing a dynaset, not the actual table. The difference between a table and a dynaset is that the table consists of all the records in the order in which they are stored on disk; the dynaset consists of a sorted list of pointers to the records, not the records themselves.

Figure 14.7
In Datasheet view, you can see that the query now includes two fields.

Query1 : Select Query

Last Name	Department
Auterman	Accounting
Baird	Accounting
Bauer	Purchasing
Baylis	Branch 3
Boxer	Accounting
Bullard	Marketing,Corporate
Dobbs	Payroll
Evich	Accounting
Hart	Marketing
Hill	Branch 2
Krasny	Accounting
Lord	Payoll
Nolan	Branch 1
O'Sullivan	Branch 3
Rhodes	Branch 1
Roberts	Branch 3

Record: 1 of 21

7 Click the View button on the toolbar.

The View button now has a different look. This step returns you to the Design view for the query. Keep the query window open in this view. You learn how to name and save the query in the next lesson.

If you would rather use the menus, you can open the **V**iew menu and select the Data**s**heet View or the **D**esign View command, instead of clicking the toolbar View buttons.

You can also add fields to the query by double-clicking the field name or by typing the field name in the Field row of the QBE grid.

You can select several fields and add them all at once from the field list. If the fields are listed next to each other, click the first field in the field list. Then hold down Shift and click the last field in the field list. Access selects the first and last fields and all fields in between. You can also select fields that aren't listed next to each other. Click the first field you want to select. Then hold down Ctrl and click the next field you want to select. Continue pressing Ctrl while you click each subsequent field. After you have selected all the fields you want, drag them to the QBE grid and place them in the first empty space in the Field row. This will add all of the selected fields to the query.

When you switch from Design view to Datasheet view, you are actually running your query. Instead of switching views, you can open the **Q**uery menu and select the **R**un command or click the Run button on the toolbar.

Lesson 3: Saving the Query

As with any object you add to a database, you must save and name the object if you want to keep it. If you want to keep the query you just created, for example, you will have to save it.

The first time you save a query, you are prompted to give it a name. After that, you can save changes to the query without retyping the name. You can open the **F**ile menu and choose the **S**ave command, or you can click the Save button on the toolbar. You can also close the query window, at which point the program will ask if you want to save the query.

In this lesson, you save the query and name it.

To Save the Query

1 The query window based on the P C Software table should still be open from the preceding lesson. Open the File menu and choose the Save command.

You see the Save As dialog box, with the name `Query1` displayed (see Figure 14.8). Access suggests Query1 as a default name, but as you can see, it isn't very descriptive. You can type a more descriptive name.

Figure 14.8
Replace the default name with a more descriptive name for the query.

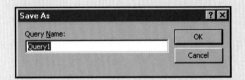

2 Type `Department Training List`.

This is the name you want to assign the query. You can type up to 64 characters, including spaces.

3 Click the OK button.

Access saves the query and the database. The name of the query is displayed in the title bar of the query window and also in the list of Queries in the database window.

4 Click the Close button in the upper-right corner of the query window.

Access closes the query window. You see the Department Training List query listed in the database window.

5 Click Department Training List on the Queries tab.

6 Click the Open button.

This step reopens the query. The query is now displayed in Datasheet view, instead of the Design view. Keep the Department Training List query open; you use it in the next lesson.

If you have problems...

If you don't like the name you used—for example, suppose that you accepted the default Query1 name—you can change the name. In Project 17, you learn how to rename objects such as tables and queries.

You don't have to save the query if you're sure you won't use it again. Just close the query window without saving. When Access prompts you to save, click the **N**o button.

If you decide to save the query, you can do so by clicking the Save button on the toolbar or by pressing Ctrl+S.

When you are given choices in a dialog box, one of the buttons will have a dark border. This is the default choice and may be activated by pressing ↵Enter. If your fingers are already on the keyboard after typing data, it is faster to press ↵Enter than to reach for the mouse. Be sure to check the default choice before pressing ↵Enter to make certain it is the action you want to take.

Lesson 4: Editing the Query

Creating a query takes some practice and a little trial and error. You choose some fields, view the query, make some changes, view the query again, and so on, until you get the results you want.

You can edit the query to add or delete fields. In this project, you add three fields and then delete a field.

To Edit the Query

1. **With the Department Training List query window displayed, click the View button on the toolbar.**

   When you opened the query in the preceding lesson, it was displayed in Datasheet view. To make changes, you first have to change to Design view. Now you should see the query window with the field list box at the top and the QBE grid at the bottom.

2. **Click the Excel field in the field list (you may have to scroll down to find it) and drag this field to the third column of the QBE grid.**

   Access adds this field to the QBE grid. You will now place the PowerPoint (labeled PP) field between the Department field and the Excel field.

3. **Click the PP field in the field list and drag this field to the third column of the QBE grid.**

   Access adds this field as the third column and moves the Excel field over one column to the right. You now have four fields in the query.

continues

To Edit the Query (continued)

If you have problems...

If the PP field appears in the wrong location, drag across the PP name in the column where it appears, and press the Del key. Then repeat step 3. If it is necessary to fill an empty column, click in the Field row of the empty column, click on the drop-down arrow and select the appropriate field for that column from the pop-up field list.

4 Double-click Access in the field list.

Access is added in the next field. You now have five fields in the query. In your window, you may not be able to see part, or even any of the fifth column, depending on the size of your computer monitor. Scroll the window to view the field you just added, if necessary.

Column selector
The area above a column in the QBE grid that enables you to select the entire column.

5 In the QBE grid, click the *column selector* (the thin gray bar just above the field names) over the PP column.

When you are in the column selector, you see a black downward arrow for the mouse pointer. When you click the mouse button, the entire column is selected (see Figure 14.9). After you select a column, you can move it or delete it. Try deleting this column.

Figure 14.9
You can select a column by clicking the column selector.

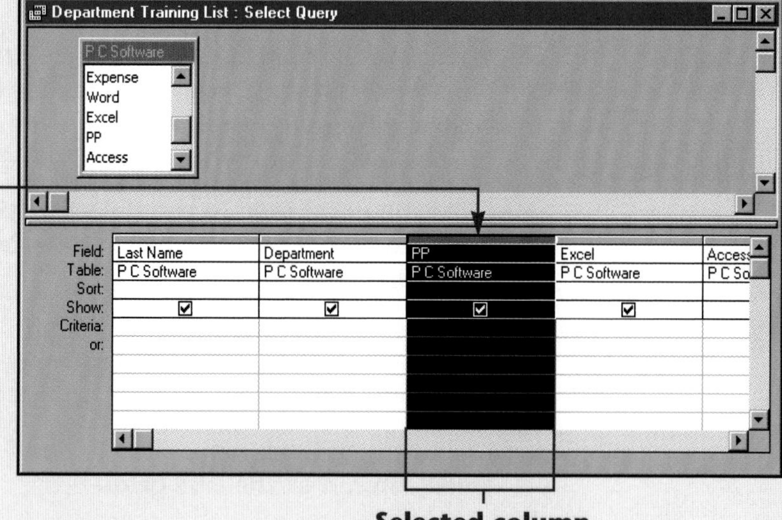

6 Open the Edit menu and choose the Delete command.

Access removes the field from the QBE grid.

7 Click the Save button on the toolbar.

Access saves the query with the changes you made. Keep the Department Training List query open in Design view. In the next lesson, you learn how to rearrange the order of the columns in your query.

If you have problems...

You cannot use the **U**ndo command to undo the deletion of a column. If you delete a column by mistake, simply add it again by dragging the name from the field list, double-clicking the field name in the field list, or using the drop-down list in the QBE grid.

After you select a field to delete it, you can press Del instead of opening the **E**dit menu and choosing the **D**elete command.

Lesson 5: Sorting the Query

The way your table is arranged depends on two factors. First, the order in which the fields are displayed is determined by the order in which you add them to the Field row in the QBE table. If you don't like the order, you can rearrange the fields into a different order, as you learn in this lesson.

Second, the default order in which the records are displayed is determined by the primary key. You can change the query's sort order by using the Sort row in the QBE grid.

To Sort the Query

1. **In the Department Training List query, click the column selector above the Department field.**

   The entire column is selected. After you select a column, you can move it or delete it.

2. **Place the pointer on the column selector and drag `Department` until it is the first column in the QBE grid.**

   A dotted box is displayed as part of the pointer to signify that you are dragging the column (see Figure 14.10). A dark vertical line also is displayed to indicate the insertion point for the selected column. When you release the mouse button, Access rearranges the columns in the new order.

continues

To Sort the Query (continued)

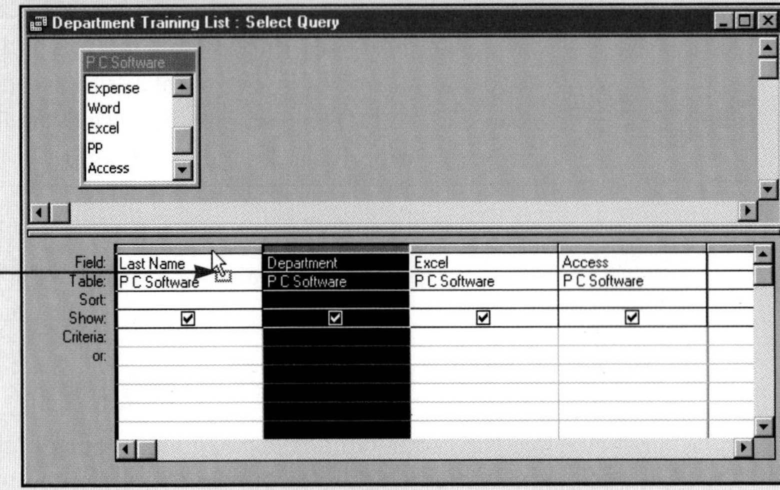

Figure 14.10
The pointer changes when you move a column in the QBE grid.

3 Click in the Sort row of the Department field.

In this example, you want to sort the query by Department. When you click in the field, Access displays a down arrow.

4 Click the down arrow.

Access displays a drop-down list of sort choices (see Figure 14.11).

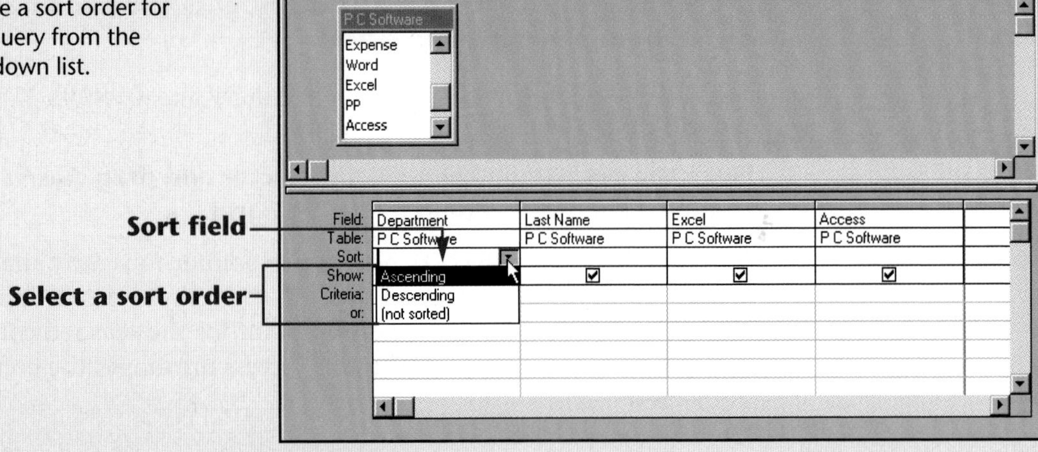

Figure 14.11
Choose a sort order for your query from the drop-down list.

5 Click Ascending.

This selects the sort order (*a* to *z*) you want to use. You can check the query by changing to Datasheet view.

6 Click the View button on the toolbar.

You can see the results of your query in the Datasheet view, as shown in Figure 14.12.

Figure 14.12
In Datasheet view, you can see that the query is now sorted by Department.

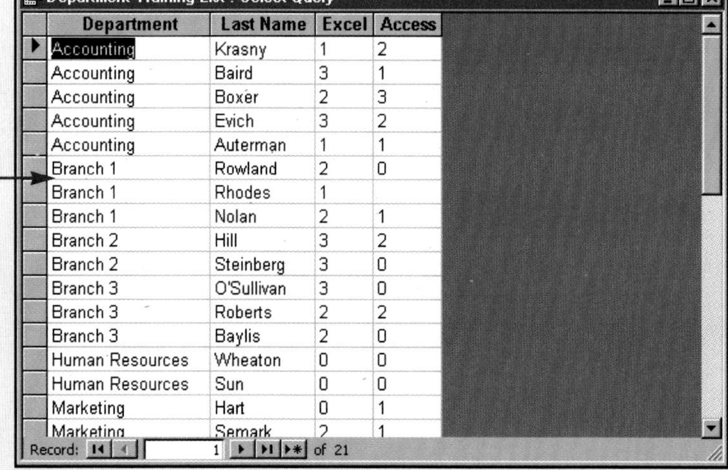

Department	Last Name	Excel	Access
Accounting	Krasny	1	2
Accounting	Baird	3	1
Accounting	Boxer	2	3
Accounting	Evich	3	2
Accounting	Auterman	1	1
Branch 1	Rowland	2	0
Branch 1	Rhodes	1	
Branch 1	Nolan	2	1
Branch 2	Hill	3	2
Branch 2	Steinberg	3	0
Branch 3	O'Sullivan	3	0
Branch 3	Roberts	2	2
Branch 3	Baylis	2	0
Human Resources	Wheaton	0	0
Human Resources	Sun	0	0
Marketing	Hart	0	1
Marketing	Semark	2	1

7 Click the View button on the toolbar again.

The query is once again displayed in Design view.

8 Click the Save button on the toolbar.

This saves the changes you made to the query. Keep the Department Training List query open in Design view as you continue with the next lesson.

Lesson 6: Matching Criteria

Criteria
A test or set of conditions that limits the records included in a query.

So far, the query you have created displays all of the records contained in the Training3 database, but only shows the fields you selected. You can also use a query to display only certain records—records that match certain *criteria*.

You can match a single criterion, such as the last names of staff members who have received training in Excel, or you can match multiple criteria, such as staff members in the Marketing or Human Resources departments who have received training in Access or Excel. In this lesson, you practice using the various types of criteria.

To Match Criteria

1 In the Design view of the Department Training List query, click the Criteria box in the Department column.

The insertion point is moved to this location of the QBE grid. Here you can type the value that you want to match.

continues

To Match Criteria (continued)

2 Type `Human Resources`.

Access automatically adds quotation marks around the criteria that has been entered (see Figure 14.13). However, in some cases, such as when entering values that contain any punctuation marks, you must add the quotation marks around the whole entry.

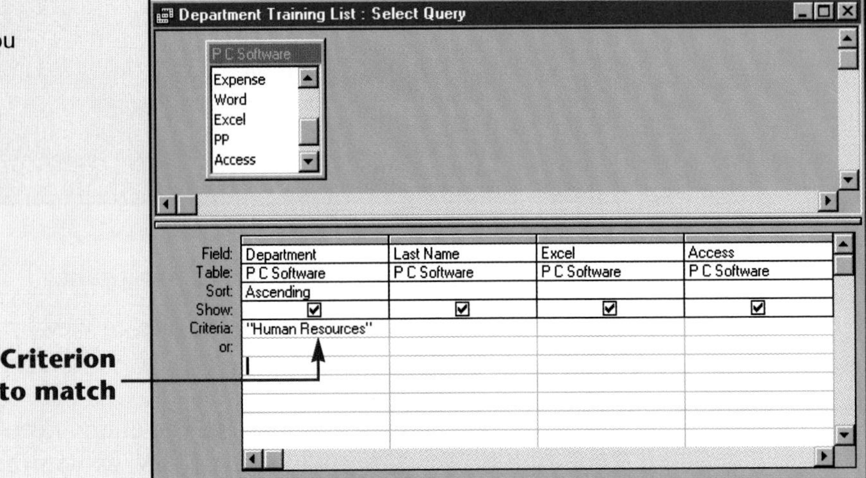

Figure 14.13
Enter the criteria you want to match.

3 Click the View button.

You see the results of the query. Notice that Access now includes only the staff members in the Human Resources Department in the query (see Figure 14.14).

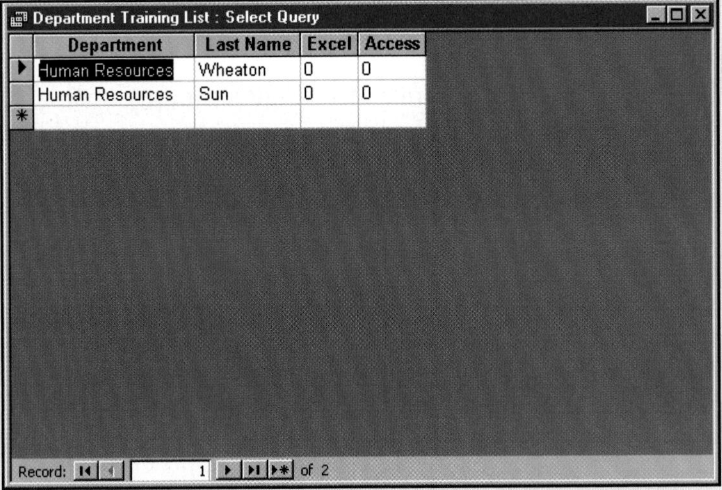

Department	Last Name	Excel	Access
Human Resources	Wheaton	0	0
Human Resources	Sun	0	0

Figure 14.14
The query now lists all the people in Human Resources who are listed in our Training table.

4 Click the View button again.

This returns you to the QBE grid so that you can make a change to the query.

5 Move to the box immediately below the Criteria box where you previously typed Human Resources. This is the `or:` row.

6 Click this box.

If you have problems...

If the window for the dialog box is not large enough to display more than one line of criteria, the window may scroll the list automatically. This will result in some of the criteria disappearing from view. Maximize this window before proceeding, if necessary.

If you want to match more than one value, you use this row to specify the second value. For this example, you might want to specify staff members in Human Resources or Accounting who have received training.

7 Type `Accounting`.

When the entry you want to match is one word and contains no punctuation, as in this example, you don't have to type quotation marks. Access will add them automatically.

8 Click the View button.

You see the results of the query. Notice that Access now includes trained staff members from Human Resources and Accounting.

9 Click the View button again.

You return to the Design view. Keep the Department Training List query open. In the next lesson, you learn how to save the query with a new name.

If you have problems...

If you see a blank table when you switch to Datasheet view, it means that Access found no matching records. Be sure that you typed the value you are trying to match exactly as you entered it in the database table. For example, you can't type `Human Resource` to match `Human Resources`. Check your typing and try again.

If, when you are entering text into the Criteria rows to make a match, Access displays a syntax error message, it means that you did not type the entry in the correct format. Remember that if the text entry contains punctuation, you must supply quotation marks.

Access has many types of queries you can use. You can, for example, match a range of values, as you would if you asked Access to display all staff members who received training in Excel at a level 2 or above. You can also create other types of queries, such as a query to display all duplicate records in a table.

There are other types of criteria that may be used besides a direct match. You can use comparisons such as <, which means *less than*, or >, which means *greater than*. If you use < to make a comparison in a text field, it uses alphabetical order. For example, if your criteria was < **Jones**, you would get all the names that came before Jones in the alphabet. Similarly, if you use **<1/1/95** in a date field, you would get all the dates before January 1, 1995. For more examples of different criteria, use the Access **H**elp index to look up help for Criteria, then explore some of the different categories.

Lesson 7: Saving the Query with a New Name and Opening Multiple Queries

In some cases, you may modify a query and then want to keep both versions of the query—the original and the modified query—for future use. In this lesson, you learn how to save a query with a new name.

You can also open a query from the database window, and you can have more than one query window open at a time. This lesson explains how to open multiple queries.

To Save the Query with a New Name and Open Multiple Queries

1. **In the Department Training List query, click the View button on the toolbar to go to the Datasheet view.**
2. **Open the File menu and choose the Save As/Export command.**

   You see the Save As dialog box, as shown in Figure 14.15, with the current name listed in the New Name text box.

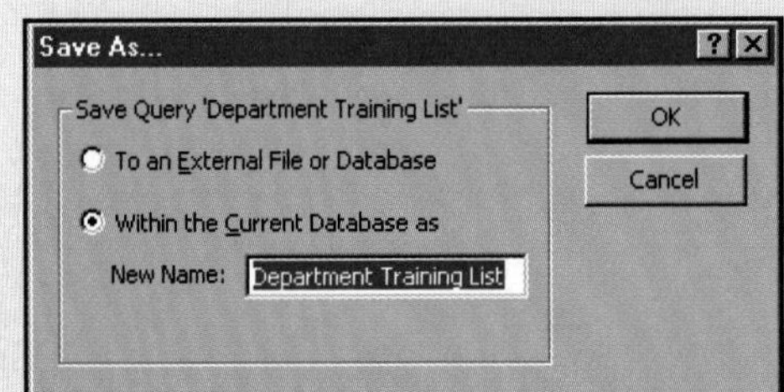

Figure 14.15
Prepare to save a query with a new name.

3. **Type HR and Accounting.**

   This is the name you want to use for the new query.
4. **Click the OK button.**

   Access saves the query with the new name, and the new name is displayed in the title bar. The original query remains unchanged on disk.

5 Close the query window.

This step closes the query window and returns you to the database window. The Queries tab should be selected, and you should see the two queries displayed in the Queries list (see Figure 14.16).

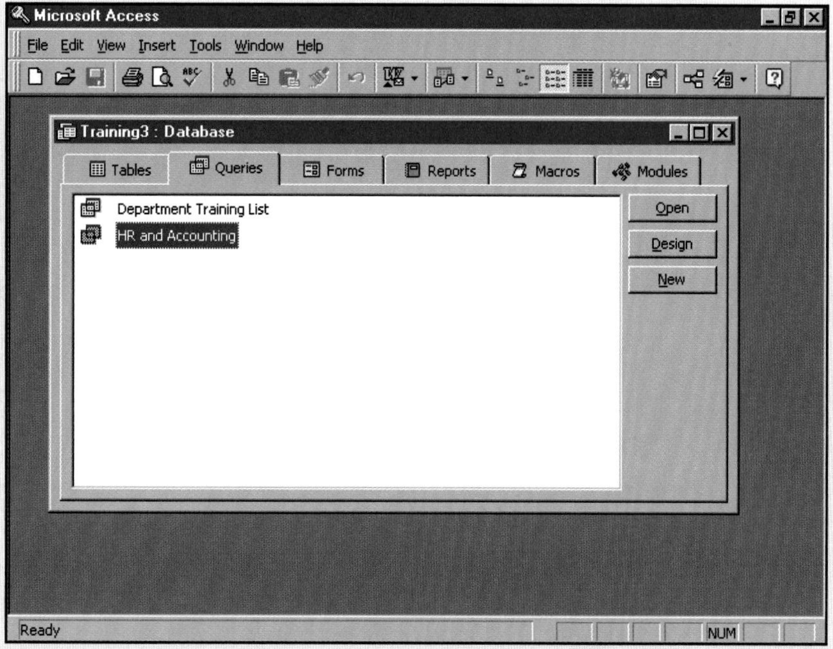

Figure 14.16 More than one query is displayed for the Training3 database.

6 Select and open the Department Training List query.

This step opens the query. Notice that the query displays all departments, not just the ones for Human Resources and Accounting.

7 Click the Database Window button on the toolbar.

8 Select and open the HR and Accounting query.

This opens your modified query. Now both queries are open onscreen, as well as the database window.

9 Open the Window menu and choose Cascade.

This step arranges the windows so that you can see which windows are currently open.

continues

To Save the Query with a New Name and Open Multiple Queries (continued)

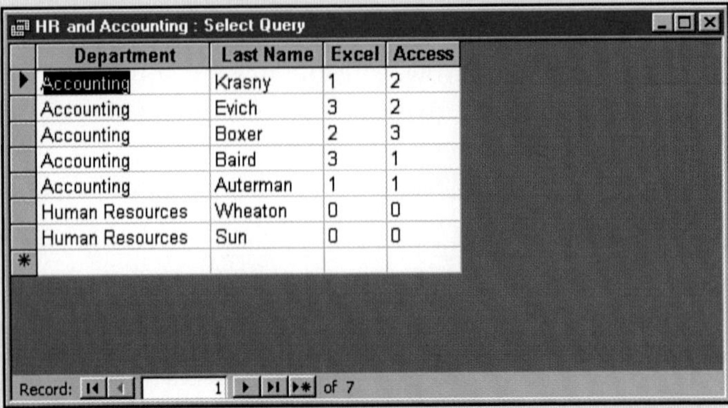

Figure 14.17
The open windows are displayed side by side.

⑩ Close both query windows and the database.

In Project 5, you create forms by using a different database. If you have completed your session on the computer, exit Access, otherwise, continue with the section "Checking Your Skills" in this project.

To open a query in Design view instead of in Datasheet view, click the query to select it in the database window. Then click the **D**esign button.

Project Summary

To	Do This
Create a new query	Open the database and click the Queries tab. Click the **N**ew button, **D**esign view, and then OK. Select the table(s) you want to use, and click **A**dd. Close the Show Table dialog box.
Choose fields for a query	Click and drag the field from the field list box to the Query By Example (QBE) grid; or, in the QBE grid, click the drop-down arrow and choose the field you want; or double-click the field in the field list box.
Save a query	Open the **F**ile menu and choose the **S**ave command. Type a descriptive name in the dialog box and click OK.
Edit a query	Work in Design view. Click and drag fields, or double-click a field to add it to the query. You can insert fields between existing fields in the QBE grid by clicking and dragging the field. Use the column selector to rearrange columns. You can delete selected columns by opening the **E**dit menu and selecting D**e**lete.
Sort a query	Work in Design view. Click in the Sort row of the QBE grid of the field to be sorted. Select Ascending or Descending order.

To	Do This
Match criteria	Work in Design view. Click in the Criteria row of the field you want to match. Type the criterion you want to match. Add a second criterion by going to the or: row in the QBE grid. Use quotation marks if punctuation is included in the criteria.
Save a query with a new name	Open the **F**ile menu and choose Save **A**s/Export command. Type a new name in the dialog box and click OK.
Open multiple queries	From the Database window, select and open first one query, then use the Database Window button to select a econd query (or more). Open the **W**indow menu and choose **C**ascade to view title bars for all queries.

Checking Your Skills

True/False

For each of the following, check *T* or *F* to indicate whether the statement is true or false.

__T __F **1.** You must include at least one field in a query.

__T __F **2.** QBE stands for Query By Example.

__T __F **3.** A dynaset is stored on disk.

__T __F **4.** You cannot include spaces or punctuation in a query name.

__T __F **5.** If you see a blank table when you run a query, Access found no matching records.

__T __F **6.** The first time you save a query, the Save As dialog box appears.

__T __F **7.** You must include all fields in a query, even though they may not be displayed.

__T __F **8.** If you accidentally delete a field from the query, you can click the Undo button to restore the field.

__T __F **9.** A query can use only one table.

__T __F **10.** As you drag a field name from the field list to the query, the mouse pointer becomes a little field box.

Multiple Choice

Circle the letter of the correct answer for each of the following questions.

1. Which of the following can you do to add a field to the query?

- **a.** Double-click the field name in the field list.
- **b.** Use the drop-down list in the Field row of the QBE grid.
- **c.** Drag the field name from the field list to the QBE grid.
- **d.** All of the above

2. Which of the following is *not* a way to run a query when you are working in the query Design view?

- **a.** Click the Run button.
- **b.** Click the Go button.
- **c.** Open the **Q**uery menu and choose the **R**un command.
- **d.** Open the **V**iew menu and choose the Data**s**heet command.

3. What is the lower half of the query window called?

- **a.** field list
- **b.** QBE grid
- **c.** Criteria box
- **d.** Query area

4. How should you enter criteria for text fields if the criterion contains punctuation?

- **a.** In all uppercase
- **b.** In all lowercase
- **c.** In bold
- **d.** Within quotation marks

5. In what order are fields included in a query?

- **a.** The order in which you add them
- **b.** The order in which they appear in the table
- **c.** Alphabetical order
- **d.** Numerical order

6. What is the column selector?

- **a.** A dialog box listing all active columns
- **b.** A drop-down list that appears when you click the down arrow in a column field
- **c.** A shortcut list of columns activated by pressing the right mouse button
- **d.** A gray box on top of the column that enables you to highlight the entire column

7. How do you change the order of the fields in a query?

- **a.** Select one field, select a second field while pressing Ctrl, and choose **S**wap from the **E**dit menu.
- **b.** Select the field and then drag it to the new location.
- **c.** Drag the field from the field list to the new location. The other reference in the query will automatically be deleted.
- **d.** You can't change the order of the fields. They must appear in the same order as in the field list.

8. Which of the following is true about a dynaset?

- **a.** It changes the table it is based on.
- **b.** When created, it can be referenced again from the Query tab.
- **c.** It can be edited, changing the data in the table it is based on.
- **d.** It removes the data from the underlying table while you are viewing it.

9. Which of the following is *not* a way of creating another query?

- **a.** Altering the current query and saving it with a new name
- **b.** Selecting **N**ew on the Query tab and building a query from scratch
- **c.** Selecting **D**uplicate from the **E**dit menu and saving the duplicate query with a new name
- **d.** Copying the query in the database window and renaming the copy with a new name

10. How long can a query name be?

- **a.** 64 characters
- **b.** 255 characters
- **c.** 8 characters
- **d.** any length

Completion

In the blank provided, write the correct answer for each of the following statements.

1. A(n) _____________ is a subset of records displayed by a query.
2. A(n) _____________ is a question you ask of the database.
3. The set of conditions or limits you use to match entries in a field is called _____________.
4. To view a query, change to the _____________ view.
5. The top half of the query window contains the _____________, which you can use to choose fields.
6. To select multiple fields in a field list that aren't next to each other, use the _____________ key when you click the fields.
7. The _____________ button changes depending on which window is open.
8. You cannot change a query in _____________ view.
9. To display only the names that start with the letters before *N*, you enter _____________ as the criterion for the name field.
10. Opening a query is the same as clicking the _____________ button.

Matching

In the blank next to each of the following terms or phrases, write the letter of the corresponding term or phrase. (Note that some letters may be used more than once.)

_____ **1.** Answers to a question that has been asked

_____ **2.** Contains locations for fields and settings for queries

_____ **3.** Contains the scope, criteria, and order of the question asked of the database

_____ **4.** Has an exclamation point on it

_____ **5.** A shortcut group of entries available by selecting a down arrow

_____ **6.** Arranges the records alphabetically in a dynaset

_____ **7.** Can be activated by pressing ↵Enter

_____ **8.** If checked, displays a field in a query

_____ **9.** Asks a question of the database

_____ **10.** A test or condition to limit a query

a. Sort Ascending

b. dark-bordered button

c. Show box

d. field list

e. query

f. QBE grid

g. dynaset

h. criterion

i. Run button

j. drop-down list

Screen ID

Identify each of the items shown in Figure 14.18.

Figure 14.18

1.______________

2.______________

3.______________

4.______________

5.______________

6.______________

7.______________

8.______________

9.______________

10.______________

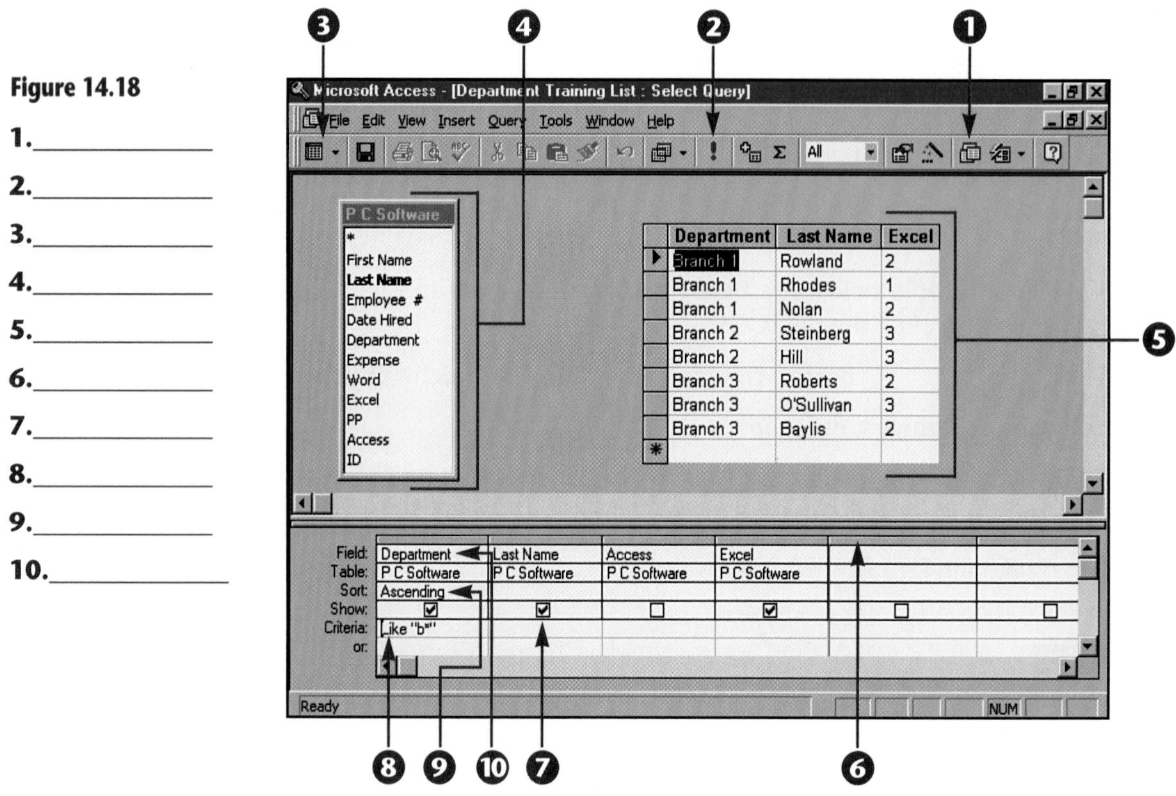

Applying Your Skills

Practice

The following exercises enable you to practice the skills you have learned in this project. Take a few minutes to work through these exercises now.

1. Querying Your Library Database

In the "Applying Your Skills" sections of Projects 12 and 13, you created a Library database with a Books table that listed the books in your library. You may be curious to see exactly what types of books you have. For instance, you may want to view a list of only book names and authors to see what your collection contains. Or you may want to determine the most common type of book in your collection. You can create a query, for example, to display only mystery books.

To Query Your Library Database

1. Copy the Proj1402 database file to **`Library3`**. Then open the Library3 database in Access.
2. Create a query and add the fields for Author Last Name and Book Title. Sort the query by Author Last Name. Then view the results of this query in Datasheet view.
3. Change back to Design view. Save the query and name it **`Book List`**.

4. Add the Type of Book field to the query. In the Criteria row for this column, type **Mystery**.
5. View the results of the query in Datasheet view. Use the Print button on the toolbar to print a copy of this view.
6. Go back to Design view and save the query with a new name, such as **Mysteries**.

2. Querying Your Record Company Database

In a previous project, you set up and then entered records for a record company database. This database includes the names of the record labels that you stock in your Sound Byte Music Store. Suppose that you are planning a trip to New York and you want to contact your sales representatives for the companies in New York. You can use a query to create the list—all record companies in New York. In this list, you can include the record company name, contact name, and phone number.

To Query Your Record Company Database

1. Copy the Proj1403 database file and rename the copy **SBMusic3**. Then return to Access and open the SBMusic3 database.
2. Create a query and add the fields for Record Company, Contact Name, and Phone.
3. View the results of this query in Datasheet view.
4. Change back to Design view and save the query with the name **NY Trip**.
5. Add the State field to the query. In the Criteria row for this column, type **NY**.
6. View the results of the query in Datasheet view. Save the query.
7. Close both query windows and the database.

3. Querying a Database to Track Personal Computer Hardware

Your company is planning to install software that takes over 200 megabytes of hard drive space. You would like to know which machines have hard drives that may be too small to handle the new software.

To Query the Database

1. Copy the file Proj1404 and rename the copy **PC3**. Open PC3.
2. Create a query, based on the PC Hardware table, that shows the PCs with hard drives of less than 500 megabytes of capacity. (The given ratings are in megabytes.) Include the following fields:

   Processor

   RAM

   Hard Drive Size

   Vendor

   Inventory Code Number

3. Sort the query by Processor.
4. Change to Datasheet view and click the Print button on the toolbar to print the query.
5. Save the query with the name **Hard Drives less than 500 meg**. Close the database.

4. Getting a Helping Hand

Queries can get complicated very quickly. It is important to understand how they are built and what they mean. The Help system provides an excellent review of queries.

To Get Help on Topics in This Project

1. With Access open, press F1. The Office Assistant opens and a dialog box in the form of a comment box opens beside it.
2. In the question area of the dialog box, type `Build a query` and press ↵Enter. The comment bubble changes, displaying a list of options that fit the statement.
3. Select the second entry, `Queries: What they are and how they work`. A help window opens that provides a three-page overview of queries. Take a few minutes and try each page by selecting the numbers at the top left of the page.
4. Close the help window. The Office Assistant remains open.
5. Click the Office Assistant once. The comment bubble reappears with your statement still in the question box.
6. Select Search. The same list of responses appears.
7. Select the first response, `Create a query`. The main help window opens, displaying the central topic covering query creation.
8. Scroll toward the bottom of the window. You will see a series of entries with buttons beside them ([>>]). The first entry, `Learn about the different types of queries I can create`, provides a good overview of the different queries. Farther down, you will find the entry `Work on my own to create a Select query`. Selecting this entry will show you more about creating your own queries.
9. Take a few minutes and explore.

5. Exploring the World of Alaska

The project file Proj1405 includes the partial Alaska database with some additional entries for pictures and sources. In Project 13, you considered how to answer questions by using sorting. Now you view the database by using queries.

To View the Database by Using Queries

1. Open the file Proj1405 as a copy.
2. Select the Queries tab and click **N**ew.
3. Select Design View and click OK.
4. Select and add the Geography table.
5. Close the Show Table dialog box.
6. From the field list, add the Object, Type, Picture, and Source fields to the QBE grid.
7. Click the Run button. A dynaset appears, including only the four fields that were chosen.
8. Return to Design view and change the sort for the Type field to Ascending.
9. Run the query again. The dynaset is now sorted so that all the geographic features are grouped by type alphabetically.
10. Return to Design view and remove the sort setting for the Type field. Instead, add a criterion to select only islands.

11. Run the query again. You should have 16 islands listing in the dynaset. Three of these islands have pictures.
12. Save the query as `Alaskan Islands`.
13. Return to Design view and try different settings and queries.

Challenge

The following challenges enable you to use your problem-solving skills. Take time to work through these exercises now.

1. Adding Club Member Names and Sorting

Open the database for tracking the members of a club or organization that you created in previous projects. Sort the table by name. Use the Print button on the toolbar to print a copy for your records. If requested by your instructor, print an extra copy to hand in.

2. Doing Customer Research

Now that you have started to receive return questionnaires, your boss seems to come into your office every five minutes wanting to know which channels are being watched and what the other numbers are. You have received four more responses and decide to build a quick query to answer your boss's questions.

To Build a Quick Query

1. Open the database Proj1406 as a copy and enter the following responses to the questionnaire:

Adults	1	2	2	2
Children	3	2	1	2
Hours	4	1	6	3
No 1	DISCOVERY	DISNEY	SCIFI	DISNEY
No 2	TNT	TNT	CNN	DISCOVERY
No 3	SCIFI	CNN		
Doing	Great	Okay	Good	Marginal

   Improvement comment for the first household: `There are many times when we have to shut off the TV because of the graphic shows.`

   Comment for the second household: `You're doing all right, though it would be great to see some other channels.`

   Comment for the third household: `Need more action stuff.`

   Comment for the fourth household: `Please block out the violence and profanity. We understand you can do that.`

2. Build a query that lists the three cable channels and sorts them based on the channels most watched.
3. Save the Query as `Boss's Lament`.

3. Owning a Vending Company

You have entered more records into your database, mostly in the Locations table. It is now time to see what some of the information can tell you.

To Query the Database

1. Open the database Proj1407 as a copy.
2. Create a query for the Locations table, including all fields, that sorts the records based on the machine type.
3. Run the query. Look through the dynaset to see which machine type is used most often.
4. Save the Query as `Earner List`.
5. Modify the query to list only that machine type.
6. Save the new query as `Big Earner`. You should have two different queries, each providing a different output.

4. Managing a Video Store

Open your video store database you created in previous projects and create a query that sorts the database by title. Save this Query as `Video List`.

Then create a query that sorts all videos by age, listing the oldest video first. This query may help you decide which videos should be replaced. Save this new query as `Replacement Candidates`.

You should also have a field that lists the number of times the video has been rented. This field should be included in the Replacement Candidate query because it tells you the wear and tear on the video. If you sort the table by both fields, age and number of rentals, you can get more information from which to base your decision on what videos need updating.

5. Taking a Home Inventory

You should have a number of records in the main table of the inventory database you created in previous projects. Build a query that sorts the inventory table based on the cost of the item. If you have included your house and car in the inventory, you should see those items at the bottom of the list (provided the list is sorted in ascending order). Save the sort as `By Dollar Listing`.

Add additional records to the table to have at least 20 records. These records will help you later in the book as you develop more complicated features for the database.

Project 15

Creating and Using Forms

Objectives

In this project, you learn how to:

- Create an AutoForm
- Enter and Edit Data Using a Form
- Save, Close, and Open a Form
- Create a New Form from Scratch
- Add Fields to Forms
- Move and Resize Fields in Forms
- Add a Form Header and Label

Why Would I Do This?

When you enter records in a table, each record is displayed in a row, and all records are displayed. If the table has many fields, you may not be able to see all of the fields in the table on-screen, and you may find it difficult to find the record you want with all the records displayed.

Form
A type of object you can create to enter, edit, and view records. Think of a form as a fill-in-the-blanks screen.

Access gives you an alternative method, using a *form*, for viewing and entering records. Using a form offers the following advantages:

- You can select the fields you want to include in the form, and you can arrange them in the order you want.
- You can choose to display only one record at a time, which makes it easier to concentrate on that record.
- You can make the form more graphically appealing.

AutoForm
A form that is created automatically by Access that includes all the fields in a table.

Access provides an *AutoForm* that you can create quickly without a great deal of work. If this form isn't what you need, you can also create a form from scratch. In this project, you learn about both methods for creating forms.

Lesson 1: Creating an AutoForm

If you want a simple form that lists each field in a single column and displays one record at a time, you can use one of the Access Form Wizards to create an AutoForm. The Form Wizards look at the structure of your database table and then create a form automatically. You simply choose the commands to start the Wizards.

To Create an AutoForm

1. **Copy the Proj1501 database file to `Address2`. Then return to Access and open the Address2 database.**

   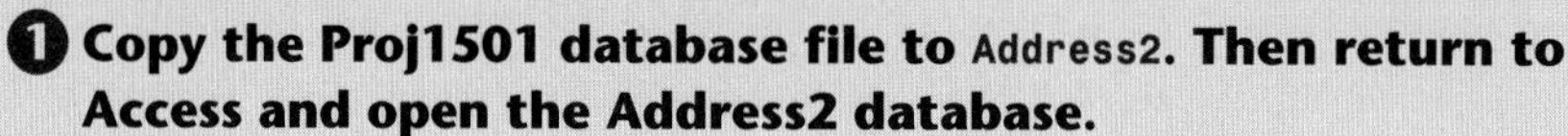

   You should see the database window, listing the Contacts table.

2.  **Click the Maximize button in the upper-right corner of the window to maximize your window before you make the new form.**

3. **Click the Forms tab.**

   The Forms list is blank because you haven't yet created and saved any forms (see Figure 15.1).

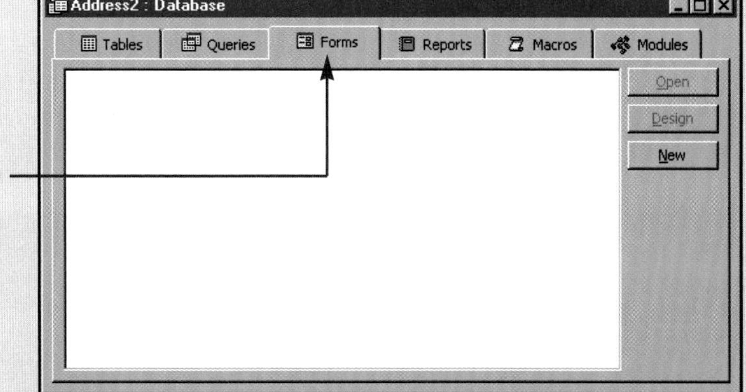

Figure 15.1
No forms are listed because you have not yet created any.

4 Click the New button.

You see the New Form dialog box. First, you have to select a table to use with the form. Then you must decide whether you want to use the Form Wizards or start with a blank form. In this lesson, you use the Form Wizards.

5 Click the down arrow in the box labeled `Choose the table or query where the object's data comes from.`

You see a list of the tables and queries available in the database (see Figure 15.2). You can base a form on either a query or a table. In this lesson, use the Contacts table.

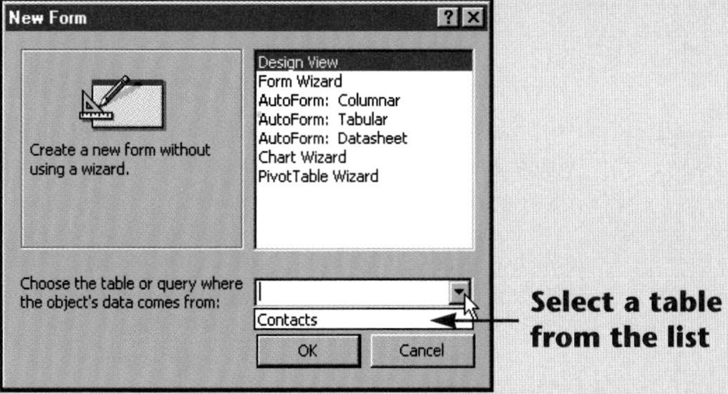

Figure 15.2
From the drop-down list, choose the table on which you want to base the form.

6 Click Contacts.

This step selects the table you want to use.

7 Click the AutoForm: Columnar option, and then click OK.

The Form Wizard creates the form; this step may take several seconds. The status bar displays the progress so that you can see that Access is working. After the AutoForm is built, Access displays the table's first record (see Figure 15.3). Notice that the fields are displayed in columns in the form. Your screen may not look exactly like the one following. This depends on the screen size and the

continues

To Create an AutoForm (continued)

background settings. The navigation buttons are displayed at the bottom of the form to enable you to move through the records. Keep this form on-screen as you continue to the next lesson, where you learn more about the navigation buttons.

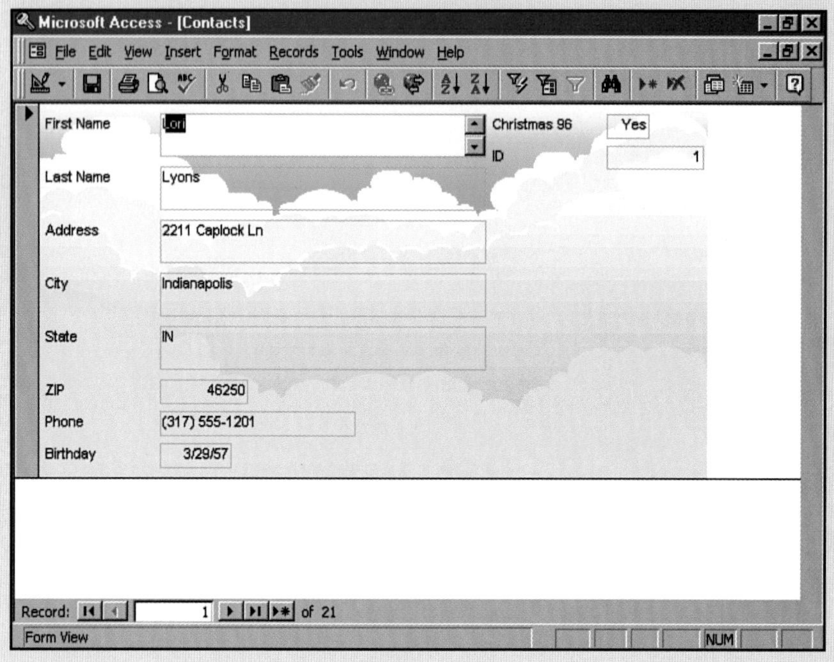

Figure 15.3
An AutoForm containing all fields displayed in a single column.

You can also create a new form by clicking the drop-down arrow to the right of the New Object button on the toolbar in the database window. When your table is in Datasheet view, you can click the New Object list button and select either the New Form button or the AutoForm button to create a new form.

Other wizard forms can be used to generate forms in different layouts, such as tabular, or to only include selected fields.

Lesson 2: Entering and Editing Data Using a Form

Forms make it easier to enter and edit data. Before you save the form, you may want to try some data entry to be sure that you like the structure of the form. If you don't like how the form is set up, you can change it or create a new one, as you learn later in this project.

You can use the same tools to enter, find, sort, and display records in a form that you use in a table. This lesson explains how to add and edit a record using a form.

To Enter and Edit Data Using a Form

1 The AutoForm based on the Contacts table should still be on your screen from the previous lesson. Click the New Record button located both on the toolbar and with the navigation buttons on the bottom of the window.

This step adds a new record, and a blank form is displayed (see Figure 15.4). The insertion point appears in the first field of the form.

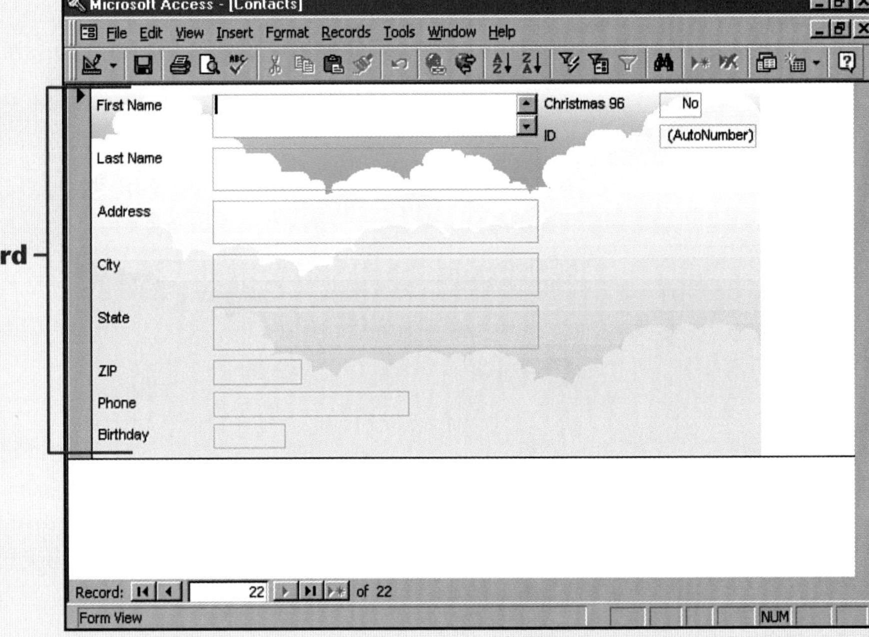

Figure 15.4 The new form is ready to have information added.

2 Type the following data, pressing Tab after each entry (not Enter) to move to the next field:

```
Janet

Eisenhut

455 Sheridan

Indianapolis

IN

46204

(317) 555-6588

3/29/60

Yes
```

Notice that when you type the phone number, Access automatically provides parentheses around the area code, moves you over so that you can type the exchange, and provides a hyphen after the exchange.

continues

To Enter and Edit Data Using a Form (continued)

You may have to scroll down to see all the fields in the form. When you reach the last field—the ID field—you don't have to enter a value because it is a counter field. Also, remember that when you move to another record, Access automatically saves the record you just entered. Keep in mind that the record is saved in the underlying Contacts table. You don't have to worry about updating the table separately.

3 Click the First Record button.

This moves you to the first record in the table.

4 Click the Next Record button until you see the record for Shelli Canady.

This is the record you want to edit. Notice that the Birthday field is blank.

5 Click in the Birthday field.

This action moves the insertion point to the field you want to edit.

6 Type 11/4/65.

This enters a birthday for Shelli.

7 Click the First Record button.

This moves you back to the first record and saves the change to the record you just edited. Keep the form open on your screen as you continue to the next lesson.

If you have problems...

If you can't find the record that you want to edit by scrolling, you can open the **E**dit menu and use the **F**ind command. (Refer to Project 13 for more information on searching records.)

If you press ↵Enter your cursor will not move to the next box. Simply press Tab instead.

If you make an editing change and want to undo it, open the **E**dit menu and choose the **U**ndo command or press the Undo button. This will undo your last change.

Besides using the navigation buttons, you can use the keyboard to move among records and fields. Press Tab or ↓ or → to move to the next field; ⇧Shift+Tab or ↑ or ← to move to the previous field; PgUp to scroll to the previous record; and PgDn to scroll to the next record. Ctrl+Home will move the insertion point to the first field in the first record and Ctrl+End will move the insertion point to the last field in the last record.

Lesson 3: Saving, Closing, and Opening a Form

If you use the form and like how it is organized, you can save the form so that you can use it again later. If you try to close the form without saving, Access reminds you to save. You don't have to save the form; you should save only if you intend to use it again.

If you have problems...

If you accidentally close the form without saving it, you can simply re-create it using the Form Wizard.

As with the other objects you have created, you are prompted to type a name the first time you save the form. You can type up to 64 characters, including spaces. After you have saved the form, you can close it and open it again when you want to use the form.

To Save, Close, and Open a Form

1 The AutoForm that uses the Contacts table should still be open on your screen. Open the File menu and choose the Save command.

You see the Save As dialog box (see Figure 15.5). Here you type the form name, which can include as many as 64 characters and spaces.

Figure 15.5 Give the form a name before you save it.

Type the name of the form

2 Type `AutoForm`**.**

This is the name you want to assign to the form.

3 Click the OK button.

Access saves the form. If you switch to Design view, you see that the form name is now displayed.

4 Click the View button on the toolbar.

Notice that the name of your form appears in the title bar.

5 Click the View button on the toolbar again.

This step returns you to your form in Form view.

6 Click the Close button in the upper-right corner of the form window to close the form.

The form window closes, and you see the database window again. Notice that your new form is now included in the Forms list when you click the Forms tab (see Figure 15.6).

continues

To Save, Close, and Open a Form (continued)

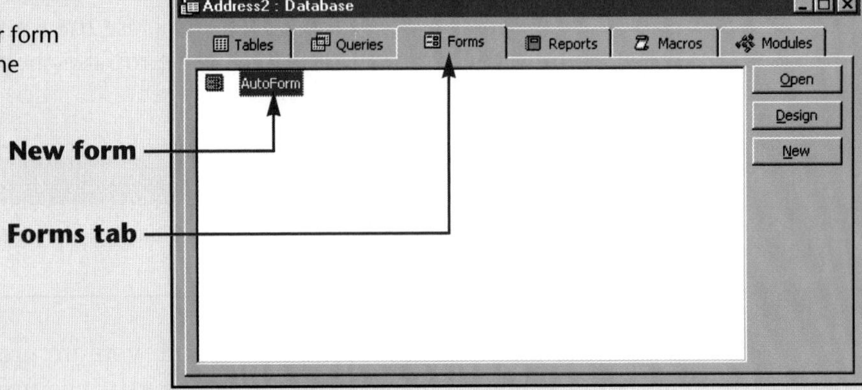

Figure 15.6
The name of your form now appears in the Forms list.

7 Double-click AutoForm to open it.

Access displays the first record in the table using the form you created. You can add, modify, or delete records. When you are finished working in the form, close it again. As you move from field to field, Access automatically saves any changes you make.

8 Click the Close button to close the form.

Access closes the form. Keep the Address2 database open and continue to the next lesson.

You can press Ctrl+S to save the form instead of using **F**ile, **S**ave.

Lesson 4: Creating a New Form from Scratch

Control
A control is any graphical object selected from the toolbox, such as a text box, checkbox, or option button that you add to a form or report.

Sometimes the Form Wizards do not create exactly the form you want. When that happens, you can start from a blank form and create the form you want. The form can include any text, fields, and other *controls* you want to incorporate.

The rest of this project covers some of the simple, common features you can use when you create a form from scratch. Keep in mind, however, that Access offers many form features, such as drop-down lists, groups of option buttons, graphic objects, and much more.

In this lesson, you create a new, blank form.

To Create a New Form from Scratch

1 In the Address2 database window, click the Forms tab.

You should see the AutoForm form listed. Next, you are going to add an additional form.

❷ **Click the New button.**

You see the New Form dialog box. Before you choose whether you want to use the Form Wizard or start with a blank form, you should select the table you want to use for the form.

❸ **Click the down arrow in the drop-down list labeled `Choose the table or query where the object's data comes from.`**

A list is displayed showing the tables and queries contained in the database. You can base the form on either a query or a table. In this lesson, use the Contacts table.

❹ **Click Contacts.**

This tells Access to use the Contacts table with the form you are creating.

❺ **Select the Design View option from the top of the list and click OK.**

You see the form in Design view. It should contain both a list of fields and the Toolbox.

❻ **If the list of fields does not appear on the screen, click the Field List button.**

❼ **If the Toolbox does not appear on the screen, click the Toolbox button.**

The Design view should now include the Toolbox and the field list (see Figure 15.7). Keep this blank form open on your screen. In the next lesson, you learn how to use the various tools in the form's Design view.

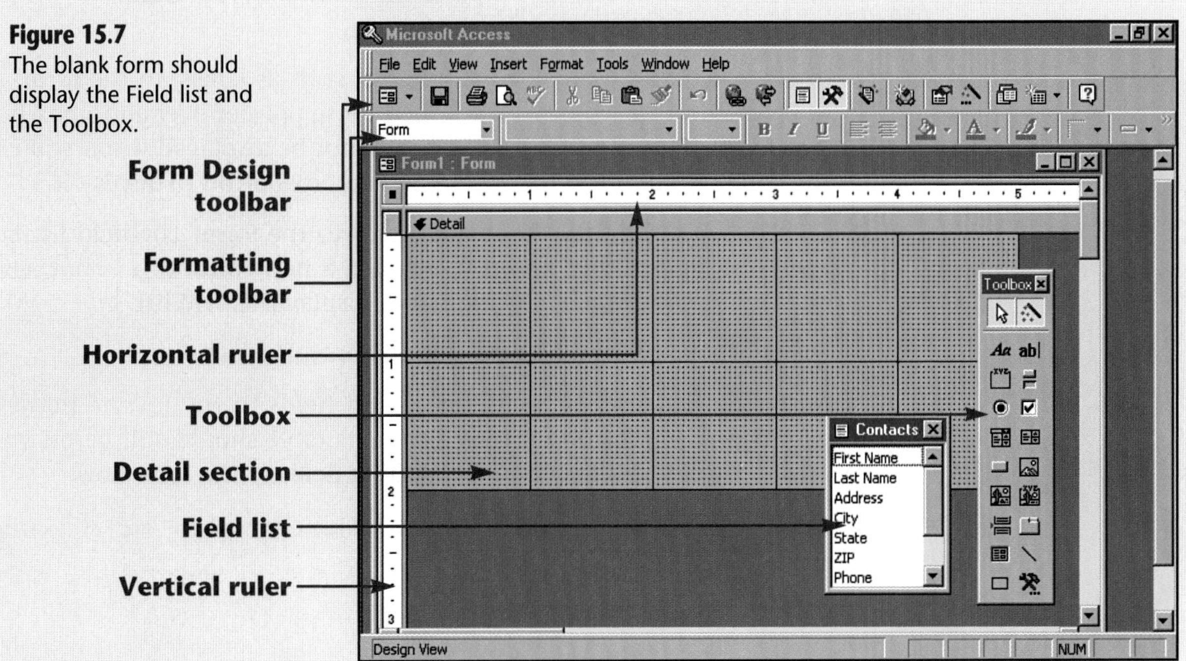

Figure 15.7
The blank form should display the Field list and the Toolbox.

Jargon Watch

A **form** consists of many different elements. Each part of the form is called a **band** or **section**. The main section is called the Detail section. This is the area in which records are displayed. You can also add **form headers** (top of form) or **form footers** (bottom of form). Anything you include in the section will be displayed on-screen in Form view when you use the form. You can also add page headers and page footers, which are not visible on-screen in Form view but will appear if you print the form.

Some controls are bound to the fields in the table. If you create a text box for a field and enter data in the field in the form, for example, the field in the table is updated. Other controls are not tied to the table but, instead, are saved with the form. For example, you may want to add a descriptive title to the form. This type of text is called a **label** and is not bound to the table.

Lesson 5: Adding Fields to Forms

You decided it would be a good idea to send birthday greetings to your customers to help maintain good relations. You added a birthday field to your Contacts table, but you have entered only the birthdays of contacts who are your customers. To make sure that birthday greetings are sent to your customers, you want to create a simple form that lists just the person's name and his or her birthday. This form will include three fields—last name, first name, and birthday—and will also include a label in the form's header.

When you want to set up or change the structure of a form, you use Design view. Access includes the following items to help you design the form:

- *Toolbar*. Use the toolbar to access some form design commands. You can click the Save button to save the form, the View button to view the form, and so on. If you place the pointer on a button, the button name appears directly under the button.
- *Toolbox*. Use the toolbox to add items, such as labels, to the form. As with the toolbar, you can place the mouse pointer over a toolbox button to see its name. The Toolbox may not be displayed when you create a new form. If it is not, click the Toolbox button to display it.
- *Field list*. Use the field list to add fields to the form. The field list box may not be displayed when you create a new form. If it is not, click the Field List button in the toolbar to display the field list.
- *Rulers*. Use the rulers to help position controls on the form.

In this lesson, you use the field list to add fields to the form. The new, blank form you are creating for the Contacts table should still be on your screen from the preceding lesson. Try adding fields to the form now.

To Add Fields to Forms

1 Select the First Name field in the field list.

This selects the first field you want to add to your form.

2 Drag the First Name field from the field list to the Detail section of the form.

Field text box
Holds a place for the contents of each field in the database.

As you drag, your pointer becomes a small, boxed field name. You can use this *field text box* to help place the field on-screen.

3 Release the mouse button and drop the field at approximately the 1-inch mark on the horizontal ruler, and down about 1/4" from the top of the detail area.

Field label
Displays the field name.

This places the field text box and *field label* on the form (see Figure 15.8).

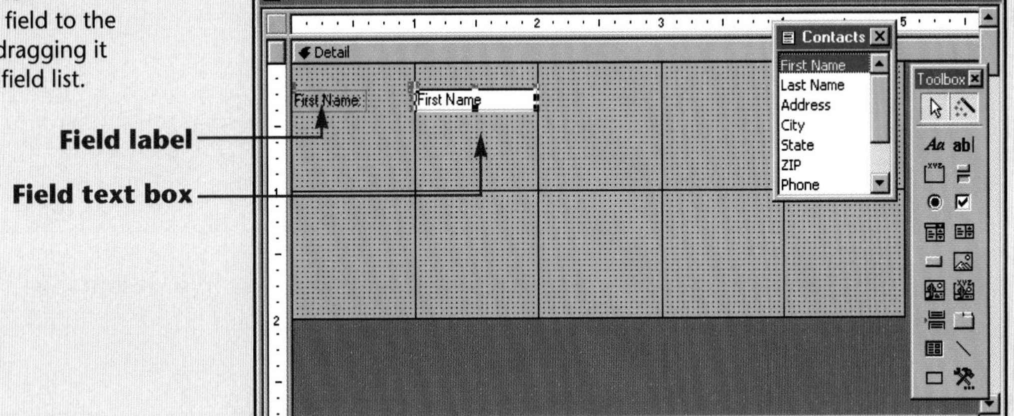

Figure 15.8
Adding a field to the form by dragging it from the field list.

4 Drag the Last Name field to the form; place this field below the First Name field, at the same horizontal location (the 1-inch mark) and about 1/4" below the First Name field.

This step adds a second field to the form. As you drag and drop the field, try to align the field with the field above it. Make sure that you leave enough room between the two fields—don't drop the fields on top of one another.

5 Drag the Birthday field to the form. Place this field below the Last Name field (also at the 1-inch horizontal mark).

Your form now includes three fields. You can save and name the form so that these changes won't be lost.

6 Open the File menu and choose the Save command.

You see the Save As dialog box, in which you can assign a name for this new form.

continues

To Add Fields to Forms (continued)

7 Type `Birthdays`.

You have now entered the name you want to give to the form.

8 Click OK.

Access saves the form and returns to Design view. You can continue building the form, or you can display the form.

9 Click the View button on the toolbar.

The form is displayed as it will appear when you use it (see Figure 15.9). You can see whether you need to make any adjustments, such as adding a label or resizing the fields. Keep the Birthdays form open and continue with the next lesson.

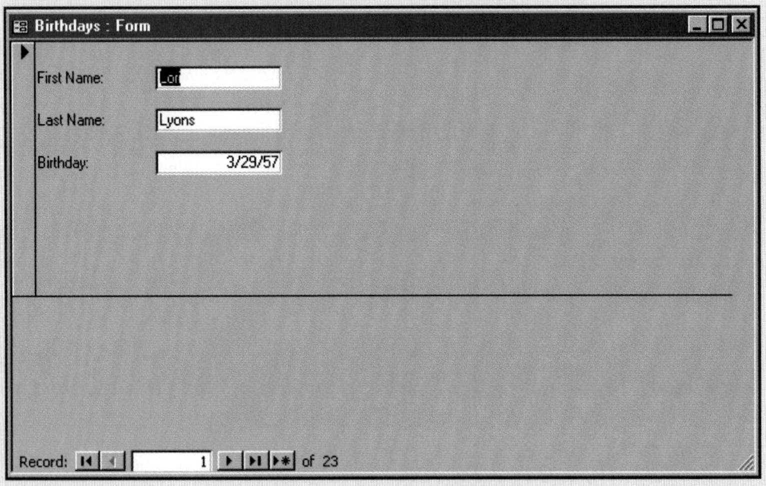

Figure 15.9
Your new form is displayed in Form view.

If you have problems...

If you see only one field box when you drag the field from the field list, you may have placed the field too far to the left (beyond the 1-inch horizontal mark, for example), or the field text box and field label may be on top of one another. You have to move or resize the field so that you can see both the field label and the field text box.

You can delete the field and start again if you run into problems. To delete a field, click it to select it and then press Del. This will remove the field from the form, but it will not delete the field or its contents from the table.

If you make changes to the form and then want to undo them, open the **E**dit menu and choose the **U**ndo command.

In addition to creating a blank form, you can use the Form Wizard to create other types of forms such as columnar, tabular, charts, and pivot tables.

To modify an existing form, click the name of the form in the database window and then click the **D**esign command button. Alternatively, you can open the form and then change to Design view by clicking the View button.

Lesson 6: Moving and Resizing Fields in Forms

When you create your form, you may find that it is difficult to get the fields in the right place the first time. That's okay; you can move or resize the fields after you have added them to the form. You can drag and place them visually, using the ruler as a guide. Or you can have Access align the fields with an underlying grid—making them an equal distance apart.

In this lesson, you move the Birthday field up next to the First Name field. Then, to make sure all the fields are aligned, you snap them to the vertical and horizontal grid.

To Move and Resize Fields in Forms

1 In the Birthdays form, click the View button.

To make changes to the form design, you must return to Design view. You cannot make changes in Form view.

2 If the Birthday field is not selected, click the field text box.

Selection handles
Small squares that appear at the corners and on the sides of boxes and that may be used to change the size of the box.

Selection handles appear around the borders (see Figure 15.10). Notice that both the field label and the field text box are selected because these two items are attached. However, handles appear all the way around only the object you clicked on. The other one (in this case the field label) has one large handle in the upper left-hand corner. Most of the time you want to keep the two together, such as when you want to move them.

Figure 15.10
You must click a field to select it before you can move it.

continues

To Move and Resize Fields in Forms (continued)

3 Place the mouse pointer on one of the borders, but not on one of the handles.

When the pointer is in the correct spot, it should resemble a small hand (see Figure 15.11). If you see arrows rather than the hand, the pointer isn't in the correct spot. Move it around until you see the hand.

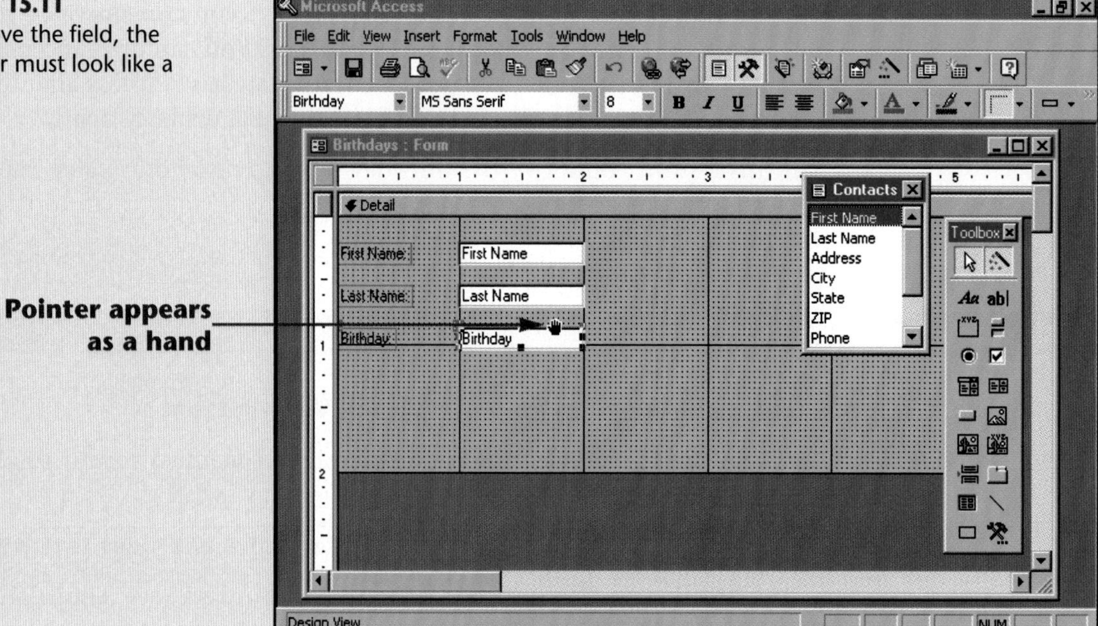

Figure 15.11
To move the field, the pointer must look like a hand.

4 Drag the Birthday field up next to the First Name field and place it so that the left edge of the Birthday field label is at approximately the 2 ½-inch mark on the horizontal ruler.

Notice as you drag that you can see the outline of both the field label and the field text box. When you release the mouse button, Access moves the field up next to the First Name field. (You may need to drag the field list box out of the way so that you can see where you are positioning the Birthday field.)

5 Move the pointer to the right side of the Birthday field and place it on the handle. The pointer turns into a two-headed arrow (see Figure 15.12).

The birthday field is longer than necessary, so you are going to change the size of the birthday field so it is approximately ½" wide.

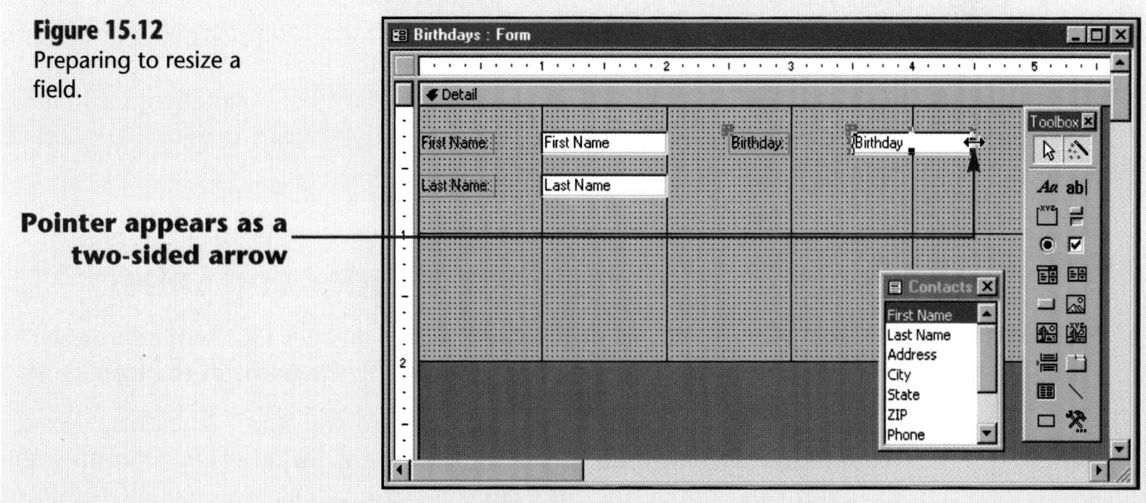

Figure 15.12 Preparing to resize a field.

6 Make the field smaller by dragging the right side of the field to the left. Stop at the 4" mark on the horizontal ruler so that the field is about ½" wide.

The Birthday field is now about the right size to contain a date.

7 Click on the View button to see if the date will fit in the new box.

8 Click the Save button.

This step saves the form with the changes you just made. Keep your Birthdays form open. In the next lesson, you learn how to add a form header to the form.

If you have problems...

If you see arrows in the form and begin to drag, you will resize the field. You resize by putting the pointer on one of the selection handles. If you resize by accident, open the **E**dit menu and choose the **U**ndo command to undo the change.

When you want to move a field, be sure to place the pointer on the edge of the field and wait until it changes to a hand; don't place the pointer on one of the selection handles.

If you want to move the label box separately from the text box, point to the larger square in the upper-left corner of the label box. When the pointer turns into a pointing finger, you can click and drag the label box to a new location. The text box can move independently from the label box by using the same technique. Point to the larger box in the upper-left corner of the text box until the pointer turns into a pointing finger, then click and drag the text box to the desired location.

When you enter data into a form, the insertion point jumps from one box to the next each time you press Tab. This is called the *Tab Order*. When you move fields around on a form, you may need to change the Tab Order. To do this, in the Design view, select **V**iew and Ta**b** Order from the menu and a list of fields will be displayed. Click once on the field that you want to move to select it, then click and drag it to the desired position on the list.

Lesson 7: Adding a Form Header and Label

The final step for this form is to add a form header that will appear at the top of the form and to include a label showing the name of the form.

In this lesson, you first add a new section to the form—the Form Header section—and then you add a label to the form. In addition to adding the label, you can change the font and font size of the text so that the form label stands out.

To Add a Form Header and Label

1 Click the View button to return to the Design view of the Birthday form.

2 Open the View menu and choose the Form Header/Footer command.

Access adds two sections to the form, a Form Header and a Form Footer (see Figure 15.13). You want to include the form label in the header, but the section is too small. Therefore, you need to adjust the size of the section.

Figure 15.13
Form Header and Form Footer sections can be added to the form.

Form Header section

Drag edge to resize

Drag edge to resize

Form Footer section

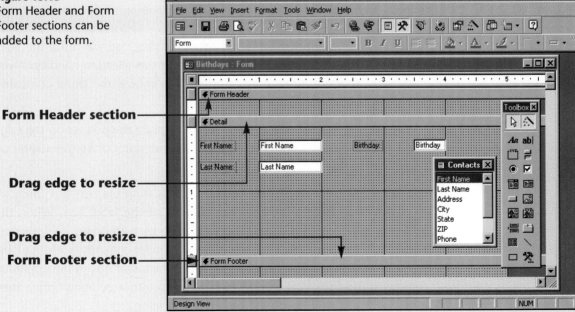

3 Place the mouse pointer on the bottom edge of the Form Header section.

The pointer should change to display a thick horizontal bar with a two-headed arrow crossbar. This pointer shape indicates that you are about to resize this section.

4 Drag down until the Form Header is about an inch tall.

You can use the rulers along the left edge of the form's Design view to gauge the size of the section. Don't worry if the size isn't exact. Now that the header is a little bigger, you can add a label to the form.

5 Click the Label button in the toolbox.

The Label button has an upper- and lowercase A on it. Remember that you can place your pointer on a button to see its name.

6 Position the crosshairs of the pointer in the upper-left corner of the Form Header section. Drag to the right and down to draw a box. Make the box approximately 2 inches wide and ½ inch tall.

The pointer should appear as a small crosshair with an A underneath while you are positioning it. When you release the mouse button, you see a label box with the insertion point inside.

7 Type `Birthdays!`

This is the text you want to include as the label. As you can see, the text is fairly small, but you can change the text size.

8 Click outside the text area to end the text-editing mode.

9 Click inside the box to select it.

Notice that the formatting toolbar displays the font and font size in the Font Name and Font Size drop-down lists. You can use these lists to change the font and the font size (see Figure 15.14).

continues

To Add a Form Header and Label (continued)

Figure 15.14
You can change the font and font size of a label using the Formatting toolbar.

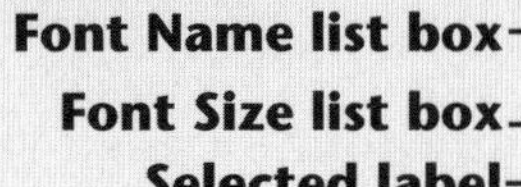

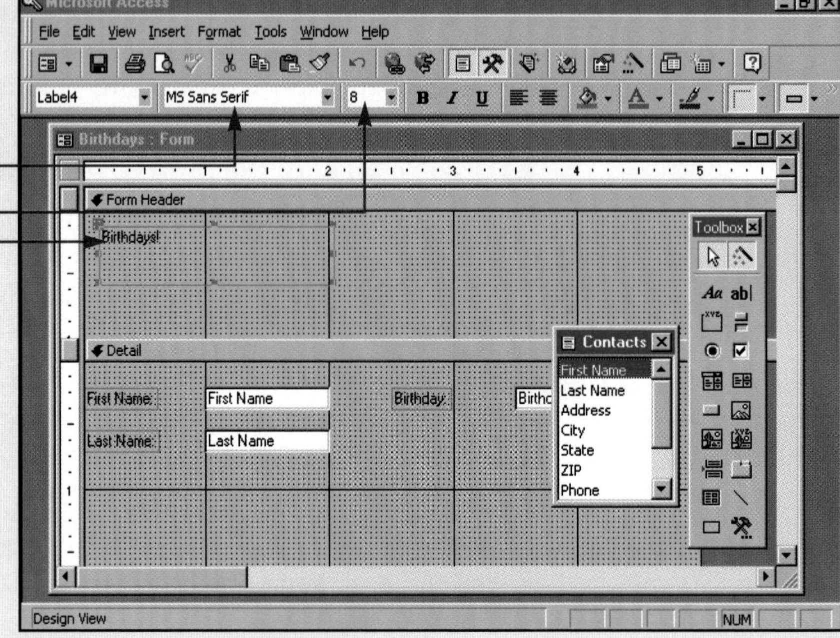

10 Click the down arrow next to the Font Size box. Click 24 (or the largest size available on your system).

This changes the font in the label box to 24-point type. You don't have to change the actual font, but you can make the text bold.

11 Click the Bold button on the toolbar.

Access makes the text bold.

12 Click the Save button on the toolbar.

The form is saved with the changes you have made.

13 Click the View button on the toolbar.

This switches you to Form view so that you can see the form you just created (see Figure 15.15).

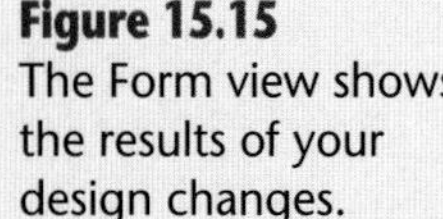

Figure 15.15
The Form view shows the results of your design changes.

Birthdays : Form

Birthdays!

First Name: Lori Birthday: 3/29/57

Last Name: Lyons

Record: 1 of 23

Close the Birthdays form and then close the Address2 database. In Project 16, you use a different database to create a report.

If you have problems...

If you make the label box too small, you can always resize it. Click the box to select it. Then place the pointer on one of the selection handles and drag to resize.

If you have completed your session on the computer, exit Access and Windows before you turn off the computer. Otherwise, continue with the section "Checking Your Skills" in this project.

Project Summary

To	Do This
Create an AutoForm	Click the Forms tab, click the **N**ew button, choose a table or a query to get the data from, and choose an AutoForm style.
Enter data using a form	Open the form in Datasheet view. Click the New Record button to add a new record.
Edit data using a form	Use the navigation buttons to move around the form. Click the field you want to edit and enter new data.
Save a form	Open the **F**ile menu and choose the **S**ave command. Type a descriptive name in the Save As dialog box. Click OK.
Close a form	Click the Close button.
Open a form	From the database window, click the Forms tab and double-click the form you want to open.
Create a new form	Click the Forms tab, click the **N**ew button, and select the table or query you want to use. Choose the Design view option from the list and click OK.
Add fields	Drag fields from the selected Field list box and place them on the grid until you have placed all the fields you need. Use the rulers to help align the fields. Save the form with a new name.
Move and resize fields	Work in Design view. Click in the field you want to move. When the pointer becomes a hand, you can click and drag the field to a new location. Click and drag the handles of a selected field text box or field label to resize it.
Add a form header and label	In Design view, use the **V**iew menu and choose Form **H**eader/Footer. Adjust the size of the header area by dragging the edge. Use the Label tool to drag a label box within the header. Type the label text inside the label box. Click elsewhere to deselect the box. Click the box to select it again, then change the font, font size, or other characteristics.

Checking Your Skills

True/False

For each of the following, check *T* or *F* to indicate whether the statement is true or false.

__T __F **1.** AutoForm creates a form with all the fields in your table.

__T __F **2.** When you use a form to enter data, that data is saved in the form. You also have to update the table.

__T __F **3.** You must save a form if you want to use it again.

__T __F **4.** You can have only one section in a form.

__T __F **5.** To delete a field from a form, click once on the field and then press Del.

__T __F **6.** By pressing Ctrl+Alt in Form view, you can use the mouse to make changes to the form while viewing the final product.

__T __F **7.** If you accidentally close a form without saving it, you can simply click the Undo button to restore the form.

__T __F **8.** In the toolbox of form Design view, the Label button has both an uppercase and a lowercase *A* on it.

__T __F **9.** When a field text box is selected, its associated label will also have selection handles around it.

__T __F **10.** After you generate a form, you cannot change it. You must generate a new form in Design view.

Multiple Choice

Circle the letter of the correct answer for each of the following questions.

1. How do you create a new record using a form?

- **a.** Scroll to the last record and then edit that record.
- **b.** Edit the first record displayed.
- **c.** Click the New Object button on the toolbar.
- **d.** Open the **I**nsert menu and choose the Ne**w** Record command.

2. Which key(s) can you use to move from field to field in a form?

- **a.** Tab
- **b.** Shift+Tab
- **c.** → or ←
- **d.** All the above

3. Which type of section includes the record information?

- **a.** Detail
- **b.** Page Header
- **c.** Page Footer
- **d.** Form Header

4. Which of the following is *not* a way to select a field in Design view?

- **a.** Double-click it.
- **b.** Click it once.
- **c.** Point to it.
- **d.** Choose Select **F**ield from the **E**dit menu.

5. What should the pointer look like to move a field?
   a. a hand
   b. a white cross
   c. a two-headed arrow
   d. a crosshair
6. Which of the following is *not* a part of a form?
   a. Form Header
   b. Page Footer
   c. Detail Area
   d. Format Area
7. To save data to the table after you have entered several forms, you must do which of the following?
   a. Choose **S**ave from the **F**ile menu.
   b. Choose **U**pdate from the **F**ile menu.
   c. Click the Save button on the toolbar.
   d. none of the above (because data is saved automatically)
8. Which of the following is *not* a way to create a form in the database window?
   a. Choose New **F**orm from the **T**ools menu.
   b. Select **F**orm from the **I**nsert menu.
   c. Click the New Object: **F**orm button on the toolbar.
   d. Click the **N**ew button on the Forms tab.
9. You can generate all the following by using the Form Wizard except which?
   a. columnar forms
   b. charts
   c. pivot tables
   d. spreadsheets
10. How can you add the toolbox to the Design View window if the toolbox is not already present?
    a. Select Open **T**oolbox from the **T**ools menu.
    b. Click the Toolbox button on the Formatting toolbar.
    c. Click the Toolbox button on the Form Design toolbar.
    d. Press F7.

Completion

In the blank provided, write the correct answer for each of the following statements.

1. A type of object you can create to enter, edit, and view records is called a(n) ____________.
2. Any graphical object (text box, checkbox, option button, and so on) that you add to a form or report is called a(n) ____________.
3. An object that holds a place for the contents of each field in the database is called a(n) ____________.
4. An object that displays the field name is called a(n) ____________.
5. A bounded object is connected to the underlying ____________.
6. The order in which fields are addressed on a form is called the ______________ Order.
7. You can create a(n) ______________ quickly without a great deal of work, and it will include all fields from your table.
8. Deleting a text box from a form will not delete the ______________ in the underlying table.
9. There are many parts to a form; each part is called a(n) ______________ or ______________.
10. The Form **H**eader/Footer menu item can be found on the ______________ menu.

Matching

In the blank next to each of the following terms or phrases, write the letter of the corresponding term or phrase. (Note that some letters may be used more than once.)

_____ **1.** A control on a form that isn't linked to anything else

_____ **2.** Used to add fields to a form

_____ **3.** The same as choosing **S**ave from the **F**ile menu

_____ **4.** Used to help position controls on a form

_____ **5.** One of two parts of a text box control

_____ **6.** Part of a form that shows up only when you are printing it

_____ **7.** Used to add items, such as labels, to a form

_____ **8.** Used to access some form design commands

_____ **9.** A tool you can use on a form just as you would on a datasheet

_____ **10.** Small squares that appear at the corners and on the sides of boxes that have been selected

a. toolbar

b. rulers

c. Ctrl+S

d. page header

e. Find

f. selection handles

g. field text box

h. field list

i. unbound

j. toolbox

Screen ID

Identify each of the items shown in Figure 15.16.

Figure 15.16

1._____________

2._____________

3._____________

4._____________

5._____________

6._____________

7._____________

8._____________

9._____________

10._____________

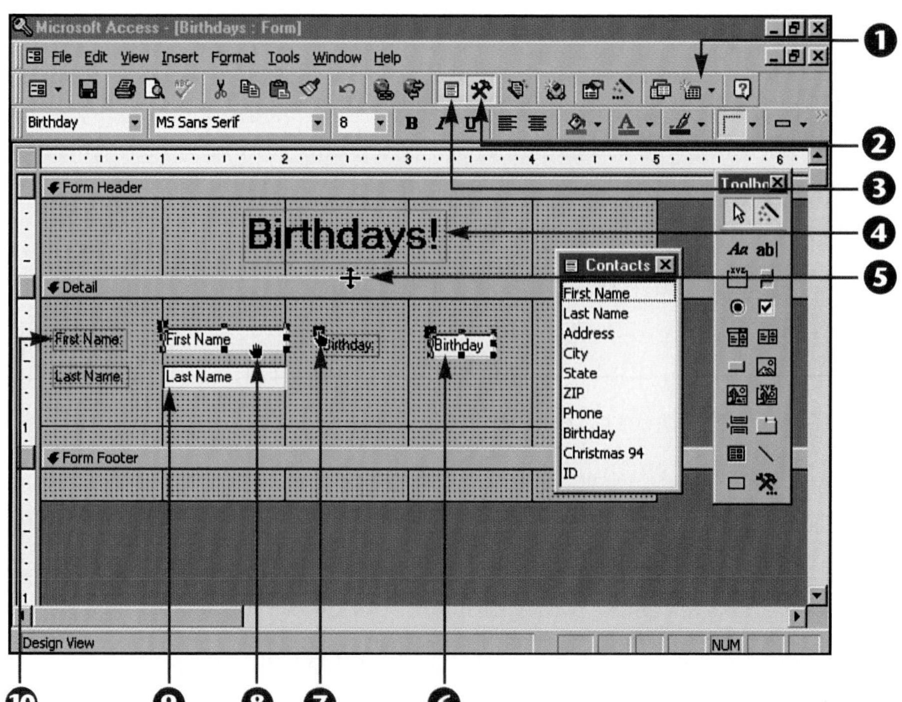

Applying Your Skills

Practice

The following exercises enable you to practice the skills you have learned in this project. Take a few minutes to work through these exercises now.

1. Creating a Form for Your Library Database

In previous Practice exercises, you created a Library database and a Books table to keep track of the books in your personal collection. To make it easy to enter the books you have in your library, you may want to create and use a form. The form is similar to a card catalog and fits more with the purpose of the database. You can create an AutoForm that includes all the fields from the table and a special quick-entry form that includes just the author's last name, first name, and book title.

To Create a Form for Your Library Database

1. Copy the Proj1502 database file to `Library4`. Then return to Access and open the Library4 database.
2. Create an AutoForm based on the Books table. Save the form as `AutoForm`.
3. Enter two new records into the form; then save and close the form.
4. Create a new form, based again on the Books table. Add fields for author last name, author first name, and book title to this form. Add a form header and include a label in this area that says `Books!`
5. Save the new form with the name `Quick Entry`. Enter two more records using the Quick Entry form.
6. Choose **F**ile, **P**rint, and select Selected **R**ecord(s) to print a copy of the form.

2. Creating a Customer Table and a Form for Customer Entry

In previous Practice exercises, you set up a database for the Sound Byte Music Store. So far, this database includes one table and one query. You can add additional tables to the database and, to make it easy to enter records into the new table, you can create an AutoForm.

In this exercise, you create a table for customers and then create a form based on the new table. Finally, you use the form to enter several records into the new table.

To Create a Customer Table and Form

1. Copy the Proj1503 database file to `SBMusic4`. Then return to Access and open the SB4Music database.
2. Create a new table and include the following text fields:

   `First Name`

   `Last Name`

   `Address`

   `City`

State

ZIP

Music Interest

3. Save the table with the name **Customers**.
4. Create an AutoForm based on the new table. Save the form with the name **AutoForm**.
5. Choose **F**ile, **P**rint, and select Selected **R**ecord(s) to print a copy of the form.
6. Using the AutoForm, enter five records for your customer table. When you are finished adding records, close the form and the database.

3. Creating Forms for the Database to Track Personal Computer Hardware

You can create forms that will help the user enter specific information about the computer hardware in the company.

To Create Forms for the Personal Computer Hardware Database

1. Copy the file Proj1504 and rename the copy **PC4**. Open PC4.
2. Create a form based on the PC Hardware table that will make data entry more convenient. Add a title and save the form as **PC Hardware Form**.
3. Create a form based on the Vendors table. Use the AutoForm to create a simple columnar form. Name it **Vendors Form**.
4. Close the form and the database.

4. Getting a Helping Hand

The Access Help system provides a number of useful topics that cover forms and Form Wizards. All of these are interrelated, and you can view them by starting with a simple statement.

To Get Help on Topics in This Project

1. In Access, choose **H**elp from the menu bar. The first menu item under **H**elp is Microsoft Access **H**elp.
2. Choose Microsoft Access **H**elp.
3. In the dialog box that appears, type the statement **create a form**. The Help system does not require a question but looks instead for key words. The simpler the interrogative, the more direct the response will be. You are then presented with a list of help topics or subject areas. The first item on the list should be Create a Form.
4. Select Create a Form. The Help program runs, and you see one of the basic topics on creating forms. This topic provides an overview with a series of selections at the bottom. Each of these selections details how to accomplish increasingly difficult tasks.
5. Take a few minutes and explore.
6. Press F1. A copy of the initial dialog box appears so that you can type another statement or question.
7. Enter **add a control**. The first entry should be Add a control to a form or report. This topic is linked to the previous topic on creating forms but is easier to approach through the main dialog box.

8. Select `Add a control to a form or report`. This topic covers some detailed information about controls and will assist you in adding very complicated features to your forms and reports.
9. Take a few minutes to review the information provided.

5. Exploring the World of Alaska

Now that you have a database of information, you may find other information that you want besides the photographs and sources. Furthermore, referring to information by simply looking at a table can be confusing.

To Create and View a Simple Form

1. Open the database Proj1505 as a copy.
2. Select the Forms tab.
3. Click the **N**ew button.
4. Select the Autoform: Columnar form type.
5. Select the Geography table from the drop-down list. Notice that the Alaskan Islands query is listed. You can create a form from a query.
6. Click OK. Access generates a simple form based on the table and loads the first record in Form view. Look the form over. It is not necessary to see the Primary Key or ID field.
7. Click the View button to switch to Design view.
8. Maximize the window, if necessary. You should have a form header and footer already attached.
9. Drag the bottom of the form header down to increase the amount of working space.
10. Add the title **`Alaskan Geographic Sites`** to the header by using the Label tool.
11. Select the field text box for the ID field. Both the text box and the field label should be selected.
12. Press Del. Both boxes disappear.
13. Click the View button to switch to Form view to observe your work.
14. Close the form and save it with the name **`Input and Viewing Form`**.

Challenge

The following challenges enable you to use your problem-solving skills. Take time to work through these exercises now.

1. Creating a Form for Your Organization

In previous Challenge exercises, you set up a database to manage information about a club or organization. Create a form to make it easier to enter data for your organization or club. Include all the fields and arrange them so that they are not in a simple column format. Add a title to the form header. Choose **F**ile, **P**rint, and select Selected **R**ecord(s) to print a copy of the form.

2. Doing Customer Research

You have been entering your data directly into the table, but you want an easier, cleaner way of entering information. It is time to build a form for inputting your data and viewing the information.

To Build a Basic Survey Input Form

1. Open the database Proj1506 as a copy (or open the database you completed in the previous project).
2. Select the Forms tab and create a new form using Design view and not one of the AutoForms. Remember to select the Questionnaire table.
3. Drag each of the fields to the new form and arrange them so that they fit in the form. Notice the size of the field as you drag each one. Not all the fields are the same size.
4. When you have completed adding and arranging your fields, add a form header and footer, and title the form `Basic Survey Input Form`.
5. Test the form in Form view by entering the following data:

Adults	2	4	2	1
Children	2	1	5	2
Hours	2	4	6	2
No 1	DISNEY	DISNEY	SCIFI	SCIFI
No 2	TNT	DISCOVERY	CNN	TNT
No 3	SCIFI			CNN
Doing	Good	Great	Okay	Okay

Improvement comment for the first household: `Need more fun programming that isn't violent or vulgar. Make it light.`

Comment for the second household: `We like what we watch, but there are days, even weeks, when we don't turn on the TV at all.`

Comment for the third household: `Less junk would be nice. How about some good old movies?`

Comment for the fourth household: `We don't really watch much though my children (both in their teens) love the SCIFI channel. I only watch CNN.`

6. Close the form and save it as `Basic Survey Input Form`.

3. Owning a Vending Company

You have three different tables that hold data for your vending business. To enter data, you will need to open each table. Instead of using the table directly, you can create an input form for each table.

To Create Input Forms for Tables

1. Open the file Proj1507 as a copy.
2. Create a new form for the Locations table using the AutoForm: Columnar option.
3. Add a title, `Machine Locations`, to the form in the form header and save the form as `Machine Locations`.
4. Create a form for the Machines table using the AutoForm: Tabular option.
5. Add the title `Machine Suppliers` to the form header above the field names. When you go to Design view, notice the differences between this form design and the previous form.
6. Save the form with the name `Machine Suppliers`.

7. Create a form for the Supplier table using the Design View option. You will have to add and position the fields.
8. Add a title, `Product Suppliers`, for the form. You will have to add the header area for the form.
9. Save the form as `Product Suppliers`.
10. Close the database.

4. Managing a Video Store

You don't need to see an entire table in order to make use of the database. If you receive a new set of videos, you don't need to see the fields for renters when you are entering the videos in the database. Likewise, when you are renting out a video and have a customer there, you don't need to see the entire history of the video.

Create an input form that enables you to enter the data for new videos without seeing the information on whether the video is rented. Save this form with the name `New Video`.

Then create a form for entering the name of a renter for a specific video. Call this form `Video Rental`.

You will not want to type the name of the video in this form; instead, you will want to search through the database for the appropriate video and then enter the name of the current renter.

5. Taking a Home Inventory

In reviewing your Home Inventory database, you should have at least two tables. The first table should have the item, purchase date, description, insurance company, cost, and so on. This is the main table, and it includes all the information you'll need for the insurance company.

The second table should list the information on the insurance company, including the company name, address, phone, agent's name, policy number, and so on.

Create a form for each of these tables. The form for the inventory should include all the fields necessary to enter a new item or modify an existing item. Name this form `Add Inventory Item`.

The form for the insurance companies will be different in that you won't modify it as much. You may want to generate this form by using the tabular AutoForm so that you can see all the companies at one time. Name this form `Company Data`.

Project 16

Creating and Printing Reports

Objectives

In this project, you learn how to:

- Print the Data in a Table
- Create a Report Using the Report Wizards
- Print and Rename a Report
- Modify a Report Design
- Save a Report with a New Name
- Add Fields to a Report
- Create a Two-Column Report

Why Would I Do This?

Report
Printed output from a database that often includes formatting, such as headings and page numbers.

There are several ways to display the information in your database. You can create printed output from your database in the form of a report. *Reports* can be as simple as a printout of a table, or as complex as a document that groups and totals information. In this project, you learn the fundamental tasks involved in creating, modifying, saving, and printing a simple report.

Before you create a report, think about why you need the printed data. Do you want to check the entries to make sure they are correct? Do you need an address list or phone list? Do you need to pass the information along to someone else? If so, what information does that person need and in what order? If you spend a few moments determining the purpose of the report, you can design a report that truly meets your needs.

Access provides many tools for creating a report—you can create an AutoReport, use the Report Wizards to create other common report types (single-column report, mailing labels, and so on), or create a blank report that you add information to later. You can also change the layout of an existing report design. This project shows you how to use the report tools included with Access.

Lesson 1: Printing the Table Data

Sometimes you don't need a fancy report; you just need a quick printout of the entries in your table. For example, you may want to print the data in a table so that you can check the accuracy of the records. In this case, you don't have to create a report; you can simply print the table.

To Print the Table Data

1. **Using the Explorer, make a copy of the Proj1601 database file and name the copy `Softball`. Then return to Access and open the Softball database.**

   The Softball database includes a table of team members and a table of game information. After you open the Softball database, you should see the two tables displayed in the Tables list. In this project, you work with the Team table.

2. **Double-click the Team table.**

   This step opens the database table in Datasheet view. You may want to scroll through the table to see how it is set up. The table includes fields for the first and last name of each player, along with his or her position, phone number, address, and dues. You can print this information; but before you print, preview the printout so that you have some idea of what the printed list will look like.

❸ Open the File menu and choose the Print Preview command.

You see a preview of the printed list (see Figure 16.1). The structure of the printout is fairly simple; each record is displayed as a row in a grid. The navigation button that enables you to scroll to the next page is active. This indicates that there is more than one page. This means that all the table columns will not fit on one page width when the report is printed.

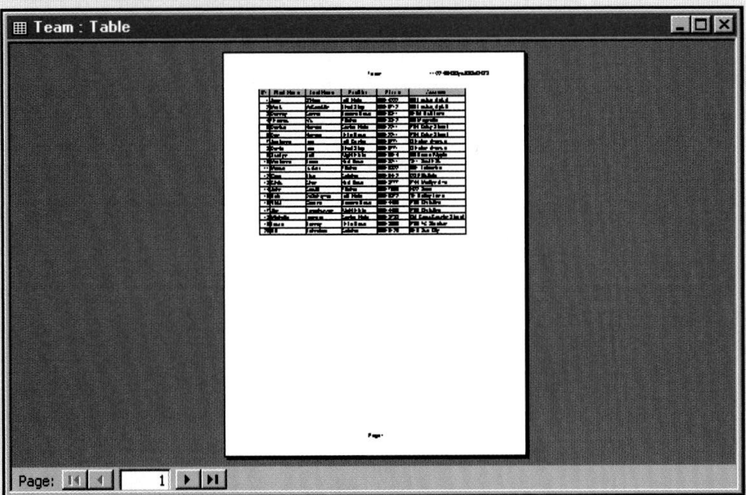

Figure 16.1
The table may be previewed before printing.

❹ Click the Next Page button.

This step displays the second page of the printout, which shows the remaining column. When your table contains many columns, you may not want to break the report into two pages. Instead, you can change the orientation of the page so that Access prints across the long edge of the page, rather than down the page. Using this orientation, you can fit more columns across the page.

❺ From the File menu, choose Page Setup.

You see the Page Setup dialog box, which lists options for setting margins and page layouts.

❻ Click the Page tab to display the page orientation (see Figure 16.2).

continues

To Print the Table Data (continued)

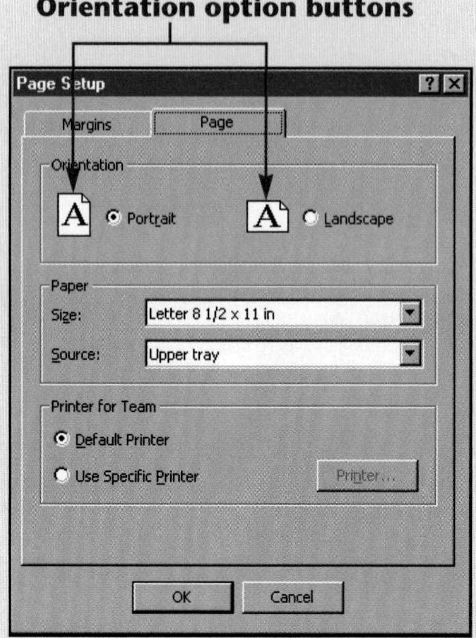

Figure 16.2
Use the Page Setup dialog box to change the page orientation.

7 In the Orientation area, click the Landscape option button and then click OK.

This step changes the orientation of the page to landscape. Now when you print the report, all the columns fit on a single page.

8 From the File menu, choose Print.

You see the Print dialog box (see Figure 16.3). Here you can control which pages are printed, how many copies are printed, and select other options. The default settings work fine for this lesson.

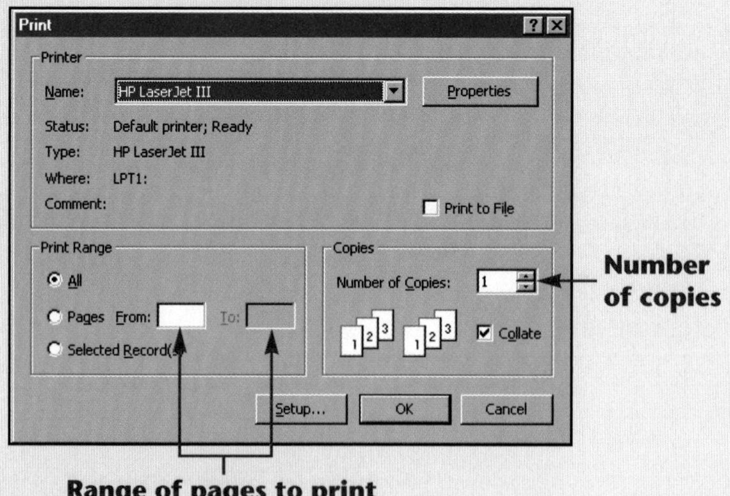

Figure 16.3
Use the Print dialog box to choose the pages and the number of copies you want to print.

9 Click OK.

Access prints the table data. If you don't have access to a printer, click Cancel.

⑩ **Open the View menu and choose the Datasheet View command.**

This step closes the preview window and returns you to Datasheet view so that, once again, you can see all the records. Keep the Team table open on your screen and continue with the next lesson.

You don't have to preview the report, but previewing is a good idea. You can print directly from Datasheet view. Simply click the Print button on the toolbar or open the **F**ile menu and choose the **P**rint command. Access then prints the data.

The keyboard shortcut for the **P**rint command is Ctrl+P.

To return to Datasheet view from the Print Preview window, you can click the **C**lose button on the toolbar instead of opening the **V**iew menu and choosing Data**s**heet View.

Lesson 2: Creating a Report Using the Report Wizards

Access provides Report Wizards to make it easy to create a report. Using the New Report feature, you can create the reports described in Table 16.1.

Table 16.1 Common Report Wizards

Type of Report Wizard	Description
Design View	Opens a design window where you can add fields or text. This option does not use the wizards.
Report Wizard	Guides you through the process of creating a report. The Report Wizard has several options for layout and grouping of data.
AutoReport: Columnar	Places all the fields in a table in a single-column report.
AutoReport: Tabular	Places all the fields of the table in a row-and-column format similar to the layout of a spreadsheet.
Chart Wizard	Guides you through the process of selecting fields that you want to summarize in a graphical form. The Chart Wizard enables you to choose from several chart types, such as pie, line, and bar.
Label Wizard	Enables you to set up and print mailing labels in more than 100 different label styles.

The wizards lead you step by step through the process of creating the report, asking you which fields to include in the report, which sort order to use, what title to print, and so on. After you make your selections, the wizards create the report.

In this lesson, you create a columnar report for your Team table in the Softball database. This report works well as an address list.

To Create a Report Using the Report Wizards

1 Open the Team table of the Softball database (if necessary).

2 Click the down arrow next to the New Object button.

A list of objects is displayed (see Figure 16.4).

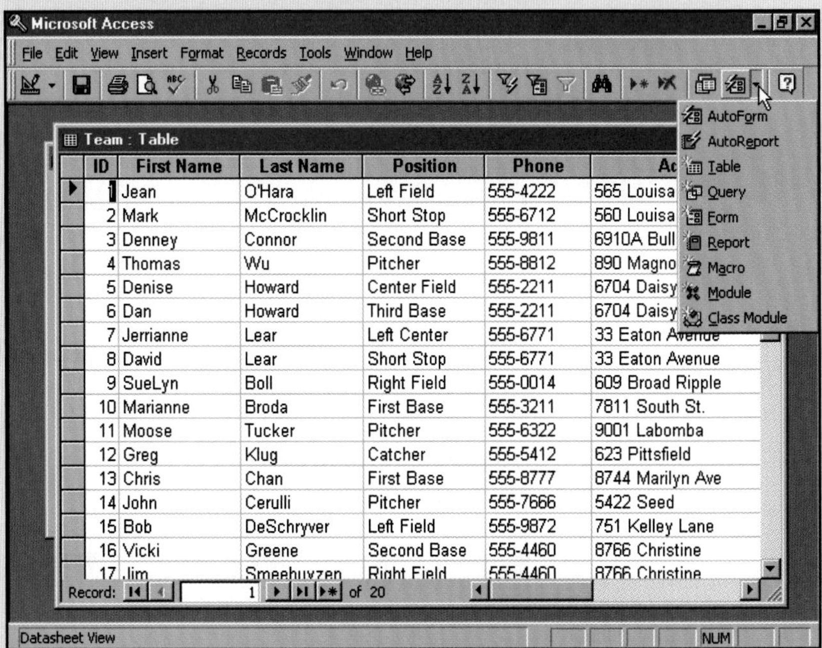

ID	First Name	Last Name	Position	Phone	Ac
1	Jean	O'Hara	Left Field	555-4222	565 Louisa
2	Mark	McCrocklin	Short Stop	555-6712	560 Louisa
3	Denney	Connor	Second Base	555-9811	6910A Bull
4	Thomas	Wu	Pitcher	555-8812	890 Magno
5	Denise	Howard	Center Field	555-2211	6704 Daisy
6	Dan	Howard	Third Base	555-2211	6704 Daisy
7	Jerrianne	Lear	Left Center	555-6771	33 Eaton Avenue
8	David	Lear	Short Stop	555-6771	33 Eaton Avenue
9	SueLyn	Boll	Right Field	555-0014	609 Broad Ripple
10	Marianne	Broda	First Base	555-3211	7811 South St.
11	Moose	Tucker	Pitcher	555-6322	9001 Labomba
12	Greg	Klug	Catcher	555-5412	623 Pittsfield
13	Chris	Chan	First Base	555-8777	8744 Marilyn Ave
14	John	Cerulli	Pitcher	555-7666	5422 Seed
15	Bob	DeSchryver	Left Field	555-9872	751 Kelley Lane
16	Vicki	Greene	Second Base	555-4460	8766 Christine
17	Jim	Smeehuyzen	Right Field	555-4460	8766 Christine

Figure 16.4
A list of available objects appears in a list.

3 Click the Report icon.

You see the New Report dialog box (see Figure 16.5). Notice that Access has already selected the table for you. You just have to tell Access whether you want to use a wizard, use an AutoReport, or start with a blank report and build it in Design view. In this lesson, you use the Report Wizard.

New Report
Create a new report without using a wizard.
Design View
Report Wizard
AutoReport: Columnar
AutoReport: Tabular
Chart Wizard
Label Wizard
Choose the table or query where the object's data comes from:
Team
OK
Cancel

Figure 16.5
In the New Report dialog box, you choose the method you want to use to create a new report.

4 Select Report Wizard and click OK.

You see the Report Wizard dialog box, as shown in Figure 16.6.

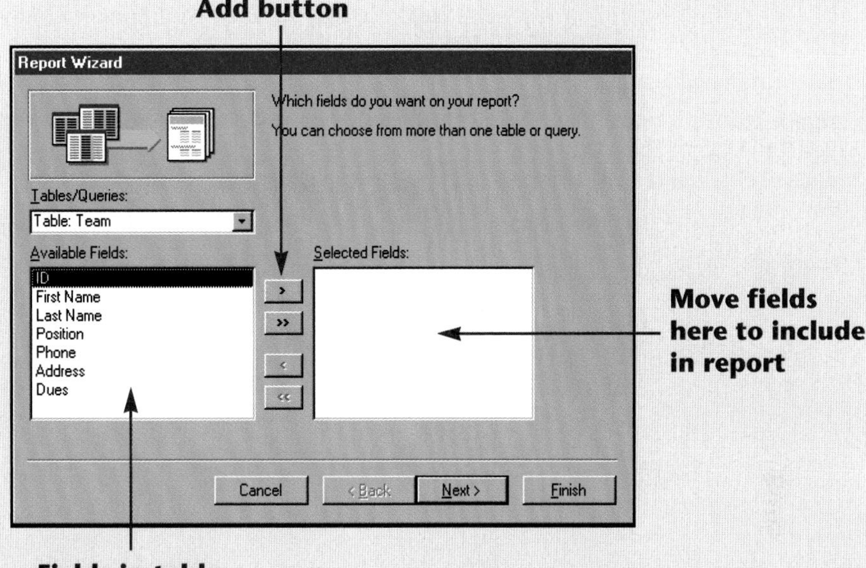

Figure 16.6
Choose which fields from the table you want to include in the report.

5 In the Available Fields list, click the First Name field. Then click the Add button (>).

The Wizard removes the field from the **A**vailable Fields list and places the field in the **S**elected Fields list. The fields will appear in the report in the order you select them. The First Name field, for example, will be the first field listed in the report.

6 Select the Last Name field and click the Add button.

The Last Name field is added to the report.

7 Select the Address field and click the Add button.

The Address field is added to the report.

8 Select the Phone field and click the Add button.

The Phone field is added to the report. Your report now includes four fields. That is all the fields you want to include for this lesson.

9 Click the Next button.

The Wizard displays a new screen for the second step. You could use this step to group similar records together, such as grouping the team by position played. In this example, we have not included any fields that need to be listed together as a group.

10 Click Next again.

The next Report Wizard dialog box enables you to sort the data on one or more fields.

continues

To Create a Report Using the Report Wizards (continued)

11 Click the list arrow next to the first sort selection to reveal the available fields. Select Last Name to sort on. Click Next.

The next Report Wizard dialog box enables you to select the layout, orientation, and fit.

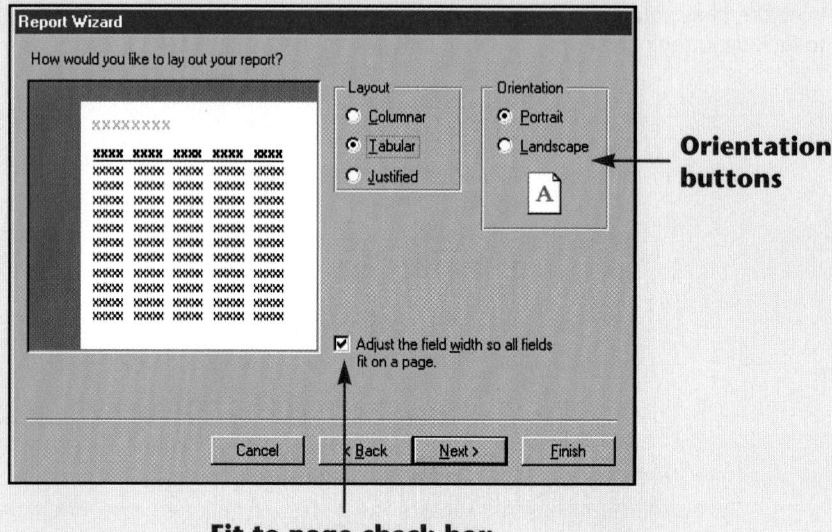

Figure 16.7
Select the layout and page orientation for your report.

12 Select a Columnar layout, Portrait orientation, and fit to one page (see Figure 16.7).

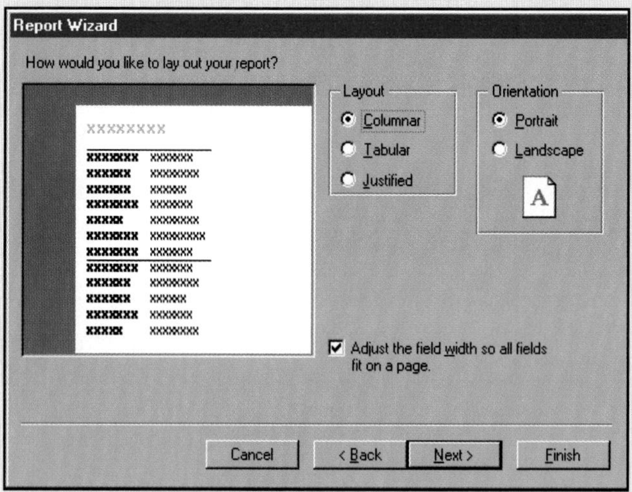

Figure 16.8
Select the layout and orientation options.

13 Click the Next button.

The Wizard displays the next step. In this screen, you select a report style. For this example, the Corporate selection works well.

14 Select the Corporate option and click the Next button.

You see the final step of the Report Wizard. In this screen, you enter the title for the report. By default, the Wizard uses the table name and prints the title on the first page. This format is OK, so you are finished with the Report Wizard.

15 **Click the Finish button.**

You see a preview of the report, as shown in Figure 16.9. You can print, zoom, and save the report, as you learn in the next lesson. Keep the report open.

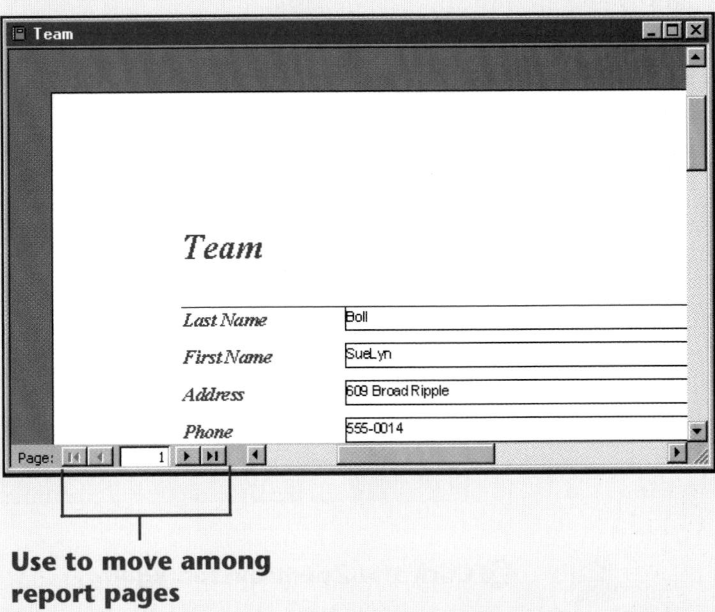

Figure 16.9
The columnar report may be reviewed on screen.

If you have problems...

If you make a mistake in the Wizard, you can back up by clicking the **B**ack button in the Wizard dialog box.

In Project 15, you used the Form Wizard to create an AutoForm. You can also create an AutoReport using the Report Wizards. An AutoReport includes all the fields from the table in the report. The report is in either a one-column or tabular format with as many records on the page as possible. The report also includes a header with the table name and current date, and a footer with the page number. To create this type of report, choose **R**eport from the list of new objects displayed in the New Objects list box.

Lesson 3: Printing and Renaming a Report

The next step is to print your report. However, before you print, it's always a good idea to preview the report. In the Print Preview mode, you can use the navigation buttons to check for unexpected additional pages, check the font, the font size, and the actual data in the report. Then, if you click the Zoom button on the toolbar, you can view the entire report to determine, generally, how the printed report will look on the page. If you do not like how the report is set up, you can make changes before you print it. This strategy can save you some time and paper.

You can also rename a report in the database window to ensure that it's not confused with other database objects with the same name.

To Print and Rename a Report

1 Click the Zoom button.

Access displays a full-page view of the report, as shown in Figure 16.10, so that you can see the entire page.

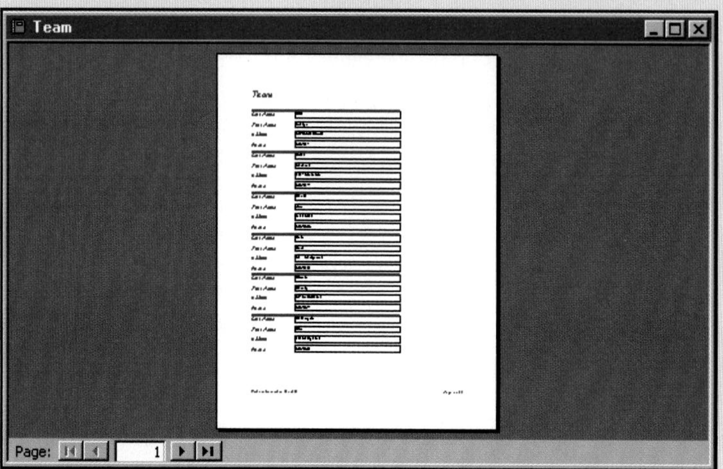

Figure 16.10
The full-page view may be used to preview the report.

2 Click the Zoom button again.

Access zooms in so that you can read the text of the report. Now you are ready to print.

3 Click the Print button on the toolbar.

Access prints the report. If you do not have access to a printer, skip this step.

Close

4 Click the Close button on the toolbar to close the report. Close the Team table as well.

The new report is shown in the database window under the Reports tab.

5 It may be confusing to use the same name for the report and the table. Click once on the name of the report to select it.

The name changes to edit mode, in which it can be changed (see Figure 16.11).

Figure 16.11
Select the report name so that it may be renamed.

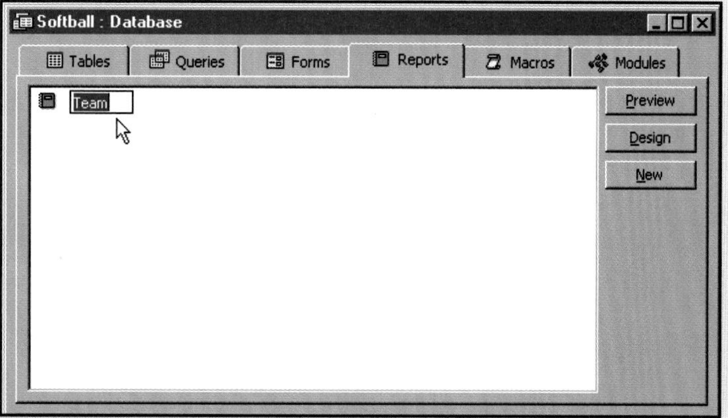

6. **Type the name `Roster`.**
7. **Press Enter or click outside the name box to indicate that you are done.**

   The report name is now Roster. Keep the database open for the next lesson.

Lesson 4: Modifying a Report Design

Once you have created a report, you may decide you want to modify it. The finished report may not be exactly what you intended. Rather than start over with a wizard or a blank form, you can modify the report design so that the report includes the information you want.

Suppose that you need a phone list in addition to the team roster. You can modify the Roster report to create this new report. Start by deleting the Address field, which you don't need in your phone list.

To Modify a Report Design

1. **Select the Roster report and click the Design button.**

   You see the report in Design view (see Figure 16.12). This view is similar to the Design view you used when you created a form. The same tools are available on-screen. You can use the ruler to place items on the report, the toolbox to add *controls*, and the field list to add fields.

continues

To Modify a Report Design (continued)

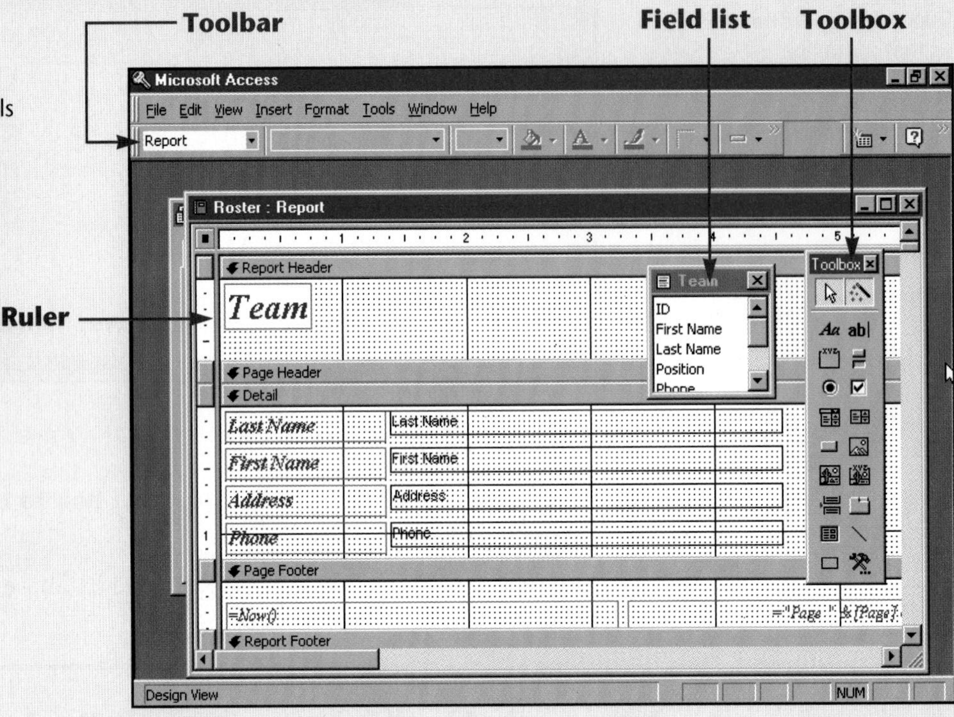

Figure 16.12
In Design mode, tools are available to help you modify your report.

❷ **Click the scroll arrows to scroll through the report and see how it is structured.**

Notice that the report includes a footer with the date and page number. The *expression* =NOW() inserts the current date. An expression is similar to a function in spreadsheet software. Access provides many expressions that you can include in your report.

Expression
A predefined formula that performs some calculations. You can include an expression in a report and in other Access objects, such as macros.

The following expression prints the current page and the total number of pages:

```
="Page" & [Page] & "Of" & [Pages]
```

The Detail section includes four fields: First Name, Last Name, Address, and Phone.

❸ **Click the Address field text box.**

The field label is on the left, and the field text box is on the right. If you click on the Address field text box, handles will appear at the sides and corners of the field text box and the field label box.

❹ **Press Del.**

Access removes the field and its label from the report. Now you have a gap between two of the fields. To fix this gap, you can move the Phone field up.

❺ **Click the Phone field to select it.**

Position the pointer on the field so that it turns into an open hand.

❻ **Drag the Phone field so that it is directly under the First Name field.**

The Phone field is now moved up closer to First Name.

❼ **Click the Print Preview button on the toolbar.**

You see a preview of the modified report. Keep the Roster report open and continue with the next lesson.

Access often provides several ways for you to perform a task. To get to another view, for example, you can use the buttons on the toolbar. In addition, you can use the list of Report Views to change views when you are in a form or table. You can use the **V**iew menu to change views when you are in a report.

Jargon Watch

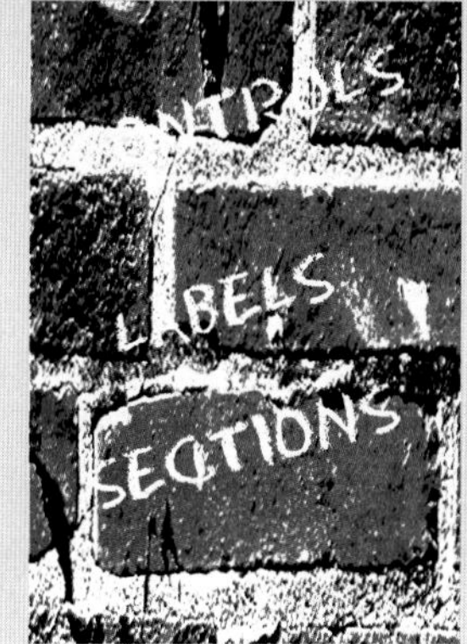

Modifying a report design is similar to creating and modifying a form. Reports and forms include controls, labels, and sections. **Controls** are the interactive elements you can add to a report or form, such as text boxes and check boxes. **Labels** have static, descriptive text you can add that is not tied to the underlying database. For example, you can include a label that provides the name of the report.

Sections are subdivisions of the form or report that control what is printed and where it is printed. Record information is printed in the Detail section, for example. Text and graphics included in the Page Header section are printed at the top of the page; information included in the Page Footer section is printed at the bottom of the page.

Lesson 5: Saving the Report with a New Name

As you modify a report, you may decide that you want to keep the original report as well as your modified version. If this is the case, you can save the modified report with a new name. Doing so enables you to use both reports.

In addition to saving the report with a new name, you should change the Report Header so that it reflects the purpose of the new report.

To Save the Report with a New Name

❶ **With the Roster report still on-screen, open the File menu and choose the Save As/Export command.**

You see the Save As dialog box, as shown in Figure 16.13, with the original name listed.

continues

To Save the Report with a New Name (continued)

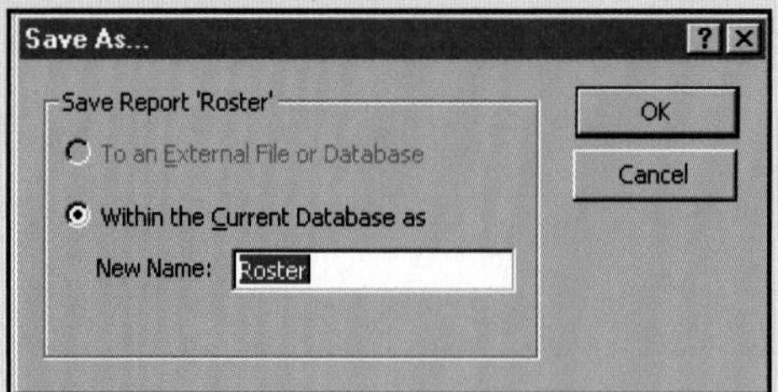

Figure 16.13
When you choose Save As/Export, Access displays the original name in the New Name box.

2. **Type `Phone List` and click OK.**

   The report is saved with a new name.

3. **From the View menu, choose Design View to switch to Design view.**

4. **Click in the label box in the Report Header section.**

   Here you want to replace the existing text, `Team`, with a more descriptive title.

5. **Drag across the text to select it; then type `Phone List`.**

   The new text replaces the selected text.

6. **Select File, Save from the menu bar.**

   This step saves your changes to the Phone List report by writing over the report with that name. Keep the Phone List report open and continue to the next lesson.

Lesson 6: Adding Fields to the Report

Just as you can delete fields you no longer need, you can add fields that you later decide you want to include in your report. For example, you may not need the players' addresses in your phone list, but suppose that you want to see the players' positions in the list. Including the position may be helpful when you are making your calls to be sure you have enough players and that all positions are covered.

In this lesson, you add the Position field and resize the Detail section.

To Add Fields

1. **With the Phone List report still open, select the Position field from the field list. (Open the field list, if necessary.)**

   This selects the field you want to add to the report.

2. **Drag the field from the field list to the Detail section of the report.**

The pointer will turn into a small field box. Place the pointer under the Phone field at the 1½-inch position on the horizontal ruler (see Figure 16.14). When you release the mouse button, the field and its label will be added to the report.

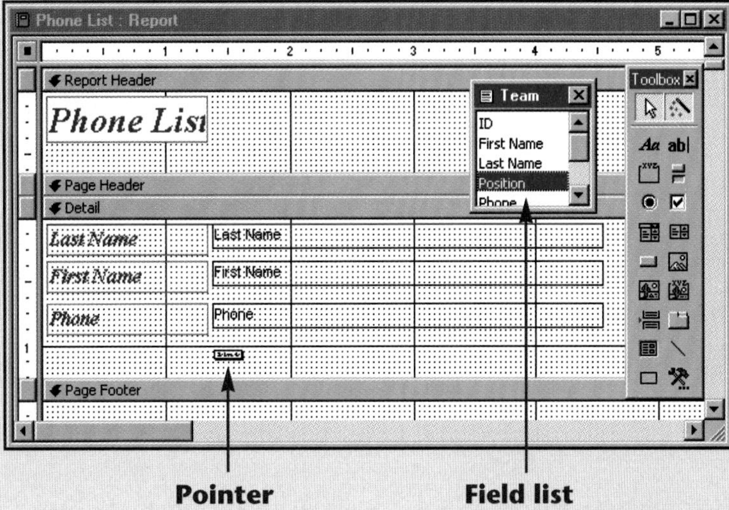

Figure 16.14 Fields may be added to a report using the field list.

The new field does not match the others in size or format.

3. **Point to the Phone text box above the new Position text box. Hold down Shift and click. The Phone and Position boxes should both be selected.**
4. **Choose Format, Size, To Widest to match the length of the two boxes.**
5. **Choose Format, Size, To Tallest to match the height of the two boxes.**
6. **Choose Format, Align, Left to match the alignment of the two boxes.**
7. **Click in an unused space in the Detail area to deselect the boxes.**
8. **Select the label boxes for Position and Phone. Repeat steps 3 through 7 to get the Position label box to match those above it in size and alignment.**

   The new field should now match the other boxes in size and alignment. However, the other text boxes have a dark border.

9. **Click the Position text box to select it.**
10. **Click the down arrow to the right of the Border Color button.**
11. **Select black for the box border (see Figure 16.15).**

   Save your changes and keep this report open for the next lesson.

continues

To Add Fields (continued)

Figure 16.15
The border of a box may be modified using the Line/Border options.

Lesson 7: Creating a Two-Column Report

When you previewed the report, you may have noticed that you have quite a bit of extra space on the page. A single-column table displays record after record in one column on the page. If you have wide fields, this format works well; but if your fields are fairly short, you end up wasting space.

If you want to include more data on the page, however, and your fields are not extremely wide, you can resize the Detail section to include two columns of records, side by side.

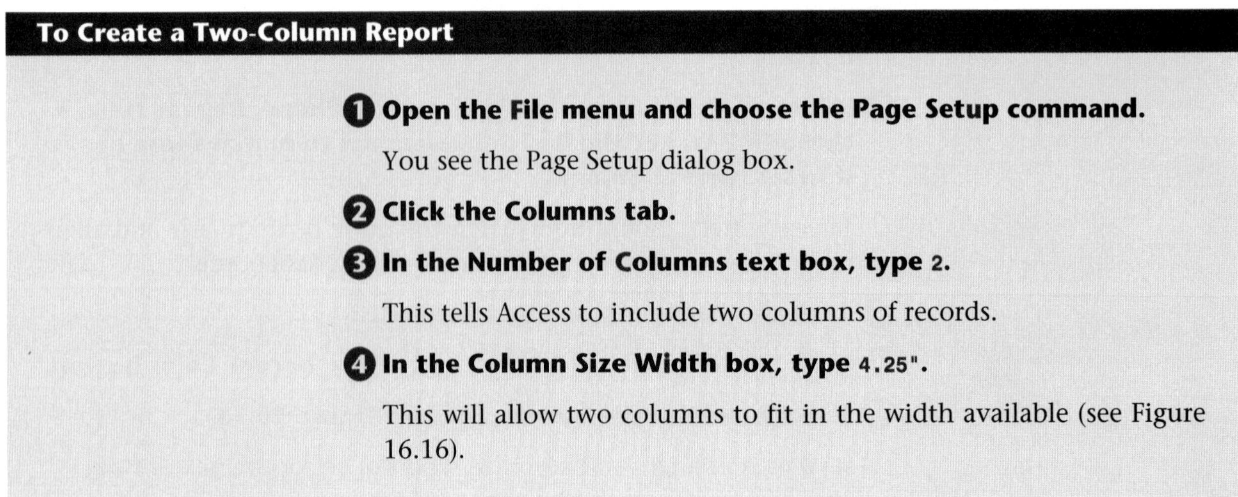

To Create a Two-Column Report

1. **Open the File menu and choose the Page Setup command.**

   You see the Page Setup dialog box.

2. **Click the Columns tab.**

3. **In the Number of Columns text box, type** `2`**.**

   This tells Access to include two columns of records.

4. **In the Column Size Width box, type** `4.25"`**.**

   This will allow two columns to fit in the width available (see Figure 16.16).

Figure 16.16
Use the Page Setup dialog box to set two columns on the page.

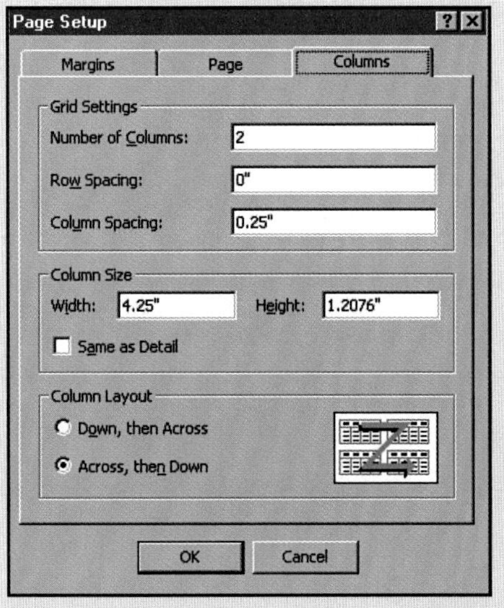

Page Setup
Margins | Page | Columns
Grid Settings
Number of Columns: 2
Row Spacing: 0"
Column Spacing: 0.25"
Column Size
Width: 4.25" Height: 1.2076"
Same as Detail
Column Layout
Down, then Across
Across, then Down
OK Cancel

5 Click the Page tab.

6 Change the orientation to Landscape and click OK. Click the Print Preview button.

The report should now show two columns of player names. Use Zoom to view the entire page, if necessary (see Figure 16.17). The text boxes are not closed at the end, which indicates that the text boxes are longer than the column width.

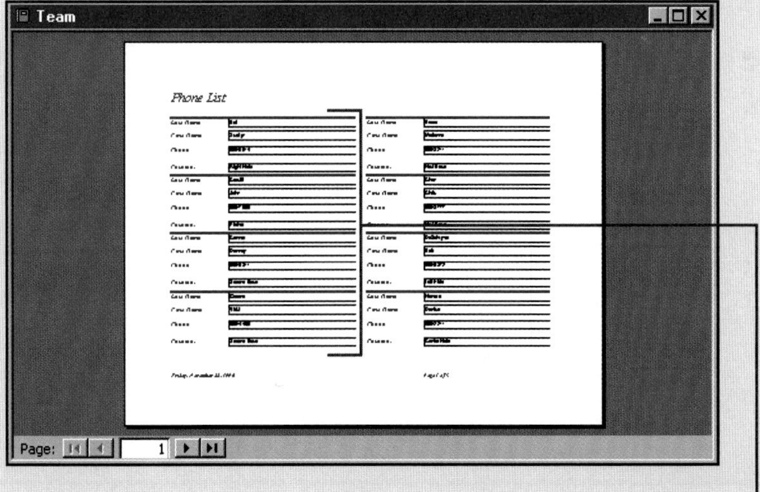

End of text boxes in original report

Figure 16.17
The report displays two columns of names. Notice that the text boxes are not closed, indicating that they are wider than the column width.

7 Click the Close button on the Print Preview toolbar, which will return the screen to the Design view.

Now you will shorten the size of the text boxes so they will fit in a 4.25-inch column.

continues

To Create a Two-Column Report (continued)

8. **Hold down Shift and click each of the four text boxes.**

   This selects all four of the boxes so that you can shorten them all at once.

9. **Move the pointer to a handle at the right edge of one of the boxes, where the pointer turns into a two-headed arrow.**

10. **Click and drag the right end of the boxes to the left to about the 4-inch mark on the horizontal ruler.**

    All four boxes are shortened together.

11. **Click the Print Preview button on the toolbar.**

    Now each text box is closed at the end.

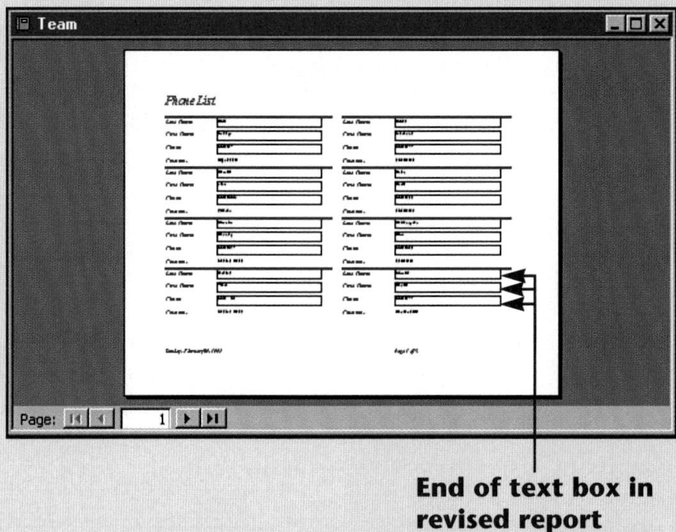

Figure 16.18
The report now shows the full width of the text boxes.

12. **Click the Close button on the Print Preview toolbar.**
13. **Select File, Save from the menu bar.**
14. **Close the Report Design view.**
15. **Close the database.**

    This saves the changes you have made to the Phone List report.

In this lesson, you modified the report to fit two columns of data on the same sheet.

If you have completed your session on the computer, exit Access and shut down Windows before you turn off the computer. Otherwise, continue with the section "Checking Your Skills" in this project.

Project Summary

To	Do This
Print the data in a table	Open the database file in Table view. Open the **F**ile menu and choose Print Pre**v**iew. Alter the layout by using the Page Set**u**p command in the **F**ile menu, if necessary. When the page appears the way you want, open the **F**ile menu and choose **P**rint.
Create a report using Report Wizards	Several wizard options are available (refer to Table 6.1). To open the Wizard you want to use, click the down arrow next to the New Object button. Select **R**eport, select Report Wizard, and click OK. Select the fields you want included in the report and click the Add button (>). Click **N**ext. The Wizard leads you through several more screens. Make your selections, click **N**ext until you reach the final screen, and click Finish.
Print a report	When you click the Finish button using the Wizard, you see a Print Preview of the report. If you are satisfied with the report, click the Print button.
Rename a report	Select the Reports tab in the database window. Click the report title you want to change. Pause and then click a second time. The box around the title will change, and you can edit the report title by typing over the existing name.
Modify a report design	Work in Design view. The same techniques used when designing a form apply here. You can start with an existing report. Click and drag the fields you want to move, add, or delete. The same tools are used in the toolbox or the Format menu to help align fields, add labels, modify fonts, or change headers and footers.
Save a report with a new name	Open the **F**ile menu and choose the Save **A**s/Export command. Type a new name in the dialog box and click OK.
Add fields	Work in Design view. In the field box, click and drag the field you want to add to the report to the desired position. Click the Print Preview button to view the report. Adjust the fields until you are satisfied with the report design.
Create a two-column report	Use the Page Set**u**p command under the **F**ile menu to change the layout to 2 Items Across. Set the column width. Use the Page tab to change the orientation to **L**andscape.

Checking Your Skills

True/False

For each of the following, check *T* or *F* to indicate whether the statement is true or false.

__T __F **1.** To print table data, you have to use a Report Wizard. You can't just print directly from the table.

__T __F **2.** You can modify the report layout in Print Preview mode.

__T __F **3.** To create a two-column report, enter **2** in the Columns text box and select a column width that is narrow enough to fit.

__T __F **4.** You cannot add new fields to an existing report.

__T __F **5.** To include two columns of records in a report, use the Print Set**u**p command in the **F**ile menu.

__T __F **6.** When you drag a field name into a report, the mouse pointer turns into a small field box.

__T __F **7.** To save a report with a new name, select Save **A**s/Export from the **F**ile menu.

__T __F **8.** If you delete a field text box, its label box will be deleted also.

__T __F **9.** The term **[#Pages]** on your form will insert the total number of pages of your report.

__T __F **10.** If the data in a report is too wide to fit in Portrait orientation, you must shorten the fields.

Multiple Choice

Circle the letter of the correct answer for each of the following questions.

1. Which of the following reports is *not* one of the Report Wizards selections?

- **a.** single-column
- **b.** double-column
- **c.** tabular
- **d.** AutoReport

2. To change the orientation of the report, which command should you use?

- **a.** Print Setup
- **b.** Print Orientation
- **c.** Page Setup
- **d.** Printer Setup

3. If you make a mistake and want to go to the previous screen in a Wizard, which button do you use?

- **a.** Next
- **b.** Back
- **c.** Previous
- **d.** Go Back

4. Which report design tool helps you precisely position controls on the report?

- **a.** toolbox
- **b.** toolbar
- **c.** field list
- **d.** ruler

5. How do you delete a control from a report?
   - a. Click it and press Del.
   - b. Drag it off the report.
   - c. Double-click it and press Del.
   - d. Press ←Backspace.
6. If you have entered all the information you need on a Wizard, you can complete the process by selecting which button?
   - a. **F**inish
   - b. Co**m**plete
   - c. **D**one
   - d. OK
7. To make a group of text boxes the same dimension from top to bottom, which menu item should you select?
   - a. **T**allest
   - b. **H**ighest
   - c. **H**eight, **T**allest
   - d. **L**argest
8. To display a full page view of a report in Print Preview, which button should you click?
   - a. Page
   - b. Zoom
   - c. Magnify
   - d. Full Page
9. An AutoReport includes which of the following?
   - a. All nonautomatic fields in the table
   - b. All fields in the database
   - c. The fields you designate in the third dialog box
   - d. All fields in the source table
10. Major parts of a report include all the following except which?
    - a. labels
    - b. commands
    - c. sections
    - d. controls

Completion

In the blank provided, write the correct answer for each of the following statements.

1. ______________ orientation prints across the long side of the page.
2. To add controls to the report (such as checkboxes, text boxes, and labels) use the ______________ in Design view.
3. Items that you add to a form or report are called ______________.
4. A(n) ______________ is a formula or function that performs a calculation.
5. To add a field to a report, drag the field from the ______________.
6. ______________ are subdivisions of a report or form.
7. You can use ______________ to see what a report will look like before you print it.
8. To have a selected group of controls line up on the report, you can select ______________ from the F**o**rmat menu.
9. You can use ______________ to help you create several graphic representations of numeric data.
10. By default, a columnar report has ______________ column(s).

Matching

In the blank next to each of the following terms or phrases, write the letter of the corresponding term or phrase. (Note that some letters may be used more than once.)

_____ **1.** Used to save a report

_____ **2.** Places all fields in a row-and-column format similar to a spreadsheet

_____ **3.** Helps you set up more than 100 different label styles

_____ **4.** Used to change the outline color of a box

_____ **5.** Menu selections to make multiple selected items the same length

_____ **6.** An electronic version of the final printed report

_____ **7.** An orientation for the report

_____ **8.** Places all of a table's fields in a single-column report

_____ **9.** Not required, but a good choice before you print a report

_____ **10.** Used to add fields from the Available Fields list

a. Landscape

b. Print Preview

c. Ctrl+S

d. F**o**rmat, **S**ize, To **W**idest

e. AutoReport: Columnar

f. AutoReport: Tabular

g. F**o**rmat, **S**ize, To **L**ength

h. Add button ([>])

i. Label Wizard

j. Border Color button

Screen ID

Identify each of the items shown in Figure 16.19.

Figure 16.19

1.______________

2.______________

3.______________

4.______________

5.______________

6.______________

7.______________

8.______________

9.______________

10.______________

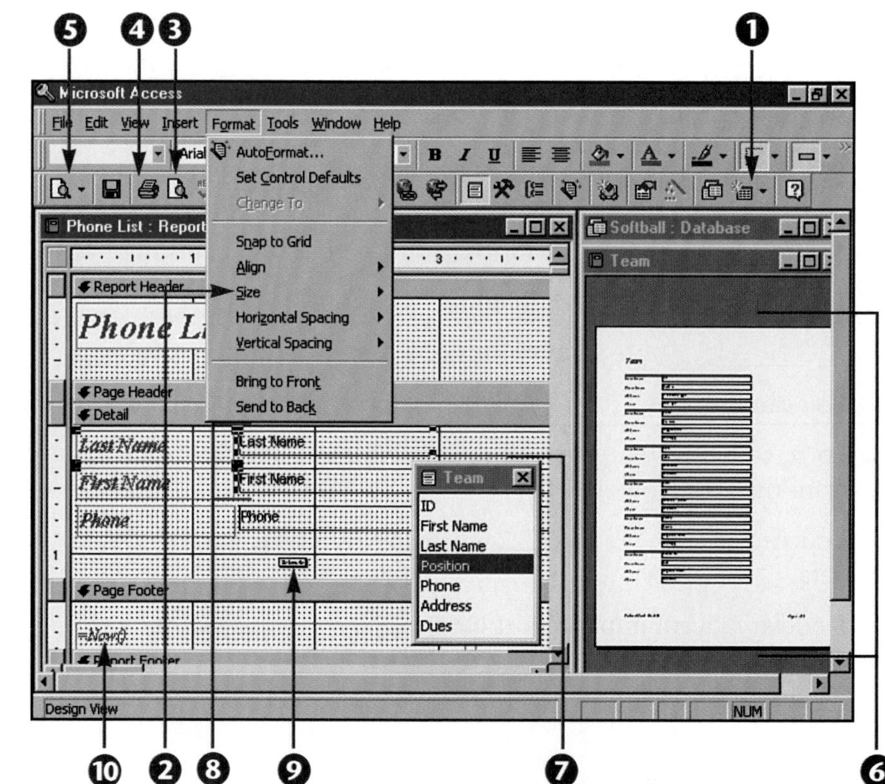

Applying Your Skills

Practice

The following exercises enable you to practice the skills you have learned in this project. Take a few minutes to work through these exercises now.

1. Creating a Book List

Printing a simple list of data in a database can be helpful in many ways. First, you usually use a database to track some item, as you have tracked your book collection by using the Library database you developed in earlier projects. You may want to have a complete list of all the entries you have made—that is, a printed copy of all the books in your collection. Second, when you want to share data in your database, you can print a report to give to someone else. For example, suppose that one of your friends wants to borrow some books to take on a trip. You can give her your book list and then let her select the titles that interest her.

To print data from your Books table, you can create a simple report. This report should include the fields for the author's last name, author's first name, and book title. You can sort the report by the author's last name.

To Create a Report for Your Library Database

1. Copy the Proj1602 database file to **`Library5`**. Then return to Access and open the **`Library5`** database and the Books table.
2. Create a single-column report using the Report Wizards. Add the Author Last Name, Author First Name, and Title fields to the report. Choose Last Name as the sort field.
3. Save the report with the name **`Book List`**.
4. Print a copy of the report. If requested by your instructor, print two copies.

2. Creating an Order Table and Printing an Order Report

In previous "Practice" exercises involving the Sound Byte Music store, you set up database tables for suppliers and for customers. In addition to tracking these two important sets of information, you may want to keep track of outstanding orders. This table can track which new products you have ordered, the number you ordered, and from whom you ordered the items. You can start by creating a new table with fields for Order Date, Order Number, Supplier Name, Item Ordered, and Quantity. Next, you can enter records for this new table. Then, to keep up-to-date on the orders, you can print a report that lists outstanding orders.

To Create an Order Table and Print an Order Report

1. Copy the Proj1603 database file and change the name of the copy to `SBMusic5`. Return to Access, open the SBMusic5 database, and create a new table that includes the following fields. All fields should have a data type of Text except for the Quantity field, which should be a Number field.

   `Order Date`

   `Order Number`

   `Supplier Name`

   `Item Ordered`

   `Quantity`

2. Make the Order Number field the primary key field.
3. Save the table with the name `Orders`.
4. Enter at least five records into the new table.
5. Create an AutoReport based on the new table. Save the form with the name `Outstanding Orders`.
6. Print the report. Close the form and the database.

3. Creating a Report Based on the Personal Computer Hardware Table

Create a report that shows the PC hardware owned by the company.

To Create the PC Hardware Report

1. Copy the file Proj1604 and rename the copy `PC5`. Open PC5.
2. Select all the fields in the table.
3. Use the tabular form in landscape orientation.
4. Go into Design view to adjust the size of the column headings so that they display the full text of each heading.
5. Save the report as `PC Hardware Report`.
6. Print the report.

4. Getting a Helping Hand

Often you have an idea of what something does, but you need to find just a little more information about it.

To Get Help on Topics in This Project

1. Open the Softball database you saved during your work earlier in this project.
2. Select the Reports tab.
3. Open the Roster report in Design view.
4. Maximize the window, if necessary. F1 opens the Office Assistant most of the time. However, if you have certain items selected, the Assistant will give you additional information about those items.
5. Select the title in the Report Header so that the control handles appear around the box.

6. With the title selected, press F1. You get a dialog box similar to What's This?, explaining what the label is. Notice at the bottom of the dialog box that you can elect to see more information.

   Now look at another example.

7. From the bottom left of the window, select the text box that contains the expression `"=Now()"`. The control handles should appear around the box.
8. Press F1. A new dialog box appears that discusses the text box. From the bottom of this dialog box, you can launch the appropriate help topic by selecting `For more information, click [>>]`.
9. Select the small button with the double greater-than symbols. Access launches the appropriate help topic. You can then get an overview or follow the links to more specific details on creating expressions.

5. Exploring the World of Alaska

Once you have a database of information, you may want to print the table so that you can check data or can file the data as a hard-copy archive. First, you want to get an idea of how the report might look.

To View and Print a Table

1. Open the database Proj1605 as a copy.
2. Open the Geography table in Datasheet view.
3. Click the Print Preview button on the toolbar. You see the first page of the report. If you click the Last Page navigation button at the bottom of the window, you should see that there are eight pages to the report. Depending on your hardware and software configuration, the total may be different.
4. Click the Multiple Pages button on the toolbar.
5. In the small window that appears, select the top-left box and drag down to the second row and across four boxes until you have a total of eight boxes selected. The complete report should appear. Notice that tables are split across pages.
6. Choose Page Set**u**p from the **F**ile menu.
7. On the Page tab, change the orientation to Landscape.
8. Select the Margins tab.
9. Change the Le**f**t and Ri**g**ht margins to 0.5 inches.
10. Click OK. The view of the report in Print Preview displays only five pages. Each one will fill the page. You can zoom in on any page to see the detail of what the report will look like.
11. Choose Print from the toolbar and close the database.

Challenge

The following challenges enable you to use your problem-solving skills. Take time to work through these exercises now.

1. Creating a Report That Lists Your Club or Organization Roster

Create a report that lists the members of your club or organization. Use the two-column format and place a title at the center of the report. Print a copy of the report.

2. Doing Customer Research

Your boss has an important meeting on the survey and wants to study the comments people have made. Your job is to create a concise report that will enable your boss to review it quickly.

To Create a Report for Quick Review

1. Open the database Proj1606 as a copy (or the database you completed in the previous project).
2. Select the Tables tab. The Questionnaire table should be highlighted.
3. Select New Report under the New Object button. The Questionnaire table should be the default table selected as the source for the report.
4. Using the Report Wizard format, create a report with the fields Adults, Children, Hours, and Improve. Don't group or sort the table, but use the Tabular format for the report. After selecting the Bold style, save the report as `Customers and their comments`.
5. View the report in Print Preview. The report you have created should be only one page and should provide a complete list of all the data your boss has requested. There is, however, a lot of wasted space for the first three fields.
6. Select Design view and shrink the width of the first three numeric fields. Be sure you move the heading as well.
7. View the revised report in Print Preview and then print a copy.

3. Owning a Vending Company

As you review your database, you realize that there are only two reports you will need. The first is a report from your Suppliers table that you can keep with you as a phone list. The second is a list of the locations that you can keep with you as you drive around town.

To Generate Two Reports

1. Open the file Proj1607 as a copy.
2. Using the New Object button on the toolbar, select Report Wizard to generate the new report.
3. Add all the fields to your report without grouping the report by any of the fields. Then sort the report by the name field and use the columnar format.
4. Choose the Soft Gray style and name the report `Supplier Phone List`.
5. After you have generated the report and viewed it with Print Preview, print a copy of the report for your notebook. Notice that the Bulk Foodstuffs supplier should now be listed at the top of the report.

6. Close the report and return to the Reports tab of the database.
7. Select New and generate an AutoReport: Tabular using the Locations table. The ID field will be included because you have created an AutoReport.
8. The ID field doesn't concern you, so change to Design view and remove the ID field and its column label in the Page Header section of the report.
9. View the report once again in Print Preview and then print a copy, using the File menu.
10. Close the report, saving it with the name `Machine Locations`.

4. Managing a Video Store

After you have generated a fairly complete database of videos for your store, you will have to conduct an inventory. Several methods for conducting the inventory are available, some taking more time than others. One effective method is to create a list of the videos, separated by type, with each type alphabetized.

With this report format, you just have to assign a person to handle one or two types. All employees can be used to conduct the inventory simultaneously.

Generate a report by using the Report Wizard. Include the video title, number, and type fields in your report. Group the report by type and sort by video title.

Save your new report as `Inventory Listing` and print a copy for your files.

5. Taking a Home Inventory

As you acquire more household items, you will see items that you need to add to your database. As you add more items, the list that the insurance company has will become out-of-date. It is important for the insurance company to have an accurate picture of what is in your household to ensure that you have set the proper level of insurance.

Create a tabular report by using your main item table, which lists specific information for the insurance company. Name the report `Periodic Update` and sort it by item name.

Then create a new report, with the same format used for the previous one, except sort the information by dollar amount, in descending order. Name this report `List by Value`. The new report will enable you to view the items that you want to ensure are covered.

Project 17

Managing Data and Files

Objectives

In this project, you learn how to:

- Switch between Applications Using the Taskbar
- Copy Tables and Queries to Microsoft Word Documents
- Copy Tables or Queries to a Spreadsheet for Data Analysis
- Merge Data from Access into Documents in Microsoft Word
- Import Tables from Databases, Spreadsheets, and Text Files
- Link Tables to Access from Other Databases

Why Would I Do This?

Although we learn computer applications one at a time, we use them simultaneously. In an office environment, you may be working on a spreadsheet to come up with the figures you need for the annual report that you are writing in a word processor. The phone rings, and you have to look up information in a database. Windows 95 was designed for this type of workplace.

Occasionally, you may need to transfer data from one application program into another. A query in Access would look good as a table in a Word document, or a spreadsheet such as Microsoft Excel may be needed to do a statistical analysis of the data in an Access table.

In some cases, the programs must work together. A common example of this type of cooperation is called *mailmerge*. The Access mailmerge feature is used to send the same letter to many people but change keywords, such as name and address, so that the letter appears to have been written to each individual. The document is written in Word, but the names and addresses come from an Access table or query.

Databases come in many forms. Some are from other database management programs, and some are from word processors, mainframe computers, or unknown sources over the Internet. The name *Access* was chosen to indicate that Microsoft Access provides powerful tools to enable the user to gain access to many forms of data. It is also possible to use Access as the user interface to large company databases that reside on the mainframe computer.

Lesson 1: Switching between Applications Using the Taskbar

Application
A computer program dedicated to one type of function, such as word processing or database management.

As you learned in Project 1, the *taskbar* displays the Start button, open applications, and the time across the bottom of the screen. The taskbar is usually visible while you are using an *application* unless it has been customized to hide itself when not in use. If the taskbar is not currently displayed on-screen, it will appear when you move the mouse to the bottom of the screen. Try using the taskbar to switch between open programs now.

To Switch between Applications Using the Taskbar

1. **With Windows 95 loaded, launch the Access program.**
2. **Move the mouse pointer to the bottom edge of the screen to reveal the taskbar if it is hidden (see Figure 17.1).**

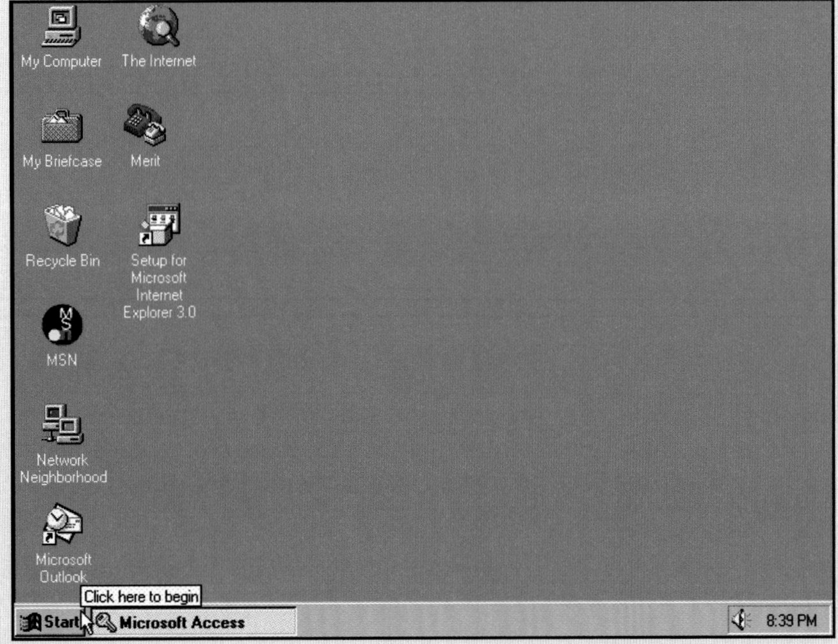

Figure 17.1
The Windows 95 taskbar showing the Access program in use.

❸ **Click the Start button and launch Microsoft Word. (Look in the Programs folder.)**

If you do not have Microsoft Word loaded on your computer, the taskbar will work with any other program launched in Windows 95.

❹ **Move the pointer to the bottom edge of the screen.**

The taskbar now shows that both Access and Word are in use (see Figure 17.2).

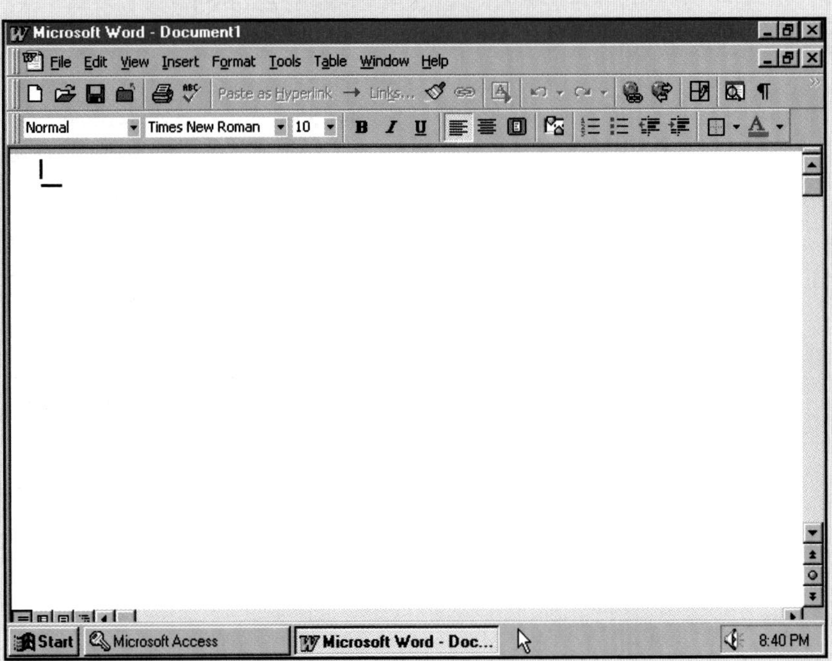

Figure 17.2
The Windows 95 taskbar showing the Access and Word programs in use.

continues

To Switch between Applications Using the Taskbar (continued)

5 To switch to the Access program, click anywhere in the rectangle that shows the Access icon.

This action does not close the Word program.

Leave the Access and Word programs open for use in the next lesson.

Lesson 2: Copying Tables and Queries to Microsoft Word Documents

At times, you may want to extract some key data from a large database and include it in a report. A convenient way to do this is to use a query in Access to create a dynaset and then copy the dynaset as a table in the Word document.

Try copying an Access query into a table in a Word document by using the steps that follow.

Jargon Watch

The term **table** has a slightly different meaning in a Word document. The data from an Access table or an Access query would be represented as a Word table. See the Help menu within the Word program for further information.

The term **dynaset** refers to a group of records in Access that includes specified fields and meets specified criteria.

To Copy an Access Query into a Table in a Word Document

1 Make a copy of the Proj1701 file and name the copy `Customer`.

This file will supply the query dynaset to be copied into the Word document.

2 Use the taskbar to switch to the Access program.

3 Open the Customer database in the Access program.

4 Click the Queries tab to reveal the queries.

5 Open the Customer List by City query.

6 From the Edit menu, choose Select All Records (see Figure 17.3).

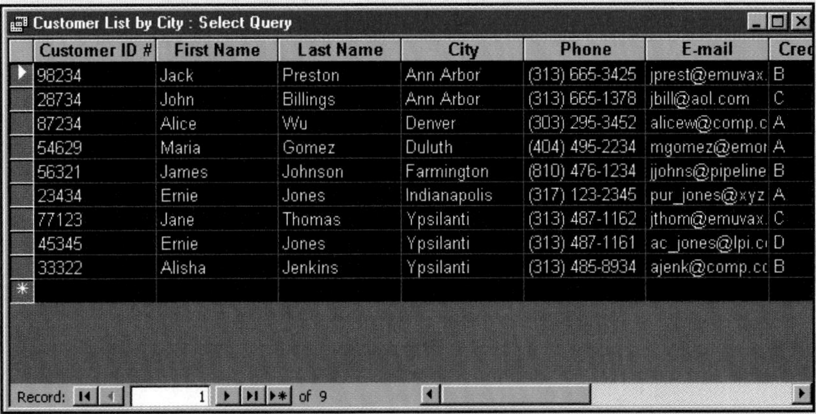

Customer ID #	First Name	Last Name	City	Phone	E-mail	Cred
98234	Jack	Preston	Ann Arbor	(313) 665-3425	jprest@emuvax.	B
28734	John	Billings	Ann Arbor	(313) 665-1378	jbill@aol.com	C
87234	Alice	Wu	Denver	(303) 295-3452	alicew@comp.c	A
54629	Maria	Gomez	Duluth	(404) 495-2234	mgomez@emor	A
56321	James	Johnson	Farmington	(810) 476-1234	jjohns@pipeline	B
23434	Ernie	Jones	Indianapolis	(317) 123-2345	pur_jones@xyz	A
77123	Jane	Thomas	Ypsilanti	(313) 487-1162	jthom@emuvax.	C
45345	Ernie	Jones	Ypsilanti	(313) 487-1161	ac_jones@lpi.c	D
33322	Alisha	Jenkins	Ypsilanti	(313) 485-8934	ajenk@comp.c	B

Figure 17.3
Select all the records in the query.

7 Click the Copy button on the toolbar.

8 Close the query but not the database.

9 Move the pointer to the taskbar at the bottom of the screen; click Microsoft Word.

10 Click the New button on the toolbar.

A new document opens to receive the query. (It is not necessary to open a new document; you can paste into an existing document just as easily.) Remember that the query will be inserted where the insertion point is located, not where the pointer may be.

11 From the Edit menu, choose Paste, or click the Paste button on the toolbar.

The table is pasted into the document (see Figure 17.4).

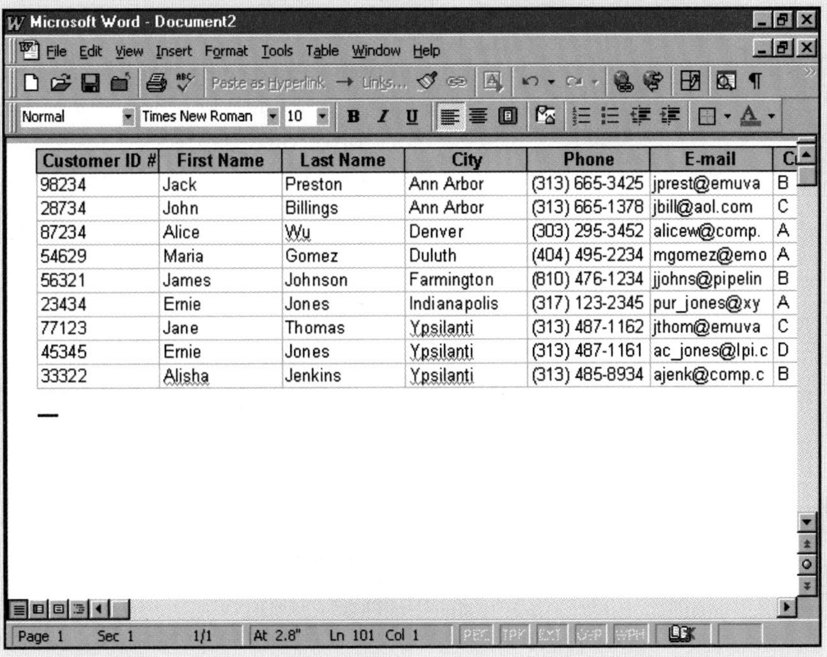

Customer ID #	First Name	Last Name	City	Phone	E-mail	C
98234	Jack	Preston	Ann Arbor	(313) 665-3425	jprest@emuva	B
28734	John	Billings	Ann Arbor	(313) 665-1378	jbill@aol.com	C
87234	Alice	Wu	Denver	(303) 295-3452	alicew@comp.	A
54629	Maria	Gomez	Duluth	(404) 495-2234	mgomez@emo	A
56321	James	Johnson	Farmington	(810) 476-1234	jjohns@pipelin	B
23434	Ernie	Jones	Indianapolis	(317) 123-2345	pur_jones@xy	A
77123	Jane	Thomas	Ypsilanti	(313) 487-1162	jthom@emuva	C
45345	Ernie	Jones	Ypsilanti	(313) 487-1161	ac_jones@lpi.c	D
33322	Alisha	Jenkins	Ypsilanti	(313) 485-8934	ajenk@comp.c	B

Figure 17.4
The Customer List by City query pasted into a Word document.

(If you have the spell checker set up to display unknown words, some of the proper names in the table will be underlined in red.)

continues

To Copy an Access Query into a Table in a Word Document (continued)

You need to change the page orientation to Landscape so that the table will fit the paper.

12 In Word, choose File and Page Setup from the menu. Click the Paper Size tab and the Landscape option button (see Figure 17.5). Click OK.

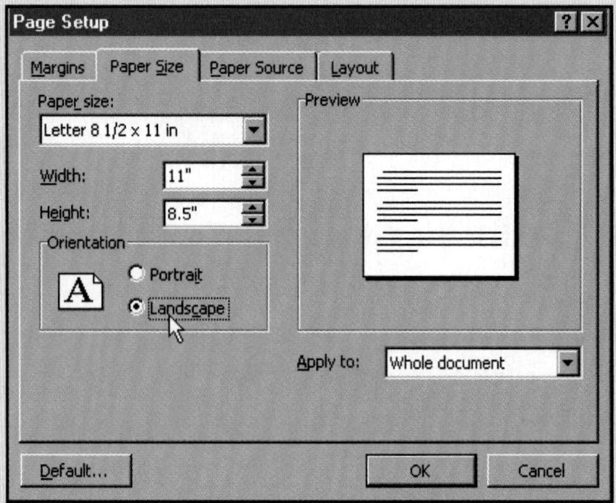

Figure 17.5
Change the orientation of the page to fit the query.

13 Click the Print button on the toolbar to print a copy for your records. (If requested by your instructor, print two copies.)

14 Close and save the document as `Customer List`.

15 Close the Word program.

If you do not want to copy a whole query dynaset, you can use the record selector buttons at the left side of the query to pick the records you want. You can select a block of records by clicking the first record selector and then selecting the last record in the block by holding down Shift while clicking. This action selects those two records *plus* all the ones between them. Access will not allow you to select records that do not make up a continuous block in a single step.

Lesson 3: Copying Tables or Queries to a Spreadsheet for Data Analysis

A spreadsheet performs certain types of data analysis more efficiently than a database management system does. If you need to take advantage of the power of your spreadsheet, you can copy the data in a table or query into most Windows-based spreadsheets.

A spreadsheet program has many more specialized financial and statistical functions than a database program has. If you use the database program to find and isolate the data according to certain criteria and then use the spreadsheet program to analyze it, you have a powerful combination of tools.

In this lesson, you copy the data from the Orders table of the Customer database into a Microsoft Excel spreadsheet. If you do not have Microsoft

Excel, try the following procedure with your Windows-based spreadsheet. If it does not work, ask your instructor for additional direction.

To Copy a Table or Query to a Spreadsheet (Microsoft Excel)

1 Use the taskbar to switch back to the Customer database in the Access program (if necessary).

2 Click the Tables tab to reveal the tables; then open the Orders table.

3 From the Edit menu, choose Select All Records.

This process is similar to the one in the preceding lesson. You may select a section of the query instead of all of it.

4 Click the Copy button on the toolbar and close the table.

If Access warns you that you have copied a large amount of data to the clipboard, click **Yes** and continue.

Next, you launch the Microsoft Excel program.

5 Click the Start button on the taskbar at the bottom of the screen.

6 Point to the Programs folder and then click Microsoft Excel.

7 Click the Paste button on the toolbar.

A copy of the Orders table is pasted into the spreadsheet (see Figure 17.6).

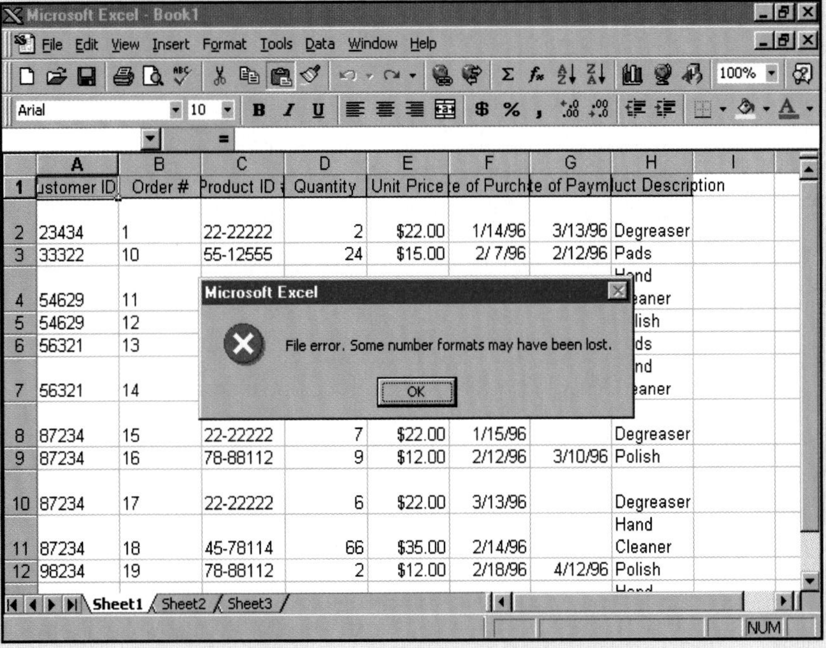

Figure 17.6 The Orders table pasted into a Microsoft Excel spreadsheet.

There are some differences in the way Access and Excel format numbers. In this case, a warning box appears because the currency format in the Unit Price field does not translate exactly. However, no data is lost. You can format the table in the Excel program.

continues

To Copy a Table or Query to a Spreadsheet (Microsoft Excel) (continued)

8. **Click OK to remove the warning box.**

9. **Click the Print button on the toolbar to print a copy for your records. (If requested by your instructor, print two copies.)**

10. **Close and save the workbook as `Orders`.**

11. **Close the Excel program.**

12. **Switch back to Access, close the Customer database, and close Access.**

Jargon Watch

The Excel program uses the term **workbook** to refer to a collection of spreadsheets. The different spreadsheets are selected by clicking their respective tabs found at the bottom of the window.

The formatting in your spreadsheet may not be exactly the same as shown in Figure 17.6. You can adjust the column widths the same way you adjust column widths in an Access table.

Lesson 4: Merging Data from Access into Documents in Microsoft Word

If you have ever received an advertising letter that referred to you personally instead of some general term such as "Occupant," you have seen the results of the merge between a word processing program and a database. This method is a common way of sending personalized letters to customers and business associates.

There are four basic steps to creating a document that merges data from a database:

- Open a new document in Word and start the Mail Merge procedure.
- Link the document to a data source.
- Type the form letter and insert field names from the database table or query into the letter.
- Preview and print the form letters.

In this lesson, you create a form letter that notifies those people who have not yet paid for their purchases. A link will be created between the form letter in Word and the Receivables query in a database similar to the one you created in Access.

To Open a Blank Document in Word and Start the Mail Merge Procedure

1. **Click the Start button and open the Microsoft Word program.**

2 Click the New button to open a new document in Word.

3 Click Tools on the menu bar and click the Mail Merge option. The Mail Merge Helper dialog box appears (see Figure 17.7).

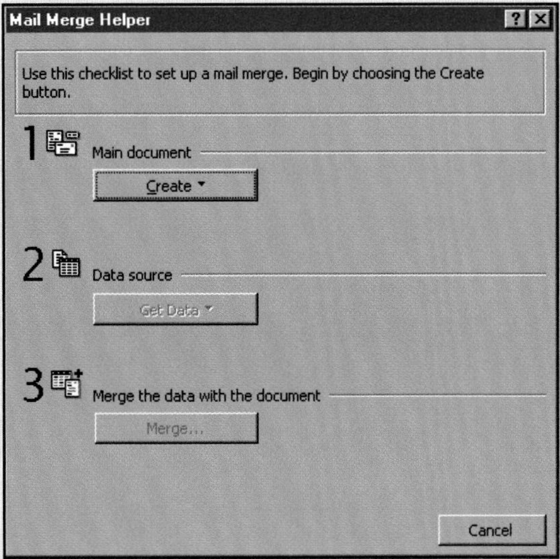

Figure 17.7
The Mail Merge Helper dialog box.

4 Click Create in the Main Document section.

A list of main document types appears.

5 Click Form Letters (see Figure 17.8).

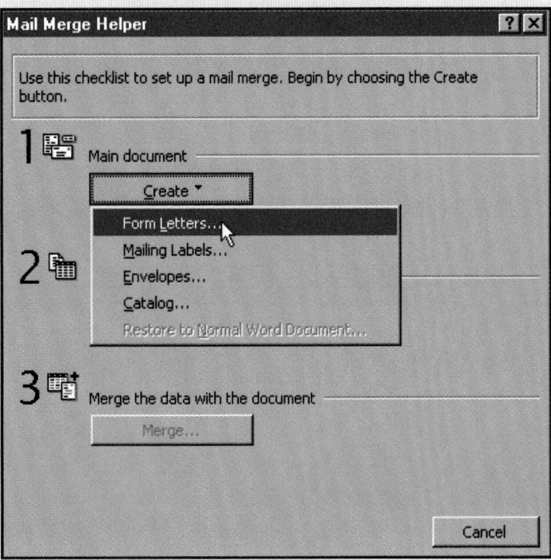

Figure 17.8
The Form Letters option.

You are presented with the option of using the current document or opening a new one to be used as the main document.

6 Click Active window to select the current blank document.

You return to the Mail Merge Helper dialog box.

The Word and Access programs are designed to work together for projects such as these. In the following tutorial, you learn how to bring the data from an Access table or query into the form letter.

To Link the Document to a Data Source

1 Click the Get Data button.

Word can use data from a variety of data sources.

2 Click Open Data Source (see Figure 17.9).

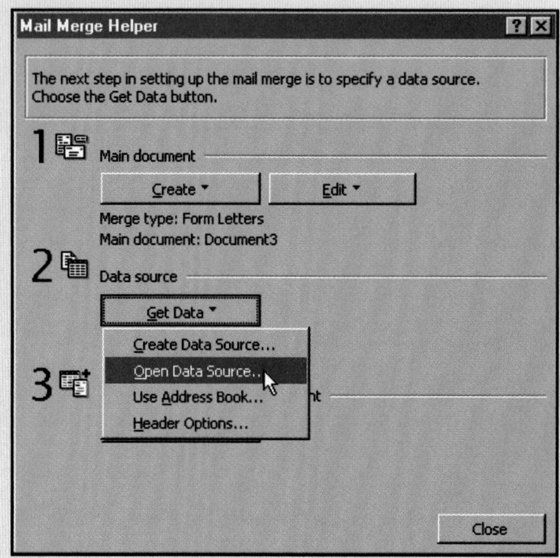

Figure 17.9 Opening a source of data.

The Open Data Source dialog box appears (see Figure 17.10).

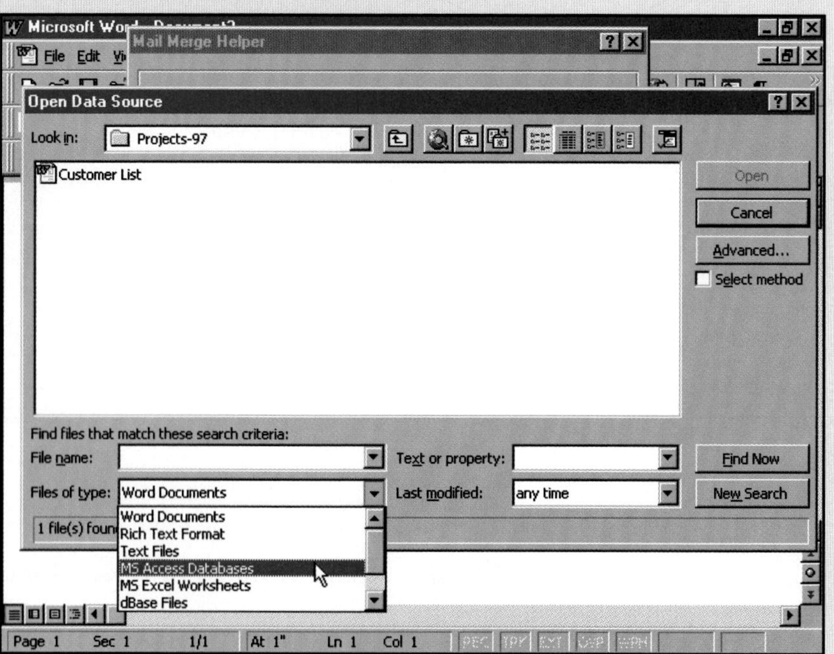

Figure 17.10 The Open Data Source dialog box.

3 In the Files of type box, click the down arrow to reveal a list of data source types.

4 Click MS Access Databases.

5 In the Look in box, find the drive and folder that contains the Customer database.

If you have problems...

If you are not in the folder that contains the Customer database, click the folder icon that has an arrow on it to move to the folder that contains the current list of files. If you do this repeatedly, you will see a list of drives and the folders they contain. Select the drive and the folder that contains the Customer database. See your instructor for further information regarding the location of this file.

6 Select the Customer database and click Open.

This opens the Microsoft Access dialog box.

7 Click the Queries tab to reveal the available queries.

8 Select the Receivables query and click OK.

This is the query that identifies the outstanding debts. The form letter will be sent to the people who owe money.

A Microsoft Word dialog box opens.

9 Click Edit Main Document.

The main document is opened with an additional toolbar for managing the link with the database (see Figure 17.11).

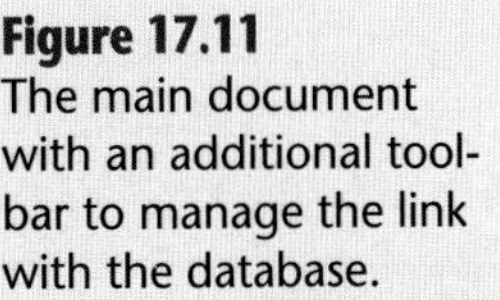

Figure 17.11
The main document with an additional toolbar to manage the link with the database.

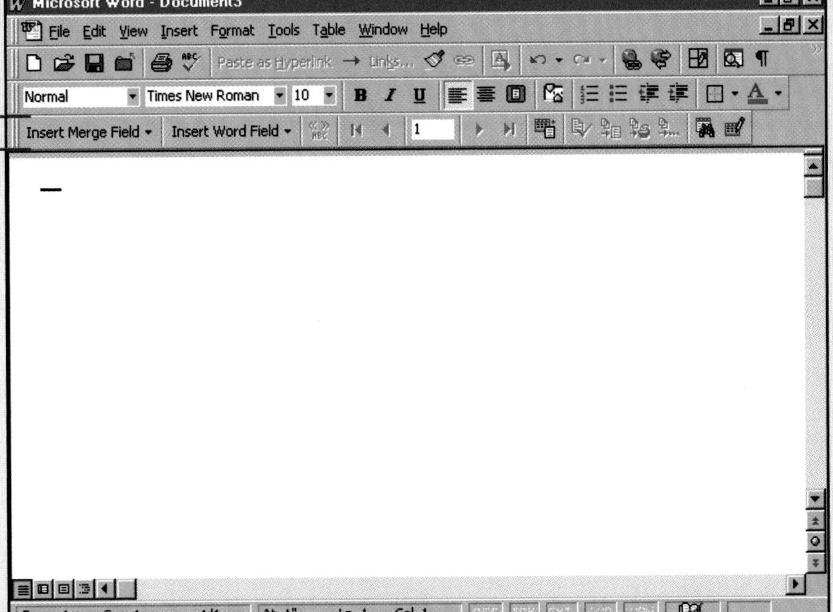

Word can use data from files created in database, spreadsheet, or text format. Word can also create its own data list and produce form letters without another program.

Next, you type the form letter and insert field names from the database into the letter.

To Type the Form Letter and Insert Field Names from the Database

1. **On the first line of the document, type the current date.**

   The process does not require this step; this example just shows a typical form letter.

2. **Press ↵Enter twice to create a blank line and move to the start of the third line.**

3. **Click the Insert Merge Field button on the toolbar.**

   A list of fields from the Access query is displayed. When you select a field from this list, the field is placed in the document at the current insertion point location.

4. **Select Title from the list of fields that appears (see Figure 17.12).**

   The field `<<Title>>` is placed in the main document.

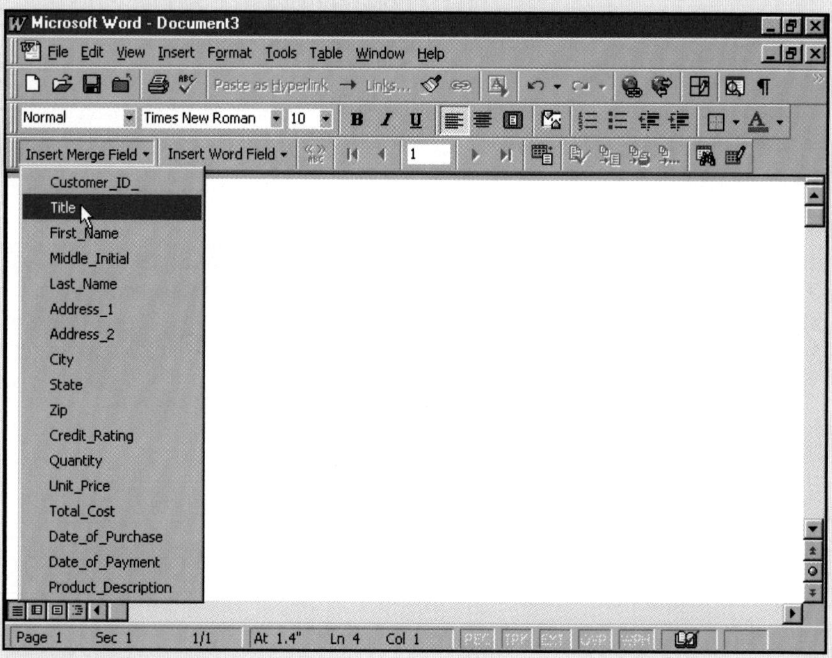

Figure 17.12
The available fields from the query.

5. **Press Spacebar to insert a space.**

6. **Click the Insert Merge Field button on the toolbar again.**

7. **Select First_Name from the list of fields.**

   The field `<<First_Name>>` is placed in the document.

8 Repeat this process to insert fields as you type the document to match the example in Figure 17.13.

Remember to add the necessary spaces and commas.

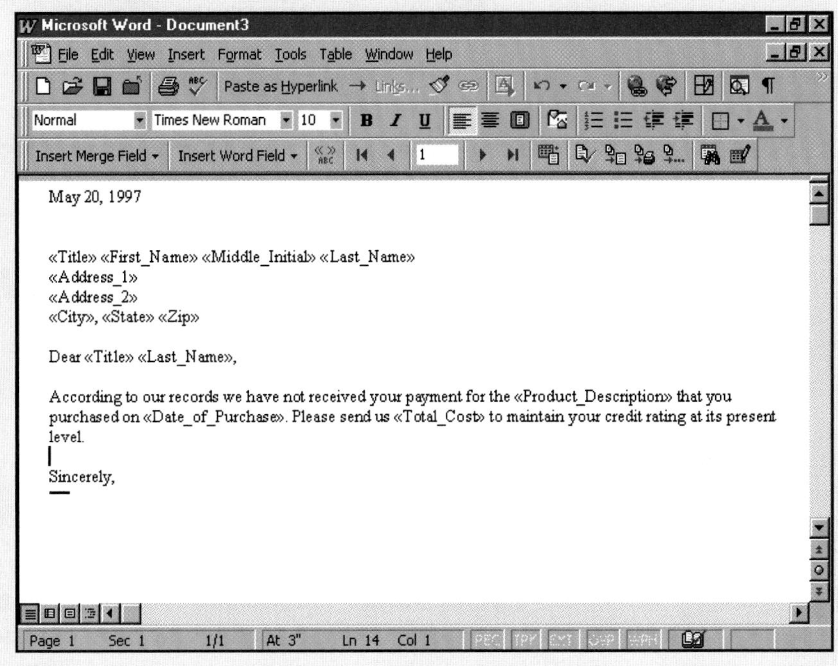

May 20, 1997

«Title» «First_Name» «Middle_Initial» «Last_Name»
«Address_1»
«Address_2»
«City», «State» «Zip»

Dear «Title» «Last_Name»,

According to our records we have not received your payment for the «Product_Description» that you purchased on «Date_of_Purchase». Please send us «Total_Cost» to maintain your credit rating at its present level.

Sincerely,

Figure 17.13
The main document with fields inserted.

If you want the date on the form letter to update itself automatically, use the Word command **I**nsert, Date and **T**ime. Click the **U**pdate Automatically checkbox in place of the first step in the preceding tutorial.

You should check the documents before you waste a lot of printing resources. In the next tutorial, you preview the records before you decide to print them.

To Preview and Print the Form Letters

1 Click the View Merged Data button on the toolbar.

This step enables you to view the contents of the query in the designated fields in the document (see Figure 17.14).

continues

To Preview and Print the Form Letters (continued)

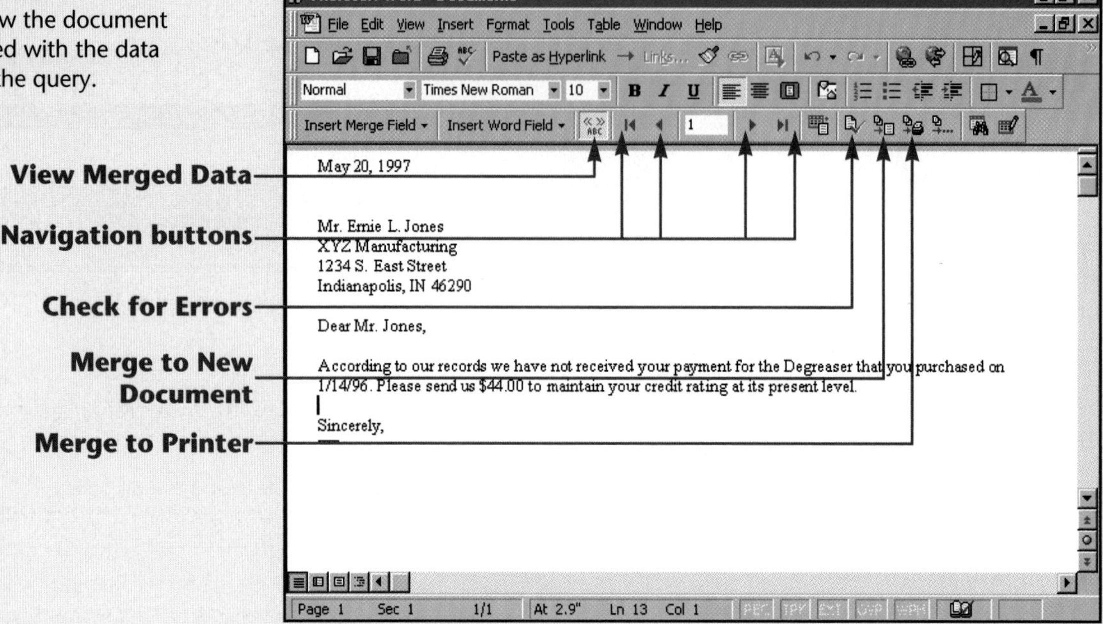

Figure 17.14
Preview the document merged with the data from the query.

2 Use the navigation buttons to scroll through the records in the query so that you can preview the form letters.

The Receivables query contains a record for each unpaid bill. In this design, a letter would be sent for each item. Do not be concerned if you have more than one letter for a person.

3 Click the Check for Errors button.

The Checking and Reporting Errors dialog box opens.

4 Select Simulate the merge and report errors in a new document, and click OK.

Word checks whether there are any problems that it recognizes.

5 A message box should appear to confirm that no errors were found. Click OK.

6 Click the Merge to New Document button to create a document that consists of a page for each of the letters.

7 Scroll through the new document.

Check for errors. Watch for inconsistent usage such as `"Dear Baker"`; you may have used the Last_Name field where you intended to use the First_Name field.

8 From the File menu, click Print.

You want to print only the first three pages.

9 Type `1-3` in the Pages box.

10 Change the number of copies to `2` if a second copy is requested by your instructor. Then click OK.

11. **Close the document but do not save it.**

    This document was used for previewing the final printout. It may be re-created from the main document and the database.

12. **Close the main document and name it `Receivables`.**

13. **Close Word.**

    The next time you need to send reminder letters to the people who owe money, this document can be opened, and the current list of people from the database will be used.

Lesson 5: Importing Tables from Databases, Spreadsheets, and Text Files

Tables are often created in spreadsheets and other database management programs. In some cases, the table of data has been created by a word processing program or has been downloaded from a mainframe computer. You may want to use the advanced, user-friendly tools in Access to work with this data.

You have two options: you can import the data into a table in an Access database, or you can leave the table in its native form and link it to an Access database. In this lesson, you learn how to import data into an Access database.

Consider three types of data tables to be imported: tables from other database management programs such as dBASE, tables from spreadsheet programs such as Microsoft Excel, and text tables of data of unknown design.

Access has been available for only a few years, and there are many valuable tables of data available in other database formats. The most commonly used database management program for personal computers in the 1980s was dBASE. Consequently, most newer database programs have been designed to read dBASE files. These files are usually identified by the extension .dbf.

To Import a Table Created by Another Database Program (dBASE)

1. **Make a copy of the Proj1702.dbf file and name the copy `MichRetl.dbf`.**

   Make sure that you type the .dbf extension. Most personal computers that use Windows or its predecessor, DOS, attach a three-letter extension to the file names. Windows 95 normally does not display these letters when it lists files created by recent versions of Microsoft programs. All dBASE databases have the .dbf extension so Access will not identify this file as a dBASE file without the extension.

2. **Open the Access program.**

   You are not required to create a new database; files can be imported as new tables into existing databases.

continues

To Import a Table Created by Another Database Program (dBASE) (continued)

3. **Select a blank database and choose OK.**
4. **Select the drive and folder where you want to save this database.**
5. **Name it `Example` and click the Create button.**

   A new database window appears.

6. **From the File menu, choose Get External Data.**
7. **Move the pointer to the right and select Import.**

   The Import dialog box appears.

8. **Move to the Files of type box. Select dBASE III from the list of possible sources (see Figure 17.15).**

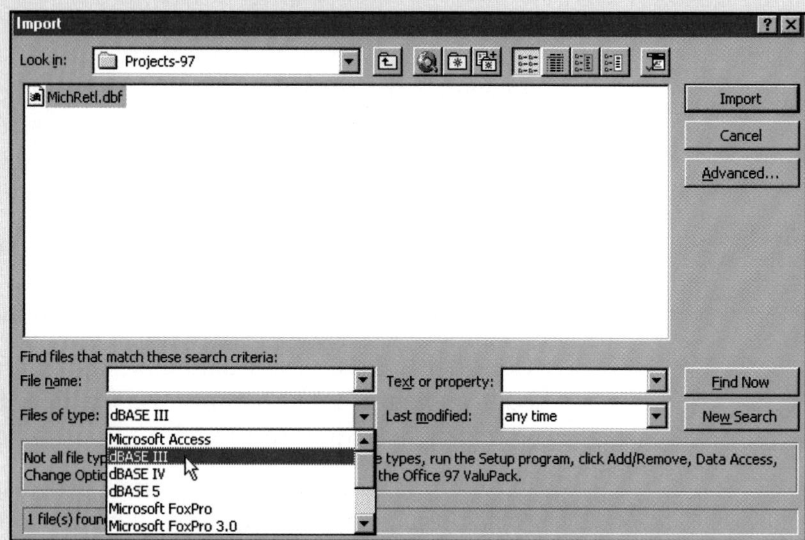

Figure 17.15
Several different types of files may be imported.

   Notice that Access can read several other types of files, including spreadsheets and text files.

9. **Find the MichRetl.dbf file that you copied earlier, select it, and click the Import button.**

   Access notifies you when it has finished importing the data.

10. **Click OK and then close the Import dialog box.**
11. **Open the new table.**

    This is a database of retail sales figures for each zip code area in Michigan for the year 1987. This type of data is available from the government on compact disc or over the Internet. In this example, the Sales and Payroll fields show numbers in the thousands. The first record is a summary for all the zip codes in the state.

12. **Print pages 1–2 for your files. (If requested by your instructor, print two copies.)**

    Close the table. Leave the Example database open for use in the next tutorial.

Next, you'll import a table from a spreadsheet. Spreadsheets are set up in rows and columns like a database table. However, in many cases, the data is interspersed with titles and formulas that do not correspond to a simple row-and-column format. If a spreadsheet is to be imported into Access as a table, the spreadsheet must have a structure that is very similar to a table.

If the first row of the spreadsheet contains labels, they can be converted into field names. The second row should contain the data for the first record in the table. If the spreadsheet that you want to import is not set up this way, copy the data from the spreadsheet and paste the data into a new spreadsheet in the simple row-and-column format, then save it.

To Import a Table from a Spreadsheet Program (Microsoft Excel)

1. **Make a copy of the file Proj1703 and name the copy `Expenses`.**
2. **Switch to Access and the Example database.**
3. **Choose File, Get External Data, Import.**
4. **Move to the Files of type box and select Microsoft Excel from the list of spreadsheets.**
5. **Find the Expenses file and click Import.**

   The Import Spreadsheet Wizard dialog box appears (see Figure 17.16).

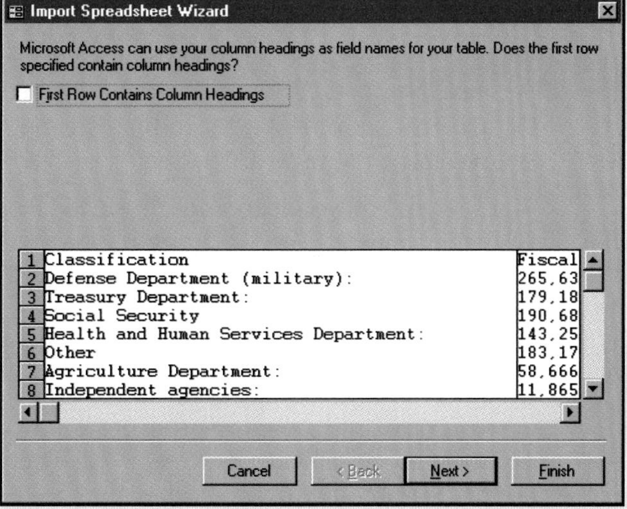

Figure 17.16
The Import Spreadsheet Wizard dialog box.

6. **Check the First Row Contains Column Headings box. Click Next.**
7. **Confirm that the data will be stored in a new table. Click Next.**
8. **Do not add indexes to any of the fields. Click Next again.**
9. **Select No Primary Key and click Next.**
10. **Name the table `Government Expenses` and click Finish.**

    A dialog box is displayed to indicate when the data has been imported.

continues

To Import a Table from a Spreadsheet Program (Microsoft Excel) (continued)

11. **Click OK.**
12. **Open the Government Expenses table.**

This is a table of the money spent by the U.S. government, in millions of dollars, from 1986 to 1989.

Close the table but leave Access and the Example database open for use in the next tutorial.

If you have problems...

If the data in the spreadsheet has been set up in a table format with one record of information per row, the data can be imported into the database. Most problems occur when the spreadsheet is not set up in a simple format. Check to see whether the column headings occupy one cell per column. Make sure that graphic characters such as dashes or asterisks that may have been used to separate sections of the table are deleted. Make sure that the data is arranged so that there is one record of information per row of the spreadsheet table.

Sometimes the data you have to work with is in simple text form. This type of table could come from a word processor, a mainframe computer, or some unknown source on the Internet.

Fixed-width fields
Fields that occupy a fixed position in the record such as characters 5 through 12. No characters are used to separate the fields.

Delimiters
The characters that separate fields; set off text from numbers; and separate parts of dates, times, and currencies.

Field separator
The delimiter that separates the fields in a row of data.

In some cases, database records are stored as continuous strings of characters and numbers. When this method is used, the fields are always the same width. For example, the second field may be the 10th through the 20th characters in the record. These are called *fixed-width field* designs.

This design can result in a lot of wasted storage space. In most designs, certain characters are used to mark the separation between fields. Special characters can also be used to designate the separation of the parts of a date, the dollars and cents of a currency field, or the minutes and seconds of a time field. These characters are called *delimiters*.

There are several ways to create separate columns of data in a table. In most word processing programs, the fields are separated by a tab character. In some database tables, a space is used. These are known as Space Delimited Fields (SDFs). Similarly, commas may be used in Comma Delimited Fields (CDFs). The type of delimiter that is used to separate the fields in a row of data is called the *field separator*.

In some database tables, the data in each field is assumed to be numeric, and text is enclosed by single or double quotation marks. These are called *text delimiters*.

The program must be told how to handle dates in the table. Many countries format dates in a Day/Month/Year sequence. For example, January 25, 1997 is written as 1/25/97 in the United States but would be written as 25.01.97 in France and 97-01-25 in Sweden. The program must also know whether zeros are used as leading characters for single-digit months and days. Access provides a dialog box where you can set these and other variables.

In the following example, the table can be read as a text file. To analyze the structure of this table, use the steps that follow.

To Identify the Structure of a Table from an Unknown Source

1 Make a copy of the file Pro1704 and name the copy `Parts`.

2 Open the Microsoft Word program.

3 Click the Open button on the toolbar and change the Files of type box to All Files.

4 Open the Parts table.

5 Click the Show/Hide button on the toolbar to reveal the tabs (see Figure 17.17).

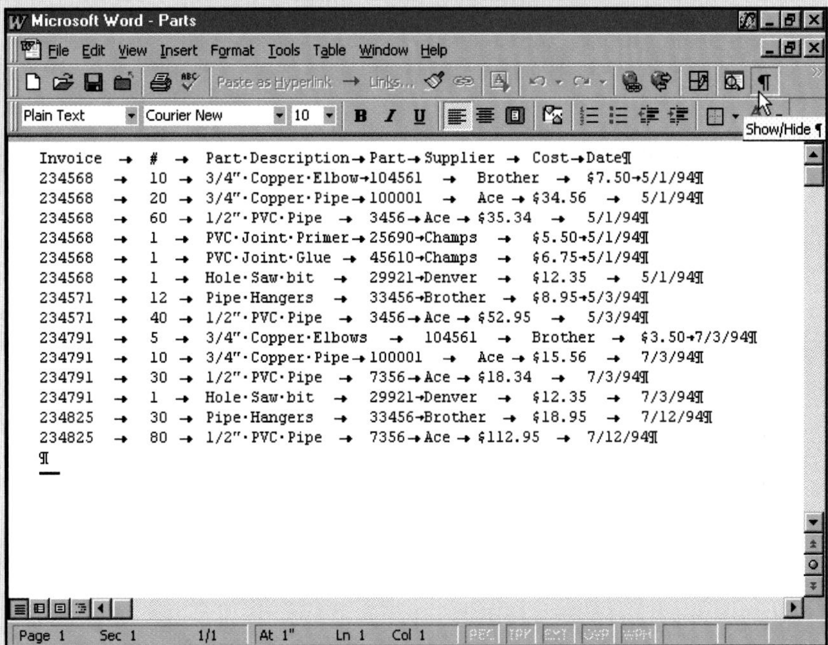

Figure 17.17
The Parts table in Word, showing the table's structure.

You will also be able to see where the spaces, paragraph marks, line breaks, and page breaks may be.

In this example, note the following features:

- The first row contains labels that can be used as field names.
- The fields are separated by tabs (indicated by the arrows).
- The text is not enclosed by quotation marks, but quotation marks are used to abbreviate inches.
- A currency field uses a decimal point to separate dollars and cents.
- None of the fields contains times with colons.
- A date field uses the Month/Day/Year method, slashes for separation, and no leading zeros.

continues

To Identify the Structure of a Table from an Unknown Source (continued)

6 Save the document as a text file. Close the document and close Microsoft Word.

If you have problems...

Word processors insert special control characters whenever you press Spacebar or ↵Enter. They also can insert special characters to force a new page (page break) or a new line (line break). These additional characters can cause problems. If they do, make a backup copy of the file, then use the find and replace function of the word processor to remove them.

After you have determined the structure of the table, you can tell the Access program what it needs to know to successfully import the table. To import a table that is in text form, use the following steps.

To Import the Table

1 Switch to Access and the Example database that is still open from the preceding tutorial.

2 Choose File, Get External Data, and Import.

The Import dialog box appears.

3 Move to the Files of type box and select Text Files.

The Import dialog box shows the available text files (see Figure 17.18).

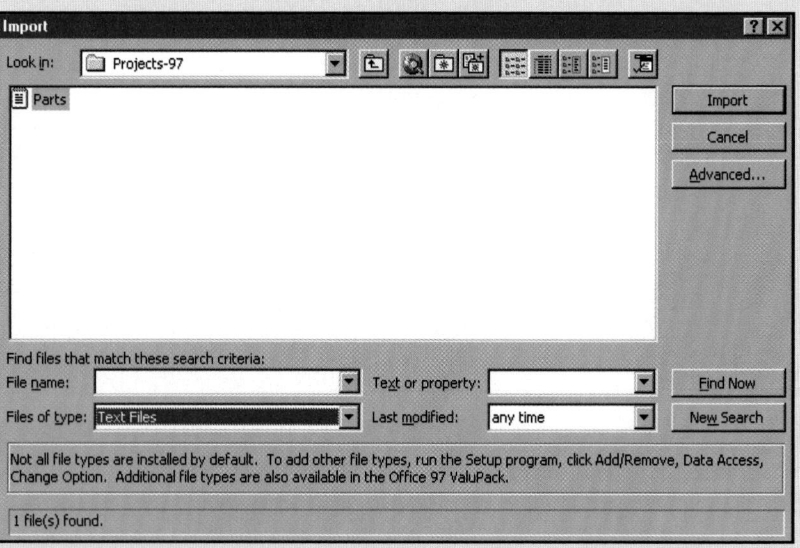

Figure 17.18
The Import dialog box displays the available text files.

4 Select the Parts file and click Import.

The Import Text Wizard dialog box appears (see Figure 17.19).

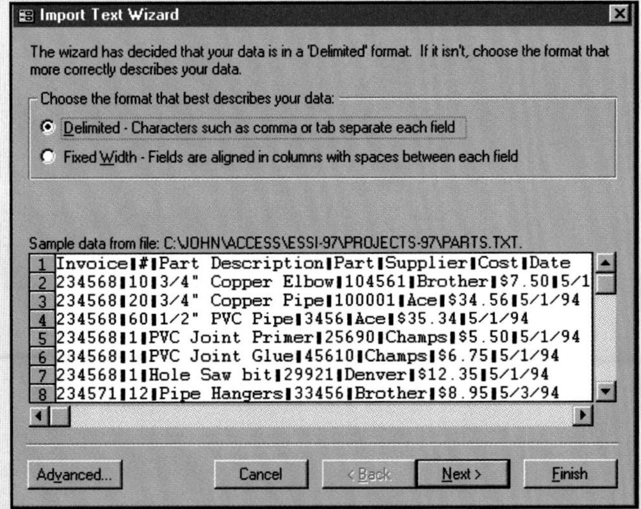

Figure 17.19
The Import Text Wizard dialog box.

❺ **Make sure that Delimited is selected. (The fields were separated by tabs.)**

❻ **Click Next.**

Another Wizard dialog box appears (see Figure 17.20).

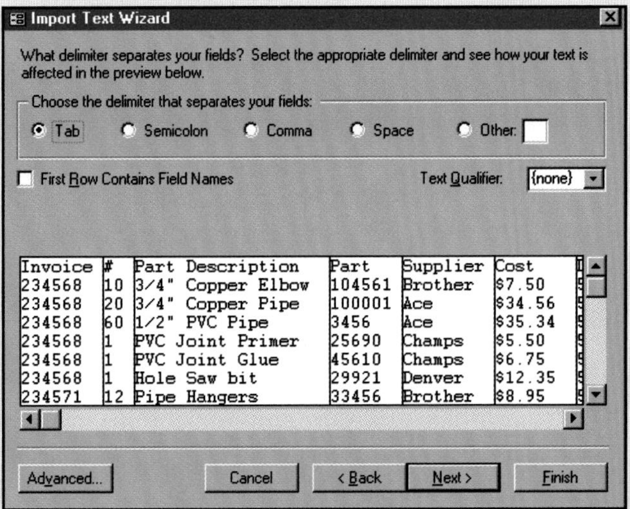

Figure 17.20
The second Import Text Wizard dialog box.

❼ **Set the following options as they are shown in Figure 17.21.**

- ➤ Confirm that the Tab delimiter is used to separate fields.
- ➤ Confirm that the Text **Q**ualifier is set to `{none}`. The text fields did not have special delimiters to distinguish them from numeric fields.
- ➤ Click the First **R**ow Contains Field Names checkbox, and then click **N**ext.

continues

To Import the Table (continued)

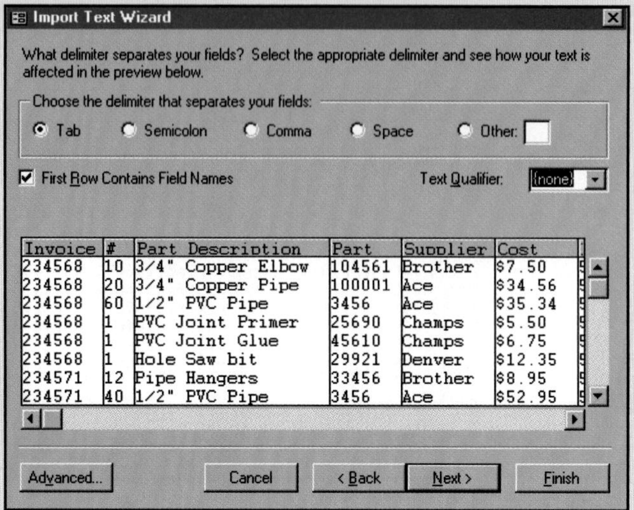

Figure 17.21
The Import Text Wizard dialog box with options.

8. **Confirm the New Table option and then click Next.**
9. **Use the default settings to import all the fields; then click Next.**
10. **Select No Primary Key and click Next.**
11. **Accept the name `Parts` and click Finish to import the table.**
12. **Click OK after you have read the import statement.**

If you have problems...

If Access does not successfully import the table, it will create a list of problems that it encountered. Because there are so many ways of storing data, the method described in this section is intended only as a guide to solving these problems, not as an exhaustive set of solutions. With these tools, you may be able to gain access (pun intended) to many other tables of data, but not necessarily all of them.

The Parts table is now a table in the Example database (see Figure 17.22).

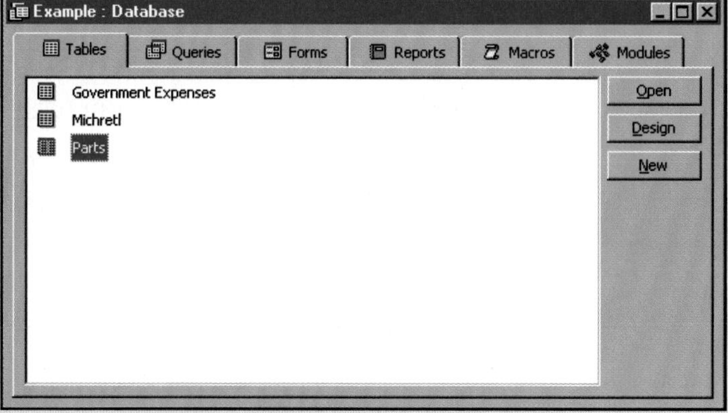

Figure 17.22
The Example database with the Parts table.

13 Open the new Parts table in the Example database (see Figure 17.23).

Figure 17.23
The new Parts table after it has been imported.

Parts : Table

Invoice	#	Part Descriptio	Part	Supplier	Cost
234568	10	3/4" Copper Elb	104561	Brother	$7
234568	20	3/4" Copper Pip	100001	Ace	$34
234568	60	1/2" PVC Pipe	3456	Ace	$35
234568	1	PVC Joint Prim	25690	Champs	$5
234568	1	PVC Joint Glue	45610	Champs	$6
234568	1	Hole Saw bit	29921	Denver	$12
234571	12	Pipe Hangers	33456	Brother	$6
234571	40	1/2" PVC Pipe	3456	Ace	$52
234791	5	3/4" Copper Elb	104561	Brother	$3
234791	10	3/4" Copper Pip	100001	Ace	$15
234791	30	1/2" PVC Pipe	7356	Ace	$16
234791	1	Hole Saw bit	29921	Denver	$12
234825	30	Pipe Hangers	33456	Brother	$16
234825	80	1/2" PVC Pipe	7356	Ace	$112

Record: 1 of 15

14 Close the table, but leave the database open for use in the next lesson.

If you ask someone from the computing division of your company for a copy of a database that you can use on your PC, request the data in one of the following formats:

- A dBASE III, dBASE IV, or dBASE V format on a floppy disk formatted for a PC
- An *ASCII* text file that uses tab delimiters as field separators on a floppy disk formatted for a PC

ASCII
A standard text format that all PCs can read.

If you need to import a table from a word processor or some unknown source, open the table in Microsoft Word and click the Show/Hide button. You can then see what type of delimiters are used. If the database is large, use the **F**ind feature to search for quotation marks, slashes, hyphens, periods, or colons that may be used to delimit text, dates, times, and currency. Search for instances that may confuse the computer. For example, if the computer is using single quotation marks to distinguish text from numbers, the use of the same character as an apostrophe in words like `John's` or `can't` can cause a problem.

One method of determining the structure of a table from an unknown source is to read the table into a word processor and reveal the hidden formatting codes. This method does not always work, but it is useful when it does.

Lesson 6: Linking Tables to Access from Other Databases

Sometimes you may want to view data from another database without importing it into Access. In this case, you can link a table from the other database to your database. This can even be done over a network and can work with mainframe databases. Now try linking a dBASE III database table to your Example database.

To Link a Table to Access from Another Database

1. **Make a copy of the file Proj1705.dbf and name the copy `MichServ.dbf`.**
2. **Use the taskbar to switch to Access and the Example database.**
3. **Choose File, Get External Data, and Link Tables.**

   The Link dialog box appears (see Figure 17.24).

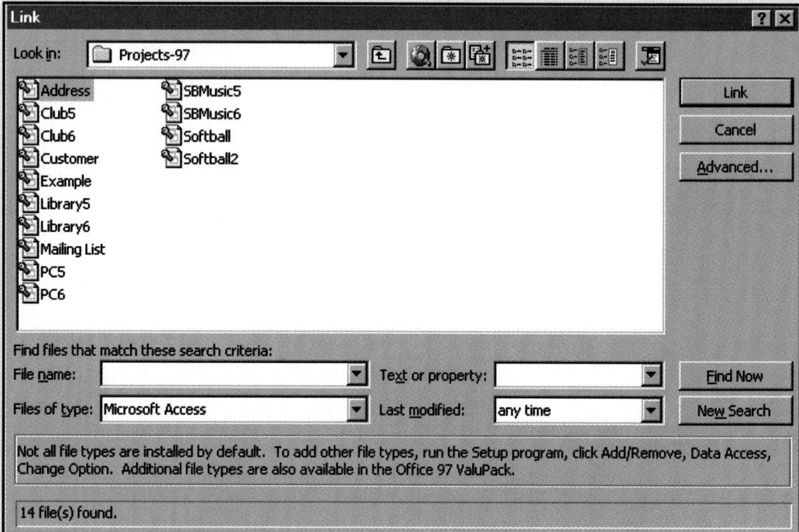

Figure 17.24
The Link dialog box.

4. **Select dBASE III in the Files of type box.**
5. **Select the database MichServ that you just copied.**
6. **Click Link.**
7. **The Select Index Files dialog box appears.**
8. **Click Cancel.**

   The dBASE program stored its indexes as separate files. There are no index files in this example.
9. **Click OK when the message appears that tells you the table has been successfully linked.**
10. **Close the Link dialog box.**

    The Example database window displays the linked table with a special icon to indicate that it is linked to a database (dB) file (see Figure 17.25).

Figure 17.25
The Example database with the MichServ table linked.

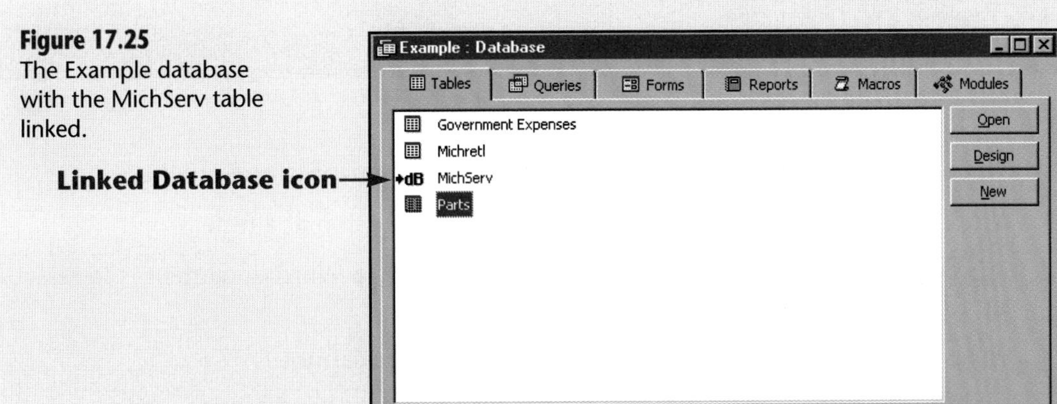

11 Open the MichServ table and view the contents.

This table contains data from 1987 about the service companies in Michigan summarized for each zip code. The Receipts (RCPT) field and the Payroll field represent thousands of dollars. The record for zip code 00000 represents the totals for the whole state.

Close the table. Close Word and Excel, if they are still open. If you have completed your session on the computer, exit Access and click the Start button on the taskbar to start the shut-down procedure. Otherwise, continue with the section "Checking Your Skills" in this project.

Project Summary

To	Do This
Switch between applications	Use the taskbar at the bottom of the screen.
Copy tables and queries to Word	Use **E**dit and Select **A**ll Records. Copy the records, switch to the Word document, and paste.
Copy tables or queries to a spreadsheet	Use **E**dit and Select **A**ll Records. Copy the records, switch to the spreadsheet, and paste.
Merge data from Access into Word	Open a new document in Word. Choose **T**ools, Mail Me**r**ge. Select a form letter. Select the database that has the information you want. Insert fields into the document. Test and merge to a single document. Print the pages you want.
Import tables from text documents	Open a database in Access. Choose **F**ile, **G**et External Data, **I**mport. Select text files as the file type and select the file. Answer the wizard's questions about delimiters, text identifiers, and column headers.
Link other database tables to Access	Open a database in Access. Choose File, Get External Data, Link Tables. Specify the type of table, select the table, and link it.

Checking Your Skills

True/False

For each of the following, check *T* or *F* to indicate whether the statement is true or false.

__T __F **1.** Windows 95 is designed to work best with one application at a time.

__T __F **2.** One way to transfer the contents of an Access table to a Word document is to select the table, and use copy and paste.

__T __F **3.** Tables can be copied to a Word document, but queries cannot.

__T __F **4.** An example of the coordination of two applications is called Mail Merge.

__T __F **5.** It is easier to import data into Access from another microcomputer database program such as dBASE than from an unknown table.

__T __F **6.** All word processors use generic character sets so that you can import data to programs such as Microsoft Access.

__T __F **7.** You can add to a form letter a date that updates itself automatically.

__T __F **8.** Microsoft Excel and Microsoft Access use identical formatting for numbers.

__T __F **9.** Microsoft Excel has many more specialized financial and statistical functions than Microsoft Access.

__T __F **10.** Before you enter Word Mail Merge, you must be in the folder that contains the source file.

Multiple Choice

Circle the letter of the correct answer for each of the following questions.

1. By default, where is the Windows 95 taskbar located?

- **a.** At the top of the screen
- **b.** On the right side of the screen
- **c.** On the left side of the screen
- **d.** At the bottom of the screen
- **e.** In the center of the screen (revealed by pressing Alt+T)

2. Which of the following statements is *not* true about copying a table from Access to Word?

- **a.** You must select the table or a range of cells in the table.
- **b.** The process copies only the cell contents; you must type the labels for each column after the table has been transferred.
- **c.** You may use the copy selection from the menu bar in Access and the paste selection from the menu bar in Word to accomplish the task.
- **d.** You may use the Copy button from the toolbar in Access and the Paste button from the toolbar in Word to accomplish the task.
- **e.** A query in Access will become a Word table after it is copied.

3. Which of the following statements is *not* true about importing an Excel spreadsheet into Access?
   - a. Any form of spreadsheet can be imported directly as a table.
   - b. The spreadsheet must be in a simple row-and-column format.
   - c. The spreadsheet may contain a row of labels that will serve as field names in the new table.
   - d. The copy-and-paste method does not work for importing spreadsheets into Access 2.0 tables.
   - e. Access can import spreadsheets that were created in the Lotus 1-2-3 spreadsheet program.
4. Which of the following is the best reason to link a table rather than import it?
   - a. The table was created by another database management software.
   - b. The table was created by (and will continue to be used by) someone else who has a different database management program.
   - c. The table is in a spreadsheet.
   - d. The table was created by a word processor.
   - e. The table was downloaded from a mainframe computer onto a floppy disk.
5. After you have set up a mail merge document linked to a table in Access, what is the next step?
   - a. Send it to the printer.
   - b. Click the View Merged Data button to see how the data looks in the document.
   - c. Save the file and close it.
   - d. Switch to Access and close the database.
   - e. None of the above
6. Which of the following is *not* one of the four basic steps in creating a document that merges data from a database?
   - a. Open a new document in Word and start the Mail Merge procedure.
   - b. Link the document to a data source.
   - c. Select AutoField Fill to place the fields in the Word document.
   - d. Preview and print the form letters.
7. Which of the following steps is *not* necessary when importing a text file to an Access table?
   - a. Determine the number of records to be imported.
   - b. Identify the file to import.
   - c. Determine whether the file is fixed-width or delimited.
   - d. Determine whether the data is to go into an existing table or a new table.
8. In Mail Merge, Word can use data from which of the following?
   - a. A database such as Access
   - b. A spreadsheet such as Excel
   - c. Another Word file
   - d. All of the above
9. Viewing data in Access without loading it is accomplished by which of the following?
   - a. Loading the data into a view table
   - b. Importing the data into a temporary database
   - c. Merging the data with a temporary file
   - d. Linking a table from another database to the current database
10. The taskbar does *not* display which of the following?
    - a. the Start button
    - b. the clock (when the option is selected)
    - c. the amount of memory used
    - d. the open applications

Completion

In the blank provided, write the correct answer for each of the following statements.

1. The bar that appears by default across the bottom of the screen to show open applications is called a(n) ______________.
2. The characters that separate fields; set off text from numbers; and separate parts of dates, times, and currencies are called ______________.
3. The menu selection that starts the process of creating a document to be combined with a database is ______________.
4. If you transform a database that was created in dBASE into a table in Access, you ______________ it.
5. If you link a table from another source to an Access database without turning the table into an Access table, you ______________ it.
6. There are ______________ basic steps to creating a document that merges data into Word from a database.
7. A standard text format that all PCs can read is called ______________.
8. Excel uses the term ______________ to refer to a collection of spreadsheets.
9. ______________ are fields that occupy a fixed position in a record and do not use characters to separate the fields.
10. The term ______________ has a slightly different meaning in Word than in Access.

Matching

In the blank next to each of the following terms or phrases, write the letter of the corresponding term or phrase. (Note that some letters may be used more than once.)

_____ **1.** Stepwise process to assist in loading ASCII data into a table

_____ **2.** Windows 95 object used to switch between active applications

_____ **3.** The delimiter that separates the fields in a row of data

_____ **4.** To associate a table from another database without loading the database

_____ **5.** **E**dit menu selection used to highlight all records in a dynaset or table

_____ **6.** Toolbar button in Word used to place a database field in a document

_____ **7.** A field designation in Mail Merge

_____ **8.** A special character used by some word processors

_____ **9.** A process for placing an Access table in an Excel spreadsheet

_____ **10.** To load external data into Access

a. import

b. <<Title>>

c. **C**opy and **P**aste

d. Text Import Wizard

e. field separator

f. page break

g. Select **A**ll Records

h. link

i. taskbar

j. Insert Merge Field button

Screen ID

Identify each of the items shown in Figure 17.26.

Figure 17.26

1.________________

2.________________

3.________________

4.________________

5.________________

6.________________

7.________________

8.________________

9.________________

10.________________

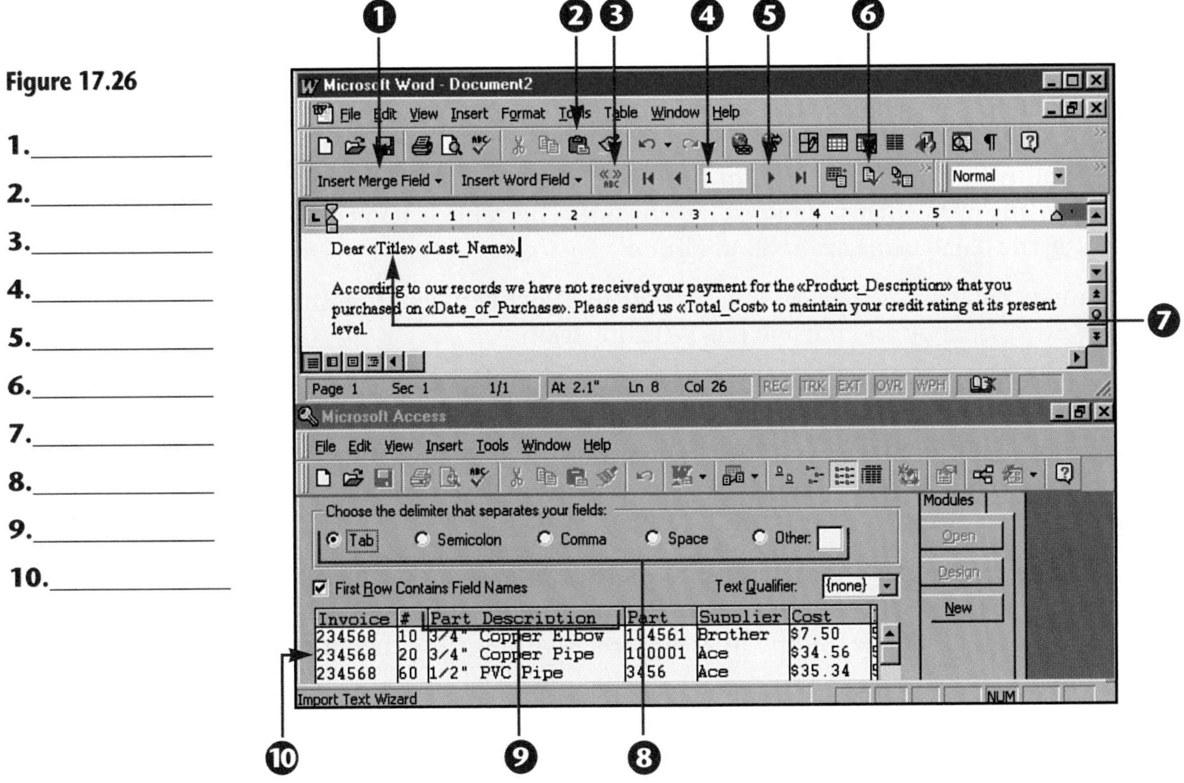

Applying Your Skills

Practice

The following exercises enable you to practice the skills you have learned in this project. Take a few minutes to work through these exercises now.

1. Copying Your Books Table to a Word Processing Program

The reports you can create using your Library database and your Books table are fine, but you may want more control over the look of your documents. You may find it easier to format and edit the list in a word processing program rather than in Access. In this case, you can copy the data from Access and paste it into a word processing program. Then you can use all the formatting and editing features of that program. Now try copying your book data to Word (or to another word processing program available to you).

To Copy Table Data from Access to Word

1. Make a copy of the Proj1706 database file and name the copy `Library7`. Then return to Access and open the `Library7` database and the `Books` table.
2. Select all the data in the table and copy the data to the Clipboard.

3. Use the Start button on the taskbar to launch Microsoft Word.
4. Paste the data from the Clipboard into the blank document. Save the document with the name **Booklist**.

2. Locating the Best Area in Michigan for a Uniform Store

Assume that you are employed by a company that sells uniforms. The company wants to locate an outlet in Michigan and wants to place the outlet where there is a concentration of retail establishments. You have obtained a table of data from the government that shows the number of retail establishments in Michigan, grouped by zip code. This table is named MichRetl.dbf, and it was created using the database program dBASE III.

Open a new database named **Uniform**. Import the MichRetl.dbf table that you have already copied and renamed, or copy and rename Proj1702.dbf again.

Create a query that is based on this table and includes all of its fields. Sort it in descending order by the number of establishments (the ESTAB field). Limit the list to those records with more than 400 establishments (enter **>400** in the Criteria box). Do not show the summary record that has a zip code of 00000 (enter **>0** in the Criteria box of the zip code field). Switch to Datasheet view. You should get a list of about 12 records.

Copy this list of records and paste it into a Microsoft Word document. Add a few lines of text to the document to explain the list of figures. Print the document. (If requested by your instructor, print two copies.) Save the document as **Uniform**. Save and close the query and database.

3. Transferring Data to a Spreadsheet for Statistical Analysis

You want to study employee wages for those in service businesses in Michigan. You have obtained a table of data from the government that shows the number of employees in each zip code area of Michigan, and the total wages paid to those employees by zip code. This table was created by the dBASE III program. To do your study, you want to perform various mathematical and statistical analyses on the data using tools that are available in Microsoft Excel.

Use the copy of MichServ.dbf that you have already made, or copy and rename Proj1705.dbf again. Open a new database in Access named **Wages** and import the MichServ table.

Create a query based on this table that contains all its fields. Eliminate the record that contains the totals for the state (zip code 00000) by entering **Not "00000"** as a criterion in the zip field. Include only the zip codes with 5,000 employees or more by entering **>5000** in the Criteria box for the EMPLOYEE field. Sort on the EMPLOYEE field in descending order. Save the query and name it **Areas With More Than 5000 Workers**.

Switch to Datasheet view and select all the records. Copy the records. Open a Microsoft Excel spreadsheet and paste the records into the spreadsheet. Then print it. (If requested by your instructor, print two copies.) Save the spreadsheet and name it **Wages**. Close the spreadsheet and close Excel. Close the database.

4. Getting a Helping Hand

Two of the common uses of Access are to store and manipulate data used in word processing or presentations. The Mail Merge feature was specifically designed to assist in the process. There are two ways to approach Mail Merge. One is from the word processor side (as with Microsoft Word, which you use in this text); the other is to view Mail Merge from the database side.

To Get Help on Topics in This Project

1. Run Microsoft Access.
2. Select Cancel in the opening dialog box.
3. Press F1. The Office Assistant opens, and the words `Type your question here, and then click Search` appear in the entry box.
4. Type the words **`mail merge`** and press ↵Enter. A list of topics appears in the comment bubble.
5. Select the first entry, `Interchange Microsoft Access data with Microsoft Word`. This topic discusses several methods of sharing data with Microsoft Word. If you are using WordPerfect, you can use many of the same methods.
6. At the bottom of the topic are references to other topics about each of the four data-sharing methods. Take a few minutes to pursue these threads.
7. Close the help topic but leave the Office Assistant open. Because most of the information you will encounter is not in Access format, you should become familiar with the different formats and understand which formats Access can use directly.
8. Press F1. The comment bubble for the Office Assistant appears, with the words you typed earlier in the type-in box.
9. Type the words **`import data`** and press ↵Enter. A list of topics appears in the comment bubble. The first of these topics discusses the basics of importing and linking data from other sources. The second topic, `Data sources Microsoft Access can import or link`, is a list of databases and data types that Access can read directly.
10. Select the topic `Data sources Microsoft Access can import or link`. The topic opens, and a list of file types is displayed.
11. Review the list and then close Access.

5. Exploring the World of Alaska

As you search for information, you often find sources that may be similar to, but not exactly like, what you already have. In gathering data on Alaska, a friend has given you a text file that includes additional geographic features (including some errors), which you don't have.

To Import a Text File

1. Open the file Proj1707 as a copy.
2. From the **F**ile menu, choose Get External **D**ata and then choose **I**mport.
3. In the Import dialog box, change the Files of **t**ype to Text Files.
4. If you are not in the folder where the student files are located, move to that folder.
5. Open the text file Proj1708. The first Import Text Wizard dialog box appears. Take a moment to study the data format.
6. Access should be able to identify the format. If it can't, select **D**elimited.
7. Select **N**ext. In the dialog box that appears, ensure that the **C**omma delimiter is selected and that the Text **Q**ualifier is set to a quotation mark. The first line does not contain the field names, so this box should not be checked.
8. Select **N**ext. The third import dialog box gives you the option of importing the data into an existing table. Although you have a table that has generally the same information, it is not a good idea to merge the data until you are sure that it is correct.

9. Select **N**ext. This dialog box gives you the option of naming each of the fields. Because you aren't sure what the fields contain, you can accept the defaults and change the names after you have imported the data.
10. Select **N**ext. This dialog box helps Access determine whether you want a primary key. In this case, you should accept the system defaults even though a primary key is not required.
11. Select **N**ext. The final dialog box appears, giving you the option of using the file name as the table name.
12. Change the name to `Additional Data` and click **F**inish. Access notifies you with an information item that it has finished the import process.
13. Open the new table and view the data. Compare the data with what you have.

For future study, see whether you can devise queries that will change the data you have imported into a form that can be merged with your base Geography table.

Challenge

The following challenges enable you to use your problem-solving skills. Take time to work through these exercises now.

1. Copying a List of Organization Members to a Word Document

Open the database that you created in earlier projects to track information about members of a club or organization. Open the main table of member information. Copy all the records. Open Microsoft Word or another Windows-compatible word processor. Paste the list into a document and print it.

2. Doing Customer Research

Your boss liked the sheet you provided earlier and wants to include the comment data in a word processing report to provide to shareholders. The intent is to demonstrate how the company is concerned about the customer and how it is addressing the customer's interests.

To Place the Comment Data in a Word Processing Report

1. Open the file Proj1709 as a copy.
2. Open the `Customers and their comments` report that you created earlier. View the report. This is the form that you need to re-create using a query.
3. Select the Queries tab and begin a **N**ew query in Design view.
4. Add the Questionnaire table and include in the query the fields Adults, Children, Hours, and Improve.
5. After you build the query, run it and select the entire dynaset, using the Select Datasheet button to the left of the Adults column selector button.
6. Copy the dynaset by using **F**ile and **C**opy.
7. Close the query, saving it with the name `Quarterly Report`, and then close Access.
8. Open Microsoft Word and paste the dynaset into a blank document. The dynaset is pasted as a table, with the column headers darkened. Notice that there is no word wrapping and that some of the text does not appear.

9. Place the insertion point in any cell of the table and click T**a**ble from the menu bar. Choose Cell Height and **W**idth. In the dialog box that appears, select the **R**ows tab, and in the Height of Rows box, select Auto. Then click OK. The table is automatically adjusted for the contents of the cells.
10. Save the Word document with the name `Quarterly Report Table` and close Microsoft Word.

3. Owning a Vending Company

Now that you have a good handle on the business, you find that you want to expand the operation to increase revenues. Instead of going with a conventional bank loan, which you may not qualify for because of the short time you've been in operation, you decide to pursue private investors. The first step is to create a portfolio showing your current operations.

To Create a Portfolio Showing Current Operations

1. Open the file Proj1710 as a copy.
2. Open the Locations table in Datasheet view. Your prospective investors don't need to know who you are dealing with, so you decide to reorganize the table.
3. Select the Owner column and drag it to the last position on the table. Then select the Site and Machine Type columns and copy them to the Clipboard.
4. Close Access.
5. Open Microsoft Word and then open the Investor file Proj1711. This file illustrates how a page in the destination file might look.
6. Highlight the text `***Enter Table Here***`.
7. Click the Paste button on the toolbar. The two-column table is pasted into the destination document and replaces the highlighted text.
8. If the table is not automatically centered, place the insertion point in any cell of the table and then choose Select T**a**ble from the T**a**ble menu. With the table selected, click the Center Align button on the toolbar.
9. Save the file as `Updated Report` and close Microsoft Word.

4. Managing a Video Store

You groan as you realize that, instead of creating a database from scratch, you could have imported the spreadsheet the owners had made. Still, you learned a lot in the process. Now the owners want a report of the current inventory. They are familiar with a specific spreadsheet format and want to see the data formatted in that way.

Open the video inventory table and copy the list to the Clipboard. If the data is beyond the size the Clipboard normally handles, Access will notify you. Click OK and continue.

Using the taskbar, open Microsoft Excel and place the insertion point in cell A1. Paste the contents of the database into the spreadsheet. You may have to adjust the size of the columns and rows for the data you have pasted.

Save the spreadsheet as `Owner's Report` and then close Excel and Access.

5. Taking a Home Inventory

It is a good thing you were prepared. You copied your inventory to your notebook computer and were away on a trip when a storm ripped through your town, damaging most of the houses. You were lucky. Lightning struck your workshop and destroyed many of your tools, but your children's toys and most of the household items remain intact.

Add a field named `damaged` to your main table. This field should be a numeric byte. Select items from your inventory and assign a damage rating from 1 to 10 for each item (a 1 means minor damage and a 10 means destroyed).

Develop a query that lists only those items that have been damaged in the dynaset, sorting them in reverse numeric order. Copy the dynaset to the Clipboard and then paste it into a blank Microsoft Word document. Save the query as `Damaged Goods`. (This might be useful later if you get reimbursed and decide to delete the items from your inventory.)

Draft a cover letter for the insurance company and save the word processing file as `Damaged Goods`.

Project 18

Getting Started with PowerPoint

Objectives

In this project, you learn how to:

- Start PowerPoint
- Create a New Presentation
- Change the View
- Move among Slides in a Presentation
- Run an Electronic Slide Show
- Save and Close Your Presentation
- Get Help
- Exit PowerPoint

Why Would I Do This?

Presentation graphics program
A software application that helps you structure, design, and present information—such as graphs or bulleted lists—to an audience so that it is visually appealing.

Presentation
A group of related slides you can create using PowerPoint.

Electronic slide show
A predefined list of slides displayed sequentially on-screen or using an LCD panel and overhead projector.

LCD projection panel
A flat-screen device that you can use to project computer images to a large screen.

PowerPoint is the *presentation graphics program* component of Microsoft Office 97. Its primary purpose is to help you create a presentation on your computer. A *presentation* is simply a series of slides that contain visual information designed to persuade an audience. Using PowerPoint, you can effectively and efficiently create professional-looking handouts, overheads, charts, and other types of visual aides for use in a group presentation.

Whether you are creating a marketing plan, reporting progress on a project, or simply conducting a meeting, PowerPoint will help you create powerful presentations. After you create the presentation, you can add and modify text, charts, clip art, and drawn objects to strengthen your arguments. PowerPoint lets you edit and refine your presentation until it's just right.

You can deliver PowerPoint presentations in all the traditional ways—as printed handouts, 35mm slides, or overhead transparencies. One of the most popular and effective ways to use PowerPoint, however, is to create an *electronic slide show*. You can run a PowerPoint slide show on a computer monitor, or you can use an *LCD projection panel* to cast the image from your computer onto a large screen.

Lesson 1: Starting PowerPoint

You can start PowerPoint a number of ways. An easy method is to use the Windows 95 taskbar, as you learn in this lesson.

To Start PowerPoint

1. **Move the mouse pointer to the Start button at the left edge of the taskbar; then click the left mouse button.**

   The Start menu appears, as shown in Figure 18.1.

2. **Point to Programs.**

   A list of available programs is displayed. The exact list depends on the programs that are installed on your system.

3. **Move the mouse pointer to Microsoft PowerPoint and click the left mouse button.**

   PowerPoint is loaded into the computer's working area—*random-access memory (RAM)*—and appears on your screen (see Figure 18.2). Note that PowerPoint's screen components are similar to those in other Windows programs and include a menu bar, a title bar, and toolbars.

Random-access memory (RAM)
The temporary storage space where the computer places a program you are using.

If you have problems...

If you don't see Microsoft PowerPoint as a program listing, move the mouse pointer to the Microsoft Office folder. Then click the PowerPoint icon from the displayed list.

Additionally, unless the feature has been turned off, the Office Assistant (a cartoon paper clip with eyes) is displayed in its own window. For now, you can turn off the Office Assistant.

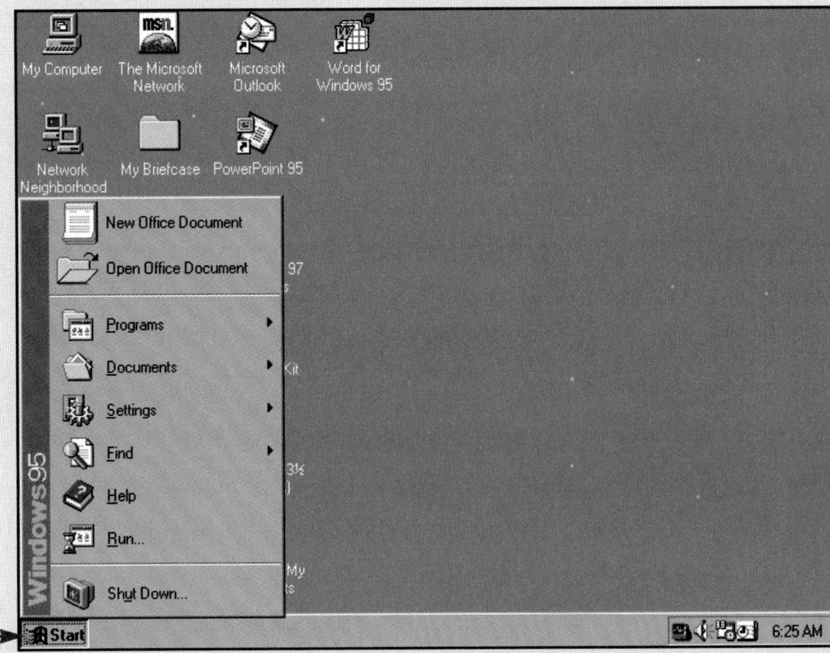

Figure 18.1
You can start PowerPoint from the Start menu.

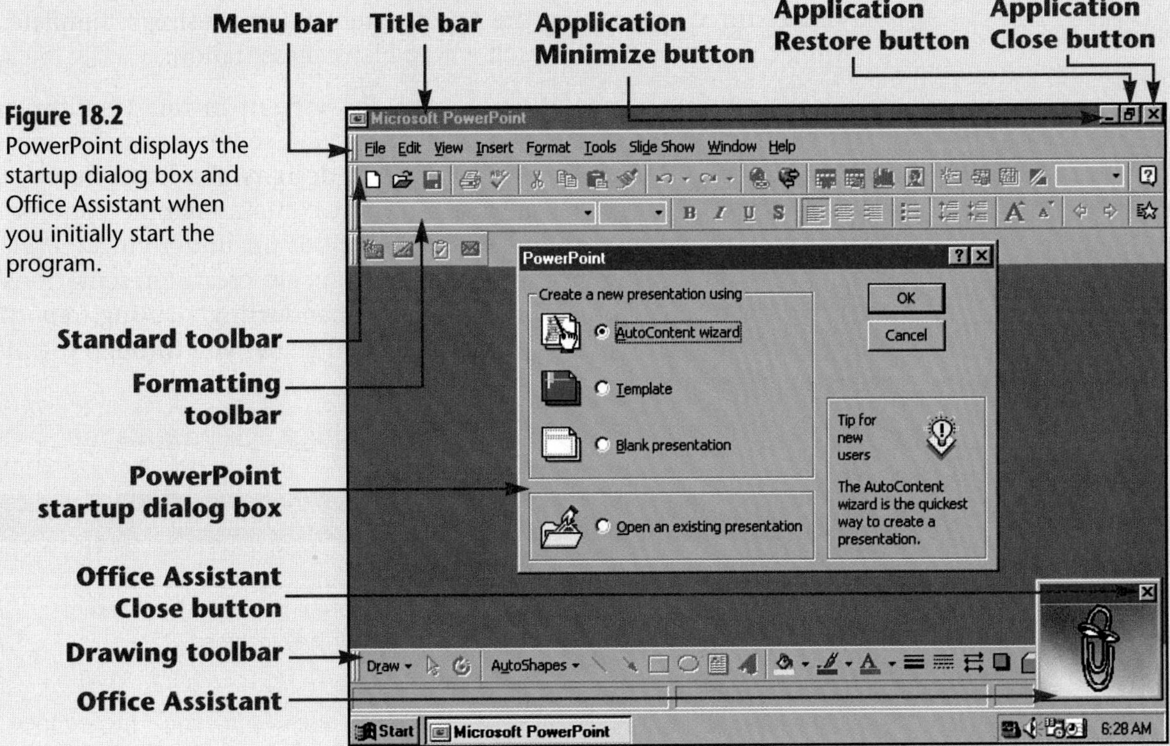

Figure 18.2
PowerPoint displays the startup dialog box and Office Assistant when you initially start the program.

continues

To Start PowerPoint (continued)

4 Click the Close button on the Office Assistant.

The Office Assistant window closes, but the PowerPoint startup dialog box remains in the PowerPoint window. This dialog box helps you either create a new presentation or open one that was created and saved earlier (an existing presentation).

Leave the screen as it is and leave PowerPoint running for the next lesson, in which you use the AutoContent Wizard to create a presentation.

If a shortcut icon for PowerPoint is displayed on your Windows 95 desktop, you can also start PowerPoint by double-clicking the icon. Alternatively, you can right-click the shortcut icon and then choose **O**pen from the displayed menu. Either method is faster than using the Start menu.

The Office 97 shortcut bar may be visible on your screen. If so, simply click the PowerPoint button in the shortcut bar to start the program.

Lesson 2: Creating a New Presentation

With the PowerPoint startup dialog box, you can create a new presentation in one of three ways: using the AutoContent Wizard, using a template, or starting completely from scratch with a blank presentation.

Template
A predefined design that includes formatting for a presentation.

AutoContent Wizard
A tool that guides you through the steps of a proposed presentation and includes suggested content.

To make creating presentations a snap, PowerPoint includes built-in presentations and *templates*. PowerPoint's *templates*, sometimes called presentation designs, include preset colors and designs but no content. The *AutoContent Wizard*, however, is a tool that contains sample content for commonly used presentation topics as well as an underlying template. Using the AutoContent Wizard, you can quickly create presentations to help you when recommending a strategy, conducting training, reporting progress, and so on. The AutoContent Wizard guides you through the planning stages by suggesting slide types, formats, and contents.

Table 18.1 summarizes the methods for creating a new presentation.

Table 18.1 Methods for Creating New Presentations

Use	To
AutoContent Wizard	Create a presentation with the sample content already included.
Template	Create a presentation using a predesigned slide layout formatted for a particular "look." Templates are also referred to as presentation designs.

Use	To
A blank presentation	Create a presentation from scratch using a blank slide and default font settings.
An existing presentation	Open a presentation that was previously created and saved.

In this lesson, you use the AutoContent Wizard to create a presentation to recommend that your entire organization upgrade to PowerPoint 97.

If you have problems...

If you accidentally close PowerPoint's startup dialog box, you can still use the AutoContent Wizard to create a presentation. Choose **F**ile, **N**ew to display the New Presentation dialog box. Click the Presentations tab and then double-click AutoContent Wizard.

To Create a New Presentation

1. **In the PowerPoint startup dialog box (which should still be open from Lesson 1), click the AutoContent wizard option and choose OK.**

   The first of six AutoContent Wizard dialog boxes is displayed, as shown in Figure 18.3. Notice that the diagram on the left side of the dialog box helps chart your progress as you create a presentation. The buttons at the bottom of the dialog box help you move between AutoContent dialog boxes or even cancel the wizard.

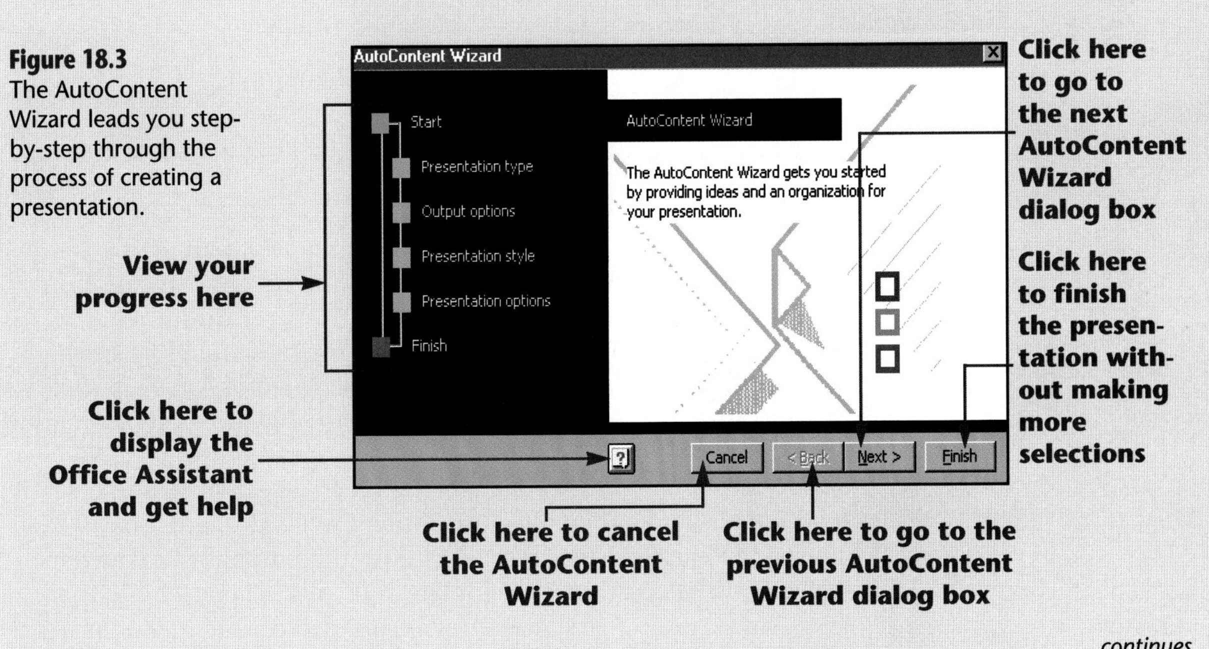

Figure 18.3
The AutoContent Wizard leads you step-by-step through the process of creating a presentation.

continues

To Create a New Presentation (continued)

2 Choose Next.

The next window of the AutoContent Wizard dialog box is displayed, as shown in Figure 18.4.

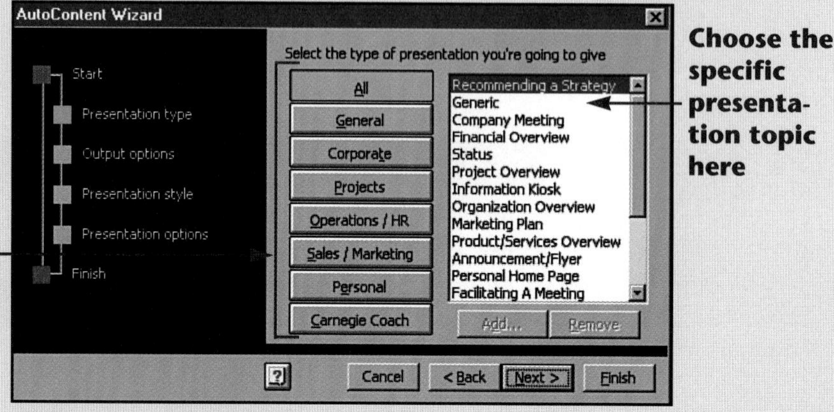

Figure 18.4
You can select a category of presentation types, then a specific presentation from that category.

You can use this window to determine the *presentation type*—the type of presentation that best fits your needs. By default, all presentation types are shown in the list on the right side of the dialog box. You can limit the type of presentations listed by clicking one of the category buttons.

3 Click several of the category buttons and take a look at the list to see what types of presentations each category contains.

4 When you're finished experimenting, choose the `Projects` category button.

In the list box, you should see all the presentations associated with this category.

5 Select `Project Overview` and choose Next.

The third window of the AutoContent dialog box is displayed. You can use this window to choose the general type of output you want. If you plan to show the presentation to others (in a meeting, for example), you can select the **P**resentations, informal meetings, handouts option. If you want to publish the presentation for others to view in your absence, you can select the **I**nternet, kiosk option.

6 Select the Presentations, informal meetings, handouts option button, if necessary; then choose Next.

The fourth window of the AutoContent Wizard dialog box is displayed. You use this window to choose the output type you want. PowerPoint selects the best template and color scheme combination to display your work, depending on the output you choose. You can also decide whether to print handouts as part of your presentation.

7 Select On-screen presentation and choose Yes; then choose Next.

The fifth window of the AutoContent Wizard dialog box is displayed, as shown in Figure 18.5. You can use this window to enter information for the first slide of your presentation—the title slide. If your computer is set up specifically for you, you are designated as the user, and your name and company probably already appear in the bottom two text boxes. If not, you can type them when you type the title.

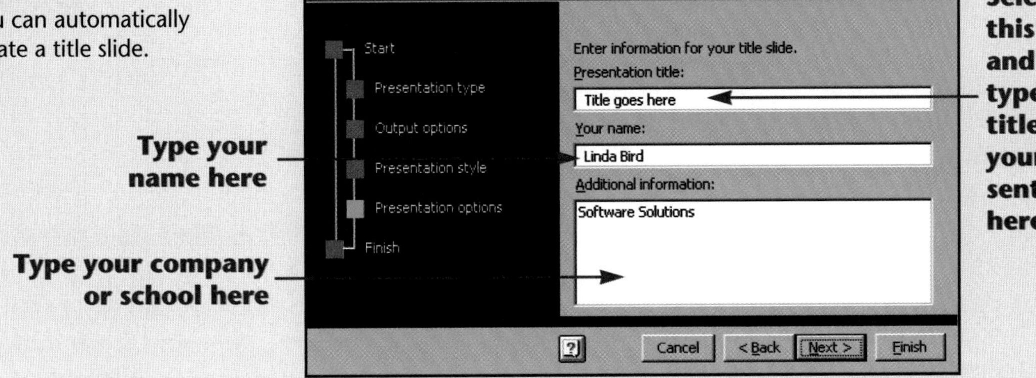

Figure 18.5
You can automatically create a title slide.

8 In the Presentation title box, select the text `Title goes here` by dragging the mouse pointer over it; then type `Project Proposal`.

The text you type replaces the selected text.

9 If necessary, select the text in the Your name and Additional information boxes, and type your name and the name of your company or school.

10 Choose Next to advance to the final window of the AutoContent Wizard dialog box.

11 Read the displayed information and then choose Finish to view your presentation.

The AutoContent Wizard creates the presentation and displays it as an outline (see Figure 18.6). Outline view is often the easiest to use when revising content. The information you typed is included in the title slide. The rest of the presentation is created as a series of slides with major topics and subpoints. These suggested topics serve as a blueprint for your presentation. Additionally, a miniature color slide, or *thumbnail*, is displayed so that you can see how the presentation will look when viewed in Slide view. Notice that PowerPoint also includes a special toolbar—the Outlining toolbar—along the left edge of the screen.

continues

To Create a New Presentation (continued)

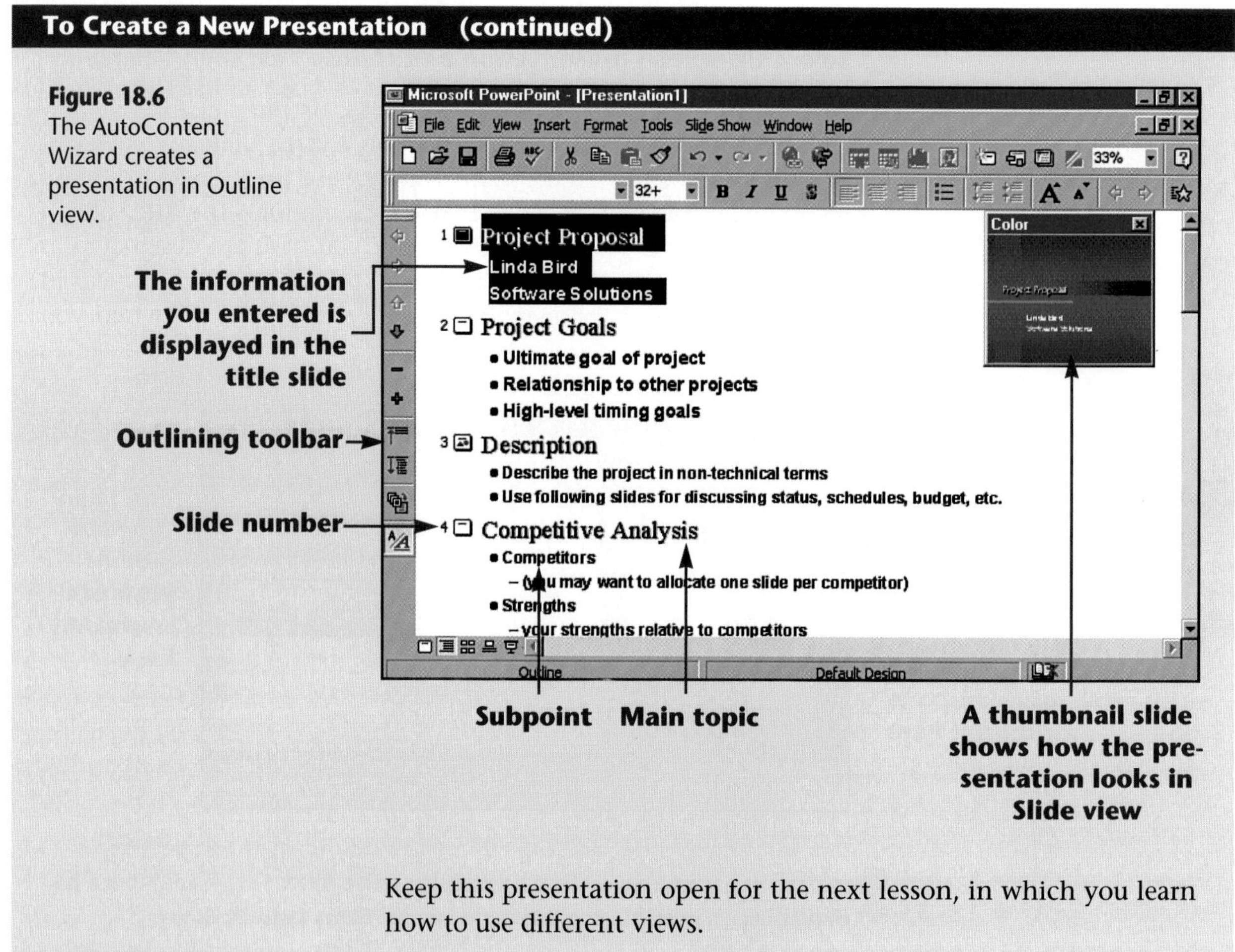

Figure 18.6
The AutoContent Wizard creates a presentation in Outline view.

Keep this presentation open for the next lesson, in which you learn how to use different views.

Lesson 3: Changing the View

After you've created a presentation, you can view it a number of different ways: Slide view, Outline view, Slide Sorter view, Notes Page view, and Slide Show. Table 18.2 describes the purpose of each of the views.

Table 18.2 Available Views in PowerPoint

Use	To
Slide view	Work with one slide at a time, add or change text and graphics, or draw shapes.
Outline view	Work with the slide title and text in traditional outline form. Graphics cannot be inserted or modified.
Slide Sorter view	Display miniature versions of all slides, including text and graphics. Use this view to change the slide order, add transitions, and set timings for electronic slide shows.
Notes Page view	Display a page where you create speaker notes for each slide.
Slide Show	Display your presentation as an on-screen electronic slide show.

The two most commonly used screen views, especially as you develop the presentation, are Outline view and Slide view. Outline view displays text only, enabling you to make quick and easy changes to the presentation's text content. Outline view is also handy for making text changes because several slides are shown at once. Additionally, you can use Outline view to change text or reorder your slides.

In contrast to Outline view, Slide view displays only one slide at a time, but displays graphics and charts as well as text. This makes Slide view a good choice when you want to modify those elements on a slide.

The sample presentation should currently be in Outline view. You can change the view by using the **V**iew menu or clicking a view button. In this exercise, you practice using both methods. Now try changing the view of the presentation.

To Change the View

ScreenTip
A description box that is displayed whenever you rest the mouse pointer on a button.

1 In the open presentation, move the mouse pointer to any of the view buttons on the left side of the status bar (see Figure 18.7).

In a second or two, a *ScreenTip* is displayed, indicating the view button's name.

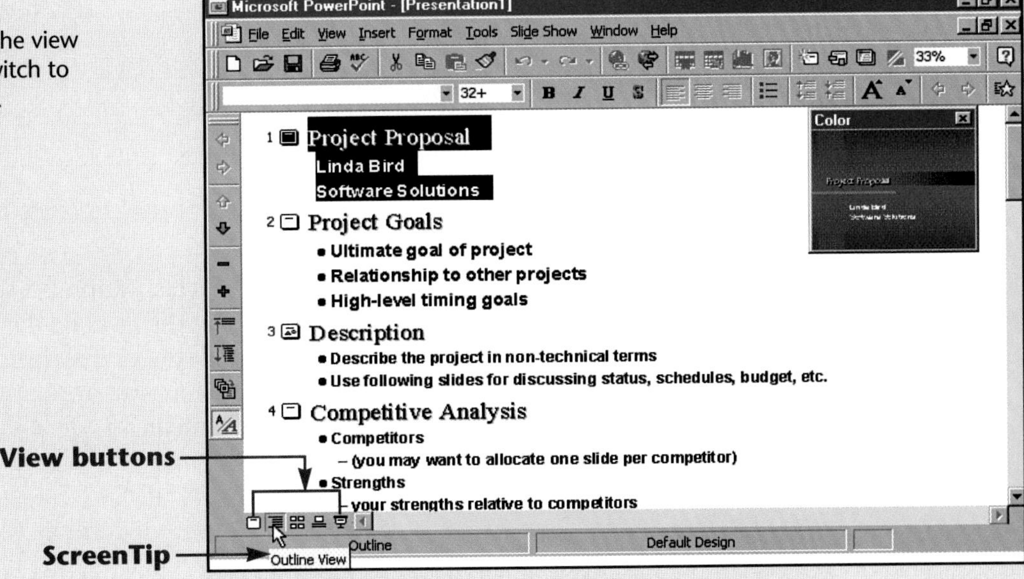

Figure 18.7
You can use the view buttons to switch to another view.

If you have problems...

If the ScreenTips aren't displayed, choose **V**iew, **T**oolbars, **C**ustomize. In the Customize dialog box, click the **O**ptions tab and select the Show ScreenTips on toolbars check box. Choose Close when you're finished.

continues

To Change the View (continued)

❷ Place the mouse pointer on each of the other view buttons.

A ScreenTip identifies each button.

❸ Click the Slide View button.

The current slide appears on-screen, displaying the color, text, and graphics (see Figure 18.8). If the horizontal and vertical rulers are displayed on your screen, you can turn them off by choosing **V**iew, **R**uler.

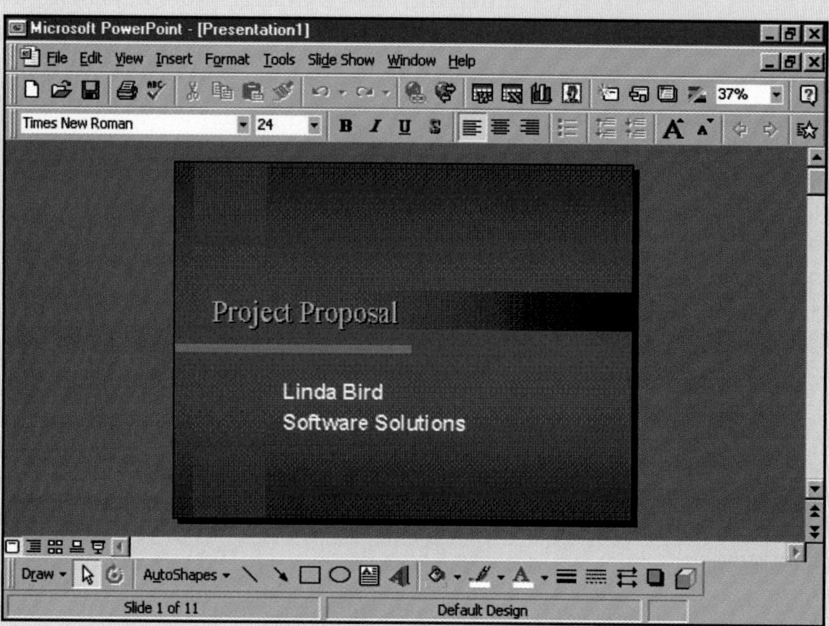

Figure 18.8
You can use Slide view to display a slide's color, text, and graphics.

❹ Click the Slide Sorter View button.

You can view the first six slides of the presentation on-screen (see Figure 18.9). Notice that the Slide Sorter displays its own toolbar. Slide Sorter view is used to add, delete, or rearrange slides. Additionally, you can add slide transitions and animation effects in this view by using the Slide Sorter toolbar.

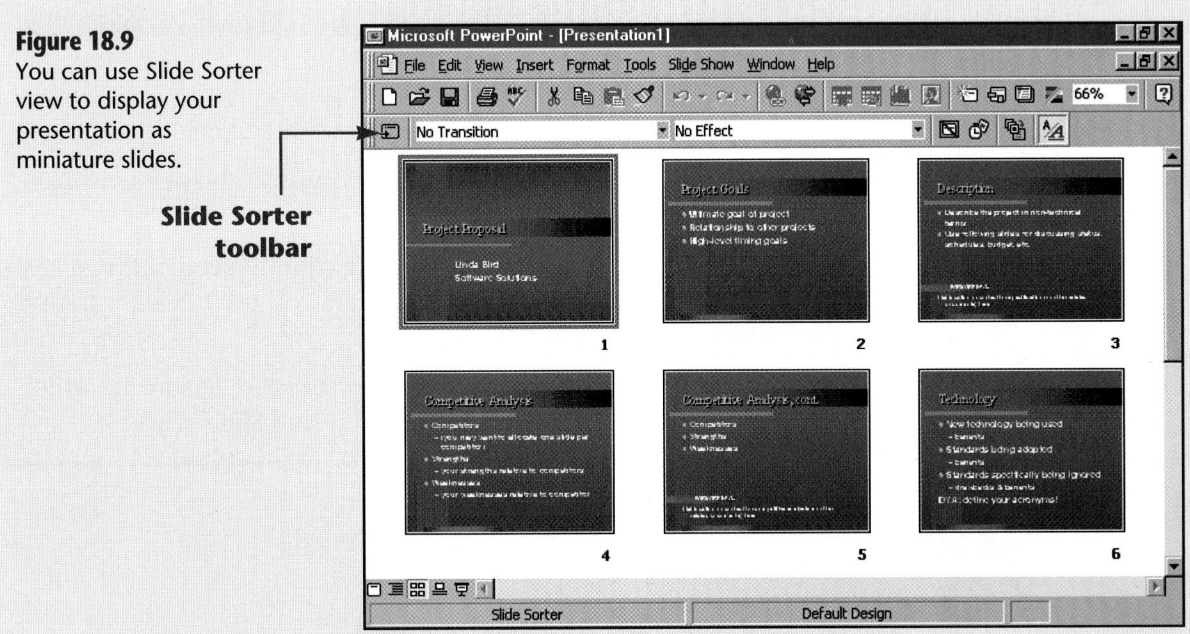

Figure 18.9
You can use Slide Sorter view to display your presentation as miniature slides.

5 Click the Notes Page View button.

Notes Page view is displayed (see Figure 18.10). This view includes miniature slides along with space for speaker notes. You can print the notes and use them to remember key points while giving your presentation.

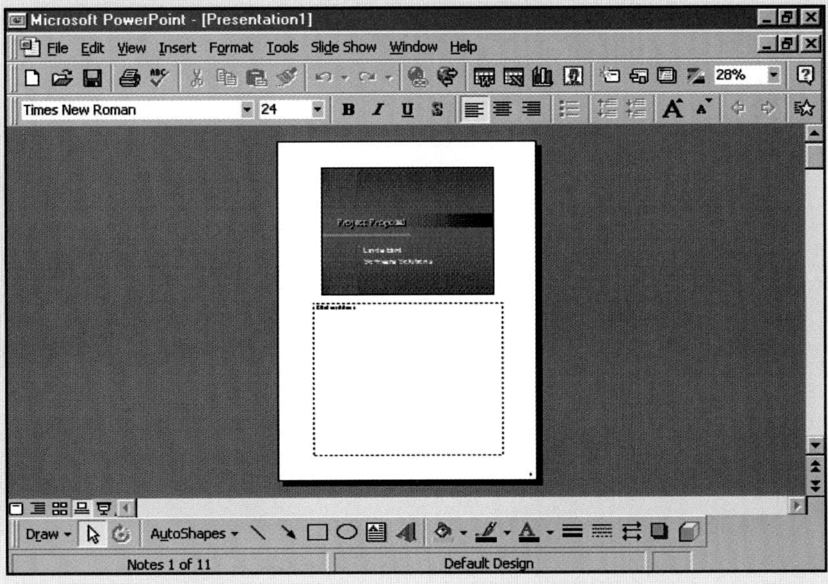

Figure 18.10
You can use Notes Page view to type speaker notes.

continues

To Change the View (continued)

6 Click the Slide Show button.

The presentation is displayed as a full-screen electronic slide show.

7 Click the left mouse button several times to advance through the slides.

Once you have viewed the entire presentation, PowerPoint displays Notes Page view, which was the last view you used before starting the slide show.

Keep this sample presentation open for the next lesson, in which you learn to move among slides in Outline and Slide views.

You can end a slide show at any time by pressing Esc.

Lesson 4: Moving among Slides in a Presentation

After you create the presentation, you need to move around in it efficiently. In this lesson, you learn to move among slides in both Outline and Slide views.

To Move among Slides in a Presentation

1 In the open presentation, click the Outline View button.

Alternatively, you can choose **V**iew, **O**utline.

The presentation returns to Outline view. Notice that not all the text is displayed on-screen at once. Note also that PowerPoint provides a vertical scroll bar on the right side of the screen that you can use to move among the slides (see Figure 18.11).

2 Click the down arrow located at the bottom of the vertical scroll bar several times.

Clicking the down arrow advances your view through the presentation one line at a time. In the same way, clicking the up arrow moves upward in the presentation one line at a time. You can also scroll continually by holding down the left mouse button while pointing to either arrow.

3 Press and hold down the mouse button while pointing to the up arrow.

The scroll box moves to the top of the scroll bar, indicating that you have moved to the top of the presentation.

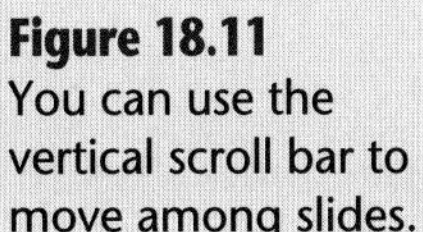

Figure 18.11
You can use the vertical scroll bar to move among slides.

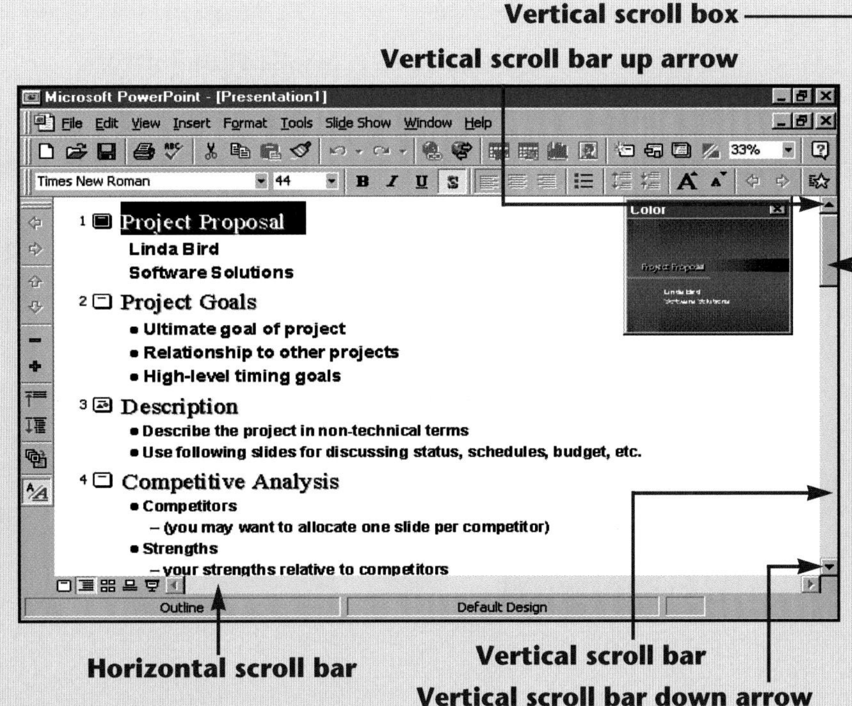

4 Press ↓ on the keyboard several times.

Insertion point
The blinking vertical bar that shows where text will appear when you type.

The *insertion point* advances one line at a time through the presentation text. In the same way, pressing ↑ moves the insertion point backward through the presentation. You can also use keyboard shortcuts to move among presentation slides.

5 Press Ctrl+Home.

PowerPoint moves the insertion point to the first slide. Using Ctrl+Home is relatively easy to remember because most Windows programs use it to move to the beginning of a document. Likewise, you can press Ctrl+End to move to the end of a document.

Now try moving among slides in Slide view.

6 Choose View, Slide.

The presentation is displayed in Slide view. You can use the vertical scroll bar to move among slides in this view as well. In addition to displaying the scroll bar elements used for Outline view, Slide view displays the Next Slide and Previous Slide buttons just below the vertical scroll bar. You can use these buttons to quickly move through the presentation.

7 Click the Next Slide button.

The second slide in your presentation is displayed.

continues

To Move among Slides in a Presentation (continued)

8 **Click the Previous Slide button.**

The first slide is now displayed.

9 **Click the vertical scroll box; then drag it up and down slowly.**

A ScreenTip appears to the left of the scroll bar. This ScreenTip shows the slide number and title (see Figure 18.12). When you release the mouse button, the slide indicated by the ScreenTip will be displayed.

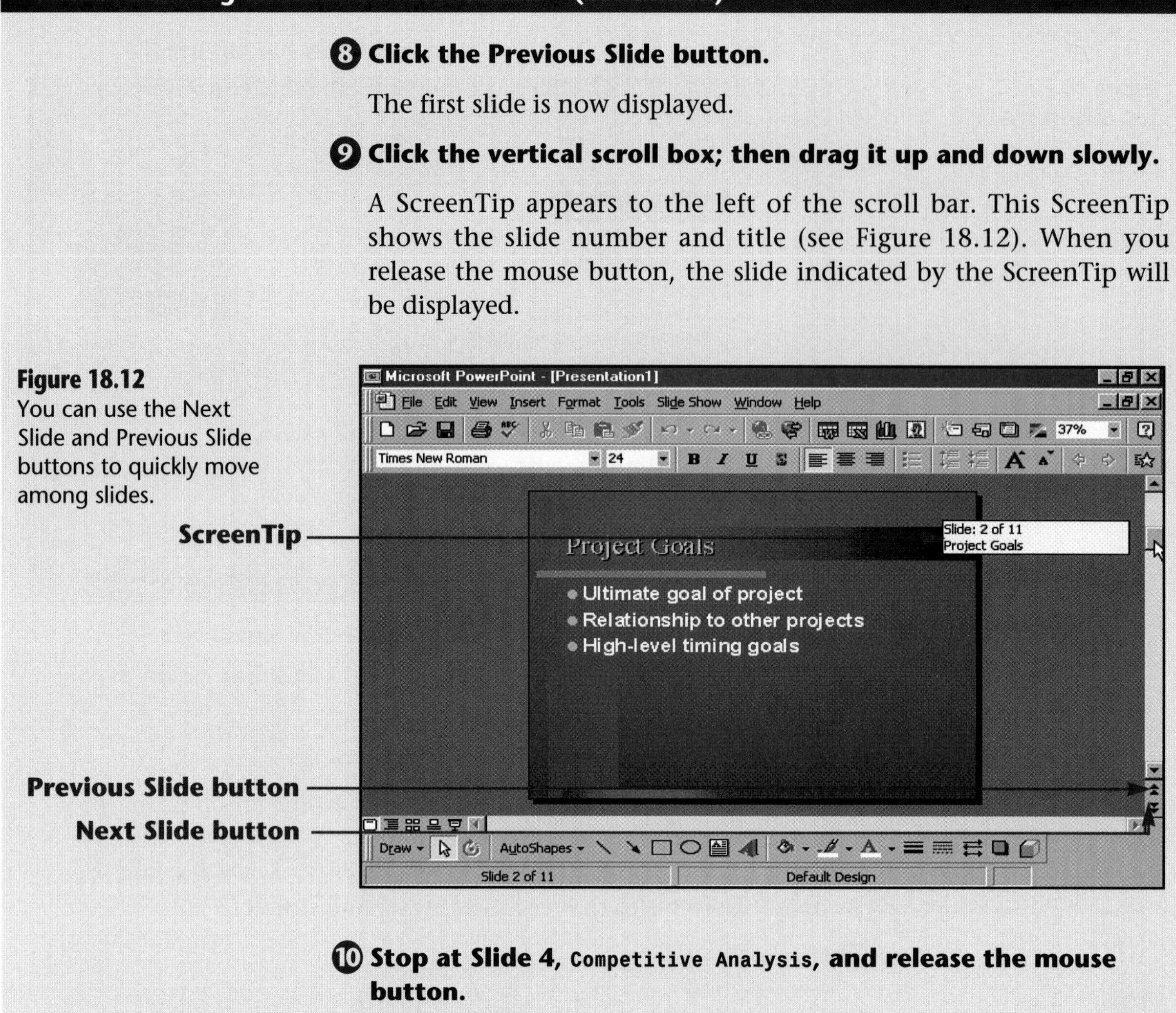

Figure 18.12 You can use the Next Slide and Previous Slide buttons to quickly move among slides.

10 **Stop at Slide 4, `Competitive Analysis`, and release the mouse button.**

The slide indicated in the ScreenTip becomes the active slide, shown in Slide view.

11 **Press PgUp three times.**

Each time you press PgUp, the previous slide is shown. Likewise, pressing PgDn moves through the presentation one slide at a time.

Leave this presentation open for the next lesson, in which you move among slides in an electronic slide show.

Table 18.3 lists the different mouse and keyboard commands you can use to move around in a presentation in Slide view.

Table 18.3 Mouse and Keyboard Commands for Moving around in Slide View

To Move To	Use This Keyboard Command	Use This Mouse Command
First slide	Ctrl+Home	Drag the vertical scroll box to the top of the scroll bar.
Last slide	Ctrl+End	Drag the vertical scroll box to the bottom of the scroll bar.
Next slide	PgDn	Click the Next Slide button.
Previous slide	PgUp	Click the Previous Slide button.

Lesson 5: Running an Electronic Slide Show

Shortcut menu
A context-sensitive menu activated by right-clicking the mouse on an object or screen area.

In Lesson 3, you learned how to activate an electronic slide show using the Slide Show button. In this lesson, you learn special commands to help you move around in a slide show. These commands are especially useful when you are conducting a presentation using an LCD display and overhead projector. One efficient way to control a running slide show is to use PowerPoint's *shortcut menu*—a context-sensitive menu you activate by right-clicking the mouse on an object or screen area.

To Run an Electronic Slide Show

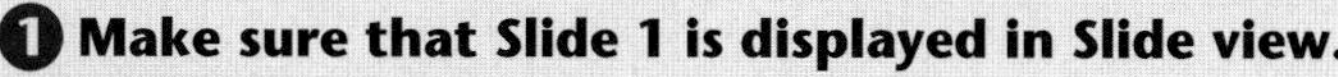

1 Make sure that Slide 1 is displayed in Slide view.

2 Click the Slide Show button.

The electronic slide show begins. Notice that the first slide displayed is the one that was active when you began the show—Slide 1. The slide now fills the entire screen, as it would during an actual electronic presentation.

3 Click the left mouse button.

The next slide in the presentation appears. If you prefer to use the keyboard, you can press ↵Enter or PgDn to advance to the next slide. You can press ←Backspace or PgUp to move back one slide.

Pop-up menu
Another term for shortcut menu.

You can also use the shortcut menu, sometimes called a *pop-up menu*, to move effectively in a slide show.

4 Click the right mouse button.

The slide show shortcut menu appears (see Figure 18.13). This menu includes commonly used commands that help you control a running slide show. Although you activated the shortcut menu by clicking the right mouse button, you choose commands with the left mouse button.

continues

To Run an Electronic Slide Show (continued)

Figure 18.13
You can control a running slide show by using the shortcut menu.

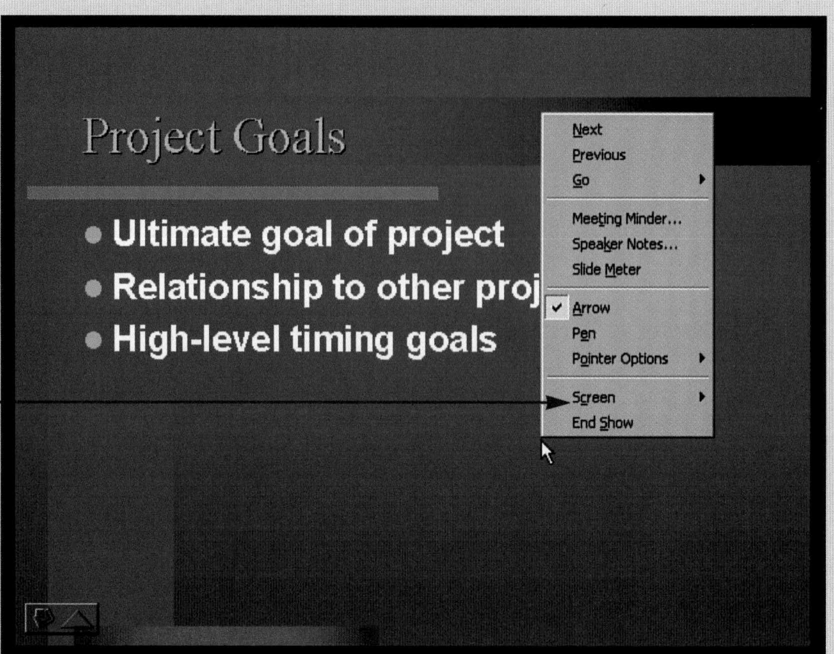

Right-click to display the shortcut menu and then choose a command by clicking the left mouse button

5 Choose Previous from the shortcut menu.

Slide 1 is displayed. Notice that you can also move forward in a presentation by choosing **N**ext from the shortcut menu.

6 Right-click the mouse to display the shortcut menu; then choose Go, Slide Navigator.

The Slide Navigator dialog box is displayed. Because this dialog box shows all the slide titles, you can use it to move quickly to any slide in your presentation.

7 Double-click Slide 7, `Team/Resources`.

The presentation jumps to Slide 7.

8 Right-click the mouse and choose End Show from the shortcut menu.

PowerPoint returns to Slide view—the one you were using just before you started the electronic slide show. You can also end a slide show by pressing Esc.

Keep this presentation open for the next lesson, in which you save the presentation.

If you have problems...

If the shortcut menu isn't displayed when you right-click the mouse, choose **T**ools, **O**ptions; then click the View tab in the Options dialog box. In the Slide Show section, check the box for **P**opup menu on right mouse click, and then choose OK.

Lesson 6: Saving and Closing Your Presentation

So far, your presentation exists only in random-access memory (RAM)—the working area of the computer. RAM retains its contents only as long as power is supplied to your computer. If power is interrupted to your computer, you lose everything in RAM.

However, when you save the presentation from RAM to one of the computer's permanent storage areas (the floppy disk, the hard drive, or a network drive), you have a stored copy. This saved file can be opened, used, and revised at a later time.

When you initially save a file, you must tell PowerPoint the name and storage location for the presentation, just as you label a file before placing it in a filing cabinet. PowerPoint 97 allows you to use long file names so that you can accurately describe a file's contents. You can use up to 255 characters, including spaces. This means that you can give a presentation descriptive names such as Annual Meeting, 1997 or Presentation to Stockholders. However, you cannot use the following characters:

/ \ > < * ? " | : ;

You use the **F**ile, **S**ave or **F**ile, Save **A**s command to save a presentation. Use **F**ile, Save **A**s when you first save a presentation or when you change the name, drive, or folder of a saved presentation. You can use **F**ile, **S**ave to quickly update a file that was previously saved. You can also click the Save button on the Standard toolbar.

After you save a presentation, you can close it—just as you clear your desk at work to make room for another project. If you made any changes since the presentation was last saved, PowerPoint prompts you to resave it. If you haven't made any revisions to a saved presentation, PowerPoint closes it. You can also close an open presentation without saving it—just as you throw away papers on your desk you no longer need.

In this lesson, you save the sample presentation to a new, formatted disk, using your floppy disk drive—usually drive A. After the presentation is saved, you close it. Before starting the tutorial, make sure you have a formatted disk in your floppy disk drive. (You should also check with your instructor in case he or she wants you to save the presentation to your hard disk or a network drive.)

To Save and Close Your Presentation

1 In the open presentation, choose File, Save As from the menu bar.

The Save As dialog box is displayed (see Figure 18.14). You use this dialog box to indicate the name and location for your file.

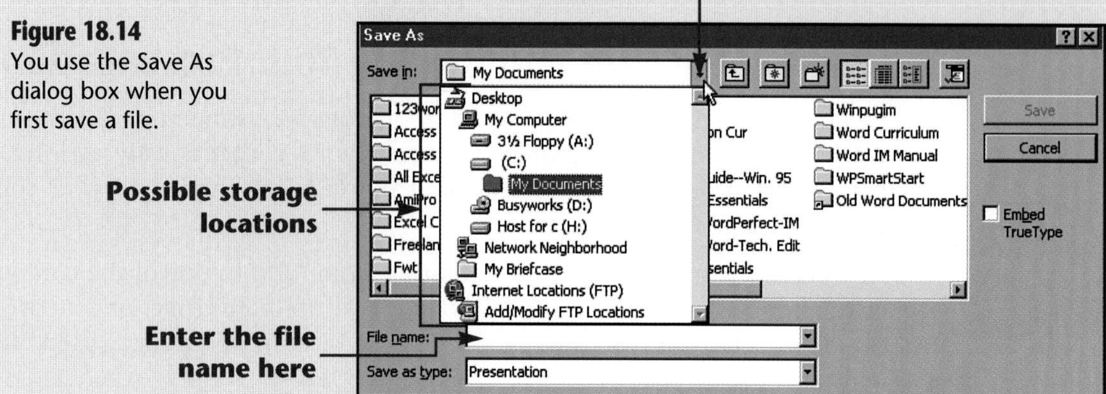

Figure 18.14
You use the Save As dialog box when you first save a file.

2 Click the Save in drop-down list arrow (see Figure 18.14).

PowerPoint displays a list of available storage locations for your computer. This list may vary from computer to computer, depending on which drives are installed.

3 Click 3 1/2 Floppy (A:).

Drive A is selected as the storage location for your presentation.

4 Move the mouse pointer into the File name text box area.

The pointer changes to an I-beam, indicating that this is an area that can accept text. However, before you can enter text, you must "set" the I-beam.

5 Click in the text box area.

This changes the I-beam to an insertion point so that you can type your file name.

6 Type `New Project Proposal` and click the Save button.

That's all there is to it! Your presentation is saved as `New Project Proposal` on the floppy disk. You now have a permanent copy stored for later use.

If you make changes to the presentation (either now or later), you can choose **F**ile, **S**ave or click the Save button to update the stored file. The file is automatically updated with the same name and location. In other words, you replace the existing file instead of creating a second copy.

Now that you have a permanent copy of the presentation, you can close the copy in memory. You can close the presentation by choosing **F**ile, **C**lose or clicking the document's Close button.

7 Choose File, Close.

The presentation closes from memory, but you have a permanent copy—the one you just saved to the floppy disk.

The next lesson focuses on using PowerPoint's Help system to quickly find information about the program. Keep PowerPoint running for this lesson.

Lesson 7: Getting Help

If you've worked with software very long, you know that sooner or later you need information about a particular feature. Fortunately, PowerPoint can provide you with help while you work. You can use the Help Topics dialog box to research a particular subject, or you can display ScreenTips using the What's This? feature. You can also use the Office Assistant to display help, tips, and messages related to the work you're performing.

In this lesson, you learn the basics of getting help in PowerPoint.

Using the Help Topics Dialog Box

One of the most straightforward methods of getting help is to use the Help Topics dialog box. You can access this dialog box by choosing **H**elp, **C**ontents and Index.

To Use the Help Topics Dialog Box

1 From the menu bar, choose Help, Contents and Index.

The Help Topics: Microsoft PowerPoint dialog box appears, as shown in Figure 18.15. The tabs represent different ways of researching your topic. You can click any tab to display the associated help page.

continues

To Use the Help Topics Dialog Box (continued)

Figure 18.15
You can get help on general topics.

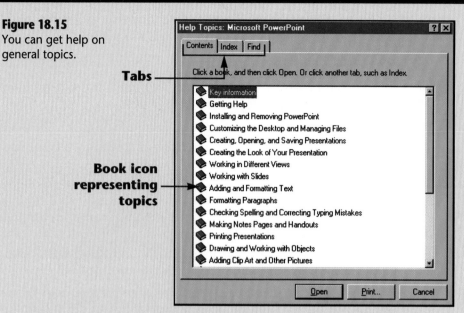

2 Click the Contents tab, if necessary.

The Contents page shows subjects topically—just like a table of contents in a book. Each topic is represented by a book icon. You can double-click the book to display subtopics related to the main topic.

3 Double-click the Getting Help book icon.

A list of subtopics appears, as shown in Figure 18.16. You can double-click any of these to show information about the topic. Alternatively, you can click to select the icon and then choose the **D**isplay button.

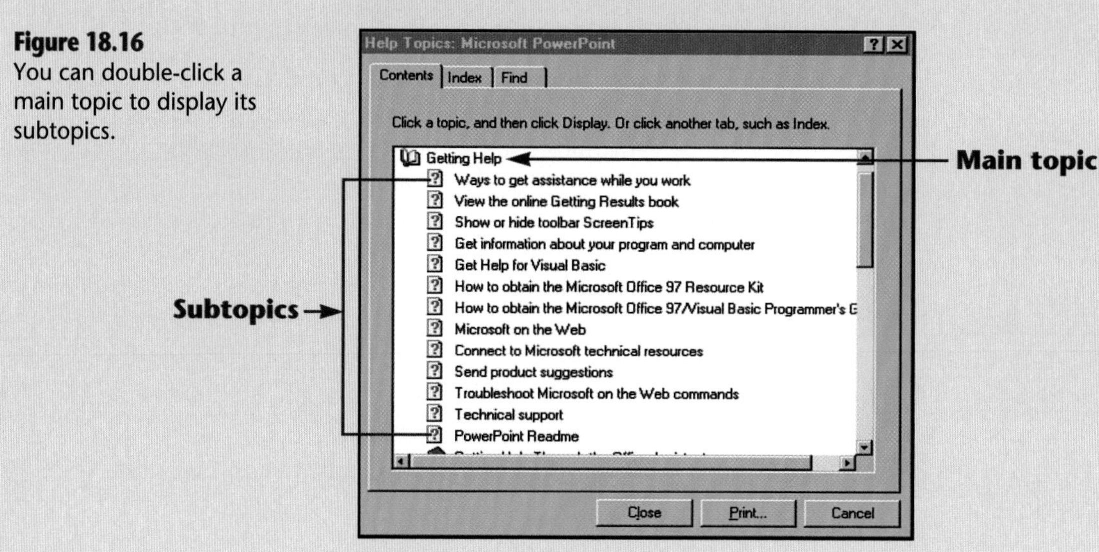

Figure 18.16
You can double-click a main topic to display its subtopics.

❹ Click Ways to get assistance while you work; then choose Display.

Hyperlinks
Areas of the screen you can click to display related information.

PowerPoint displays a dialog box that graphically depicts the ways you can get assistance (see Figure 18.17). This screen contains *hyperlinks*—areas of the screen you can click to display related information. You can find a hyperlink by moving the mouse pointer until a hand pointer appears, and then click.

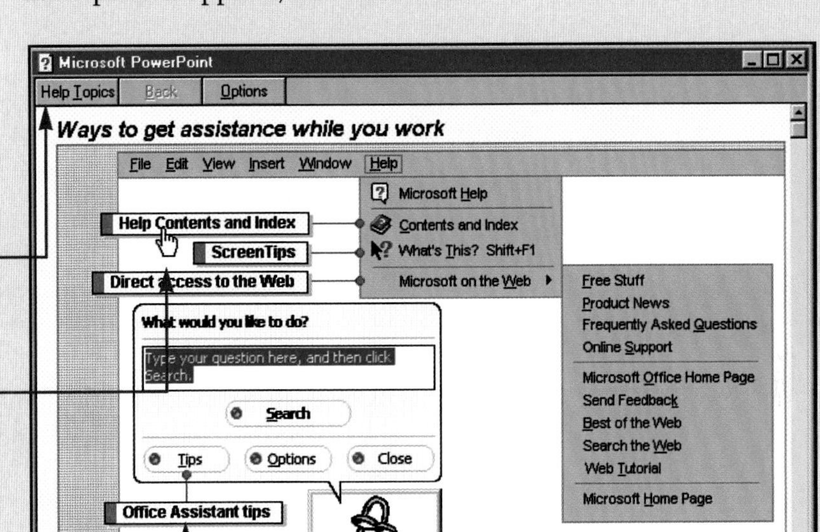

Figure 18.17
You can use Power-Point's graphical screens to get assistance.

Click this button to return to the Help Topics dialog box

You can activate a hyperlink by clicking the hand pointer

Hyperlink

❺ Move the mouse pointer to the Help Contents and Index hyperlink and then click.

Information related to this topic is displayed as a ScreenTip. You can clear the tip by clicking anywhere in the dialog box.

❻ Click in the dialog box to clear the tip; then click the Help Topics button (see Figure 18.17).

The Contents page of the Help Topics dialog box appears again. Now try using the Index page, which includes an alphabetical list of topics. Using the Index, you can search for a topic you want, and then display information about it.

❼ Click the Index tab.

The Index page appears. Notice that the insertion point is already in the **T**ype the first few letters of the word you're looking for text box. You can use this text box to indicate the topic you want.

❽ Type `creating presentations` in the Type the first few letters of the word you're looking for text box.

PowerPoint highlights the topic you indicated. You can choose **D**isplay to view the subtopics associated with this subject.

continues

To Use the Help Topics Dialog Box (continued)

9. **Click Display.**

   The Topics Found dialog box is displayed, with a list of subtopics. You can double-click any topic to display specific help about it.

10. **Double-click** `Create a new presentation.`

    PowerPoint displays information about creating a new presentation.

11. **Read the displayed information and then click the Close button in the upper-right corner of the dialog box.**

    PowerPoint closes the dialog box and displays the presentation. If you want, take a few minutes to research other topics by using the Help Topics dialog box.

    In the next tutorial, you learn how to use the Office Assistant to get tips and help while you work.

PowerPoint provides ScreenTips to give you information about different items on-screen. In any dialog box, click the question mark (?) and then click the dialog box command you want to research. To find information about a toolbar button, menu command, or screen area, choose **H**elp, What's **T**his? and then click the object.

Using the Office Assistant

Did you ever wish for a personal computer trainer—someone to personally guide you through a new software program? Fortunately, PowerPoint 97 includes an electronic version of such a person: the Office Assistant. Although not a substitute for a personal trainer, the Office Assistant can display tips related to the feature you're using. Additionally, the Office Assistant can provide a list of subjects related to a question you type.

You can choose **H**elp, Microsoft PowerPoint **H**elp to display the Office Assistant. Alternatively, you can click the Office Assistant button on the Standard toolbar. When the Assistant is displayed, you can type the question you want, or display a tip. When you're finished, you can close the Office Assistant window by clicking its Close button.

To Use the Office Assistant

1. **Choose Help, Microsoft PowerPoint Help.**

   The Office Assistant is displayed in its own window (see Figure 18.18). The bubble shows how to use the Assistant to get help.

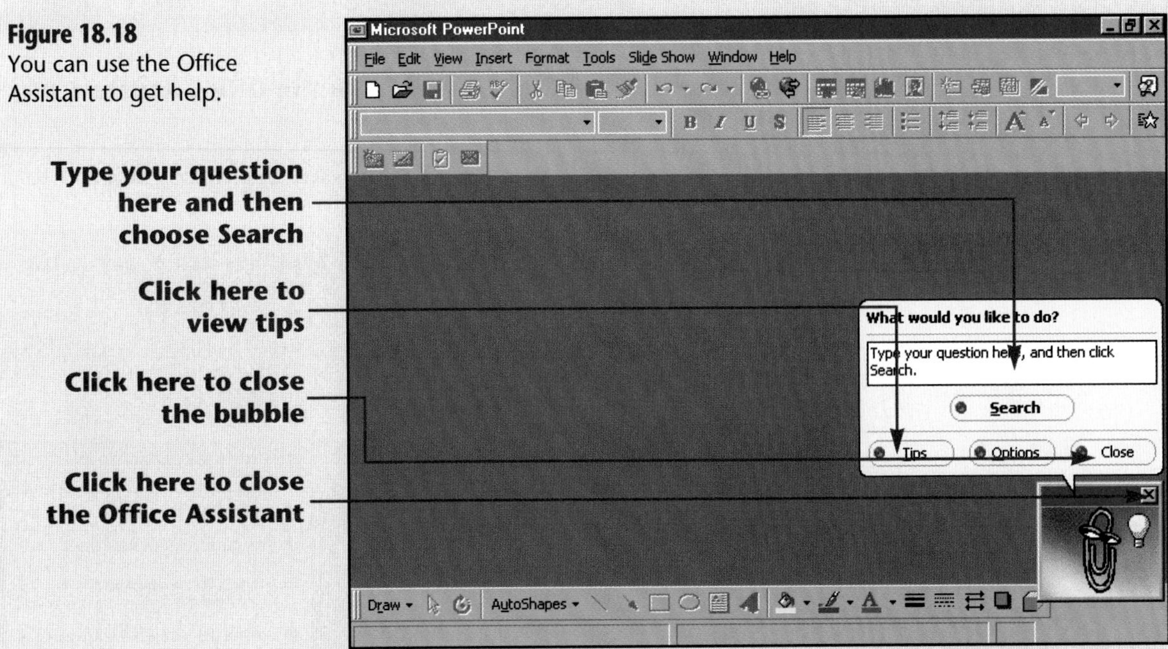

Figure 18.18
You can use the Office Assistant to get help.

❷ Click Tips in the Office Assistant bubble.

The Assistant displays a tip (see Figure 18.19). You can also click the **N**ext or **B**ack button to scroll through a list of tips. When you're finished, you click Close in the tip bubble.

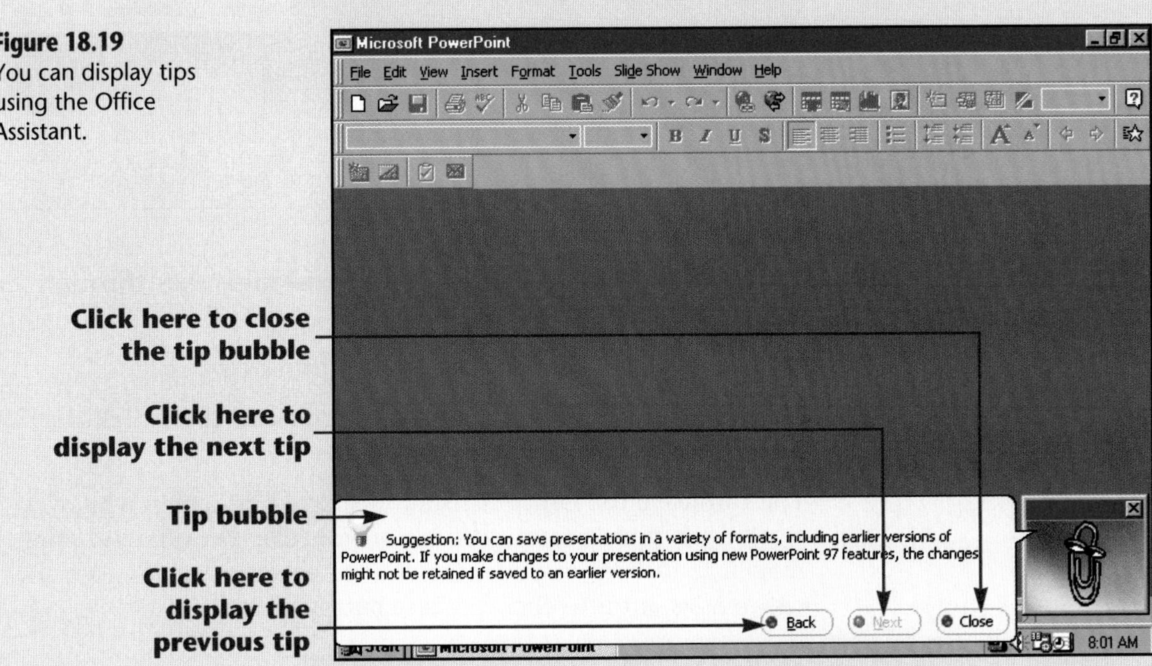

Figure 18.19
You can display tips using the Office Assistant.

continues

To Use the Office Assistant (continued)

3 Click Close to close the tip; then click the Office Assistant to display the bubble.

Besides displaying tips, the Assistant can list topics related to a question you type.

4 In the Office Assistant text box area, type `How can I get help?` and choose Search.

A list of related topics is displayed (see Figure 18.20). You can click the topic for which you want help.

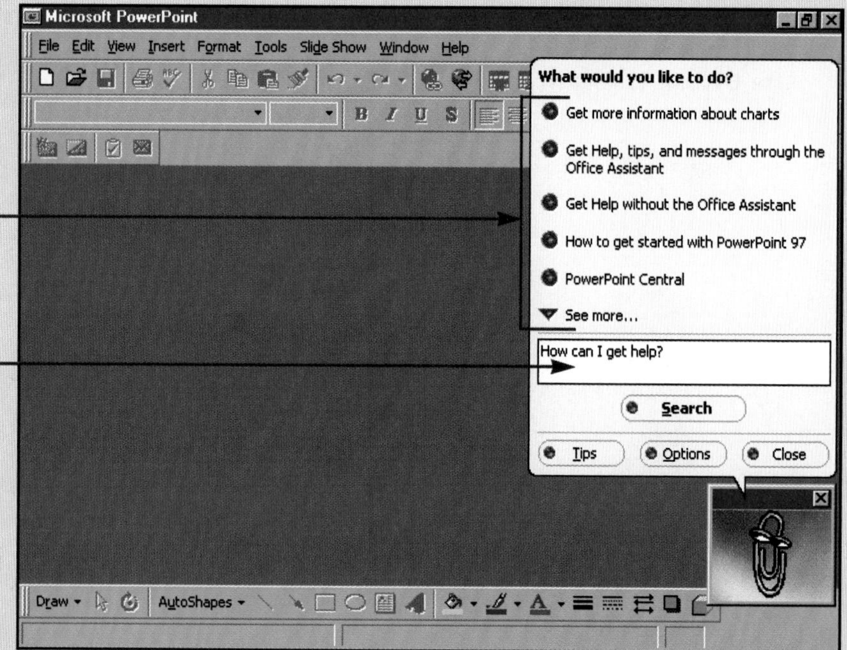

Figure 18.20
The Office Assistant answers your question by displaying related topics.

5 From the list, choose Get Help, tips and messages through the Office Assistant.

The help dialog box about this topic is displayed.

6 Read the information in the dialog box and then click the Close button in the upper-right corner.

You can leave the Office Assistant displayed on-screen while you work with your presentations, or you can close it and then reopen it just when you need it. The easiest way to close the Office Assistant is to click its Close button.

7 Click the Office Assistant Close button.

The Office Assistant window closes.

Keep PowerPoint running for the next lesson, in which you learn how to exit the program correctly.

The default Office Assistant is displayed as a personified paper clip, called "Clippit." However, you can change the Office Assistant's appearance to suit your personality. Insert your Office 97 CD in the CD-ROM drive. In the Assistant bubble, choose **O**ptions to display the Options dialog box, and then click the **G**allery tab. Click the **N**ext and **B**ack buttons to scroll through the available Assistants. When you're finished, click OK.

Lesson 8: Exiting PowerPoint

Closing a presentation, as you did in Lesson 6, is like clearing a project from your desk. Exiting the entire program is like leaving your office. When you exit PowerPoint, you clear the program from memory and return to the Windows 95 desktop.

You can exit PowerPoint by clicking the Application Close button or choosing **F**ile, E**x**it from the menu. Once you've exited the program, you can start it again, especially if you plan to complete the Applying Your Skills exercises at the end of this project. However, if you're finished working, you should also shut down Windows 95 and turn off the computer. Try exiting PowerPoint and Windows 95 now.

To Exit PowerPoint

1. **Click the Application Close button (see Figure 18.21).**

   Alternatively, you can choose **F**ile, E**x**it from the menu. If you don't have any unsaved presentations, PowerPoint is cleared from RAM, and the Window 95 desktop is displayed. If you have a presentation in memory that contains unsaved work, PowerPoint prompts you to save it before exiting the program.

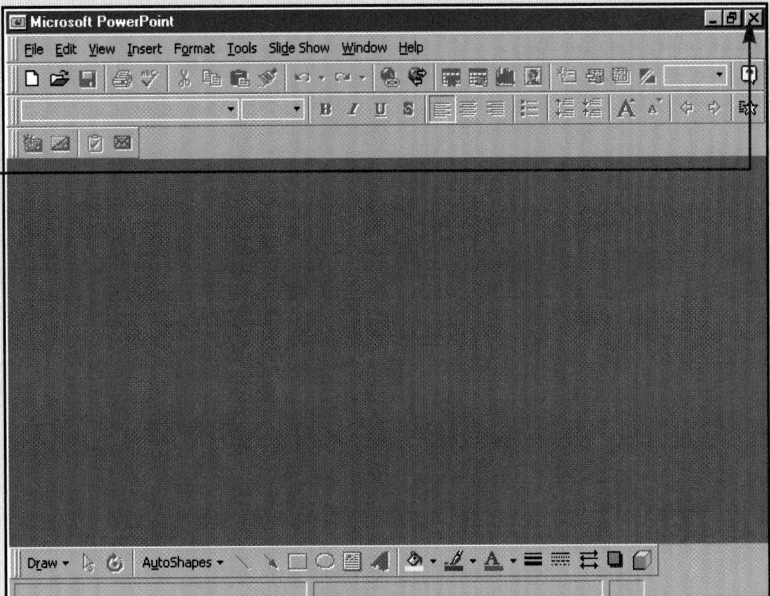

Figure 18.21
PowerPoint is easy to exit.

Click the Application Close button to exit the program

continues

To Exit PowerPoint (continued)

It's also important to exit Windows 95 correctly before turning off the computer. The best way to do this is to use (ironically enough) the Start button.

2. **Click the Start button and choose Shut Down from the menu.**

   The Shut Down Windows dialog box is displayed (see Figure 18.22). You use this dialog box to control how to shut down or restart Windows.

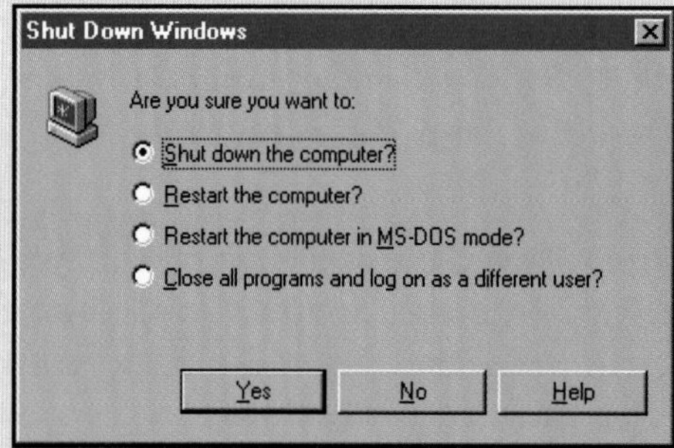

Figure 18.22
Be sure to shut down Windows 95 correctly.

3. **Make sure that the Shut down the computer? option button is selected; then click Yes.**

   Windows 95 closes temporary files and is cleared from memory. This process generally takes a few seconds, so be patient. It's important to wait until Windows 95 indicates that you can turn off the computer.

4. **Wait until the `It's now safe to turn off your computer` message appears.**

   When you see the message, you can turn off your computer.

5. **Turn off your computer monitor, main unit, and any other hardware (such as speakers or a printer).**

Project Summary

To	Do This
Start PowerPoint	Choose the Start button, **P**rograms, Microsoft PowerPoint.
Use the AutoContent Wizard	Choose **F**ile, **N**ew; then click the Presentations tab and double-click AutoContent Wizard.
Use different views	Click the PowerPoint view buttons.
Move to the first slide	Drag the scroll box to the top of the vertical scroll bar.
Move to the last slide	Drag the scroll box to the bottom of the vertical scroll bar.
Move to the next slide	Click the Next Slide button.
Move to the previous slide	Click the Previous Slide button.

continues

To	Do This
End a running slide show	Press Esc.
Use the Slide Navigator	Right-click in the slide show screen and choose **G**o, Slide **N**avigator.
Display general help topics	Choose **H**elp, **C**ontents and Index.
Display the Office Assistant	Click the Office Assistant button.
Save a presentation	Choose **S**ave or Save **A**s from the **F**ile menu.
Close a presentation	Choose **F**ile, **C**lose.
Exit PowerPoint	Choose **F**ile, E**x**it.
Shut down Windows 95	Choose the Start button, Sh**u**t Down.

Checking Your Skills

True/False

For each of the following, check *T* or *F* to indicate whether the statement is true or false.

__T __F **1.** You can view a presentation using one of ten views.

__T __F **2.** The Slide Sorter View button automatically sorts the slides alphabetically.

__T __F **3.** Outline view, Slide view, and Slide Show are just different ways of viewing the same set of slides.

__T __F **4.** The AutoContent Wizard creates the structure and suggested content based on choices you make.

__T __F **5.** You can get help by using the PowerPoint Window Assistant.

__T __F **6.** The first time you save a presentation you must name it.

__T __F **7.** Closing a presentation and exiting PowerPoint are the same.

__T __F **8.** You shut down Windows 95 by using the Start button.

__T __F **9.** To move among PowerPoint slides in Slide view, you must use the mouse.

__T __F **10.** If power is interrupted to your computer you lose everything in Random Access Memory.

Multiple Choice

Circle the letter of the correct answer for each of the following questions.

1. Which of the following views is the best to view *only* the text contained in a presentation?

a. Slide view

b. Slide Sorter view

c. Outline view

d. Notes Page view

2. Which of the following can you use to quickly create a presentation that already contains sample content?

a. Template Wizard

b. AutoContent Wizard

c. Outline view

d. Answer Wizard

3. Which of the following describes an LCD panel?

- **a.** A device used with an overhead projector to display images from the computer to a screen
- **b.** Another name for a toolbar
- **c.** A list of special effects for transition from one slide to another
- **d.** The Learning Center Display panel shown when you use the Office Assistant

4. One way to move among slides is to use which of the following?

- **a.** The Search feature on the **H**elp menu
- **b.** The Office Assistant
- **c.** The horizontal scroll bar
- **d.** The vertical scroll bar

5. You can use the Office Assistant to do which of the following?

- **a.** To display tips
- **b.** To automatically create a presentation with sample content
- **c.** To move among slides
- **d.** To end an electronic slide show

6. A presentation you create using the AutoContent Wizard initially displays in which of the following?

- **a.** Slide view
- **b.** Outline view
- **c.** AutoContent Wizard view
- **d.** Slide Sorter view

7. You can quickly move to the first presentation slide in Slide view by doing which of the following?

- **a.** Clicking the First Slide button on the vertical scroll bar
- **b.** Pressing Ctrl+Home
- **c.** Pressing Home
- **d.** Dragging the scroll box to the bottom of the vertical scroll bar

8. Which of the following views does PowerPoint provide?

- **a.** Outline
- **b.** Slide Sorter
- **c.** Notes Page
- **d.** All the above

9. When you initially save a new presentation, which of the following is true?

- **a.** You can use only eight characters in the file name.
- **b.** You must save to the hard drive.
- **c.** You indicate a file name and location for the presentation.
- **d.** You can use characters such as < > ? :.

10. When you're finished working with PowerPoint, you should do which of the following?

- **a.** Simply turn off the computer.
- **b.** Choose **F**ile, E**x**it from the menu.
- **c.** Click the Application Close button.
- **d.** Both b and c

Completion

In the blank provided, write the correct answer for each of the following statements .

1. The temporary working area that the computer uses to run programs is called _____________.
2. _____________ view shows six slides on-screen at once.
3. You can use _____________ view to add notes to your presentation.
4. A group of related slides you can create using PowerPoint is called a(n) _____________.
5. A software application that helps you structure, design, and present information (such as graphs) to an audience so that it is visually appealing is called _____________ software.
6. A predefined list of slides displayed sequentially on-screen or using an LCD panel and overhead projector is called a(n) _____________.
7. The _____________ is a tool that guides you through the steps of a proposed presentation and includes suggested content.
8. A _____________ is a predefined design that includes formatting for a presentation.
9. The _____________ is the blinking vertical bar that shows where text will appear when you type.
10. You can right-click the mouse in a slide show to display a _____________.

Matching

In the blank next to each of the following terms or phrases, write the letter of the corresponding term or phrase. (Note that some letters may be use more than once.)

____ **1.** A series of related slides

____ **2.** A flat-screen device used to project computer images on a screen

____ **3.** The computer's temporary memory

____ **4.** A permanent storage location on your computer

____ **5.** A PowerPoint feature you can use to find information

____ **6.** A tool for creating a new presentation with content

____ **7.** A presentation design that contains formatting but no content

____ **8.** A description box that is displayed when you rest the mouse pointer on a button

____ **9.** The result of right-clicking the mouse

____ **10.** A blinking vertical bar that shows where text will next appear

a. AutoContent Wizard

b. RAM

c. ScreenTip

d. shortcut menu

e. presentation

f. hard drive

g. insertion point

h. template

i. Office Assistant

j. LCD projection panel

Screen ID

Identify each of the items shown in Figure 18.23.

Figure 18.23

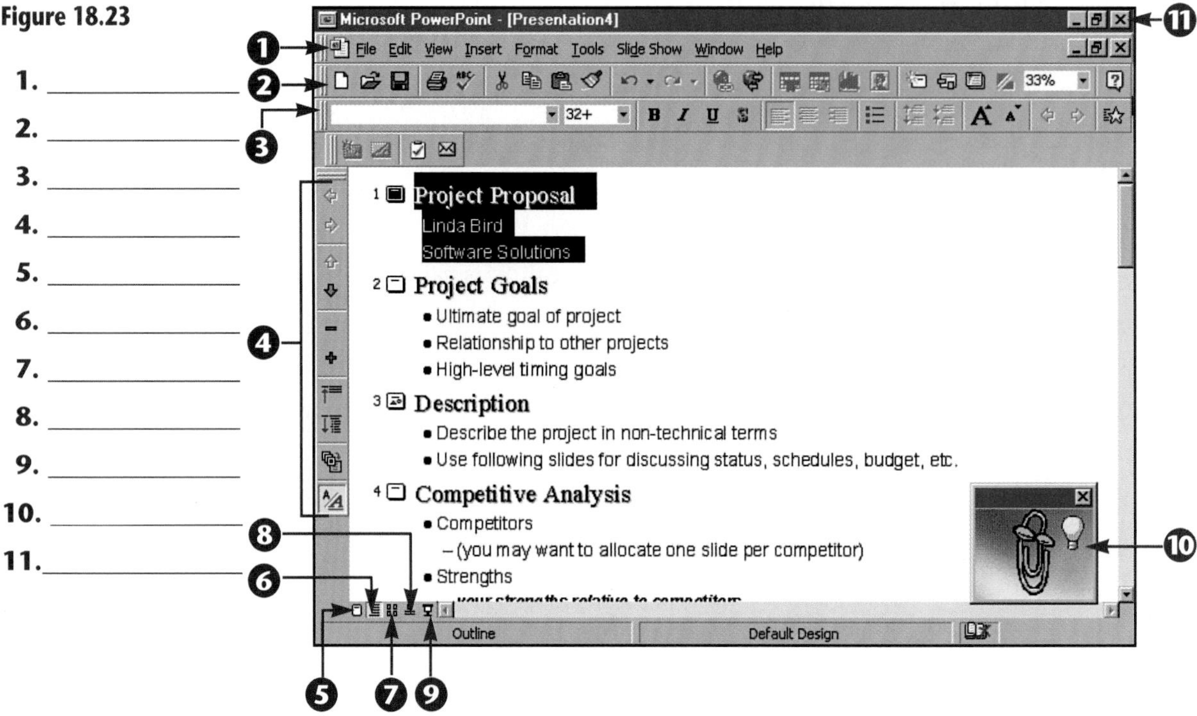

Applying Your Skills

Practice

The following exercises enable you to practice the skills you have learned in this project. Take a few minutes to work through these exercises now.

1. Creating a Presentation

Because you have attended a PowerPoint class, everyone in your department now considers you a PowerPoint expert. For this reason, your coworkers want you to convince management to buy the latest and greatest computers for them. You decide to use PowerPoint to present your ideas at tomorrow's meeting to show that purchasing new computers would be cost-effective. Because you need to prepare the presentation by tomorrow, you decide to use the AutoContent Wizard. After creating the presentation, you can practice displaying it in different views and running an electronic slide show.

To Create a Presentation

1. Start PowerPoint, if necessary.
2. Choose **A**utoContent Wizard in the startup dialog box. (If this dialog box is not displayed, choose **F**ile, **N**ew, click the Presentations tab, and double-click AutoContent Wizard.)

3. Choose Selling Your Ideas as the presentation type.
4. Choose an on-screen presentation for an informal meeting. Also indicate that you'd like PowerPoint to produce handouts.
5. Type `Improving Productivity` as your presentation title. Enter your name and company, if necessary.
6. Use the view buttons to observe the presentation in each of the five views.
7. Use the methods listed in Table 18.3 to move among slides in Slide view and Outline view.
8. Run the electronic slide show. Use the shortcut menu to move to the previous and next slides as well as to end the show.
9. Save the presentation as `Our Plan for Getting New Computers` and then close it.

2. Creating a Marketing Plan Presentation

As Marketing Manager, you've just found out that your boss wants you to present your new marketing plan at the upcoming annual company meeting. Because the meeting is only two days away, you decide to use the AutoContent Wizard to quickly create an on-screen presentation.

To Create a Marketing Plan Presentation

1. Start PowerPoint, if necessary, and choose the **A**utoContent Wizard from the startup dialog box. (If this dialog box is not displayed, choose **F**ile, **N**ew, click the Presentations tab, and double-click AutoContent Wizard.)
2. Choose Marketing Plan as the presentation type and click the **F**inish button.
3. View the text contents of the presentation in Outline view; then choose **V**iew, **S**lide to switch to Slide view.
4. Use the vertical scroll bar to move through the slides in Slide view.
5. Run the electronic slide show. Use the shortcut menu to move among the slides and end the show.
6. Save the presentation as `Marketing Plan for the Annual Meeting` and then close it.

3. Creating a Presentation with the AutoContent Wizard

You are working for a company that deals in computer ergonomics products—products designed to help people work more effectively at the computer. You want to create a presentation to promote your products for a sales meeting. You decide to use the AutoContent Wizard to create the basic framework and suggested slide content.

To Create a Presentation with the AutoContent Wizard

1. Start PowerPoint, if necessary, and choose the **A**utoContent Wizard from the startup dialog box. (If this dialog box is not displayed, choose **F**ile, **N**ew, click the Presentations tab, and double-click AutoContent Wizard.)
2. Choose Product/Services Overview as the presentation type and choose **F**inish.
3. Click the Slide Show button to run the presentation as an electronic slide show.
4. Press ↵Enter to advance through the presentation one slide at a time.
5. Press Esc to end the show.
6. Save the presentation as `Company Products` and close it.

4. Using the Office Assistant

You stay late one night at the office to learn a few new features in PowerPoint. In order to use your time efficiently, you decide to use PowerPoint 97's Office Assistant to find the information you need.

To Use the Office Assistant

1. In the open PowerPoint screen, click the Office Assistant button on the Standard toolbar.
2. Click the **T**ips button to view a tip.
3. In the tip bubble, scroll through the available tips by clicking the Next and **B**ack buttons.
4. Close the tip bubble by clicking the Close button.
5. Display the Assistant's bubble by clicking the Office Assistant window.
6. Type `How do I create a presentation?` in the text box area; then choose **S**earch.
7. Choose a subject from those displayed. When you're finished reading the information, close the help dialog box.
8. Close the Office Assistant window by clicking the Close button.

5. Using the AutoContent Wizard

As part of one of your business classes you need to give a speech on a software program. Because you are familiar with PowerPoint 97, you decide to create a PowerPoint presentation to use along with your speech.

To Use the AutoContent Wizard

1. Start PowerPoint if necessary; then choose **F**ile, **N**ew to display the New Presentations dialog box.
2. Click the Presentations tab to display that page.
3. Double-click the AutoContent Wizard icon to start the AutoContent Wizard.
4. Read the opening AutoContent Wizard dialog box; then click **N**ext.
5. Choose **G**eneral as the type of presentation and choose Generic from the list; then click **N**ext.
6. Click the **P**resentations, informal meetings, handouts option button and then click **N**ext.
7. Click the On-**s**creen presentation and **Y**es option buttons in the Presentation style step; then click **N**ext.
8. In the Presentation options screen, type `PowerPoint 97` in the **P**resentation title text box. Press Tab to move to the **Y**our name text box and enter your name. Also enter the school you attend in the **A**dditional information text box. When you're finished entering text, click **N**ext.
9. Click **F**inish in the last AutoContent screen to view your presentation as an outline.
10. Save the presentation as `PowerPoint 97 Speech`; then close it.

Challenge

The following challenges enable you to use your problem-solving skills. Take time to work through these exercises now.

1. Using the AutoContent Wizard

You are president of your university's Biking Club. As such, you are frequently asked to give presentations on the activities in which your club participates. To quickly develop a presentation of this type, you decide to use the AutoContent Wizard.

To Use the AutoContent Wizard

1. Start PowerPoint and display the New Presentations dialog box.
2. Launch the AutoContent Wizard.
3. Choose the Product/Services Overview as the Presentation type.
4. Choose the option that creates a presentation for meetings. Also choose to create an on-screen presentation.
5. Enter `University Biking Club` as the Presentation title. Also enter your name and school in the appropriate locations in the AutoContent Wizard screens.
6. View the presentation in Outline, Slide, Slide Sorter and Slide Show views.
7. Save the presentation as `Biking Club Presentation`; then close it.

2. Using Different PowerPoint Views

You are helping a friend create a presentation for the first time and learn the basics of using the PowerPoint views. To do so, you use the AutoContent Wizard.

To Use Different PowerPoint Views

1. Start PowerPoint and display the New Presentations dialog box.
2. Start the AutoContent Wizard.
3. Choose whichever presentation type you wish; then click **F**inish.
4. Click PowerPoint's view buttons to display the presentation in Outline, Slide Sorter, Slide, Notes Page, and Slide Show views.
5. Use the **V**iew menu to display the presentation in the various views.
6. Close the presentation without saving it.

3. Using the AutoContent Wizard to Create an Announcement

You're planning a birthday party for a friend. To create the invitations in a snap, you decide to use the AutoContent Wizard.

To Use the AutoContent Wizard to Create an Announcement

1. Start PowerPoint and display the New Presentations dialog box.
2. Launch the AutoContent Wizard.
3. Choose the Announcement/Flyer presentation type in the Personal Category.
4. Choose the **P**resentations, informal meetings, handouts option in the Output options screen.

5. Choose to display the presentation on-screen and to print handouts.
6. In the Presentation options screen, type `Birthday Party!` in the **P**resentation title text box. Delete entries in the other text boxes.
7. View the presentation in Outline, Slide, Slide Sorter and Slide Show views.
8. Save the presentation as `Birthday Party`.
9. Close the presentation.

4. Using Help and the Office Assistant

You have some extra time after class and decide to research a few PowerPoint topics. You use PowerPoint's help system and Office Assistant to do so.

To Use Help and the Office Assistant

1. Start PowerPoint if necessary, then choose **H**elp, **C**ontents and Index to display the Help Topics: Microsoft PowerPoint dialog box.
2. Double-click the Key information book icon; then research the following topics:
   a. What's new in PowerPoint 97
   b. How to get started with PowerPoint 97
3. Write down at least one new thing you learned for each topic.
4. On the Contents page of the Help Topics: Microsoft PowerPoint dialog box, double-click the Working in Different Views book icon.
5. Double-click PowerPoint Views sub-topic; then click each of the hyperlink buttons to display information about the views.
6. Click the Close button in the Microsoft PowerPoint dialog box to close it.
7. Click the Office Assistant button on the Standard toolbar.
8. Type `How do I run a slide show?` in the text box area of the Assistant's bubble; then choose **S**earch.
9. Click the "Ways to run a slide show" option button and read the displayed information. Close the Microsoft PowerPoint dialog box.
10. Close the Office Assistant.

5. Moving among Presentation Slides

Because you have learned PowerPoint so quickly, your instructor has hired you as a tutor for those students who are struggling. To brush up on your skills before a tutorial session, you work through the following steps:

To Move among Presentation Slides

1. Create a new presentation using the AutoContent Wizard.
2. Use the view buttons to display the presentation in Outline, Slide Sorter, Slide and Notes Page views.
3. Display the presentation in Slide view.
4. Use the mouse and keyboard commands listed in Table 18.3 to move among slides.

5. Move to slide 1 in the presentation; then start the electronic slide show.
6. Click the left mouse button several times to move through the entire presentation.
7. Click the right mouse button to display the slide show shortcut menu; then use its commands to move forward and backward through the slide show.
8. Choose End **S**how from the shortcut menu to stop the slide show.
9. Close your presentation without saving it.

Project 19

Changing the Appearance of a Presentation

Objectives

In this project, you learn how to:

- Use Templates
- Work with Color Schemes
- Change the Slide Background
- Work with a Slide Master
- Create Drawn Objects
- Select and Modify Drawn Objects
- Use Clip Art

Why Would I Do This?

You can strengthen the impact of your presentations by enhancing the color and design. PowerPoint contains a number of color schemes and design layouts created by graphic artists to make your presentation truly outstanding. You can use these preset color schemes or create your own. You can also use PowerPoint's Slide Master to add design elements, such as date and time, to every slide in your presentation.

Another way to spice up a presentation is to include drawings and illustrations. PowerPoint comes with a set of electronic pictures, called clip art, that you can add to emphasize parts of your presentation. You can also use PowerPoint's drawing tools to create simple or complex illustrations. By combining these features, you can produce an impressive presentation quickly and easily. Try using these features to create an exciting presentation now.

Lesson 1: Using Templates

Template
A blueprint that PowerPoint uses to create slides. The template includes the formatting, color, and graphics necessary to create a particular look.

PowerPoint provides an extensive group of predesigned *templates* (sometimes called *design templates*) that you can use for your presentation. Because these templates have been created by professional graphic artists, the templates can help you create a presentation with a consistent, well-designed look. By using the templates, you can concentrate on content rather than on layout and design.

You can use a template at any time while working with a presentation. You can choose a template when you initially create the presentation, or you can apply a template later. For example, if you have already created a presentation but want to see some other "looks," you can apply various templates until you find one you like. Try working with templates now.

To Use Templates

1. **Start PowerPoint, if necessary, and close the PowerPoint startup dialog box; then choose File, New.**

   The New Presentation dialog box is displayed, as shown in Figure 19.1.

   You can click the General, Presentations, Presentation Designs, or Web Pages tab to display the associated page and create that type of presentation.

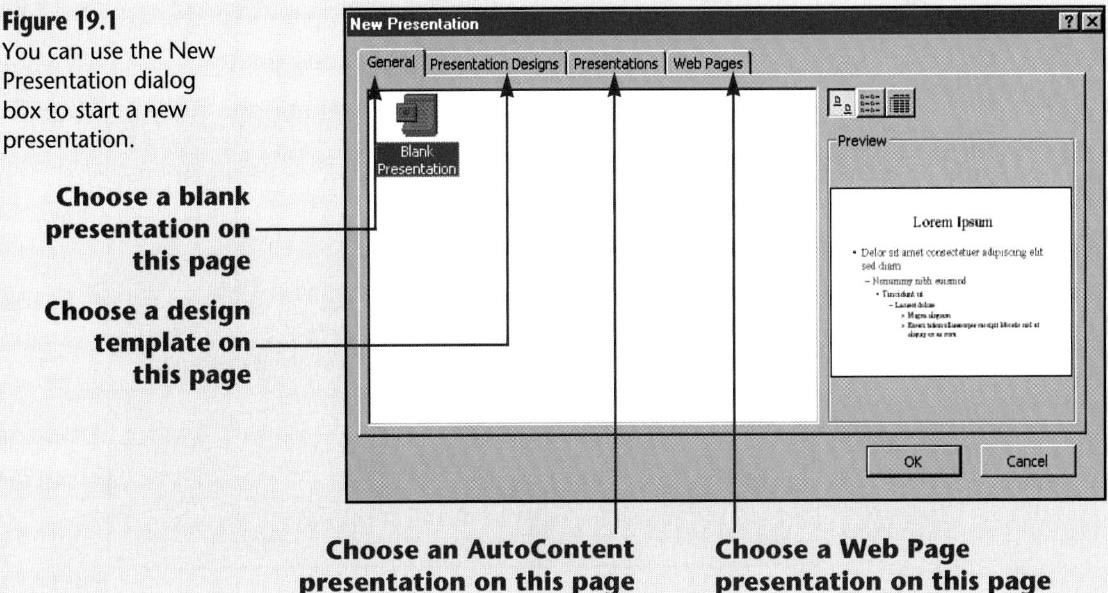

Figure 19.1
You can use the New Presentation dialog box to start a new presentation.

The General tab, used to create a blank presentation, has no particular template associated with it. The Presentations tab provides a list of files that the AutoContent Wizard uses to make presentations with sample content already included. The Web Pages page helps you design a home page for the World Wide Web. Finally, the Presentation Designs tab includes a list of available templates. You use this page to select a template.

2 Click the Presentation Designs tab.

This brings the Presentation Designs page to the front. The templates available are shown (see Figure 19.2). You can use this page to preview and choose a template for your presentation.

If you have problems...

If your templates look different from those shown in Figure 19.2, don't worry—your system probably is showing the files in List view or Details view rather than in Large Icons view. You can click the Large Icons button to display the templates in Large Icons view.

continues

To Use Templates (continued)

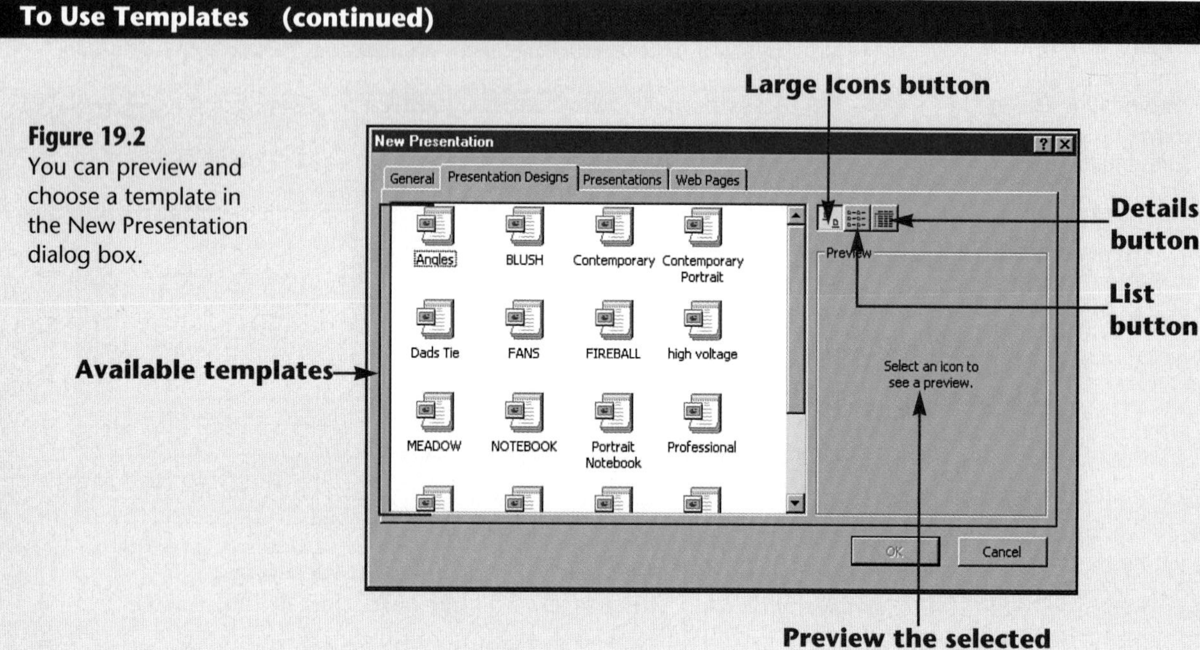

Figure 19.2
You can preview and choose a template in the New Presentation dialog box.

3 Click the Angles template icon.

The preview area displays an example of the selected template. If you want, click several templates to preview them and then proceed with the tutorial.

4 Choose the Fireball template and click OK.

The New Slide dialog box is displayed so that you can select an AutoLayout.

5 Make sure the Title Slide AutoLayout is selected; then choose OK.

A title slide with the selected template is created. All slides that you add to this presentation will use the same template.

6 In the title placeholder, type your company name and enter your own name in the subtitle area.

You can choose a template when you initially create a presentation, or you can apply another template to an existing presentation. Try changing design templates now.

7 Right-click the mouse on the slide, and from the shortcut menu, choose Apply Design.

The Apply Design dialog box is displayed, showing a list of all available templates (see Figure 19.3). Notice that this is the same list of templates you saw in the New Presentation dialog box. Additionally, you can preview a template by clicking it, just as you did earlier.

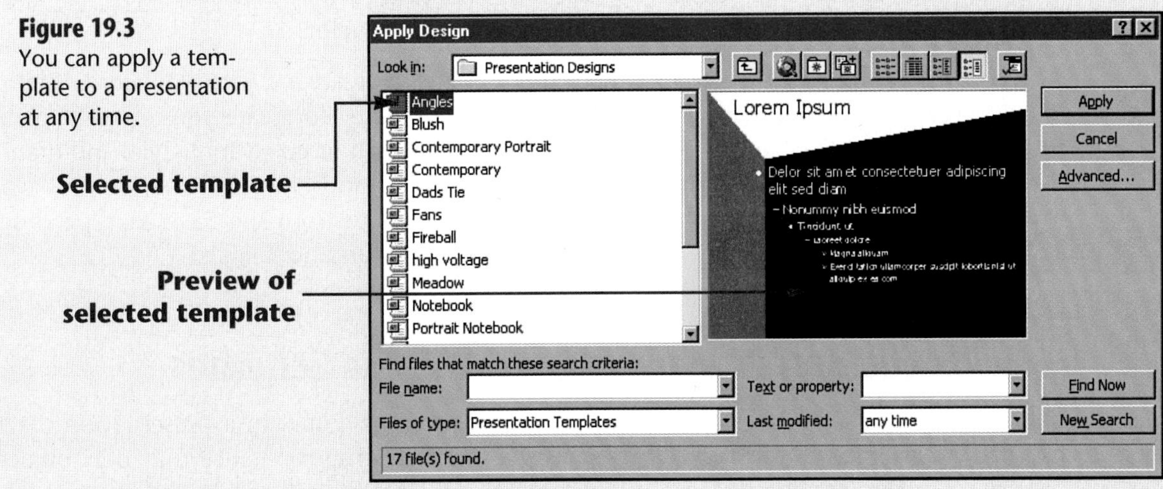

Figure 19.3
You can apply a template to a presentation at any time.

8 Choose the Notebook template and click Apply.

The new template design is applied to the presentation (see Figure 19.4). If you want, try applying other templates. When you're finished, close the presentation without saving it.

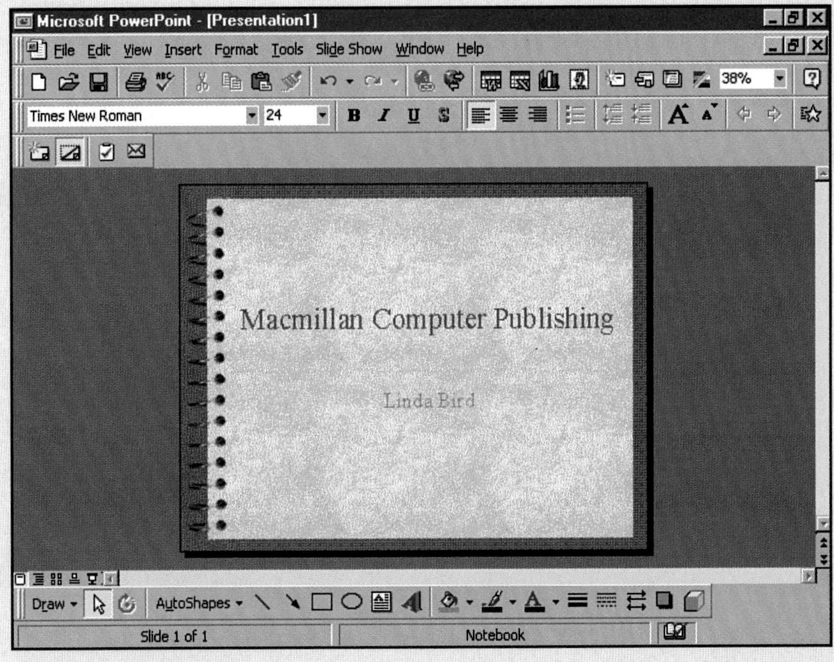

Figure 19.4
You can change design templates for a different appearance.

Keep PowerPoint running for the next lesson, in which you work with color schemes.

You can apply design templates by choosing F**o**rmat, Appl**y** Design or by clicking the Apply Design button on the Standard toolbar.

If you are artistically inclined (or just want to create a custom look for your presentations), you can design your own template. To create your own template, change whatever slide features you'd like—such as color, font style, and graphics—of a presentation. Choose **F**ile, Save **A**s and enter a name for your new template. Then choose Presentation Template from the Save as **t**ype drop-down list so that it will be saved as a template and not a file.

Lesson 2: Working with Color Schemes

Color scheme
A set of eight coordinated colors you can use in your presentation.

A color scheme is the underlying set of eight colors in a presentation. Each template that you use includes a color scheme to ensure that new objects you create or recolor will match those already in place. For example, when you change font color, the colors initially displayed are from the underlying color scheme.

In addition to using the color scheme in place, you can change the color scheme for all slides in a presentation or for just the current slide.

Changing color schemes for the entire presentation is handy for a couple of reasons. You might be about to give a presentation on the road, and the LCD or computer screen doesn't have the same contrast as your office computer. Being able to change the color scheme could create a better contrast and literally save your presentation (or job)!

You may also have similar presentations but have added customized slides for different audiences—one set for sales, one for marketing, one for advertising, and so on. By changing the color scheme for each audience, you can instantly tell that you are running the correct version of your presentation.

You can also change the color scheme for only one slide in order to highlight certain information. For example, you might want to highlight a new proposal or agenda. Changing color schemes for that slide is a subtle but effective attention-grabber.

Try customizing the color scheme of an existing presentation now.

To Work with Color Schemes

1. **Open Proj1901 and save it as `Hickory`.**

2. **Display the presentation in Slide Sorter view.**

   Color schemes are easy to see in Slide view or Slide Sorter view.

3. **Choose Format, Slide Color Scheme.**

   The Color Scheme dialog box is displayed, as shown in Figure 19.5. If you are working in Slide view, you can also open this dialog box by choosing Slide **C**olor Scheme from the shortcut menu.

Figure 19.5
You can quickly change color schemes in the Color Scheme dialog box.

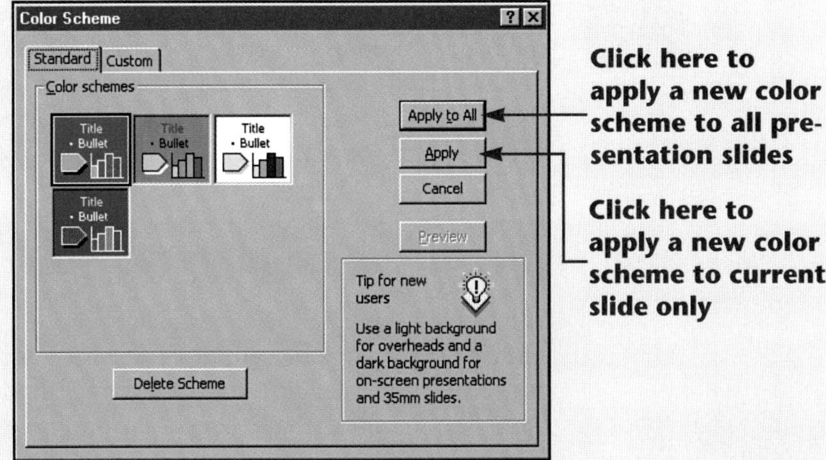

In general, you should select a scheme with a light background and dark text for overheads. Select a dark background with contrasting text for on-screen display and 35mm slides. Try selecting a color scheme for on-screen display now.

4. **Select the dark maroon color scheme on the second row; then choose Apply to All.**

The presentation is shown with the dark maroon color scheme applied to all slides. However, if you chose **A**pply, the color scheme for only the displayed slide would change. Try changing the color scheme for just one slide now.

5. **Select Slide 3, `Our Customer's Needs`, and choose Format, Slide Color Scheme.**

6. **In the Color Scheme dialog box, choose the light blue color scheme (the middle box) on the first row and then choose Apply.**

The selected color scheme is applied to the selected slide only. Notice that the slide elements, such as graphics and font style, remain consistent on all slides (because they are created by the underlying template) but that the color combinations are different.

7. **Save the `Hickory` presentation and then close it.**

Keep PowerPoint running for the next lesson, in which you change the background color.

If you have problems...

Make sure you choose **A**pply rather than Apply **t**o All if you want to change the color scheme for the current slide only.

If you like the overall color scheme but want to change color for one color element, click the Custom tab in the Color Scheme dialog box to display the colors that make up the scheme. Click the **S**cheme color you want to change; then choose Change C**o**lor. Choose a color in the Color dialog box and then choose OK. You can choose **A**pply to place the modified color scheme on the currently displayed slide, or Apply **t**o All to change the color scheme on all slides.

Lesson 3: Changing the Slide Background

You can also change the slide background. By changing the background, you add pizzazz to your presentation and get your audience's attention. You can customize your background by adding shadow effects, textures, and patterns. Try changing the slide background now.

To Change the Slide Background

1. **Open Proj1902 and save it as `Appalachian Logging Company`.**

2. **With Slide 1, `Business Overview`, in Slide view, choose Format, Background.**

   The Background dialog box is displayed, as shown in Figure 19.6.

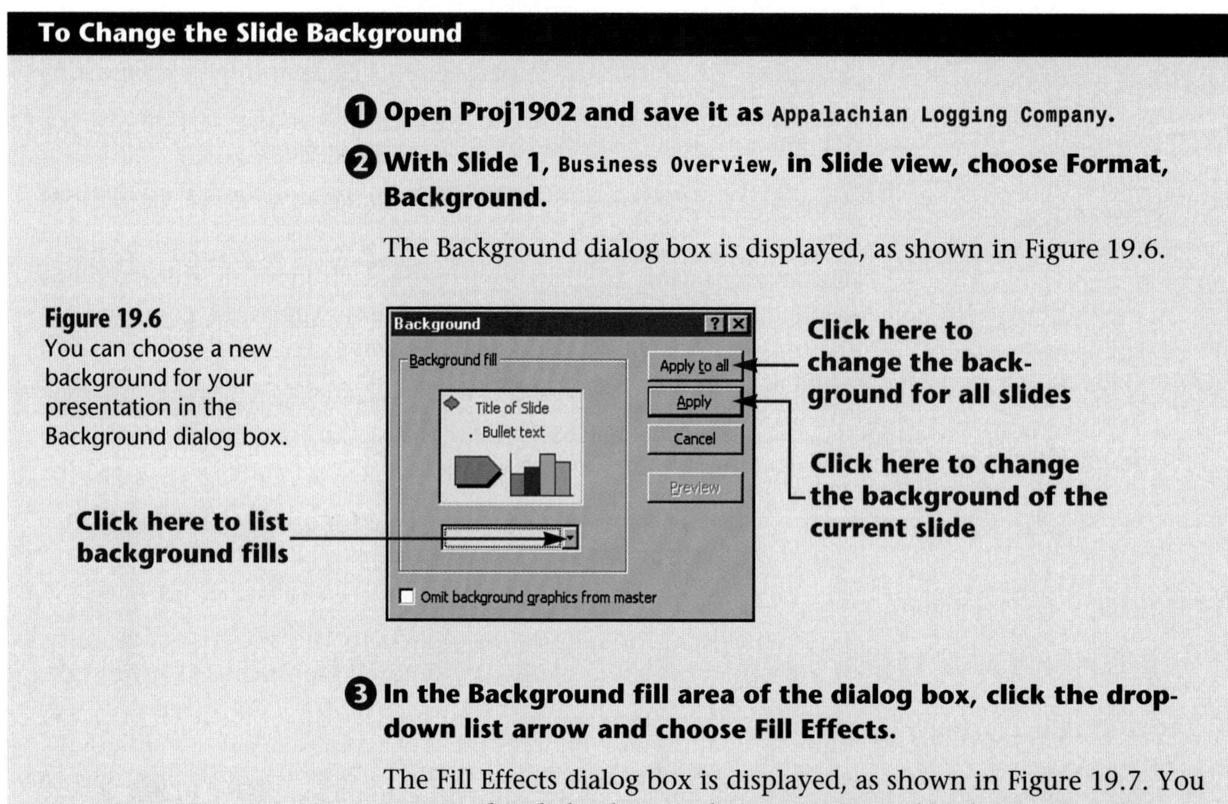

Figure 19.6
You can choose a new background for your presentation in the Background dialog box.

3. **In the Background fill area of the dialog box, click the drop-down list arrow and choose Fill Effects.**

   The Fill Effects dialog box is displayed, as shown in Figure 19.7. You can use this dialog box to choose a variety of background styles.

Figure 19.7
You can choose a variety of gradient patterns.

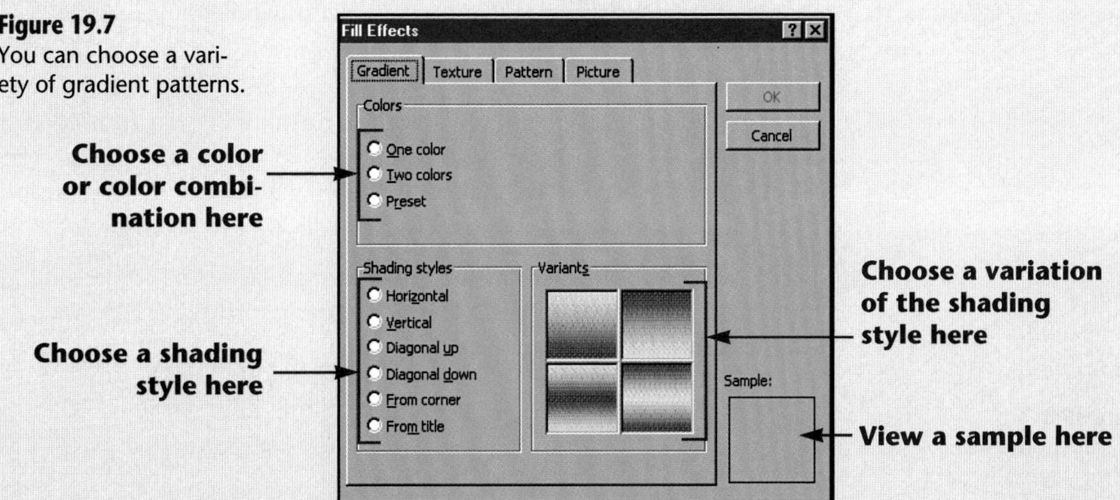

4 Click the Gradient tab, if necessary, and then click the Preset option button in the Colors area.

PowerPoint selects a color scheme pattern consistent with the underlying template. You can also choose variations of the pattern.

5 Click the Diagonal up option button and preview your choice in the Sample box.

6 Choose OK and then choose Apply to all in the Background dialog box.

The new background style is applied to all slides. (If you want to confirm this, scroll through all the slides. Display Slide 1, `Business Overview`, before proceeding.)

PowerPoint also provides a number of textures you can use as a background. Try using these now.

7 Right-click Slide 1, `Business Overview`, to display the shortcut menu; then choose Background.

The Background dialog box is displayed.

If you have problems...

Make sure you right-click on the slide background and not on a placeholder area so that the correct shortcut menu is displayed.

8 Choose Fill Effects from the drop-down list of available backgrounds.

The Fill Effects dialog box is displayed.

continues

To Change the Slide Background (continued)

9 In the Fill Effects dialog box, click the Texture tab.

The Texture page is displayed with a number of natural-looking backgrounds, such as wood and stone, that you can use. If you want, click several of the textures to preview them in the Sample box before proceeding with the next steps.

10 Scroll through the available textures and choose Oak, as shown in Figure 19.8; then click OK to close the Fill Effects dialog box.

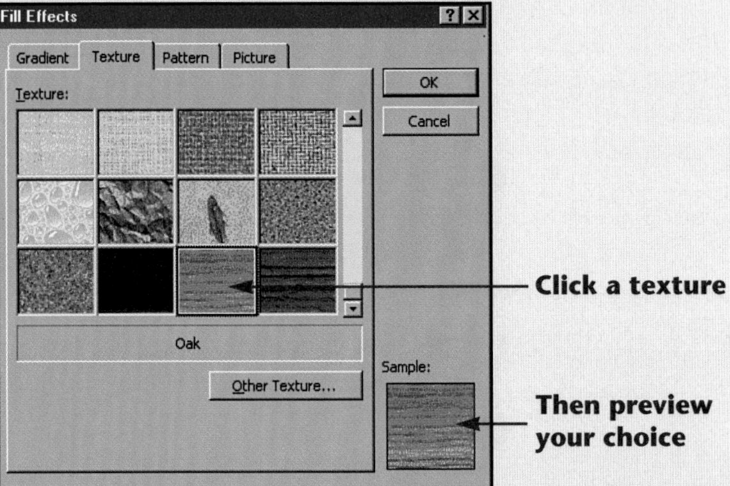

Figure 19.8
You can choose a texture for your slide background.

11 Choose Apply to all in the Background dialog box.

The textured oak wood background is applied to all slides in the presentation.

12 Save and close the file.

Keep PowerPoint running for the next lesson, in which you work with a Slide Master.

Lesson 4: Working with a Slide Master

Slide Master
A framework slide that controls how a slide will look and enables you to place items such as date, name, and logo on each slide automatically.

The *Slide Master* controls the elements displayed on each slide. Every presentation that you create automatically includes the Slide Master. This master works "behind the scenes" and contains instructions so that the same objects are included on every presentation slide. You can change the Slide Master so that different elements are included in a specific presentation. For example, once you place a logo or the date on the Slide Master, that element is displayed on all slides in the presentation.

You can use four masters in PowerPoint: Slide Master, Title Master, Handout Master, and Notes Master. Each dictates the elements included on the associated slide type. In this lesson, you use and modify a Slide Master. Try working with a Slide Master now.

To Work with a Slide Master

1 Open Proj1903 and save it as `Star Manufacturing`.

2 Choose View, Master, Slide Master.

The master slide for the presentation is displayed (see Figure 19.9). It contains a title object and a body object that you can use to specify the default format for the title and body text. You can also add other objects, such as the date, to the Slide Master to be included on all slides.

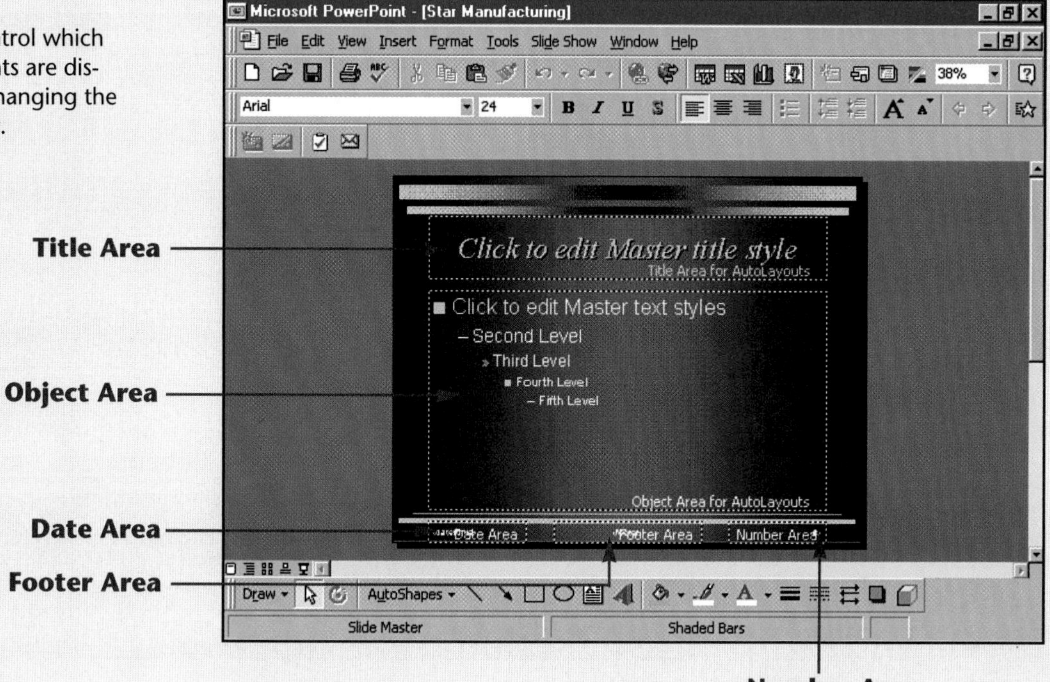

Figure 19.9
You can control which slide elements are displayed by changing the Slide Master.

3 Click the object `Click to edit Master title style.`

The title area is selected, as indicated by the thickened border. The text in this area is currently formatted in italic.

4 Click the Italic button.

Italic is removed from the title area text. Because you made this change on the Slide Master rather than on an individual slide, the change affects all the presentation slides.

You can also customize the presentation by including information such as your name, department, or company name in the footer area of the Slide Master. When you place this information on the Slide Master, the information is automatically placed on all slides.

To work more effectively with the Slide Master, you can use the Zoom button on the Standard toolbar to enlarge the view.

continues

To Work with a Slide Master (continued)

5 Click the Zoom button drop-down list arrow and choose 66%.

Your view is enlarged, enabling you to see the Slide Master objects more easily.

6 Use the vertical scroll bar to scroll to the bottom of the Slide Master; then click the footer area object.

The footer area is selected (see Figure 19.10). You also see a field for footer text. You can select this field and then enter your own text.

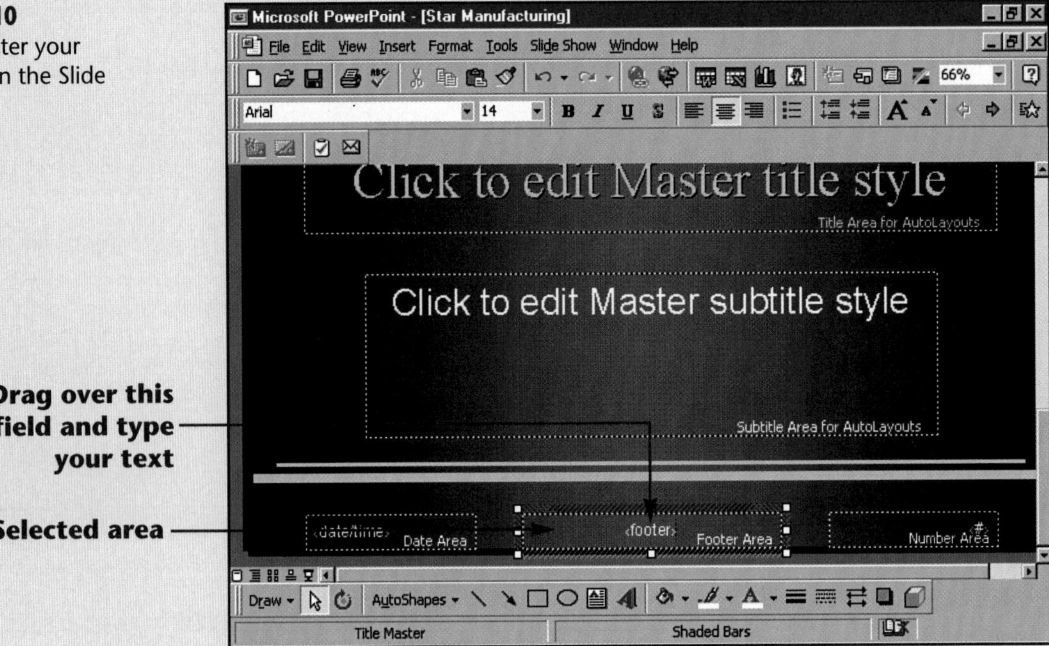

Figure 19.10
You can enter your own text on the Slide Master.

7 Drag over the <footer> field and type `Joyce Parks, Management.`

The text that you type is entered in the footer area so that it can be included on every slide. Before you switch to Slide view, change the view percentage so that you can see an entire slide on-screen.

8 Click the Zoom button drop-down list arrow and choose Fit.

The entire Slide Master is displayed on-screen. Switch to Slide view so that you can see the change on your presentation slides.

9 Choose View, Slide.

The footer text is inserted on each slide in the presentation. Scroll through the slides to see the text at the bottom of each slide.

10 Save and close the presentation.

Keep PowerPoint running for the next lesson, in which you create drawn objects.

To toggle quickly between the Slide Master and Slide view, rest the mouse pointer on the Slide View button. Press and hold down ⇧Shift and click the Slide View button. The Slide Master is displayed. You can click the Slide View button again to return the presentation to Slide view.

Lesson 5: Creating Drawn Objects

With PowerPoint, you can add drawn objects—such as rectangles, ovals, lines, and arrows—to your presentation. PowerPoint has a variety of drawing tools that enable you to create simple to complex illustrations. You can use these tools to jazz up a slide or emphasize specific information (see Figure 19.11). Once the objects are created, you can move, resize, and modify them. By using graphics in your presentation, you make it a cut above the rest and help get your audience's attention.

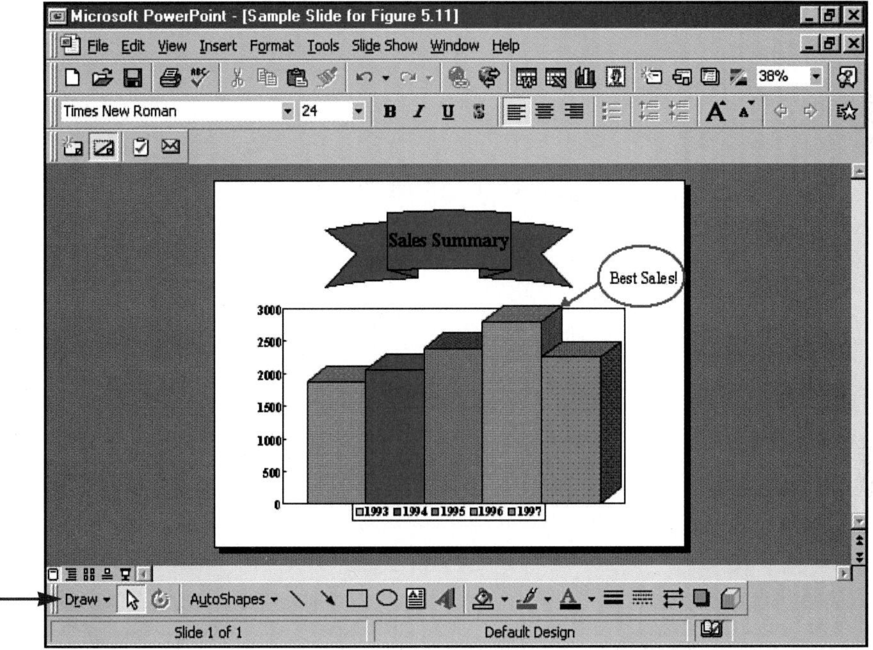

Figure 19.11
You can jazz up a slide with drawn objects.

In this lesson, you learn how to create basic objects by using the tools on the Drawing toolbar. Table 19.1 describes these tools. You can use this table as a handy reference when you create and modify drawings.

Table 19.1 The Drawing Tools

Tool	Name	Use
	Select Objects	Select drawn objects
	Free Rotate	Rotate a selected object
AutoShapes	AutoShape	Display menu options for inserting a predesigned shape
	Line	Draw a line

continues

Table 19.1 Continued

Tool	Name	Use
	Arrow	Draw an arrow
	Rectangle	Draw rectangles and squares
	Oval	Draw ellipses and circles
	Text Box	Draw a text box where you click and drag so that you can enter text
	Insert WordArt	Start the WordArt program
	Fill Color	Add, remove, or modify the texture, color, or pattern for a selected object
	Line Color	Add, remove, or modify the line color for a selected object
	Font Color	Change font color for a selected object
	Line Style	Change line thickness
	Dash Style	Change line appearance
	Arrow Style	Change arrowhead appearance
	Shadow	Add, remove, or modify shadow formatting for a selected object
	3-D	Add, remove, or modify 3-D formatting for a selected object

To Create Drawn Objects

1 Start a new presentation and display a blank slide.

You can use PowerPoint's horizontal and vertical rulers in order to help you accurately place drawn objects. You can turn the rulers on or off by choosing **V**iew, **R**uler. When turned on, the rulers appear in Slide view and Notes Page view, at the top and left side of the slide window. The 0" marks on the horizontal and vertical rulers represent the center of the slide. When you draw an object, the movement reflects on the rulers to show your exact location on the slide.

2 Choose View, Ruler.

The rulers are displayed (see Figure 19.12).

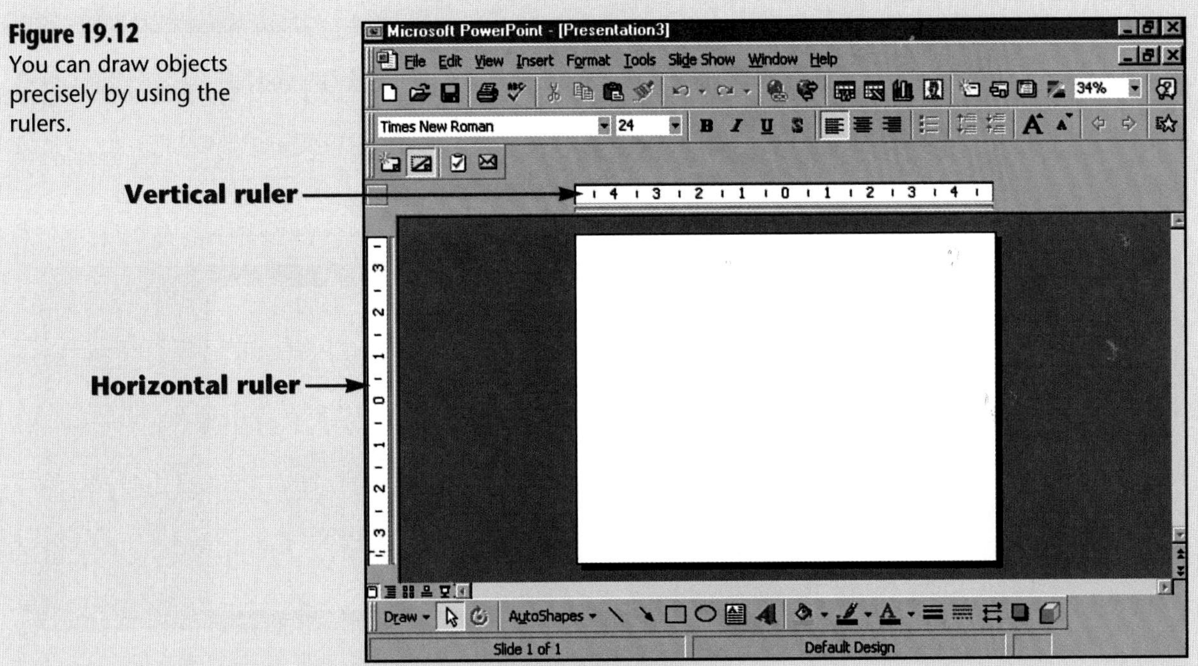

Figure 19.12
You can draw objects precisely by using the rulers.

3 Click the Rectangle tool on the Drawing toolbar and move the mouse pointer to the slide area.

The mouse pointer changes to a crosshair so that you can accurately place the drawn object.

4 On the slide, position the crosshair where the two 0" marks intersect; then click and drag until the lower-right corner of the rectangle is at the place where the 3" horizontal ruler mark and the 2" vertical ruler mark intersect.

A rectangle is added to your presentation (see Figure 19.13). The fill color and line colors used for the object are whatever was used most recently for the Fill Color and Line Color tools. Additionally, white selection handles appear around the object to indicate that it is selected. When you click on the slide or draw another object, the rectangle is deselected.

continues

To Create Drawn Objects (continued)

Figure 19.13
You can add drawings to your presentation.

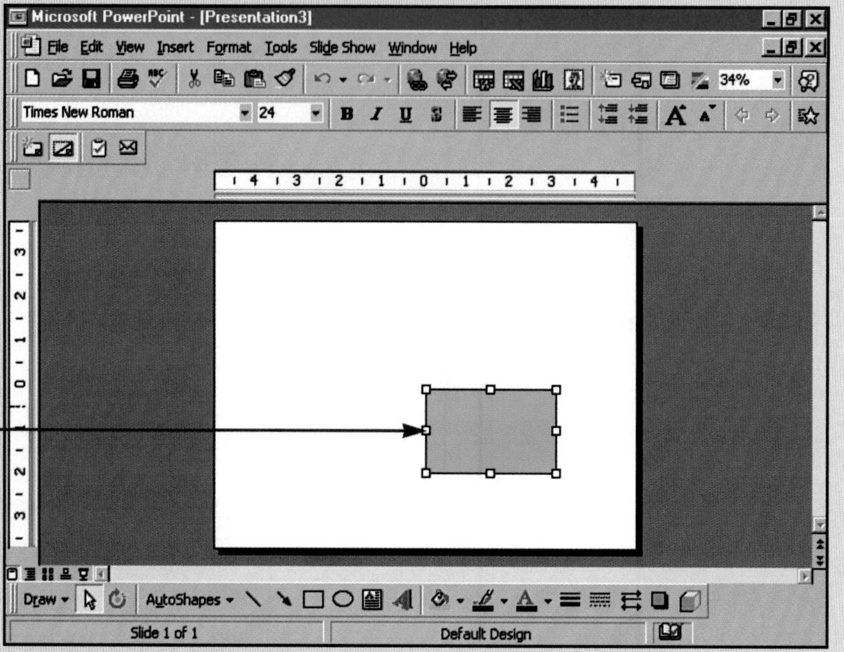

Selection handle

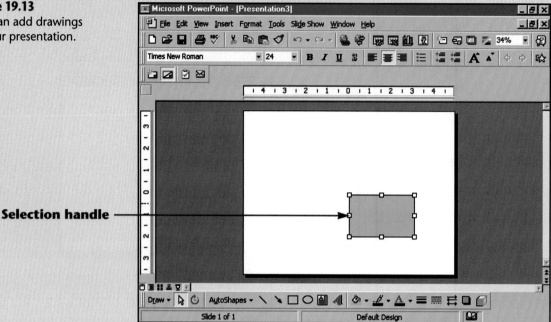

You can use other tools in the same manner. You click the tool and then drag to draw the object on the slide. Try drawing an oval, or an ellipse, now.

5 Click the Oval tool and drag to draw an oval in the upper-left corner of the slide.

You can also make an object symmetrical by pressing Shift as you draw it. For example, pressing Shift while using the Rectangle tool produces a perfect square; pressing Shift while using the Oval tool creates a perfect circle. Try drawing a circle now.

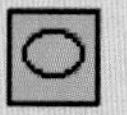

6 Click the Oval tool, press Shift, and drag to draw a circle in the lower-left corner of the slide.

If you have problems...

Make sure you release the mouse button before you release Shift, or your object may skew into an oval.

You can also use the Line tool to create lines. To make the line straight, press Shift while you draw it.

7 Click the Line tool and draw a line from the oval to the rectangle (see Figure 19.14).

Figure 19.14
You can draw lines on your slide.

Select the Line tool and drag from here...

to here

A drawing tool is automatically turned off once you draw an object with it. However, you can double-click the tool to keep it active so that you can draw multiple objects. You turn the tool off by clicking it a second time or pressing Esc. Try drawing multiple ovals now with the Oval tool.

8 Double-click the Oval tool and draw several small ovals in the upper-right corner of the slide.

Your slide should look similar to that in Figure 19.15.

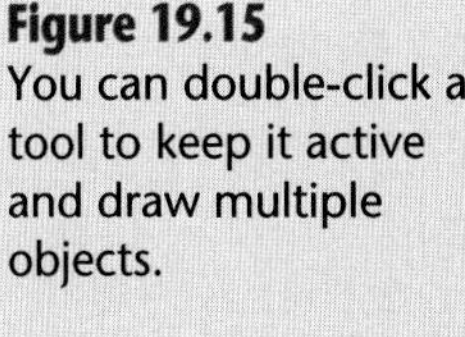

Figure 19.15
You can double-click a tool to keep it active and draw multiple objects.

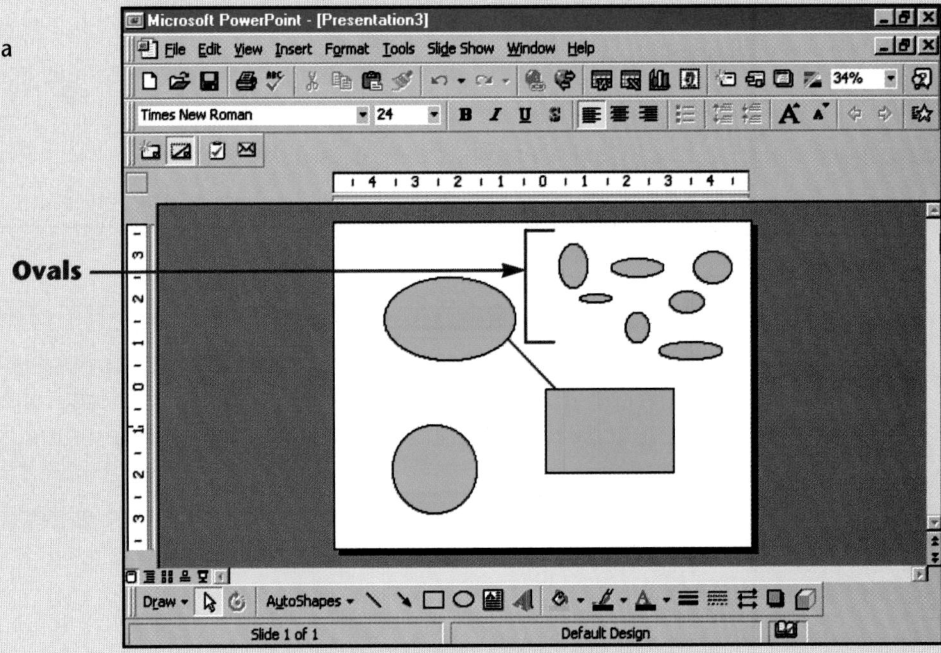

continues

To Create Drawn Objects (continued)

9 Click the Oval tool to turn it off.

If you want, practice using the various drawing tools. When you're finished, close your presentation without saving it. Keep PowerPoint open for the next lesson, in which you select and modify objects.

If you're not very artistic, or you simply want some help when you create drawings, you can use PowerPoint's AutoShapes feature to create professionally designed shapes. Click the A**u**toShapes tool on the Drawing toolbar to display the AutoShapes menu. Move your mouse pointer to a menu item to display a graphical submenu; then click the shape you want. You drag to draw the shape on a slide, just as you created rectangles, ovals, and lines in the preceding lesson.

Lesson 6: Selecting and Modifying Drawn Objects

After you have created drawn objects, you can modify them in a number of ways. You can move, resize, recolor, or delete objects. However, before you modify an object, you must first select it. You can use Table 19.2 as a handy reference for selecting and deselecting objects.

Table 19.2 Methods of Selecting Objects

To	Do This
Select an object	Click the object.
Select multiple objects	Press and hold down Shift while clicking objects.
	Using the Select Objects tool, draw a box around all objects.
Deselect one object	Hold down Shift, click the object, and release Shift.
Deselect all objects	Click outside selected objects.

Selecting, Resizing, Moving, and Deleting Drawn Objects

In this lesson, you learn how to select drawn objects by using some of the techniques listed in Table 19.2. Once the objects are selected, you can modify them in various ways. Try selecting and modifying objects now.

To Select, Resize, Move, and Delete Drawn Objects

1 Open Proj1904 and save it as `Drawing`.

2 Click the diamond object.

The diamond is selected, as indicated by the white selection handles that surround it.

3 Press and hold down Shift, click the rectangle object, and then release Shift.

The rectangle is selected in addition to the diamond.

4 Click the Select Objects tool on the Drawing toolbar, if necessary, and drag from above and to the left of the diamond object down to the lower-right corner of the slide.

A dashed border indicates the area being selected (see Figure 19.16).

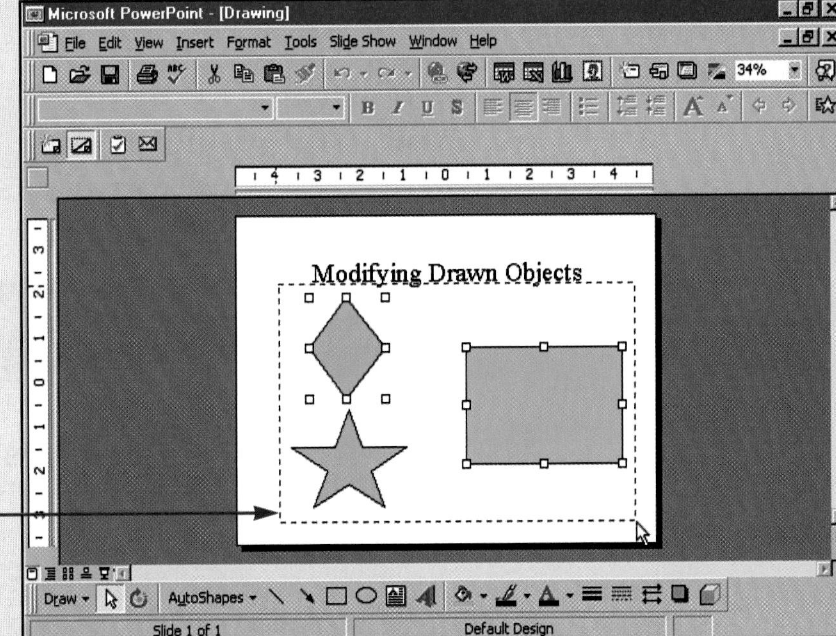

Figure 19.16 You can select multiple objects.

5 Release the mouse button.

When you release the mouse button, all the objects within the area are selected, indicated by white selection handles.

If you have problems...

Make sure you start drawing the selection box above and to the left of all the objects. If you start in the middle of an object, that object won't be selected.

continues

To Select, Resize, Move, and Delete Drawn Objects (continued)

6 Click outside the objects.

All objects are deselected. Next, you learn to resize an object.

7 Click the rectangle to select it and then move the mouse pointer across the top-center handle until it becomes a two-sided resizing arrow (see Figure 19.17).

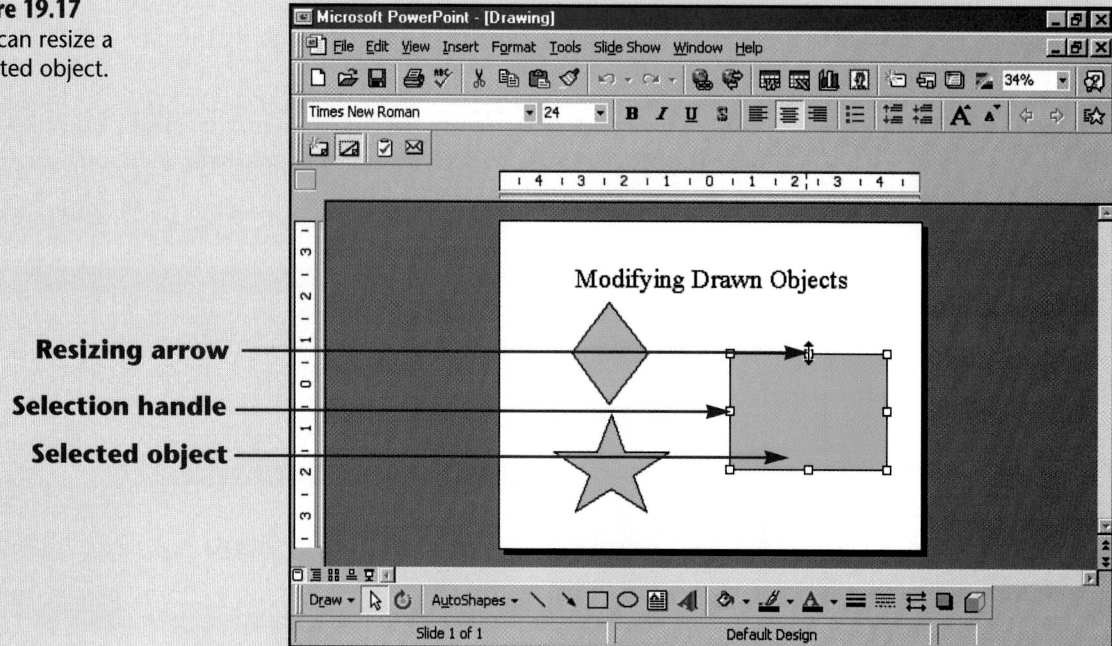

Figure 19.17
You can resize a selected object.

8 Drag the upper border of the rectangle downward to resize it to about half the original size; then release the mouse button.

The rectangle is resized. You can also move a selected object.

9 With the rectangle still selected, move the mouse pointer inside the rectangle until the pointer changes to a four-sided arrow.

10 Click and drag the rectangle object until it touches the bottom border of the slide; then release the mouse button.

The drawn object is moved. If you make a mistake as you move or resize an object, choose **E**dit, **U**ndo to reverse the action. You can also delete objects.

11 Select the rectangle if it isn't already selected and press Del.

The selected object is deleted. Selecting several objects before pressing Del erases all the objects at once. If you accidentally delete an object, click the Undo button. Keep the presentation open for the next tutorial.

Changing Lines and Colors on a Drawn Object

After the objects are selected, you can change the color and lines associated with them. Changing lines and colors helps to emphasize certain information in your presentation or to create a different "look." Try changing lines and colors now.

To Change Lines and Colors on a Drawn Object

1 In the Drawing presentation that you revised in the preceding tutorial, select the star object.

As usual, you must first select an object before you can modify it.

2 Click the Fill Color tool drop-down arrow.

A color palette is displayed (see Figure 19.18). You can use this palette to select a coordinating color or a fill effect. You can also click the **M**ore Fill Colors button to see additional colors.

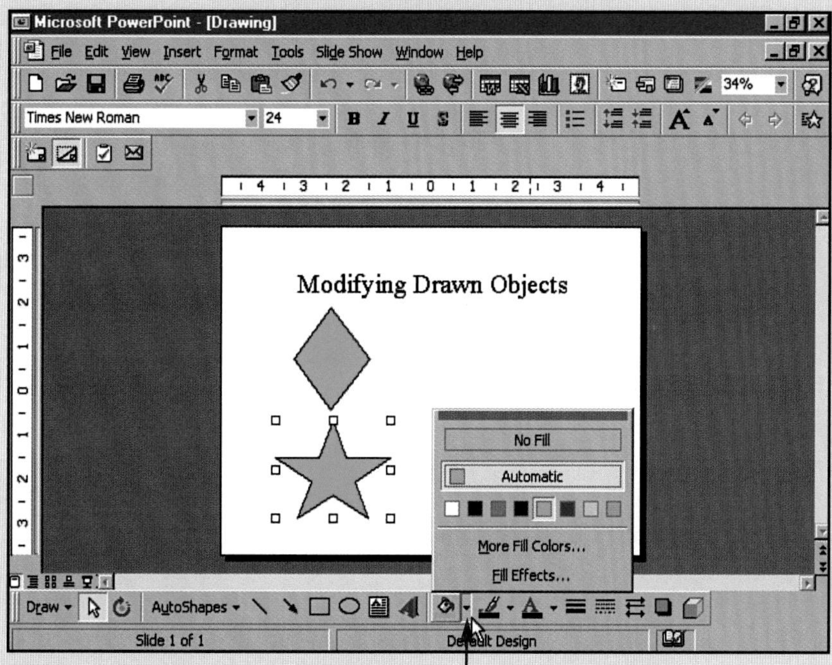

Figure 19.18
You can quickly change fill color or effects.

Click this arrow to display a palette of color and fill effects

3 Click the blue color (the third box from the right).

The Fill Color palette closes, and the selected color is applied to the star.

4 With the star object still selected, click the Line Style tool.

A palette of line styles is displayed (see Figure 19.19). You can choose a line style from this palette to apply to the selected object.

continues

To Change Lines and Colors on a Drawn Object (continued)

Figure 19.19
You can select a new line style for your object.

Choose this line style

5 Click the 6-point triple line (refer to Figure 19.19).

The selected line style applies to the star. (If you want to see the effect better, choose **V**iew, **Z**oom, **6**6%. When you're finished viewing your changes, choose **V**iew, **Z**oom, **F**it to see the entire slide.)

You can also change the line color.

6 Click the Line Color tool drop-down arrow and choose gray (the third color from the left).

The star's outline border appears in gray.

7 Save the `Drawing` presentation and then close it.

You can apply color and line options to several objects at once by selecting them and then applying the attributes to the entire group.

Lesson 7: Using Clip Art

Clip art
A collection of electronic pictures, stored on disk and available for use by PowerPoint.

The PowerPoint program includes a good selection of electronic *clip art* in its Clip Gallery that you can use to enhance your presentation. Including clip art on a slide can help hold audience attention and reinforce your main points. The Clip Gallery that comes with PowerPoint includes a variety of pictures for personal and business use. You can also purchase additional clip art if you want more choices.

After clip art is placed on a slide, you can change its location, size, and appearance. Clip art can also be ungrouped into its component parts so that you can work with each part as an individual object. For example, you can recolor parts of a map to highlight data associated with it. Try your hand at clip art now.

To Use Clip Art

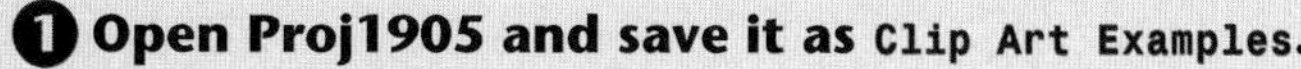

1 Open Proj1905 and save it as `Clip Art Examples`.

2 Display Slide 2, `Financial Stability`, in Slide view, and click the New Slide button.

3 In the New Slide dialog box, click the Text & Clip Art AutoLayout (the first slide on the third row) and choose OK.

A new slide is inserted with a clip art placeholder (see Figure 19.20). You can double-click this placeholder object to display the Clip Gallery and then choose a picture.

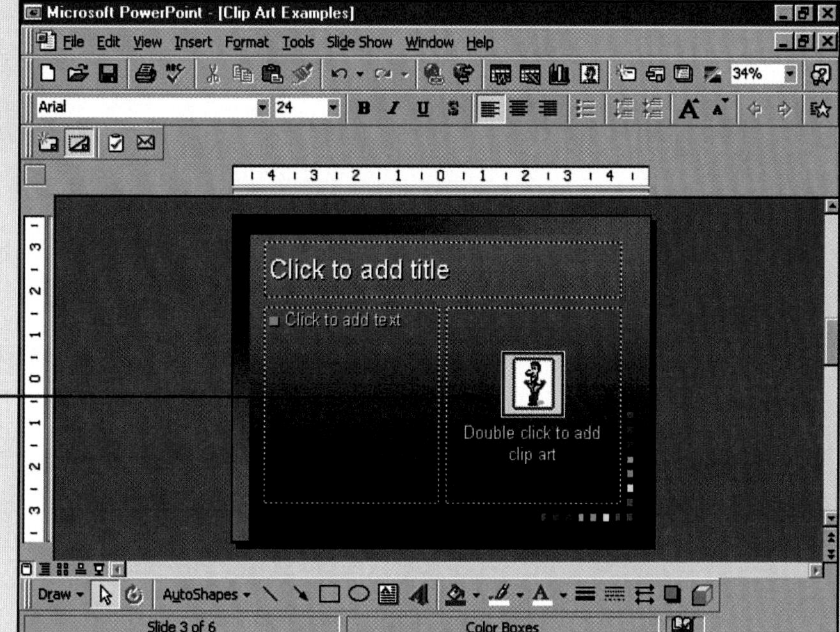

Figure 19.20
You can use the clip art placeholder to access the Clip Gallery.

4 Double-click the clip art placeholder.

The Microsoft Clip Gallery dialog box is displayed, with a graphical list of available images, as shown in Figure 19.21. (The Clip Gallery on your computer may list different pictures from those illustrated in this project, depending on what art has been installed.) Once you are in the Clip Gallery, you can view all the available clip art or select a specific category to limit the display.

continues

To Use Clip Art (continued)

Figure 19.21
The Microsoft Clip Gallery dialog box displays the available images.

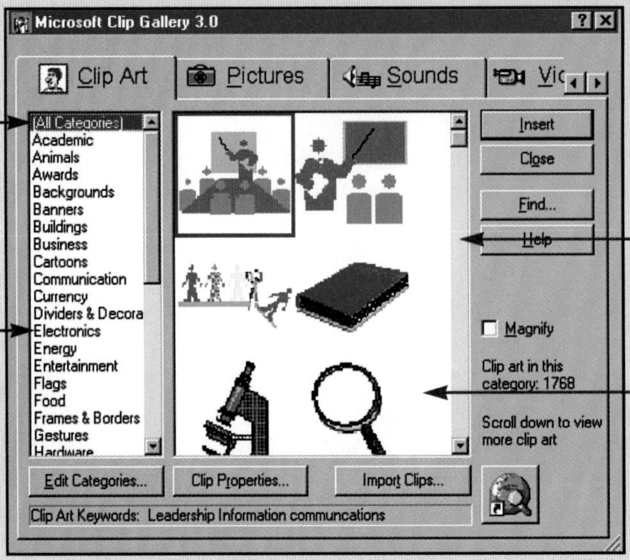

Click here to display all pictures

Click a category to limit the display

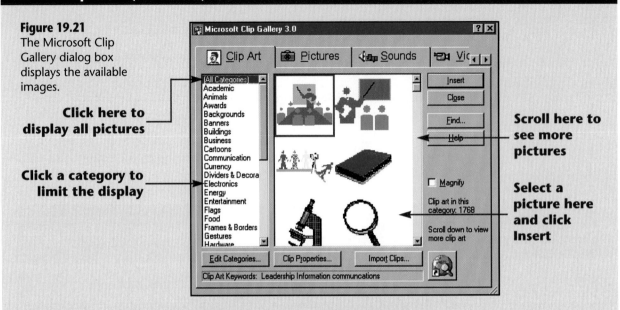

Scroll here to see more pictures

Select a picture here and click Insert

❺ **Click the Buildings category, select the image indicated in Figure 19.22, and choose Insert.**

Figure 19.22
You can choose from a variety of clip art.

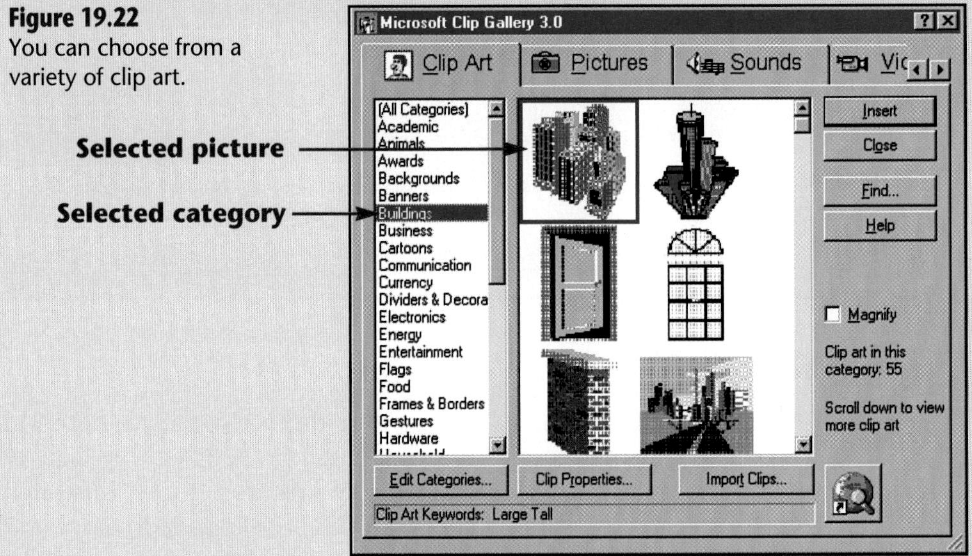

The selected image is placed on the slide. The white selection handles indicate that the image can currently be resized, moved, or deleted in the same way as the drawn objects in Lesson 6.

You can easily replace the clip art on your slide with another clip art image. Just double-click the clip art to access the Clip Gallery; then choose another image. Try replacing the picture now.

❻ **Double-click the clip art on your slide.**

The Clip Gallery is displayed.

7 Choose any category and picture you want; then choose Insert.

The clip art you originally selected is replaced by the new image.

You can also insert clip art on a slide that doesn't have a clip art placeholder. To do this, you use the Insert Clip Art button. Try this now.

8 Move to Slide 2, `Financial Stability`, and click the Insert Clip Art button.

The Clip Gallery is displayed so that you can choose a picture. You can quickly insert the picture on your slide by double-clicking the picture.

9 In the Currency category, double-click to insert the Money Bags with the Dollar Sign picture on your slide. (If this image isn't available on your computer, choose a similar one.)

The picture is placed on the slide. If you don't like the placement or size of the picture, you can easily move or resize it, just as you moved and resized the drawn objects. Click to select the picture; then drag it to a new location or use the resizing handles to change the size.

10 Move the picture so that it is displayed in a blank area of the slide.

11 Save and close the presentation.

If you have finished your work session, exit PowerPoint and shut down Windows 95 before turning off your computer. Otherwise, complete the "Applying Your Skills" exercises at the end of this project.

After the picture is on the slide, you can recolor the picture to emphasize information. Select the image and choose Format, Picture. Click the Picture tab in the Format Picture dialog box and choose Recolor. In the New area, click the drop-down arrows for the colors you want to change; then choose a new color. You can preview your changes in the Recolor Picture dialog box. When you're satisfied with your choices, close the Recolor Picture and Format Picture dialog boxes.

Project Summary

To	Do This
Apply a template	Click the Apply Design button on the Standard toolbar.
Apply a color scheme	Select Format, Slide Color Scheme.
	Right-click a slide to activate the shortcut menu; select Slide Color Scheme.

continues

To	Do This
Change the slide background	Choose Format, Background.
View the Slide Master	Choose **V**iew, **M**aster, **S**lide Master.
Insert a footer into a Slide Master	Select the footer area placeholder on the Slide Master and then type the text.
Modify a Slide Master	Select the placeholder and then format or change the text.
Create a drawn object	Select the tool from the Drawing toolbar; then click and drag to draw.
Select a drawn object	Click the object.
Select multiple objects	Hold down Shift while clicking objects.
	Use the Select Objects tool and draw a box around all objects.
Deselect one object	Hold down Shift, click the object, and release Shift.
Deselect all objects	Click outside selected objects.
Resize an object	Rest the mouse pointer on a selection handle until the pointer turns into a two-sided arrow; then drag to resize.
Move an object	Move the mouse pointer to the middle of the selected object; then drag to move.
Delete an object	Select the object and press Del.
Change an object's colors	Click the Fill Color tool drop-down arrow on the Drawing toolbar.
Change an object's line style	Click the Line Style tool on the Drawing toolbar.
Insert clip art	Double-click a clip art placeholder.
	Click the Insert Clip Art button on the Standard toolbar.
Replace clip art picture	Double-click a clip art object.
Recolor clip art	Select a picture and choose Format, Picture; then click the Picture tab and choose Recolor.

Checking Your Skills

True/False

For each of the following, check *T* or *F* to indicate whether the statement is true or false.

__T __F **1.** You create drawn objects in your presentation by using the Design toolbar.

__T __F **2.** Changes to the Slide Master, such as adding footer text, apply only to the current slide.

__T __F **3.** The design template enables you to select and print handouts for a presentation.

__T __F **4.** Customizing the template design before building your presentation is usually best because you can't change the template later.

__T __F **5.** You can add clip art to a slide even if it doesn't have a clip art placeholder.

__T __F **6.** You can preview a template before choosing it.

__T __F **7.** You can apply a color scheme to the current slide or to all slides in your presentation.

__T __F **8.** You should carefully draw any objects on a slide because they can't be resized later.

__T __F **9.** You can toggle between the Slide Master and Slide view by pressing Ctrl while clicking the Slide View button.

__T __F **10.** You can double-click a drawing tool to keep it active and create multiple drawings.

Multiple Choice

Circle the letter of the correct answer for each of the following questions.

1. Which of the following is a good reason for changing color schemes?

- **a.** To change display contrast when using an LCD panel and overhead projector
- **b.** To emphasize a particular slide
- **c.** To keep track of similar but slightly different presentations you created for different audiences
- **d.** All the above

2. Which of the following is true regarding Design templates?

- **a.** They are the same as a Slide Master.
- **b.** They are a "blueprint" that PowerPoint uses to determine the overall look of a presentation.
- **c.** They can't be changed once selected.
- **d.** None of the above

3. You can select multiple objects and then do which of the following?

- **a.** Apply the same color or line style to them at the same time.
- **b.** Apply AutoShapes to them.
- **c.** Delete them.
- **d.** Both a and c

4. Using the Slide Master, you can change which of the following?

- **a.** The footer area text
- **b.** Font sizes or styles
- **c.** The date area data
- **d.** All the above

5. You can create a perfect square by doing which of the following?

- **a.** Pressing Shift while using the Rectangle tool
- **b.** Pressing Ctrl while using the Rectangle tool
- **c.** Using the Square tool on the Drawing toolbar
- **d.** Selecting an existing rectangle and then choosing F**o**rmat, S**q**uare

6. When you draw an object on a slide, which of the following occurs?

- **a.** White resizing handles appear to indicate that the object is selected.
- **b.** You use the tools on the Formatting toolbar.
- **c.** You can hold down Ctrl while drawing to make an object symmetrical.
- **d.** All the above

7. Drawn objects are usually used in a PowerPoint presentation to do which of the following?
   a. Create organization charts
   b. Create data charts
   c. Emphasize specific information
   d. All the above
8. You can select multiple drawn objects by doing which of the following?
   a. Double-clicking each of them
   b. Pressing Ctrl while clicking them
   c. Pressing Shift while clicking them
   d. None of the above
9. Which of the following is true in relation to clip art?
   a. PowerPoint displays available pictures in the Clip Gallery.
   b. You can use a toolbar button or a placeholder to insert clip art.
   c. You can recolor clip art.
   d. All the above
10. Which of the following is true regarding the Slide Master?
   a. It controls the way elements on a slide display.
   b. It is the same as a Title Master.
   c. It cannot be changed.
   d. None of the above

Completion

In the blank provided, write the correct answer for each of the following statements.

1. You can select several objects by pressing ______________ while clicking them.
2. You can tell that a drawn object is selected because it has ______________ around its borders.
3. The set of eight colors associated with a slide design is called its ______________.
4. PowerPoint contains electronic pictures referred to as ______________.
5. A blueprint or pattern for slide design is called a(n) ______________.
6. The ______________ dictates the components that display on a slide.
7. You can change the slide ______________ by adding various fill effects (such as wood and stone).
8. You can use vertical and horizontal ______________ to help you draw objects precisely.
9. You can select objects by using the ______________ tool to draw a box around them.
10. You can remove a selected object by pressing ______________.

Matching

In the blank next to each of the following terms or phrases, write the letter of the corresponding term or phrase. (Note that some of the letters may be used more than once.)

____ **1.** Electronic pictures

____ **2.** The drawing tool used to create squares

____ **3.** The drawing tool used to create circles

____ **4.** Eight colors that coordinate with your template

____ **5.** Using a shading style on an entire slide

____ **6.** Enables you to place a logo or footer on each slide

____ **7.** Professionally designed drawn shapes

____ **8.** Indicates that an object is selected

____ **9.** Changes fill color of selected object

____ **10.** Changes line color of selected object

a. AutoShapes

b. handles

c. Slide Master

d. clip art

e. Fill Color button

f. Rectangle

g. Oval

h. Line Color button

i. slide background

j. color scheme

Screen ID

Identify each of the items shown in Figure 19.23.

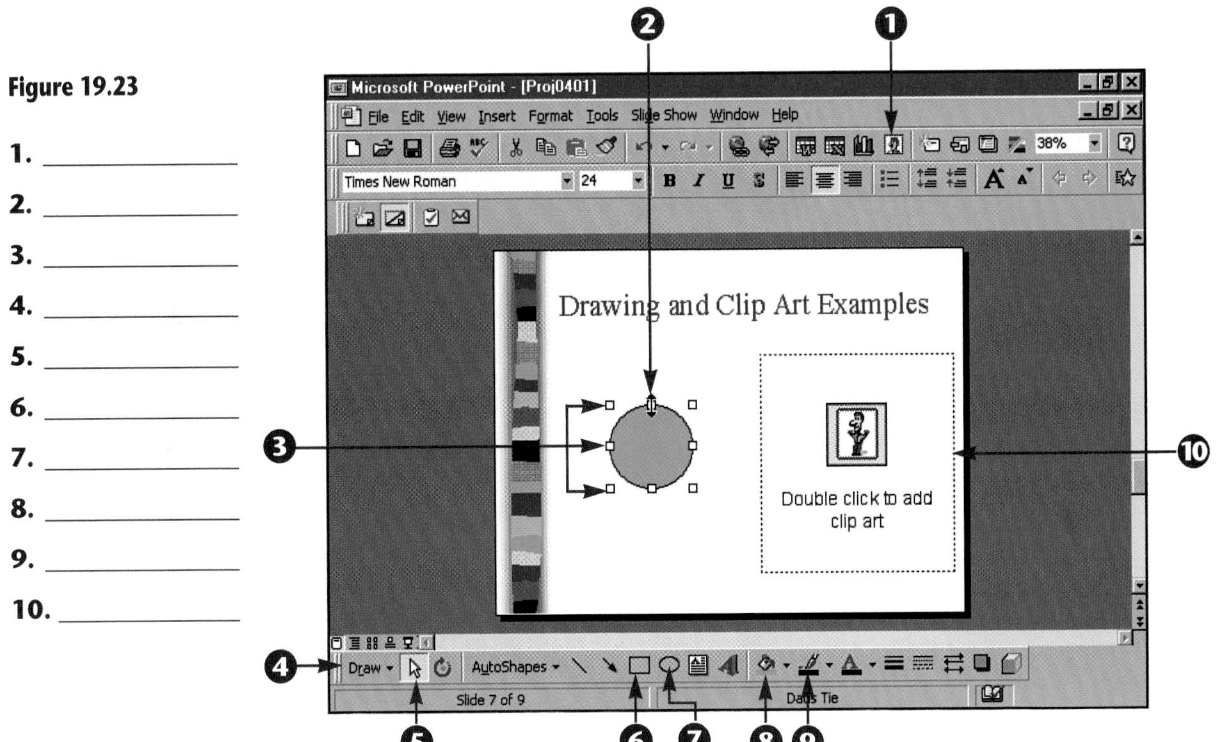

Figure 19.23

1. ____________

2. ____________

3. ____________

4. ____________

5. ____________

6. ____________

7. ____________

8. ____________

9. ____________

10. ____________

Applying Your Skills

Practice

The following exercises enable you to practice the skills you have learned in this project. Take a few minutes to work through these exercises now.

1. Working with Templates, Slide Masters, and Color Schemes

Your boss has asked that you revise a presentation she previously created and that you add some elements to jazz it up. To do this, you decide to apply a different design template. You also add clip art and add a footer to the Slide Master.

To Work with Templates, Slide Masters, and Color Schemes

1. Open Proj1906 and save it as `Company Overview`.
2. Choose F**o**rmat, Appl**y** Design to view the Apply Design dialog box. Then preview the presentation with different design templates such as Dad's Tie, Angles, and Meadow.
3. Apply the Ribbons template to the entire presentation.
4. Add a footer that reads `Report developed by B. Cory` to the Slide Master.
5. Add a clip art image to Slide 2, `Financial Stability`. Select the stacked coins picture from the Currency category (or a similar image).
6. Save and close the presentation.

2. Working with Drawn Objects

As the owner of a small company, you develop your own publicity materials. You decide to practice using PowerPoint's drawing tools so that you can easily create logos, flyers, and other publicity materials.

To Work with Drawn Objects

1. Create a new presentation with a blank slide.
2. Use the Rectangle tool on the Drawing toolbar to create a rectangle and a perfect square.
3. Use the Oval tool to create an ellipse and a perfect circle.
4. Use the Fill Color tool to change the color of each object to blue.
5. Change the line style of each object to a 4½-pt single line. Change the line color of each object to gray.
6. Delete the circle.
7. Resize the rectangle so that it is approximately half the original size.
8. Close the presentation without saving it.

3. Selecting and Modifying Drawn Objects

Your boss has told you that she wants you to use PowerPoint to develop flowcharts and other diagrams for a training manual. In preparation for the project, you decide to practice selecting and modifying drawn objects.

To Select and Modify Drawn Objects

1. Open Proj1907 and save it as `Working with Objects`.
2. Select each of the objects on the slide.
3. Click outside the objects to deselect them.
4. Use the Select Objects tool to select all the objects simultaneously.
5. Deselect the rectangle.
6. Change the fill color for the star and diamond to blue. Change the line style to a 6-pt single line.
7. Click outside the objects to deselect them.
8. Save the presentation and then close it.

4. Using Clip Art

Your company gives a certificate to employees who successfully complete a safety training course. To make the certificate, you decide to insert and recolor clip art on a PowerPoint slide.

To Use Clip Art

1. Create a new presentation with a blank slide.
2. Click the Insert Clip Art button to display the Clip Gallery.
3. Choose the Academic category and double-click any picture that looks like a book.
4. Double-click the clip art picture on your slide to access the Clip Gallery again.
5. Select the picture that looks like a diploma and choose **I**nsert.
6. With the clip art image selected on your slide, choose F**o**rmat, P**i**cture. Click the Picture tab and choose R**e**color.
7. Change the red ribbon to blue.
8. Close the Recolor Picture and Format Picture dialog boxes.
9. View your changes and close the presentation without saving it.

5. Enhancing a Presentation

You need to create a presentation to convince management to buy new software. In order to do this, you use a predesigned presentation; then apply different templates and color schemes to it.

Creating and Enhancing a Presentation

1. Choose **F**ile, **N**ew to create a new presentation.
2. In the New Presentation dialog box, click the Presentations tab. Select the Selling Your Ideas—Dale Carnegie Training® presentation and click OK.
3. Choose F**o**rmat, Appl**y** Design to display the Apply Design dialog box. Preview each of the design templates PowerPoint provides.

4. Apply the Fans template to the entire presentation.
5. Choose Format, Slide Color Scheme to display the Color Scheme dialog box.
6. Choose the third color scheme in the third row; then choose Apply to All.
7. Close the presentation without saving it.

Challenge

The following challenges enable you to use your problem-solving skills. Take time to work through these exercises now.

1. Working with Design Templates

As president of the University Biking Club you are preparing for an upcoming meeting. In order to find the best template for your presentation, you preview several before choosing one.

To Work with Design Templates

1. Open Proj1908 and save it as `Revised Biking Club Presentation`.
2. Preview the presentation with each of the design templates listed in the Apply Design dialog box.
3. Apply the High Voltage template to the presentation.
4. View the presentation as a slide show.
5. Save the presentation; then close it.

2. Working with a Slide Master

To make the elements appear more uniform on your biking club presentation, you decide to change the Slide Master.

To Work with a Slide Master

1. Open Proj1909 and save it as `Slide Master Changes`.
2. Display the Slide Master.
3. Make the Master Title Style italic.
4. Add the current date in the Date Area.
5. Add May Meeting in the Footer Area.
6. Display the presentation in Slide view; then scroll through your presentation to see the changes.
7. Save the presentation; then close it.

3. Working with Clip Art

To spice up your presentation to the biking club, you add some clip art. Then, for added interest, you recolor it.

To Work with Clip Art

1. Open Proj1910 and save it as `Adding Clip Art`.
2. Display Slide 1 in Slide view; then open the Clip Gallery.

3. In the Sports & Leisure category, choose the bicyclist clip art.
4. Move and resize the clip art picture so that it displays in the lower right corner of the slide.
5. Right-click the picture; then choose Format Picture.
6. In the Format Picture dialog box, click the Picture tab and choose Recolor.
7. Change the color of the clip art to dark maroon.
8. Display your presentation as an electronic slide show to see your changes.
9. Save your presentation; then close it.

4. Using Drawing Tools and Clip Art

As part of your biking club presentation, you need to provide directions to the club activity. You decide to use PowerPoint's drawing tools and clip art to do so.

To Use Drawing Tools and Clip Art

1. Open Proj1911 and save it as `Ride and Picnic`.
2. Using PowerPoint's drawing tools, clip art and the following diagram as a guide, create a flyer for the upcoming club activity. (Hint: Use the Text Box tool to create the text.)

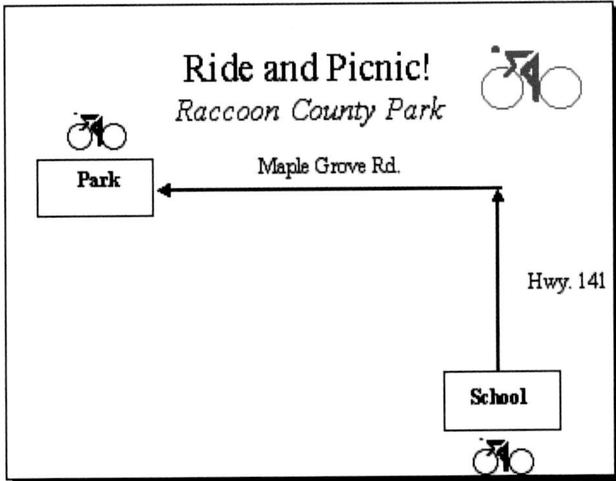

3. Print a copy of the slide.
4. Save the presentation; then close it.

5. Using Color Schemes

You arrive at the biking club meeting to give your presentation when you discover that the presentation's template and color scheme don't display properly using the LCD projector and overhead. Rather than panicking, you decide to quickly change to another color scheme so that the contrast on-screen is more marked.

To Use Color Schemes

1. Open Proj1912 and save it as `Color Scheme Changes`.
2. Change to each of the color schemes available for the presentation.

3. Apply the second color scheme on the first row of the Color Scheme dialog box to the entire presentation.
4. View the presentation as an electronic slide show.
5. Save the presentation; then close it.

Project 20

Integrating Office Applications

Creating a Binder of Rollerblading Club Documents

In this project, you learn how to:

- Merge an Access Table with a Word Letter
- Create an Access Report Using an Excel List
- Create a PowerPoint Presentation from a Word Outline
- Create a Word Handout from a PowerPoint Presentation
- Create and Print a Binder

Why Would I Do This?

Office integration is using one program's features as you work in a document in another program. For example, you can start a Word Wizard from Access to create a form letter, or you can enter data into an Excel worksheet using an Access form. Although conceptually these tasks may sound complex, in reality, Office makes it very simple to integrate its applications.

In this project, you use sample documents concerning an increase in Rollerblading Club dues to explore the ways you can integrate the features of different applications. You integrate Access with Word and Excel—first to create a mailing for the Rollerblading Club, and then to create an Access report from an Excel list. You create a PowerPoint presentation from a Word outline, and then use the presentation to create an accompanying handout in Word. Finally, you use an Office binder to organize these related files.

Lesson 1: Merging an Access Table with a Word Letter

When you want to send a personalized letter to a number of people, you can use Word's Merge feature. For example, if you need to send your resume to a number of people, you can save time by setting up the cover letter as a form letter and then merging the names and addresses of the recipients. The result, a personalized letter, gives the impression that you typed each letter individually. In reality, you only typed the letter once.

Although you can create a document in Word that contains the recipients' names and addresses, Access is much more suited to storing that kind of information. If you have a table of names and addresses in Access, you can make it available for use in a Word Merge without wasting time reentering all of that data.

In this lesson, you merge an existing form letter in Word with the names and addresses of Rollerblading Club members stored in Access. Try starting a merge from Access now.

To Merge an Access Table with a Word Letter

1. **In Windows, copy the PROJ2001 file and name it `Rollerblading Club 3`; then copy the PROJ2002 file and name it `Merge Letter`.**

   You need these two files to conduct the merge. The Rollerblading Club 3 database file contains a table of club members' names and addresses, and the Merge Letter file is a letter informing club members of an increase in dues.

2 Start Access, then open the Rollerblading Club 3 database and the Addresses table.

You want to use the Addresses table as a *data source* in the merge.

Data source
The document that contains the variable data used in a merge.

Main document
The document that contains the data that does not change in a merge.

3 Open the Tools menu, move the mouse pointer to the OfficeLinks command, and choose MergeIt from the submenu.

The Word Mail Merge Wizard dialog box appears on-screen, as shown in Figure 20.1. You can choose to use an existing *main document* in Word, or you can create a new main document. Because the letter document already exists, keep the default selection.

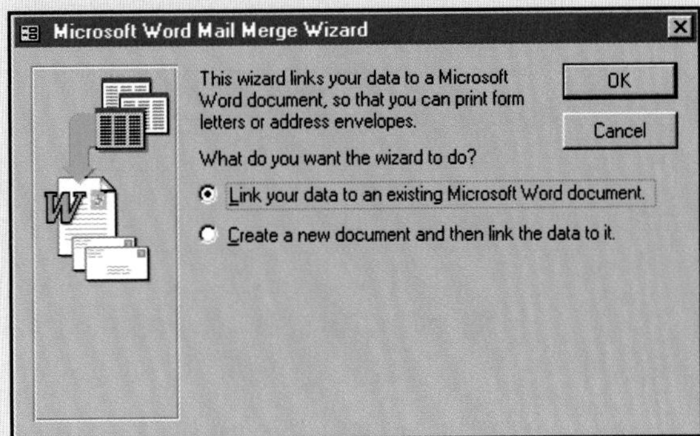

Figure 20.1
The Mail Merge Wizard dialog box.

4 Choose OK.

The Select Microsoft Word Document dialog box appears (see Figure 20.2). This dialog box works similar to the Open dialog box you use to open existing files. By default, all Office files stored in the My Documents folder are displayed.

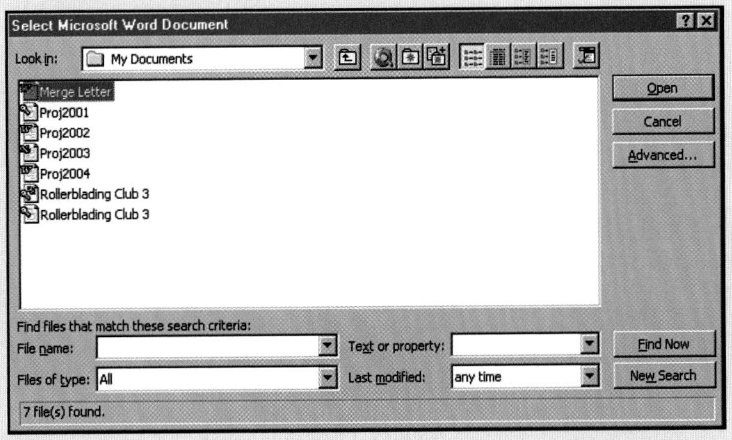

Figure 20.2
The Select Microsoft Word Document dialog box.

continues

To Merge an Access Table with a Word Letter (continued)

5 Double-click the Merge Letter file.

This step selects the Merge Letter file as the main document for the merge. The Mail Merge Wizard opens the selected document in Word, and opens a new, temporary Access window in the background. Notice that the Merge toolbar appears. You use the buttons on the Merge toolbar to set up the Merge Letter for the merge and to conduct the merge. You may need to maximize the Word window in order to see the document clearly. Now, try inserting merge fields into the document.

Figure 20.3
The Merge Letter document.

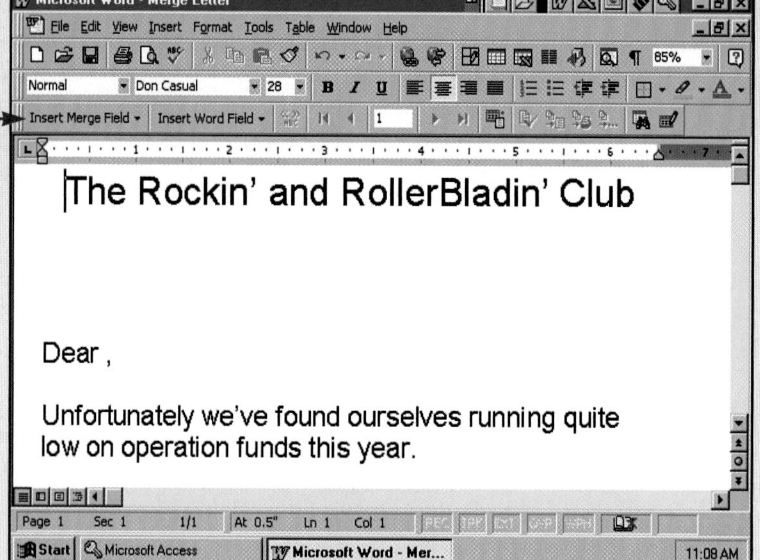

6 Position the mouse pointer two lines below the title.

You want to insert the first *merge field* here.

Merge field
A nonprinting placeholder in the merge main document that identifies what data gets inserted, and where it goes.

7 Click the Insert Merge Field button on the Merge toolbar.

A list appears with fields corresponding to the fields in the Access table, as shown in Figure 20.4.

8 Click First_Name.

The First_Name merge field appears in the document at the insertion point location (see Figure 20.5). During the merge, the data from the First Name field in the Access table replaces the merge field. Now, continue inserting fields to complete the main document.

Figure 20.4
The list of merge fields.

Insert Merge Field button

Select First_Name here

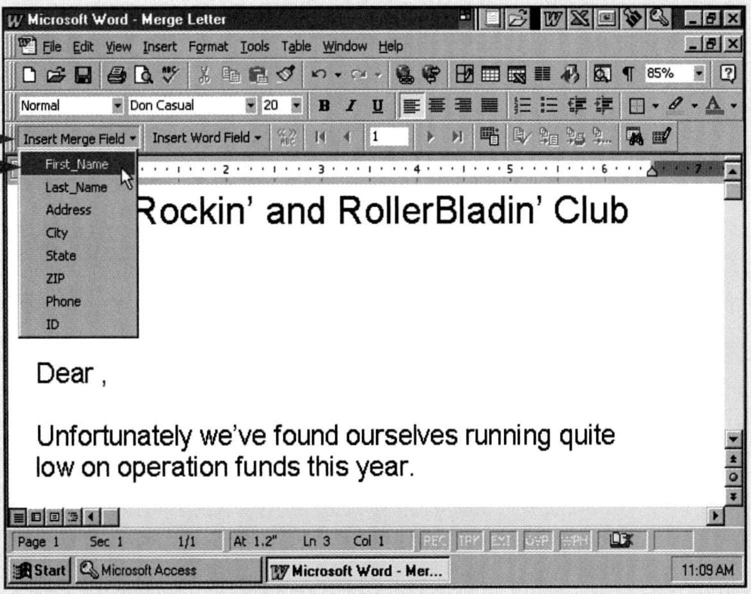

Figure 20.5
The First_Name merge field in the document.

The First_Name Merge field

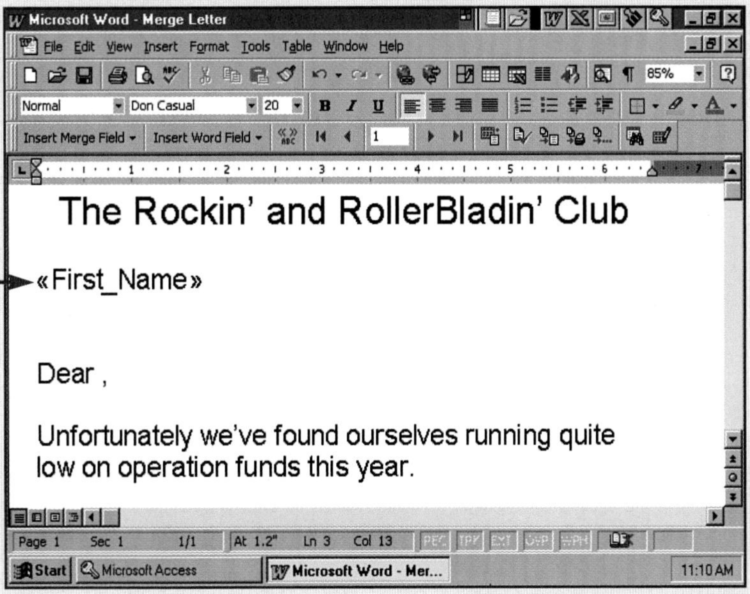

9 Press the Spacebar once, then click the Insert Merge Field button, and choose the Last_Name field.

This step inserts a space after the first name and adds the last name field. When the documents merge, the data source data appears exactly where you position the merge field. If you want to leave a space between the first name and the last name, you must leave a space between the First_Name field and the Last_Name field.

continues

To Merge an Access Table with a Word Letter (continued)

Likewise, if you want any additional characters—such as commas or exclamation points—to appear on every letter printed, you must make sure to insert them into the main document.

10 Press Enter, and choose `Address` from the Insert Merge Field drop-down list; then press Enter again, and choose `City` from the Insert Merge Field drop-down list.

This step completes the first and second lines of the recipient's address information and starts the third line.

11 Type a comma (,), press the Spacebar, and insert the State merge field. Then press the Spacebar, and insert the ZIP code field.

This step completes the recipient's address information. Now, insert a field in the greeting.

12 Position the insertion point to the left of the comma on the greeting line, and choose `First_Name` from the Insert Merge Field drop-down list.

All merge fields are now inserted, as shown in Figure 20.6. You can insert as many merge fields as necessary, and you can use a merge field more than once. You have now finished setting up the main document. Before you actually print the letters, however, you should take a look to see whether they are set up correctly. To do this, you can merge the letters into a file and then look at them in the file.

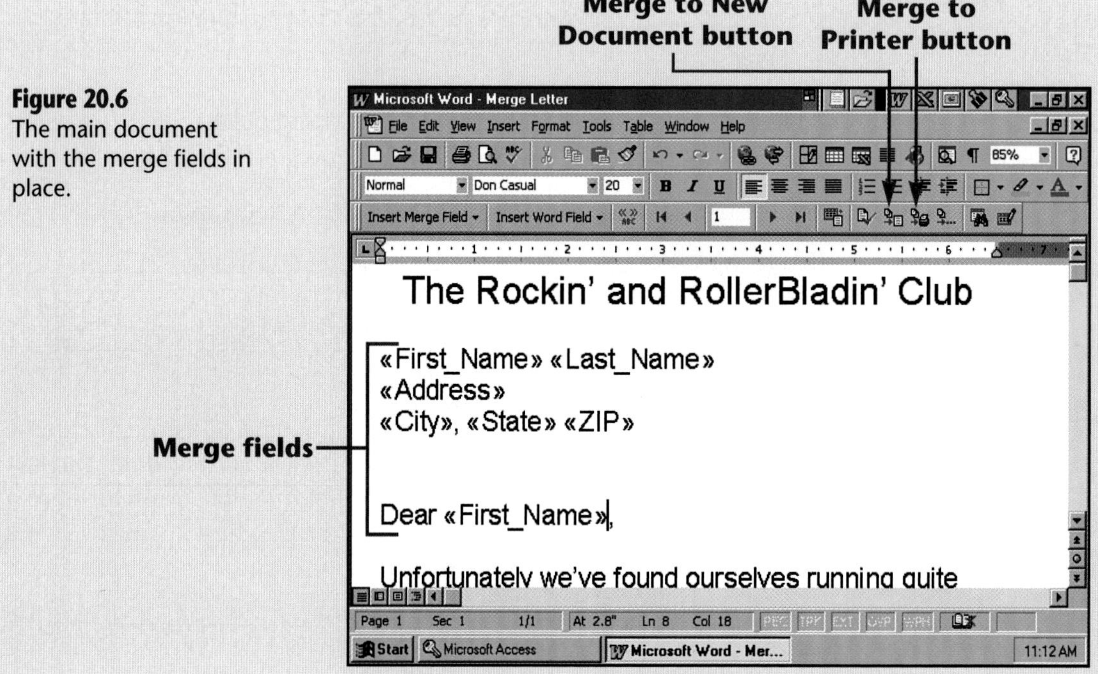

Figure 20.6
The main document with the merge fields in place.

⓭ **Click the Merge to New Document button on the Merge toolbar.**

Word performs the merge, and displays on-screen all of the letters, in a file called Form Letters1 (see Figure 20.7). You can scroll down through the document to see how the Access field data appears in place of the merge fields in every letter.

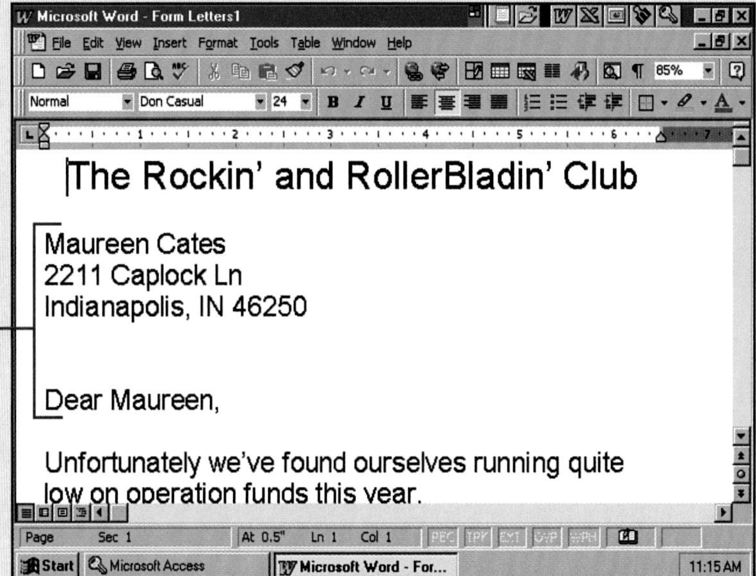

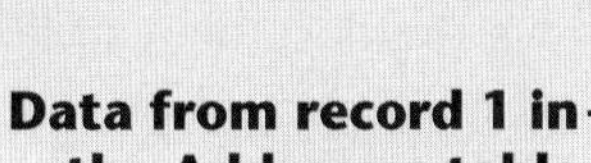

Figure 20.7
When merged, the Access data replaces the merge fields in the main document.

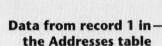

⓮ **Click the Document Close button to close the Form Letters1 document. Choose No when Word prompts you to save the changes.**

The Merge Letter document appears on-screen. If necessary, you can adjust the spacing, format, or merge fields in the document. If everything looks fine, you can print the letters.

⓯ **Click the Merge to Printer button on the Merge toolbar.**

Word prints all of the form letters. Save and close the Merge Letter document. The Mail Merge Wizard closes Word and the background session of Access. The Rollerblading Club 3 database window and the Address table still appear on-screen. Close the table and the database window, but leave Access open to use in the next lesson, where you learn how to create an Access report using an Excel list.

Jargon Watch

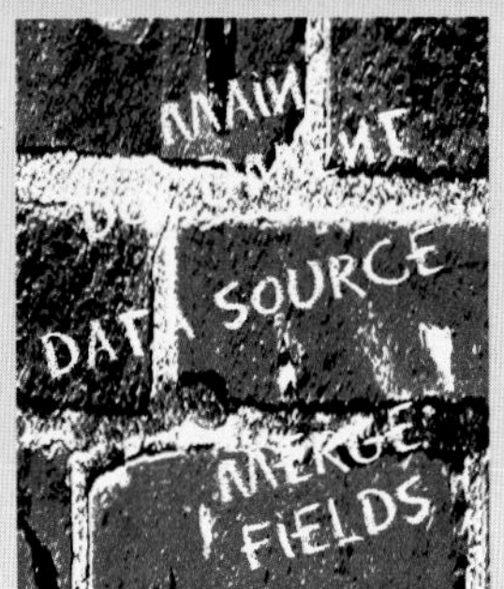

A merge has two types of files: a **main document** and a **data source**. The main document contains the information that stays the same for all the recipients—in this case, the notice. The data source contains the information that changes for each recipient—in this case, the names and addresses.

Merge fields identify where in the main document you want to insert data from the data source. Merge fields correspond to field labels; for example, if you have a First_Name field in the data source, you can place a First_Name merge field in the main document. During the merge, the data from the data source replaces the merge field in the main document.

If you have problems...

If a merge doesn't produce the desired results, just close the document that contains the results of the merge. (Don't save the document.) Make the necessary corrections in the data source and main documents, then perform the merge again.

First, make sure you didn't accidentally delete part of the merge field in the main document—the << >> and the field names are very important. If you have deleted any part of the merge field, delete the rest of it, then reinsert the merge field. You can't type these codes from the keyboard.

Second, make sure you included the correct spacing and punctuation in the main document. All spacing and punctuation should be included in the main document, not the data source.

Third, make sure the names of the merge fields in both files match exactly. If they don't, Word can't match up the merge fields and insert the information.

To start a merge from Word, choose **T**ools, Mail Me**r**ge. Identify the main document and the data source, then proceed to insert the merge fields and merge the documents.

You can use the Access Report Label Wizard to create corresponding mailing labels from your Addresses table. Refer to Project 16 for more information about creating Access reports.

Lesson 2: Creating an Access Report from an Excel List

With Office, you can link data in Excel with Access in order to create Access reports. For example, you can use the Access Label Report Wizard to create mailing labels from data stored in an Excel worksheet.

Access reports are much more comprehensive and flexible than the reports you can create in Excel. You can select which fields to include, as well as how to group and sort the data. Also, once you link the Excel data to an

Access database, you can use the data to create additional reports, queries, and forms. You can use the objects created with linked data the same way you use other Access objects. For example, you can modify the designs or print them.

An Excel worksheet is organized in columns and rows, very much like an Access table, so Access can easily work with worksheet data. Some limitations exist, however. The Excel worksheet you want to link must be set up as a list, which means it must have column headings across the first row, like a table, and the worksheet must not have any blank rows.

In this lesson, you use a list of banks stored in Excel to create a telephone list in Access.

To Create an Access Report from an Excel List

1. **Start Excel, open the PROJ2003 file, and save it as `Bank Contacts`.**

   This file contains the Excel list you want to use to create an Access report.

2. **Click anywhere within the Excel list, then open the Data menu and choose Access Report.**

   The Create Microsoft Access Report dialog box appears, as shown in Figure 20.8. You can choose to create the report in a new database, or you can use an existing database. You want to store the report with other Rollerblading Club data, so the Rollerblading Club 3 database that already exists is appropriate.

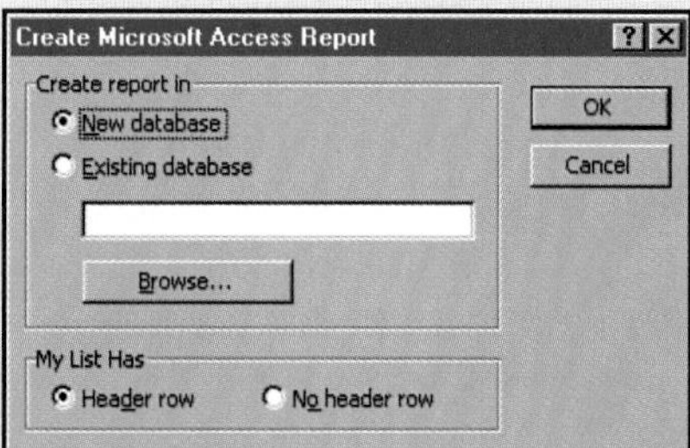

Figure 20.8
The Create Microsoft Access Report dialog box.

If you have problems...

If the Access Report command appears dimmed on the **D**ata menu, you may not have installed the necessary add-in programs. First, choose Add-**I**ns from the **T**ools menu to open the Add-Ins dialog box, and make sure the Access Links Add-Ins check box is selected. Then click OK. If the command still appears dimmed on the **D**ata menu, use Office set up to install the Excel Add-ins.

continues

To Create an Access Report from an Excel List (continued)

3 Click the Existing database option button, then click the Browse button.

The Choose Database dialog box appears, as shown in Figure 20.9. This dialog box works similar to the Open dialog boxes you use to open files in Office applications. The files in the My Documents folder appear.

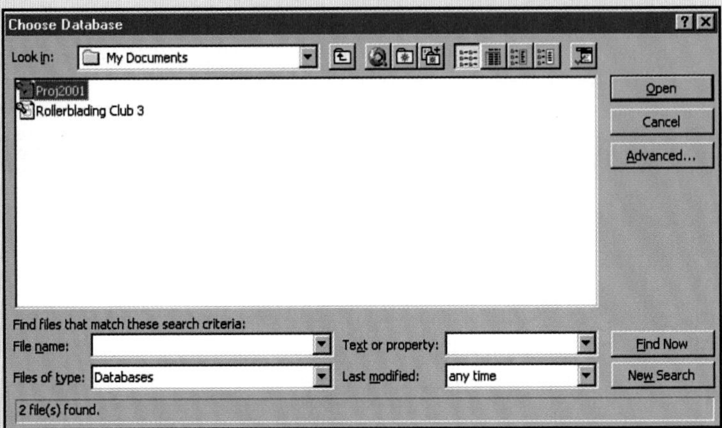

Figure 20.9
The Choose Database dialog box.

4 Double-click the Rollerblading Club 3 database file.

This action enters the database name and location into the Create Microsoft Access Report dialog box.

5 Choose OK.

Office starts or switches to Access, and begins the process of linking the Excel file to Access to create the report. This step may take a few minutes, as Access sets up a new table from the Excel data and starts the Report Wizard. Finally, you see the Report Wizard on-screen (see Figure 20.10). You use the Report Wizard to create the report just as you did in Project 16. If you need a refresher on creating Access reports, refer back to Project 16.

6 Choose to include the Bank, Contact Name, and Phone fields in the report, then choose Next.

You want these fields in the phone list. The default values in the Report Wizard are fine, so continue to choose **N**ext until the last Wizard screen is displayed.

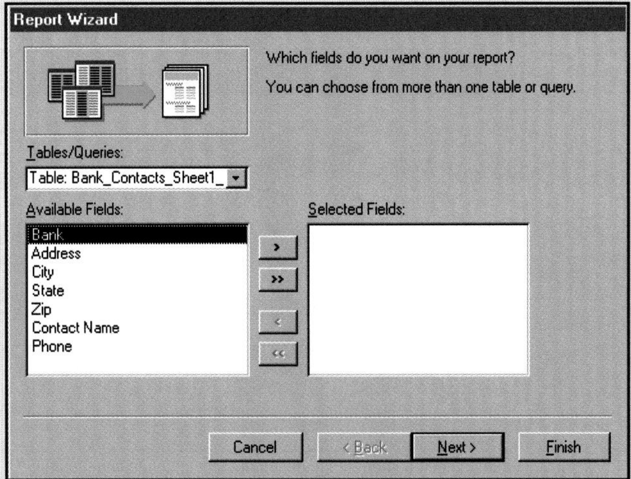

Figure 20.10
The Access Report Wizard opens from Excel.

7 In the Report Title text box, type `Bank Contact Phone List`, then choose Finish.

Access creates the report. This process may take a few minutes, so be patient. Finally, the report appears on-screen (see Figure 20.11). You may need to maximize the window to see it clearly. You can modify the design or print the report if you want, just as you do with reports created with Access table data.

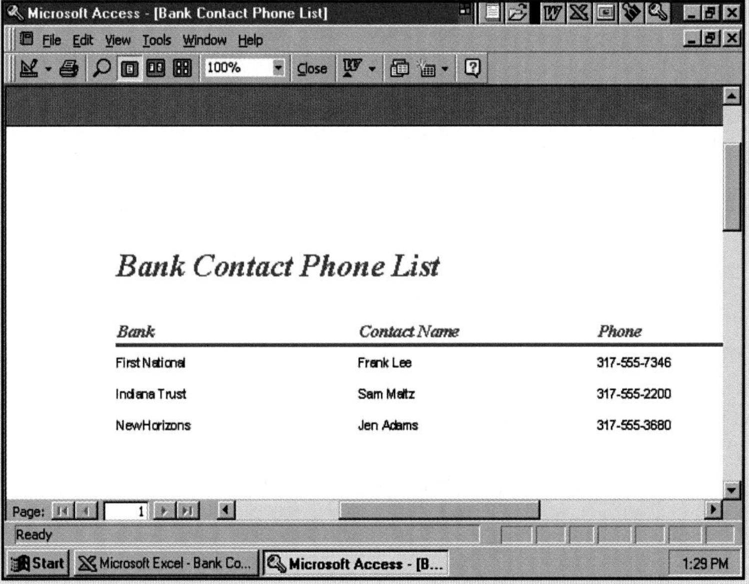

Figure 20.11
The Access report created with Excel data.

continues

To Create an Access Report from an Excel List (continued)

If you have problems...

If it seems that nothing is happening while you wait for Access to create the report, your computer may not have enough memory available for Access to complete the task. You can close the Excel window to free up memory if necessary, but make sure to give Access a chance to finish the job first. If you close Excel too soon, the link may not be established, and you will have to start creating the report all over again. If after waiting five minutes or so, you feel that you must close Excel, click the Excel button on the Taskbar, then click the Excel application Close button.

8 Click the application Close button to close Access.

This action closes Access, the report, and the Rollerblading Club 3 database. Save changes if prompted. The Bank Contacts file in Excel is still open on your screen. Notice the View MS Access Report button that appears at the end of the first row (see Figure 20.12). You use this button to view and use the Access report any time you work with the file in Excel. Try viewing the report now.

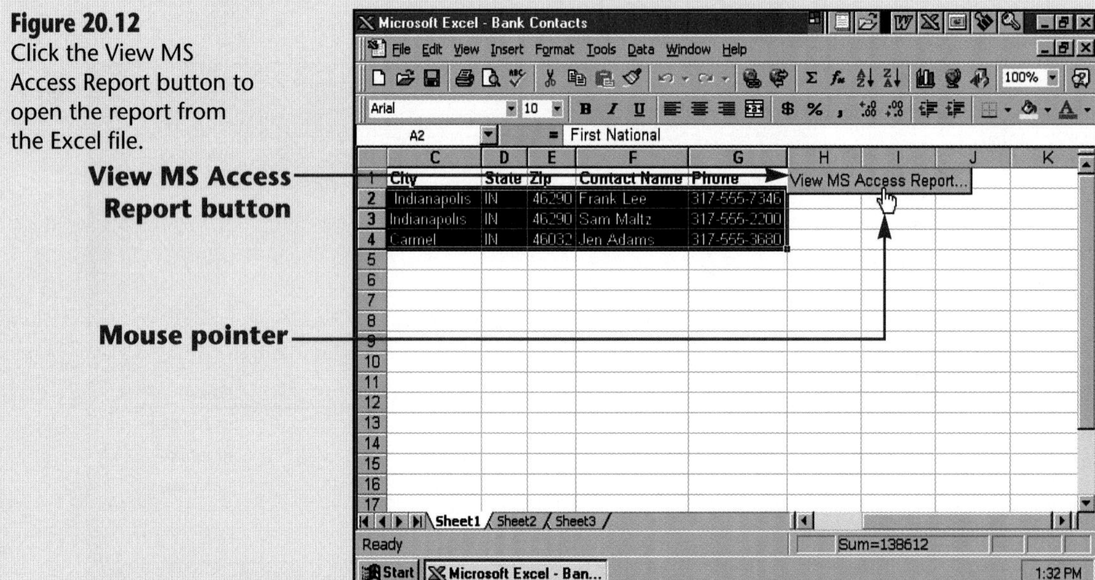

Figure 20.12
Click the View MS Access Report button to open the report from the Excel file.

9 Click the View MS Access Report button in the Excel file.

Excel uses the link to start Access, open the correct database, and display the report (you may need to maximize the Access window to see the report clearly). Of course, this process may take a few minutes. Be patient! The report will appear on-screen. Close Access and Excel, and save changes if prompted. In the next lesson, you use a Word outline to create a PowerPoint presentation.

If you have problems...

If the Excel title bar and taskbar button start to blink while you are waiting for Access to open the report, it means an Excel warning message is displayed. Click the Excel button on the taskbar to switch to Excel. The message probably says that Excel is waiting for another application to establish OLE links. Click OK, then switch back to Access. Excel doesn't like waiting for Access anymore than you do!

You can create Access forms to use with Excel lists in much the same way that you create Access reports. Forms can be useful for entering data, one record or row at a time, and for looking at data, one record at a time. To create a form from an Excel list, choose **A**ccess Form from the Excel **D**ata menu, and choose the database you want to use; then, use the Form Wizard to create the form (see Project 15 for information on creating forms).

If you have already linked an Excel file to a database, you do not have to link it again in order to create additional reports, forms, or queries. Simply select the table in Access that is linked to Excel, then create the object in Access the same way you would with an regular Access table.

Lesson 3: Creating a PowerPoint Presentation from a Word Outline

Another integration feature that can save you some time and effort is creating a PowerPoint presentation from a Word outline. If you have created an outline in Word using the standard outline headings, you can simply open the Word outline in PowerPoint. You then format and enhance the slides to complete the presentation. Try creating a presentation from a Word outline now.

To Create a PowerPoint Presentation from a Word Outline

1. **Start Word, open the PROJ2004 file, and save it as `Club Dues`. Then close Word.**

   You want to convert this outline to a PowerPoint presentation. The file must be closed so that you can open it in PowerPoint.

2. **Start PowerPoint, and choose to open an existing presentation.**

   The File Open dialog box appears. The existing PowerPoint documents stored in the My Documents folder are displayed.

3. **Click the drop-down arrow next to the Files of type text box, and choose All Outlines.**

   The file list in the dialog box changes to display Word and Excel files, as shown in Figure 20.13. Now you can choose to open the Club Dues file.

continues

To Create a PowerPoint Presentation from a Word Outline (continued)

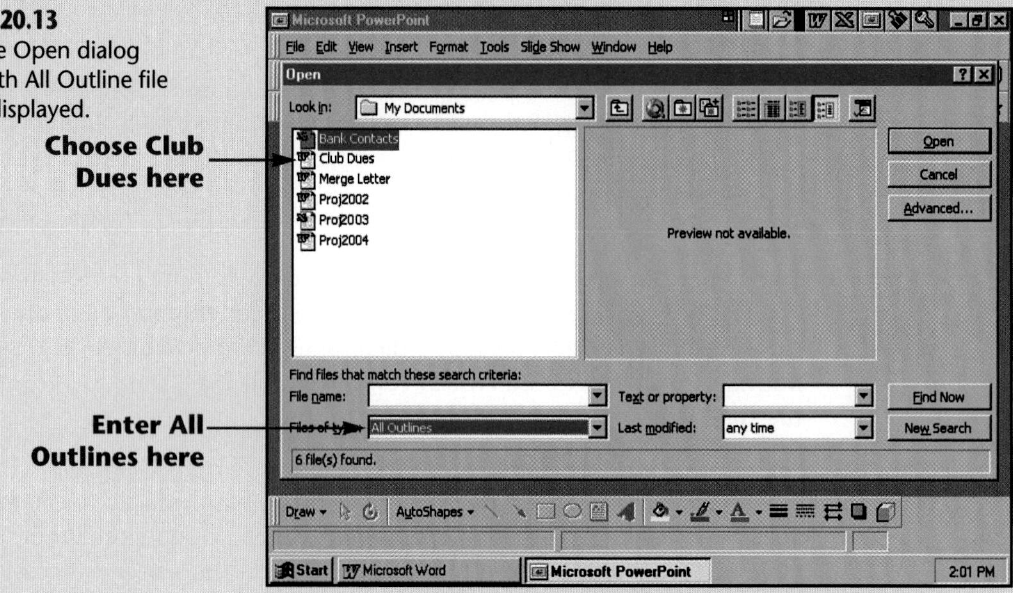

Figure 20.13
The File Open dialog box with All Outline file types displayed.

❹ **Double-click the Club Dues file.**

PowerPoint converts the Club Dues outline text and opens it in a presentation file in Outline view (see Figure 20.14). Notice that all of the outline text appears on only one slide. The first step in editing and enhancing the presentation is to use the Promote and Demote buttons to create additional slides.

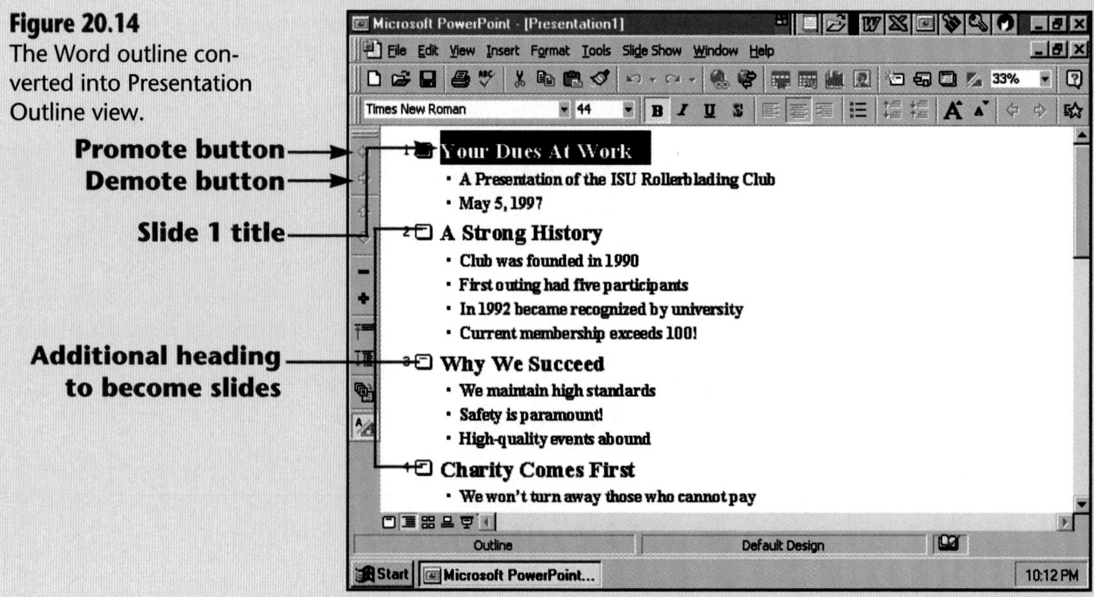

Figure 20.14
The Word outline converted into Presentation Outline view.

❺ **Select the heading `A Strong History`, and the four lines below it.**

You want to put this text on Slide 2.

6 Click the Promote button on the Outline toolbar.

This step moves the selected text up one level, creating a new slide with four bulleted lines of text (see Figure 20.15).

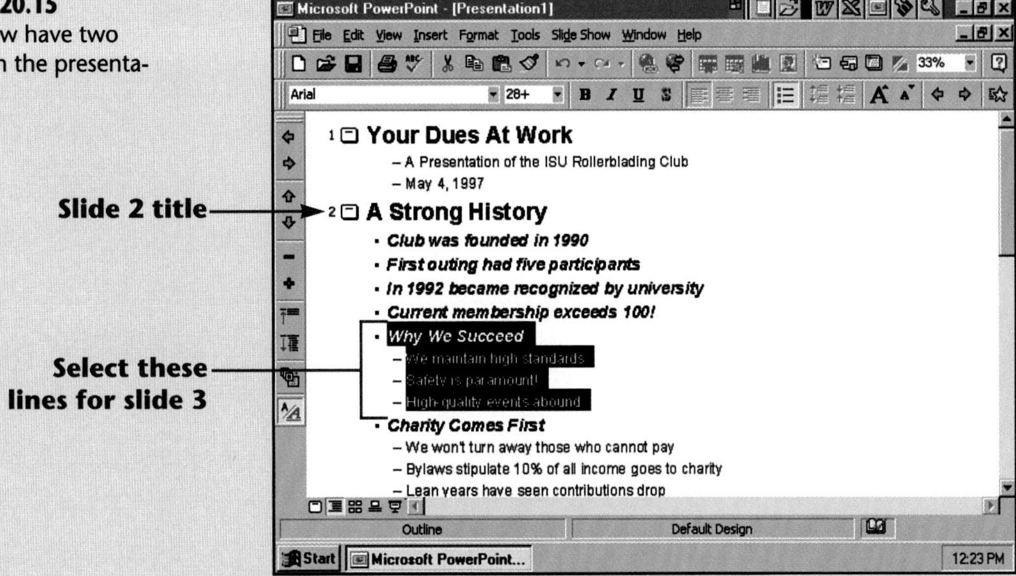

Figure 20.15
You now have two slides in the presentation.

7 Select the four lines beginning with the heading `Why We Succeed`, and click the Promote button.

You now have three slides in your presentation. Repeat these steps for each of the original bulleted items until you have a total of six slides in your presentation. Now, apply a template design to give the presentation some color and formatting.

8 Click the Slide view button on the View toolbar.

Now you can see the presentation—one slide at a time.

9 From the Format menu, choose Apply Design Template.

The Apply Design Template dialog box appears. You can choose any of the templates in the Name list. When you select one, a preview appears on the right side of the dialog box (see Figure 20.16).

10 Click the Cheers template (or any other available template) in the Name list, then choose Apply.

PowerPoint applies the color, layout, and formatting of the Cheers template to all of the slides in the presentation.

continues

To Create a PowerPoint Presentation from a Word Outline (continued)

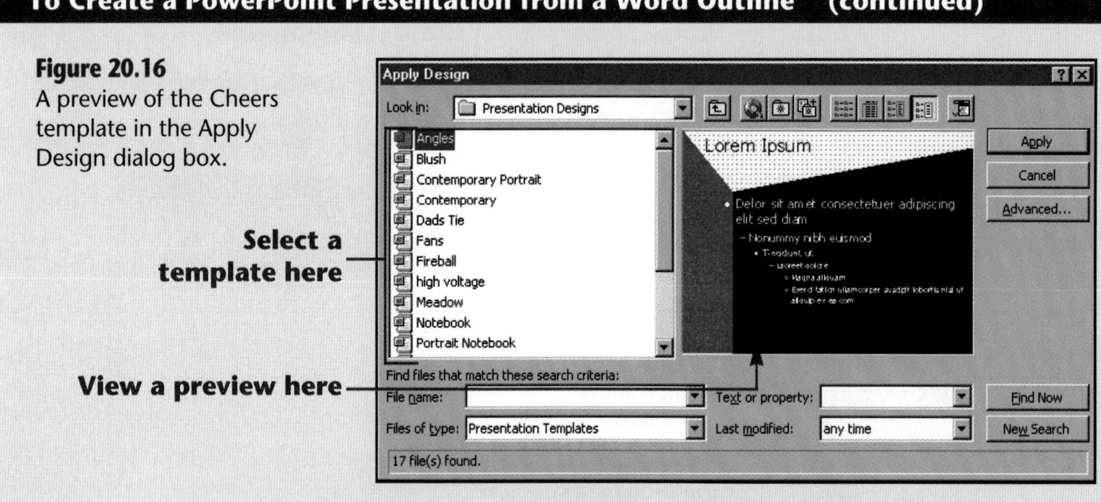

Figure 20.16
A preview of the Cheers template in the Apply Design dialog box.

⓫ **Open the File menu and choose Save. Save the presentation with the name `Higher Dues`.**

You have now turned the Word outline into a PowerPoint presentation. You can continue to enhance the presentation with additional slides, text, and graphics just as you would a presentation you create from scratch or with the Presentation Wizard. Leave the Higher Dues presentation open. In the next lesson, you learn how to turn a presentation into a Word document you can use as an accompanying handout.

Lesson 4: Creating a Word Handout from a PowerPoint Presentation

Often when you show a presentation, you want to be able to provide printed information to support your ideas. You can use PowerPoint to create notes and handouts that will complement your presentation. You can create a handout that includes all of the data from your presentation, including slides, text, and notes, or you can export the contents of the slides, but not the slides themselves.

In this lesson, you learn how to export all data from a presentation into a Word document.

To Create a Word Handout from a PowerPoint Presentation

1 With the Higher Dues presentation open in PowerPoint, choose File, Send To, Microsoft Word.

The Write-Up dialog box appears (see Figure 20.17). You can choose from four different layouts for your Word document, and you can choose to simply paste the data into the Word document, or link it as well. If you link the data, when you make changes to the presentation in PowerPoint, the data in the Word document is automatically updated. If you simply paste the data, you must make changes manually. For this example, the default option of simply pasting the data is fine.

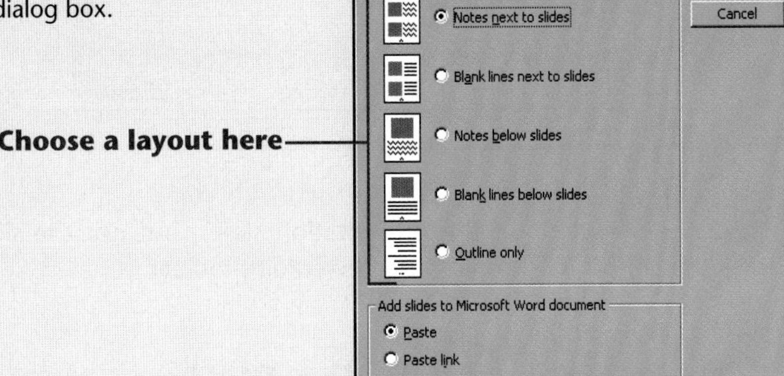

Figure 20.17 The Write-Up dialog box.

2 Click the second layout option: Blank Lines Next to Slides. Choose OK.

PowerPoint starts Word, and after a few minutes, creates a new document where it inserts replicas of the slides in the layout you selected (see Figure 20.18). You can edit the document using any Word feature.

3 Open the File menu and choose Save, then save the document with the name `Dues Handout`.

You now have a document that you can print and hand out to accompany your presentation. Close all open files and applications. In the next lesson, you learn how to create a Binder for a group of related documents.

continues

To Create a Word Handout from a PowerPoint Presentation (continued)

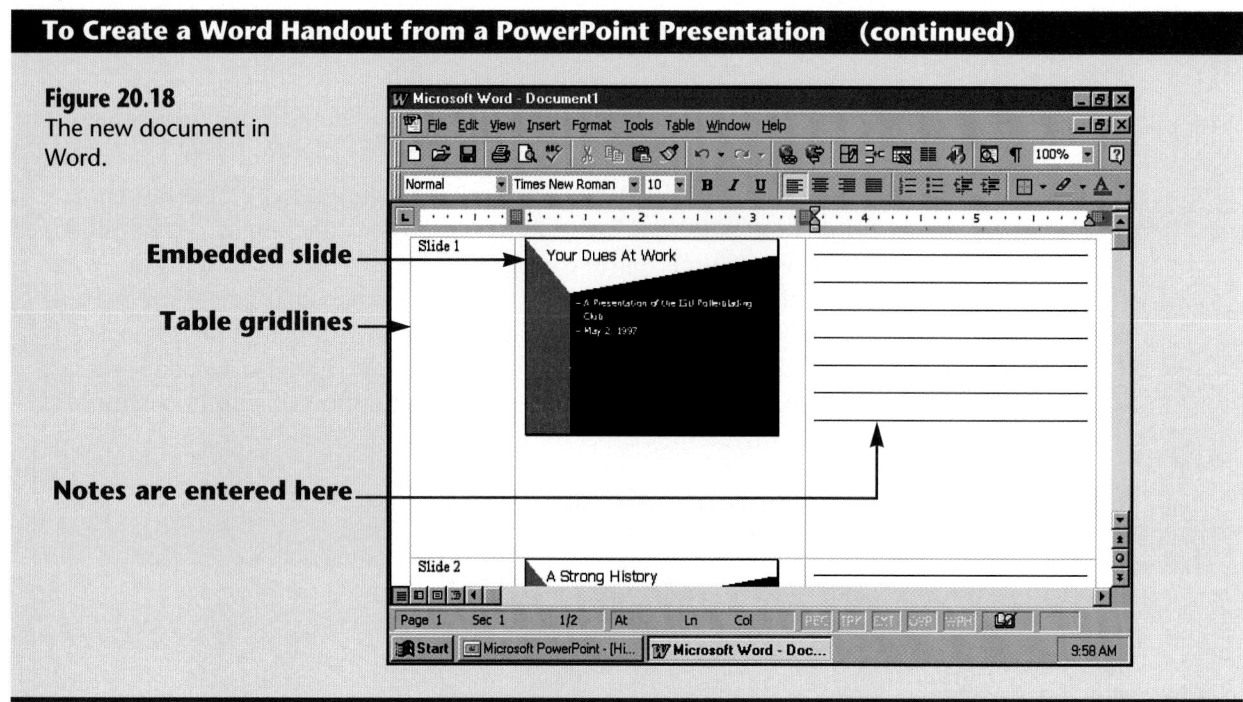

Figure 20.18
The new document in Word.

To quickly export the contents of the presentation slides, but not the slides themselves, click the Report It button on the PowerPoint toolbar.

Lesson 5: Creating and Printing Binders

When you work on a project, it often ends up requiring many different documents. Even if the documents are all created with one application, you may have difficulty keeping track of them all, and if the documents are created with different applications, your task can become almost impossible. For example, to create a training course, you may start with a Word outline and then create a longer document or a presentation. You probably develop charts using Excel worksheet data, and keep a list of students in an Access database.

If you are very organized, you may have your folders and disks set up so that you can always find the documents you need, but you can easily store a document in the wrong folder, or with the wrong project. If you print the documents, you have to remember to label them carefully so that you know which go together.

Binder
In Office, one file that contains other files.

Section
In an Office Binder, one document.

With Office 97, you no longer have to rely on paper clips to keep all of your documents organized because you can create *binders*. A binder is a master file into which you can group many different documents created with different applications. Each document gets placed in its own *section* in the binder, but you can open, close, save, and print the binder as one file, no matter how many sections it has.

You can move from section to section to see the different documents, and you can rearrange the sections. Although you can edit the documents in a binder, it is much easier to edit them outside the binder; therefore, you want to add documents to a binder once they are complete.

If you have problems...

The only type of Office application files that cannot be included in a binder are Access files. If you want to keep Access data with other documents in a binder, you must first export it into another application format, such as Excel. You can include documents that are linked to Access databases—such as a merge letter. Unless Access and the linked Access database are available to the binder file, however, you cannot use the information usually supplied by the link.

In this lesson, you use a binder to group the documents you have created regarding the increase in Rollerblading Club dues.

Try creating a binder now.

To Create and Print Binders

1 Click the Start button on the Taskbar, move the mouse pointer to Programs, and choose Microsoft Binder from the Programs menu.

A new blank binder document appears on-screen, as shown in Figure 20.19. The document has two panes: On the left is a narrow area called the Binder pane, and on the right is the Section window pane. The document in the active section appears in the Section window pane. Right now, the binder is empty, so both panes appear empty.

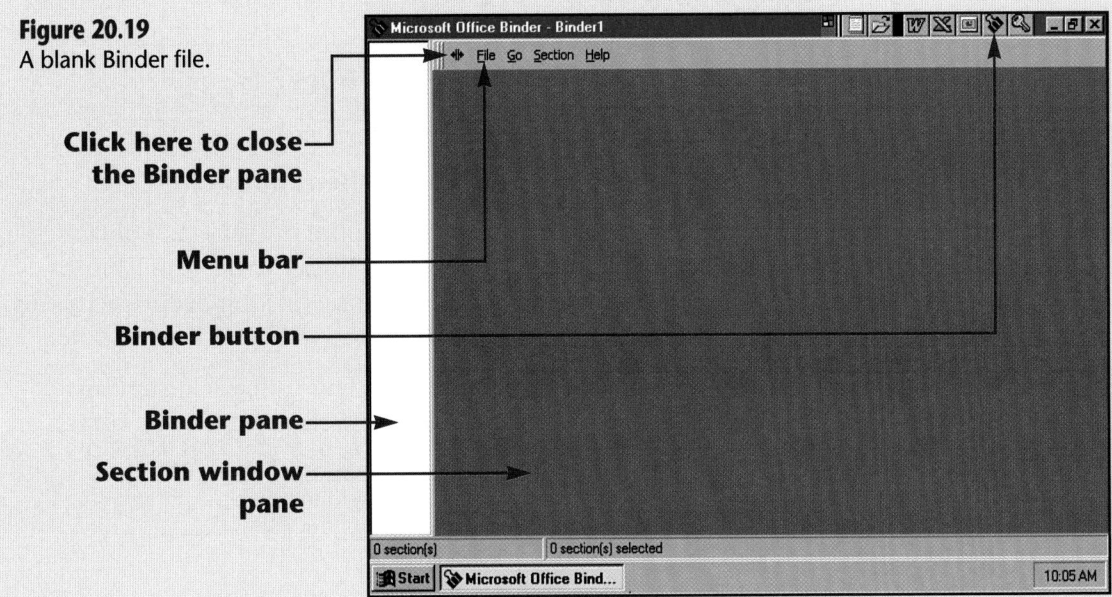

Figure 20.19
A blank Binder file.

continues

To Create and Print Binders (continued)

2 From the Section menu, choose Add from File.

The Add from File dialog box appears, as shown in Figure 20.20. This dialog box works similar to the Open File dialog boxes you use in the other Office applications. All Office files (except Access files) appear.

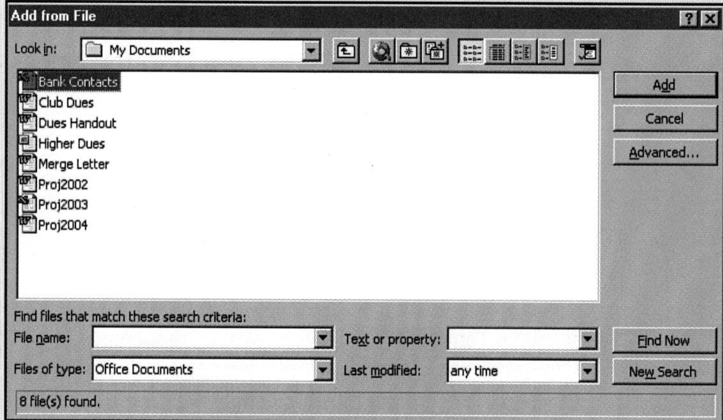

Figure 20.20
The Add from File dialog box.

3 Choose the Club Dues Letter document; then choose Add.

Office adds the Club Dues Letter document to the binder. A section icon for the document appears in the Binder pane. Because the icon is selected, the document itself appears in the active Section window pane (see Figure 20.21). Notice that the menu bar now contains menu items for Word (the section application), as well as for the binder. You can use the Word menus to edit the section document if you want, but it will be slower than editing the document out of the binder.

4 From the Section menu, choose Add from File again.

The Add from File dialog box appears.

5 Choose the Higher Dues document, then choose Add.

You have now added two documents to the binder. Each document is represented by a section icon in the Binder pane. The Club Dues section remains selected. Now, continue adding sections to the binder.

6 Use the Add a File dialog box to add the following sections to the binder: Dues Handout, Bank Contacts, and Merge Letter.

Your binder now contains five sections: one presentation, one worksheet, and three Word documents.

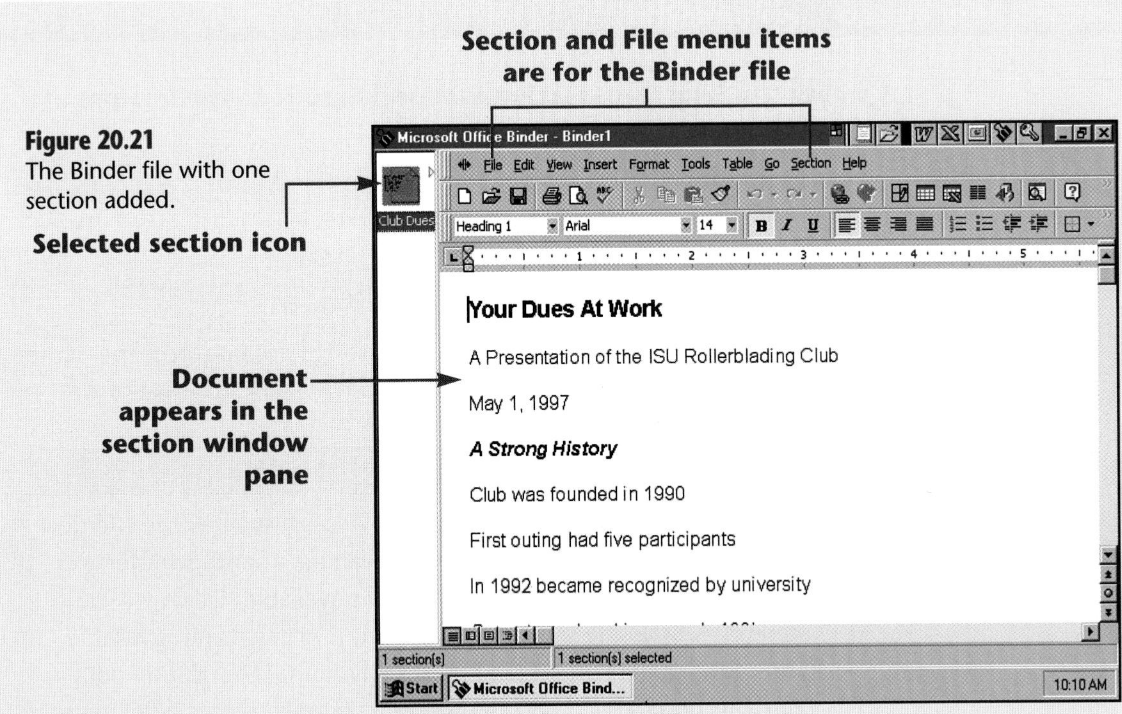

Figure 20.21
The Binder file with one section added.

❼ **Click the Higher Dues section icon in the Binder pane.**

This step activates the Higher Dues section. Office activates PowerPoint, and the presentation appears in the Section pane, as shown in Figure 20.22. To view a section, you select the Section icon.

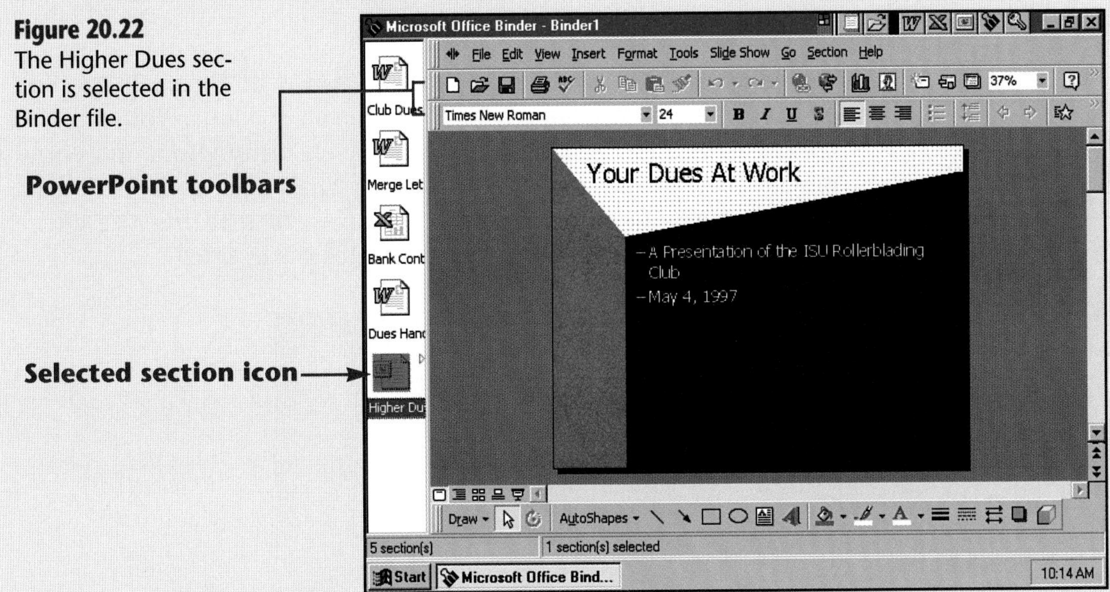

Figure 20.22
The Higher Dues section is selected in the Binder file.

continues

To Create and Print Binders (continued)

8 Click the Club Dues section icon and drag it to the bottom of the Binder pane.

This step moves the Club Dues section to the end of the binder. To move a section, drag the section icon to a new location in the binder pane. Now save the binder.

9 Open the File menu and choose Save Binder.

The Save As dialog box appears. You use this dialog box the same way you use the Save As dialog box in other Office applications.

If you have problems...

If you select a section that is linked to Access, such as the Merge Letter section, you may find yourself waiting a long time for the document to appear. As long as Access is available, Office will activate it as well as the section application. If Access is not available, a message appears on-screen informing you that the section document can be opened, but that any data supplied by the link cannot be used.

10 In the File Name text box, type `Club Dues Documents`, then choose Save.

This step saves the Binder file. Now, try printing the Club Dues Documents binder.

11 Choose File, Print Binder.

The Print Binder dialog box opens, as shown in Figure 20.23. You can print the entire binder, or just selected sections. You can also choose to number each page consecutively throughout the entire binder, or you can have numbering begin all over again with each new section. For now, the default option of printing the entire binder with consecutively numbered pages works fine.

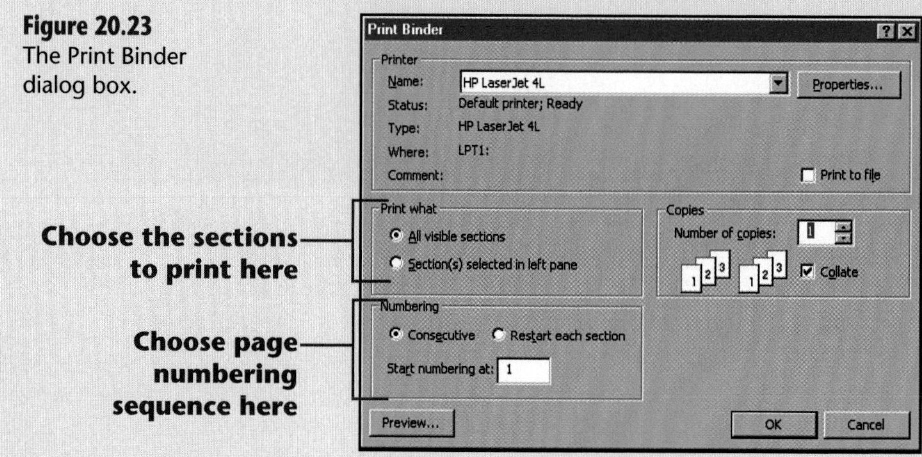

Figure 20.23
The Print Binder dialog box.

⓬ **Choose OK.**

Office prints all five sections of the binder.

⓭ **Open the File menu and choose Close.**

Office closes the Binder file. Save the changes if prompted. If you have completed your session on the computer, exit all open applications and Windows 95 before turning off the computer. Otherwise, continue with the "Applying Your Skills" exercises at the end of this project.

Checking Your Skills

True/False

For each of the following, check *T* or *F* to indicate whether the statement is true or false.

__T __F **1.** You can integrate features of different Office applications to create new documents.

__T __F **2.** Merge fields in both the main document and the data source must match exactly.

__T __F **3.** You can create an Access report from any Excel file.

__T __F **4.** You cannot add Access files to a binder.

__T __F **5.** You can use a Word outline to create a PowerPoint presentation.

__T __F **6.** When you create an Access report from Excel data, Access stores the Excel data as a Query object.

__T __F **7.** When you set up a form letter using merge fields, you don't have to worry about spacing and punctuation because Word adds them automatically.

__T __F **8.** You can print all of the sections of a Binder file together.

__T __F **9.** When you create a presentation from a Word outline, you cannot format the presentation.

__T __F **10.** You can create a Word outline from a PowerPoint presentation.

Multiple Choice

Circle the letter of the correct answer for each of the following questions.

1. Which document contains the information you want to insert when you merge files?

- **a.** main document
- **b.** data source document
- **c.** file manager document
- **d.** merge file document

2. What is each document in a binder called?

- **a.** pane
- **b.** window
- **c.** section
- **d.** document

3. In what format must Excel data be organized to be used with Access reports?
   a. worksheet
   b. chart
   c. map
   d. list
4. You can create mailing labels with Access data using which wizard?
   a. Label Merge Wizard
   b. Form Label Wizard
   c. Report Label Wizard
   d. AutoLabel Wizard
5. How many slides are created when you convert a Word outline into a PowerPoint presentation?
   a. 1
   b. 6
   c. 8
   d. It depends on how many outline headings there are.
6. What acts as the placeholder for data in a Mail Merge main document?
   a. data source fields
   b. merge fields
   c. space fields
   d. holder fields
7. In which pane of a Binder file can you view the icons representing the binder contents?
   a. section pane
   b. binder pane
   c. document pane
   d. icon pane
8. If you want to embed PowerPoint slides in a Word document handout created from a presentation document, which option should you select in the Write-Up dialog box?
   a. Paste
   b. Link
   c. Embed
   d. Paste Link
9. In which view is a presentation created from a Word outline initially displayed?
   a. Slide view
   b. Outline view
   c. Slide Sorter view
   d. Slide Show view
10. Which application should you export Access data to if you want to include it in a Binder?
    a. Word
    b. Powerpoint
    c. Outlook
    d. Excel

Completion

In the blank provided, write the correct answer for each of the following statements.

1. To view an existing Access report from the linked Excel file, click the ______________ button.
2. The ______________ file contains merge fields where the information from the data source is inserted.
3. To view a document in a binder, click the ______________ icon.
4. You can have as many ______________ in a binder as you want.
5. Use the Write-Up dialog box in PowerPoint to create a __________ in Word to accompany a presentation.

6. When you create an Access Report from an Excel document, the Excel data is ____________ to a table in Access.
7. If the ____________ command is dimmed on the Excel **D**ata menu, make sure the AccessLinks add-in has been installed.
8. The View MS Access Report button in an Excel file is a ____________ that you can use to jump to the Access report.
9. To create additional slides from an outline in a presentation, select the lines of data, then click the ____________ button.
10. In a Binder file, the selected section is displayed in the __________ pane.

Applying Your Skills

The following exercises enable you to practice the skills you have learned in this project. Take a few minutes to work through these exercises now.

Practice

1. Creating a Mass Mailing for Club Members

You want to notify the club members of upcoming events. You can easily merge your Member List database with a form letter to create a mass mailing.

To Create a Mass Mailing for Club Members

1. Copy the `PROJ2005` database file, and name the copy `Member Source`.
2. Copy the `PROJ2006` document file, and name the copy `Member Letter`.
3. Open the `Member Source` database in Access, then open the Addresses table.
4. Start the Mail Merge Wizard by choosing **T**ools, Office **L**inks, **M**ergeIt with MS Word.
5. Choose to use an existing Word document.
6. Open the `Member Letter` document.
7. Insert the Merge Fields to set up a recipient's name, mailing address, and a greeting line.
8. Click the Merge to New Document button on the Merge toolbar.
9. Save the `FormLetter` document as `Member Merge`, then close it.
10. Click the Merge to Printer button on the Merge toolbar to print the letters.
11. Save and close all open files and applications.

2. Creating a Handout to Accompany the Presentation to Your Parents

You can quickly create a handout to accompany the presentation to your parents. You can include slides and notes, or leave room for your parents to make their own notes. Choose the layout you think serves your presentation the best.

To Create the Handout

1. In PowerPoint open the file `Proj2007`, and save it as `Parents 4`.
2. Use the **F**ile, Sen**d** To, Microsoft **W**ord command to create the handout.
3. Choose the layout you think works best.
4. Save the handout as `Parents Handout`.
5. Print the `Parents Handout` document.
6. Save and close all open files and applications.

3. Creating an Access Report from Your Course List

You think it will be easier to keep track of what courses you are taking if you have a nicely printed report of your course list. Although your course list is stored in Excel, use Access to create the report. Use a new database to store the report.

To Create an Access Report from Your Course List

1. In Excel, open the file `Proj2008` and save it as `Course List 3`.
2. Use the **D**ata, MS A**c**cess Report command to start the Report Wizard.
3. Choose to use a new database (by default, Access names it `Course List 3`).
4. Include the following fields in the report: Semester, Class, Days, Time.
5. Choose the options you want in the Report Wizard. For example, sort the report by semester, and give it the title `Course List`.
6. If necessary, modify the report design. For example, decrease the width of the Days field so you can increase the width of the Time field.
7. When the report is complete, print it.
8. Save and close all files and applications.

4. Creating a Club Presentation from a Word Outline

The club has asked you to create a presentation explaining membership rules. You already have an outline in Word that you can use as the basis.

To Create a Club Presentation from a Word Outline

1. Open `PROJ2009` in Word, save it as `Club Rules`, then close it.
2. Start PowerPoint, and choose to open an existing presentation.
3. Display All Outline file types in the Open dialog box.
4. Open the `Club Rules` outline document.
5. Apply a design to the presentation.
6. Modify or enhance any of the features of the slides that you want.

7. Save the presentation with the name `Membership Presentation`.
8. Save and close all open files and applications.

5. Creating a Binder of Your Club Documents

To keep your club documents organized, you can store them together in a Binder file.

To Create a Binder of Your Club Documents

1. Create a new Binder file.
2. Add the following documents to the Binder: `Member Letter`, `Club Rules`, `Rules Presentation`.
3. Arrange the sections in the following order: Club Rules, Member Letter, Membership Rules.
4. Save the Binder file with the name `Club Binder`.
5. Print the entire Binder file.
6. Save and close all open files and applications.

Challenge

The following challenges enable you to use your problem-solving skills. Take time to work through these exercises now.

1. Creating a Mailing List Report from an Excel List of Investors

You have a list of potential investors stored in an Excel worksheet. You can use Access to create a report that includes the investors' mailing information.

To Create a Mailing List Report from an Excel List

1. Open the file PRO2010 in Excel, and save it as `Investor List`.
2. In Excel, start the Access Report Wizard, then select to use a new database. By default, Access names the database `Investor List`.
3. Include all the fields you need for a complete mailing list. (Hint: You'll need all but the phone field.)
4. Select appropriate options in the Report Wizard to complete the report. For example, you can sort the report by last name, and, since there are so many fields, you can select Landscape orientation.
5. Title the report `Investor Mailing List`.
6. Print the report.
7. Save and close all open files and applications.

2. Creating a Form Letter to Send to the List of Investors

You want to send a letter to investors asking if you can arrange a meeting when you could show a presentation. You can merge an addresses table in an Access database with a letter created in Word.

To Create the Form Letter

1. Use Windows to copy the database file PROJ2011, and name the copy `Investor Database`.
2. Copy the Word file `PROJ2012`, and name the copy `Investor Letter`. Be sure that Word is closed.
3. Open the `Investor Database` in Access, and open the Addresses table.
4. In Access, start the Mail Merge Wizard.
5. Use the `Investor Letter` as the main document, and insert the merge fields to set up the recipient's name and address. Since this is a formal letter, be sure to include the title field (Mr., Ms., or Mrs.). Also, insert the recipient's title and last name on the greeting line, between the word *Dear* and the comma.
6. Preview the merged documents to see how they look, and save the `FormLetter` document as `Investor Merge`.
7. If necessary, make adjustments to the main document.
8. Print the merged documents.
9. Save and close all open files and applications.

3. Creating a Handout to Accompany the Investors Presentation

Now that you have meetings arranged with the investors, you want to be able to hand out information about the presentation so they can refer to it after you have gone.

To Create a Handout to Accompany the Investors Presentation

1. Open the file `PROJ2013` in PowerPoint, and save it as `Final Presentation`.
2. Use the **F**ile, Sen**d** To command to open the Write-Up dialog box.
3. Select a layout, then create the handout. You can simply paste the slides into the Word document.
4. Save the Word handout document with the name `Investor Handout`.
5. Print `Investor Handout`.
6. Save and close all open files and applications.

4. Creating a Marketing Presentation from a Word Outline

You are so pleased with the investors presentation that you want to create a presentation to use for marketing. You have already started outlining some basic marketing tips and suggestions in a Word document. Use that outline to create the presentation.

To Create a Marketing Presentation from a Word Outline

1. Open the file `Proj2014` in Word, save it as `Marketing Outline`, then close it.
2. Start PowerPoint, and open `Marketing Outline` as an existing presentation.
3. Apply a design to the presentation.
4. Modify or enhance the slides with other PowerPoint features.

5. Save the presentation as **`Marketing Presentation`**.
6. Save and close all open files and applications.

5. Creating a Binder

To keep track of all the documents you have created regarding the investors, store them in one binder.

To Create a Binder

1. Create a blank binder.
2. Add the following documents:

   `Investor List`

   `Investor Letter`

   `Final Presentation`

   `Investor Handout`
3. Save the binder as **`Investor Binder`**.
4. Print the binder.
5. Save and close all open files and applications.

Working with Windows 95

In this appendix, you learn how to:

- Start Windows
- Use the mouse
- Understand the Start Menu
- Identify the Elements of a Window
- Manipulate Windows
- Exit the Windows Program

Why Would I Do This?

Graphical user interface (GUI)
A computer application that uses pictures, graphics, menus, and commands to help users communicate with their computers.

Microsoft Windows 95 is a powerful operating environment that enables you to access the power of DOS without memorizing DOS commands and syntax. Windows 95 uses a *graphical user interface* (GUI) so that you can easily see on-screen the tools that you need to complete specific file- and program-management tasks.

This appendix, an overview of the Windows 95 environment, is designed to help you learn the basics of Windows 95.

Lesson 1: Starting Windows 95

Desktop
The background of the Windows screen, on which windows, icons, and dialog boxes appear.

Icon
A picture that represents an application, a file, or a system resource.

Shortcut
Gives you quick access to frequently used objects so you don't have to look through menus each time you need to use that object.

Taskbar
Contains the Start button, buttons for each open window, and the current time.

Start button
A click of the Start button opens the Start menu.

The first thing you need to know about Windows 95 is how to start the software. However, before you can start Windows, it must be installed on your computer. If you need to install it, refer to your Windows 95 manual or ask your instructor for assistance.

In most cases, Windows starts automatically when you turn on your computer. If your system is set up differently, you must start Windows from the DOS prompt (such as `C:\>`). Try starting Windows 95 now.

To Start Windows 95

1. Turn on your computer and monitor.

   Most computers display technical information about the computer and the operating software installed on it.

   If Windows starts, you can skip step 2. Otherwise, you will see the DOS prompt `C:\>`.

2. At the DOS prompt, type **win** and then press ↵Enter.

   When you start the Windows program, a Microsoft Windows 95 banner displays for a few seconds; then, the *desktop* appears (see Figure A.1).

Program *icons* that were created during installation (such as My Computer, Recycle Bin, and Network Neighborhood) are displayed on the desktop. Other icons may also appear, depending on how your system is set up. *Shortcuts* to frequently used objects (such as documents, printers, and network drives) can be placed on the desktop. The *taskbar* appears along the bottom edge of the desktop. The *Start button* appears at the left end of the taskbar.

Figure A.1
The Windows 95 desktop appears a few seconds after a Windows 95 banner.

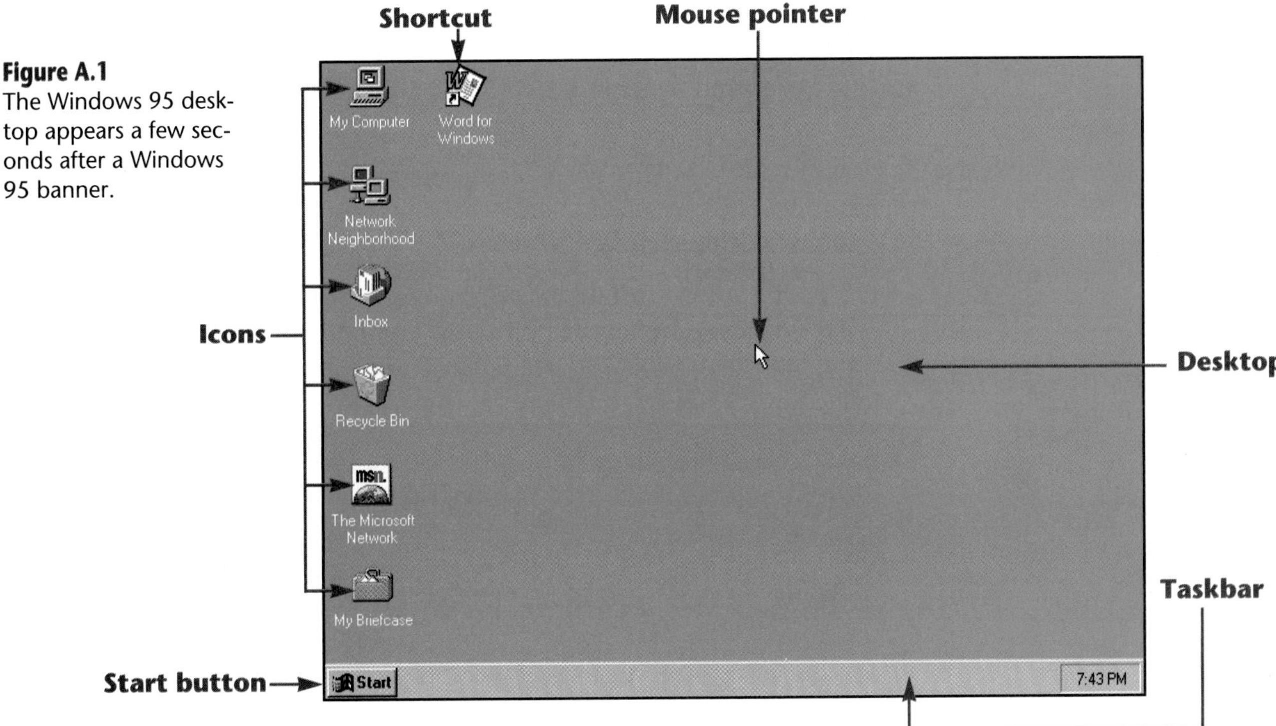

Lesson 2: Using the Mouse

Pull-down menus
Menus that cascade downward into the screen whenever you select a command from the menu bar.

Dialog box
A window that opens on-screen to provide information about the current action or to ask the user to provide additional information to complete the action.

Mouse
A pointing device used in many programs to make choices, select data, and otherwise communicate with the computer.

Mouse pointer
A symbol that appears on-screen that is controlled by the mouse.

Mouse pad
A pad that provides a uniform surface for the mouse to slide on.

Windows is designed to be used with a *mouse*, so it's important that you learn how to use a mouse correctly. With a little practice, using a mouse is as easy as pointing to something with your finger. You can use the mouse to select icons, to make selections from *pull-down menus* and *dialog boxes*, and to select objects that you want to move or resize.

In the Windows desktop, you can use a mouse to

- Open windows
- Close windows
- Open menus
- Choose menu commands
- Rearrange on-screen items, such as icons and windows

The position of the mouse is indicated on-screen by a *mouse pointer*. Usually, the mouse pointer is an arrow, but it sometimes changes shape depending on the current action.

On-screen, the mouse pointer moves according to the movements of the mouse on your desk or on a *mouse pad*. To move the mouse pointer, simply move the mouse.

There are four basic mouse actions:

- *Click*. To point to an item and then press and quickly release the left mouse button. You click to select an item, such as an option on a menu. To cancel a selection, click an empty area of the desktop. Unless otherwise specified, you use the left mouse button for all mouse actions.

Context menu
A menu that gives you a shortcut to frequently used commands.

- *Double-click.* To point to an item and then press and release the left mouse button twice, as quickly as possible. You double-click to open or close windows and to start applications from icons.
- *Right-click.* To point to an item and then press and release the right mouse button. This opens a *context menu,* which gives you a shortcut to frequently used commands. To cancel a context menu, click the left mouse button outside the menu.
- *Drag.* To point to an item, then press and hold down the left mouse button as you move the pointer to another location, and then release the mouse button. You drag to resize windows, move icons, and scroll.

If you have problems...

If you try to double-click but nothing happens, you may not be clicking fast enough. Try again.

Lesson 3: Understanding the Start Menu

Program folder
Represented by an icon of a file folder with an application window in front of it, program folders contain shortcut icons and other program folders.

The Start button on the taskbar gives you access to your applications, settings, recently opened documents, the Find utility, the **R**un command, the Help system, and the Sh**u**t Down command. Clicking the Start button opens the Start menu. Choosing the **P**rograms option at the top of the Start menu displays the **P**rograms menu, which lists the *program folders* on your system. Program folders are listed first, followed by shortcuts (see Figure A.2).

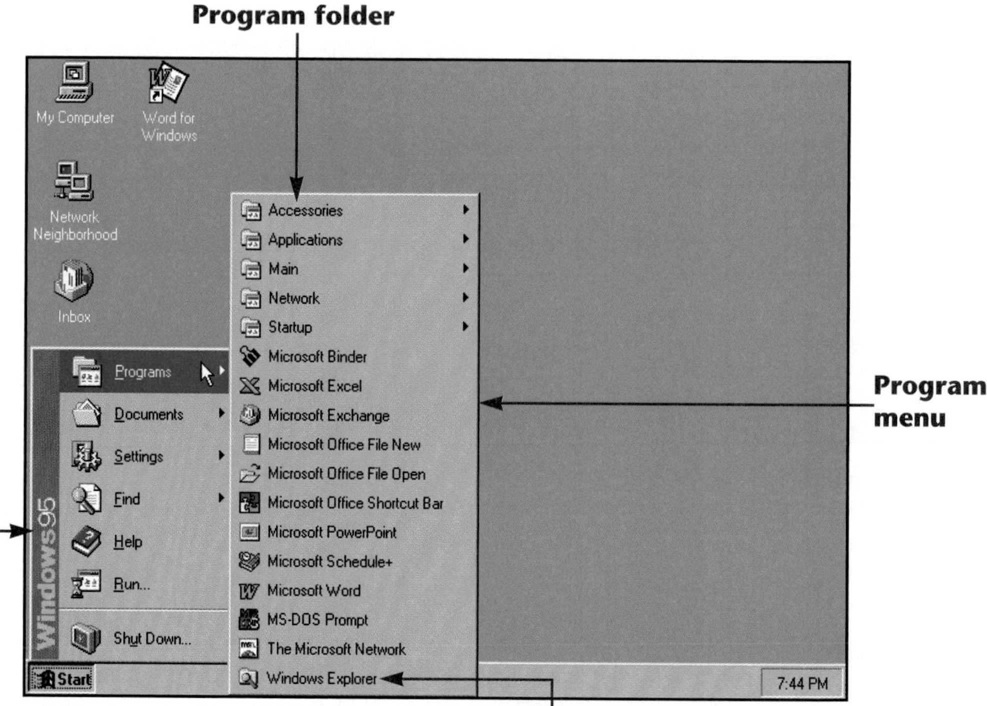

Figure A.2
Click the Start button to open the Start menu. All your programs are grouped together in the Programs menu.

When the Start menu is open, moving the mouse pointer moves a selection bar through the menu options. When the selection bar highlights a menu command with a right-facing triangle, a submenu opens. Click the shortcut icon to start an application. If a menu command is followed by an ellipsis (...), then clicking that command opens a dialog box.

Lesson 4: Identifying the Elements of a Window

In Windows 95, everything opens in a window. Applications, documents, and dialog boxes all open in windows. For example, double-clicking the My Computer icon opens the My Computer application into a window. Because window elements stay the same for all Windows applications, this section uses the My Computer window for illustration.

Title Bar

Across the top of each window is its title bar. A title bar contains the name of the open window as well as three buttons to manipulate windows. The Minimize button reduces windows to a button on the taskbar. The Maximize button expands windows to fill the desktop. The Close button closes the window.

Menu Bar

The menu bar gives you access to the application's menus. Menus enable you to select options that perform functions or carry out commands (see Figure A.3). The **F**ile menu in My Computer, for example, enables you to open, save, and print files.

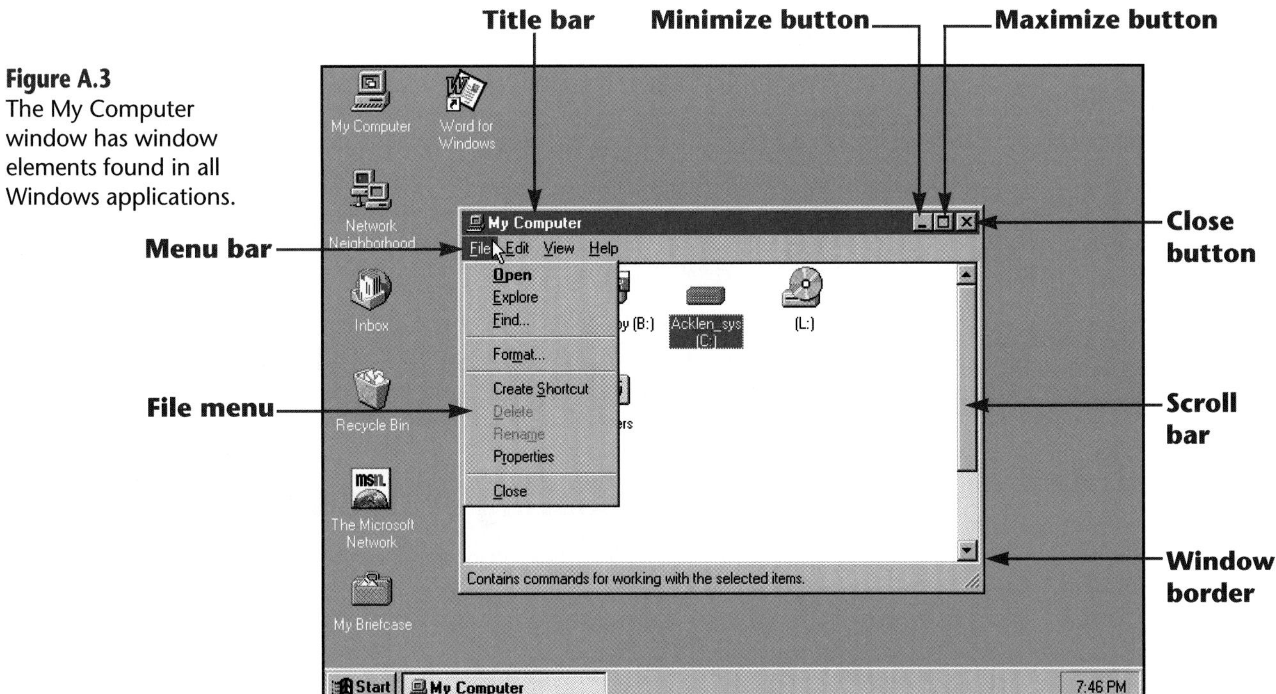

Figure A.3
The My Computer window has window elements found in all Windows applications.

Some menu options require you to enter additional information. When you select one of these options, a dialog box opens (see Figure A.4). You type the additional information, select from a list of options, or select a button. Most dialog boxes have a Cancel button, which closes the dialog box without saving the changes; an OK button, which closes the dialog box and saves the changes; and a Help button, which opens a Help window.

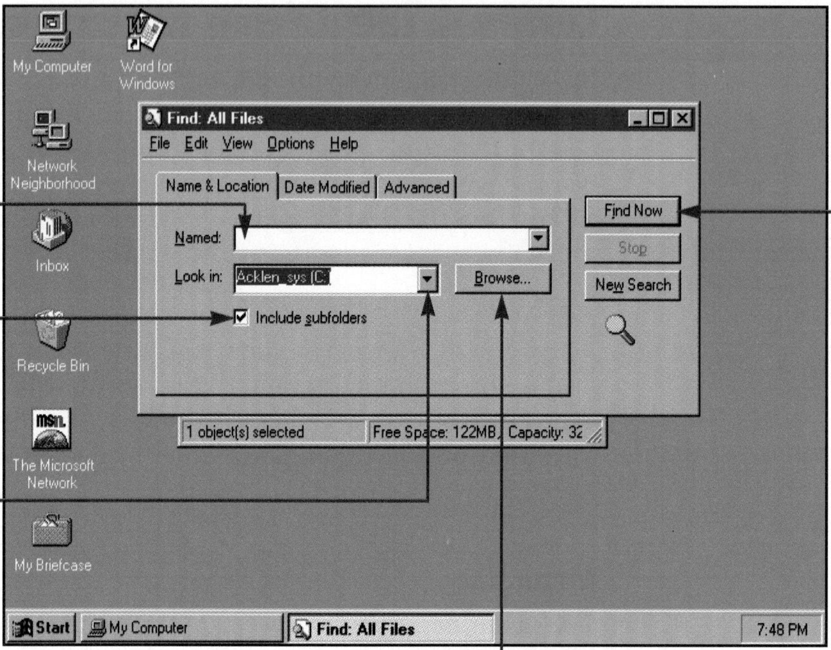

Figure A.4
You can use the options in the Find dialog box to search for a file.

Scroll Bar

Scroll bars appear when you have more information in a window than is currently displayed on-screen. A horizontal scroll bar appears along the bottom of a window, and a vertical scroll bar appears along the right side of a window.

Window Border

The window border identifies the edge of the window. In most windows, it can be used to change the size of a window. The window corner is used to resize a window on two sides at the same time.

Lesson 5: Manipulating Windows

When you work with windows, you need to know how to arrange them. You can shrink the window into an icon or enlarge the window to fill the desktop. You can stack windows together or give them each an equal slice of the desktop.

Maximizing a Window

Maximize
To increase the size of a window so that it fills the entire screen.

You can *maximize* a window so that it fills the desktop. Maximizing a window gives you more space to work in. To maximize a window, click the Maximize button on the title bar.

Minimizing a Window

Minimize
To reduce a window to an icon.

When you *minimize* a window, it shrinks the window to an icon on the taskbar. Even though you can't see the window anymore, the application stays loaded in the computer's memory. To minimize a window, click the Minimize button on the title bar.

Restoring a Window

When a window is maximized, the Maximize button changes into a Restore button. Clicking the Restore button restores the window back to the original size and position before the window was maximized.

Closing a Window

When you are finished working in a window, you can close the window by clicking the Close button. Closing an application window exits the program, removing it from memory. When you click the Close button, the window (on the desktop) and the window button (on the taskbar) disappear.

Arranging Windows

Changing the size and position of a window enables you to see more than one application window, which makes copying and pasting data between programs much easier. You can also move a window to any location on the desktop. By moving application windows, you can arrange your work on the Windows desktop just as you arrange papers on your desk.

Tile
To arrange open windows on the desktop so that they do not overlap.

Cascade
To arrange open windows on the desktop so that they overlap, with only the title bar of each window (behind the top window) displayed.

Use one of the following options to arrange windows:

- Right-click the taskbar and choose Tile **H**orizontally.
- Right-click the taskbar and choose Tile **V**ertically. See Figure A.5 for an example.
- Right-click the taskbar and choose **C**ascade. See Figure A.6 for an example.
- Click and drag the window's title bar to move the window on the desktop.
- Click and drag a window border (or corner) to increase or decrease the size of the window.

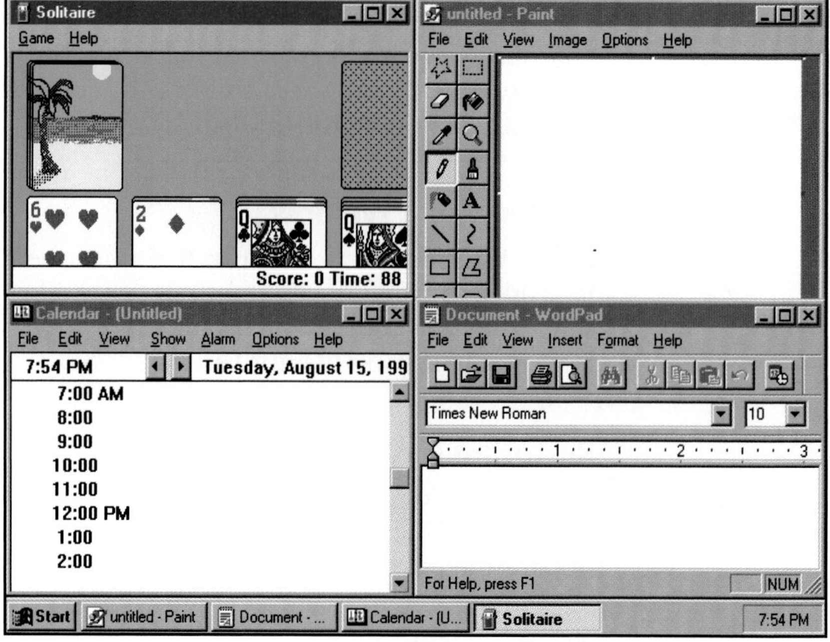

Figure A.5
The windows are tiled vertically across the desktop.

Figure A.6
The windows are cascaded on the desktop.

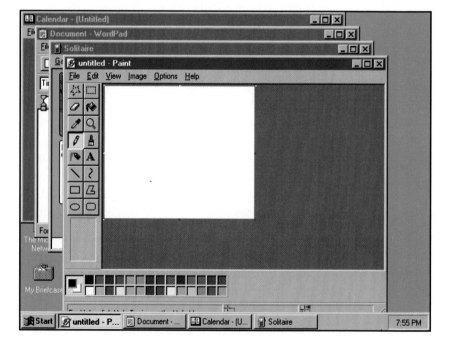

Lesson 6: Exiting Windows 95

In Windows 95, you use the Shut Down command to exit the Windows program. You should always use this command, which closes all open applications and files, before you turn off the computer. If you haven't saved your work in an application when you choose this command, you'll be prompted to save your changes before Windows 95 shuts down.

To Exit Windows 95

1. Click the Start button on the taskbar.
2. Choose Sh**u**t Down.
3. Choose **S**hut Down the Computer.
4. Choose **Y**es.

Windows 95 displays a message asking you to wait while the computer is shutting down. When this process is complete, a message appears telling you that you can safely turn off your computer now.

Getting Started with Microsoft Outlook 97

Learning the Basics

In this project, you learn how to:

- Start Outlook
- Explore the Outlook Screen
- Use Menus and Dialog Boxes
- Customize Outlook
- Use Office Assistant for Help
- Exit Outlook

Why Would I Do This?

You live and work in the information age. Businesses and individuals rely on information to remain competitive, to communicate with customers and vendors, and to stay informed of competitors' products and services. In any business, many individuals are responsible for keeping track of this constant flow of information—including managers, assistants, and executives.

Many people rely on several different types of computer software to manage and organize information, share that information with others, and integrate information with their business documents. On any given day, you might have several such information-management programs running on your computer at the same time. These programs include contact information managers, calendar and scheduling programs, and others.

Desktop information manager
A single computer program that helps you manage e-mail messages, contact information, schedules, tasks, and other vital personal and business information.

Electronic mail (e-mail)
Messages that are electronically created and sent between individuals and groups. E-mail is the electronic equivalent of sending mail through the U.S. Postal Service.

Microsoft Outlook 97 is designed to help you organize and manage information from one central application. Outlook 97 is a *desktop information manager* that enables you to manage and organize several different types of information. You can communicate with others using *electronic mail* (usually called *e-mail*), store and update contact lists, keep a journal, maintain a to-do list, schedule personal and team activities, and create notes to "stick" on your desktop.

In this project, you learn the fundamentals of Outlook. You first learn how to start Outlook if it is not already running on your machine. You then explore the features of the Outlook screen, and get an introduction to Outlook's menus and dialog boxes. Then you learn how to customize Outlook in basic ways, such as turning on and off the standard Outlook toolbar. You also learn how to access Outlook's extensive Help system, including the new Office Assistant utility. Finally, you learn how to exit Outlook.

Lesson 1: Starting Outlook

On some computers, Outlook may be set up to start when you boot your computer and Windows 95 starts. This is the case if Outlook is placed inside the Windows 95 Startup folder. If Outlook is already started on your computer, you do not need to perform steps 1 or 2 in this lesson.

If Outlook does not start automatically when Windows 95 starts on your computer, then you need to start Outlook manually. But like other Windows 95 applications, Outlook is easy to start.

To Start Outlook

1 Start Windows 95, if it is not already running on your computer.

You must have Windows 95 running to use Outlook.

2 Click the Start button.

The Start button is located at the bottom left corner of the Windows 95 screen on the Windows 95 *taskbar*. When you click the Start button, the Start menu displays (see Figure B.1).

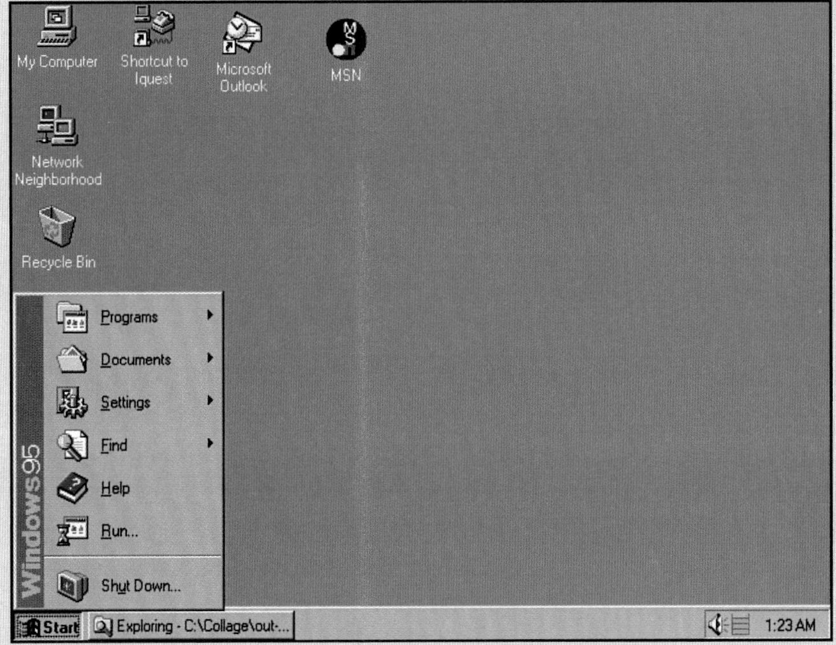

Figure B.1
The Windows 95 desktop, with the Start menu displayed.

3 Choose Programs.

When you choose **P**rograms, the Programs submenu opens to the right of the Start menu. The Programs submenu contains *icons* for the programs installed on your computer.

4 Click the Microsoft Outlook icon.

The Outlook program starts on the Windows 95 desktop, and the Choose Profile dialog box appears (see Figure B.2), if Outlook is set up to let you choose a profile each time you start Outlook.

If you have problems...

You can have Outlook set up to automatically start when you launch Windows 95. To do this, place a shortcut to the OUTLOOK.EXE program in the Windows 95 StartUp folder. The next time you start Windows 95, Outlook will start automatically.

continues

To Start Outlook (continued)

If Outlook is not set up to let you choose a profile, the Choose Profile dialog box does not appear when you start Outlook. Instead, the Outlook window appears. If the Choose Profile dialog box does not appear on your screen, skip to the explanation following step 6 to continue.

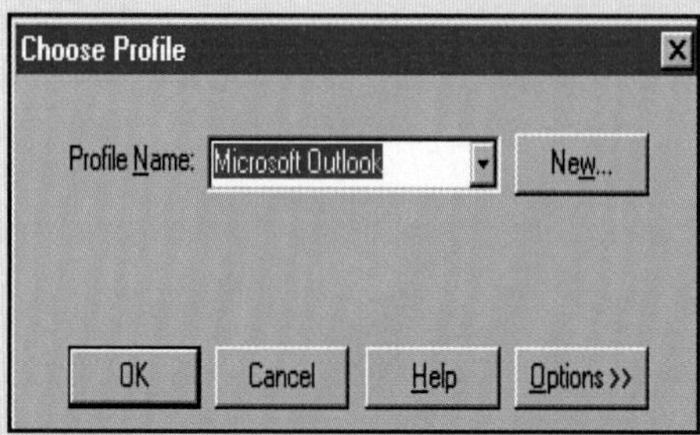

Figure B.2
The Choose Profile dialog box.

An Outlook profile is a group of settings that defines how Outlook is configured for a user, including how Outlook looks, which e-mail services are set up for that user, and other settings. More than one profile per user can be set up on a computer.

5 Click the drop-down arrow next to the Profile Name box.

A drop-down list appears, listing the profiles that have been set up on your computer. Depending on the number of profiles set up for the computer you are using, this list may contain one or several profile names.

6 Select the profile name that you want to use from the drop-down list.

Your instructor will tell you which profile to use. In most cases, the default profile (the one that Outlook sets up automatically) is called Microsoft Outlook. Select this profile unless your instructor tells you to select a different one.

7 Choose OK.

The Choose Profile dialog box closes, and the Outlook window appears, as shown in Figure B.3. When Outlook first starts, you see a screen with a title bar, a menu bar, a toolbar, the Outlook Bar, and the information viewer. On some systems, Outlook may be set up to display a Folder List, which displays between the Outlook Bar and the information viewer.

Leave Outlook as it is for the next lesson, where you learn about the different areas of the Outlook window.

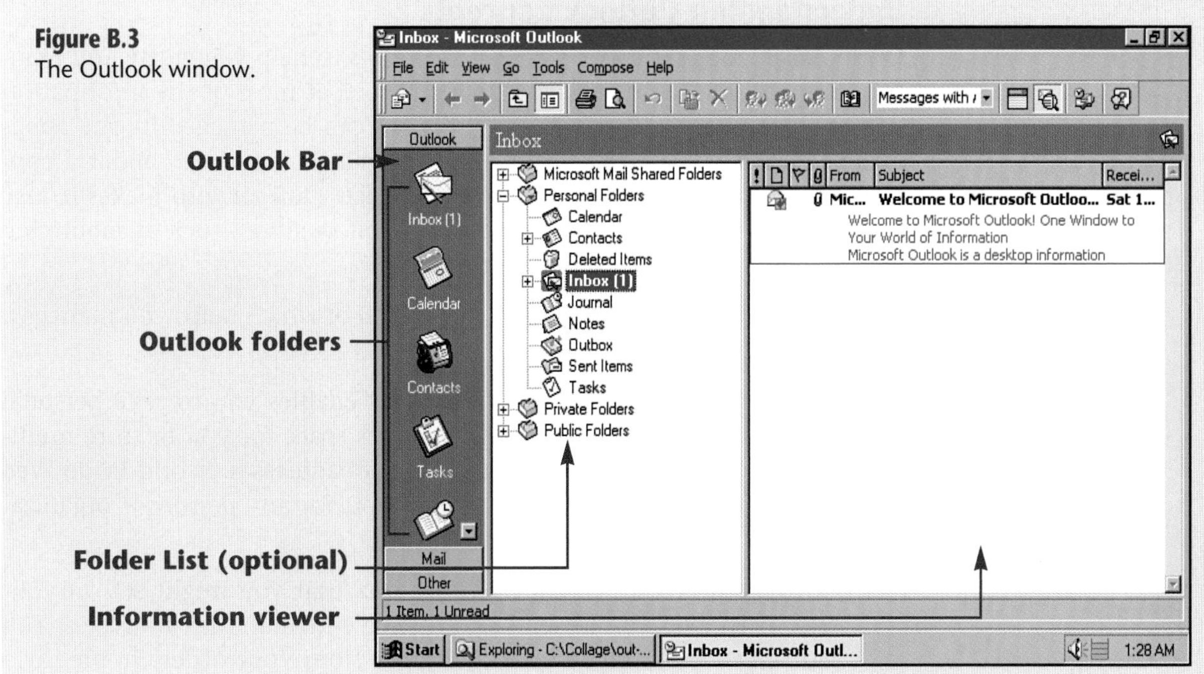

Figure B.3
The Outlook window.

If you have problems...

If your screen does not look exactly like the one shown in Figure B.3, you can change it by clicking the Inbox folder shortcut in the Outlook Bar. This changes the content of the information viewer to display those items stored in the Inbox folder, duplicating the appearance of Figure B.3.

Jargon Watch

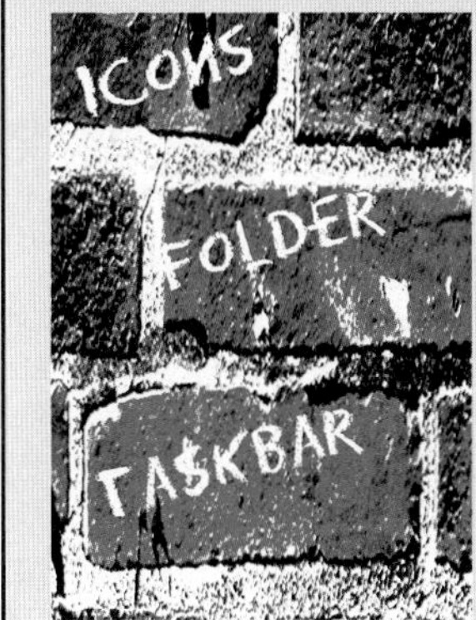

Although this workbook assumes you have working knowledge of Windows 95, you may need a refresher of some of the terms used in this first lesson. The Windows 95 ***taskbar*** sits at the bottom of the Windows 95 screen and displays the Start button, icons for any applications that are currently running, and the taskbar tray (which displays the clock, for instance). A Windows 95 ***folder*** includes applications, documents, printers, and other items stored on your computer. ***Icons*** are small graphics that represent another object or item on your computer. An icon can be used to represent printers, modems, files, folders, programs, and shortcuts. When you click or double-click an icon, you activate the action of the item associated with it. When you clicked the Outlook icon in step 3 in Lesson 1, for instance, you started the Outlook program, which is the associated action of the icon.

Understanding Outlook Concepts

Outlook is made up of six organizational tools to help you create and manage information. These tools are designed so that most of the information you manage in several separate applications can be managed in one application. This makes it easy to find the information you need about a contact, appointment, or task in one central place. Outlook also makes it easy to update existing information or add new information, such as modifying contact data or changing a meeting time.

Outlook provides the following six tools, each of which helps you manage a specific type of information:

- **Contacts.** Outlook's contact manager enables you to save personal and business contacts. Outlook provides space for you to store multiple telephone numbers, addresses, e-mail addresses, World Wide Web addresses, and other contact information for any person or organization.
- **Inbox.** The Inbox is just like an inbox that you might set on your desk. It enables you to send and receive e-mail and fax messages. You can send and receive e-mail messages from your office, home, or a remote site using Outlook.
- **Calendar.** The Outlook Calendar keeps track of your activities, appointments, and meetings. You can schedule new appointments, quickly see your upcoming appointments, and schedule recurring appointments. You also can use the Meeting Planner to set up meetings with other people in your office.
- **Tasks.** The Task Manager provides an electronic to-do list for your business and personal tasks. You can create new tasks, set reminders for tasks, and prioritize your tasks.
- **Journal.** The Journal feature enables you to record interactions with your contacts and keep track of items in Outlook. You can automatically keep track of your activities by using AutoJournal.
- **Notes.** The Notes feature provides electronic sticky notes you can display on-screen and store in the Notes folder. You can use Notes to quickly write down ideas, notes, or reminders and keep them on your desktop as you are working.

Lesson 2: Exploring the Outlook Window

Once you have Outlook started and on-screen, you may be somewhat overwhelmed by what you see. Some of the elements of the Outlook window, however, should be familiar to you if you use other Windows 95 applications. The title bar, menu bar, and toolbar, for instance, should look familiar to you. These items are common to almost every Windows 95 application. Also, the Minimize, Maximize, and Close buttons on the far right side of the title bar are found on most Windows 95 applications. Some Outlook-specific window elements include the Outlook Bar, information viewer, and Folder List (if it is turned on). These parts of the Outlook window help you manage and view the information you store in Outlook.

You can control the Outlook window in much the same way you control any other Windows 95 application. This includes maximizing and minimizing the window, resizing the window, moving the window, and switching between Outlook and other applications that are running on your desktop. Figure B.4 shows the Outlook window with all parts of the screen denoted.

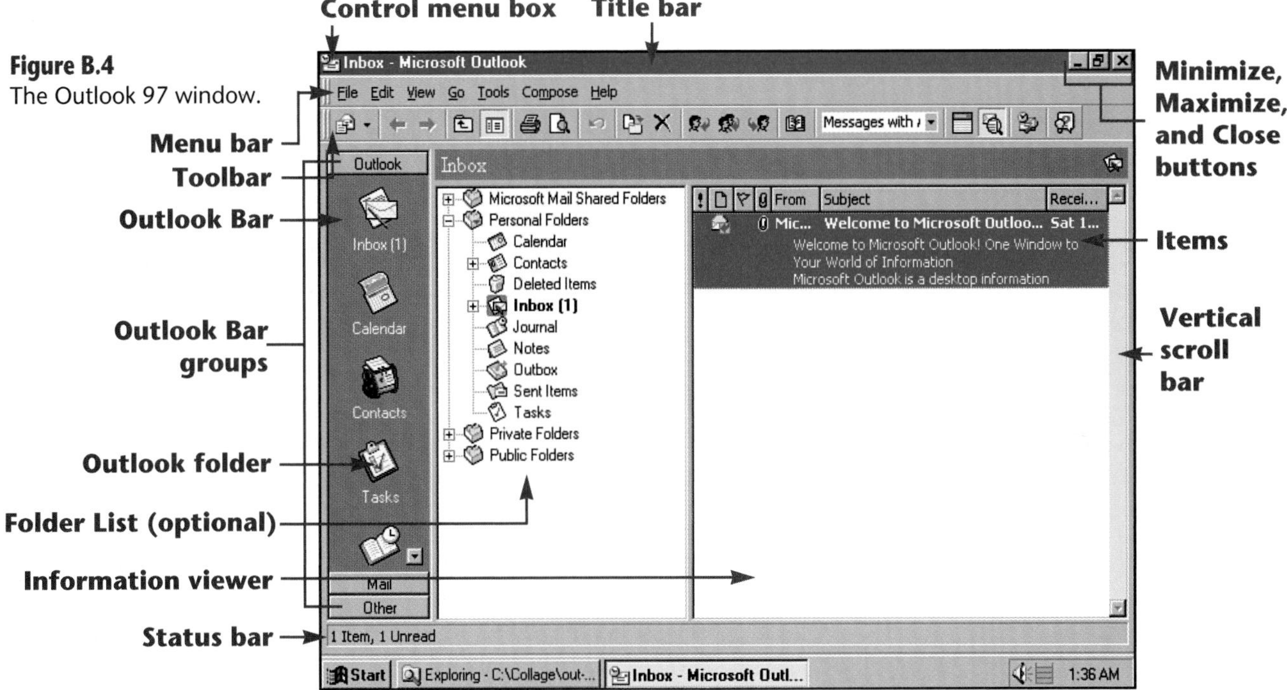

Figure B.4
The Outlook 97 window.

Table B.1 lists and describes each Outlook 97 window element.

Table B.1 Outlook 97 Window Elements

Element	Description
Title bar	Displays the current folder name (such as Inbox, Calendar, and so on) and the name of the application (Microsoft Outlook).
Control menu box	Provides access to the application control menu, which includes common Windows 95 commands that quickly resize, move, restore, maximize, minimize, and close the Outlook window.
Minimize, Maximize, Close buttons	Enable you to minimize, maximize, and close the Outlook window.
Menu bar	Displays available menus for you to access Outlook's commands. To access items in a menu, click the desired menu's name to open the menu and display the commands or options it contains. Use the mouse to click menu items. You also can use the keyboard to select menus and menu items.

continues

Table B.1 Continued

Element	Description
	To do this, press Alt on the keyboard and then press the underlined letter for the menu you want to display (such as Alt+F to display the **F**ile menu). Next, press the underlined letter for the menu item you want to display.
Toolbar	Displays icons for common or frequently used Outlook commands. The toolbar gives you quick access to these commands; simply click the toolbar. A picture on the toolbar button illustrates the feature of the button, such as a printer picture to illustrate what action the Print toolbar button performs.
Outlook Bar	Provides *shortcuts* to your Outlook folders and groups. To display a folder, click the folder shortcut name in the Outlook Bar. If a folder resides in a different group, such as the Mail or Other group, click the group name to display the folder shortcuts in the selected group, then click the folder shortcut you want to display. You can add folders and groups to the Outlook Bar, or you can hide the Outlook Bar.
Outlook Bar groups	Contain a set of shortcuts to *items*, all having something in common. The Mail group, for instance, contains shortcuts to e-mail related folders. The default groups are named Outlook, Mail, and Other.
Folder List (optional)	Displays all your folders in Outlook in a list view. If the Folder List is not displaying on your screen, select **V**iew, Fold**e**r List from the Outlook main menu. The lessons in the remainder of this project have the Folder List turned off.
Outlook folders	Contain items you create or store in Outlook groups. Default *folders* in the Outlook group are: Inbox, Calendar, Contacts, Tasks, Journal, Notes, and Deleted Items. You can create and delete folders in Outlook.
Information viewer	Displays items in a selected folder. Columns can be added or deleted in the information viewer to help you manage your information. You also can sort, filter, and group items in the information viewer.
Items	Individual pieces of information created or stored in Outlook, such as mail messages, journal entries, calendar appointments, contacts, tasks, and notes. *Items* are organized in folders to help you manage and keep track of each item. All e-mail messages, for instance, are stored in the Inbox folder.
Vertical scroll bar	Enables you to move up and down in the information viewer.
Status bar	Displays the number of items in the selected folder. If, for instance, you have 10 e-mail messages in the Inbox folder, the status bar indicates you have 10 items, as well as the number of unread items in the folder.

Shortcut
Shortcuts provide a quick way to access frequently used items, such as folders, documents, or other objects.

Folder
A folder contains items you store in Outlook, such as e-mail messages, calendar information, files, and other information.

Items
Items are the information you create or store in Outlook, such as individual mail messages, journal entries, calendar appointments, contacts, tasks, and notes.

Now explore the Outlook screen on your own.

To Explore the Outlook Window

1 Open the File menu.

The **F**ile menu opens. The **F**ile menu is common to most Windows programs, including Outlook. You can use menus to select commands to execute in Outlook. To select an item on the menu, move the mouse pointer to the item you want to execute and click it. If you want to close a menu, click the name of the menu again, or click anywhere on the Outlook window. You also can press Esc twice to close an open pull-down menu.

2 Click the File menu name again to close the menu.

When you cancel a menu using this method, make sure you do not click a menu item. If you do, the command associated with that menu item executes.

3 Move the mouse pointer to the toolbar and rest the pointer over the Print Preview tool.

The Print Preview tool is the seventh button from the left on the Outlook toolbar (refer to Figure B.4). These buttons are used to access commonly used Outlook commands quickly. When you let the mouse pointer hover over a tool without clicking, a ToolTip displays, which is a short description of the tool and the action associated with it.

4 Move the mouse pointer to the Outlook Bar and click the Calendar folder shortcut.

When you click a folder shortcut in Outlook, the contents (items) of that folder display in the information viewer, such as the Calendar folder shown in Figure B.5. Any time you want to view or manipulate items in a folder, click the selected folder shortcut in the Outlook Bar and examine its contents in the information viewer.

continues

To Explore the Outlook Window (continued)

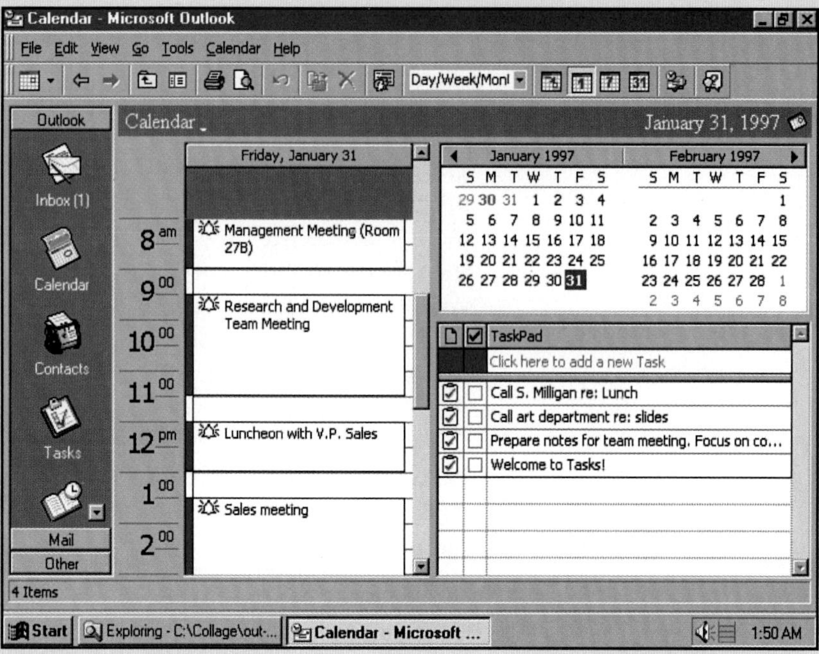

Figure B.5
The contents of any Outlook folder appear in the information viewer.

If you have problems...

When you click on the Calendar folder shortcut, you are shown the contents of your calendar in the information viewer. However, the contents in your calendar may not be the same as shown in Figure B.5. The data shown in Figure B.5 is used to illustrate the way the information viewer displays items stored in the Calendar folder.

5 Click the Mail group in the Outlook Bar.

This displays the Mail group and its contents in the Outlook Bar (see Figure B.6). The Mail group in Figure B.6 contains five shortcuts—Inbox(1), Sent Items, Outbox, Deleted Items, and Shared Public. (Your display may not show the Shared Public shortcut if you are not set up in a networked environment.) When you want to select a shortcut in a group, you must click the group name from the Outlook Bar. Notice that the Outlook group name appears above the Mail group after you select the Mail group. You can view the contents of the Outlook group again by clicking it.

Notice also that when you display a new group, the contents of the information viewer do not change. You must click a folder inside a group for the contents of that folder to display in the information viewer.

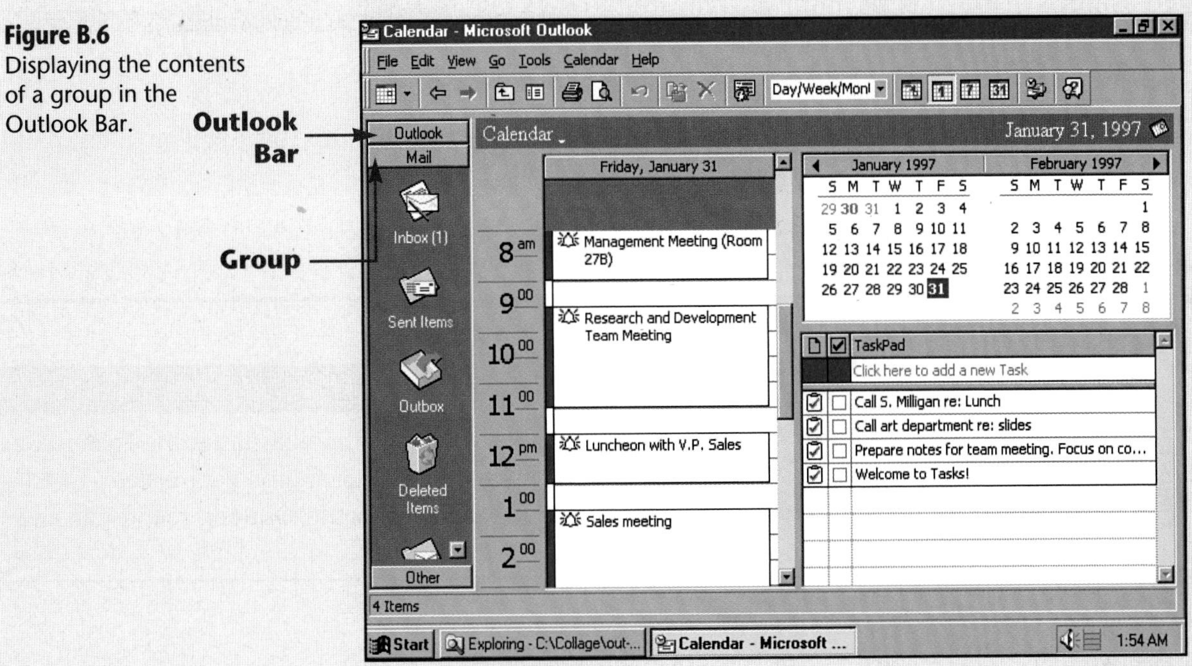

Figure B.6
Displaying the contents of a group in the Outlook Bar.

❻ Click the Outlook group.

This displays the Outlook group's contents again. A small down-arrow button appears at the bottom of the Outlook group (see Figure B.7). This button lets you know that the group includes additional shortcuts that you cannot currently see. When you click this arrow button, the view of the group slides up to reveal additional folder shortcuts. When you do this, a small up-arrow button displays at the top of the Outlook group, letting you know that additional shortcuts are "above" the ones currently showing.

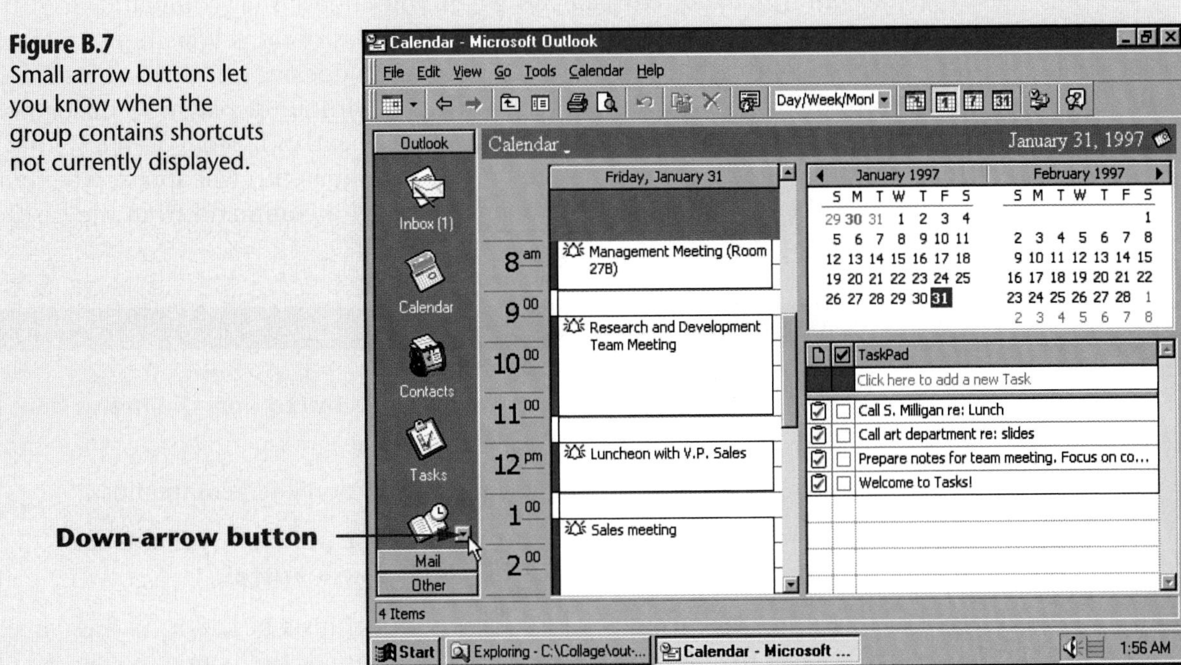

Figure B.7
Small arrow buttons let you know when the group contains shortcuts not currently displayed.

continues

To Explore the Outlook Window (continued)

7 Click the small down-arrow button.

The contents of the Outlook group slide up to show you additional shortcuts in the group.

Leave the Outlook window as it is for the next lesson, where you learn how to use menus and dialog boxes.

If you have problems...

As mentioned in Table B.1 in Lesson 1, this book assumes the Folder List view is turned off. If the Folder List view is showing on your system, turn it off now by selecting the **V**iew menu from the Outlook menu bar and choosing Fold**e**r List.

Lesson 3: Using Menus and Dialog Boxes

The menu bar appears below the title bar on the Outlook window and includes the menu names. Menus are the primary way for users to access Outlook's commands. Outlook commands enable you to compose new e-mail messages, create new folders, keep track of your contacts, and perform other Outlook tasks.

Dialog box
A dialog box is a window in which you enter additional information for a command or to complete a process.

When you click a menu's name in the menu bar, a pull-down menu appears, displaying a list of related commands and options. You then choose a command from the list. If a menu command has an ellipsis (...) next to it, a *dialog box* displays when you choose that command from the menu. A dialog box is a window that includes options you choose to complete a command. When a menu command does not have an ellipsis next to it, the command executes immediately, without displaying a dialog box. A menu command that has a small arrow next to it lets you know that a cascading menu (sometimes referred to as a submenu) will appear when you select that menu choice. You then can select a command from the cascading menu.

To Use Menus and Dialog Boxes

1 Move the mouse pointer to the Tools button on the menu bar and click the left mouse button.

The **T**ools menu opens, displaying a set of related commands.

2 Choose Options by moving the mouse pointer over the command name and clicking the left mouse button.

Notice the **O**ptions command has an ellipsis beside it, telling you that a dialog box will appear if you choose the command. In this case, the dialog box is named Options (see Figure B.8). The Options

Tab
In dialog boxes, tabs contain options you can set for Outlook.

dialog box contains several options you can set to configure Outlook, such as e-mail options, spelling preferences, and more. The Options dialog box also includes *tabs*, which display separate pages of options you can set.

Figure B.8
The Options dialog box.

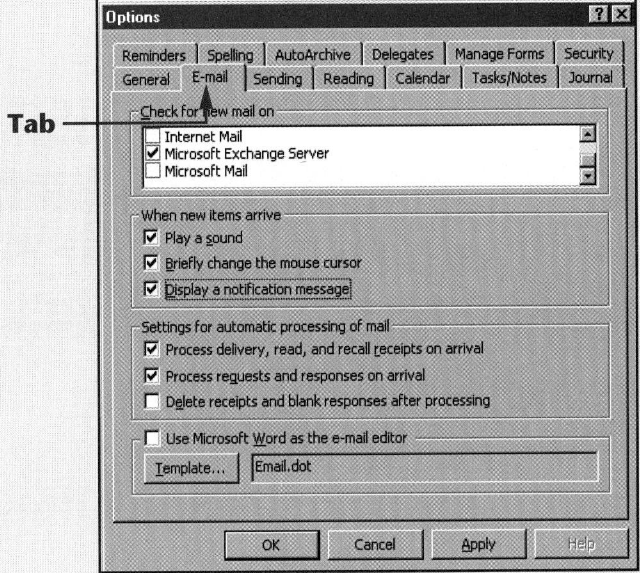

3 Click the Calendar tab.

The Calendar tab displays, enabling you to set options relating to the Calendar tool of Outlook.

4 Choose Cancel.

When you click the Cancel button, you close the dialog box without making any of the changes you select in the dialog box. You also can press Esc to cancel a dialog box.

5 Choose File from the menu bar.

The **F**ile menu displays. Notice that the Ne**w** command has a small arrow next to it. This means a submenu with additional commands relating to the Ne**w** command will display when you select it.

6 Choose New.

A submenu appears (see Figure B.9). You can select commands from this menu the same as you can from Outlook's main menus.

continues

To Use Menus and Dialog Boxes (continued)

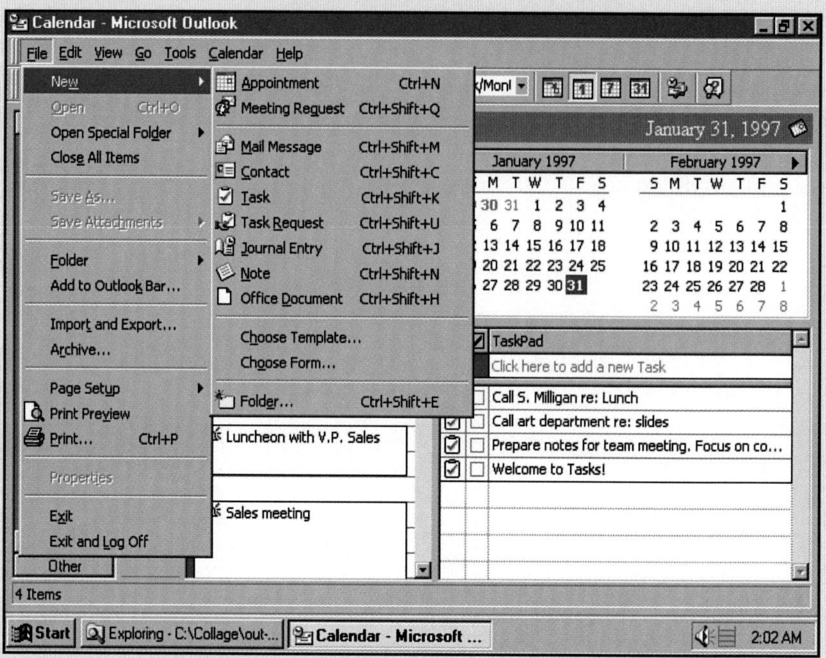

Figure B.9
A submenu.

7 Click the mouse pointer any place in the Outlook window away from the New command submenu.

This closes the New menu and submenu without selecting a command. In the next lesson, you learn how to customize Outlook.

As you begin using different components of Outlook such as Contacts, Inbox, and so on, you'll notice that the menu commands change depending on the component you use. This is referred to as *Smart Menus* in Outlook. Outlook's Smart Menus provide the user with commands that are relevant to the functions and actions of the selected component.

Lesson 4: Customizing Outlook

Outlook is highly customizable, letting you add folders, turn the standard toolbar on or off, hide or display the Outlook Bar, and change to different views. You also can customize the way the six organizational tools look and behave. You can, for instance, set the Calendar tool so that your work week starts on Tuesday and ends on Saturday instead of the traditional Monday through Friday work week.

In this lesson, you learn how to turn the Standard toolbar off and on, as well as how to hide and display the Outlook Bar.

To Customize Outlook

1 Select View from the Outlook menu bar.

The **V**iew menu displays showing you different Outlook viewing options.

2 Select Toolbars from the View menu.

A cascading menu displays, with the Standard command showing (see Figure B.10). Notice the checkmark next to the Standard command. This lets you know that the Standard toolbar is turned on.

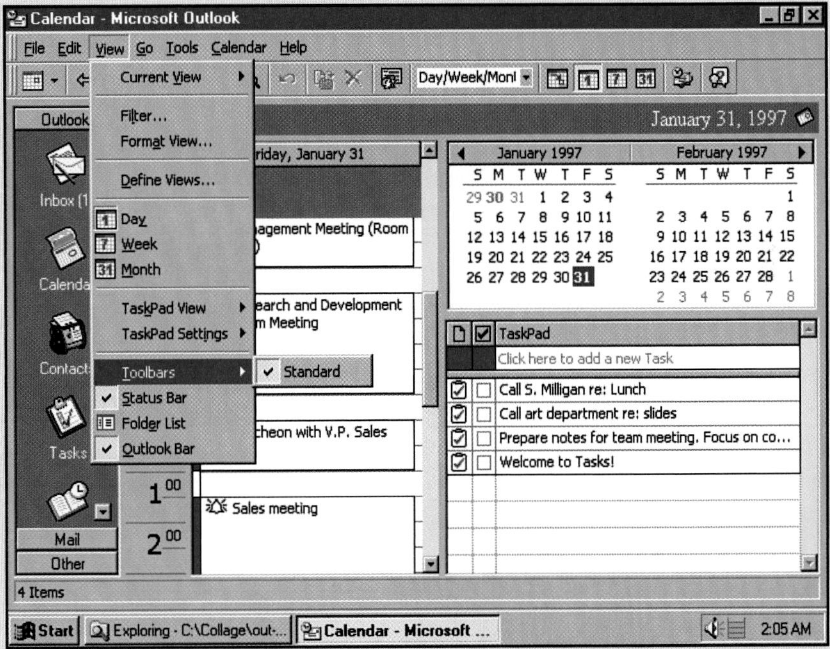

Figure B.10
The **T**oolbars command's cascading menu.

3 Choose Standard from the Toolbars cascading menu.

The checkmark next to the Standard command disappears, the cascading and **V**iew menus close, and the Standard toolbar is no longer showing on the Outlook screen. You've turned off the Standard toolbar. Now see how easy it is to turn it back on.

4 Choose View, Toolbars, Standard.

This displays the **V**iew menu and **T**oolbars cascading menu, places a checkmark next to the Standard command, closes the menus, and displays the standard toolbar on the Outlook screen.

5 Move the mouse pointer to the Outlook Bar.

The Outlook Bar is the vertical area on the far left side of the screen that displays folder shortcuts and groups. Refer to Figure B.4 for a reminder of where the Outlook Bar is.

continues

To Customize Outlook (continued)

Right-clicking
The process of clicking the right mouse button, usually to display a context menu.

Context menu
A context menu is a menu of commands that displays when you right-click an object in Windows 95 or right-click anywhere in many Windows 95 applications.

6 Click once with the right mouse button.

When you click with the right mouse button (known as *right-clicking*), a context menu displays off the tip of the mouse pointer. The *context menu* contains commands you can execute quickly using the mouse instead of moving the mouse to the top of the screen to click toolbar buttons or access main menu items. Using the right mouse button to display a context menu is a feature of many Windows 95 applications, including Outlook.

7 Choose Hide Outlook Bar from the context menu.

When you choose **H**ide Outlook Bar, the Outlook Bar disappears from the Outlook screen (see Figure B.11). The information viewer now displays across the entire Outlook window underneath the Standard toolbar and above the status bar. This is handy when you need to free up some room on your screen to see more of an item in the information viewer. Now see how easy it is to turn the Outlook Bar back on.

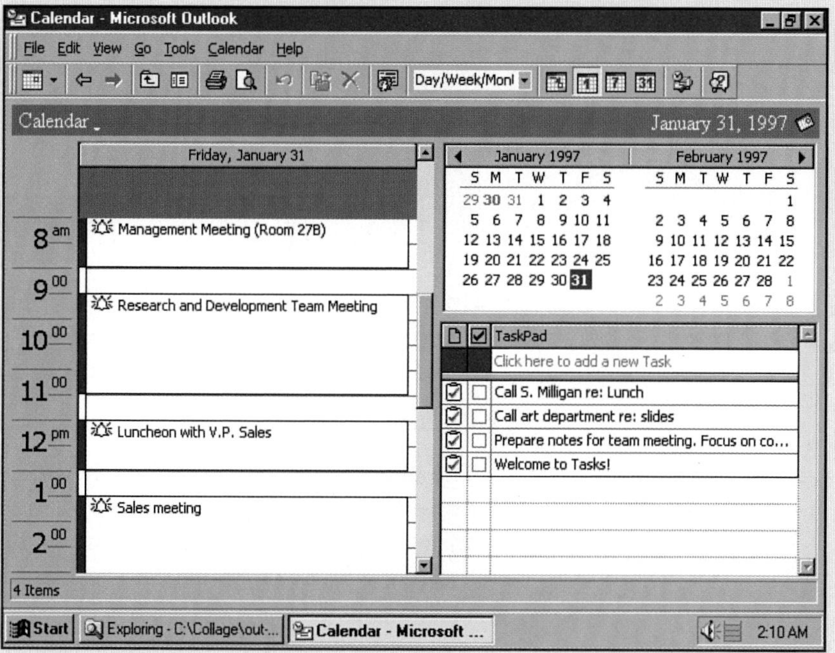

Figure B.11
The Outlook screen, with the Outlook Bar hidden.

8 Choose View, Outlook Bar.

The Outlook Bar reappears on the Outlook screen. Your screen should now have the Outlook Bar and Standard toolbar displayed.

Leave the Outlook window like this for the next lesson, where you learn how to get help in Outlook.

Lesson 5: Using the Office Assistant for Help

As you work with Outlook, you are bound to run into problems with a feature, forget how to perform a task, or need a tip on how to perform a task more quickly or easily. Outlook provides an easy-to-use help feature known as the Office Assistant for you to use during these times. The Office Assistant is an animated Help system that answers questions, provides helpful tips, displays helpful reminders, and offers help when you need it most.

In this lesson, you are introduced to the Office Assistant and are shown how easy it is to search for help on a topic.

To Use the Office Assistant for Help

1 Click once inside the TaskPad in the information viewer.

This changes the focus to the TaskPad so the Office Assistant displays information about the TaskPad.

2 Click the Office Assistant tool on the Outlook Standard toolbar.

The Office Assistant toolbar button is the last button on the far right of the toolbar. It looks like a question mark with a light bulb sitting atop it. When you click the Office Assistant button, the Office Assistant screens display (see Figure B.12). One screen displays a cartoon-like character and another screen displays Help options and a search field. You can click one of the blue buttons next to the options under `What would you like to do?` to get information about that topic. You can click the See more option to display additional help items. Or you can enter search criteria to have the Office Assistant search for a specific help topic. If you want to view helpful tips, click the **T**ips button at the bottom of the Office Assistant screen.

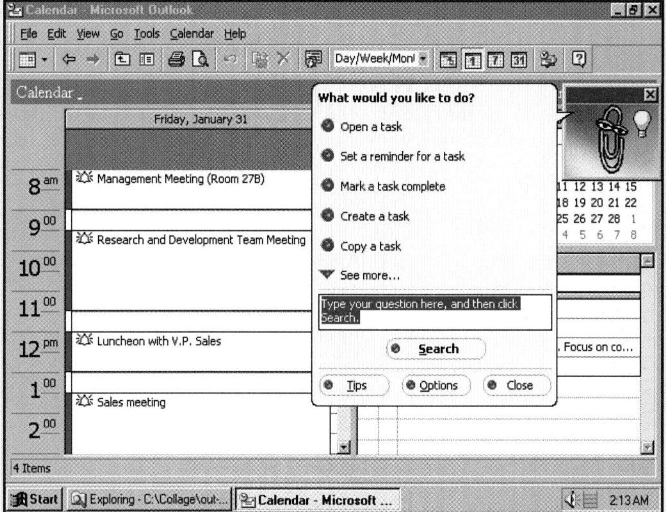

Figure B.12
The Office Assistant provides tips, help, and steps on how to complete tasks in Outlook.

continues

To Use the Office Assistant for Help (continued)

3 Click the blue button next to the help topic `Open a task`.

When you do this, a Microsoft Outlook Help window displays (see Figure B.13) with the contents of the help topic, which in this case is the topic describing how to open tasks in Outlook. In the Help window, some help text appears in green with a dashed underline. These are hypertext glossary terms, which are terms you click to display a pop-up window with a definition of that term.

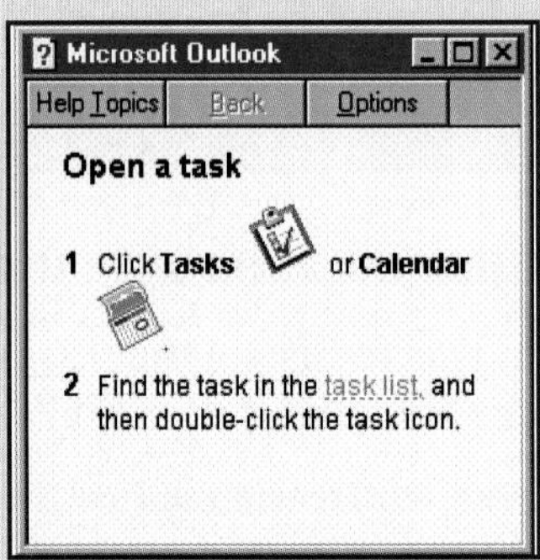

Figure B.13
The Open a task help topic explains how to open tasks in Outlook.

If you have problems...

If your Office Assistant screen shows different options from the ones shown here, you have a different folder selected than the one assumed in these steps. Make sure you have the Calendar folder selected and that the Calender items appear in the information viewer. To do this, click the Calendar item in the Outlook group in the Outlook Bar.

4 Click the Help Topics button on the Help window menu bar.

Clicking the Help Topics button displays the Help Topics dialog box, from which you can look for additional help. On the Index tab of the Help Topics dialog box (see Figure B.14), you can enter letters, words, or phrases to search for specific help items.

Figure B.14
The Help Topics dialog box provides access to Outlook's online help system.

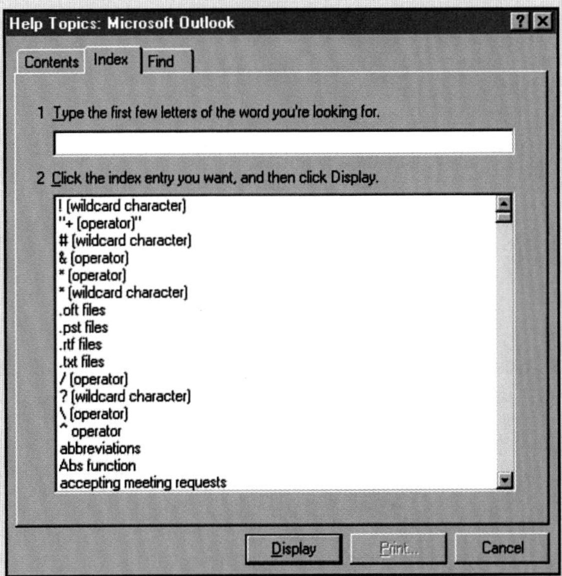

5 Click the Cancel button in the Help Topics dialog box.

Clicking the Cancel button closes the Help Topics dialog box. Notice the Office Assistant window with the animated character remains on-screen. You can click the Close window button on the title bar of this window to close it, or you can click anywhere on the window to display the other Office Assistant window, as previously shown in Figure B.12.

6 Click the Office Assistant window.

This displays the Office Assistant window with selected Help topics. If there is not a help topic you are interested in reading in this window, you can type in a search word or phrase to locate additional Help items.

7 Type `Reminders` in the box above the Search button.

The words `Type your question here, and then click Search` appear in the box above the Search button and are highlighted. You need to type over these words to enter your new search criteria. Typing words or phrases in this box enables you to specify the Help topic about which you want to read.

8 Click the Search button.

Clicking the **S**earch button displays a window with the results of your search. If Office Assistant cannot find any Help items relating to your topic, it displays a window telling you `I don't know what you mean. Please rephrase your question.` You need to enter a new word or phrase and click the **S**earch button again if you receive this message.

continues

To Use the Office Assistant for Help (continued)

9 Click the Close button.

Clicking the Close button closes the Office Assistant window that contains the Help items.

10 Click the Close window button on the Office Assistant window that has the animated character in it.

Clicking the Close window button closes the Office Assistant. In the next lesson, you learn how to exit Outlook.

The Office Assistant is shared by other Microsoft Office 97 applications, such as Microsoft Word 97, Excel 97, PowerPoint 97, and Access 97. Any settings you make to the Office Assistant in Outlook are reflected in other Office applications.

Another way to access Help in Outlook is to select the **H**elp menu on the Outlook menu bar and choose **C**ontents and Index. This displays the Help Topics dialog box. Table B.2 describes the Help commands you can choose from Outlook's **H**elp menu.

Table B.2 Outlook Help Menu Commands

Menu Command	Description
Microsoft Outlook **H**elp	Displays the Office Assistant.
The Microsoft Network He**l**p Topics	Enables you to connect to the Microsoft Network (MSN) for online help. You must have a modem installed and an MSN account for this feature to work.
Contents and Index	Displays the Help Topics dialog box.
What's **T**his?	Enables you to display screen tips for a menu command, screen item, or toolbar button.
Microsoft on the **W**eb	Provides links to sites on the World Wide Web for online help and assistance. You must have a modem installed and access to the Internet, or have a network connection that connects you directly to the Internet. This help command has a cascading menu with specific sites listed, such as Frequently Asked Questions and Microsoft Office Home Page.
About Microsoft Outlook	Displays product information about Outlook, your computer's system information, and technical support information.

Lesson 6: Exiting Outlook

If you are finished using Outlook and Windows 95, you should exit Outlook and shut down Windows. This way you do not inadvertently lose data or information that you are working on. Finish this project by exiting Outlook and shutting down Windows 95.

To Exit Outlook

1 Choose File, Exit.

Choosing the Exit command shuts down Outlook and returns you to the Windows 95 desktop. If the option Exit and Log Off is available on the File menu, choose that command instead of Exit. The Exit and Log Off command ensures that you log off from any network connection you may have as you close down Outlook.

2 Click the Start menu on the Windows 95 taskbar and choose the Shut Down command.

When you do this, the Shut Down Windows dialog box displays.

3 Select the Shut down the computer? option.

Usually, this option is selected by default so you may not need to select it.

4 Click Yes on the Shut Down Windows dialog box.

When you do this, Windows 95 starts its shut-down process. A screen displays instructing you to wait as the computer shuts down. Do not turn off your computer until Windows 95 displays a message telling you it is OK to turn off your computer.

If you are finished using the computer, turn off the computer. Otherwise, reboot the computer, start Windows 95, and start Outlook. Finally, continue with the next section, "Checking Your Skills."

Project Summary

To	Do This
Start Outlook for Windows 95	Start Windows 95, choose the Start button, and select **P**rograms. Click the Microsoft Outlook icon.
Choose a profile when starting Outlook	Perform the same steps as above. When the Choose a Profile dialog box appears, select a profile from the Profile **N**ame drop-down list. Click OK.
Select a menu command	Move mouse pointer to Outlook menu bar and click on menu. From drop-down list of commands, click on command.
Display a ToolTip	Move mouse pointer over a toolbar button and let it hover for a second or two.
Open folder items in information viewer	Click folder in Outlook Bar.
Display Outlook group	Click group name in Outlook Bar.
Cancel a dialog box	Click Cancel on the dialog box, or press Esc.
Turn off Standard Outlook toolbar	Select the **V**iew menu, choose **T**oolbars, and click Standard from the cascading menu.
Turn on Standard Outlook toolbar	Select the **V**iew menu, choose **T**oolbars, and click Standard from the cascading menu.
Hide Outlook Bar	Right-click on Outlook Bar and select **H**ide Outlook Bar from context-menu.
Display Outlook Bar	Select the **V**iew menu and choose **O**utlook Bar.
Start Office Assistant	Click the Office Assistant toolbar button on the Standard toolbar. Or, select **H**elp and choose Microsoft Outlook **H**elp.
Search Help topic	Enter search word or phrase in search box in Outlook Assistant and click **S**earch button.
Exit Outlook	Select **F**ile and choose **E**xit (or Exit and **L**og Off).

Checking Your Skills

True/False

For each of the following, check *T* or *F* to indicate whether the statement is true or false.

__T __F **1.** You can start Outlook before Windows 95 starts.

__T __F **2.** Outlook enables you to use the right mouse button to display a context menu.

__T __F **3.** Outlook's Standard toolbar must always display when you use Outlook.

__T __F **4.** You use the Office Assistant to gather names and phone numbers of users in your office.

__T __F **5.** Dialog boxes can be cancelled without making any changes in them.

Multiple Choice

Circle the letter of the correct answer for each of the following questions.

1. The Office Assistant can be started using which **H**elp menu command?

- **a.** Office Assistant
- **b.** Microsoft Outlook **H**elp
- **c.** Microsoft Office 97 Help
- **d.** **A**bout Microsoft Outlook

2. Outlook profiles include what type of information?

- **a.** Information about Outlook technical support
- **b.** Settings for how Windows 95 starts when you turn on your computer
- **c.** Information about each user on the network
- **d.** Settings for how Outlook is configured for a user

3. Which function does the information viewer perform?

- **a.** Displays the contents of selected folders
- **b.** Enables you to see Help information for a topic
- **c.** Displays Outlook folders and groups
- **d.** Contains the **O**ptions command

4. The Windows 95 taskbar can usually be found where on the screen?

- **a.** Inside the Start menu
- **b.** Below the Standard toolbar in Outlook
- **c.** Within the Shut Down dialog box
- **d.** At the bottom of the Windows 95 screen

5. The Outlook Bar contains which types of components?

- **a.** Options and tabs
- **b.** Folder shortcuts and group buttons
- **c.** Dialog boxes and menus
- **d.** Help topics and Office Assistant characters

Completion

In the blank(s) provided, write the correct answer for each of the following statements.

1. Outlook is a desktop ____________ manager.

2. Outlook provides these six tools: ________________, ______________, ____________, ____________, ___________, ___________.

3. You can use the __________ feature in Help or Office Assistant to specify a Help topic or phrase you want to view.

4. A menu command with an ellipsis (...) next to it means a ______ box appears after selecting the command.

5. In the Outlook Bar, you choose the ______________ command from the context menu to hide the Outlook Bar.

Applying Your Skills

Practice

Work through the following exercises to practice the skills you learned in Appendix B.

To Select Menu Options

1. From the Outlook menu bar, choose **V**iew.
2. Choose Fold**e**r List.
3. Choose **T**ools from the menu bar.
4. Choose the **O**ptions command.
5. Click the Spelling tab on the Options dialog box.
6. Click the Always **c**heck spelling before sending option.
7. Click OK.
8. Select the **V**iew menu and choose the Folder List option (to turn off the Folder List view).

To Get Help

1. From the Outlook menu bar, choose **H**elp.
2. Choose **C**ontents and Index.
3. Click the Index tab.
4. Type **`Outlook`** in the search field at the top of the tab.
5. Click OK.
6. Double-click on the word `Outlook (Microsoft)` in the bottom window of the tab. This is where your search results appear.
7. In the Topics Found dialog box, click the `Control what happens when you start Outlook` topic. Click OK.
8. Read the help topic.
9. Click the Close window button on the help screen.

To Specify a Different Office Assistant Character

1. From the Outlook Standard toolbar, click the Office Assistant button.
2. Click the **O**ptions button.
3. From the Office Assistant dialog box, click the Gallery tab.
4. Click the **N**ext button until the Shakespeare character appears.
5. Click Cancel without making any changes. (To choose this item, the Outlook 97 or Office 97 CD-ROM must be available and placed in the CD-ROM drive of the computer.)

Access key The underlined letter in a menu command name.

Alignment The placement of text along the left margin, right margin, or both margins.

Animate To create the illusion of movement during an electronic slide show by controlling how text is displayed.

Annotate To draw or write a comment. In a PowerPoint slide show, annotation refers to using the electronic pen to write or draw.

Application A computer program dedicated to one type of function, such as word processing or database management.

Arguments The values on which the function performs its calculations. An argument can be a single cell, a range of cells, or any value you enter.

ASCII A standard text format that all PCs can read.

AutoContent Wizard A tool that guides you through the steps of a proposed presentation and includes suggested content.

AutoForm A form that is created automatically by Access that includes all the fields in a table.

Bullet An object, such as a circle or square, which is used to set off items in a list.

Character attribute An enhancement you add to a font, such as bold, italic, or underline.

Chart A pictorial representation of data. A chart is also sometimes referred to as a graph.

Clipboard A temporary storage area in Windows that stores copied data and from which you can paste that data.

Color scheme A set of eight coordinated colors you can use in your presentation.

Column selector The area above a column in the QBE grid in Access that enables you to select the entire column.

Conditional Statement A function that returns different results depending on whether a specified condition is true or false.

Control Any graphical object selected from the toolbox, such as a text box, checkbox, or option button that you add to a form or report.

Criteria A test or set of conditions that limits the records included in a query.

Current worksheet The worksheet containing the active cell.

Data The information that you work with in a spreadsheet, including text, numbers, and graphic images.

Data Form A dialog box that displays only one row of your list—in other words, one record. Column headings appear as field labels. You can enter data or work with existing data using a data form.

Datasheet A grid of columns and rows that enables you to enter numerical data into a PowerPoint chart.

Datasheet view The view of the table you use when you enter or exit records. The field names you enter appear in the first row, followed by any records you have entered in the table.

Default An automatic setting that the computer uses unless you specify another setting.

Delimiter the characters that separate fields; set off text from numbers; and separate parts of dates, times, and currencies.

Demote To indent a line of text more that the previous line, indicating a lower level of importance.

Design view The view of the table you use when you are creating or changing fields. You see columns for the field name, data type, and description.

Document A file containing work that has already been created, such as a report, memo, or worksheet.

Drag-and-drop To perform a move on a PowerPoint slide icon by selecting and dragging it to another location and then releasing the mouse button.

Dynaset A subset of records created as a result of a query in Access.

Electronic slide show A predefined list of slides displayed sequentially on-screen or using an LCD panel and overhead projector.

Embedded chart A graphical representation of worksheet data created within the worksheet rather than as a separate worksheet.

Expression A predefined formula that performs some calculations. You can include an expression in a report and in other Access objects, such as macros.

Field label Displays the field name.

Field separator The delimiter that separates the fields in a row of data.

Field text box Holds a place for the contents of each field in a database.

File Information you enter in your computer and save for future use, such as a document or workbook.

Filter A method for controlling which records are extracted from the database and displayed in the worksheet.

Fixed-width fields Fields that occupy a fixed position in the record, such as characters 5 through 12. No characters are used to separate the fields.

Folder An icon that represents a group of files.

Font The typeface, type size, and type attributes of text or numbers.

Font size The size of a font is actually the height of a character, which is measured in points. A 72-point font has characters that are roughly one inch high.

Footer Text or graphics that appear at the bottom of every page.

Form A type of object you can create to enter, edit, and view records. Think of a form as a fill-in-the-blanks screen.

Format To change the appearance of text or numbers.

Formatting To arrange text and other page elements so the information is easier to read and appears polished.

Function A built-in formula that automatically performs calculations.

Graphic Graphic images come in all shapes and sizes. Typical graphics include clip art images, drawings, photographs, scanned images, signature files, and so on.

Header Text or graphics that appear at the top of every page.

Icon A pictorial representation of a program, a file, or other element.

Insertion point A blinking vertical line that appears on-screen at a location where you can enter data. The insertion point is sometimes called a *cursor*. Characters that you type appear to the left of the insertion point.

Integration Using two or more software applications together to create a single document.

Internet Service provider (ISP) A company that provides a connection between your computer and the other computers on the Internet.

Join The manner in which the common fields between two tables are associated.

LCD projection panel A flat-screen device that you can use to project computer images to a large screen.

Merge A feature that enables you to combine information, such as names and addresses, with a form document, such as a letter. The result of a typical merge is personalized letters and envelopes.

Modem A device that enables your computer to communicate with other computers using traditional phone lines.

Multitasking The execution of more than one program at a time on a computer system.

Notes Master A PowerPoint feature that controls the components and formatting of all notes pages.

Object Linking and Embedding (OLE) A set of standards that enable you to insert objects, such as pictures or spreadsheets, from one document created with one application into documents created with another application.

Office Assistant An animated guide that helps you search for help.

Online Directly connected to a computer and ready for use.

Page Setup The way data is arranged on a printed page.

Peripheral program Sometimes called an applet, this is a program with a specific function that is started every time a feature is accessed.

Personal Computer A stand-alone computer (sometimes called a microcomputer) equipped with all the system, utility, application software and input/output devices needed to perform one or more tasks.

Placeholder On a PowerPoint slide, an area that can accept text, graphics, or objects (such as charts).

Point A unit of measurement used in printing and publishing to designate the height of type. There are roughly 72 points in an inch.

Presentation A group of related slides you can create using PowerPoint.

Presentation graphics program A software application that helps you structure, design, and present information-such as graphs or bulleted lists- to an audience so that it is visually appealing.

Primary key field A field that contains a unique value for each record in the table.

Promote To indent a line of text less than the previous line, indicating a greater level of importance.

Property An attribute or a field that you can use to define characteristics of that field.

Query A question posed to the database that determines what information is retrieved.

Random-Access Memory (RAM) The temporary storage space where the computer places a program you are using.

Range A cell or a rectangular group of adjacent cells.

Range Finder A feature of Excel that helps you locate cells referenced in a formula by color coding them. The range in the formula is highlighted in the same color as the range in the worksheet.

ScreenTip A description box that is displayed whenever you rest the mouse pointer on a button.

Search criteria A defined pattern or detail used to find matching records.

Select To define a section of text so that you can take action on it, such as copying, moving, or formatting.

Selecting Designating an item on-screen so you can do something with it. Also called *highlighting*.

Shortcut key The keystroke combination that can be used to quickly execute Word commands (rather than opening a menu and choosing a command).

Slide Master A framework slide that controls how a slide will look and enables you to place items such as date, name, and logo on each slide automatically.

Slide transition A special effect used to introduce a slide during an electronic slide show.

Sort A function that rearranges the data in a list so that it appears in alphabetical or numerical order.

Sort fields The fields used to determine the order in which a list is sorted.

Speaker notes Notes that help you document and present your speech.

Spreadsheet An accounting form that contains rows and columns. The intersection of a row and column is called a cell.

Spreadsheet functions In spreadsheet programs, the most commonly performed numeric calculations (such as adding a column of numbers and averaging) are already set up for you to use.

Submenu A list of options that appears when you point at some menu items in Windows 95 and in applications designed for use with Windows 95. A small, right-pointing arrowhead appears to the right of menu items that have submenus.

Table A series of rows and columns. The intersection of a row and column is called a cell, which is where you type text and numbers.

Template A blueprint that PowerPoint uses to create slides. The template includes the formatting options, color, and graphics necessary to create a particular look.

Toggle switch A single menu command used to turn a feature on and off. If the feature is already on, selecting the menu command turns it off, and vice versa.

Value A numeric cell entry.

Workbook An Excel file that contains one or more worksheets.

Worksheet One page of your work in an Excel workbook.

Worksheet frame The horizontal bar containing the column letters and the vertical bar containing the row numbers, located in the worksheet area.

Symbols

C

D

F

G

H

I

N

O

P

S

T

U-V

X-Y-Z

Technical Support:

If you cannot get the CD/Disk to install properly, or you need assistance with a particular situation in the book, please feel free to check out the Knowledge Base on our Web site at **http://www.superlibrary.com/general/support**. We have answers to our most Frequently Asked Questions listed there. If you do not find your specific question answered, please contact Macmillan Technical Support at **(317) 581-3833.** We can also be reached by email at **support@mcp.com**.